The Environment and Society Reader

R. Scott Frey, Editor
University of North Florida

Allyn and Bacon
Boston • London • Toronto • Tokyo • Sydney • Singapore

For My Parents

Senior Editor: Sarah Kelbaugh
Editor in Chief, Social Sciences: Karen Hanson
Editorial Assistant: Lori Flickinger
Marketing Manager: Jude Hall
Editorial Production Service: Chestnut Hill Enterprises, Inc.
Manufacturing Buyer: Megan Cochran
Cover Administrator: Brian Gogolin
Electronic Composition: Omegatype Typography, Inc.

Internet: www.abacon.com

Between the time Website information is gathered and published, some sites may have closed. Also, the transcription of URLs can result in typographical errors. The publisher would appreciate notification where these occur so that they may be corrected in subsequent editions.

Library of Congress Cataloging-in-Publication Data

The environment and society reader / R. Scott Frey, editor.
    p. cm.
   Includes bibliographical references and index.
   ISBN 0-205-30876-7
    1. Environmentalism—Social aspects. 2. Environmental policy. 3. Social ecology. 4. Human ecology. I. Frey, Richard Scott.

GE195 .E58 2000
304.2—dc21
                                                         00-057615

Printed in the United States of America
10 9 8 7 6 5 4 3 2 1   05 04 03 02 01 00

Contents

Preface   v

About the Editor   xii

PART I   NATURE AND CHARACTER OF ENVIRONMENTAL PROBLEMS   1

Chapter 1   **Environmental Problems from the Local to the Global**   3
1: Environmental Problems *R. Scott Frey*   4

Chapter 2   **Environmental Sociology: Past, Present, and Back to the Future**   26
2: Sociology as if Nature Did Not Matter: An Ecological Critique
Raymond Murphy   27
3: The Evolution of Environmental Sociology: A Brief History and
Assessment of the American Experience *Riley E. Dunlap*   43
4: Marx's Theory of Metabolic Rift: Classical Foundations for
Environmental Sociology *John Bellamy Foster*   63

Chapter 3   **Environmental Justice within and between Countries**   96
5: Anatomy of Environmental Racism and the Environmental Justice
Movement *Robert D. Bullard*   97
6: The Hazardous Waste Stream in the World-System *R. Scott Frey*   106
7: Principles of Environmental Justice *The First National People of Color
Environmental Leadership Summit*   121

Chapter 4   **Driving Forces of Environmental Problems**   123
8: Rethinking the Environmental Impacts of Population, Affluence,
and Technology *Thomas Dietz and Eugene A. Rosa*   124
9: Uneven and Combined Development and Ecological Crisis: A
Theoretical Introduction *James O'Connor*   151

PART II   HUMAN RESPONSES TO ENVIRONMENTAL PROBLEMS   161

Chapter 5   **Environmental Beliefs and Attitudes**   163
10: The Social Bases of Environmental Concern: Have They Changed
over Time? *Robert Emmet Jones and Riley E. Dunlap*   164

11: Culture and the Environment in the Pacific Northwest *Richard J. Ellis and Fred Thompson*   180
12: Global Concern for the Environment: Is Affluence a Prerequisite? *Riley E. Dunlap and Angela G. Mertig*   202

Chapter 6   The Environmental Movement   216
13: Environmental Discourse and Social Movement Organizations: A Historical and Rhetorical Perspective on the Development of U.S. Environmental Organizations *Robert J. Brulle*   217
14: Development, Poverty and the Growth of the Green Movement in India *Jayanta Bandyopadhyay and Vandana Shiva*   238
15: Science, Nature, and the Globalization of the Environment, 1870–1990 *David John Frank*   249

Chapter 7   Environmental Assessment and Management   271
16: Risk Assessment and Management *Thomas Dietz, R. Scott Frey, and Eugene Rosa*   272

Chapter 8   Science, Democracy, and the Environment   300
17: Popular Epidemiology and Toxic Waste Contamination: Lay and Professional Ways of Knowing *Phil Brown*   301
18: Science for the Post-Normal Age *Silvio O. Funtowicz and Jerome R. Ravetz*   320

PART III   ENVISIONING A SUSTAINABLE AND EQUITABLE FUTURE   337

Chapter 9   Toward a New Worldview   339
19: A New Ecological Paradigm for Post-Exuberant Sociology *William R. Catton, Jr. and Riley E. Dunlap*   340

Chapter 10   From Growth to Sustainable and Equitable Development   361
20: What Does Sustainability Really Mean?: The Search for Useful Indicators *Alex Farrell and Maureen Hart*   362

Chapter 11   Attaining Sustainable and Equitable Development   378
21: A Declaration of Sustainability *Paul Hawken*   379

Preface

Resource availability and the limited absorptive capacity of the biophysical environment are increasingly important to humans. Consider the fact that the majority of living Nobel Prize winners signed the *World Scientists' Warning to Humanity* in 1992. This proclamation stated that "If not checked, many of our current practices...may so alter the living world that it will be unable to sustain life in the manner that we know" (Union of Concerned Scientists 1992). Never before had a majority of Nobel Laureates agreed to a single statement on any issue, but then again the extent of resource depletion and pollution problems, as well as their consequences, are startling (see e.g., Brown 2000; McNeill 2000; National Research Council 1999; Wackernagel and Rees 1996). It is estimated, for instance, that *each day* humans:

- Appropriate 40 to 50 percent of the products of photosynthesis (Giampietro and Pimentel 1993; Vitousek et al. 1986; see also Vitousek et al. 1997);
- Consume around 54 percent of the accessible runoff water on earth (Postel et al. 1996);
- Mine more material from the earth than the natural erosion of all the Earth's rivers (Young 1992);
- Add over 15 million tons of carbon to the atmosphere (Brown et al. 2000:67);
- Destroy 180 square miles of tropical rain forest (Miller 1994:264);
- Create over 60 square miles of desert (Miller 1994:324);
- Eliminate at least 74 animal and plant species (Wilson 1992:280);
- Erode 70 to 80 million tons of topsoil (Pimentel et al. 1995);
- Add around 1,400 tons of CFCs to the stratosphere (Brown et al. 1995:63).

These and a host of other environmental problems (including catastrophic events such as Bhopal, Chernobyl, Exxon Valdez, and the Gulf War oil spill) have aroused worldwide concern. This concern has been expressed in several ways: public anxiety and demand for a physically attractive, biologically healthy, and productive environment (Dunlap 1998; Dunlap and Mertig 1995; Freudenburg 1993); scientific debate and controversy over the nature, scope, and management of environmental problems (National Research Council 1999, 2000; Rosa and Dietz 1998); political controversy, conflict, and litigation among various industry, government, and public groups (Dryzek 1997); and mitigative and regulatory efforts by numerous governmental and nongovernmental organizations at the local, national, regional, and global levels (Elliott 1998; Fiorino 1995; Frank 1999). The problems are so severe that German sociologist Ulrich Beck (1992, 1999) has argued that the modern world is a "risk society" in which exposure to environmental risk is as important a determinant of life as class, race, and gender.

Current concerns with environmental problems can best be summarized in six interrelated questions:

1. What is the actual nature and scope of depletion and pollution problems at the local, national, regional, and global levels?
2. How are threats to humans created by problems of depletion and pollution distributed within and between countries?
3. What are the human causes or driving forces of environmental problems?
4. What kinds of human responses (individual, organizational, cultural, societal,

and international) have these environmental problems produced?

5. Because human responses are embedded in a larger social context, how have they been influenced by psychological, economic, political, and social and cultural forces?

6. How can we deal more effectively with environmental problems?

Despite the pressing importance and sociological relevance of these questions, there is no comprehensive introduction to the issues in sociology. This reader provides such an introduction for advanced undergraduate and beginning graduate students. It consists of twenty-one papers that are organized into eleven chapters. Part I (Chapters 1–4) examines the scope, nature, and human causes of environmental problems. Part II (Chapters 5–8) provides an overview of various human responses to environmental problems. Part III (Chapters 9–11) outlines an emerging view referred to as *sustainable development* that not only represents an alternative way of thinking about environmental problems but provides concrete suggestions for action.

PART 1: NATURE AND CHARACTER OF ENVIRONMENTAL PROBLEMS

Chapter 1 Environmental problems are problems of resource depletion and pollution created by human activities. Specific examples include the depletion and degradation of soil, water, and marine resources that are important for food production; air and water pollution; devegetation of land by deforestation and desertification; stratospheric ozone depletion; acidic precipitation; global climate change; destruction of natural habitats; loss of biodiversity. Such problems affect human health and sociocultural production and other species, as well as disrupt the overall integrity of the biosphere. The nature and character of environmental problems are examined in this chapter.

This chapter consists of a paper that discusses the nature of environmental problems and identifies their effects on humans and the larger biosphere (Frey). The paper also examines three specific environmental problems (ranging from the local to the global) to illustrate major points: (1) toxic wastes at the local level in the United States; (2) environmental degradation in the former Soviet Union; and (3) global climate change. It concludes with discussion of a basic model for thinking about the human causes and responses to environmental problems.

Chapter 2 Environmental sociology as a distinct subdiscipline centered on the study of "societal–environmental interactions" emerged in the late 1970s. Although sociologists studied environmental topics (including public opinion, resource management issues, and the environmental movement) for several decades prior to this, they did so typically from a disciplinary tradition grounded in what some have called the "Human Exemptionalist Paradigm." This paradigm assumes that humans are exempt from constraints imposed by the biophysical environment because of culture, science, and technology. Environmental sociology (or the new human ecology as some prefer to call it) challenges this idea by insisting that the biophysical environment shapes and is shaped by human activities. The implications that this assumption has for sociology are explored in Chapter 2.

Three papers are included in this chapter. The first paper argues that mainstream sociology ignores the relationship between the biophysical environment and society at the risk of increasing irrelevancy (Murphy). The second paper outlines the conceptual underpinnings and theoretical core of U.S.-based environmental sociology, examines its history and current status, and discusses existing theoretical shortcomings and possible new directions (Dunlap). The chapter concludes with a paper that explores the potential contribution of the Marxist narrative (and other classical theoretical narratives) to the development of a deeper understanding of environmental problems (Foster).

Chapter 3 Environmental problems are embedded in stratification systems that exist within and between countries. Consequently, the human benefits (economic and other) and the threats of environmental problems (such as exposure to pollution and the attendant health risks, economic problems like unemployment resulting from resource depletion, and the protection from such problems) are not equitably distributed within and between countries. Rather, they tend to reflect power–dependency relations between various social groups (based on class, gender, and race), communities and regions within countries, as well as between countries. The threats of environmental problems, therefore, tend to vary inversely across groups and geographic areas within countries by economic and other considerations and between countries by position in the world-economic system. Despite widespread recognition of the problem, social science research is limited. We have little understanding of how the threats of environmental problems are distributed across class, gender and racial groups, communities, countries, and other meaningful human categories such as generations. The general issue is examined in this chapter by concentrating on the specific problem of differential exposure to environmental hazards and the attendant health risks.

This chapter consists of three papers. The first paper examines how exposure to environmental hazards and the attendant health risks vary by racial–ethnic group status in the United States (Bullard). (Among other things, this paper examines what is known about the differential location of locally unwanted land uses [LULUs] in poor and minority communities and how these contribute to the problem of health risks.) The second paper examines how the export of hazardous wastes to less developed coun-

tries by transnational corporations (based in the industrialized or core countries) contributes to health, safety, and environmental risks in the periphery (Frey). The chapter concludes with the statement of environmental justice principles adopted by The First National People of Color Environmental Leadership Summit in 1991.

Chapter 4 Environmental problems have been linked to various driving forces or human causes. Major forces include population growth, economic growth and poverty, technological change, the structure of political–economic institutions, and cultural attitudes and beliefs. Population growth is thought to result in greater aggregate demand placed on the resource base and absorptive capacity of the environment. Economic growth (or increased production and consumption of goods) results in increased resource withdrawals and waste creation. Poverty fosters population growth and increases human demands on local environments. Technological change affects the environment in several interrelated ways: It not only creates new ways for using resources, but it changes the efficiency of production and consumption patterns. Characteristics of political–economic institutions (the existence or absence of markets, centralization of power, and the like) have been linked to environmental problems in various ways. Cultural attitudes and beliefs (often referred to as *worldviews*) emphasizing domination, growth, progress, and a world without physical limits are thought to underlie short-sighted, self-interested human activities linked to environmental degradation. Little consensus exists in the scientific literature on the nature of the relationship between these driving forces and environmental problems. In fact, considerable controversy has emerged around several of these factors.

This chapter consists of two papers. The first paper reports an important effort to synthesize and make sense of the seemingly disparate (but highly conventional) views outlined above, especially population growth, affluence, and technology (Dietz and Rosa). The second paper represents a neo-Marxian effort to link environmental problems (especially those of the periphery) to global capitalism (O'Connor).

PART II: HUMAN RESPONSES TO ENVIRONMENTAL PROBLEMS

Chapter 5 Research in the United States and many developed and less developed countries indicates that the public is concerned with environmental quality. The public perceives a deterioration in environmental quality and is concerned with the threats to human health and well-being posed by this deterioration. Furthermore, there has been a reduction in public confidence in the state's ability to protect them from environmental threats. The intent of this chapter is to summarize what is known about environmental beliefs and attitudes.

This chapter consists of three papers. The first paper examines the social bases of environmental concern in the United States (Jones and Dunlap). The second paper examines one interesting (but highly controversial) effort to explain why humans differ in their views of the environment and the nature of environmental problems (Ellis and Thompson). The third paper discusses the nature and recent trends in public concerns with the environment in twenty-four developed and less developed countries (Dunlap and Mertig).

Chapter 6 The contemporary environmental movement can be viewed as a political response to environmental problems. It has been described by several commentators as a "new social movement" because its origins, tactics, and goals differ substantially from traditional class and economic-based social movements. Regardless of the accuracy of this characterization, the environmental movement has challenged the underlying goals and structure of the ad-

vanced industrial countries and become an important actor in the political process in many industrialized countries. There has also been a dramatic increase in environmental movement activity throughout the less developed world and the emergence of what can be described as a global environmental movement.

This chapter consists of three papers. Attention in the first paper is directed to the contemporary environmental movement in the United States (Brulle). It examines the contemporary U.S. environmental movement sector: its ideology, support bases, motivational dynamics, organizational structures, and the political styles of the increasingly diverse movement organizations (ranging from mainstream organizations such as the Sierra Club to community grassroots organizations and other local groups fighting LULUs as well as more radical groups such as Earth First!) that have emerged at the local and national levels. The second paper discusses the environmental movement in the less developed world; specifically, the authors discuss the distinguishing characteristics, political styles, and direction of the environmental movement in India (Bandyopadhyay and Shiva). The chapter concludes with a paper examining the emergence of global-level environmental discourse and activity (Frank).

Chapter 7 Environmental problems generate conflict between various actors about appropriate state policy. In response, industry and government have developed formal techniques for assessing and managing environmental problems. These include economic cost-benefit analysis, risk analysis, environmental impact assessment, and related procedures. Proponents of these techniques maintain that they are rational scientific tools that facilitate environmental assessment and management. Critics contend that these techniques have numerous limitations that may produce flawed environmental assessment and management practices. One such technique, risk assessment, is discussed in this chapter.

This chapter consists of a paper outlining the distinguishing characteristics and major shortcomings of risk assessment (and management), as well as the sociological implications of risk (Dietz, Frey, and Rosa). Risk assessment is characterized by scientific uncertainty resulting from inadequate data and methods and the values surrounding risk assessment and management are often in dispute. These problems are compounded as the spatial and temporal horizons of environmental problems become more distant.

Chapter 8 Many people in the United States and other countries are concerned with environmental quality, and they appear to have lost confidence in the state's ability to protect them from environmental threats. Although several commentators have described laypersons and environmentalists as victims of "near-clinical paranoia," a number of observers have argued that the public's response is reasonable and predictable given the way that environmental assessment and management have been conducted by government and industry. Interested parties are often disenfranchised. They are either excluded from participating in the assessment and management process or they are consulted after the assessment has been conducted and management decisions have been made. This chapter examines the problem and outlines ways for improving the process.

The chapter begins with a paper that discusses the dynamic tension between science and democracy that seems to underlie the problems discussed in papers in the previous two chapters: This tension can best be described as the conflict between expertness and popular rule (Brown). The authors of the second paper argue that the traditional view of science (a practice conducted by a peer community of experts) is outmoded given the scientific uncertainties

and value disputes discussed earlier and that an extended community of peers or interested parties (including both experts and nonexperts) is needed in the assessment and management of environmental problems (Funtowicz and Ravetz). The argument is not based on a rejection of science as a means of generating valid information or normative considerations regarding the moral superiority of democracy over technocratic rule by experts, but on pragmatic grounds: By broadening the peer community, the quality of assessment information may improve, confidence and trust among key actors may increase, and consensus about appropriate management strategies may emerge.

PART III: ENVISIONING A SUSTAINABLE AND EQUITABLE FUTURE

Discussions of environmental problems often have a pessimistic tone because the problems are large and often seem intractable. This collection concludes with a discussion of an emerging perspective (referred to as *sustainable development*) that provides a means for thinking more clearly about and dealing more effectively with environmental problems. *Sustainability* is typically defined as the responsibility of the current generation to ensure the ability of future generations to meet their material needs and experience a healthy environment. Beyond this, however, there is little consensus about the conceptual and operational content of sustainability. Ecologists, for instance, see sustainablity as the preservation of ecological systems, whereas most economists (and sociologists) see it as the maintenance and improvement of living standards for humans. Disagreements over the meaning of *sustainability* represent more than a debate between economics and ecology; they are based on different views regarding the nature of the relationship between the biophysical environment and human society. The utility of the sustainability concept for thinking about and dealing with environmental problems is discussed in Chapters 9–11.

Chapter 9 The Western conception of development is critically reviewed in this chapter. The chapter consists of a paper that outlines the historical origins of the Western view of development; discusses the major social components of this conception (or dominant social paradigm as some have called it); discusses how it has become embedded in much of the contemporary social, economic, and political thought and practice; and presents an alternative view (Catton and Dunlap). In other words, the Western conception of development as economic growth is considered illusory because it is neither sustainable nor morally defensible.

Chapter 10 Chapter 10 consists of a paper that addresses several important issues surrounding the concept of *sustainable development* (Farrell and Hart). It examines the conceptual and operational core of sustainable development by critically reviewing existing conceptions. It outlines a synthetic conception of sustainable development that incorporates important dimensions from existing conceptions and responds to criticisms raised by critics. It also discusses what sustainable development might look like and ways for assessing progress at different spatial levels and across time.

Chapter 11 The book concludes on an upbeat note by discussing specific changes (including transformations in technology, economic and political institutions, and lifestyles) required for the emergence of a sustainable and equitable future. The role of both science and politics in shaping the future and the place that human agency plays in shaping future human–biophysical environment interactions are emphasized in the discussion. A paper is included that draws together the understanding developed in previous chapters and discusses specific ways

in which humans can reduce environmental problems (Hawken).

I want to thank reviewer Thomas Dietz, George Mason University, for his helpful comments and suggestions.

REFERENCES

Beck, Ulrich. 1992. *Risk Society: Towards a New Modernity.* Newbury Park, CA: Sage.
———. 1999. *World Risk Society.* Malden, MA: Blackwell.
Brown, Lester R., Christopher Flavin, and Hal Kane. 1995. *Vital Signs, 1995: Trends That Are Shaping Our Future.* New York: W. W. Norton.
Brown, Lester R., editor. 2000. *State of the World, 2000.* New York: W. W. Norton.
Brown, Lester R., Michael Renner, and Brian Halwell. 2000. *Vital Signs 2000: The Environmental Trends That Are Shaping Our Future.* New York: W. W. Norton.
Dryzek, John S. 1997. *The Politics of the Earth: Environmental Discourses.* New York: Oxford University Press.
Dunlap, Riley E. 1998. "Lay Perceptions of Global Risk: Public Views of Global Warming in Cross-National Context." *International Sociology* 13:473–498.
Dunlap, Riley E. and Angela G. Mertig. 1995. "Global Concern for the Environment: Is Affluence a Prerequisite?" *Journal of Social Issues* 51:121–137.
Elliott, Lorraine. 1998. *The Global Politics of the Environment.* New York: New York University Press.
Fiorino, Daniel J. 1995. *Making Environmental Policy.* Berkeley: University of California Press.
Frank, David John. 1999. "The Social Bases of Environmental Treaty Ratification, 1870–1990." *Sociological Inquiry* 69:523–550.
Freudenburg, William R. 1993. "Risk and Recreancy: Weber, the Division of Labor, and the Rationality of Risk Perceptions." *Social Forces* 71:909–932.
Giampietro, M. and D. Pimentel. 1993. "The Tightening Conflict: Population, Energy Use, and the Ecology of Agriculture." In *NPG Forum.* Teanek, NJ: Negative Population Growth.
McNeill, J. R. 2000. *Something New Under the Sun: An Environmental History of the Twentieth-Century World.* New York: W. W. Norton.
Miller, G. Tyler. 1994. *Living in the Environment.* (Eighth Edition.) Belmont, CA: Wadsworth.
National Research Council. 1999. *Our Common Journey: A Transition to Sustainability.* Washington, D.C.: National Academy Press.
———. 2000. *Reconciling Observations of Global Temperature.* Washington, D.C.: National Academy Press.
Pimentel, David, C. Harvey, P. Resosudarmo, K. Sinclair, D. Kurtz, M. McNair, S. Crist, L. Shpritz, L. Fitton, R. Saffouri, and R. Blair. 1995. "Environmental and Economic Costs of Soil Erosion and Conservation Benefits." *Science* 267:1117–1123.
Postel, Sandra L., Gretchen C. Daily, and Paul R. Ehrlich. 1996. "Human Appropriation of Renewable Fresh Water." *Science* 271 (9 February):785–788.

Rosa, Eugene A. and Thomas Dietz. 1998. "Climate Change and Society: Speculation, Construction and Scientific Investigation." *International Sociology* 13:421–455.

Union of Concerned Scientists. 1992. *World Scientists' Warning to Humanity.* Cambridge, MA: Union of Concerned Scientists.

Vitousek, Peter M., Paul R. Ehrlich, Anne H. Ehrlich, and Pamela A. Matson. 1986. "Human Appropriation of the Products of Photosynthesis." *BioScience* 36:368–373.

Vitousek, Peter M., Harold A. Mooney, Jane Lubcheno, and Jerry M. Melillo. 1997. "Human Domination of Earth's Ecosystems." *Science* 277:494–499

Wackernagel, Mathis and William Rees. 1996. *Our Ecological Footprint: Reducing Human Impact on the Earth.* Gabriola Island, BC: New Society Publishers.

Wilson, Edward. 1992. *The Diversity of Life.* Cambridge, MA: Harvard University Press.

Young, John J. 1992. *Mining of the Earth.* (Worldwatch Paper 109.) Washington, D.C.: Worldwatch Institute.

ACKNOWLEDGMENTS

Copyright holders have kindly granted permission to reprint material in this book.

Raymond Murphy. 1995. "Sociology as if Nature Did Not Matter: An Ecological Critique." *British Journal of Sociology* 46:688–707.

Riley E. Dunlap. 1997. "The Evolution of Environmental Sociology: A Brief History and Assessment of the American Experience," from *The International Handbook of Environmental Sociology* by Michael Redclift and Graham Woodgate, editors (Cheltenham, UK and Northampton, MA: Edward Elgar), 21–39.

John Bellamy Foster. 1999. "Marx's Theory of Metabolic Rift: Classical Foundations for Environmental Sociology." *American Journal of Sociology* 105:366–405, revised version. Copyright (c) 1999 by The University of Chicago Press.

Robert D. Bullard. 1993. "Anatomy of Environmental Racism and the Environmental Justice Movement," from *Confronting Environmental Racism: Voices from the Grassroots* by Robert Bullard, editor (Boston: South End Press), 15–39, excerpts.

R. Scott Frey. 1998. "The Hazardous Waste Stream in the World-System," from *Space and Transport in the World-System,* by Paul S. Ciccantell and Stephen G. Bunker, editors (Westport, CT: Greenwood Press), 84–103, revised version. Copyright (c) 1998 by Paul S. Ciccantell and Stephen G. Bunker. Reproduced with permission of Greenwood Publishing Group, Inc.

The First National People of Color Environmental Leadership Summit. 1991. "Principles of Environmental Justice" (Adopted 27 October 1991, The First National People of Color Environmental Leadership Summit, Washington, D.C.).

Thomas Dietz and Eugene A. Rosa. 1994. "Rethinking the Environmental Impacts of Population, Affluence, and Technology." *Human Ecology Review* 1:277–300, revised version.

James O'Connor. 1989. "Uneven and Combined Development and Ecological Crisis: A Theoretical Introduction." *Race and Class* 30:1–11.

Robert Emmet Jones and Riley E. Dunlap. 1992. "The Social Bases of Environmental Concern: Have They Changed over Time?" Reprinted from *Rural Sociology* 57:28–47 by permission granted by the Rural Sociological Society.

Richard J. Ellis and Fred Thompson. 1997. "Culture and the Environment in the Pacific Northwest." *American Political Science Review* 91:885–897.

Riley E. Dunlap and Angela G. Mertig. 1995. "Global Concern for the Environment: Is Affluence a Prerequisite?" *Journal of Social Issues* 51:121–137. Copyright (c) 1995 by the Society for the Psychological Study of Social Issues.

Robert J. Brulle. 1996. "Environmental Discourse and Social Movement Organizations: A Historical and Rhetorical Perspective on the Development of U.S. Environmental Organizations." *Sociological Inquiry* 66:58–83. Copyright (c) 1996 by the University of Texas Press, P.O. Box 7819, Austin, TX 78713-7819.

Jayanta Bandyopadhyay and Vandana Shiva. 1989. "Development, Poverty and the Growth of the Green Movement in India." *The Ecologist* 19 (May/June):111–117, excerpts, Unit 18, Chelsea Wharf, 15 Lots Road, London, UK.

David John Frank. "Science, Nature, and the Globalization of the Environment, 1870–1990." Reprinted from *Social Forces* (76, December, 1997, pp. 409–435). Copyright (c) The University of North Carolina Press.

Thomas Dietz, R. Scott Frey, and Eugene Rosa. "Risk Assessment and Management." Copyright (c) 2000 by Thomas Dietz, R. Scott Frey, and Eugene Rosa.

Phil Brown. 1992. "Popular Epidemiology and Toxic Waste Contamination: Lay and Professional Ways of Knowing." *Journal of Health and Social Behavior* 33:267–281, revised version.

Silvio O. Funtowicz and Jerome R. Ravetz. 1993. "Science for a Post-Normal Age." *Futures* 25:739–755, with permission from Elsevier Science.

William R. Catton, Jr. and Riley E. Dunlap. 1980. "A New Ecological Paradigm for Post-Exuberant Sociology." *American Behavioral Scientist* 24 (1):15–47, copyright (c) 1980 by Sage Publications, Inc. Reprinted by permission of Sage Publications, Inc.

Alex Farrell and Maureen Hart. 1998. "What Does Sustainability Really Mean?: The Search for Useful Indicators." *Environment* 40 (November):4–9, 26–31. Reprinted with permission of the Helen Dwight Reid Educational Foundation. Published by Heldref Publications, 1319 Eighteenth St., NW, Washington, DC 20036-1802. Copyright (c) 1998.

Paul Hawken. 1993. "A Declaration of Sustainability." *Utne Reader* 59 (September/October): 54–61.

About the Editor

R. Scott Frey is currently Professor and Chair in the Department of Sociology, Anthropology, and Criminal Justice at the University of North Florida. He has held appointments at Argonne National Laboratory, The George Washington University, Kansas State University, and the National Science Foundation. He has contributed chapters to recent books on environmental issues and he has published his work in numerous periodicals, including the *American Journal of Sociology* and the *American Sociological Review.* His work has been funded by the Ford Foundation and the U.S. Department of Agriculture.

PART I

Nature and Character
of Environmental Problems

Chapter 1

Environmental Problems from the Local to the Global

1. Environmental Problems

R. SCOTT FREY

What are environmental problems? At the most abstract level, environmental problems occur when the state of the biophysical environment has adverse consequences on things people value. We can think of two general kinds of problems. One occurs when a resource that people value is in short supply or disappears entirely. This is resource depletion. The other is when human actions change ecosystems in undesirable ways. We think of this as pollution.

As we proceed into the twenty-first century, we are faced with a host of severe environmental problems (National Research Council 1999:186–224). Specific examples include:

- The depletion and degradation of soil, water, and marine resources that are considered important for human food production;
- Air and water pollution;
- Land devegetation resulting from deforestation and desertification;
- Stratospheric ozone depletion;
- Accumulation of greenhouse gases in the upper atmosphere;
- Acidic precipitation;
- Destruction of natural habitats;
- Species extinction and the loss of biodiversity.

The U.S. Environmental Protection Agency (EPA) (1987, 1990) and other organizations and analysts (see especially National Research Council 1999:190–191) have published numerous lists of the most important environmental problems facing humanity. The EPA list of environmental problems of concern is presented in Table 1.1. Some of these problems have very adverse effects on human health and economic welfare. They can also affect other species and disrupt the overall integrity of natural ecosystems, crucial bio-geochemical cycles, and the larger biosphere. The EPA's expert-based ranking of the most important environmental problems in terms of their human health and ecological risks is presented in Table 1.2.

With so many different kinds of environmental problems, we need to have some way to sort them into categories. This sorting, if done in meaningful ways, can help us understand the character of the problems. Sometimes it is useful to look at environmental problems in terms of their causes. At other times it is useful to consider whether the problems are based on the depletion of resources or pollution. It is also useful to consider the spatial scope of an environmental problem, which can range from the local to the global. Another concern centers on whether the consequences are mostly for humans or for nonhumans and the larger biosphere. We may also be concerned about the time scope of environmental problems, because some problems have immediate effects while others will not make themselves

TABLE 1.1   Environmental Problems Identified by the U.S. Environmental Protection Agency (not in rank order)

1. Urban air pollution
2. Regional air pollution, including acid rain
3. Hazardous air pollutants
4. Indoor radon
5. Indoor air pollutants other than radon
6. Radiation other than radon
7. Depletion of stratospheric ozone associated with CFCs and other substances
8. Global climate change associated with carbon dioxide and other greenhouse gases
9. Water pollution associated with direct and indirect point source discharges from industrial and other facilities to surface waters
10. Water pollution associated with nonpoint source discharges to surface waters
11. Contaminated sludge
12. Pollution of estuaries, coastal waters, and oceans from all sources
13. Deterioration of wetlands from all sources
14. Pollution of drinking water as it arrives at the tap from chemicals, lead in pipes, biological contaminants, and radiation
15. Pollution of groundwater and soil at hazardous sites, both sites with continuing disposal and those no longer in use
16. Pollution of groundwater and other media at nonhazardous waste sites, including municipal landfills and industrial sites
17. Exhaustion of landfills
18. Groundwater contamination from septic systems, road salts, injection wells, leaking storage tanks, and other sources
19. Wastes and tailings from mining and other extractive activities
20. Accidental releases of toxic substances
21. Oil spills and other accidental releases of environmentally damaging materials and substances
22. Pesticide residues on foods eaten by humans and wildlife, and risks to applicators of pesticides
23. Risks to air and water from pesticides and other agricultural chemicals as a result of leaching and runoff, aerial spraying, and other sources
24. New toxic chemicals
25. Undesirable environmental release of genetically altered materials
26. Exposure to consumer products
27. Worker exposure to chemicals
28. Reductions in biodiversity
29. Deforestation
30. Desertification

Source: U.S. Environmental Protection Agency (1987).

TABLE 1.2   U.S. Environmental Protection Agency Relative Ranking of Environmental Problems in Terms of Ecological and Human Health Risks

Relatively High-Risk Ecological Problems

Wildlife habitat alteration and destruction
Species extinction and loss of biodiversity
Stratospheric ozone depletion
Global climate change

Relatively Medium-Risk Ecological Problems

Herbicides/Pesticides
Toxic chemicals, nutrients, biochemical
    oxygen demand, and sediment in
    surface waters
Acid deposition
Airborne toxics

Relatively Low-Risk Ecological Problems

Oil spills
Groundwater pollution
Radionuclides
Acid runoff to surface waters
Thermal pollution

Relatively High-Risk Health Problems

Indoor air pollution
Outdoor air pollution
Worker exposure to industrial or
    farm chemicals
Pollutants in drinking water
Pesticide residues on food
Toxic chemicals in consumer products

Source: U.S. Environmental Protection Agency
(1990:13ff)

felt for a generation or more. Finally, we can classify problems in terms of their severity (as the EPA has done in Table 1.2) or we can classify problems in terms of how certain

they are to occur, how many people or other plants and animals will be affected, and whether or not the consequences of the problem can be reversed.

The purpose of this chapter is to introduce you to the nature and scope of environmental problems. The distinguishing features of environmental problems are first examined. This is followed by an examination of the claim that we are in the midst of an environmental crisis. A brief discussion of three specific environmental problems is then presented to illustrate the major points developed in this and subsequent chapters. The chapter concludes with the examination of a conceptual model that provides a basis for thinking about the causes and human responses to environmental problems, as well as possible solutions to such problems.

THE NATURE OF ENVIRONMENTAL PROBLEMS

Human societies are dependent on the biophysical environment (Daily 1997). The biophysical environment is the system of living and nonliving physical elements (including matter and energy) found on Earth (for further details, see Catton et al. 1984; Cottrell 1970/1955; Daly 1996; Ehrlich et al. 1977). Sunlight and fossil fuels, plant and animal protein, genetic material, water, soil, and related physical materials are the material base on which all human societies are constructed. This natural system in turn acts as a sink for wastes created by human activities.

Environmental problems exist when the stock of physical resources is depleted or degraded or when the absorptive capacity of natural sinks is exceeded (Daly 1996; Schnaiberg, 1980:9–43; Schnaiberg and Gould 1994: Chapter 1).[1] People may exploit resources at rates that cannot be continued.

We may emit wastes at rates that exceed the absorptive capacity of the environment. In either case, depletion of resources and pollution create threats for humans and nonhuman species, and in some cases threaten the integrity of ecosystems and the larger biosphere.

Source Limits: Resource Depletion and Degradation

Natural resources (anything produced naturally) are either material or nonmaterial in nature. Material resources include physical substances such as oil, copper, and clean water. Nonmaterial resources include amenities like peace, solitude, biological diversity, and beauty. A special case is the genetic diversity contained in the ecosystems around the world, which is an information resource. Generally, we know how to measure the amount of resources available, though measurements may over or underestimate the actual supply. It is much more difficult, perhaps impossible, to estimate the supply of nonmaterial resources. And we are just beginning to think about the amount of genetic information available in the biosphere and specific ecosystems.

Before a substance can be considered a resource, the necessary human skills for capturing and processing it must exist and there must be a human demand for it. Consequently, the meaning of resources has changed over time as a result of improvements in knowledge and technical capabilities and changes in production costs and human demands (Rees 1990). For example, the yew tree that grows in undisturbed forest habitats in the Pacific Northwest of the United States and Canada has been known to scientists for more than a century, but only in the last decade have scientists realized that it contains a substance (taxol) that

can be used as an anticancer drug. Whale oil and baleen were resources of tremendous economic importance, but are no longer of much economic value.

Material resources can be divided into two basic types: nonrenewable and renewable resources. Nonrenewable resources are substances that are fixed in amount and are regenerated very slowly, if at all, through natural processes. Oil, copper, and coal are examples of nonrenewable resources. A further distinction can be made among nonrenewable resources. Some can be consumed only once (such as oil and coal when burned as fuel). Others can be used more than once or recycled. Most metals, such as copper, cadmium, and zinc are in the category of potentially recyclable resources. On the other hand, renewable resources are substances that are not fixed in supply and are generated fairly quickly in the environment. These include clean water, clean air, animal and plant life, wind, ocean waves, and solar radiation.

Of course the distinction between renewable and nonrenewable resources is one of time scale. The earth regenerates the supply of fossil fuels such as coal and oil. But the pace of that regeneration, through the geologic transformation of buried plant and animal matter, is so slow compared to human rates of consumption that we have to consider such fossil fuels nonrenewable. In other cases, ecosystem processes can restore a resource to a useable form. If a fish species is overfished, it will decline in numbers to the point where it can no longer be relied on as part of the human food supply. But if there are enough of the fish left in the ecosystem it inhabits, and if fishing stops for a long enough period of time, then the population of fish can return to its original level and be used again. On the other hand, if the population becomes too small, it may never recover. Soil is an interesting and important example that sits somewhere between a renewable and a nonrenewable resource. Soil is generated by geological and biological processes that convert rock into small particles ("dirt") and then create a microecosystem made up of the small particles of rock, organic matter from plants and animals, and a variety of microorganisms. While we think of soil as dead, inorganic material, soil is actually a miniature ecosystem. It has been estimated that soil is generated by natural processes around the world at a slower rate than current levels of erosion (Pimentel et al. 1995). Under this pattern of loss and regeneration, we must consider soil a nonrenewable resource. But if erosion was better controlled, soil could be classified as a renewable resource.

Herman Daly (e.g., 1990, 1993, 1996) has emphasized this concept of renewable rates of resources use and talks about the sustainability rate of resource use. He says that the sustainable rate at which a renewable resource can be used is no greater than the natural regeneration rate of the resource. In turn, the sustainable use rate of a nonrenewable resource is no greater than the rate at which a renewable resource (used in a sustainable fashion) can be substituted for it. This is the essence of those environmental problems that involve resource depletion. Resource use rates of humans exceed natural regeneration rates for many critical resources.

Sink Limits: Pollution

Pollutants or wastes are by-products of resource extraction, processing, and use that are threats to the health and survival of humans, nonhuman species, ecosystems, and the biosphere. Pollution is a problem when pollutants are emitted to the air, water, or soil at rates greater than the rates at which they can be recycled, absorbed, or otherwise rendered harmless by the natural processes of the environment. Sewage, for example, can be added to streams at a rate at which the local ecosystem can absorb the nutrients contained in it without changing the character of the stream ecosystem. But if too much sewage is emitted, the nutrients and other substances in the sewage change the structure of the ecosystem. For example, a clear stream containing trout may be converted into an algae-filled stream in which carp are the dominant species. In effect, pollution exists when wastes are emitted at rates that exceed the absorptive capacity of the environment.

Many substances that we consider pollutants occur naturally in the environment (Ames et al. 1987), but humans are a major source of pollution. Human sources of pollution can be categorized as either point or nonpoint in nature. Fixed point sources, as the term implies, come from identifiable places and activities. Examples include the smokestack of a factory, the tailpipe of an automobile, and the drainage pipe of a slaughterhouse. Nonpoint sources are dispersed and cannot be attributed to a single point in space or a single activity. These include sources that are hard to identify and that are dispersed across space and, possibly, time. Current U.S. agricultural practices (including beef production in large feedlots and the use of pesticides, fertilizers, and other chemicals) are nonpoint dispersed sources of problems such as groundwater contamination, pesticide residues on food, and the like (McDuffie et al. 1995; National Research Council 1989; Rifkin 1992). Of course, the distinction is somewhat arbitrary. A single auto tailpipe is a point source but auto emissions in the Los Angeles area are a nonpoint source. A single feedlot is a point source, but the runoff from agricultural activities in an entire watershed must be treated as a nonpoint source.

The severity of the harmful effects of pollutants in the air, water, and soil is a function of several interrelated factors. First, the potency of the pollutant is an important consideration. Some substances are highly toxic, generating adverse effects even at very low concentrations. Others are relatively benign, and produce bad effects only in large concentration. The second consideration is the level of concentration of the pollutant in the environment. And the final condition is the persistence of the pollutant in the environment. Natural processes dilute or break down some pollutants rather quickly. Others are immune to breakdown by most biological processes, remain active in ecosystems, and may even be concentrated by biological processes so that their effects are multiplied. Pollutants that are potent, highly concentrated, and nondegradable pose serious environmental threats to humans, other species, and the larger environment.

Nonhuman and Human Threats from Environmental Problems

There are limits to the rates at which resources can be used and pollutants can be emitted without threatening plant and animal species, natural ecosystems, and the larger biosphere, as well as the health and economic well-being of humans.

Nonhuman and ecological threats. Nonhuman threats refer to plant and animal health and the disruption of natural life-support systems such as the atmosphere, the oceans, tropical rain forests, and so on. Plant and animal health suffers as pollutants are added to the environment and re-

sources are extracted. The extinction rate of many species (including not only exotic animals but many species of plants, insects, and animals) is at an all-time high according to many scholars (Wilson 1992). Natural life-support systems at the local, regional, and global levels in turn have increasingly been degraded. Climate change and the dispersion of pollutants throughout the biosphere lead to changes in ecosystems that most people find undesirable: a loss of species, a loss of aesthetic quality, and in many cases a loss of the ability to use the ecosystem for productive purposes.

Human threats. Source and sink problems create hazards that increase the health risks of humans. Health risks are typically defined as the adverse health effects resulting from exposure to hazards. Adverse effects to human health include death, disease, and injury. Such effects can be either acute or chronic. *Acute* refers to adverse effects that manifest themselves quickly, such as the catastrophic release of cyanide in the Bhopal, India disaster. *Chronic* refers to adverse effects that take a long time to manifest themselves, such as cancers induced by long-term exposure to low doses of toxic chemicals in drinking water (Ward et al. 1995). As with all the distinctions made here, the distinction can be arbitrary, depending on the time scale chosen. And, unfortunately, most substances that produce acute effects can also produce chronic effects. Specific hazards of concern here include the disruption of natural life-support systems, as well as toxic chemicals and other pollutants in the air, water, and soil.

Adverse consequences resulting from disrupted natural life-support systems (like climate change, increased acidic precipitation, and ozone depletion and ultraviolet radiation) increase human health risks such as skin cancer, infectious diseases, and the like. Adverse effects to human health resulting from exposure to toxic chemicals and other environmental pollutants include diseases of the respiratory system, genetic and reproductive problems, reduced ability of the immune system to cope with invading viruses and bacteria, and various types of cancer. Environmental disruptions associated with various source and sink problems have also led to concerns with the possibility of increased viral traffic and infectious diseases, resulting from the transfer of animal diseases to humans (Daszak et al. 2000; Epstein, 1995; Morse, 1993).

Environmental problems also affect humans by constraining sociocultural production through increased prices resulting from reduced resource stocks. Unemployment, reduced incomes, decreased profitability and capital formation, and decreased availability of public services often result from resource scarcities and increased production costs (Bunker 1985; Freudenburg 1992; Schnaiberg 1980). Sink problems, in turn, result in property damage (including metal corrosion, weathering of buildings, and the like) and increased nuisance and aesthetic damage such as unpleasant smells and reduced visibility (U.S. Environmental Protection Agency 1987). Human exposure to pollution is unequal: some groups (especially those marginalized by gender, age, class, race/ethnicity, and geographic location) are at high risk of exposure (Bryant 1995; Bryant and Mohai 1992; Bullard 1994a, 1994b; Camacho 1998; Cohen 1997). Human responses to such problems in the past have included population migration, political controversy, and violent conflict between those who benefit and those who lose from source and sink problems (Camacho 1998; Homer-Dixon 1999).

Environmental Problems in Historical and Comparative Perspective

Depletion of the quantity of resources and degradation of the quality of resources and pollution have been problems throughout human history (Ponting 1991; Redman 1999). Overcultivation, overgrazing, deforestation, various irrigation practices, and soil erosion have degraded land and led to the destruction of several civilizations in the Mediterranean Basin and the Near East and the jungles of Meso-America. Although pollution has existed for thousands of years, serious pollution problems and the attendant human and nonhuman threats are of more recent origin and they are tied to industrial production (Foster 1999; Markham 1994; Ponting 1991: Chapter 16).

Problems of pollution and resource depletion/degradation exist throughout the world, but the nature and mix of problems varies by country. Production and especially consumption practices in the developed countries (DCs) lead to serious problems of pollution; production practices in the newly industrializing countries and the Eastern European countries lead to very serious problems of pollution; and resource extraction and poverty in the less developed countries (LDCs) lead to serious problems of resource depletion and degradation. Environmental problems are becoming increasingly global in nature and scope as we will see below (National Research Council 1999; Rosa and Dietz 1998; Stern et al. 1992)

IS THERE AN ENVIRONMENTAL CRISIS?

Cornucopians and Neo-Malthusians

Humans have demonstrated an ability to substitute new resources for declining ones and to reduce the pollution associated with various agricultural, industrial, and other types of activities to minimal levels. It is therefore only natural to conclude that environmental problems can be solved through the proper application of science and the development of new technologies. In fact, many people contend that technological advances occur more quickly than rates of resource source and sink exhaustion (Bailey, 1993, 1995, 2000; Easterbrook 1995; Ray 1990; Simon 1981). But do they? Is there really an environmental crisis? Let's turn to a discussion of these interrelated questions.

Two polarized views have emerged around the question of the severity of environmental problems. These are often referred to as the Cornucopian and the Neo-Malthusian views (Dryzek, 1987: Chapter 2). Cornucopians (Simon 1981) and many of their sympathizers (Bailey 1993, 1995, 2000; Douglas and Wildavsky 1982) admit that environmental problems exist, but they argue that an environmental crisis does not. In fact, one noted critic has referred to environmental problems as "less a crisis than a nuisance" (Bailey 1993:121). They contend that existing stocks of many resources are greater than current estimates indicate. They also point to advances in technology and the development of alternative or substitute resources, declining prices, and declines in the levels of certain pollutants. If we run out of energy sources such as coal, petroleum, and natural gas they argue, we will develop alternative sources such as breeder reactors on which to base economic welfare. Enthusiasts such as Ronald Bailey (1993, 2000), Julian Simon (1981), and Herman Kahn (Simon and Kahn, 1984) point to declining levels of various pollutants and declining costs of many natural resources. They reject the pessimistic conclusions of Malthus and the neo-Malthusians

and envision a future state of human well-being.

Neo-Malthusians and their sympathizers (Brown et al. 2000; Carson 1962; Catton 1980; Commoner 1990; Ehrlich and Ehrlich 1990; Hardin 1993; Meadows et al. 1992), on the other hand, argue that serious environmental problems exist for which there are few viable solutions. Technological fixes, resource substitutions, and the like will not ultimately solve crucial environmental problems. They maintain that critical resource shortages and pollution problems lie in the not too distant human future. And while they acknowledge that recent history has been one of declining resources prices and no absolute shortage of key resources, they contend that this trend will not continue because we are taxing the biosphere to its limits (Meadows et al. 1992).

They argue that human actions are changing the world much more quickly than would otherwise occur and at rates never before experienced on Earth (Stern et al. 1992). By analogy, think of driving down a curvy mountain road at night. As you encounter each new twist at 30 miles per hour, you may be able to steer enough to get around the curves. There are ways to cope with the changes in the road and the danger they entail at that pace. But if you accelerate to 60 miles an hour, the changes come too quickly for you to steer, and you plummet off a cliff. Many environmental scientists think that the current situation is more like driving the road at 60 than at 30.

Problem Solution or Displacement?

How do we begin to assess these polarized positions? If we accept the fact that human societies are dependent on a finite biophysical environment (in terms of sources and

sinks), we soon realize that there is no ultimate solution to environmental problems.
And once we realize this, it becomes increasingly clear that human societies cannot
grow beyond their physical limits without
adverse consequences. Dryzek (1987: Chapter 2), Schnaiberg (1980:23–26), Schnaiberg
and Gould (1994), and Commoner (1990),
for instance, make a very convincing argument that current policies and technological
efforts have not solved crucial or pending
environmental problems, but simply redi-
rected or displaced them across space, various media, and time. Selected examples
clearly illustrate the problem:

- Enactment of environmental laws in
  the United States and Western Europe
  has promoted the transfer of many hazardous production processes, products,
  and wastes across state and national
  boundaries (Covello and Frey 1990;
  Frey 1995, 1997, 1998, 1999). DDT is a
  good example of the problem. Production and use have been outlawed in the
  United States and Western Europe since
  the early 1970s, but worldwide production and use is dominated by U.S. and
  Western European companies and it is
  being used at record levels around the
  world (Frey 1995). Or consider the
  movement of hazardous production
  from the United States and other industrialized countries to the export processing zones located in the periphery
  of the world-system (Frey 1999).
- The technologies used to solve one environmental problem often generate
  another problem. For example, greenhouse gases are emitted when we burn
  fossil fuels, such as coal and oil, so
  many people have advocated increased
  use of nuclear power, which does not
  produce greenhouse emissions. But nu-

clear power does involve pollution
problems from radioactive wastes; we
simply trade one form of pollution for
another.
- Some solutions to environmental problems involve passing the problem to
  future generations. Because nuclear
  wastes are so long-lived, most current
  schemes for "disposing" of them involve
  storing them in places where they will
  remain for hundreds, thousands, or
  even tens of thousands of years. Thus
  our children, grandchildren, and great-
  great-great-great-grandchildren will have
  to be cautious about the potential hazards of these storage sites (Hamilton and
  Viscusi 1999; Shrader-Frechette 1993).

SELECTED CASE STUDIES
OF ENVIRONMENTAL PROBLEMS

Let's examine three examples of important
depletion and pollution problems at the local, regional, and global levels to illustrate
some of the ideas that have been discussed.
The first example is toxic pollution at the
community level in the United States. Environmental deterioration in the former Soviet Union is the second example. The third
example is the specter of global climate
change.

Contaminated Communities
in the United States

Estimates indicate that as many as 750 million tons of toxic wastes were dumped in
thousands of sites around the United States
between the late 1950s and the early 1990s
by various actors (U.S. Environmental Protection Agency 1991). The major actors
tended to be profit-based companies, but the
U.S. military and other government agencies
contributed to this problem by producing

and stockpiling toxic materials at facilities located throughout the country (Shulman 1992). The human health effects associated with these toxic materials are not fully known, but the available evidence indicates that the problem is serious (National Research Council 1991). Griffith et al. (1989) in an important early study, for instance, found that rates for certain site-specific cancers were inflated in U.S. counties with hazardous waste sites. The authors of an important National Research Council (1991:20) report concluded that there "is sufficient evidence that hazardous wastes have produced serious health effects in some populations," but "that populations may be at risk that have not been adequately identified, because of the inadequate program of site identification and assessment." Other researchers report that those exposed to toxic wastes have experienced negative psychological and social consequences (Brown and Mikkelsen 1997; Edelstein 1988). Some contaminated communities have also experienced declining property values (Kohlhase 1991). A particularly troubling fact is that toxic wastes often end up in poor minority neighborhoods and communities. This puts some of the most disadvantaged members of our society at greater health and economic risk than their more affluent and politically powerful neighbors (see, e.g., Bryant 1995; Bryant and Mohai 1992; Bullard 1994a, 1994b; Camacho 1998; Cohen 1997; Daniels and Friedman 1999).

Harvest of Environmental Sorrow: Environmental Deterioration in the Former Soviet Union

The political and human rights abuses in the former Soviet Union (FSU) have been fully documented (e.g., Conquest 1986, 1990, 1999), but the environmental abuses of the country have only recently come to light. Several Soviet (Komarov 1980) and Western (Cockerham 1999; Feshbach 1995; Feshbach and Friendly 1992; Peterson 1993; Weiner 1988) observers have documented the scope of environmental deterioration and the declining state of public health in the FSU and conclude that an environmental crisis exists. Observers describe the situation as "death by ecocide" and note that, "No other great industrial civilization so systematically and so long poisoned its land, air, water and people" (Feshbach and Friendly, 1992:1). The actual human and nonhuman costs are staggering.

Numerous examples of the problem abound. Consider the following: "only 15 percent of the urban population of Russia lives in areas with 'ecologically acceptable levels of pollution'" (Feshbach 1995:67); official Russian sources suggest that 75 percent of all surface water in the FSU was polluted in 1989 and most rivers, lakes, and seas are thought to be at risk of dying due to oxygen deprivation (Feshbach 1995:53); "Atmospheric pollution…is now estimated to be responsible for 20 to 30 percent of the overall illness rate of the population (Feshbach 1995:67); during the 1980s a third of the world's industrial accidents occurred in the FSU (Feshbach 1995:68); and the number of "Yellow Children"—a condition marked by a yellowing of skin and diseases of the blood (such as anemia and reduced platelets and red blood cells) and the central nervous system—is on the rise in various areas of the country and is linked to chemical contaminants in food and water (Cockerham 1999; Feshbach 1995:73–74). Efforts to alleviate such problems will take decades, cost hundreds of billions of dollars, and require coordinated international action (Feshbach and Friendly 1992; Feshbach 1995:82–83; Schreiber 1991:366–367).

Given the scope of the problem, it is ironic that one early commentator on the environmental threats posed by human activity was the noted Russian scientist Vlaidimir Vernadsky (1945, 1986/1926). Vernadsky coined the concept of "biosphere" and argued that human activity needs to be balanced with the absorptive and stock (or carrying) capacity of the biosphere. How the post-Lenin FSU authorities came to violate such advice is a tragic tale that cannot be told here (see, e.g., Foster 1999:394–395; Pryde 1991; Weiner 1988), but the basic causes are sketched.

Environmental problems (despite the existence of environmental laws more stringent than those of the West) can be traced to state efforts to promote rapid economic growth and military strength. The values underlying the socialist command economy of the FSU have been variously described as "make it big; keep it secret; meet production at any cost; reward many for success but make no one responsible for failure" (Feshbach 1995:100) and "Big was better, huge was best, and science could solve the problems" (Peterson 1993:11).

Environmental destruction in the FSU is often linked to production and pollution inefficiencies associated with socialist command economies. And, of course, many Western analysts have promoted the market as the means for overcoming such inefficiencies. But one noted ecological economist cautions:

> *capitalist market systems and socialist command systems both remain committed to the same preanalytic vision of infinite sources and sinks. Relative efficiencies of market systems, compared with command economies, enable capitalist economies to get away with this faulty vision* longer *[emphasis added]. Command economies, with their production and pollution inefficiencies, have* collapsed

> *sooner [emphasis added]. The danger is that the East thinks that once it adopts a market system it can grow forever—that market efficiency will permit an ever expanding scale (Townsend 1993:290).*

Several Worlds, but Only One Earth: Global Climate Change

Existing geological and historical records indicate that the earth's climate has fluctuated naturally over time. Such fluctuations have in turn affected human societies in dramatic and unusual ways (see, e.g., Ingram and Farmer 1981; Intergovernmental Panel on Climate Change 1990, 1992; Rosa and Dietz 1998). Climate change contributed to such human tragedies as the Irish potato famine of 1845–1847, which resulted in mass starvation and outmigration (O'Grada 1989); the Dust Bowl of the 1930s in the U.S. Great Plains and the ensuing socioeconomic problems and outmigration (Gregory 1989; Worster 1979); and the drought and famine experienced by a number of sub-Saharan African countries in the last several decades (Timberlake 1988).

It is increasingly clear that humans are adding "greenhouse gases" (e.g., carbon dioxide, chloroflourocarbons or CFCs, methane, nitrous oxide, sulfur oxides, etc.) to the earth's atmosphere at rates that exceed the absorptive capacity of the atmosphere (Intergovernmental Panel on Climate Change 1996; Kerr 2000). These gases act like glass in a parked automobile; the glass allows most of the sun's energy to reach the interior of the car but prevents heat from escaping back into space. On a sunny day, the interior of the car will be much warmer than the air outside. This phenomenon is referred to as the "greenhouse effect."

Increases in greenhouse gases are attributed to human industrial and agricultural activities, including the burning of fossil fuels and increased use of CFCs in various production processes, as well as such methane- and nitrous oxide-producing agricultural activities as nitrogen fertilizer use, cattle raising, and rice cultivation. The problem is compounded by deforestation, which reduces the ability of the earth to remove carbon dioxide through photosynthesis and adds substantial amounts of carbon dioxide to the atmosphere through burning and natural decay (Intergovernmental Panel on Climate Change 1990, 1992).

Greenhouse gases are the effluents of affluence (industrial production and automobiles) and poverty (the burning of vegetation, farming of paddy rice, which both release methane). Both the developed and less developed countries are contributing to the problem (Dietz and Rosa 1997), though several developed countries are contributing more than their fair share (Redclift and Sage 1998; see also Roberts and Grimes 1997). Estimates indicate that the United States contributed approximately 18 percent of the total greenhouse gases added to the earth's atmosphere in the late 1980s and early 1990s, while the Soviet Union (13.5%), China (9.1%), Japan (4.7%), India (4.7), Brazil (3.9%), and Germany (3.4%) combined contributed slightly more than 39 percent of the total greenhouse gases added during this period (Intergovernmental Panel on Climate Change 1990).

The global average surface temperature has warmed by 0.5 to 0.6 degrees Celsius over the past century (Intergovernmental Panel on Climate Change 1996; National Research Council 2000). The degree to which the earth's temperature has increased over the past century and will increase as a result of human generated greenhouse gases is somewhat uncertain. But there is a very strong consensus among the world's leading experts that the process has begun (Intergovernmental Panel on Climate Change

1996; Kerr 1999; National Research Council 2000). The Intergovernmental Panel on Climate Change (a group of distinguished scientists assembled by the World Meteorological Organization and the United Nations' Environmental Programme) believes that the earth's average temperature will increase anywhere from 1.0 to 4.5 degrees Celsius by the year 2100 (Intergovernmental Panel on Climate Change 1996; Kerr 1999). Other estimates are even higher.

You may wonder why there is so much concern about an increase of only a few degrees. Such a change is the average global temperature change and does not reflect the regional variations that would result. Actually, such average changes could have dramatic regional effects. Historian Barbara Tuchman's (1978:24) description of the Little Ice Age in *A Distant Mirror* conveys a sense of the impact that a change of only a few degrees in temperature can make:

> *A physical chill settled on the 14th Century at its very start, initiating the miseries to come. The Baltic Sea froze over twice, in 1303 and 1306–7; years followed of unreasonable cold, storms and rains, and a rise in the level of the Caspian Sea. Contemporaries could not have known that it was the onset of what has since been recognized as the Little Ice Age, caused by an advance of polar and alpine glaciers and lasting until about 1700. Nor were they yet aware that, owing to the climatic change, communication with Greenland was gradually being lost, that the Norse settlements there were being extinguished, that cultivation of grain was disappearing from Iceland and being severely reduced in Scandinavia. But they could feel the colder weather, and mark with fear its result: a shorter growing season.*

The consequences (understood in terms of the effects and the magnitude and timing

of such effects) of global warming are uncertain. Several skeptical economists (Mendelsohn and Neuman 1999; Nordhaus
1992, 1994) have applied traditional economic reasoning to the problem of global
warming and concluded that the consequences will be minimal and some suggest
the consequences will be positive. Despite
the scientific uncertainties and the claims of
skeptical economists and other "greenhouse
dissenters" (e.g., Bailey 1993: Chapter 9;
Easterbrook 1995; Ray 1990, 1993), there is
strong scientific consensus that the surface
temperature of the earth has increased due
to human activities and that the consequences of global warming will be substantial for humans, nonhumans, and natural
ecosystems (Intergovernmental Panel on
Climate Change 1996; Melillo 1999; Silver
and Defries 1990; see also National Research Council 2000). Likely consequences
of global warming include:

- Rising sea levels resulting from increased temperatures and the melting
  of alpine glaciers and polar ice caps. The
  potential impacts (including flooding,
  salination of fresh waters, and coastal
  erosion) on human populations are
  staggering because a large human population resides along the coastlines
  throughout the world (Mintzer 1992;
  Silver and Defries 1990:90–102).
- Increased temperatures will affect
  storm patterns and possibly even increase weather-related disasters such as
  hurricanes (Mintzer 1992).
- Changes in jet streams, prevailing
  winds, and ocean currents could alter
  the distribution of rainfall in many areas, making some areas drier and others
  wetter. The U.S. Great Plains is one
  region that is expected to get drier,
  leading to a dramatic reduction in crop

production in an already dry region and
questions about the viability of many
rural communities in the area (Glantz
and Ausubel 1988; Opie 1993). Other
hard-hit areas are parts of the Sahel,
the Middle East, the steppes of Asia and
the former Soviet Union, and Australia.
These areas (which are all major grain
producers) will be increasingly subject
to degradation through soil erosion and
fire (Silver and DeFries 1990:78–89).
Such changes would cause severe disruptions in agricultural production, creating refugees and starvation, as well as
increasing political conflict between
and within nations (Homer-Dixon et al.
1999).

- Increased temperatures and changes in
  precipitation patterns will also reduce
  the global range of forests because they
  cannot disperse quickly enough to pursue their optimal climatic conditions
  (Melillo 1999; Peters and Lovejoy 1992;
  Wilson 1992).
- Rapidly shifting, shrinking, and disap-
  pearing habitats would surpass the capacity of many animal species to adapt
  and survive, resulting in increased rates
  of plant and animal extinction (Peters
  and Lovejoy 1992; Wilson 1992).
- Human morbidity and mortality will
  rise because of heat stress and increased
  incidence of infectious and other diseases. Temperature change will affect
  the range and life cycle of plants, animals, insects, bacteria, and viruses, resulting in increased geographic ranges
  for certain infectious diseases (including malaria, river blindness, yellow
  fever, sleeping sickness, etc.) and increased viral traffic across species or the
  transfer of animal diseases to humans
  or vice versa (Epstein 1995; Morse
  1993; see also Daszak et al. 2000).

Although critical scientific uncertainties exist, there is reason to believe that the two other environmental problems discussed above will be influenced dramatically by changes in the earth's temperature. Toxic pollution at the local level in the United States through increased use of pesticides and fertilizers might increase if various pests gain an advantage from temperature changes. Climate change in the former Soviet Union is likely to contribute to the many environmental problems of the area. Finally, many of the consequences associated with global climate change are not going to be distributed equitably: Some areas and countries will suffer, while others will benefit (Kasperson and Dow 1991). The LDCs are more vulnerable to climate change than their developed counterparts, because they have fewer resources to expend in dealing with the negative consequences posed by climate change (Redclift and Sage 1998). The end result of this process is an increased probability of conflict within and between countries over resource scarcities (see, e.g., Homer-Dixon 1999).

THINKING MORE DEEPLY ABOUT ENVIRONMENTAL PROBLEMS[2]

What causes environmental problems of the sort outlined above? Why are people so concerned with them? How do humans respond to them? What can we do about them? Scholars working at the intersection between the social and environmental sciences are addressing these questions and creating what Stern (1993) has called "the second environmental science," and others call the "new human ecology" or the "new ecological paradigm" (Dunlap 1997; Dunlap and Catton 1994). It is the study of the interrelationships between humans and their biological and physical environment.

Figure 1.1 provides a conceptual base for understanding such interrelationships. It sketches the links between humans and their environment. Like all such diagrams it oversimplifies a complex reality. It should not be taken as a model that accurately describes the world, but as a conceptual device that helps us think through the human causes of environmental problems and the responses humans make to those problems, as well as provide a basis for thinking about possible solutions.

Let's start at the top of the diagram. The two boxes at 12 o'clock in the top center ("Sources of Change within and between Environmental Systems" and "Environmental Systems") are linked to indicate an important point: The environment would change even if there were no humans on Earth. We must be aware of this if we want

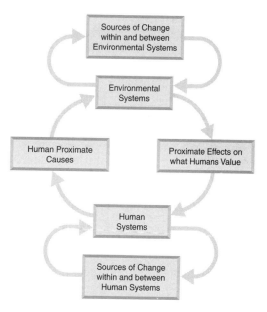

FIGURE 1.1   Relationship between Human and Environmental Systems

Adapted from Stern et al. (1992:34).

to understand the role played by humans in the creation of environmental problems. For example, a critical issue in the study of climate change is separating the effects of natural changes from changes caused by humans (Intergovernmental Panel on Climate Change 1996; National Research Council 2000). As discussed earlier, human activities release very large amounts of "greenhouse gases," chemicals that tend to trap heat in the atmosphere and cause the earth's climate to grow warmer. But it is possible that the amount of energy being emitted by the sun is changing over time. If so, such changes in solar radiation will also affect the climate. Volcanoes and other natural processes release both greenhouse gases that increase the earth's temperature and dust particles that, in the short run at least, cool the Earth.

When dealing with environmental problems we often slip into a shorthand by using terms such as "nature," "natural processes," or "ecological balance." There is no doubt that human activities are producing massive changes in ecosystems throughout the world, and in the biosphere itself (Meyer 1996; Turner et al. 1990). But such massive changes have happened in the past, long before humans evolved from our primate forbearers. What is critical about the current situation is not that we are disturbing a pristine and constant natural world that would be in perfect harmony were it not for humans. Rather, there are two causes for concern. The first is that we are producing changes at a pace that seems unparalleled in the history of the planet (McNeill 2000; Stern et al. 1992). For example, the pace of extinctions going on at present is probably faster than the extinction of the dinosaurs or any other major transformation in the history of life on earth (Sala et al. 2000; Swanson 1995; Wilson 1992).

The second, related cause for concern is described in the next box in the diagram, moving clockwise ("Proximate Effects on What Humans Value"). The environmental changes that humans cause are affecting things we value. It is unlikely that human activity will lead to the extinction of all life on earth. Evolutionary processes will continue, bur we are destroying some of the things we value most. We are threatening our own health, the ability of ecosystems to support a reasonable quality of human life, and the diversity and complexity of life that shares the planet with us (McNeill 2000; National Research Council 1999; Turner et al. 1990; Wilson 1992). The biosphere will persist whatever we do, but the quality of human life may not.

There is a reason the box is labelled "Effects on Things *Humans Value*" rather than "important things," "critical environmental processes," or some other term that may seem more scientific. Concentrating on "things humans value" emphasizes people's perceptions, which may differ from reality as described by environmental science. Perceptions may highlight some things and ignore others. Much of the concern about endangered species is focused on large, exotic species that are aesthetically pleasing. The plight of whales, elephants, and gorillas attracts attention, while threats to the existence of various species of grasses, frogs, or fungi do not. Human perceptions (what sociologists like to call the "social construction of reality") is part of human responses to environmental problems. But while we emphasize human values, there is a strong argument that animals, plants, ecosystems, and the biosphere have a value of their own, whether or not humans think them important or make use of them (Nash 1989).

The bottom two boxes ("Sources of Change within and between Human Systems" and "Human Systems") suggest that not all social change is driven by environmental change. Indeed, until recently most social scientists would have argued that *all* important social change is generated within and between human systems, that the environment has little effect on us (see, e.g., Dunlap 1997; Dunlap and Catton 1994; Foster 1999; Murphy 1995). (This issue will be taken up in much greater detail in Chapter 2.) The point to draw from this pair of boxes is that in understanding how people respond to environmental change and what they do to cause environmental problems, we must take account of the changes in human systems that are occurring independently of the physical and biological environment. For example, some people argue we must preserve tropical rain forests because of the rich library of genetic information that is preserved in the diversity of plant and animal species found there (Swanson 1995; Wilson 1992). They argue that this genetic information may be among the most valuable natural resources available to us, a basis for future curative drugs, new foods, and other great benefits. But others suggest that technological progress will soon make it possible to reengineer DNA molecules so as to create whatever genes we need. We will no longer need the library (Easterbrook 1995:593–598). In other words, changes in human systems can affect the values we assign to the physical and biological environment.

A more positive example is the decline in commercial whaling from the nineteenth century to the twentieth. The whaling industry was driven by the use of whale oil for household lighting and by the use of whalebone (baleen) for corsets. The development of gas and electrical lighting reduced the demand for whale oil for illumination. The development of cellulose and other plastics reduced the demand for whalebone in corsets. Although some whaling continued, the economic value of products from whales plummeted, and whaling was transformed from a central industry in many regions of the world to a cruel and unnecessary anachronism.

Continuing around the inner circle, we can distinguish proximate causes of environmental change from all the other actions of human systems. Proximate causes are the actual physical activities that affect the environment: burning fossil fuels, cutting down trees, dumping toxic substances into a river. One of the challenges for environmental science is to identify and monitor the proximate causes of environmental problems. The environmental movement has grown substantially since the late 1960s in part because we have learned much more about proximate causes (Hays 1987): the effects of pesticides on most animal species, including humans; the effects of CFCs on the protective ozone layer; the prevalence of high levels of radioactive radon in many homes; and so on.

The ecological anthropologist Andrew Vayda (1988) has argued that looking at the proximate causes is the best way to examine environmental problems. If you want to understand the loss of tropical forests, go to the forests and see who is cutting trees and try to understand why. Certainly much important work needs to be done along these lines. This would include the identification of who is doing what and what effect it has on the environment. But as Vayda notes, we cannot stop there. It is important to understand what lies behind proximate causes: Why are those people cutting the trees? Why did we develop and continue to use pesticides and CFCs? Answers to these questions can be complex and require careful thought. There is usually a commonsense answer, but the commonsense answer is usually only half the truth. For example, the commonsense answer we often hear about the causes of tropical deforestation is that poor people cut trees to clear land for crops. But in Kalimantan, Vayda (1988) and his colleagues found that most cutting was done under contract to affluent people in the cities, who were selling the logs on the international timber market. So the proximate cause of deforestation in Kalimantan was forestry, but that was driven by the demand for tropical wood in the richer nations of the world-system.

CODA

Environmental problems occur when the stock of physical resources is depleted or degraded and the absorptive capacity of natural sinks is exceeded. These problems have adverse effects on human health and economic welfare and other species, as well as disrupt the overall integrity of ecosystems, crucial life-support processes, and the larger biosphere. Such problems are pervasive and they are increasingly global in nature. What causes environmental problems? Why are people concerned with environmental problems? How do humans respond to environmental problems? What can we do about environmental problems? The authors of the remaining ten chapters of the reader address these important questions in some detail.

ENDNOTES

1. Several commentators suggest that the definition of environmental problems is not as clear-cut as suggested here. They maintain that the selection of environmental problems is a social process in which cultural, political, economic, and related factors influence definitions (see, e.g.,

the discussions of Bird [1987], Douglas and Wildavsky [1982], Hannigan [1995], Thompson et al. [1990], Yearley [1991]). While I acknowledge that there is an element of truth to the view that environmental and other types of social problems are socially constructed, I embrace a critical-realist position that maintains that environmental problems have a basis in physical reality that is independent of human construction. The more important question seems to center on defining the point at which pollution and depletion become problems. This, of course, is a normative question.

2. The last section of this chapter ("Thinking More Deeply about Environmental Problems") draws extensively from an earlier unpublished manuscript coauthored with Tom Dietz.

REFERENCES

Ames, Bruce, Renae Magaw, and Louis Swirsky Gold. 1987. "Ranking Possible Carcinogenic Hazards." *Science* 236:271–277.

Bailey, Ronald. 1993. *Eco-Scam: The False Prophets of Ecological Apocalypse.* New York: St. Martin's Press.

———, editor. 1995. *The True State of the Planet.* New York: Harper-Perennial.

———, editor. 2000. *Earth Report 2000.* New York: McGraw-Hill.

Bird, Elizabeth Ann R. 1987. "The Social Construction of Nature: Theoretical Approaches to the History of Environmental Problems." *Environmental Review* 11:255–264.

Brown, Lester R., editor. 2000. *State of the World, 2000.* New York: W. W. Norton.

Brown, Phil and Edwin J. Mikkelsen. 1997. *No Safe Place: Toxic Waste, Leukemia, and Community Action.* (Revised Edition.) Berkeley: University of California Press.

Bryant, Bunyan, editor. 1995. *Environmental Justice: Issues, Policies, and Solutions.* Washington, D.C.: Island Press.

Bryant, Bunyan and Paul Mohai, editors. 1992. *Race and the Incidence of Environmental Hazards: A Time for Discourse.* Boulder, CO: Westview Press.

Bullard, Robert D. 1994a. *Dumping in Dixie: Race, Class, and Environmental Quality.* (Second Edition.) Boulder, CO: Westview Press.

Bullard, Robert D., editor. 1994b. *Unequal Justice: Environmental Justice and Communities of Color.* San Francisco, CA: Sierra Book Club.

Bunker, Stephen. 1985. *Underdeveloping the Amazon: Extraction, Unequal Exchange, and the Failure of the Modern State.* Urbana: University of Illinois Press.

Camacho, David E., editor. 1998. *Environmental Injustices, Political Struggles.* Durham, NC: Duke University Press.

Carson, Rachel. 1962. *Silent Spring.* Boston: Houghton Mifflin.

Catton, Jr., William R. 1980. *Overshoot: The Ecological Basis of Revolutionary Change.* Urbana, IL: University of Illinois Press.

Catton, Jr., William R., Gerhard Lenski, and Frederick H. Buttel. 1984. "To What Degree Is a Social System Dependent on Its Resource Base?" Pp. 165–186 in *The Social Fabric: Dimensions and Issues,* edited by James Short. Beverly Hills, CA: Sage.

Cockerham, William C. 1999. *Health and Social Change in Russia and Eastern Europe.* New York: Routledge.

Cohen, Maurie J. 1997. "The Spatial Distribution of Toxic Chemical Emissions: Implications for Nonmetropolitan Areas." *Society and Natural Resources* 10:17–41.

Commoner, Barry. 1990. *Making Peace with the Planet.* New York: Pantheon Books.

Conquest, Robert. 1986. *The Harvest of Sorrow: Soviet Collectivization and the Terror-Famine.* New York: Oxford University Press.

———. 1990. *The Great Terror: A Reassessment.* New York: Oxford University Press.

———. 1999. *Reflections on a Ravaged Century.* New York: W. W. Norton.

Cook, Earl. 1976. *Man, Energy, Society.* San Francisco: W. H. Freeman.

Cottrell, W. Fred. 1970/1955. *Energy and Society.* Westport, CT: Greenwood Press.

Covello, Vincent T. and R. Scott Frey. 1990. "Technology-Based Environmental Health Risks in Developing Nations." *Technological Forecasting and Social Change* 37:159–179.

Daily, Gretchen C., editor. 1997. *Nature's Services: Societal Dependence on Natural Ecosystems.* Washington, D.C.: Island Press.

Daly, Herman. 1990. "Toward Some Operational Principles of Sustainable Development." *Ecological Economics* 2:1–6.

———. 1993. "Sustainable Growth: An Impossibility Theorem." Pp. 267–273 in *Valuing the Earth: Economics, Ecology, Ethics,* edited by Herman E. Daly and Kenneth N. Townsend. Cambridge, MA: MIT Press.

———. 1996. *Beyond Growth: The Economics of Sustainable Development.* Boston: Beacon Press.

Daniels, Glynis and Samantha Friedman. 1999. "Spatial Inequality and the Distribution of Industrial Toxic Releases: Evidence from the 1990 TRI." *Social Science Quarterly* 80:244–262.

Daszak, Peter, Andrew A. Cunningham, and Alex D. Hyatt. 2000. "Emerging Infectious Diseases of Wildlife—Threats to Biodiversity and Human Health." *Science* 287 (21 January):443–449.

Dietz, Thomas and Eugene A. Rosa. 1997. "Effects of Population and Affluence on CO_2 Emissions." *Proceedings of the National Academy of Sciences, USA* 94:175–179.

Douglas, Mary and Aaron Wildavsky. 1982. *Risk and Culture: An Essay on the Selection of Technical and Environmental Dangers.* Berkeley: University of California Press.

Dryzek, John S. 1987. *Rational Ecology: Environment and Political Economy.* Oxford: Basil Blackwell.

Dunlap, Riley. 1997. "The Evolution of Environmental Sociology: A Brief History and Assessment of the American Experience." Pp. 21–39 in *The International Handbook of Environmental Sociology,* edited by Michael Redclift and Graham Woodgate. Cheltenham, UK: Edward Elgar.

Dunlap, Riley E. and William R. Catton. 1994. "Struggling with Human Exemptionalism: The Rise, Decline and Revitalization of Environmental Sociology." *American Sociologist* 25 (Spring):5–30.

Easterbrook, Gregg. 1995. *A Moment on Earth: The Coming Age of Environmental Optimism.* New York: Viking.

Edelstein, Michael. 1988. *Contaminated Communities: The Social and Psychological Impacts of Residential Toxic Exposure.* Boulder, CO: Westview Press.

Ehrlich, Paul R. and Anne H. Ehrlich. 1990. *The Population Explosion.* New York: Simon and Schuster.

Ehrlich, Paul R., Anne H. Ehrlich, and John P. Holdren. 1977. *Ecoscience: Population, Resources, Environment.* San Francisco: Freeman.

Epstein, Paul R. 1995. "Emerging Diseases and Ecosystem Instability: New Threats to Public Health." *American Journal of Public Health* 85:168–172.

Feshbach, Murray. 1995. *Ecological Disaster: Cleaning Up the Hidden Legacy of the Soviet Regime.* New York: Twentieth Century Fund.

Feshbach, Murray and Alfred Friendly, Jr. 1992. *Ecocide in the USSR: Health and Nature Under Siege.* New York: Basic Books.

Foster, John Bellamy. 1999. "Marx's Theory of Metabolic Rift: Classical Foundations for Environmental Sociology." *American Journal of Sociology* 105:366–405.

Freudenburg, William R. 1992. "Addictive Economies: Extractive Industries and Vulnerable Localities in a Changing World Economy." *Rural Sociology* 57:305–332.

Frey, R. Scott. 1995. "The International Traffic in Pesticides." *Technological Forecasting and Social Change* 50:151–169.

———. 1997. "The International Traffic in Tobacco." *Third World Quarterly* 18:303–319.

———. 1998. "The Hazardous Waste Stream in the World-System." Pp. 84–103 in *Space and Transport in the World-System,* edited by Paul Ciccantell and Stephen G. Bunker. Westport, CT: Greenwood Press.

———. 1999. "The Migration of Hazardous Industries to the *Maquiladora* Centers of Northern Mexico." Paper presented at the annual meeting of the American Sociological Association, Chicago, IL.

Glantz, Michael H. and Jesse H. Ausubel. 1988. "Impact Assessment by Analogy: Comparing the Impacts of the Ogallala Aquifer Depletion and CO2-Induced Climate Change." Pp. 113–142 in *Societal Responses to Regional Climate Change: Forecasting by Analogy,* edited

by Michael H. Glantz. Boulder, CO: Westview Press.

Gregory, James N. 1989. *American Exodus: The Dust Bowl Migration and Okie Culture in California.* New York: Oxford University Press.

Griffith, Jack, Robert C. Duncan, Wilson B. Riggan, and Alvin C. Pellom. 1989. "Cancer Mortality in U.S. Counties with Hazardous Waste Sites and Ground Water Pollution." *Archives of Environmental Health* 44:69–74.

Hamilton, James T. and W. Viscusi. 1999. *Calculating Risks?: The Spatial and Political Dimensions of Hazardous Waste Policy.* Cambridge, MA: MIT Press.

Hannigan, John A. 1995. *Environmental Sociology: A Social Constructionist Perspective.* London: Routledge.

Hardin, Garret. 1993. *Living within Limits: Ecology, Economics, and Population Taboos.* New York: Oxford University Press.

Hays, Samuel P. 1987. *Beauty, Health, and Permanence: Environmental Politics in the United States, 1955–1985.* New York: Cambridge University Press.

Homer-Dixon, Thomas F. 1999. *Environment, Scarcity, and Violence.* Princeton, NJ: Princeton University Press.

Ingram, M. J. and G. Farmer. 1981. *Climate and History: Studies on Past Climate and Their Impact on Man.* Cambridge, UK: Cambridge University Press.

Intergovernmental Panel on Climate Change. 1990. *Climate Change: The IPCC Scientific Assessment,* edited by G. J. Jenkins and J. J. Ephramus. Cambridge, UK: Cambridge University Press.

———. 1992. *Climate Change, 1992,* edited by J. T. Houghton, B. A. Callander, and S. K. Varney. Cambridge, UK: Cambridge University Press.

———. 1996. *Climate Change 1995,* edited by J. T. Houghton et al. Cambridge, UK: Cambridge University Press.

Kasperson, Roger E. and Kirstin M. Dow. 1991. "Developmental and Geographic Equity in Global Environmental Change." *Evaluation Review* 15:149–171.

Kerr, Richard A. 2000. "Draft Report Affirms Human Influence." *Science* 288:589–590.

Kohlhase, Janet E. 1991. "The Impact of Toxic Waste Sites on Housing Values." *Journal of Urban Economics* 30:1–26.

Komarov, Boris. 1980. *The Destruction of Nature in the Soviet Union.* White Plains, NY: M. E. Sharpe.

Markham, Adam. 1994. *A Brief History of Pollution.* London: Earthscan.

McDuffie, Helen H., James A. Dosman, Karen M. Semchuk, Stephen A. Olenchock, and Ambikapakan Senthilselvan, editors. 1995. *Agricultural Health and Safety: Workplace, Environment, Stability.* Boca Raton, FL: CRC Press.

McNeill, J. R. 2000. *Something New Under the Sun: An Environmental History of the Twentieth-Century World.* New York: W. W. Norton.

Meadows, Donella H., Dennis L. Meadows, and Jorgen Randers. 1992. *Beyond the Limits: Confronting Global Collapse, Envisioning a Sustainable Future.* Post Mills, VT: Chelsea Green.

Melillo, Jerry M. 1999. "Warm, Warm on the Range." *Science* 283 (8 January):183–184.

Mendelsohn, Robert and James E. Neumann, editors. 1999. *The Impact of Climate Change on the United States Economy.* New York: Cambridge University Press.

Meyer, William B. 1996. *Human Impact on the Earth.* New York: Cambridge University Press.

Mintzer, Irving M., editor. 1992. *Confronting Global Climate Change: Risks, Implications, and Responses.* New York: Cambridge University Press.

Morse, Stephen S. 1993. *Emerging Viruses.* New York: Oxford University Press.

Murphy, Raymond. 1995. "Sociology as if Nature Did Not Matter: An Ecological Critique." *British Journal of Sociology* 46:688–707.

Nash, Roderick Frazier. 1989. *The Rights of Nature: A History of Environmental Ethics.* Madison: University of Wisconsin Press.

National Research Council. 1989. *Alternative Agriculture.* Washington, D.C.: National Academy Press.

———. 1991. *Environmental Epidemiology: Public Health and Hazardous Wastes.* Washington, D.C.: National Academy Press.

———. 1999. *Our Common Journey: A Transition toward Sustainability.* Washington, D.C.: National Academy Press.

———. 2000. *Reconciling Observations of Global Temperature.* Washington, D.C.: National Academy Press.

Nordhaus, William D. 1992. "An Optimal Transition Path for Controlling Greenhouse Gases." *Science* 258:1315–1319.

———. 1994. *Managing the Global Commons: The Economics of Climate Change.* Cambridge, MA: MIT Press.

O'Grada, Cormac. 1989. *The Great Irish Potato Famine.* Dublin: Gill and Macmillan.

Opie, John. 1993. *Ogallala: Water for a Dry Land.* Lincoln: University of Nebraska Press.

Peters, Robert L. and Thomas E. Lovejoy. 1992. *Global Warming and Biological Diversity.* New Haven, CT: Yale University Press.

Peterson, D. J. 1993. *Troubled Lands: The Legacy of Soviet Environmental Destruction.* Boulder, CO: Westview Press.

Pimentel, David, C. Harvey, P. Resosudarmo, K. Sinclair, D. Kurtz, M. McNair, S. Crist, L. Shpritz, L. Fitton, R. Saffouri, and R. Blair. 1995. "Environmental and Economic Costs of Soil Erosion and Conservation Benefits." *Science* 267:1117–1123.

Ponting, Clive. 1991. *A Green History of the World: The Environment and the Collapse of Great Civilizations.* New York: Penguin Books.

Pryde, Philip R. 1991. *Environmental Management in the Soviet Union.* Cambridge: Cambridge University Press.

Ray, Dixy Lee, with Lou Guzzon. 1990. *Trashing the Planet.* Chicago: Regnery Gateway.

———. 1993. *Environmental Overkill: What Ever Happened to Common Sense.* New York: Harper Perennial.

Redclift, Michael and Colin Sage. 1998. "Global Environmental Change and Global Inequality: North/South Perspectives." *International Sociology* 13:499–516.

Redman, Charles L. 1999. *Human Impact on Ancient Environments.* Tucson: University of Arizona Press.

Rees, Judith. 1990. *Natural Resources: Allocation, Economics, and Policy.* (Second Edition.) London: Routledge.

Rifkin, Jeremy. 1992. *Beyond Beef: The Rise and Fall of Cattle Culture.* New York: Dutton Books.

Roberts, J. Timmons and Peter E. Grimes. 1997. "Carbon Intensity and Economic Development 1962–91: A Brief Exploration of the Environmental Kuznets Curve." *World Development* 25:191–198.

Rosa, Eugene A. and Thomas Dietz. 1998. "Climate Change and Society: Speculation, Construction and Scientific Investigation." *International Sociology* 13:421–455.

Sala, Osvaldo et al. 2000. "Global Biodiversity Scenarios for the Year 2100." *Science* 287:1770–1774.

Schnaiberg, Allan. 1980. *The Environment: From Surplus to Scarcity.* New York: Oxford University Press.

Schnaiberg, Allan and Kenneth Alan Gould. 1994. *Environment and Society: The Enduring Conflict.* New York: St. Martin's Press.

Schreiber, Helmut. 1991. "The Threat from Environmental Destruction in Eastern Europe." *Journal of International Affairs* 44:359–391.

Shrader-Frechette, K. S. 1993. *Burying Uncertainty: Risk and the Case against Geological Disposal of Nuclear Waste.* Berkeley: University of California Press.

Shulman, Seth. 1992. *The Threat at Home: Confronting the Toxic Legacy of the U.S. Military.* Boston: Beacon Press.

Silver, Cheryl Simon and Ruth S. DeFries. 1990. *One Earth, One Future: Our Changing Global Environment.* Washington, D.C.: National Academy Press.

Simon, Julian. 1981. *The Ultimate Resource.* Princeton, NJ: Princeton University Press.

Simon, Julian and Herman Kahn, editors. 1984. *The Resourceful Earth: A Response to Global 2000.* New York: Basil Blackwell.

Stern, Paul C. 1993. "The Second Environmental Science: Human–Environment Interactions." *Science* 260:1897–1899.

Stern, P. C., O. R. Young, and D. Druckman, editors. 1992. *Global Environmental Change: Understanding the Human Dimensions.* Washington, D.C.: National Academy Press.

Swanson, Paul C., editor. 1995. *The Economics and Ecology of Biodiversity Decline.* New York: Cambridge University Press.

Thompson, Michael, Richard Ellis, and Aaron Wildavsky. 1990. *Cultural Theory.* Boulder, CO: Westview Press.

Timberlake, Lloyd. 1988. *Africa in Crisis: The Causes, the Cures of Environmental Bankruptcy.* London: Earthscan.

Townsend, Kenneth N. 1993. "Steady-State Economies and the Command Economy." Pp. 275–296 in *Valuing the Earth: Economics, Ecology, and Ethics,* edited by Herman K. Daly and Kenneth N. Townsend. Cambridge, MA: MIT Press.

Tuchman, Barbara W. 1978. *A Distant Mirror: The Calamitous Fourteenth Century.* New York: Knopf.

Turner, B. L., H. W. C. Clark, R. W. Kates, J. F. Richards, J. T. Mathews, and W. B. Meyer, editors. 1990. *The Earth as Transformed by Human Action.* Cambridge: Cambridge University Press.

U.S. Environmental Protection Agency. 1987. *Unfinished Business: A Comparative Assessment of Environmental Problems.* Washington, D.C.: Environmental Protection Agency.

———. 1990. *Reducing Risk: Setting Priorities and Strategies for Environmental Protection.* Washington, D.C.: Environmental Protection Agency.

———. 1991. *Toxics in the Community: National and Local Perspectives.* Washington, D.C.: Government Printing Office.

Vayda, Andrew P. 1988. "Actions and Consequences as Objects of Explanation in Human Ecology." Pp 9–18 in *Human Ecology: Research and Applications,* edited by Richard J. Borden, Jamien Jacobs, and Gerald L. Young. College Park, MD: Society for Human Ecology.

Vernadsky, Vlaidimir. 1945. "The Biosphere and Noosphere." *American Scientist* 33 (January):1–12.

———. 1986/1926. *The Biosphere.* Oracle, AZ: Synergetic Press.

Ward, M. H., S. H. Zahm, D. D. Weisenburger, K. P. Cantor, R. C. Saal, and A. Blair. 1995. "Diet and Drinking Water Source: Association with Non-Hodgkin's Lymphoma in Eastern Nebraska." Pp. 143–150 in *Agricultural*

Health and Safety: Workplace, Environment, Sustainability, edited by Helen H. McDuffie, James A. Dosman, Karen M. Semchuk, Stephen A. Olenchock, and Ambikaipakan Senthilselvan. Boca Raton, FL: CRC.

Weiner, Douglas R. 1988. *Models of Nature: Ecology, Conservation, and Cultural Revolution in Soviet Russia.* Bloomington: Indiana University Press.

Wilson, E. O. 1992. *The Diversity of Life.* Cambridge, MA: Harvard University Press.

Worster, Donald. 1979. *Dust Bowl: The Southern Plains in the 1930s.* New York: Oxford University Press.

Yearley, Steven. 1991. *The Green Case: A Sociology of Environmental Issues: Arguments and Politics.* London: Harper-Collins.

Chapter 2

Environmental Sociology:
Past, Present, and Back to the Future

2. Sociology as If Nature Did Not Matter: An Ecological Critique*

RAYMOND MURPHY

The social ecologist Bookchin (1987: 72) argues convincingly that

> the view we hold of the natural world profoundly shapes the image we develop of the social worlds, even as we assert the 'supremacy' and 'autonomy' of culture over nature.

His argument applies with force to sociology. The assumptions made by sociologists about the natural world have profoundly shaped Sociology itself.

PRE-ECOLOGICAL SOCIOLOGY: SOCIOLOGY AS IF NATURE DID NOT MATTER

Berger and Luckmann (1967: 1) summarized the core argument of their influential book *The Social Construction of Reality* as follows.

> The basic contentions of the argument of this book are implicit in its title and subtitle, namely, that reality is socially constructed and that the sociology of knowledge must analyse the processes in which this occurs.... It will be enough, for our purposes, to define 'reality' as a quality appertaining to phenomena that we recognize as having a being independent of our own volition (we cannot 'wish them away').

In short, phenomena that we recognize as beyond being 'wished away' are socially constructed. Nature is conspicuous by its absence in this sociological construction.

This thesis is based on the following assumptions:

> the human organism manifests an immense plasticity in its response to the environmental forces at work on it.... While it is possible to say that man has a nature, it is more significant to say that man constructs his own nature, or more simply, that man produces himself. (Bergar and Luckmann 1967: 48–9)

This in turn is based on the premise of a radical discontinuity between humans and non-human animals.

> It refers to the biologically fixed character of their [non-human animals] relationship to the environment, even if geographical variation is introduced. In this sense, all non-human animals, as species and as individuals, live in closed worlds whose structures are predetermined by the biological equipment of the several animal species. By contrast, man's relationship to his environment is characterized by world-openness. (Bergar and Luckmann 1967: 47)

*Reprinted by permission of *Routledge* Volume no. 46 Issue no. 4 December 1995.

27

Catton and Dunlap (1978: 41–9) concluded that sociology has been based on the assumption that the exceptional traits of humans have rendered them exempt from the constraints of nature. For example, Lipset (1979: 1–35) and Nisbet (1979: 2–6, 55) willfully neglected ecological limits and Bell (1977: 13–26) claimed that limits to growth are social not ecological.

The search for intelligible connections between the two 'sides' of human nature—between what we share with other animals, and, what makes us distinctive—was to be replaced by a view of human nature as constituted by the latter. (Benton 1991: 11)

This supports Bookchin's (1987: 51) conclusion that 'sociology sees itself as the analysis of "man's" ascent from "animality" ...these self-definitions...[try to] impart a unique autonomy to cultural development and social evolution'. And try they do. In the epistemology of the social construction of knowledge,

truth and objectivity are seen as nothing but human products and man rather than Nature is seen as the ultimate author of 'knowledge' and 'reality'. Any attempt to appeal to an external 'reality' in order to support claims for the superiority of one way of seeing over another is dismissed as ideological'. (Whitty 1977: 37)

Prus (1990: 356) argues 'that there are as many varieties of reality as might be experienced by people'. Baldus (1990: 470) suggests that this 'sociology assumes that reality exists only in human experience'. Fox (1991: 23–4) observed that

sociology has been suspicious of anything claiming to be grounded in nature, and its positioning has been in direct opposition to any claims that the natural has influence over human relations.... Sociology typically 'brackets' the natural world.... Either 'nature' is asserted to be ineffectual in influencing social relations...[or] it is asserted that basically the natural world is unchanging.

Hence Sessions (1985: 255) concludes that

the dominant trend of the academic social sciences (especially psychology and sociology) have by-and-large both reinforced anthropocentrism and promoted a view of humans as being malleable and totally conditioned by the social environment.

The classical illustration of the argument for ignoring nature, presented in sociology textbooks (Spector and Kitsuse 1977: 43), is the case of marijuana. In the USA, marijuana was officially classified as dangerous and addictive in the 1930s, but was no longer classified as addictive in the 1960s. This changing classification cannot be explained by the chemical nature of marijuana, since it did not change, and can only be explained by changing notions of addiction and political strategies and tactics.

An area that, one would think, would deal with the relationship between social action and the processes of nature is that of the sociology of science. Yet most contemporary studies in the sociology of science have focused solely on how scientific knowledge is socially constructed and neglected the role of nature as a source of that knowledge (see Murphy 1994a: Chapter 9 and Murphy 1994b).

Even the sociology of environmental issues has often not investigated the relationship between the processes of nature and social action. Instead much of it has interpreted environmental issues as socially constructed 'social scares' and has deflected attention away from their connection to changes in ecosystems (Dunlap and Catton 1994a). Where the social—natural relationship has been discussed, it has been in terms of unidirectional causality from the social to the natural.

There may have been a time when human ecological systems were embedded in natural ecosystems; today the opposite is the case: all existing natural ecosystems are embedded in the global human ecological system. (Carlo Jaeger quoted in Brulle and Dietz 1993: 2)

AN ECOLOGICAL CRITIQUE OF SOCIOLOGY AS IF NATURE DID NOT MATTER

These postulates are far removed from an ecological emphasis on what humans share with other forms of life (Devall and Sessions 1985; Sale 1988: 670–5; Ehrlich and Ehrlich 1983; Blea 1986: 13–4; Catton 1980; Naess 1988; Fox 1990), on the finite character of our planet as a stock of resources and sink for waste (Meadows *et al.* 1972; Ophuls 1977), on the requirements of a human-sustaining ecosystem (World Commission on Environment and Development 1987; Bookchin 1971, 1980, 1987; Commoner 1971; Dryzek 1987), and hence on the implasticity of the relationship between humans and their natural environment (Perrow 1984). The supposedly holistic discipline of sociology has been quite partial, abstracting social action out of its context within the processes of nature (Benton 1991).

Although social constructions are particularly important, focusing only on them results in theoretical myopia. The feminist Biehl (1991: 19) has now concluded that

in dissolving 'women and nature' into metaphors or subjective attributes, social-constructionist ecofeminists obscure both nonhuman nature and women's relationship to it.

The problem is greater than that of self-aggrandizing exaggeration of the social by sociologists. The exemptionalist emphasis on what distinguishes humans from other species obscures what we share—ecosystem-dependence—and this too is crucial for understanding social action (Catton and Dunlap 1978; Dunlap and Catton 1994a). Sociology as if nature did not matter mystifies what Benton (1991: 7) refers to as 'the causal importance of the *non-social* materials, objects and relations which fall within the spatial limits of human societies'. The assumption that the embeddedness of human society in nature was true only in the past is a false assumption. The mutual exclusiveness constructed by some sociologists—between human embeddedness in nature and nature's (or more accurately that infinitesimal fragment of it on planet Earth) growing embeddedness in social constructions—is equally false. Social constructions remain grounded in a dynamic ecological system, even as Earth's ecosystems become increasingly affected by human constructions. Human constructors who neglect the ecological system operating behind their backs do so at the risk of unintentional human self-destruction.

Sociological theory that deflects attention away from this part of reality, which cannot be reduced to a social construction but which interacts with social constructions, takes sociology in a misleading direction. Weber was well aware of this, and hence, despite his emphasis on values and agency, he did not propose a reductionism to the social. He held that 'culture was grounded in, even if not determined by, nature and to take the social out of the realm of natural causality altogether was to confuse the ideal and dogmatic formulations of jurists [and we might add, sociologists] with empirical reality' (Albrow 1990: 257).

Humans do reshape nature more than other species and thereby influence their own nature. Humans are, nevertheless, creatures of nature dependent on its processes, like other forms of life. By focusing on differences between humans and other animals, sociologists have lost sight of all that we share with them. For example, the social-construction-of-reality premise has, as its name indicates, been particularly one-sided. Constructivist sociologists have excluded nature in order to construct their purely social sense of reality.[1]

Woolgar (1983: 251–3) concludes that the marijuana illustration (paraphrased above) presented in sociology textbooks reveals a profound commitment to epistemological realism—the unchanging character of nature—that is hidden by proclamations of relativism. But a very different conclusion is warranted, namely, that this misleading illustration and others like it are used as rhetorical devices by sociologists to treat nature (in this case, marijuana) as a constant and therefore to ignore it. Sociologists have selected such examples in isolation in order to avoid the incorporation of nature into sociological theory. Had researchers used a comparative approach, for example comparing heroin with water, they would have been forced to conclude that the chemical nature of these two substances tends to affect notions of their addictive effect as well as the social construction of laws forbidding their ingestion. It is through rhetorical avoidance devices such as these that sociologists have constructed their sense of reality, one which excludes nature. Furthermore, selective illustrations of the unchanging character of nature have misled

sociologists into ignoring the dynamic character of nature.

Burns and Dietz (1992: 274) conclude that sociological indifference to the effects of nature, as well as the overbearing emphasis of contemporary sociology on agency, have left it unconvincing.

In the short run, deciding that lead in drinking water is harmless is within the scope of agency, but in the long run individual and collective actors who adopt such a rule tend to be at a strong disadvantage compared to those who believe otherwise, and it will be hard for the rule to persist.

Disadvantage to be sure, since proponents of such water who believe their own rhetoric and drink it will get confused or die off, leading to a shortage of proponents. This defect has rendered sociology indifferent and mute concerning important socio-environmental problems. Deconstructing particular representations of environmental problems has been the facile sociological substitute for solving such problems (Dunlap 1993).

People can have the erroneous conception, and even perception, that they will live forever in their bodily form. Such conceptions and perceptions tend to be extremely rare because they are tangibly contradicted by the processes of nature: all living organisms constructed by nature, including the human body, have a finite existence. Processes of nature influence perceptions and conceptions. Sociological theory that fails to incorporate this fundamental insight is a very partial theory indeed.

Sociology as if nature did not matter is theory in a vacuum, interactive and interpretive work having nothing to work with, on, or against. It is a sociological theory of Disneyworld: a synthetic world inhabited by artificial creatures, including humans, constructed by humans. It postulates all-powerful interpretation that creates what little reality it perceives. It is a contemporary variant of idealism, of the almighty role of ideas in history and of 'an idealist or dualist anthropocentrism' (Benton 1991: 18). Nature as a dynamic force has thereby been evacuated from sociology.

Humans only gradually become aware of the interaction of their constructions with nature's constructions. The depletion of the ozone layer was occurring before humans observed it. There might well be something now occurring in nature, including nature's reaction to what humans are doing, that will affect or is affecting our lives, but of which we are presently unaware. What exists is not limited to what we are conscious of. Sociologists who construct theory as if nature did not matter are like the Berkeleyian philosopher sitting under a tree in a storm, meditating on the idea that reality consists of what humans construct conceptually, unaware of the lightning bolt about to strike.

The misconception that reality is socially constructed, and the illusion that the relationship between the social and the natural can be characterized by plasticity, have taken on a life of their own in sociology as objective, taken-for-granted facts. Sociological overstatement of the social construction of reality has resulted in as much reification in sociology as its understatement ever did.

Sociology as if nature did not matter misses the distinguishing feature of the contemporary period, namely, the manipulation of nature by means of science and technology to attain material goals, thereby disrupting the equilibrium constructed by nature and unleashing nature's dynamic reaction, which in turn threatens human constructions. Beck (1992: 80–1) argues that

nature can no longer be understood outside of *society, or society* outside of *nature…in advanced modernity, society with all its subsystems of the economy, politics, culture and the family can no longer be understood as autonomous of nature.*

Sociology has correctly emphasized the importance of the social. But there is a point beyond which the rightful place of the social becomes the exaggerated sense of the social, beyond which the enlightened focus on the social becomes a blindness to the relationship between the processes of nature and social action, beyond which sociology becomes sociologism. The assumed dualism between social action and the processes of nature, with sociology focusing solely on the social as independent variable, has misled sociology into ignoring the dialectical relationship between the two.

The evolution of society out of nature and the ongoing interaction between the two tend to be lost in words that do not tell us enough about the vital association between nature and society and about the importance of defining such disciplines as economics, psychology, and sociology in natural as well as social terms. (Bookchin 1987: 59 fn.)

By confronting sociological theory with the growing recognition of the importance of the processes of nature for social action, environmental problems and the ecological movement can help correct the excesses of sociologism in sociology.

A synthesis of both the social and natural construction of reality involves going beyond Durkheim's narrow fixation with the social to a more inclusive Weberian perspective: 'unlike his contemporary Durkheim, Weber had no reluctance to admit the causal significance of non-social factors for social processes' (Albrow 1990: 146).

The neglect of nature is one important element of the dissolution of sociology into relativistic discourse focused on the social contingencies of the human observer, rather than on what he or she is observing. 'If social reality exists only in the perception of the observer, there are no other criteria to rank one perception against the next' (Baldus 1990: 474). Since 'any particular claim to the truth is merely one alternative among several such possibilities' (Cheal 1990: 133), the proper academic credentials and apprenticeship of the sociologist (Prus 1990: 361) become the sole basis for evaluating affirmations in this sociological discursive practice unfettered by external criteria of truth. Sociology thereby degenerates into the field *par excellence* where Collins's (1975, 1979) theory of credentials as pseudo-ethnicity, political labour, professional closure, and status-cultural sinecures holds true. This 'is the ultimate step in the conversion of sociology into a self-policing professional paradise whose inhabitants are safely sheltered from the ill winds of criticism. But it also takes no special predictive powers to see that such a sociology is on its way toward becoming utterly irrelevant' (Baldus 1990: 474). The utter irrelevance of sociology constructed as if nature did not matter has recently been dramatically underscored by increasingly severe environmental problems resulting from the interaction of social constructions with nature's constructions, as well as the looming social consequences of those problems.

Mainstream sociologists have reacted to criticisms like these by treating the critics as environmental specialists, working within a sociological subspeciality with no particular relevance for social theory.[2] This rhetorical device successfully fended off the earlier

challenges of Catton and Dunlap,[3] but at great cost to the field of sociology. The strategy allowed sociology to shelve the rectification of its assumptions about nature and to continue with the shortcomings of its theoretical constructions, even as environmental problems intensified and the environmental movement grew. This avoidance tactic prevented sociology from correcting its self-destructive mistakes.

The assumptions of sociology as if nature did not matter—that nature is constant, that nature and the relationship of humans to it are plastic, and that humans, in contrast to non-human animals, do not live in a closed natural world—are not simplifying assumptions necessary for disciplinary specialization. Simplifying assumptions are correct as far as they go, but they do not capture the full complexity of a phenomenon. Their simplicity does not invalidate theories based on them (Gluckman 1964). The above assumptions are instead erroneous assumptions about nature that invalidate theories requiring them to conclude that reality is a social construction *rather than* a construction of nature. The less extreme approaches based on the pragmatic choice of examining only social action in order to carve out a professional niche of expertise are not invalidated, but they can be criticized for neglecting an important influence on social action.

WHY WAS SOCIOLOGY CONSTRUCTED AS IF NATURE DID NOT MATTER?

Factors Internal to Sociology

i) ***Disciplinary specialization.*** The first and most obvious reason why sociology was constructed as if nature did not matter involves disciplinary specialization. Sociologists specialize in the social.

It is the bread and butter of sociologists. We have material and ideal interests in drawing attention to the importance of social action, even at the expense of the relationship between it and the processes of nature. This has hitherto been the approach of mainstream sociology, short-sighted though it has been.

It is not that sociologists have tried to take the dynamics of nature into account in their theories but were prevented from doing so by obstacles to interdisciplinary research;[4] rather the vast majority have not tried. In order to give added importance to social action, sociologists have assumed that the effect of nature on social action can be ignored. They have obscured the context of social action, thereby de-naturing humans, their society and culture. Sociologists assuming the social construction of reality has the same epistemological status as carpenters assuming the world is made of wood. To each his or her own fetish.

Although sociologists like to present their field as holistic scholarship that perceives the larger picture and develops a synthesis of elements other disciplines investigate in a narrow, specialized fashion, we have failed to incorporate the relationship between processes of nature and social action into our synthetic whole. The specialization of knowledge has misled sociology into excluding nature and arriving at premature analytic closure. This professional bias restricting analysis to the social has rendered sociology synthetic in the pejorative sense of the word. The creation of interdisciplinary fields, such as environmental studies including a few sociologists, has been a stopgap measure that left unrectified the deficient assumptions about nature in the discipline of sociology.

ii) **Revulsion and repulsion.** There have, nevertheless, been some attempts to explain the social by the natural, but they have had the effect of distancing sociology even further from the investigation of the relationship between the processes of nature and social action. For example, Social Darwinism (Spencer 1898–9) borrowed concepts of competition, natural selection, survival of the fittest, etc., from Darwin's theory of the evolution of nature and applied them to social processes. According to Social Darwinism, competition weeds out weaker individuals and groups not fit to survive and results in social progress whereas social welfare measures protect the weak and lead to an inferior population. Even though this doctrine still has appeal in some circles of society, sociologists (Ward 1897) reacted swiftly and strongly to its ultra-conservative implications such that it has had virtually no proponents among sociologists since the 1880s.

It is important to note that Social Darwinism was not a theory of the relationship between social action and the processes of nature. Rather Social Darwinists borrowed the theory of evolution from Darwin, who had developed it for processes of nature, and they used it analogously to infer a theory of social progress. Runciman (1989: 296, 449) discards the assumptions of progress and of a predetermined goal in his construction of a different version of social evolutionary theory based on struggle for power, but he too only peripherally takes into account the processes of nature. Although the word 'ecology' appears in the label of the Human Ecology approach (Park *et al.* 1925) to sociology, Michelson (1970) and Catton (1992) showed that nature was largely absent from its analyses as well. Rather concepts, such as concentration, segregation, invasion, succession, and especially competition, were borrowed from fields that studied nature, for example biological ecology, and were used to explain social action by analogy. 'Natural areas' and 'natural processes' had more to do with what human ecologists regarded as normal social processes than with the interaction between society and nature. Despite its label, Human Ecology glossed over the relationship between the dynamics of nature and social action.

Theories have also been proposed of genetically based differences, at times even between races and ethnic groups, in criminality (Sheldon 1949; Glueck and Glueck 1966), in I.Q., educational attainment and aspirations (Jensen 1969; Herrnstein 1971; Eysenck 1971; Rushton 1988), and hence in economic success. The contrast between these questionable sociobiological explanations of social inequality and an appreciation of nature as a powerful force interacting with social action was highlighted recently in Canada when the main opponent of Rushton's biological determinism turned out to be none other than the environmentalist (and geneticist) David Suzuki. Another example is the important exposé of fallacies in biological determinism presented by the evolutionary biologist Gould (1981).

Sociologists (Kamin 1974; Halsey 1977) too have found biological determinism less than appealing and have correctly brought sociobiological explanations under close critical scrutiny. They have reacted, and rightly so,

against crude explanations of the social by the natural. They have criticized the tendency to 'naturalize' and 'reify' social processes by which inequalities in privilege and power are generated. The history of questionable attempts to reduce the social to the natural is the second reason explaining the reluctance of sociologists to examine the relationship between the two. The revulsion those explanations have aroused among sociologists has repelled the investigation of that relationship.

Benton (1991) has shown that Durkheim developed his social reductionism as a result of his reaction to biological reductionism. The current wave of social constructivism in sociology followed the development of sociobiology. Sociology has repeatedly reacted to the imperialistic thrusts of biology by regressing to the opposite extreme of constructing its own equally narrow social imperialism. Sociolgists will have to learn from feminists who are now beginning to question

> the belief that gender is socially constructed was the only alternative to a belief in biological determinism. If you did not agree with one, then by implication, you must believe in the other. This opposition has had dire consequences, both for feminism and for the Left in general. (Birke 1986: x)

iii) An aggravating tendency. The analysis of the *social* production of reality has been the dominant focus of sociology all along. A recent development has aggravated the tendency of sociology to neglect the relationship between the processes of nature and social action.

I would argue that the relative weight of two kinds of sociology (Dawe

1978)—social-system and human-agency—has shifted over time. Until the late 1960s, there was widespread agreement, although not unanimity, that the task of sociology was to investigate systems working behind the backs of humans. By this was meant the social forces—or even laws, according to some sociologists—that shape human action. On the micro-level there was an effort to detect recurring patterns of interaction in small groups in order to discover the salient variables and develop empirical generalizations concerning their interrelationships. On the macro-level the focus was on the large-scale forces that were determining social structures and social change. Functionalists concentrated on differentiation and modernization, Marxists on the transformation from feudalism to liberal capitalism and then to monopoly capitalism. Others, less easy to classify but often associated with functionalism, saw the most important dynamics to be industrialization or urbanization.

For example, the classical interpretation of Marx is based on the premise

that social reality and its trajectory can be explained in terms that remove human visions, cultural influences, and most significantly, ethical goals from the social process. Indeed, Marxism elucidates the function of these cultural, psychological, and ethical 'forces' in terms that make them contingent on 'laws' which act behind human wills.' (Bookchin 1980:198)

The process is one of compulsion, not aims.

The question is not what this or that proletarian, or even the whole proletariat at the moment, considers as its aim. The question

is what the proletariat is, and what, consequent on that being, it will be compelled to do. (Marx and Engels 1956: 52–3)

Althusser (1979: 180) presented the ideal type of this approach

the structure of the relations of production determines the places and functions occupied and adopted by the agents of production, who are never anything more than the occupants of these places... The true subjects are these definers and distributors: the relations of production.

Within Marxism, the reply to 'scientific Marxists' such as Althusser was given by E. P. Thompson (1963, 1978). He referred to Althusser's work as an 'orrery of errors' and presented his alternative in which the working class was seen not as determined and overdetermined by large-scale impersonal forces but rather as self-made in the context of the local contingencies it faced.

This interpretive shift went well beyond Marxism. Berger and Luckmann (1967: 186–7) reacted against structural-functionalism in general, and against its Parsonian version in particular. 'We cannot agree that sociology has as its object the alleged "dynamics" of social and psychological "systems"'. They shifted sociology away from the study of systemic forces toward the study of meaningful interpretation (including notions of such systems). Garfinkel (1967) and Cicourel (1964) developed an ethnomethodological approach for the analysis of the methods used by people to negotiate and construct reality in their everyday taken-for-granted interaction. Neo-Weberians such as Collins objected to the functionalist interpretation of Weber by sociologists like Parsons (1964, 1966, 1971). Collins (1971, 1975, 1979, 1981, 1986) was influenced by ethnomethodological assumptions and claimed that the 'social construction of reality is a key to all of sociology' (Collins 1975: 470). In the sociology of science Mulkay (1980) followed a similar intellectual trajectory. Much of the sociology of science since the 1970s has been based on the premise that science is a social construction fabricated and negotiated by scientists according to their local contingencies *rather than* factual principles. Parkin (1979) reacted strongly against the Marxian structuralism of Althusser and Poulantzas, then developed his own Weberian closure theory employing what Giddens (1980: 887) refers to as 'a strongly voluntaristic vocabulary'. The 'new directions' sociology of education (Whitty and Young 1976; Young and Whitty 1977) consisted of a social constructivist view of formal education. Whereas previous work in the sociology of the professions investigated the evolving knowledge base that distinguishes professions from other occupations, present work focuses on the methods negotiated by members to construct and maintain their occupation as a profession (see Murphy 1988: Ch. 8 and Murphy 1990).

Although there are many different variants of both social-system sociology and human-agency sociology as well as exceptions to the general tendency, it is impossible to avoid the conclusion that there has been an overall shift in sociology over, the past-quarter century in which the attraction of structural determinism, of functionalism, and of systems theory has diminished as a result of the growing emphasis on human

agency (see also Alexander 1988: esp. 89, 92–3). This has consisted of a displacement of the centre of sociology from the thesis of a system working behind the backs of humans to an up-front, human-making-of-reality antithesis, which has become shared by those who differ along other lines of theoretical demarcation. This development originated especially in reaction against the systems theory and structural functionalism of Parsons (1964, 1966, 1971) and against the structuralism of Althusser (1970, 1979) and Poulantzas (1978).

The attempt to highlight creative humans making their world according to their intentions and projects rather than being pushed around by external forces has induced sociology to neglect still more the relationship between the external forces of nature and social action. The emphasis in sociology has shifted from the *social* construction of reality to the social *construction* of reality, and the interaction between the natural and the social has been further obscured in the shuffle. The accent on human-agency sociology—in reaction to structuralism, systems theory, and functionalism—has aggravated the problem of failing to incorporate into sociological theory the relationship between the dynamic processes of the ecosystem of nature and social action.

Factors External to Sociology

The conception of the plasticity of the relationship of humans to nature, the belief in the feasibility of the goal of mastering nature,[5] and faith that technology has rendered humans exempt from the constraints of the dynamics of nature (Dunlap and Catton 1994a) arose in human culture in a brief intervening period of exuberance in human history between the age when humans could not manipulate nature and the age when the reaction of nature to the constructions of humans became evident. These beliefs, characteristic of this fleeting period of manipulating nature with apparent impunity, penetrated many areas of thought, including sociology. Far from being an unbiased observation of society and its culture, sociology has been socially constructed in a specific cultural context and has been influenced by prevailing plasticity and exemptionalist assumptions. During this period, the premises of sociologists— that nature is constant and plastic and that humans, in contrast to non-human animals, do not live in a closed natural world— structurally corresponded to the assumptions and practices of capitalists, bureaucrats, and politicians, as manifested by the economic and political actions of the latter as well as by their discursive practices. 'Reagan's explicit rejection of the idea of "ecological limits" may have been the one theme of his administration that resonated with mainstream sociology' (Dunlap and Catton 1994a: 22). Like capitalists, sociologists have stressed 'producing' and 'constructing' rather than adapting to nature. The dominant assumptions of a formally rationalized world have been the assumptions underlying sociology.

At this early point on the environmental degradation curve, the world could be dealt with as an open sewer and it seemed, as Berger and Luckmann (1967: 47) assumed, that 'man's relationship to his environment is characterized by world-openness'. The mastery-of-nature assumption of human progress was represented within sociology in terms of the ideology of world-openness instead of a closed planet, of the immense plasticity of humans to environmental forces, of the overbearing emphasis on what distinguishes humans from other species rather than on what they share, and of humans

producing their own nature rather than it being produced by the processes of nature. These were the sociological expressions of modern societies careless of nature, a sociology developed in the wealthiest nations during the period when their citizens shared the illusion of being capable of reshaping nature at will (Catton and Dunlap 1978; Dunlap and Catton 1994a). The Age of Exuberance (Catton 1980) led to a socially exuberant sociology. The above postulates were taken for granted by sociologists before the cumulative reaction of nature to social constructions became evident.

At a later point on the waste accumulation curve, however, the interaction between social constructions and the dynamic processes of nature resulted in tangible consequences even at the global planetary level. Humans faced the disturbing observation that they too exist with a fixed nature in a closed world to which they must adjust, or perish. All-too-rare sociologists began to transcend sociology as if nature did not matter in order to investigate new social relationships mediated by nature, for example, 'diachronic competition, a relationship whereby contemporary well-being is achieved at the expense of our descendants' (Catton 1980: 3). The growing awareness that social constructions unleash dynamic processes of nature that bear on social action has the potential of radically transforming sociology.

TOWARD SOCIOLOGY IN WHICH NATURE MATTERS

Beck (1992) argues that environmental problems, which are produced and knowable by science, are provoking a risk society and reflexive modernization. In the earliest phase of primary scientization, science was applied only to nature, people, and society.

In the emerging phase of reflexive scientization, scientific scepticism is also applied to science itself. Rather than constituting self-destruction, self-criticism by the sciences is probably the only way that their mistakes can be caught early. Reflexive scientization threatens to shake the foundations of science, demonopolize scientific knowledge, and diminish barriers between experts and lay people. It is engendering, none the less, a new expansion of science because the problems created by science can only be understood and solved by science.

Beck's argument can be extended to sociology. The phase of primary sociology consisted in the elaboration of a sceptical approach to society, its values and its institutions, including science. In this phase the foundations of sociology were excluded from sociological scepticism. Such sociology was based on the naivete that scepticism could be restricted to the objects of sociology, that is, to the terrain of others. The demystifier was to remain exempt from the process of demystification. Throwing stones at others from this glass house of sociology proved dangerous, however, because sociology promoted the development of standards of scepticism concerning science and society that could just as logically be applied to sociology itself.

In the emerging reflexive phase, sociologists are beginning to apply sociological scepticism to sociology. The construction of science according to the principles of career and social acceptance is finally seen as applying to sociology as well, with sociology having carved out its own characteristic niche of expertise like other disciplines, a niche focusing exclusively on the social construction of reality. The agents of the transition from primary to reflexive sociology are those who critically apply sociology to itself, thereby eroding the self-dogmatization of the discipline and questioning its limitations. In this self-critical sociology the principle of fallibilism is applied not only to other sciences but also to sociology, rendering sociology less partial. Sociology opposing sociology constitutes not its self-destruction; it is on the contrary the way that self-destructive mistakes can be detected and corrected. As with science in general, criticism from within threatens to undermine the claim to distinctive expert status in a specialized niche of knowledge, but it also has the potential to lead to a more complete sociology and expand it in new directions.

In particular, as society runs the risk of environmental problems, the construction of sociology as if nature did not matter meets with increasing scepticism from the wider public and from sociologists themselves. The critique of sociology's misleading assumptions about nature and the exposure of the self-contradiction of sociological scepticism concerning scientific knowledge seek to broaden sociology by integrating into sociological theory the embeddedness of social action in the processes of nature.

Environmental problems are challenging sociology to transcend its parochial focus on the social.

The point is not to deify nature or to 'go back' to it, but to take account of a simple fact: human activity finds in the natural world its external limits. Disregarding these limits sets off a backlash whose effects we are already experiencing in specific, though still widely misunderstood, ways. (Gorz 1980: 13)

Even in its suggested integration of the natural world into sociological theory, this formulation by Gorz underestimates the significance of nature. Human activity finds in the natural world not only external limits but also external possibilities. Taking into account the effects of the natural world on human activity would extend sociology beyond its present partial conception, as if nature did not matter, to a more complete conception of what humans are experiencing.

The preceding criticism does not imply that sociologists need to become expert in physics and biology, rather that they should broaden their sociological theories to situate explicitly social action in its context, namely, in the processes of nature. For example, rather than treating the depletion of the ozone layer or the threat of nuclear energy as media-based social scares or the equivalent of parapsychology, sociologists have a special competence to examine the social causes and consequences of these interactions with the processes of nature. Nuclear energy as a source of empowerment—very different from magic—of the Communist Party in the Soviet Union, and the explosive reaction of nature at Chernobyl as a contributing factor in the disintegration of the Soviet empire, are examples of research topics for which sociologists are eminently qualified, with the results informing sociological theory about how social projects are rooted in the dynamic processes of nature. Sociologists will have to rethink causation as an interaction between social action and the processes of nature (Halsey 1977: 3), and deal with a range of questions much broader than the overworked and unproductive ones emanating from the nature *versus* nurture debate.

Nature consists not only of static limits, but also of a dynamic development, of processes and not just conditions, of relationships as well as constraints. Ecologists have demonstrated that humans enter into a relationship with the powerful, active forces

of nature. A simple example is the development, use, and overuse of antibiotics, which have provoked the unintended emergence of drug-resistant strains of bacteria in turn affecting social, and in particular sexual, relations among humans. Unidirectional determinisms and reductionisms—of the social by the natural or the reverse—need to be replaced by a perception of the dialectical relationship between the two.

The synthesis of systemic sociology and human-agency sociology is crucial for the advancement of the field. Alexander (1988: 96 fn. 26) argues that the younger generation of theorists is currently engaged in an effort to achieve such a synthesis. Although Collins was an important contributor to shifting the mainstream of sociology from a systemic approach to a constructivist, human-agency one based on political labour, he now argues that the shift has gone too far

> although there is a culturally constructed component in any knowledge, it also can be knowledge of something. Indeed, any argument about the social basis of knowledge is self-undermining if it doesn't have some external truth-reference as well—otherwise why should we believe that this social basis itself exists? We need to get beyond polemically one-sided epistemologies, of either the subjectivist or the objectivist sort; a multidimensional epistemology can take account of the way we live in a cultural tunnel of our own history, but still we can cumulate objective knowledge about the world. (Collins 1989: 132)

Similarly, Alexander (1988: 93) concludes that if the opposite mistakes of idealism and of the preemption of individual creativity can be avoided, 'the new movement in sociology will have a chance to develop a truly multidimensional theory'.

Humans construct their sense of reality and their understanding of it. They exert an effect on nature by manipulating it according to their goals, and in the process unleash unexpected forces of nature and new forms of social-natural interaction, which affect social action. Humans are shaping the world more than any other species, and are being shaped by nature in ways never before experienced. Human choice and human activity take place within a dynamic ecosystem in which human activity is but one element. A less partial analysis would grasp the embeddedness of social action in the processes of nature thereby capturing how reality is both a social construction and a construction of nature. Research on this theme (Catton 1980; Catton and Dunlap 1980; Devall and Sessions 1985; Bookchin 1971, 1980, 1987; Perrow 1984; Benton 1991, 1993; Dickens 1992; Jones 1990; Newby 1991; Beck 1992; Dunlap 1993; Dunlap and Catton 1994a, 1994b), much too rare and poorly integrated into mainstream sociology, has only recently begun. This research has not yet influenced general sociological theory, which continues to proceed as if nature did not matter. The effect of nature on social action remains an undertheorized area in sociology. And yet the thesis of social construction is viable only if tempered by an ecosystemic sociology that incorporates into sociological theory the effect of an objective world of nature with its own processes that react to and against human constructions.[6]

ENDNOTES

1. A detailed critique of this flaw in the sociology of science has been developed in Murphy 1994b.
2. Buttel (1987: 465–88) documents how this has occurred.

3. See Dunlap and Catton (1994b: 19) for their sense of failure to remedy the deficiencies of sociology.
4. Sherif and Sherif (1969) have specified such obstacles.
5. The perverse effects of such conceptions, beliefs, and goals in society generally—particularly as held by capitalists, bureaucrats, and their spokespersons—are examined in detail in Murphy (1994a).
6. For my own elaboration of a synthesis that I refer to as an 'ecology of social action', see Murphy (1994a).

BIBLIOGRAPHY

Albrow, M. 1990 *Max Weber's Construction of Social Theory,* London: Macmillan.

Alexander, J. 1988 'The New Theoretical Movement' in N. Smelser (ed.) *Handbook of Sociology,* Newbury Park: Sage.

Althusser, L. 1970 'Idéologie et Appareils Idéologiques d'Etat', La Pensée 151.

Althusser, L. 1979 (1968) 'The Object of Capital', in L. Althusser and E. Balibar *Reading Capital,* London: Verso.

Baldus, B. 1990 'In defense of theory', *Canadian Journal of Sociology* 15: 470–5.

Beck, U. 1992 *Risk Society: Towards a New Modernity,* London: Sage.

Bell, D. 1977 'Are There "Social Limits" to Growth?' in K. D. Wilson (ed.) *Prospects for Growth,* New York: Praeger.

Benton, T. 1991 'Biology and Social Science' *Sociology* 25: 1–29.

Benton, T. 1993 *Natural Relations,* London: Verso.

Berger, P. and Lucianann, T. 1967 (1966) *The Social Construction of Reality,* Garden City: Anchor.

Biehl, J. 1991 *Rethinking Ecofeminist Politics,* Boston: South End Press.

Birke, L. 1986 *Women, Feminism and Biology,* Brighton: Wheatsheaf.

Blea, C. 1986 'Animal Rights and Deep Ecology Movements', *Synthesis* 23: 13–4.

Bookchin, M. 1971 *Post-Scarcity Anarchism,* Montreal: Black Rose.

Bookchin, M. 1980 *Toward an Ecological Society,* Montreal: Black Rose.

Bookchin, M. 1987 *The Modern Crisis,* Montreal: Black Rose.

Bruile, R. and Dietr, T. 1993 'A Rhetoric for Nature'. Paper presented at the International Conference'. 'The Social Functions of Nature'. Chantilly, France, March 8–12.

Burns, T. and Dietz, T. 1992 'Cultural Evolution', *International Sociology* 7: 259–83.

Buttel, F. 1987 'New Directions in Environmental Sociology', *Annual Review of Sociology* 13:465–88.

Catton, W. 1980 *Overshoot,* Urbana: University of Illinois Press.

Catton, W. 1992 'Separation Versus Unification in Sociological Human Ecology', in L. Freese (ed.) *Advances in Human Ecology,* Vol. 1. Greenwich: JAI Press.

Catton, W. and Dunlap, R. 1978 'Environmental Sociology', *American Sociological* 13: 41–9.

Catton, W. and Dunlap, R. 1980 'A New Ecological Paradigm for Post-Exuberant Sociology', *American Behavioral Scientist* 24: 15–48.

Cheal, D. 1990 'Authority and incredulity', *Canadian Journal of Sociology* 15: 129–47.

Cicourel, A. 1964 *Method and Measurement in Sociology,* New York: The Free Press.

Collins, R. 1971 'Functional and Conflict Theories of Educational Stratification', *American Sociological Review* 36: 1002–19.

Collins, R. 1975 *Conflict Sociology,* New York: Academic Press.

Collins, R. 1979 *The Credential Society,* New York: Academic.

Collins, R. 1981 *Sociology Since Midcentury,* New York: Academic.

Collins, R. 1986 *Weberian Sociological Theory,* Cambridge: Cambridge University Press.

Collins, R. 1989 'Sociology: Proscience or Antiscience?', *American Sociological Review* 54: 124–39.

Commoner, B. 1971 *The Closing Circle: Nature, Man, and Technology,* New York: Alfred A. Knopf.

Dawe, A. 1978 'Theories of Social Action', in T. Bottomore and R. Nisbet (eds) *A History of Sociological Analysis,* New York: Basic Books.

Devall, B. and Sessions, G. 1985 *Deep Ecology,* Salt Lake City: Peregrine Smith.

Dickens, P. 1992 *Science and Nature,* Philadelphia: Temple University Press.

Dryzek J. 1987 *Rational Ecology,* Oxford: Basil Blackwell.

Dunlap, R. 1993 'From Environmental to Ecological Problems.' in C. Calhoun and G. Ritzer (eds) *Social Problems,* New York: McGraw-Hill.

Dunlap, R. and Catton, W. 1994a 'Struggling with Human Exemptionalism', *American Sociologist* 25:5–30.

Dunlap, R. and Catton, W. 1994b 'Toward an Ecological Sociology', Chapter 2 in W. D'Antonio, M. Sasaki, and Y. Yonegayashi (eds) *Ecology, Society and the Quality of Social Life,* London: Transaction.

Ehrlich, P. and Ehrlich, A. 1983 *Extinction.* New York: Random House.

Eysenck, J. 1971 *The I.Q. Argument,* New York: Library Press.

Fox, N. 1991 'Green Sociology', *Network* (Newsletter of the British Sociological Association), No. 50: 23–4.

Fox, W. 1990 *Toward A Transpersonal Ecology,* Boston: Shambhala.

Garfinkel, H. 1967 *Studies in Ethnomethodology,* Englewood Cliffs: Prentice-Hall.

Giddens, A. 1980 'Classes, Capitalism, and the State', *Theory and Society* 9: 877–90.

Gluckman, M. (ed.) 1964 *Closed Systems and Open Minds,* Chicago: Aldine.

Glueck, S. and Glueck, E. 1966 *Physique and Delinquency,* New York: Harper and Row.

Gorz, A. 1980 *Ecology as Politics,* Montreal: Black Rose Press.

Gould, S. 1981 *The Mismeasure of Man,* New York: Norton.

Halsey, A. H. (ed.) 1977 *Heredity and Environment,* London: Methuen.

Herrnstein, R. 1971 '"I.Q."' *Atlantic Monthly* 228: 43–64.

Jensen, A. 1969 'How much can we boost I.Q. and Scholastic Achievement?', *Harvard Educational Review* 39: 1–123.

Jones, A. 1990 'Social Symbiosis', *The Ecologist* 20: 108–13.

Kamin, L. 1974 *The Science and Politics of I.Q.,* Potomac: Erlbaum.

Lipset, S. M. 1979 'Predicting the Future of Post-Industrial Society: Can We Do It?', in S. M. Lipset (ed.) *The Third Century,* Stanford: Hoover Institution Press.

Marx, K. and Engels, F. 1956 *The Holy Family,* Progress Publishers.

Meadows, D. *et al.* 1972 *The Limits to Growth,* New York: New American Library.

Michelson, W. 1970 *Man and His Urban Environment,* Reading: Addison-Wesley.

Mulkay, M. 1980 'Sociology of Science in the West', *Current Sociology* 28: 1–116.

Murphy, R. 1988 Social Closure: *The Theory of Monopolization and Exclusion,* Oxford: Oxford University Press (Clarendon).

Murphy, R. 1990 'Proletarianization or Bureaucratization: The Fall of the Professional?', Chapter 5 in R. Torstendahl and M. Burrage (eds) *The Formation of Professions: Knowledge, State and Strategy,* London: Sage.

Murphy, R. 1994a *Rationality and Nature,* Boulder; Westview.

Murphy, R. 1994b 'The Sociological Construction of Science Without Nature', *Sociology* 28: 957–74.

Naess, A. 1988 *Ecology, Community and Lifestyles,* Cambridge: Cambridge University Press.

Newby, H. 1991 'One World, Two Cultures: Sociology and the Environment', *Network* 50: 1–8.

Nisbet, R. 1979 'The Rape of Progress', *Public Opinion* 2: 2–6, 55.

Ophuls, W. 1977 *Ecology and the Politics of Scarcity,* San Francisco: W. H. Freeman and Co.

Park, R., Burgess, E. and McKenzie, R. (eds) 1925 *The City,* Chicago: University of Chicago Press.

Parkin, F. 1979 *Marxism and Class Theory: A Bourgeois Critique,* London: Tavistock.

Parsons, T. 1964 (1951) *The Social System,* New York: Free Press.

Parsons, T. 1966 *Societies,* Englewood Cliffs: Prentice-Hall.

Parsons, T. 1971 *The System of Modern Societies,* Englewood Cliffs: Prentice-Hall.

Perrow, C. 1984 *Normal Accidents,* New York: Basic Books.

Poulantzas, N. 1978 *Classes in Contemporary Capitalism,* London: Verso.

Prus, R. 1990 'The interpretive challenge', *The Canadian Journal of Sociology* 15: 355–63.

Runciman, W. G. 1989 *A Treatise an Social Theory: Volume II Substantive Social Theory,* Cambridge: Cambridge University Press.

Rushton, P. 1988 'Race differences in behaviour', *Personality and Individual Differences* 9: 1009–24.

Sale, K. 1988 'Deep Ecology And Its Critics', *The Nation* May 14: 670–5.

Senions, G. 1985 'A Postscript', Appendix H in B. Devall and G. Sessions *Deep Ecology,* Salt Lake City: Peregrine Smith.

Sheldon, W. 1949 *Varietiey of Delinquent Youth,* New York: Harper and Row.

Sherif, M. and Sherif, C. (eds) 1969 *Interdisciplinary Relationships in the Social Sciences,* Chicago: Aldine.

Spector, M. And Kitsuse, J. 1977 *Constructing Social Problems,* Menlo Park: Cummings.

Spencer, H. 1898–9 *Principles of Sociology,* New York: Appleton.

Thompson, E. P. 1963 *The Making of the English Working Class,* Harmondsworth: Penguin.

Thompson, E. P. 1978 *The Poverty of Theory and Other Essays,* London: Merlin.

Ward, L. 1897 *Outlines of Sociology,* New York: Macmillan.

Whitty, G. 1977 'Sociology and the Problem of Radical Educational Change', in M. F. D. Young and G. Whitty (eds) *Society, State, and Schooling,* Ringmer: Falmer Press.

Whitty, G. and Young, M. F. D. (eds) 1976 *Explorations in the Politics of School Knowledge,* Nefferton: Nefferton Books.

Woolgar, S. 1983 'Irony in the Social Study of Science', in K. Knorr-Cetina and M. Mulkay (eds) *Science Observed,* London: Sage.

World Commission on Environment and Development 1987 *Our Common Future,* Oxford: Oxford University Press.

Young, M. F. D. and Whitty, G. (eds) 1977 *Society, State, and Schooling,* Ringmer: Falmer Press.

3. The Evolution of Environmental Sociology: A Brief History and Assessment of the American Experience*

RILEY E. DUNLAP

INTRODUCTION

Nearly two decades ago Catton and I tried to codify the burgeoning but diverse body of sociological work on environmental issues being conducted primarily but not exclusively in the United States by providing an explicit definition of the field of environmental sociology. Included in a thematic issue of *The American Sociologist* devoted to 'New Theoretical Perspectives in Sociology', our article defined the field as 'the study of interaction between the environment and society' (Catton and Dunlap, 1978). We also contended that examining such interaction would require overcoming sociology's traditional and deep-seated reluctance to acknowledge the relevance of the physical environment for understanding contemporary societies.

We argued that in particular the Durkheimian tradition of explaining social phenomena only in terms of other 'social facts', plus an aversion to earlier excesses of biological and geographical 'determinism',

had led sociologists to ignore the physical world in which humans live. These disciplinary traditions were further strengthened, we suggested, by the emergence of sociology during an era of unprecedented growth and prosperity, fuelled by resource abundance and technological progress. Along with increased urbanization, which reduced contact with nature, these societal trends made it easy for sociologists to assume that, at least within industrial societies, human life was becoming increasingly independent of the physical world. Consequently, we claimed that our discipline had come to assume that the exceptional features of homo sapiens—language, technology, science and culture more generally—made industrialized societies 'exempt' from the constraints of nature. We concluded by claiming that changing circumstances (such as the 1973–4 energy crisis) necessitated shedding the 'blinkers' imposed by exemptionalism and adopting an ecological paradigm or world view that acknowledges the ecosystem-dependence of all human societies.[1]

It is clear, in retrospect, that our call for a paradigmatic revolution was issued during an exuberant period for the new field of environmental sociology. It had been formally recognized via establishment of a 'Section' within the American Sociological

*Reprinted by permission of the author, the editors of *The International Handbook of Environmental Sociology* (1997) Michael Redclift and Graham Woodgate, and the publisher, Edward Elgar, Cheltenham, England.

43

Association (ASA) in 1976, following similar developments in the Rural Sociological Society (RSS) and the Society for the Study of Social Problems (SSSP) (Dunlap and Catton, 1979). Buttel (1987:466) has described this period as one in which 'there was a vibrant *esprit de corps* that a new sociology was being nurtured.... Environmental sociologists sought nothing less than the reorientation of sociology toward a more holistic perspective that would conceptualise social processes within the context of the biosphere.' Writing a decade ago, Buttel (ibid.) went on to argue, 'These lofty intentions...have largely failed to come to fruition. The discipline at large has handily withstood the challenges to its theoretical assumptions posed by environmental sociologists.' While not challenging the accuracy of Buttel's appraisal of the situation at that time, I believe his pessimistic assessment of environmental sociology and his apparent confidence in the continuing hegemony of exemptionalist thinking within the larger discipline were heavily influenced by the period in which he was writing. The late 1970s were indeed a 'vibrant' period for environmental sociology, but the 1980s saw a significant decline of interest in the field, reaching its nadir at mid-decade, when Buttel wrote his overview. Since the late 1980s there has been a resurgence of interest in environmental sociology within the USA and internationally, and the larger discipline's misplaced faith in human exemptionalism has been increasingly called into question by environmental sociologists as well as by societal developments. Thus a new assessment of the field and its paradigmatic implications seems in order.

The first goal of this chapter is to trace the broad contours of the emergence, decline and revitalization of American environmental sociology, and to demonstrate linkages between these disciplinary developments and major trends in societal attention to environmental problems of the past quarter-century.[2] Having described major emphases of American work over time, and how these were influenced by societal events, the chapter's second goal will be to provide a brief assessment of the strengths and weaknesses of American environmental sociology via comparisons with discernible trends abroad. We will conclude by assessing the state of the field internationally *vis-à-vis* our original call for greater sociological attention to the environment and the importance of shedding the exemptionalist assumptions that were inhibiting such attention.

EMERGENCE OF ENVIRONMENTAL SOCIOLOGY IN THE 1970s

Although there was minor sociological interest in environmental topics prior to the 1970s, consisting primarily of research on natural resources by rural sociologists (see Burch *et al.*, 1972) and on built environments by urban sociologists (see Michelson, 1970), it is generally agreed that the field of environmental sociology developed largely in response to the emergence of widespread societal attention to environmental problems in the early 1970s (Buttel, 1987; Dunlap and Catton, 1979; Freudenburg and Gramling, 1989; Humphrey and Buttel, 1982). Not surprisingly, the bulk of this early work focused on the environmental movement, public attitudes towards environmental issues, environmental policy making and the development of environmental quality as a social problem. This work involved the application of mainstream sociological perspectives, especially analyses of the importance of various claims-making activities in generating societal interest in environmental degradation, to environmental topics. It was a 'normal science' approach and was labelled the 'sociology of environmental issues' (Dunlap and Catton, 1979).

As sociologists paid more attention to environmental issues, some began to look beyond societal attention to environmental problems to the underlying relationships between modern, industrialized societies and the physical environments they inhabit. Concern with the societal causes of environmental pollution (Molotch and Follett, 1971) was supplemented by a focus on the social impacts of pollution and resource constraints (Catton, 1972). In some cases there was explicit attention to the reciprocal relationships between societies and their environments, or to the 'ecosystem-dependence' of modern societies (Burch, 1971).

It is apparent, in hindsight, that the widespread attention received by *The Limits to Growth* (Meadows *et al.,* 1972) and the 1973–4 energy crisis that appeared to validate its thesis led to a preoccupation with the societal impacts of resource scarcity. Sociological research on energy in the 1970s focused far more attention on the impacts of energy shortages than on the social forces influencing energy use (Rosa *et al.,* 1988). Likewise, there was considerable sociological interest in the societal impacts of resource scarcity in general, especially the inequitable manner in which these impacts would likely be distributed among social strata (Morrison, 1976). While some attention was given to the social mechanisms driving the rapid growth leading to scarcity (Schnaiberg, 1975), the dominant theme was that we were entering an era of ecological limits, exemplified by publication of an issue of *Social Science Quarterly* (September, 1976) devoted to 'Scarcity and Society' that included several contributions by environmental sociologists.

Sociological interest in the impacts of energy and other resource scarcities contributed to the emergence of environmental sociology as a distinct specialization by increasing awareness that 'environment' was more than just another social problem, and that environmental conditions could indeed affect society. While many energy researchers probably never gave much thought to the fact that their work involved examining 'society–environment interactions', and thus violated Durkheim's dictum that the causes of social facts must be sought in other social facts, the general concern with the societal impacts of scarcity facilitated the transition from a 'sociology of environmental issues' to a self-conscious 'environmental sociology' focused explicitly on such interactions. That concern also contributed to a somewhat one-sided view of these interactions, however, as it was the effects of resource constraints on society that received emphasis rather than the impacts of society on the environment (for example, Morrison, 1976).

Sociological attention to the societal impacts of resource limits was very much in tune with the *Weltanschauung* of the mid- to late-1970s, highlighted by President Carter's energy policy and his sponsorship of *The Global 2000 Report* (Barney, 1980), but an emphasis on ecological constraints was clearly at odds with the discipline's ingrained exemptionalist orientation. Thus it is not surprising that sociological work on resource scarcity never appeared in the discipline's top journals, or that several leading American sociologists directly challenged the notion of ecological limits (Bell, 1977; Lipset, 1979; Nisbet, 1980). Indeed, Daniel Bell (1977) provided the quintessential exemptionalist response by arguing that, *if* there are limits to growth, they are surely *social* rather than physical! It is also not surprising that environmental sociology's critique of human exemptionalism had little impact on the discipline at large.

Despite a low profile within the larger discipline, environmental sociology ended the 1970s with a good deal of momentum. Research on topics such as environmental attitudes and the environmental movement, along with energy and natural resources, had increased throughout the 1970s. The ASA Section on Environmental Sociology grew from 290 members in 1976 to 321 in 1979, attracting members with a wide range of interests such as housing and the built environment, social impact assessment and natural hazards, as well as environmentalism, energy and natural resources. In addition, numerous environmental sociology courses sprang up and a few graduate programmes began to offer students the opportunity to specialize in the field (Freudenburg and Gramling, 1989: 447). The situation looked quite promising, but not for long.

THE DECLINE OF ENVIRONMENTAL SOCIOLOGY IN THE 1980s

Even though the events of the 1970s had caused the public to give some credence to the idea of limited natural resources (Yankelovich and Lefkowitz, 1980), the notion of limits remained unpalatable—for expectations of endless growth and prosperity were deeply ingrained in the American psyche (Dunlap and Van Liere, 1984; Milbrath, 1982). Part of the appeal of Ronald Reagan's promise to 'make America great again' was his explicit rejection of the reality of limits. As one analyst put it during the 1980 election campaign:

> For voters terrified by the implications of an era of limits, the expansive ideology of the American Century carries powerful political force. While President Carter has suggested that the challenges ahead are extremely complicated and may require national sacrifice, [Reagan] insists that happy days are just around the corner. (Viviano, 1980)

As another analyst wrote eight years later, 'Carter's humiliating defeat sealed the end of the poor misspent '70s, a decade of limits and frustration and malaise' (Barol, 1988: 41).

From the perspective of those who conceptualized core American values and beliefs such as individualism, free enterprise, abundance, growth and prosperity as a 'dominant social paradigm' or 'DSP' (Dunlap and Van Liere, 1984; Milbrath, 1982), the Reagan Revolution was a natural reaction to the emergence of unconventional social paradigms or world views in the 1970s that were premised on the existence of limits (such as 'voluntary simplicity': Elgin, 1981). Just as adherents of dominant scientific paradigms seldom surrender quickly to challengers, so adherents of the DSP fought back. The anomaly of energy shortages was quickly 'solved' by freeing the market from government restraints, and the idea of limits lost currency. In the intellectual arena explicit rejections of limits-to-growth arguments were put forth with increased frequency. Julian Simon's (1981) argument that population growth was desirable because human ingenuity makes people 'the ultimate resource' (epitomizing a human exemptionalist perspective) resonated particularly well with Reagan's perspective and contributed to the administration's reversal of long-term US support for population control at the 1984 World Population Conference. Similarly, Simon's subsequent book with Herman Kahn, *The Resourceful Earth* (1984), was cited in support of the administration's dismissal of the Carter-sponsored *Global 2000 Report* (Boggs, 1985).

Was environmental sociology affected by this dramatic change in national mood? A variety of evidence certainly suggests so. After three years of growth, membership in the ASA Section on Environmental Sociology dropped below 300 by late 1980 and declined to 274 by 1983. The two books most widely used as texts (Schnaiberg, 1980; Humphrey and Buttel, 1982) went out of print, and were not replaced by new ones. Fewer papers on environmental topics were presented at professional meetings and this reflected a decline in sociological work, not only on energy, but on topics such as environmental attitudes and environmentalism as well. In particular, very few contributions to what Buttel (1987: 467–72) called the 'core' of environmental sociology—its theoretical critique of mainstream sociology's neglect of the physical environment—were made after 1980, and none were published in the leading sociology journals. Similarly, limited success was achieved in bringing the major 'factions' of the field, such as those involved in research on housing and the built environment and those concerned with natural resources (Dunlap and Catton, 1983), into a cohesive intellectual community (Buttel, 1987; Freudenburg and Gramling, 1989: 449).

Environmental sociology courses often suffered declining enrollments, the few existing graduate programmes experienced a levelling of student interest and there were very few job advertisements for environmental sociologists in the 1980s. Such problems were partially shared with sociology (and social science) as a whole, which came under severe attack from the Reagan administration and suffered declining enrolments due to student migration to other fields. However, not only did this situation make it especially hard to maintain the momentum needed to institutionalize a new area of specialization in the discipline, but environmental sociology's emphasis on the ecosystem-dependence of modern, industrialized societies seemed particularly out of step with the tenor of the times. It is therefore understandable that Buttel's mid-1980s appraisal of the progress of the field was less than optimistic about its future.

There were some countervailing trends in the 1980s. Problems afflicting resource-dependent communities (for example, mining, timber and fishing towns) received increasing attention from rural sociologists (Freudenburg and Gramling, 1994). The rise of citizen concern over exposure to toxic and other hazardous wastes stimulated even more attention. Levine's (1982) classic study of the controversy at Love Canal (which began at the end of the 1970s) was the first of numerous sociological investigations of community responses to local environmental hazards (Couch and Kroll-Smith, 1991). Likewise, the major accidents at Three-Mile Island (1979), Bophal, India (1984) and Chernobyl (1986) dramatized the importance of the social impacts and human responses to technological accidents.[3] The fact that exposure to such hazards was typically distributed quite unevenly across social strata also renewed interest in the distributional impacts of environmental problems (Schnaiberg *et al.,* 1986), while growing awareness of such hazards in blue-collar and minority communities stimulated research on a new form of environmentalism—local, grassroots environmental action (Bullard, 1983). More generally, increased attention to environmental and technological hazards stimulated sociological interest in the nature and role of risk in modern societies (Short, 1984).

In addition to their societal significance, work on local hazards had strong appeal to sociologists. The problems were obviously human-created, their recognition and resolution typically involved enormous levels of social controversy in which competing claims-making activities were quite apparent, and conflict over the problems could often be linked to existing patterns of social stratification and political power. They also allowed for micro-level investigations of individual communities employing a wide array of standard data collection efforts (surveys, field work, content analyses and so on). In short, sociologists' research on environmental (and technological) hazards was inherently sociological (Couch and Kroll-Smith, 1991; Levine, 1982). Although this work focused on societal–environmental interactions, the environmental conditions were often viewed as 'socially constructed' and even when taken as objectively hazardous to human health the delimited nature of the problems did not raise questions about the future of homo sapiens, as did earlier work on the impacts of limits to growth. Yet, as in the 1970s, with the emphasis on the social impacts of scarcity, work in the 1980s was initially more concerned with understanding the impacts of environmental conditions *on* humans (especially as mediated by perceptions, collective definitions and community networks) than with the impacts of humans on the environment.

THE LATE 1980s AND EARLY 1990s: REVITALIZATION OF THE FIELD

By the late 1980s, increased societal attention was again focused on what humans were doing *to* the environment, as was true when environmental quality emerged as a social problem in the late 1960s. In 1988 and 1989 alone, three major news magazines—*Time, Newsweek* and *U.S. News and World Report*—carried several cover stories on environmental problems such as the

contamination of the Atlantic coast with hospital wastes, acid rain, ozone depletion, rainforest destruction and global warming (Mazur and Lee, 1993). *Time* went so far as to name the 'Endangered Earth' as 'Planet of the Year' in lieu of its 'man of the year' for 1988. The exceptionally hot summer of 1988 appeared to validate the notion of global warming in the eyes of the public, much as the 1973–4 energy crisis had done for limits to growth (Ungar, 1992). Thus, although the threat of energy (and other resource) shortages had receded during the 1980s, the quality of the environment was widely seen as worsening.

The renewed salience of environmental problems in the USA was given great impetus by the mobilization of public support for the 20th anniversary of Earth Day, 22 April 1990, an event that attracted unprecedented public involvement and also helped swell the memberships of environmental organizations (Dunlap and Mertig, 1992). In fact, by 1990 the American public was expressing greater concern over the state of the environment and more support for environmental protection than it had in the early 1970s. In particular, majorities felt that environmental quality had declined in recent years and expected it to continue to do so, and large majorities supported increased government spending and regulations for environmental protection (ibid.). Not long after the enthusiasm surrounding the 20th Earth Day began to subside, a new wave of interest was stimulated by preparations for the June 1992 'Earth Summit' in Rio de Janeiro (technically known as the United Nations Conference on Environment and Development).

The visibility of the 20th Earth Day and the Earth Summit, combined with media attention to issues such as the *Exxon Valdez* oil spill, tropical rainforest destruction and the environmental devastation found in Eastern Europe, resulted in an unprecedented level of societal interest in environmental issues—not only in the USA but throughout much of the world (Dunlap *et al.,* 1993)—in the early 1990s. Inevitably, as the result of 'ceiling effects' and the difficulties of keeping an issue on the public agenda, environment was bound to decline in public importance and it did by mid-decade (Dunlap, 1995). However, the recent attacks on environmental protection policies by the Republican Congress have led to a resurgence of public support (Shabecoff, 1996), reminiscent of what happened in the Reagan era (Dunlap and Mertig, 1992).

THE CHANGING NATURE OF ENVIRONMENTAL PROBLEMS

The growing salience of environmental problems over the past decade stemmed, not only from increased attention to them by scientists, media and policy makers, but from discernible changes in the nature of the problems. Contemporary environmental problems differ from earlier ones such as litter, loss of natural areas and air and water pollution in a number of critical respects. First, the scale of such problems has increased from typically localized problems (such as urban air pollution and pollution of rivers) to the regional level (as with acid rain) and even global level (for example, ozone depletion), thereby potentially affecting far more people. Second, localized problems such as contaminated water supplies and inadequate solid waste repositories occur (and are reported in the media) with enough frequency for them to be seen as generalized problems, adding to the sense that environmental deterioration is pervasive. Third, environmental problems are increasingly recognized as often having origins

that are poorly understood and consequences that are difficult to detect and predict, with the result that they appear 'riskier' than earlier predecessors (Ungar, 1995). Fourth, the impacts of many problems pose serious consequences for the health and welfare of humans (including future generations) as well as for other species, and some of these impacts may be irreversible. In short, environmental problems appear to have increased in frequency, scale and seriousness (Dunlap, 1993). Whereas in the 1960s and early 1970s environmental degradation often seemed an aesthetic issue (or, at most, an irritant affecting outdoor activities), it is increasingly seen as a direct threat to human health and well-being, from the local level (for example, toxic wastes) to the global level (for example, ozone depletion).

To summarize, the past decade has seen the emergence of widespread societal recognition of the fact that human activities are causing a deterioration in the quality of the environment, *and* that environmental deterioration in turn has negative impacts on people (Dunlap and Mertig, 1992). Thus the fundamental subject matter of environmental sociology—the relationship between humans and the environment—is much more obvious and seen as far more significant than when Buttel wrote his pessimistic appraisal of the field in the mid-1980s or even when the field was emerging in the 1970s. In addition, growing recognition of the health threat posed by many environmental conditions makes it apparent that not only do human–environment interactions occur at the symbolic or cognitive level, once posited as the core of environmental sociology (Klausner, 1971), but that such conditions can have direct (and deleterious) impacts on human behaviour and well-being.

Especially significant have been the gradual development of scientific consensus and widespread public concern over the reality of human-induced global environmental change such as ozone depletion, loss of biodiversity and, to a lesser extent, global climate change (Dunlap, 1996). The finite ability of ecosystems to absorb the by-products of industrialization without disruption is increasingly seen as a more pressing limit than is scarcity of natural resources. Global environmental change highlights the fact that ecosystems serve not only as 're-source depot' and 'waste repository' for human societies, but as our 'living space' as well, and that these three uses are increasingly in conflict (Dunlap, 1993). For example, ozone depletion and global warming—both the result of the global ecosystem's inability to absorb industrial pollutants without being altered—may affect where humans can live safely as well as the availability of agricultural crops and other resources. Ultimately, ecological limits on humans stem from the finite ability of ecosystems (from local to global) to fulfil these three increasingly competing functions.

Widespread recognition of the human origins and consequences of global environmental change (GEC) represents an enormous opportunity for environmental sociology, as well as an obvious anomaly for human exemptionalism. Examining the human dimensions of GEC necessitates study of society–environment interactions, including a balanced examination of the impacts of humans on the environment as well as the effects of ecological constraints on human societies (Stern, 1993). Further, the range of potential societal responses to such change (denial, adaptation, mitigation and so on) highlights the vital role of human agency in responding to ecological constraints. In fact, we must acknowledge that our original call for the abandonment of the exemptionalist paradigm tended to empha-

size the importance of ecological constraints and to play down the potential of modern reflexive societies to cope with (but not escape) such constraints (Spaargaren and Mol, 1992).

REVITALIZATION OF ENVIRONMENTAL SOCIOLOGY

Given the dramatic increase in the societal salience of environmental issues—measured by environmental activism, media attention, public opinion and policy making—in the USA since the late 1980s, it is not surprising that sociological interest in these topics was also rekindled. This is apparent from a variety of indicators, including membership in the ASA Section on Environment and Technology. After bottoming out from 1983 to 1985 and increasing only slightly over the next three years, section membership grew rapidly in the late 1980s and early 1990s, reaching its peak in 1993 and levelling off to around 400 since then. The field's revitalization is also confirmed by the publication of several new texts (Cable and Cable, 1995; Cylke, 1993; Foster, 1994; Harper, 1996; Schnaiberg and Gould, 1994), an obvious indicator of growing interest among both faculty and students. Finally, the few departments offering formal graduate training in the field have experienced a sharp increase in student interest.

Most significantly, unlike the situation in the 1970s, environmental sociology is now receiving a good deal of attention internationally, as evidenced by this volume. Indeed, in the 1990s a majority of the potential texts written in English have been written by Canadians (Hannigan, 1995; Mehta and Ouellet, 1995; Murphy, 1994) and Europeans (Dickens, 1992; 1996; Goldblatt, 1996; Martell, 1994; Yearley, 1991). Recent years have also seen the formation of environmental sociology organizations in countries such as the UK and Japan, and the formation of 'environmental social science associations' in Scandinavia, Brazil and Canada. In addition, a Working Group on Environment and Society, launched within the International Sociological Association in 1990, grew rapidly and achieved research committee status in record time.[4] In short, in the 1990s environmental sociology is being institutionalized internationally along the same lines as occurred in the USA in the 1970s. This likely reflects, in part, the fact that environmental conditions are now viewed as problematic in virtually all nations, as well as being inherently global in nature (Dunlap *et al.*, 1993).

Much of this new and renewed interest in environmental issues, both in the USA and elsewhere, has taken the form of sociological analyses of societal reaction to environmental problems in the form of studies of public opinion and perceptions, environmentalism, green politics and environmental policy making (see, for example, Hannigan, 1995; Martell, 1994; Yearley, 1991). The political economy of environmental problems and sociological contributions to risk analyses, both discerned as emerging areas by Buttel (1987), have continued to attract increasing attention. While some traditional sub-areas such as housing and the built environment and social impact assessment have apparently not yet benefited much from the revitalization of sociological interest in the environment (perhaps because they are only indirectly affected by the upturn in societal interest in environmental problems), new research emphases have emerged. Most obvious in the USA has been the virtual explosion of interest in issues related to growing awareness of the pervasiveness of environmental hazards at the local level: studies of community reaction to local hazards; the rapidly spreading NIMBY ('Not In My Back Yard') syndrome; the emergence of local, grassroots environmental groups; and the interrelated phenomena of 'environmental racism' (the location of hazards in predominantly minority areas) and the emerging 'environmental justice' movement among minorities.[5]

In addition to the wide range of work noted above, the revitalization of environmental sociology is particularly apparent from a recent spate of publications self-consciously designed as contributions to the methodological, conceptual and theoretical 'core' of the field—something that was notably absent during the 1980s. Many of these contributions involve efforts to apply insights from traditional theoretical perspectives, ranging from symbolic interactionism to Marxism, to help understand human–environment relations, yet their authors (who are often British) frequently acknowledge the limitations imposed by the 'exemptionalist' nature of these perspectives and call for a reorientation away from our traditional disciplinary assumption that the biophysical environment is irrelevant to modern, industrialized societies (Benton, 1991; Dickens, 1992, 1996; Goldblatt, 1996; Jones, 1990; Murphy, 1994; Weigert, 1991). In addition to these efforts at 'greening' sociological theory, renewed attention is also being paid to conceptual and methodological issues involved in examining society–environment interactions, primarily by empirically oriented American scholars (Freudenburg and Gramling, 1993; Gramling and Freudenburg, 1996; Freudenburg *et al.*, 1995; Kroll-Smith and Couch, 1991; Kroll-Smith *et al.*, 1996). The eventual merging of these theoretical and empirical efforts promises to yield important advances in understanding the nature of society–environment relations.

In sum, although most of the 1980s, the so-called 'Decade of Greed', was a difficult time for environmental sociology in the USA, recent years have seen a dramatic resurgence of interest in the field and signs of its intellectual revitalization. Despite Reagan-era efforts to define environmental conditions as non-problematic, they continued to worsen and their significant impacts on humans became increasingly apparent. In other words, real-world conditions (and, of course, societal attention to them) seem to have stimulated renewed sociological attention to the environment (see, for example, Foster, 1994: 8).

CHARACTERISTICS OF AMERICAN ENVIRONMENTAL SOCIOLOGY

While environmental sociology may have emerged in the USA, it has now taken root throughout much of the world. This raises the question of whether American environmental sociology retains any distinct characteristics. It appears to us that in addition to— and often as a result of—its longer history, American environmental sociology has some unique features. We highlight them via a comparison of apparent strengths and weaknesses of the field in the USA relative to the situation in Europe, particularly the UK, where environmental sociology seems to be flourishing.

Empirical Orientation

As is true of the larger discipline in the USA, American environmental sociology has a strong empirical orientation. Whether one traces its roots to research on natural resources or to studies of the emergence of environmentalism, one finds large bodies of empirical studies. In terms of the latter, for example, there are careful longitudinal analyses both of the evolution of public attitudes towards environmental issues and of membership in national environmental organizations (Dunlap and Mertig, 1992). Scores of studies of the social bases of support for various forms of environmentalism reveal that, although members of major national organizations such as the Sierra Club tend to be above average in socioeconomic status, the charge of 'environmental elitism' does not fit either the memberships of local, grassroots organizations or public support for environmental protection, which is widely distributed among social strata (Morrison and Dunlap, 1986). In short, American environmental sociology has produced a wealth of information on the nature, sources and evolution of societal concern with environmental problems.

The empirical orientation is also obvious from the body of knowledge that has accumulated concerning the sociocultural factors that influence both energy consumption and conservation (Lutzenhiser, 1993). Similarly, the rush to develop domestic sources of energy such as coal in the 1970s led to numerous studies of the social impacts of rapid growth in western US 'energy boomtowns' and findings useful for predicting the effects of rapid growth in rural areas regardless of its source (Freudenburg and Jones, 1991). Another body of research suggests that environmentally hazardous facilities such as landfills tend to be located disproportionately in lower-income and especially minorities communities, leading to charges of 'environmental racism' and pleas for 'environmental justice' (Bryant and Mohai, 1992). The validity and generalizability of this claim have recently been challenged (Oakes *et al.*, 1996) but, despite the politically charged nature of the debate, I expect that it will eventually be settled via additional and more carefully designed empirical work.

Systematic empirical research has also documented that community impacts of manmade or 'technological' disasters (such as leakage from a toxic waste site) tend to differ dramatically from those of 'natural' disasters such as floods, earthquakes and hurricanes: whereas the latter stimulate a cooperative, 'therapeutic' community, the former tend to generate controversy, conflict and community fragmentation (Couch and Kroll-Smith, 1991). More recently, researchers have discerned differing reactions to proposals to locate potentially hazardous facilities from those to discoveries of already-existing hazards within communities. While siting proposals often lead to a fairly unified 'NIMBY' reaction, discoveries of hazards tend to produce great conflict (Couch and Kroll-Smith, 1994).

This small sampling of empirical research (see Dunlap and Michelson, 1997, for reviews of additional research emphases) demonstrates that American environmental sociologists have developed a range of empirical generalizations that are proving to have considerable validity and reliability as well as policy relevance. Their work involves both a 'sociology of environmental issues' (for example, studies of environmental attitudes) and an 'environmental sociology' that examines the relations between social variables (such as race and socioeconomic status) and environmental variables (such as levels of pollution). In fact, now that it is no longer difficult to justify incorporating environmental variables into sociological research (Gramling and Freudenburg, 1996) and given the difficulty at times in distinguishing between social and physical phenomena (Buttel, 1996; Redclift, 1996), this distinction seems to have lost its utility. Thus we agree with Buttel (1987) that we should treat environmental sociology as consisting of the body of sociological work being conducted on environmental topics.

Cautious Constructionism

Related to American environmental sociologists' strong empirical orientation is their tendency to avoid the strong or strict social–constructionist perspective that has evolved over the past quarter-century in social problems theory and the sociology of science[6] and that was given additional impetus by the emergence of postmodernism. This view 'asserts that the environment (and our relations with it) is a purely social construction' in that 'it is simply a product of language, discourse and power-plays' (Dickens, 1996: 71). As a consequence, strong constructionism 'denies the importance of nature as an object external to human experience' (ibid.: 73). Such a perspective eschews the possibility of examining society–environment relations, since it acknowledges nothing (at least nothing knowable) external to human society, and thereby suggests a very restricted role for sociological analyses of environmental problems.[7]

A strong constructionist orientation, typically derived from the sociology of science and postmodernist discourse analysis, has been quite influential among European environmental sociologists and clearly offers important insights (see, for example, McNaughton and Urry, 1995; Wynne, 1994).[8] Yet, thus far, strong constructionism seems to have had less appeal to Americans. Greider and Garkovich's (1994: 5) recent call for environmental sociologists to move 'away from an increasingly dominant focus on the world that is there' towards a 'focus on how humans actors creatively use culture as a resource to construct symbols and meanings that define nature, the environment and human–environment relationships' has thus far generated little enthusiasm. More telling, perhaps, was Buttel's disavowal of his apparent endorsement of a strong constructionist perspective (most notable in

Taylor and Buttel, 1992) shortly after it was challenged (in an early version of Dunlap and Catton, 1994a; see also Murphy, 1994): 'Neither a "strong program" dissection of environmental knowledge nor a gratuitous postmodernist cultural sociology of environmental beliefs will or should change the reality of global environmental problems' (Buttel, 1993: 10).

In contrast, weaker forms of constructionism that analyse the important roles played by various actors such as activists, scientists and policy makers in generating societal recognition and definition of environmental conditions as 'problems'—without denying the objective existence of such problems or the possibility of discerning the relative validity of competing claims about them—have been widely used in the USA. In fact, a great deal of American environmental sociologists' work has focused on the activities of various 'claims makers' (environmentalists, industrialists and so on), the manner in which their competing claims about the environment are received by the public and policy makers, and the resulting dynamics of environmental issues in the policy arena (see, for example, Albrecht, 1975; Dietz et al., 1989; Schoenfeld et al., 1979). Typically, however, these analyses assume (and at times assert) the objective existence of environmental problems, rather than treating them as mere social constructions. Even Canadian John Hannigan (1995: 3), the author of an excellent book-length explication of the utility of a social constructivist approach to environmental sociology, disavows 'an extreme constructionist position which insists that the global ensemble of problems is purely a creation of the media (or science or ecological activists) with little basis in objective conditions'.

I am not trying to portray American scholars as naive objectivists (or as all of one mind in such matters). Indeed, recent cutting-edge efforts to understand the complexities of society–environment interactions explicitly combine consideration of the material/biophysical and symbolic/sociocultural dimensions of environmental issues in innovative ways that reveal the influences of both (for example, Freudenburg and Gramling, 1994; Freudenburg et al., 1995; Couch and Kroll-Smith, 1994; Kroll-Smith and Couch, 1991; Kroll-Smith et al., 1996). I do, however, think it is a strength of American environmental sociology that it has clearly not limited itself to treating the environment solely or even primarily as a social construction.

The influence of Americans' scepticism regarding the merits of a strong constructionist orientation, as well as their empirical orientation, has become apparent in recent work, on GEC. While Americans (Mazur and Lee, 1993) and Canadians (Ungar, 1992, 1995) have conducted a variety of constructionist-based analyses of various aspects of GEC, they have seldom offered 'deconstructions' of the concept as the latest environmental ideology à la Taylor and Buttel (1992). More importantly, such work has been complemented by empirical analyses of the social roots of tropical deforestation and greenhouse gas emissions (for example, Lutzenhiser and Hackett, 1993; Grimes and Roberts, 1993; Rudel with Horowitz, 1993). In contrast, most of the sociological work on GEC being conducted in Europe seems confined to theoretical analyses and investigations of the roles of various claims makers (especially environmentalists and scientists) in GEC policy debates (for a nice overview of UK work on GEC, see Redclift and Benton, 1994).

Insular and Atheoretical

While I think the cautious constructionism and empirical orientation of environmental sociology in the USA has been beneficial, this is less the case with two other interrelated characteristics that have been attributed to the field: that it has remained isolated from the larger discipline and, in part as a result, that it remains highly atheoretical (Buttel, 1987, 1996; Spaargaren and Mol, 1992). Both charges have some merit and I think they stem partially from unique aspects of the American situation.

First, regarding the presumed insularity, the lack of an 'intellectual core' within American sociology is frequently noted, and the growth of numerous specializations has led to what some term the 'Balkanization' of the discipline (Buttel, 1987). Given this, we wonder whether environmental sociology is truly more insular than many other (especially the newer) specialities in the American Sociological Association. If the field is indeed more insular in the USA than in other nations, this may stem from its earlier emergence in an era of sociological neglect of environmental issues and consequent scepticism of their relevance (they were seen as 'faddish') as well as the hostile societal situation during the 1980s. In such circumstances it is perhaps not surprising that environmental sociologists felt more comfortable, despite their differences, talking to one another rather than to the larger discipline. In contrast, by the time the field 'took off' abroad, perhaps acid rain, ozone depletion, toxic contamination and so on had made the significance of the 'ecological problématique' obvious to society (as suggested by the enormous attention accorded to the Brundtland Report) and, therefore, to the social sciences as well as funding bodies.

In terms of lack of theoretical development, a similar phenomenon may have operated along with the obvious preference for empirical over theoretical work among American sociologists. In the 1970s, leading American sociologists and influential theorists either ignored environmental issues or, as previously noted in the cases of Bell, Nisbet and Lipset, dismissed their significance (admittedly in part because of the overemphasis on 'limits to growth' at the time). In contrast, a decade later, leading European theorists such as Giddens, Luhmann, Beck and Touraine recognized the vital role of environmental issues and problems and began to assign them key roles in their theoretical schemas. Indeed, ecological matters have now become a central aspect of European theorizing on the nature of modernization leading Mol (1995: 23) to argue that 'the environment has moved from the periphery to the centre of sociological attention and is now acknowledged, as a major factor in triggering institutional transformations'. Interestingly, however, leading American theorists such as Jeffrey Alexander have not yet tackled the environmental question.

Finally, Catton's and my own call (1978, 1980) for a paradigmatic revolution has been criticized for contributing to environmental sociology's failure to engage the larger discipline (Spaargaren and Mol, 1992). To the extent that our plea for shedding the exemptionalist blinkers of mainstream sociology in lieu of a more ecological paradigm admittedly played down the continuing importance of sociological theories for providing insight into environmental issues, I must plead guilty. However, besides being sceptical of having had that much influence, I note that several theoretically insightful analyses building upon mainstream political economy perspectives— Schnaiberg's (1980) analysis of the 'treadmill of production', Buttel's (1985) examination of environmental regulation via theories of the state and O'Connor's (1988) explication of environmental problems as the 'second contradiction' of capitalism— have failed to attract attention from scholars outside environmental sociology. Thus, once again, we face the ironic possibility (given the early emergence of environmental sociology in the USA) that American sociology in general has been an infertile field for the growth of environmental sociology. Perhaps unique characteristics of the American experience, especially resource abundance and rapid growth (Potter, 1954), continue to make the notion that human societies are free from ecological constraints particularly appealing in the USA.

In sum, environmental sociology in the USA has both strengths and weaknesses. In terms of the latter, I suspect that the increasing internationalization of sociological interest in environmental matters (both by self-identified environmental sociologists and by leading theorists), along with the globalization of environmental problems, will inevitably overcome the presumed insularity of American environmental sociology. I also think that the marriage of the strong empirical orientation apparent in the USA with the stronger theoretical orientation of our colleagues in Europe and elsewhere augurs well for the future of the field.

CONCLUDING OBSERVATIONS

I conclude by assessing the current standing of sociological interest in environmental issues relative to Catton's and my original call for the development of environmental sociology as a distinct area of specialization and for adoption of an ecological paradigm to guide it. In terms of the former, it is obvious that, despite some ups and downs, environmental sociology has established itself as a viable area of specialization, not only in the USA but throughout much of the world. Indeed, it has become institutionalized at the international level. Moreover, at least in Europe, environmental issues have begun

to receive considerable attention and are increasingly assigned theoretical import in the larger discipline. Overall, our hope for increased sociological attention to the environment has been exceeded.

Our plea for replacing the discipline's human exemptionalism paradigm with an ecological one is more difficult to assess, in part because it was inherently more ambiguous as well as provocative. One's assessment clearly depends upon one's interpretation of our call for a paradigmatic shift, which in turn is heavily influenced by one's conception of 'paradigm'. It appears to me that there are at least three possibilities (see, for example, various chapters in Mehta and Ouellet, 1995). I label them the 'strong', 'moderate' and 'weak' interpretations, reflecting differing levels of expectation for the utility of an ecological, versus exemptionalist, perspective.

The *strong* interpretation, used by our critics, treats paradigms as essentially synonymous with theories and thereby criticizes our formulation of the 'new ecological paradigm' (NEP) as lacking sufficient specificity to lead to testable hypotheses (Buttel, 1978, 1987, 1996). Our response was, and remains, that our depictions of both the dominant exemptionalist paradigm and our proposed ecological alternative represent sets of broad background assumptions (or world views) that influence the kinds of issues that are seen as appropriate for sociological scholarship, and were never intended to be logically interrelated sets of propositions from which testable hypotheses can be deduced (Catton and Dunlap, 1980; Dunlap and Catton, 1994b). We made ourselves vulnerable to this charge by de-emphasizing the obvious diversity and continuing utility of sociological theories (see, for example, Sunderlin. 1995) while emphasizing the hegemonic nature of their shared exemptionalism, and by vaguely (and somewhat over-zealously) implying that the NEP might supplant them. We subsequently noted that we expected the NEP *not* to replace Marxist, Weberian or other perspectives, but to stimulate development of more ecologically sensitive or 'greener' versions of them, which is precisely what is being done with Marxist (Benton, 1996; Dickens, 1992) Weberian (Murphy, 1994) and symbolic interactionist (Weigert, 1991) theories. Nonetheless, because we apparently created unrealistic expectations concerning the NEP's utility in guiding empirical research, it continues to receive criticism (Buttel, 1996; Spaargaren and Mol, 1992).

The *weak* interpretation of our argument would be that we were calling for sociology to shed the blinkers we labelled the 'human exemptionalism paradigm' (HEP) in order to recognize the significance of environmental problems. Judged by this criterion, our argument has fared much better. Our portrayal of sociology's exemptionalist orientation seems to have resonated with a number of previously cited colleagues whose efforts to 'green' one or more theoretical perspectives represent (in our view) reasonable operationalizations of our plea to adopt an ecological perspective, and Vaillancourt (1995) even discerns the emergence of 'ecosociology'. Other theorists have come to compatible conclusions regarding the degree to which sociological traditions have inhibited serious concern with environmental issues (for example, Beck, 1995: ch. 10; Goldblatt, 1996; Redclift and Woodgate, 1994).

Far more important, however, is the growing attention to environmental issues within the larger discipline, particularly in theoretical efforts to understand modernization and postmodernity (Mol, 1995). While obviously a response to the increased salience of ecological conditions throughout society, the attention being given to ideas such as the 'risk society' challenges Buttel's gloomy assessment of a decade ago. While it is likely that sociology 'has handily withstood the challenges to its theoretical assumptions posed by environmental sociologists' (Buttel, 1987: 366), it has apparently been less able to withstand the challenges posed by the heightened visibility of environmental degradation. One need only compare current theorising on postmodernization with the modernization theories of two or three decades ago (see Hannigan, 1995: 9–10) to see the declining credibility of exemptionalism in our discipline.

The *moderate* interpretation of our argument is that we were trying to justify incorporation of environmental variables or 'non-social facts' into sociological analyses, something that our exemptionalist traditions prohibited.[9] Like Gramling and Freudenburg (1996) I think that this has clearly been accomplished via numerous empirical investigations by environmental sociologists, such as the studies of communities' experiences with toxic wastes and minorities' exposure to environmental hazards, cited above. And, I hasten to add, analyses of society–environment interactions have clearly been enriched (albeit often complicated) by enhanced awareness of the sociocultural and symbolic meanings attached to various aspects of the environment emphasized by those with a constructionist bent. It is only when a strong constructionist orientation leads to dismissal of the possibility of studying human interaction with the environment that sociologists remain within the confines of the exemptionalist premise that the physical environment is irrelevant to modern humans.

In conclusion, while it has a long way to go, I think sociology has made considerable progress towards recognizing the importance of the ecological dimension of human existence during the past two decades. If the trend continues, I suspect that analyses of ecological matters—both empirical and theoretical—may eventually become so common among sociologists that there will no longer be a need for an 'environmental sociology' per se. This would represent the ultimate demise of human exemptionalism in our discipline.

ENDNOTES

1. We originally labelled the dominant disciplinary perspective the 'human *exceptionalist* paradigm', but subsequently shifted to the 'human *exemptionalist* paradigm' to acknowledge that we were not questioning that homo sapiens possessed 'exceptional' characteristics, but only that these characteristics 'exempted' our species from ecological constraints. Likewise, we revised the call for a 'new *environmental* paradigm' to that for a 'new *ecological* paradigm' (Dunlap and Catton, 1979; Catton and Dunlap, 1980). For an update of the HEP–NEP Intent, see Dunlap and Catton (1994b).

2. This section will draw heavily on Dunlap and Catton (1994a). We are using 'American' in the narrow sense of applying to the United States. While there are many similarities between environmental sociology in Canada and the USA, we do not purport to describe the development of the field in Canada. For insight into the Canadian situation, see Mehta and Ouellet (1995), particularly the chapter by Vaillancourt (1995).

3. The growing importance of technological accidents and hazards, along with recognition of the technological component inherent in most environmental problems, led the ASA Section to change its name to 'Section on Environment and Technology' in 1988, parallel to the SSSP Division's 1983 change to 'Division on Environment and Technology'.

4. This was accomplished by a merger with the existing Research Committee on Social Ecology.

5. See, for example, the special issue of *Social Problems* (February 1993) devoted to 'environmental justice', the special issue of *Sociological Spectrum* (January–March 1993) devoted to 'New Directions in Hazard, Risk and Disaster Research' and the special issue of *Sociological Perspectives* (Summer 1996) devoted to 'Environmental Conflicts'.

6. Yearley (1991) offers a rare usage of both perspectives. Both are variously labelled 'constructivist' and 'constructionist' and we treat the two labels as synonymous.

7. Space constraints prevent us from discussing the growing debate over the relative strengths and weaknesses of the constructionist/ relativist versus objectivist/realist perspectives on environmental problems, so we refer interested readers to Buttel (1996). Dickens (1996: ch. 3), Dunlap and Catton (1994a), Greider and Garkovich (1994), McNaughton and Urry (1995) and Murphy (1994) for various perspectives on it within environmental sociology, and to Soper (1995) for a broader-ranging analysis of the two views. For useful efforts to move beyond the debate, see Rosa's (forthcoming) discussion of risk and Redclift's (1996) discussion of sustainable development.

8. Ironically, however, British 'realists' such as Benton (1993) and Dickens (1996) have been among its most vocal critics.

9. An indication of the strength of this 'taboo' at the time we were writing can be seen in debates over the appropriateness of employing environmental variables in sociological analyses of agriculture (Dunlap and Martin, 1983).

REFERENCES

Albrecht, Stan L. (1975), 'The Environment as a Social Problem', in A. L. Mauss (ed.), *Social Problems as Social Movements*, Philadelphia: J. P. Lippincott.

Barney, Gerald O. (1980), *The Global 2000 Report to the President of the U.S.*, Elmsford, NY: Pergamon Press.

Barol, Bill (1988), 'The Eighties Are Over', *Newsweek*, January, 48.

Beck, Ulrich (1995), *Ecological Enlightenment*, Atlantic Highlands, NJ: Humanities Press.

Bell, Daniel (1977), 'Are There "Social Limits" to Growth?', in K. D. Wilson (ed.), *Prospects for Growth: Changing Expectations for the Future*, New York: Praeger.

Benton, Ted (1991), 'Biology and Social Science: Why the Return of the Repressed Should Be Given A (Cautious) Welcome', *Sociology*, 25, 1–29.

Benton, Ted (1993), *Natural Relations: Ecology, Animals Rights & Social Justice*, London/New York: Verso.

Benton, Ted (ed.) (1996), *The Greening of Marxism*, New York: Guilford.

Boggs, Danny J. (1985), 'When Governments Forecast', *Futures*, 17, 435–9.

Bryant, Bunyan and Paul Mohai (eds) (1992), *Race and the Incidence of Environmental Hazards*, Boulder, CO: Westview.

Bullard, Robert D. (1983), 'Solid Waste Sites and the Black Houston Community', *Sociological Inquiry*, 53, 273–88.

Burch, William R. (1971), *Daydreams and Nightmares: A Sociological Essay on the American Environment*, New York: Harper & Row.

Burch, William R., Neil H. Cheek and Lee Taylor (eds) (1972), *Social Behavior Natural Resources, and the Environment*, New York: Harper & Row.

Buttel, Frederick H. (1978), 'Environmental Sociology: A New Paradigm?', *The American Sociologist*, 13, 252–6.

Buttel, Frederick H. (1985), 'Environmental Quality and the State: Some Political–Sociological Observations on Environmental Regulation', *Research in Political Sociology*, 1, 167–88.

Buttel, Frederick H. (1987), 'New Directions in Environmental Sociology', *Annual Review of Sociology*, 13, 465–88.

Buttel, Frederick H. (1993), 'Environmental Sociology as Science and Social Movement', *Environment, Technology and Society* (Newsletter of the ASA Section on Environment and Technology), no. 73, Fall, 101–11.

Buttel, Frederick H. (1996), 'Environmental and Resource Sociology: Theoretical Issues and Opportunities for Synthesis', *Rural Sociology*, 61, 56–76.

Cable, Sherry and Charles Cable (1995), *Environmental Problems/Grassroots Solutions*, New York: St Martin's Press.

Catton, William R. (1972), 'Sociology in an Age of Fifth Wheels', *Social Forces*, 50, 436–47.

Catton, William R. and Riley E. Dunlap (1978), 'Environmental Sociology: A New Paradigm', *The American Sociologist*, 13, 41–9.

Catton, William R. and Riley E. Dunlap (1980), 'A New Ecological Paradigm for Post-Exuberant Sociology', *American Behavioral Scientist*, 24, 15–47.

Couch, Stephen R. and J. Stephen Kroll-Smith (eds) (1991), *Communities at Risk: Collective Responses to Technological Hazards*, New York: Peter Lang.

Couch, Stephen R. and J. Stephen Kroll-Smith (1994), 'Environmental Controversies, Interactional Resources and Rural Communities: Siting Versus Exposure Disputes', *Rural Sociology*, 59, 1–24.

Cylke, F. Kurt (1993), *The Environment*, New York: Harper Collins.

Dickens, Peter (1992), *Society and Nature: Towards a Green Social Theory*, Philadelphia: Temple University Press.

Dickens, Peter (1996), *Reconstructing Nature: Alienation, Emancipation and the Division of Labour*, London/New York: Routledge.

Dietz, Thomas, Paul C. Stern and Robert W. Rycroft (1989), 'Definitions of Conflict and Legitimation of Resources: The Case of Environmental Risk', *Sociological Forum*, 4, 47–70.

Dunlap, Riley E. (1993), 'From Environmental to Ecological Problems', in C. Calhoun and G. Ritzer (eds), *Social Problems*, New York: McGraw-Hill; reprinted in M. Redclift and G. Woodgate (eds), *The Sociology of the Environment*, Vol. 1, Aldershot/Brookfield: Edward Elgar, 1995.

Dunlap, Riley E. (1995), 'Public Opinion and Environmental Policy', in J. P. Lester (ed.), *Environmental Politics & Policy*, 2nd ed., Durham, NC: Duke University Press.

Dunlap, Riley E. (1996), 'Public Perceptions of Global Warming: A Cross-National Comparison', in Human Dimensions of Global Environmental Change Program (ed.), *Global Change, Local Challenge*, Vol. 2, Geneva: Human Dimensions Program.

Dunlap, Riley E. and William R. Catton (1979), 'Environmental Sociology', *Annual Review of Sociology*, 5, 243–73.

Dunlap, Riley E. and William R. Catton (1983), 'What Environmental Sociologists Have in Common (Whether Concerned with "Built" or "Natural" Environments)', *Sociological Inquiry*, 53, 113–35.

Dunlap, Riley E. and William R. Catton (1994a), 'Struggling with Human Exemptionalism: The Rise, Decline and Revitalization of Environmental Sociology', *The American Sociologist*, 25, 5–30.

Dunlap, Riley E. and William R. Catton (1994b), 'Toward an Ecological Sociology: The Development, Current Status and Probable Future of Environmental Sociology', in W. V. D'Antonio, M. Sasaki and Y. Yonchayashi (eds), *Ecology, Society and The Quality of Social Life*, New Brunswick/London: Transaction Publishers.

Dunlap, Riley E. and Kenneth E. Martin (1983), 'Bringing Environment into the Study of Agriculture', *Rural Sociology*, 48, 201–18.

Dunlap, Riley E. and Angela G. Mertig (eds) (1992), *American Environmentalism: The U.S. Environmental Movement, 1970–1990*, Washington, DC: Taylor and Francis.

Dunlap, Riley E. and William Michelson (eds) (1997), *Handbook of Environmental Sociology*, Westport, CT: Greenwood.

Dunlap, Riley E. and Kent D. Van Liere (1984), 'Commitment to the Dominant Social Paradigm and Concern for Environmental Quality', *Social Science Quarterly*, 65, 1013–28.

Dunlap, Riley E., George H. Gallup and Alec M. Gallup (1993), 'Of Global Concern: Results of the Health of the Planet Survey', *Environment*, 35, November, 6–15, 33–9.

Elgin, Duane (1981), *Voluntary Simplicity*, New York: William Morrow.

Foster, John Bellamy (1994), *The Vulnerable Planet*, New York: Monthly Review Press.

Freudenburg, William R. and Robert Gramling (1989), 'The Emergence of Environmental Sociology', *Sociological Inquiry*, 59, 439–52.

Freudenburg, William R. and Robert Gramling (1993), 'Socioenvironmental Factors and Development Policy: Understanding Opposition and Support for Offshore Oil Development', *Sociological Forum*, 8, 341–64.

Freudenburg, William R. and Robert Gramling (1994), 'Natural Resources and Rural Poverty: A Closer Look', *Society and Natural Resources*, 7, 5–22.

Freudenburg, William R. and Robert Emmett Jones (1991), 'Criminal Behavior and Rapid Community Growth: Examining the Evidence', *Rural Sociology*, 56, 619–45.

Freudenburg, William R., Scott Frickel and Robert Gramling (1995), 'Beyond the Nature/Society Divide: Learning to Think About a Mountain', *Sociological Forum*, 10, 361–92.

Goldblatt, David (1996), *Social Theory and the Environment*, Boulder, CO: Westview.

Gramling, Robert and William R. Freudenburg (1996), 'Environmental Sociology: Toward a Paradigm for the 21st Century', *Sociological Spectrum*, 16, 47–60.

Greider, Thomas and Lorraine Garkovich (1994), 'Landscapes: The Social Construction of Nature and the Environment', *Rural Sociology*, 59, 1–24.

Grimes, Peter and J. Timmons Roberts (1993), 'Social Roots of Environmental Damage: A World-Systems Analysis of Global Warming and Deforestation', Paper presented at the Annual Meeting of the American Sociological Association, Miami Beach, August.

Hannigan, John A. (1995), *Environmental Sociology: A Social Constructionist Perspective*, London/New York: Routledge.

Harper, Charles L. (1996), *Environment and Society*, Upper Saddle River, NJ: Prentice-Hall.

Humphrey, Craig R. and Frederick H. Buttel (1982), *Environment, Energy, and Society*, Belmont, CA: Wadsworth.

Jones, Alwyn (1990), 'Social Symbiosis: A Gaian Critique of Contemporary Social Theory', *The Ecologist*, 20,108–13.

Klausner, Samuel Z. (1971), *On Man in His Environment*, San Francisco: Jossey-Bass.

Kroll-Smith, J. Stephen and Stephen R. Couch (1991), 'What is a Disaster? An Ecological–Symbolic Approach to Resolving the Definitional Debate', *International Journal of Mass Emergencies and Disasters*, 9, 355–66.

Kroll-Smith, Steve, Valerie Gunter and Shirley Laska (1996), 'The Symbolic, the Physical and Sociology: How We Theorize Environments', Paper presented at the Annual Meeting of the American Sociological Association, New York, August.

Levine, Adeline Gordon (1982), *Love Canal: Science, Politics, and People*, Lexington, MA: Lexington Books.

Lipset, Seymour Martin (1979), 'Predicting the Future of Post-Industrial Society: Can We Do It?', in S. M. Lipset (ed.), *The Third Century: America as a Post-Industrial Society*, Stanford, CA: Hoover Institution Press.

Lutzenhiser, Loren (1993). 'Social and Behavioral Aspects of Energy Use', *Annual Review of Energy and Environment*, 18: 247–89.

Lutzenhiser, Loren and Bruce Hackett (1993), 'Social Stratification and Environmental Degradation: Understanding Household CO_2 Production', *Social Problems*, 40, 50–73.

McNaughton, Phil and John Urry (1995), 'Towards a Sociology of Nature', *Sociology*, 29, 203–20.

Martell, Luke (1994), *Environment and Society*, Amherst: University of Massachusetts Press.

Mazur, Allan and Jinling Lee (1993), 'Sounding the Global Alarm: Environmental Issues in the U.S. National News', *Social Studies of Science*, 23, 681–720.

Meadows, Donella H., Dennis L Meadows, Jorgen Randers and William W. Behrens (1972), *The Limits to Growth*, Washington, DC: Universe Books.

Mehta, Michael D. and Eric Ouellet (eds) (1995), *Environmental Sociology: Theory and Practice*, North York: Captus Press.

Michelson, William H. (1970), *Man and His Urban Environment*, Reading, MA: Addison-Wesley.

Milbrath, Lester (1982), *Environmentalists: Vanguard for a New Society*, Albany: State University of New York Press.

Mol, Arthur P. J. (1995), *The Refinement of Production: Ecological Modernization Theory and the Chemical Industry*, Utrecht, the Netherlands: Van Arkel.

Molotch, Harvey and Ross Charles Follett (1971), 'Air Pollution as a Problem for Sociological Research', in P. B. Downing (ed.), *Air Pollution and the Social Sciences*, New York: Praeger.

Morrison, Denton E. (1976), 'Growth, Environment, Equity and Scarcity', *Social Science Quarterly*, 57, 292–306.

Morrison, Denton E. and Riley E. Dunlap (1986), 'Environmentalism and Elitism: A Conceptual and Empirical Analysis', *Environmental Management*, 10, 581–9.

Murphy, Raymond (1994), *Rationality & Nature*, Boulder, CO: Westview.

Nisbet, Robert (1980), *History of the Idea of Progress*, New York: Basic Books.

Oakes, John Michael, Douglas L. Anderton and Andy B. Anderson (1996), 'A Longitudinal Analysis of Environmental Equity in Communities with Hazardous Waste Facilities', *Social Science Research*, 25, 125–48.

O'Connor, James (1988), 'Capitalism, Nature, Socialism: A Theoretical Introduction', *Capitalism/Nature/Socialism*, 1, 11–38.

Potter, David M. (1954), *People of Plenty: Economic Abundance and the American Character*, Chicago: University of Chicago Press.

Redclift, Michael (1996). 'Sociology and Sustainability: Northern Preoccupations', unpublished paper, University of London, Wye College.

Redclift, Michael and Ted Benton (eds) (1994), *Social Theory and the Global Environment*, London and New York: Routledge.

Redclift, Michael and Graham Woodgate (1994), 'Sociology and the Environment: Discordant Discourse?' in M. Redclift and T. Benton (eds), *Social Theory and the Global Environment*, London/New York: Routledge.

Rosa, Eugene A. (forthcoming), 'Metatheoretical Foundations for Post-Normal Risk', *Journal of Risk Research*, 1.

Rosa, Eugene A., Gary E. Machlis and Kenneth M. Keating (1988), 'Energy and Society', *Annual Review of Sociology*, 14, 149–72.

Rudel, Thomas K. with Bruce Horowitz (1993), *Tropical Deforestation: Small Farmers and Land*

Clearing in the Ecuadorian Amazon, New York: Columbia University Press.

Schnaiberg, Allan (1975), 'Social Syntheses of the Societal–Environmental Dialectic: The Role of Distributional Impacts', *Social Science Quarterly,* 56, 5–20.

Schnaiberg, Allan (1980), *The Environment: From Surplus to Scarcity,* New York: Oxford University Press.

Schnaiberg, Allan and Kenneth Alan Gould (1994), *Environment and Society: The Enduring Conflict,* New York: St. Martin's Press.

Schnaiberg, Allan, Nicholas Watts and Klaus Zimmerman (eds) (1986), *Distributional Conflicts in Environmental Resource Policy,* New York: St. Martin's Press.

Schoenfeld, A. Clay, Robert F. Meier and Robert J. Griffin (1979), 'Constructing a Social Problem: The Press and the Environment', *Social Problems,* 27, 38–61.

Shabecoff, Philip (1996), 'Greens vs. Congress: A Play-By-Play', *The Amicus Journal,* 18, Summer, 24–9.

Short James F. (1984), 'The Social Fabric at Risk: Toward the Social Transformation of Risk Analysis', *American Sociological Review,* 49, 711–25.

Simon, Julian L. (1981), *The Ultimate Resource,* Champaign: University of Illinois Press.

Simon, Julian L. and Herman Kahn (eds) (1984), *The Resourceful Earth,* New York: Basil Blackwell.

Soper, Kate (1995), *What is Nature?,* Oxford: Blackwell.

Spaargaren, Gert and Arthur P. J. Mol (1992), 'Sociology, Environment and Modernity: Ecological Modernization as a Theory of Social Change', *Society and Natural Resources,* 5, 323–44.

Stern, Paul C. (1993), 'A Second Environmental Science: Human–Environment Interactions', *Science,* 260, 1897–9.

Sunderlin, William D. (1995), 'Global Environmental Change, Sociology and Paradigm Isolation', *Global Environmental Change,* 5, 211–20.

Taylor, Peter J. and Frederick H. Buttel (1992), 'How Do We Know We Have Global Environmental Problems?', *Geoforum,* 23, 405–16.

Ungar, Sheldon (1992), 'The Rise and (Relative) Decline of Global Warming as a Social Problem', *Sociological Quarterly,* 33, 483–501.

Ungar, Sheldon (1995), 'Social Scares and Global Warming: Beyond the Rio Convention', *Society and Natural Resources,* 8, 443–56.

Vaillancourt, Jean-Guy (1995), 'Sociology of the Environment: From Human Ecology to Ecosociology', in M. D. Mehta and E. Ouellet (eds), *Environmental Sociology: Theory and Practice,* North York: Captus Press.

Viviano, Frank (1980), 'Happy Days Again', *Lewiston Tribune,* 8 June, 2B.

Weigert, Andrew J. (1991), 'Transverse Interaction: A Pragmatic Perspective on Environment as Other', *Symbolic Interaction,* 14, 353–63.

Wynne, Brian (1994), 'Scientific Knowledge and the Global Environment', in M. Redclift and T. Benton (eds), *Social Theory and the Global Environment,* London/New York: Routledge.

Yankelovich, Daniel and Bernard Lefkowitz (1980), 'The Public Debate on Growth: Preparing for Resolution', *Technological Forecasting and Social Change,* 17, 95–140.

Yearley, Steven (1991), *The Green Case: A Sociology of Environmental Issues, Arguments and Politics,* London: Harper-Collins.

4. Marx's Theory of Metabolic Rift: Classical Foundations for Environmental Sociology[1]*

JOHN BELLAMY FOSTER

CLASSICAL BARRIERS TO ENVIRONMENTAL SOCIOLOGY

In recent decades, we have witnessed a significant transformation in social thought as various disciplines have sought to incorporate ecological awareness into their core paradigms in response to the challenge raised by environmentalism and by what is now widely perceived as a global ecological crisis. This transformation has involved a twofold process of rejecting much of previous thought as ecologically unsound, together with an attempt to build on the past, where possible. This can be seen as occurring with unequal degrees of success in the various disciplines. Geography, with its long history of focusing on the development of the natural landscape and on biogeography (see Sauer 1963), was the social science that adapted most easily to growing environmental concerns. Anthropology, with a tradition of investigating cultural survival and its relation to ecological conditions (see Geertz 1963; Milton 1996), also adjusted quickly to a period of greater environmental awareness. In other social science disciplines, significant progress in incorporating ecological ideas has been made, yet with less discernible effect on the core understandings of these fields. Economics, which was able to draw on the theoretical foundations provided by A. C. Pigou's *Economics of Welfare* (1920), has seen the rapid development of a distinctive, if limited, approach to environmental issues focusing on the internalization of "externalities"—making "environmental economics…one of the fastest-growing academic sub-disciplines throughout the industrial world" (Jacobs 1994, p. 67). As a relatively atheoretical field, political science has had little difficulty in incorporating environmental issues into its analysis of public policy, its focus on pluralist interest groups, its social contract theory, and more recently its emphasis on rational choice (Dryzek 1997)—though the pragmatic character of most political science in the United States, together with the lack of a strong Green political party and the absence of a clear connection between identification with environmental causes and voting behavior, has kept the politics of the environment on the margins of the discipline.

In sociology too, dramatic progress has been made, as seen by the rapid growth of the subfield of environmental sociology in the 1970s and again (after a period of quiescence) in the late 1980s and 1990s (see

*This is a slightly revised article that first appeared in the *American Journal of Sociology* Volume 105, Number 2 (September 1999): 366–405. Copyright © 1999 by the University of Chicago Press.

Dunlap 1997). Nevertheless, sociology is perhaps unique within the social sciences in the degree of resistance to environmental issues. An early barrier erected between society and nature, sociology and biology—dividing the classical sociologies of Marx, Weber, and Durkheim from the biological and naturalistic concerns that played a central role in the preclassical sociology of the social Darwinists—has hindered the incorporation of environmental sociology within the mainstream of the discipline, according to an interpretation repeatedly voiced by prominent environmental sociologists over the last two and a half decades (Burch 1971, pp. 14–20; Dunlap and Catton 1979, pp. 58–59; Benton 1994, pp. 28–30; Murphy 1994, pp. ix–x; Beck 1995, pp. 117–20; Buttel 1996, pp. 57–58; Murphy 1996).

Hence, until recently "there has…been general agreement among environmental sociologists that the classical sociological tradition has been inhospitable to the nurturing of ecologically-informed sociological theory" (Buttel 1986, p. 338). "From an environmental-sociological point of view," Buttel (1996, p. 57) has argued, "the classical tradition can be said to be 'radically sociological,' in that in their quest to liberate social thought and sociology from reductionisms, prejudices, power relations, and magic, the classical theorists (and, arguably more so, the 20th century interpreters of the classical tradition) wound up exaggerating the autonomy of social processes from the natural world." Likewise, Benton (1994, p. 29) has observed that "the conceptual structure or 'disciplinary matrix' by which sociology came to define itself, especially in relation to potentially competing disciplines such as biology and psychology, effectively excluded or forced to the margins of the discipline questions about the relations between society and its 'natural' or 'material' substrate." "Sociology," according to one

prominent environmental sociologist, "was constructed as if nature didn't matter" (Murphy 1996, p. 10). Such marginalization of the physical environment was made possible, in part, through the enormous economic and technological successes of the industrial revolution, which have long given the impression that human society is independent of its natural environment (Dunlap and Martin 1983, pp. 202-3). This is seen as offering an explanation for the fact that "sociological work on resource scarcity never appeared in the discipline's top journals" in the United States (Dunlap 1997, p. 23; also Dunlap and Catton 1994, p. 8).

Modern sociology in its classical period, according to the prevailing outlook within environmental sociology, was consolidated around a humanistic worldview that emphasized human distinctiveness in relation to nature. This has been referred to by some as the old "human exemptionalist paradigm" in contrast to the "new environmental paradigm," which rejects the anthropocentrism supposedly characteristic of the former view (Catton and Dunlap 1978; Dunlap and Catton 1994). With respect to Durkheim, for example, it has been argued that the social constituted a distinct reality, relatively autonomous from the physical individual and from psychological and biological pressures (Benton and Redclift 1994, p. 3; Dunlap and Catton 1979, p. 58). "The thrust of Durkheim's and Weber's methodological arguments," according to Goldblatt (1996, p. 3), "was to cordon off sociology from biology and nature, rejecting "all forms of biological determinism"; while Marx's treatment of such issues, though considerable, was largely confined to the "marginal" realm of agricultural economics.

In the language of contemporary environmentalism, then, sociology is a discipline that is "anthropocentric" in orientation, allowing little room for consideration of society's relation to nature, much less the thorough-going "ecocentrism" proposed by many environmentalists. It is rooted in a "sociocultural determinism" that effectively excludes ecological issues (Dunlap and Martin 1983, p. 204). For Dunlap and Catton (1994, p. 6), sociology needs to shed "the 'blinders' imposed by [human] exceptionalism" and to acknowledge "the ecosystem dependence of all human societies."

One result of this problem of theoretical dissonance is that environmental sociology, despite important innovations, has continued to have only a marginal role within the discipline as a whole. Although an environmental sociology section of the American Sociological Association was launched in 1976, it did not have the paradigm-shifting effect on sociology that leading figures in the section expected. Neither was sociology as a whole much affected by the rise of environmental sociology, nor did environmental issues gain much notice within the profession. As one leading practitioner of environmental sociology observed in 1987, "The discipline at large has handily withstood the challenges to its theoretical assumptions posed by environmental sociologists" (Buttel 1987, p. 466).

Where the core sociological discipline has been most ready to acknowledge environmental issues is in the area of environmental movements. There the literature has rapidly expanded in recent years through the growth of the environmental justice movement, concerned with the impact of environmental degradation on distinct sociological groupings, conceived in terms of race, class, gender, and international hierarchy. But this literature owes much more to social movement theory than to the environmentalist challenge to traditional sociological conceptions.

One way in which environmental sociologists have sought to address this problem of what are generally perceived as barriers within classical sociology to any consideration of the physical environment is by reaching out to the preclassical social Darwinist tradition: thinkers such as Malthus and Sumner (Catton 1982). Recently, however, there has been a great deal of research within environmental sociology directed not at circumventing the main classical sociological theorists but at unearthing alternative foundations within the classical literature, neglected in later interpretations. For example, an impressive attempt has been made by Murphy (1994) to establish a neo-Weberian sociology by applying Weber's critique of rationalization to the ecological realm and developing an "ecology of social action." Järvikoski (1996) has argued that we should reject the view that Durkheim simply neglected nature, choosing to address instead Durkheim's social constructionism with respect to nature, while examining how society fit within the hierarchical conception of nature that he generally envisioned. Others have stressed Durkheim's use of biological analogies and the demographic basis that he gave to his social morphology of the division of labor and urbanism, which seemed to foreshadow the urban-oriented human ecology of Park and other Chicago sociologists (Buttel 1986, pp. 341–42). The most dramatic growth of literature in relation to classical sociology, however, has centered on Marx's ecological contributions, which were. more extensive than in the other classical theorists, and which have spawned a vast and many-sided international debate, encompassing all stages of Marx's work (e.g., Schmidt 1971; Parsons 1977; Giddens 1981; Redclift 1984; Clark 1989; Benton 1989; McLaughlin 1990, Mayumi 1991; Grundmann 1991; Eckersley 1992; Perelman 1993; Hayward 1994; Harvey 1996; Burkett 1997; Foster 1997; Dickens 1997; O'Connor 1998).

Significantly, this growing literature on the relation of classical sociolological theorists to environmental analysis has caused some of the original critics of classical sociology within environmental sociology to soften their criticisms. Buttel, one of the founders of the subdiscipline, has gone so far as to suggest that, despite all of their deficiencies in this respect, "a meaningful environmental sociology can be fashioned from the works of the three classical theorists" (1986, pp. 340–41). We now know, for example, that Weber, writing as early as 1909 in his critique of Wilhelm Ostwald's social energetics, demonstrated some concern over the continued availability of scarce natural resources and anticipated the ecological economist Georgescu-Roegen in arguing that the entropy law applied to materials as well as energy (Martinez-Alier 1987, pp. 183–92). Durkheim's analysis of the implications of Darwinian evolutionary theory—as we shall see below—pointed toward a complex, coevolutionary perspective. Nevertheless, the widespread impression of rigid classical barriers to environmental sociology continues to exert its influence on most environmental sociologists, leaving them somewhat in the state of the mythical centaur, with the head of one creature and the body of another, unable fully to reconcile their theoretical commitment to classical sociology with their environmental sociology, which demands that an emphasis be placed on the relations between society and the natural environment.

The following will focus on addressing the seemingly paradoxical relation of classical sociological theory and environmental sociology by centering on the work of Marx, while referring only tangentially to the cases of Weber and Durkheim. It will be argued that neglected but crucial elements within Marx's social theory offer firm foundations for the development of a strong environmental sociology. In contrast to most treatments of Marx's ecological writings, emphasis will be placed not on his early philosophical works but rather on his later political economy. It is in the latter that Marx provided his systematic treatment of such issues as soil fertility, organic recycling, and sustainability in response to the investigations of the great German chemist Justus von Liebig—and in which we find the larger conceptual framework, emphasizing the metabolic rift between human production and its natural conditions.[2]

It may seem ironic, given Marx's peculiar dual status as an insider-founder and outsider-critic of classical sociology (not to mention his reputation in some quarters as an enemy of nature), to turn to him in order to help rescue sociology from the embarrassing dilemma of having paid insufficient attention to the relation between nature and human society. Yet, the discovery or rediscovery of previously neglected features of Marx's vast intellectual corpus has served in the past to revitalize sociology in relation to such critical issues as alienation, the labor process, and, more recently, globalization. The irony may seem less, in fact, when one considers that there already exists "a vast neo-Marxist literature in environmental sociology, and [that] there are few other areas of sociology today that remain so strongly influenced by Marxism" (Buttel 1996, p. 61).

In constructing this argument around Marx, an attempt will be made to comment more broadly on the paradox of the existence—as we are now discovering—of a rich body of material on environmental issues within classical sociological theory, on the one hand, and the widespread perception that the classical tradition excluded any serious consideration of these issues, and itself constitutes a barrier inhibiting the development of environmental sociology, on the other. Here two hypotheses will be advanced arising out of the treatment of Marx. First, the apparent blindness of classical sociological theory to ecological issues is partly a manifestation of the way classical sociology was appropriated in the late 20th century. This can be viewed as *the approbation problem*. Second, environmental sociology's critique of classical traditions has itself often been rooted in an overly restrictive conception of what constitutes environmental theorizing, reducing it to a narrow "dark green" perspective (as exemplified by the deep ecology tradition).[3] This can be thought of as *the definitional problem.*

THE DEBATE ON MARX AND THE ENVIRONMENT

It is a sign of the growing influence of environmental issues that in recent years numerous thinkers, from Plato to Gandhi, have had their work re-evaluated in relation to ecological analysis. Yet it is in relation to Marx's work that the largest and most controversial body of literature can be found, far overshadowing the debate over all other thinkers. This literature (insofar as it takes environmental issues seriously) has fallen into four camps: (1) those who contend that Marx's thought was antiecological from beginning to end and indistinguishable from Soviet practice (Clark 1989; Ferkiss 1993); (2) those who claim that Marx provided illuminating insights into ecology but ultimately succumbed to "Prometheanism" (protechnological, antiecological views)—a corollary being that he believed that environmental problems would be eliminated as a result of the "abundance" that would characterize postcapitalist society (Giddens 1981; Nove 1987; Redclift 1984; Benton

1989; McLaughlin 1990; Eckersley 1992; Deléage 1994; Goldblatt 1996); (3) those who argue that Marx provided an analysis of ecological degradation within agriculture, which remained, however, segregated off from his core social analysis (O'Connor 1998); and (4) those who insist that Marx developed a systematic approach to nature and to environmental degradation (particularly in relation to the fertility of the soil) that was intricately bound to the rest of his thought and raised the question of ecological sustainability (Parsons 1977; Perelman 1993; Mayumi 1991; Lebowitz 1992; Altvater 1993; Foster 1997; Burkett 1997).

Some of the sharpest criticisms of Marx from an environmentalist standpoint have come from leading sociologists (both non-Marxist and Marxist), particularly in Britain. Giddens (1981, p. 60) has contended that Marx, although demonstrating considerable ecological sensitivity in his earliest writings, later adopted a "Promethean attitude" toward nature. Marx's "concern with transforming the exploitative human social relations expressed in class systems does not extend," Giddens writes, "to the exploitation of nature" (1981, p. 59). Similarly, Redclift (1984, p. 7) has observed that for Marx the environment served "an enabling function but all value was derived from labor power. It was impossible to conceive of a 'natural' limit to the material productive forces of society. The barriers that existed to the full realization of resource potential were imposed by property relations and legal obligations rather than resource endowments." More recently, Redclift and Woodgate (1994, p. 53) have added that, "while Marx considered our relations with the environment as essentially social, he also regarded them as ubiquitous and unchanging, common to each phase of social existence. Hence, for Marx, the relationship between people and nature cannot provide a source of change in society.... Such a perspective does not fully acknowledge the role of technology, and its effects on the environment." Finally, Nove (1987, p. 399) has contended that Marx believed that "the problem of production had been 'solved'" by capitalism and that the future society of associated producers therefore would not have "to take seriously the problem of the allocation of scarce resources," which meant that there was no need for an "ecologically conscious" socialism.

Marx thus stands accused of wearing *blinders* in relation to the following: (1) the exploitation of nature, (2) nature's role in the creation of value, (3) the existence of distinct natural limits, (4) nature's changing character and the impact of this on human society, (5) the role of technology in environmental degradation, and (6) the inability of mere economic abundance to solve environmental problems. If these criticisms were valid, Marx's work could be expected to offer no significant insights into problems of ecological crisis and indeed would itself constitute a major obstacle to the understanding of environmental problems.

In contrast, an attempt will be made here, in the context of a systematic reconstruction of Marx's theory of metabolic rift, that these ecological blinders are not in fact present in Marx's thought—and that each of the problems listed above were addressed to some extent in his theory. Of more significance, it will be contended that Marx provided a powerful analysis of the main ecological crisis of his day—the problem of soil fertility within capitalist agriculture—as well as commenting on the other major ecological crises of his time (the loss of forests, the pollution of the cities, and the Malthusian specter of overpopulation). In doing so, he raised fundamental issues about the antagonism of town and country, the necessity of ecological sustainability, and what he called the "metabolic" relation between human beings and nature. In his theory of metabolic rift and his response to Darwinian evolutionary theory, Marx went a considerable way toward a historical-environmental-materialism that took into account the co-evolution of nature and human society.

MARX AND THE SECOND AGRICULTURAL REVOLUTION: THE METABOLIC RIFT

The Concept of the Second Agricultural Revolution

Although it is still common for historians to refer to a single agricultural revolution that took place in Britain in the 17th and 18th centuries and that laid the foundation for the industrial revolution that followed, agricultural historians commonly refer to a second and even a third agricultural revolution. The first agricultural revolution was a gradual process occurring over several centuries, associated with the enclosures and the growing centrality of market relations; technical changes included improved techniques of crop rotation, manuring, drainage, and livestock management. In contrast, the second agricultural revolution (Thompson 1968) occurred over a shorter period (1830–80) and was characterized by the growth of a fertilizer industry and a revolution in soil chemistry, associated in particular with the work of the great German agricultural chemist Justus von Liebig.[4] The third agricultural revolution was to occur still later, in the 20th century, and involved the replacement of animal traction with machine traction on the farm and the eventual concentration of animals in massive feedlots, together with the genetic alteration of plants (resulting in narrower monocultures) and the more intensive use of chemical inputs—such as fertilizers and pesticides.

Marx's critique of capitalist agriculture and his main contributions to ecological thought have to be understood in relation to the second agricultural revolution occurring in his time. For Marx, writing in *Capital* in the 1860s, there was a gulf separating the treatment of agricultural productivity and soil fertility in the work of classical economists like Malthus and Ricardo, and the understanding of these problems in his own day. In Marx's ([1863–65] 1981, pp. 915–16) words, "The actual causes of the exhaustion of the land…were unknown to any of the economists who wrote about differential rent, on account of the state of agricultural chemistry in their time."

The source of the differential fertility from which rent was derived was, in the work of Malthus and Ricardo in the opening decades of the 19th century, attributed almost entirely to the natural or absolute productivity of the soil—with agricultural improvement (or degradation) playing only a marginal role. As Ricardo (1951, p. 67) observed, rent could be defined as "that portion of the produce of the earth, which is paid to the landlord for the use of the original and indestructible powers of the soil." These thinkers argued—with the presumed backing of natural law—that lands that were naturally the most fertile were the first to be brought into production and that rising rent on these lands and decreasing agricultural productivity overall were the result of lands of more and more marginal fertility being brought into cultivation, in response to increasing demographic pressures. Further, while some agricultural improvement was possible, it was quite limited, since the increases in productivity to be derived from successive applications of capital and labor to any given plot of land were said to be of diminishing character, thereby helping to account for the slowdown in growth of productivity in agriculture. All of this pointed to the Malthusian dilemma of a tendency of population to outgrow food supply—a tendency only countered as a result of vice and misery that served to lower fecundity and increase mortality, as Malthus emphasized in his original essay on population, or through possible moral restraint, as he was to add in later editions of that work.

Classical Marxism, in contrast, relied from the beginning on the fact that rapid historical improvement in soil fertility was possible, though not inevitable, given existing social relations. In his "Outlines of a Critique of Political Economy," published in 1844, a young Friedrich Engels was to point to revolutions in science and particularly soil chemistry—singling out the discoveries of such figures as Humphry Davy and Liebig—as constituting the main reason why Malthus and Ricardo would be proven wrong about the possibilities for rapidly improving the fertility of the soil and thereby promoting a favorable relation between the growth of food and the growth of population. Engels (1964, pp. 208–10) went on to observe that, "To make earth an object of huckstering—the earth which is our one and all, the first condition of our existence—was the last step toward making oneself an object of huckstering." Three years later in *The Poverty of Philosophy,* Marx (1963, pp. 162–63) wrote that at "every moment the modern application of chemistry is changing the nature of the soil, and geological knowledge is just now, in our days, beginning to revolutionize all the old estimates of relative fertility…. Fertility is not so natural a quality as might be thought; it is closely bound up with the so-cial relations of the time."

This emphasis on historical changes in soil fertility in the direction of agricultural improvement was to be a continuing theme in Marx's thought, though it eventually came to be coupled with an understanding of how capitalist agriculture could un-dermine the conditions of soil fertility, re-sulting in soil degradation rather than improvement. Thus in his later writings, increasing emphasis came to be placed on the exploitation of the earth in the sense of the failure to sustain the conditions of its reproduction.

Liebig and the Depletion of the Soil

During 1830–70 the depletion of soil fertil-ity through the loss of soil nutrients was the overriding environmental concern of capi-talist society in both Europe and North America, comparable only to concerns over the growing pollution of the cities, defores-tation of whole continents, and the Malthu-sian fears of overpopulation (Foster 1997; O'Connor 1998, p. 3). In the 1820s and 1830s in Britain, and shortly afterward in the other developing capitalist economies of Europe and North America, widespread concerns about "soil exhaustion" led to a phenomenal increase in the demand for fertilizer. The value of bone imports to Brit-ain increased from £14,400 in 1823 to to £254,600 in 1837. The first boat carrying Peruvian guano (accumulated dung of sea birds) unloaded its cargo in Liverpool in 1835; by 1841, 1,700 tons were imported, and by 1847, 220,000 (Ernle [1912] 1961, p. 369). European farmers in this period raided Napoleonic battlefields such as Wa-terloo and Austerlitz, so desperate were they for bones to spread over their fields (Hillel 1991, pp. 131–32).

The second agricultural revolution asso-ciated with the rise of modern soil science was closely correlated with this demand for increased soil fertility to support capitalist agriculture. In 1837, the British Association for the Advancement of Science commis-sioned Liebig to write a work on the rela-tionship between agriculture and chemistry. The following year saw the founding of the Royal Agricultural Society of England, viewed by economic historians as a leading organization in the British high-farming movement—a movement of wealthy land-owners to improve farm management. In 1840, Liebig published his *Organic Chemistry in Its Applications to Agriculture and Physiology,* which provided the first convincing expla-nation of the role of soil nutrients, such as nitrogen, phosphorous, and potassium, in the growth of plants. One of the figures most influenced by Liebig's ideas was the wealthy English landowner and agronomist J. B. Lawes. In 1842, Lawes invented a means of making phosphate soluble, en-abling him to introduce the first artificial fer-tilizer, and in 1843, he built a factory for the production of his new "superphosphates." With the repeal of the Corn Laws in 1846, Liebig's organic chemistry was seen by the large agricultural interests in England as the key to obtaining larger crop yields (Brock 1997, pp. 149–50).

In the 1840s, this scientific revolution in soil chemistry, together with the rise of a fertilizer industry, promised to generate a faster rate of agricultural improvement—impressing many contemporary observers, including Marx and Engels, who up to the 1860s believed that progress in agriculture might soon outpace the development of in-dustry in general. Still, capital's ability to take advantage of these scientific break-throughs in soil chemistry was limited by development of the division of labor inherent to the system, specifically the growing antagonism between town and country. By the 1860s, when he wrote *Capital,* Marx had become convinced of the contradictory and unsustainable nature of capitalist agriculture, due to two historical developments in his time: (1) the widening sense of crisis in agriculture in both Europe and North America associated with the depletion of the natural fertility of the soil, which was in no way alleviated, but rather given added impetus by the breakthroughs in soil science; and (2) a shift in Liebig's own work in the late 1850s and early 1860s toward an ecological critique of capitalist development.

The discoveries by Liebig and other soil scientists, while holding out hope to farmers, also intensified in some ways the sense of crisis within capitalist agriculture, making farmers more acutely aware of the depletion of soil minerals and the paucity of fertilizers. The contradiction was experienced with particular severity in the United States— especially among farmers in New York and in the plantation economy of the Southeast. Blocked from ready access to guano (which was high in both nitrogen and phosphates) by the British monopoly of Peruvian guano supplies, U.S. capitalists spread across the globe looking for alternative supplies. Nevertheless, the quantity and quality of natural fertilizer obtained in this way fell far short of U.S. needs (Skaggs 1994).

Peruvian guano was largely exhausted in the 1860s and had to be replaced by Chilean nitrates. Potassium salts discovered in Europe gave ample access to that mineral, and phosphates became more readily available through both natural and artificial supplies. Yet prior to the development of a process for producing synthetic nitrogen fertilizer in 1913, fertilizer nitrogen continued to be in chronically short supply. It was in this context that Liebig was to state that

what was needed to overcome this barrier was the discovery of "deposits of manure or guano…in volumes approximating to those of the English coalfields" (quoted in Kautsky [(1899) 1988], vol. 1, p. 53).

The second agricultural revolution, associated with the application of scientific chemistry to agriculture, was therefore at the same time a period of intense contradictions. The decline in the natural fertility of the soil due to the disruption of the soil nutrient cycle, the expanding scientific knowledge of the need for specific soil nutrients, and the simultaneous limitations in the supply of both natural and synthetic fertilizers, all served to generate serious concerns about present and future soil fertility under capitalist agriculture.

In upstate New York, increased competition from farmers to the west in the decades following the opening of the Erie Canal in 1825 intensified the concern over the "worn-out soil." In 1850, the British soil chemist, James F. W. Johnston, whom Marx (Marx and Engels *1975a,* vol. 38, p. 476) was to call "the English Liebig," visited the United States. In his *Notes on North America,* Johnston (1851, pp. 356–65) recorded the depleted condition of the soil in upstate New York, comparing it unfavorably to the more fertile, less exhausted farmlands to the west. These issues were taken up by the U.S. economist Henry Carey, who in the late 1840s and 1850s laid stress on the fact that long-distance trade, which he associated with the separation of town from country and of agricultural producers from consumers ([1847] 1967*a,* pp. 298–99, 304–8), was the major factor in the net loss of nutrients to the soil and in the growing soil fertility crisis. "As the whole energies of the country," Carey wrote of the United States in his *Principles of Social Science,* "are given to the enlargement of the trader's power, it is no matter of surprise that its people are everywhere seen employed in 'robbing the earth of its capital stock'" ([1858–59] 1867, p. 215; also Carey [1853] 1967b, p. 199).

Carey's views were to have an important impact on Liebig. In his *Letters on Modern Agriculture* (1859), Liebig argued that the "empirical agriculture" of the trader gave rise to a "spoliation system" in which the "conditions of reproduction" of the soil were undermined. "A field from which something is permanently taken away," he wrote, "cannot possibly increase or even continue equal in its productive power." Indeed, "every system of farming based on the spoliation of the land leads to poverty" (1859, pp. 175–78). "Rational agriculture, in contrast to the spoliation system of farming, is based on the principle of restitution; by giving back to the fields the conditions of their fertility, the farmer insures the permanence of the latter." For Liebig, English "high farming" was "not the open system of robbery of the American farmer...but is a more refined species of spoliation which at first glance does not look like robbery" (1859, p. 183). Echoing Carey (1858), Liebig (1859, p. 220) observed that there were hundreds, sometimes thousands, of miles in the United States between the centers of grain production and their markets. The constituent elements of the soil were thus shipped to locations far removed from their points of origin, making the reproduction of soil fertility that much more difficult.

The problem of the pollution of the cities with human and animal wastes was also tied to the depletion of the soil. In Liebig's (1863, p. 261) words, "If it were practicable to collect, with the least loss, all the solid and fluid excrements of the inhabitants of the town, and return to each farmer the portion arising from produce originally supplied by him to the town, the productiveness of the land might be maintained almost unimpaired for ages to come, and the existing store of mineral elements in every fertile field would be amply sufficient for the wants of increasing populations." In his influential *Letters on the Subject of the Utilization of the Municipal Sewage* (1865) Liebig argued—basing his analysis on the condition of the Thames—that organic recycling that would return the nutrients contained in sewage to the soil was an indispensable part of a rational urban-agricultural system.

Marx and the Metabolic Rift

When working on *Capital* in the early 1860s, Marx was deeply affected by Liebig's analysis. In 1866, he wrote to Engels that in developing his critique of capitalist ground rent, "I had to plough through the new agricultural chemistry in Germany, in particular Liebig and Schönbein, which is more important for this matter than all the economists put together" (Marx and Engels 1975a, vol. 42, p. 227). Indeed, "to have developed from the point of view of natural science the negative, i.e., destructive side of modern agriculture," Marx was to note in *Capital*, "is one of Liebig's immortal merits" ([1867] 1976, p. 638). Far from having ecological blinders with regard to the exploitation of the earth, Marx, under the influence of Liebig's work of the late 1850s and early 1860s, was to develop a systematic critique of capitalist "exploitation" (in the sense of robbery, i.e., failing to maintain the means of reproduction) of the soil.

Marx concluded both of his two main discussions of capitalist agriculture with an explanation of how large-scale industry and large-scale agriculture combined to impoverish the soil and the worker. Much of the resulting critique was distilled in a remarkable passage at the end of Marx's treatment of "The Genesis of Capitalist Ground Rent" in *Capital*, volume 3, where he wrote:

> *Large landed property reduces the agricultural population to an ever decreasing minimum and confronts it with an ever growing industrial population crammed together in large towns; in this way it produces conditions that provoke an irreparable rift in the interdependent process of the social metabolism, a metabolism prescribed by the natural laws of life itself. The result of this is a squandering of the vitality of the soil, which is carried by trade far beyond the bounds of a single country. (Liebig.)…Large-scale industry and industrially pursued large-scale agriculture have the same effect. If they are originally distinguished by the fact that the former lays waste and ruins the labour-power and thus the natural power of man, whereas the latter does the same to the natural power of the soil, they link up in the later course of development, since the industrial system applied to agriculture also enervates the workers there, while industry and trade for their part provide agriculture with the means of exhausting the soil. (Marx 1981, pp. 949–50)*

Marx provided a similar and no less important distillation of his critique in this area in his discussion of "Large scale Industry and Agriculture" in volume 1 of *Capital*.

> *Capitalist production collects the population together in great centres, and causes the urban population to achieve an ever-growing preponderance. This has two results. On the one hand it concentrates the historical motive force of society; on the other hand, it disturbs the metabolic interaction between man and the earth, i.e. it prevents the return to the soil of its constituent elements consumed by man*

> *in the form of food and clothing; hence it hinders the operation of the eternal natural condition for the lasting fertility of the soil…. But by destroying the circumstances surrounding that metabolism…it compels its systematic restoration as a regulative law of social production, and in a form adequate to the full development of the human race…. All progress in capitalist agriculture is a progress in the art, not only of robbing the worker, but of robbing the soil; all progress in increasing the fertility of the soil for a given time is a progress toward ruining the more long-lasting sources of that fertility…. Capitalist production, therefore only develops the techniques and the degree of combination of the social process of production by simultaneously undermining the original sources of all wealth—the soil and the worker. (Marx 1976, pp. 637–38)*

In both of these passages from Marx's *Capital*—the first concluding his discussion of capitalist ground rent in volume 3 and the second concluding his discussion of large-scale agriculture in volume 1—the central theoretical construct is that of a "rift" in the "metabolic interaction between man and the earth," or in the "social metabolism prescribed by the natural laws of life," through the removal from the soil of its constituent elements, requiring its "systematic restoration." This contradiction is associated with the growth simultaneously of large-scale industry and large-scale agriculture under capitalism, with the former providing agriculture with the means of the intensive exploitation of the soil. Following Liebig, Marx argued that long-distance trade in food and clothing made the problem of the alienation of the constituent elements of the soil that much more of an "irreparable rift." As he indicated elsewhere in *Capital* (vol. 1), the fact that "the blind desire for profit" had "exhausted the soil" of England could be seen daily in the conditions that "forced the manuring of English fields with guano" imported from Peru (1976, p. 348). Central to Marx's argument was the notion that capitalist large-scale agriculture prevents any truly rational application of the new science of soil management. Despite all of its scientific and technological development in the area of agriculture, capitalism was unable to maintain those conditions necessary for the recycling of the constituent elements of the soil.

The key to Marx's entire theoretical approach in this area is the concept of social-ecological metabolism (*Stoffwechsel*), which was rooted in his understanding of the labor process. Defining the labor process in general (as opposed to its historically specific manifestations), Marx employed the concept of metabolism to describe the human relation to nature through labor:

Labour is, first of all, a process between man and nature, a process by which man, through his own actions, mediates, regulates and controls the metabolism between himself and nature. He confronts the materials of nature as a force of nature. He sets in motion the natural forces which belong to his own body, his arms, legs, head and hands, in order to appropriate the materials of nature in a form adapted to his own needs. Through this movement he acts upon external nature and changes it, and in this way he simultaneously changes his own nature.... It [the labor process] is the universal condition for the metabolic interaction [Stoffwechsel] between man and nature, the everlasting nature-imposed condition of human existence. (Marx 1976, pp. 283, 290)

Only a few years before this, Marx had written in his *Economic Manuscript of 1861–63*

that "actual labour is the appropriation of nature for the satisfaction of human needs, the activity through which the metabolism between man and nature is mediated." It followed that the actual activity of labor was never independent of nature's own wealth-creating potential, "since material wealth, the world of use values, exclusively consists of natural materials modified by labour" (Marx and Engels 1975a, vol. 30, p. 40).[5]

Much of this discussion of the metabolic relation between human beings and nature reflected Marx's early, more directly philosophical attempts to account for the complex interdependence between human beings and nature. In the *Economic and Philosophical Manuscripts* of 1844, Marx had explained that, "Man *lives* from nature, i.e., nature is his *body,* and he must maintain a continuing dialogue with it if he is not to die. To say that man's physical and mental life is linked to nature simply means that nature is linked to itself, for man is a part of nature" (1974, p. 328; emphasis in original). But the later introduction of the concept of metabolism gave Marx a more solid—and scientific—way in which to depict the complex, dynamic interchange between human beings and nature, resulting from human labor. The material exchanges and regulatory action associated with the concept of metabolism encompassed both "nature-imposed conditions" and the capacity of human beings to affect this process. According to Hayward (1994, p. 116), Marx's concept of socio-ecological metabolism "captures fundamental aspects of humans' existence as both natural and physical beings: these include the energetic and material exchanges which occur between human beings and their natural environment.... This metabolism is regulated from the side of nature by natural laws governing the various physical processes involved, and from the side of society by institutionalized norms governing the division of labor and distribution of wealth etc."

Given the fundamental way in which Marx conceived of the concept of metabolism—as constituting the complex, interdependent process linking human society to nature—it should not surprise us that this concept enters into Marx's vision of a future society of associated producers: "Freedom, in this sphere [the realm of natural necessity]," he wrote in *Capital* (volume 3), "can consist only in this, that socialized man, the associated producers, govern the human metabolism with nature in a rational way, bringing it under their own collective control rather than being dominated by it as a blind power; accomplishing it with the least expenditure of energy and in conditions most worthy and appropriate for their human nature" (1981, p. 959).

Just as the introduction of the concept of "metabolism" allowed Marx to provide a firmer, scientific grounding for his ideas, so the central position that this concept came to occupy in his theory encouraged him to draw out some of its larger implications. The term "metabolism" (*Stoffwechsel*) was introduced as early as 1815 and was adopted by German physiologists in the 1830s and 1840s to refer to material exchanges within the body, related to respiration (Bing 1971; Caneva 1993). But the term was given a somewhat wider application (and therefore greater currency) in 1842 by Liebig in his *Animal Chemistry*, the great work that followed his earlier work on the soil, where he introduced the notion of metabolic process (in the context of tissue degradation). It was subsequently generalized still further and emerged as one of the key concepts, applicable both at the cellular level and in the analysis of entire organisms, in the development of biochemistry (Liebig [1842] 1964; Brock 1997, p. 193; Caneva 1993, p. 117).

Within biological and ecological analysis, the concept of metabolism, beginning in the 1840s and extending down to the present day, has been used as a central category in the systems-theory approach to the relation of organisms to their environments. It refers to a complex process of metabolic exchange, whereby an organism (or a given cell) draws upon materials and energy from its environment and converts these by way of various metabolic reactions into the building blocks of proteins and other compounds necessary for growth. The concept of metabolism is also used to refer to the regulatory processes that govern this complex interchange between organisms and their environment (Fischer-Kowalski 1997, p. 120). Leading system ecologists like Odum (1969, p. 7) employ "metabolism" to refer to all biological levels, beginning with the single cell and ending with the ecosystem.

Recently, the notion of metabolism has become what Fischer-Kowalski (1997, pp. 119–20) has called "a rising conceptual star" within social-ecological thought, as a result of the emergence of cross-disciplinary research in "industrial metabolism." For some thinkers, it offers a way out of one the core dilemmas of environmental sociology raised by Dunlap and Catton (1979) and Schnaiberg (1980), which requires a way of envisioning the complex interaction between society and nature (Hayward 1994, pp. 116–17; Fischer-Kowalski 1997). Further, the concept of metabolism has long been employed to analyze the material interchange between city and country, in a manner similar to the way in which Liebig and Marx used the concept (Wolman 1965; Giradet 1997). Within this rapidly growing body of literature on social-ecological metabolism, it is now well recognized that "within the nineteenth-century foundations of social theory, it was Marx and Engels who applied the term 'metabolism' to society" (Fischer-Kowalski 1997, p. 122).

Indeed, environmental sociologists and others exploring the concept of "industrial metabolism" today argue that just as the materials that birds use to build their nests can be seen as material flows associated with the metabolism of birds, so similar material flows can be seen as part of the human metabolism. Fischer-Kowalski has thus suggested "considering as part of the metabolism of a social system *those material and energetic flows that sustain the material compartments of the system*" (1997, pp. 121, 131; emphasis in original). The tough question, however, is how such a human metabolism with nature is regulated on the side of society. For Marx, the answer was human labor and its development within historical social formations.

MARX AND SUSTAINABILITY

An essential aspect of the concept of metabolism is the notion that it constitutes the basis on which life is sustained and growth and reproduction become possible. Contrary to those who believe that he wore an ecological blinder that prevented him from perceiving natural limits to production, Marx employed the concept of metabolic rift to capture the material estrangement of human beings in capitalist society from the natural conditions of their existence. To argue that large-scale capitalist agriculture created such a metabolic rift between human beings and the soil was to argue that basic conditions of sustainability had been violated. "Capitalist production" Marx ([1861–63] 1971*b*, p. 301) wrote, "turns toward the land only after its influence has exhausted it and after it has devastated its natural qualities." Moreover, this could be seen as related not only to the soil but to the antagonism between town and country. For Marx, like Liebig, the failure to recycle nutrients to the soil had its counterpart in the pollution of the cities and the irrationality of modern sewage systems. In *Capital* (volume 3), he observed: "In London... they can do nothing better with the excrement produced by 4½ million people than pollute the Thames with it, at monstrous expense" (1981, p. 195). Engels was no less explicit on this point. In addressing the need to transcend the antagonism between the town and country, he referred, following Liebig, to the fact that "in London alone a greater quantity of manure than is produced by the whole kingdom of Saxony is poured away every day into the sea with an expenditure of enormous sums" and to the consequent need to reestablish an "intimate connection between industrial and agricultural production" along with "as uniform a distribution as possible of the population over the whole country" (Engels [1872] 1975, p. 92). For Marx, the "excrement produced by man's natural metabolism," along with the waste of industrial production and consumption, needed to be recycled back into the production, as part of a complete metabolic cycle (1981, p. 195).

The antagonistic division between town and country, and the metabolic rift that it entailed, was also evident at a more global level: whole colonies saw their land, resources, *and soil* robbed to support the industrialization of the colonizing countries. "For a century and a half," Marx wrote, "England has indirectly exported the soil of Ireland, without as much as allowing its cultivators the means for making up the constituents of the soil that had been exhausted" (1976, p. 860).

Marx's view of capitalist agriculture and of the necessity of cycling the nutrients of the soil (including the organic wastes of the city) thus led him to a wider concept of eco-logical sustainability—a notion that he thought of very limited practical relevance to capitalist society, which was incapable of such consistent rational action, but essential for a future society of associated producers. "The way that the cultivation of particular crops depends on fluctuations in market prices and the constant change in cultivation with these prices—the entire spirit of capital-ist production, which is oriented towards the most immediate monetary profits—stands in contradiction to agriculture, which has to concern itself with the whole gamut of per-manent conditions of life required by the chain of successive generations" (Marx 1981, p. 754).[6]

In emphasizing the need to maintain the earth for "successive generations," Marx cap-tured the essence of the contemporary no-tion of sustainable development, defined most famously by the Brundtland Commis-sion as "development which meets the needs of the present without compromising the ability of future generations to meet their needs" (World Commission on Environment and Development 1987, p. 43). For Marx, the "conscious and rational treatment of the land as permanent communal property" is "the inalienable condition for the existence and reproduction of the chain of human generations" (1981, pp. 948–49). Indeed, in a remarkable, and deservedly famous, pas-sage in *Capital* (vol. 3), Marx wrote, "From the standpoint of a higher socio-economic formation, the private property of particular individuals in the earth will appear just as absurd as the private property of one man in other men. Even an entire society, a na-tion, or all simultaneously existing societies taken together, are not owners of the earth, they are simply its possessors, its beneficia-ries, and have to bequeath it in an im-proved state to succeeding generations as

boni patres familias [good heads of the household]" (1981, p. 911).

This took on greater significance near the end of Marx's life, when, as a result of his investigations into the revolutionary po-tential of the archaic Russian commune (the Mir), he argued that it would be possible to develop an agricultural system "organized on a vast scale and managed by cooperative labor" through the introduction of "modern agronomic methods." The value of such a system, he argued, would be that it would be "in a position to incorporate all the posi-tive acquisitions devised by the capitalist system" without falling prey to the purely exploitative relation to the soil, that is, the robbery, that characterized the latter (Marx and Engels 1975*a*, vol. 24, p. 356). Marx's absorption in the literature of the Russian populists at the end of his life, and his grow-ing conviction that the revolution would emerge first within Russia—where eco-nomic, and more specifically agricultural, abundance could not be assumed—forced him to focus on agricultural underdevelop-ment and the ecological requirements of a more rational agricultural system.[7]

Marx and Engels did not restrict their discussions of environmental degradation to the robbing of the soil but also acknowl-edged other aspects of this problem, includ-ing the depletion of coal reserves, the destruction of forests, and so on. As Engels observed in a letter to Marx, "the working individual is not only a stabaliser of *present* but also, and to a far greater extent, a squanderer of *past*, solar heat. As to what we have done in the way of squandering our reserves of energy, our coal, ore, forests, etc., you are better informed than I am" (Marx and Engels 1975*a*, vol. 46, p. 411; emphasis in original). Marx referred to the "devastating" effects of "deforestation" (Marx and Engels 1975*a*, vol. 42, p. 559) and saw this as a long-term result of an exploitative relation to nature (not simply confined to capitalism): "The development of civilization and industry in general," Marx wrote, "has always shown itself so active in the destruction of forests that everything that has been done for their conservation and production is completely insignificant in comparison" ([1865–70] 1978, p. 322). He lamented the fact that the forests in England were not "true forests" since "the deer in the parks of the great are demure domestic cattle, as fat as London aldermen"; while in Scotland, the so-called "deer-forests" that were established for the benefit of huntsmen (at the expense of rural laborers) contained deer but no trees (1976, pp. 892–93). Under the influence of Darwin, Marx and Engels repudiated the age-old view that human beings were at the center of the natural universe. Engels expressed "a withering contempt for the idealistic exaltation of man over the other animals" (Marx and Engels 1975*b*, p. 102).

Some critics attribute to Marx an ecological blinder associated with an overly optimistic faith in the cornucopian conditions supposedly made possible by the forces of production under capitalism. In this view, he relied so much on the assumption of abundance in his conception of a future society that ecological factors such as the scarcity of natural resources were simply nonexistent. Yet whatever Marx may have thought in his more "utopian" conceptions, it is clear from his discussions of both capitalism and of the transition to socialism that he was far from believing, as Nove (1987, p. 399) contends, "that the problem of production" had already been "solved" under capitalism or that natural resources were "inexhaustible." Rather, capitalism, as he emphasized again and again, was beset with a chronic problem of production in agriculture, which ultimately had to do with an unsustainable form of production in relation to natural conditions. Agriculture, Marx observed, "when it progresses spontaneously and is not *consciously controlled...* leaves deserts behind it" (Marx and Engels 1975*b*, p. 190; emphasis in original). Within industry too, Marx was concerned about the enormous waste generated and emphasized the "reduction" and "re-use" of waste—particularly in a section of *Capital* (volume 3), entitled, "Utilization of the Refuse of Production" (1981, pp. 195–97). Moreover, he gave every indication that these problems would continue to beset any society attempting to construct socialism (or communism). Hence, although some critics, such as McLaughlin (1990, p. 95), assert that Marx envisioned "a general material abundance as the substratum of communism," and therefore saw "no basis for recognizing any interest in the liberation of nature from human domination," overwhelming evidence to the contrary (much of it referred to above) suggests that Marx was deeply concerned with issues of ecological limits and sustainability.

Moreover, there is simply no indication anywhere in Marx's writings that he believed that a sustainable relation to the earth would come automatically with the transition to socialism. Rather, he emphasized the need for planning in this area, including such measures as the elimination of the antagonism between town and country through the more even dispersal of the population (Marx and Engels [1848] 1967, pp. 40–41) and the restoration and improvement of the soil through the recycling of soil nutrients. All of this demanded a radical transformation in the human relation to the earth via changed production relations. Capitalism, Marx wrote, "creates the material conditions for a new and higher synthesis, a union of agriculture and industry on the basis of the forms that have developed during the period of their antagonistic isolation" (1976, p. 637). But in order to achieve this "higher synthesis" in a society of freely associated producers, he argued, it would be necessary for the associated producers to "govern the human metabolism with nature in a rational way"—a requirement that raised fundamental challenges for postcapitalist society (1981, p. 959; 1976, pp. 637–38).

Another ecological blinder commonly attributed to Marx is that he denied the role of nature in the creation of wealth by developing a labor theory of value that saw all value as derived from labor, and by referring to nature as a "free gift" to capital, lacking any intrinsic value of its own (Deléage 1994, p. 48; Churchill 1996, pp. 467–68; Georgescu-Roegen 1971, p. 2). Yet this criticism is based on a misunderstanding of Marx's political economy. Marx did not invent the idea that the earth was a "gift" of nature to capital. This notion was advanced as a key proposition by Malthus and Ricardo in their economic works (Malthus 1970, p. 185). It was taken up later on by the great neoclassical economist Alfred Marshall (1920) and persisted in neoclassical economics textbooks into the 1980s. Thus, in the 10th edition of a widely used introductory economics textbook, we discover the following: "Land refers to all natural resources—all 'free gifts of nature'— which are usable in the production process." And further on we read, "Land has no production cost; it is a 'free and nonreproducible gifts of nature'" (McConnell 1987, pp. 20, 672). Marx was aware of the social-ecological contradictions embedded in such views, and in his *Economic Manuscript of 1861–63* he attacked Malthus repeatedly for falling back on the "physiocratic" notion

that the environment was "a gift of nature to man," while ignoring how this was connected to the definite set of social relations brought into being by capital (Marx and Engels 1975a, vol. 34, pp. 151–59).

To be sure, Marx agreed with liberal economics that under the law of value of capitalism nature was accorded no value. "The earth…is active as agent of production in the production of a use-value, a material product, say wheat," he wrote. "But it has nothing to do with producing the *value of the wheat*" (1981, p. 955). The value of the wheat as in the case of any commodity under capitalism was derived from labor. For Marx, however, this merely reflected the narrow, limited conception of wealth embodied in capitalist commodity relations and in a system built around exchange value. Genuine wealth consisted of use values— the characteristic of production in general, transcending its capitalist form. Hence, nature, which contributed to the production of use values, was just as much a source of wealth labor. "What Lucretius says," Marx wrote in *Capital* (1976, p. 323), "is self-evident: *nil posse creari de nihilo*, out of nothing, nothing can be created…. Labour-power itself is, above all else, the material of nature transposed into a human organism."

It follows that "labour," as Marx stated at the beginning of *Capital*, "is not the only source of material wealth, that is, of the use-values it produces…As William Petty says, labour is the father of material wealth, and the earth is its mother" (1976, p. 134). In the *Critique of the Gotha Programme*, Marx criticized those socialists who had attributed what he called "*supernatural creative power* to labour" ([1875] 1971a, p. 11; emphasis in original) by viewing it as the sole source of wealth and disregarding the role of nature. Under communism, he argued, wealth would need to be conceived in far more universal terms, as consisting of those material use values that constituted the basis for the full development of human creative powers, "the development of the rich individuality which is all sided in its production as in its consumption"—expanding the wealth of connections allowed for by nature, while at the same time reflecting the developing human metabolism with nature ([1857–58] 1973, p. 325).

Marx therefore set himself in opposition to all those who thought the contribution of nature to the production of wealth could be disregarded, or that nature could be completely subordinated to human ends regardless of their character. Commenting in the *Grundrisse* on Bacon's ([1620] 1994, pp. 29, 43) great maxim that "nature is only overcome by obeying her"—on the basis of which Bacon also proposed to "subjugate" nature—Marx replied that for capitalism the theoretical discovery of nature's "autonomous laws appears merely as a ruse so as to subjugate it under human needs, whether as an object of consumption or a means of production" (1973, pp. 409–10).

For Engels too, it was clear that to construct a society built on the vain hope of the total conquest of external nature was sheer folly. As he wrote in *The Dialectics of Nature* ([1874–80] 1940, pp. 291–92), "Let us not, however, flatter ourselves overmuch on account of our human conquest of nature. For each such conquest takes revenge on us.... At every step we are reminded that we by no means rule over nature like a conqueror over a foreign people, like someone standing outside nature—but that we, with flesh, blood, and brain, belong to nature, and exist in its midst, and that all our mastery of it consists in the fact that we have the advantage of all other beings of being able to know and correctly apply its laws."

For Marx, "the human metabolism with nature" was a highly dynamic rela-

tionship, reflecting changes in the ways human beings mediated between nature and society through production. Engels and Marx read *The Origin of Species* soon after it appeared in 1859 and were enthusiastic supporters of Darwin's theory of natural selection. Marx (1976, p. 461) called Darwin's book an "epoch-making work," and in January 1861, Marx wrote a letter to the German socialist Lasalle stating that Darwin had dealt the "death blow" to "'teleology' in the natural sciences" (Marx and Engels 1975a, vol. 41, pp. 246–47). Marx expressed no reservations about Darwin's fundamental theory itself—not even with regard to Darwin's application of the Malthusian "struggle for existence" to the world of plants and animals—yet he was sharply critical of all attempts by social Darwinists to carry this analysis beyond its proper domain and to apply it to human history. Unfortunately, some critics have viewed his cautionary notes in this respect as criticisms of Darwin himself.[8]

Darwin's evolutionary theory led Marx and Engels to what would now be called a "cautious constructionism" (Dunlap 1997, pp. 31–32). For Marx, human evolution, that is, human history, was distinct from evolution as it occurred among plants and animals, in that the natural evolution of the physical organs of the latter, that is, "the history of natural technology," had its counterpart in human history in the conscious development of the "productive organs of man in society" (technology), which helped establish the conditions for the human mediation between nature and society via production (Marx 1976, p. 493). Marx was of course aware that the Greek word organ (organon) also meant tool, and that organs were initially viewed as "grown-on" tools of animals—an approach that was utilized by Darwin himself, who compared the development of specialized organs to the development of specialized tools (see Pannekoek 1912; Darwin [1859] 1968, pp. 187–88).

Engels was later to add to this an analysis of "The Part Played by Labour in the Transition from Ape to Man" (Engels 1940, pp. 279–96). According to this theory (verified in the 20th century by the discovery of *Australopithecus*), erect posture developed first (prior to the evolution of the human brain), freeing the hands for tools. In this way, the human (hominid) relation to the local environment was radically changed, altering the basis of natural selection. Those hominids that were most successful at tool-making were best able to adapt, which meant that the evolutionary process exerted selective pressures toward the development of the brain, eventually leading to the rise of modern humans. The human brain, according to Engels, evolved then through a complex, interactive process, now referred to as "gene-culture evolution." As biologist and paleontologist Stephen Jay Gould has observed, all scientific explanations of the evolution of the human brain thus far have taken the form of gene-culture coevolution, and "the best nineteenth-century case for gene-culture coevolution was made by Friedrich Engels" (Gould 1987, pp. 111–12). The analysis of Marx and Engels thus pointed to coevolution (Norgaard 1994), neither reducing society to nature, nor nature to society, but exploring their interactions. Indeed, the view that "nature reacts on man and natural conditions everywhere exclusively determined his historical development," Engels observed, "is…one-sided and forgets that man also reacts on nature, changing it and creating new conditions of existence for himself" (1940, p. 172).

The key to the metabolic relation of human beings to nature then is technology, but technology as conditioned by both social relations and natural conditions. Contrary to those who argue that Marx wore an ecolog-

ical blinder when it came to envisioning the limitations of technology in surmounting ecological problems, he explicitly argued in his critique of capitalist agriculture, that while capitalism served to promote "technical development in agriculture," it also brought into being social relations that were "incompatible" with a sustainable agriculture (1981, p. 216). The solution thus lay less in the application of a given technology than in the transformation of social relations. Moreover, even if the most advanced technical means available were in the hands of the associated producers, nature, for Marx, sets certain limits. The reproduction of "plant and animal products," for example, is conditioned by "certain organic laws involving naturally determined periods of time" (1981, p. 213). Marx reiterated the Italian political economist Pietro Verri's statement that human production was not properly an act of creation but merely "the reordering of matter" and was thus dependent on what the earth provided (1976, p. 132). The human interaction with nature always had to take the form of a metabolic cycle that needed to be sustained for the sake of successive generations. Technological improvements were a necessary but insufficient means for the "improvement" in the human relation to the earth. For Marx, human beings transformed their relation to nature but not exactly as they pleased; they did so in accordance with conditions inherited from the past and as a result of a complex process of historical development that reflected a changing relation to a natural world, which was itself dynamic in character. Redclift and Woodgate (1994, p. 53) are therefore wrong when they say that Marx wore blinders in relation to the coevolution of nature and society, viewing the human relation to nature as an "unchanging" one. Engels began his *Dialectics of Nature* with a dramatic description of the historic defeat of

18th-century conceptions of nature in which the natural world existed only in space not in time; "in which all change, all development of nature was denied" (1940, p. 6).

BEYOND THE APPROPRIATION AND DEFINITIONAL PROBLEMS

The foregoing suggests that Marx's analysis provides a multilayered and multivalent basis for linking sociology (and in particular the classical tradition of sociology) with environmental issues. Yet, if this is so, why has this concern with ecological issues not found a strong echo in the Marxist tradition throughout its development, and why has our understanding of Marx so often excluded these issues? Why has environmental sociology, which is concerned directly with these questions, been so slow to acknowledge Marx's importance in this respect? The first question relates to what we referred to at the beginning of this article as "the appropriation problem," the second to what was labeled "the definitional problem."

The Appropriation Problem

Marx's reputation as an ecological thinker was no doubt affected by the fact that, as Massimo Quaini (1982, p. 136) has pointed out, he "denounced the spoliation of nature before a modern bourgeois ecological conscience was born." Nevertheless, Marx's ecological critique was fairly well-known and had a direct impact on Marxism in the decades immediately following his death. It came to be discarded only later on, particularly within Soviet ideology, as the expansion of production at virtually any cost became the overriding goal of the Communist movement. The influence of Marx's cri-

tique in this respect can be seen in the writings of such leading Marxist thinkers as Kautsky, Lenin, and Bukharin.

Kautsky's great work, *The Agrarian Question*, published in 1899, contained a section on "The Exploitation of the Countryside by the Town" in which he held that the net external flow of value from countryside to town "corresponds to a constantly mounting loss of nutrients in the form of corn, meat, milk and so forth which the farmer has to sell to pay taxes, debt-interest and rent.... Although such a flow does not signify an exploitation of agriculture in terms of the law of value [of the capitalist economy], it does nevertheless lead...to its material exploitation, to the impoverishment of the land of its nutrients" (Kautsky 1988 [1899], p. 214)[9] Arguing at a time when the fertilizer industry was further developed than in Marx's day, Kautsky discussed the fertilizer treadmill resulting from the metabolic rift:

> *Supplementary fertilisers...allow the reduction in soil fertility to be avoided, but the necessity of using them in larger and larger amounts simply adds a further burden to agriculture—not one unavoidably imposed by nature, but a direct result of current social organization. By overcoming the antithesis between town and country... the materials removed from the soil would be able to flow back in full. Supplementary fertilisers would then, at most, have the task of enriching the soil, not staving off its impoverishment. Advances in cultivation would signify an increase in the amount of soluble nutrients in the soil without the need to add artificial fertilisers. (Kautsky 1988, vol. 2, pp. 214–15)*

Some of the same concerns were evident in Lenin's work. In *The Agrarian Ques-*

tion and the "Critics of Marx," written in 1901, he observed that, "The possibility of substituting artificial for natural manures and the fact that this is already being done (partly) do not in the least refute the irrationality of wasting natural fertilisers and thereby polluting the rivers and the air in suburban and factory districts. Even at the present time there are sewage farms in the vicinity of large cities which utilise city refuse with enormous benefit to agriculture; but by this system only an infinitesimal part of the refuse is utilized" (1961, pp. 155–56).

It was Bukharin, however, who developed the most systematic approach to ecological issues in his chapter on "The Equilibrium between Society and Nature" in *Historical Materialism* his important work of the 1920s. Cohen (1980, p. 118) has characterized Bukharin's position as one of "'naturalistic' materialism," because of its emphasis on the interaction between society and nature. As Bukharin wrote,

> This material process of "metabolism" between society and nature is the fundamental relation between environment and system, between "external conditions" and human society.... The metabolism between man and nature consists, as we have seen, in the transfer of material energy from external nature to society.... Thus, the interrelation between society and nature is a process of social reproduction. In this process, society applies its human labor energy and obtains a certain quantity of energy from nature ("nature's material," in the words of Marx). The balance *between expenditures and receipts is here obviously the decisive element for the growth of society. If what is obtained exceeds the loss by labor, important consequences obviously follow for society, which vary with the amount of this excess. (Bukharin 1925, pp. 108–12)

For Bukharin, technology was the chief mediating force in this metabolic relationship between nature and society. The human metabolism with nature was thus an "unstable equilibrium," one which could be progressive or regressive from the standpoint of human society. "The productivity of labor," he wrote, "is a precise measure of the 'balance' between society and nature." An increase in social productivity was seen as a progressive development; conversely, if the productivity of labor decreased—here Bukharin cited "the exhaustion of the soil" as a possible cause of such a decline—the relationship was a regressive one. Such a decline in social productivity resulting from an ill-adapted metabolic relation between society and nature could, he argued, lead to society being "barbarianized" (1925, pp. 77, 111–13).

Thus the whole "process of social production," Bukharin (1925, p. 111) wrote, "is an adaptation of human society to external nature." "Nothing could be more incorrect than to regard nature from the teleological point of view: man, the lord of creation, with nature created for his use, and all things adapted to human needs" (1925, p. 104). Instead, human beings were engaged in a constant, active struggle to adapt. "Man, as an animal form, as well as human society, are products of nature, part of this great, endless whole. Man can never escape from nature, and even when he 'controls' nature, he is merely making use of the laws of *nature* for his own ends" (1925, p. 104). "No system, including that of human society," Bukharin (1925, p. 89) insisted, "can exist in empty space; it is surrounded by an 'environment,' on which all its conditions ultimately depend. If human society is not adapted to its environment, it is not meant for this world." "For the tree in the forest, the environment means all the other trees, the brook, the earth, the ferns, the grass, the bushes, together with all their properties. Man's environment is society, in the midst of which he lives; the environment of human society is external nature" (1925, p. 75). Indeed, human beings, as Bukharin emphasized in 1931, need to be conceived as "living and working in the biosphere" (1971, p. 17).[10]

Other early Soviet thinkers connected to Bukharin demonstrated a similar concern for ecological issues. Komrov (1935, pp. 230–32) quoted at length from the long passage on the illusion of the conquest of nature in Engels's *Dialectics of Nature* and went on to observe that, "The private owner or employer, however necessary it may be to make the changing of the world comply with the laws of Nature, cannot do so since he aims at profit and only profit. By creating crisis upon crisis in industry he lays waste natural wealth in agriculture, leaving behind a barren soil and in mountain districts bare rocks and stony slopes." Similarly, Uranovsky (1935, p. 147) placed heavy emphasis, in a discussion of Marxism and science, on Marx's research into Liebig and "the theory of the exhaustion of the soil."[11]

Burkharin's ecological work and that of those associated with him was a product of the early Soviet era. The tragedy of the Soviet relation to the environment, which was eventually to take a form that has been characterized as "ecocide" (Feshbach and Friendly 1992; Peterson 1993), has tended to obscure the enormous dynamism of early Soviet ecology of the 1920s and the role that Lenin personally played in promoting conservation. In his writings and pronouncements, Lenin insisted that human labor could never substitute for the forces of nature and that a "rational exploitation" of the environment, or the scientific management of natural resources, was essential. As the principal leader of the young Soviet state, he argued for "preservation of the monuments of nature" and appointed the dedicated environmentalist Anatolii Vasil'evich Lunacharskii as head of the People's Commissariat of Education (Enlightenment), which was put in charge of conservation matters for all of Soviet Russia (Weiner 1988a, pp. 4, 22–28, 259; Weiner 1988b, pp. 254–55; Bailes 1990, pp. 151–58). Lenin had considerable respect for V. I. Vernadsky, the founder of the science of geochemistry (or biogeochemistry) and the author of *The Biosphere*. It was in response to the urging of Vernadsky and mineralogist E. A. Fersman that Lenin in 1919 established in the southern Urals the first nature preserve in the USSR—and indeed the first reserve anywhere by a government exclusively aimed at the scientific study of nature (Weiner 1988a, p. 29; Bailes 1990, p. 127). Under Lenin's protection, the Soviet conservation movement prospered, particularly during the New Economic Policy period (1921–28). But with the early death of Lenin and the triumph of Stalinism in the late 1920s, conservationists were attacked for being "bourgeois." Worse still, with the rise of Trofim Denisovich Lysenko, as an arbiter of biological science, "scientific" attacks were launched first on ecology and then genetics. By the late 1930s, the conservation movement in the Soviet Union had been completely decimated (Weiner 1988b, pp. 255–56).

The disconnection of Soviet thought from ecological issues, from the 1930s on, was severe and affected Marxism in the West as well, which between the 1930s and the 1970s tended to ignore ecological issues, though there was a revival of interest in this area in Marxism as well with the renewal of environmentalism following the publication of Rachel Carson's *Silent Spring* in 1962.

To be sure, when Western Marxism had first emerged as a distinct tradition in the 1920s and 1930s, one of the major influences was the Frankfurt School, which developed an ecological critique (Horkheimer and Adorno 1972). But this critique was largely philosophical, and while it recognized the ecological insights in Marx's *Economic and Philosophical Manuscripts,* it lost sight of the ecological argument embedded in *Capital.* Hence, it generally concluded that classical Marxism (beginning with the later Marx) supported a "Promethean" philosophy of the straightforward domination of nature. Not until the 1960s and 1970s did a more complex interpretation begin to emerge in the writings of the thinkers influenced by the Frankfurt tradition (Schmidt 1971; Leiss 1974). And it was not until the late 1980s and 1990s that scholars began to resurrect Marx's argument on soil fertility and organic recycling (Perelman 1988; Hayward 1994; Foster 1997; Fischer-Kowalski 1997). Much of the renewed emphasis on Marx's (and Liebig's) treatment of soil fertility and its ecological implications has come from agronomists and ecologists concerned directly with the debates around the evolution of soil science and the struggles over agribusiness versus organic agriculture (Mayumi 1991; Magdoff, Lanyon, and Liebhardt 1997; Gardner 1997).

It is scarcely surprising, then, that interpretations of Marx within sociology, and environmental sociology in particular, have been affected by an "appropriation problem." Sociologists in general tend to have little knowledge of volume 3 of Marx's *Capital,* where his critique of capitalist agriculture (and of the undermining of soil fertility) is most fully developed, and while these issues were well-known to the generations of Marxist thinkers who immediately followed Marx, they largely vanished

within Marxist thought in the 1930s. Even today, treatments of Marx's relation to ecology that purport to be comprehensive focus on his early writings, largely ignoring *Capital* (Dickens 1992). This appropriation problem had important ramifications. It left the appearance that there were no explicit linkages between human society and the natural world within classical Marxism, thus facilitating the notion that there was an unbridgeable gulf between classical sociology and environmental sociology.

Analogous appropriation problems might be raised with respect to the other classical theorists. Martinez-Alier (1987, pp. 183–92) has argued that Weber's important essay on Ostwald's social energetics has also been neglected; indeed it has yet to be translated into English. This has left the false impression that Weber had nothing to say in this area. Durkheim discussed the sociological origins of the classification of nature within what he called the "first philosophy of nature," and related this to modem scientific evolutionism. He also commented in profound ways about Darwinian evolutionary theory, the indestructibility of matter, the conservation of energy, and so on (Durkheim and Mauss 1968, pp. 81–88; Durkheim [1893] 1984, pp. 208–9; Durkheim [1911–12] 1983, pp. 21–27, 69–70). The systematic character of his more naturalistic thinking has never been properly addressed, and works like *Pragmatism and Sociology,* in which he presents some of his more complex views in this regard, have generally been ignored. Nevertheless, it is clear that his analysis pointed toward a complex, coevolutionary perspective. "Sociology," he wrote, "introduces a relativism that rests on the relation between the physical environment on the one hand and man on the other. The physical environment presents a relative fixity.

It undergoes evolution, of course; but reality never ceases to be what it was in order to give way to a reality of a new kind, or to one constituting new elements.... The organic world does not abolish the physical world and the social world has not been formed in contradistinction to the organic world, but together with it" (Durkheim 1983, pp. 69–70).

The Definitional Problem

Along with the appropriation problem, which deals with how received sociology has been affected by the selective appropriation of the classical tradition, there is also the definitional problem, which stands for the fact that sociology's (specifically environmental sociology's) failure to address the classical inheritance in this regard is at least partly due to overly narrow, preconceived definitions as to what constitutes genuinely environmental thought.

Here a major role was assumed by the contrast, drawn by Catton and Dunlap (1978), between the "human exceptionalist paradigm" and the "new environmental paradigm." All of the competing perspectives in sociology, such as "functionalism, symbolic interactionism, ethnomethodology, conflict theory, Marxism, and so forth" were seen as sharing a common trait of belonging to a "human exceptionalist paradigm" (later renamed "human exemptionalist paradigm"), and thus the "apparent diversity" of these theories was "not as important as the fundamental anthropocentrism underlying *all* of them" (Catton and Dunlap 1978, p. 42). The human exemptionalist paradigm was depicted as embracing the following assumptions: (1) the existence of culture makes human beings unique among the creatures of the earth, (2) culture evolves much more rapidly than biology, (3) most human characteristics are culturally based and hence can be socially altered, and (4) a process of cultural accumulation means that human progress can be cumulative and without limit. The habits of mind produced by this human exemptionalist paradigm, Catton and Dunlap (1978, pp. 42–43) argued, led to an overly optimistic faith in human progress, a failure to acknowledge ecological scarcity, and a tendency to neglect fundamental physical laws such as the entropy law.

For Catton and Dunlap, this "human exemptionalist paradigm," which encompassed nearly all of existing sociology could be contrasted to what they termed the "new environmental paradigm" emerging from environmental sociology, which was based on the following assumptions: (1) human beings are one of many species that are interdependently connected within the biotic community; (2) the biotic community consists of an intricate web of nature, with complex linkages of cause and effect; and (3) the world itself is finite, there are natural (physical, biological) limits to social and economic progress (1978, p. 45). In contrast to the "anthropocentrism" that characterized the human exemptionalist paradigm, the new environmental paradigm represented a shift toward what is now called an "ecocentric" point of view in which human beings are seen as part of nature, interconnected with other species and subject to the natural limits of the biosphere.

Ironically, the chief problem with this contrast between the human exemptionalist paradigm and the new environmental paradigm is that, even while emphasizing environmental factors, it tended to perpetuate a dualistic view of society versus the physical environment, anthropocentrism versus ecocentrism, and thus easily fell into the fallacy of the excluded middle (or a false dichotomy). There is a tendency in this view to see any theory that emphasizes socioeconomic progress or cultural accumulation as thereby "anthropocentric" and opposed to an "ecocentric" perspective, which seeks to decenter the human world and human interests. Nevertheless, logic suggests that there is no reason for such a stark opposition, since there are numerous ways in which sociology can embrace a concern for ecological sustainability without abandoning its emphasis on the development of human culture and production. Moreover, extreme ecocentrism runs the risk of losing sight of the sociological construction of much of the "natural world." Although classical sociology may have been anthropocentric to some extent in its focus on socioeconomic advance and its relative neglect of external nature, it was not necessarily antiecological (in the sense of ignoring natural limits) insofar as it acknowledged ecological sustainability as a requirement of social progress. The current preoccupation with sustainable development and coevolutionary theories within environmental discussions suggests that there have always been complex views that attempted to transcend the dualisms of humanity versus nature, anthropocentrism versus ecocentrism, socioeconomic progress versus natural limits.

Marx in particular has been criticized for being "anthropocentric" rather than "ecocentric" in orientation and hence outside of the framework of green theory (Eckersley 1992, pp. 75–95). Yet this kind of dualistic conception would have made little sense from his more dialectical perspective, which emphasized the quality (and sustainablilty) of the *interaction* between society and its natural conditions. It is the commitment to ecological sustainability, not the abstract notion of "ecocentrism," which most

clearly defines whether a theory is part of ecological discourse. Moreover, a comprehensive *sociology* of the environment must by definition be coevolutionary in perspective, taking into account changes in both society and nature and their mutual interaction.

CONCLUSION: THE ELEMENTS OF ENVIRONMENTAL SOCIOLOGY

The burden of argument in this article has been to demonstrate, using the case of Marx, that it is wrong to contend that classical sociology "was constructed as if nature didn't matter" (Murphy 1996, p. 10). A central claim of this article, backed up by logic and evidence, has been that each of the six ecological blinders commonly attributed to Marx—namely his alleged inability to perceive (1) the exploitation of nature, (2) nature's role in the creation of wealth, (3) the existence of natural limits, (4) nature's changing character, (5) the role of technology in environmental degradation, and (6) the inability of mere economic abundance to solve environmental problems—are in fact wrongly (or misleadingly) attributed to him. The point of course is not that Marx provided definitive treatments of all of these problems but rather that he was sufficiently cognizant of these issues to elude the main traps and to work the vitally important notion of the "human metabolism with nature" into his overall theoretical framework. Hence his work constitutes a possible starting point for a comprehensive sociology of the environment. No doubt some will still insist, despite the argument presented above, that Marx did not place sufficient *emphasis* on natural conditions, or that his approach was too anthropocentric, more along the lines of utilitarian-conservationism that genuine green radicalism. Some will still say that he in fact never entirely renounced economic development despite his insistence on a sustainable relation to the earth. But the evidence regarding his concern with ecological issues—particularly the crisis of the soil as it was perceived in the mid-19th century—is too extensive, and too much a part of his overall critique of capitalism, to be simply disregarded. Marx certainly argued *as if nature mattered,* and his sociology thus takes on a whole new dimension when viewed from this standpoint.

Just as Marx translated his early theory of the alienation of labor into more material terms through his later analysis of exploitation and the degradation of work, so he translated his early notion of the alienation of nature (part of the Feuerbachian naturalism that pervaded his *Economic and Philosophical Manuscripts* into more material terms through his later concept of a metabolic rift. Without the latter concept, it is impossible to understand Marx's developed analysis of the antagonism of town and country, his critique of capitalist agriculture, or his calls for the "restoration" of the necessary metabolic relation between humanity and the earth, that is, his basic notion of sustainability. Marx's response to Liebig's critique of capitalist agriculture was coupled, moreover, with a sophisticated response to Darwin's evolutionary theory. What emerges from this is a historical materialism that is ultimately connected to natural history; one that rejects the crude, one-sided traditions of mechanical materialism, vitalism, and social Darwinism that existed in Marx's day. Yet, at the same time, Marx avoided falling into the trap of Engels's later "dialectical materialism," which, ironically, drew too heavily on both Hegel's *Logic* and his *Philosophy of Nature,* abstractly superimposing a despiritualized Hegelian dialectic (i.e., con-

ceived in purely logical terms, divorced from Hegel's self-mediating spirit) on top of what was otherwise a mechanical view of the universe. Instead, Marx provides, as we have seen, a cautious constructionism, fully in tune with his own practical materialism, which always emphasized the role of human praxis, while remaining sensitive to natural conditions, evolutionary change, and the metabolic interaction of humanity and the earth.

Marx's main contribution in this area was methodological. He saw "the economic formation of society" as part of a process of "natural history" and struggled within his critique of political economy to take account of both natural conditions and the human transformation of nature (1976, p. 92). In the process, he applied a dialectical mode of analysis not to external nature itself (recognizing that the dialectic had no meaning aside from the self-mediating role of human beings as the agents of history) but rather to the *interaction* between nature and humanity, emphasizing the alienation of nature in existing forms of reproduction and the contradictory, nonsustainable character of the metabolic rift between nature and society that capitalism in particular had generated. Moreover, Marx conceived this metabolic rift not simply in abstract terms but in terms of the concrete crisis represented by the degradation of the soil and by the problem of human and animal "wastes" that engulfed the cities. Both were equal indications, in his analysis, of the metabolic rift between humanity and the soil, reflected in the antagonism of town and country.

The way in which Marx's analysis prefigured some of the most advanced ecological analysis of the late 20th century— particularly in relation to issues of the soil and the ecology of cities—is nothing less than startling. Much of the recent work on the ecology of the soil (Magdoff et al. 1997; Mayumi 1991; Gardner 1997) has focused on successive, historical breaks in nutrient cycling. The first such break, associated with the second agricultural revolution, is often conceived in essentially the same terms in which it was originally discussed by Liebig and Marx and is seen as related to the physical removal of human beings from the land. This resulted in the failure to recycle human organic wastes back to the land, as well as the associated break in the metabolic cycle and the net loss to the soil arising from the transfer of organic products (food and fiber) over hundreds and thousands of miles. It was these developments that made the creation of a fertilizer industry necessary. A subsequent break occurred with the third agricultural revolution (the rise of agribusiness), which was associated in its early stages with the removal of large animals from farms, the creation of centralized feedlots, and the replacement of animal traction with farm machinery. No longer was it necessary to grow legumes, which had the beneficial effect of naturally fixing nitrogen in the soil, in order to feed ruminant animals. Hence, the dependence on fertilizer nitrogen increased, with all sorts of negative environmental consequences, including the contamination of ground water, the "death" of lakes, and so on. These developments, and other related processes, are now seen as related to the distorted pattern of development that has characterized capitalism (and other social systems such as the Soviet Union that replicated this pattern of development, sometimes in even more distorted fashion), taking the form of a more and more extreme metabolic rift between city and country—between what is now a mechanized humanity and a mechanized nature. Similarly, the ecological prob-

lem of the city is increasingly viewed in terms of its metabolic relationship to its external environment (focusing on the flows of organic nutrients, energy, etc.) and the ecological distortions that this entails (Wolman 1965; Giradet 1997; Fischer-Kowalski 1997; Opschoor 1997).

The fact that Marx was able to conceive a sociological approach that pointed to these developments when they were still in their very early stages represents one of the great triumphs of classical sociological analysis. It stands as a indication of how sociology could be extended into the ecological realm. It reinforces the view that ecological analysis, devoid of sociological insight, is incapable of dealing with the contemporary crisis of the earth—a crisis which has its source and its meaning ultimately in society itself.

It is not just Marxist sociology that is in a position to draw on Marx's insights in this respect, which are sociological as much as they are Marxist. Moreover, other paradigms within classical sociology have much more to contribute to the analysis of the natural environmental context of human social development than is commonly supposed. There is no doubt that Weber and Durkheim were both concerned in their own ways with the metabolic interaction between nature and society. Although systematic investigations into the work of Weber and Durkheim in this respect still have to be undertaken, it is not to be doubted that embedded in their sociologies were important insights into ecological problems. When Weber wrote at the end of *The Protestant Ethic and the Spirit of Capitalism* of a civilization characterized by "mechanized petrification" that might continue along the same course—that of formal or instrumental rationality—"until the last ton of fossilized coal" was burnt, he was suggesting the possibility of a wider social and environmental critique of this civilization (Weber [1904–5] 1930, pp. 181–82). Likewise, Durkheim's discussions of Darwinian theory and its implications for social analysis pointed the way toward a sociological understanding of the coevolution of nature and society. In the cases of Weber and Durkheim—as in Marx—we may surmise that an appropriation problem, coupled with a definitional problem, has hindered the appreciation of the way in which their sociologies took natural conditions into account.

Today, even among leading environmental sociologists who criticized the classical traditions of sociology for failing to take into account the physical environment, there is a dawning recognition that these classical traditions have proven themselves to be resilient in the face of challenges of environmental sociologists and are open to reinterpretation and reformulation along lines that give greater weight to ecological factors. Dunlap points to the emergence, in recent years, of "'greener' versions of Marxist, Weberian and symbolic interactionist theories" (1997, p. 34). Ironically, it is coming to be recognized that the problem of "human exemptionalism," that is, the neglect of the physical environment, may have been less characteristic of classical sociology than it was of the sociology that predominated after World War II—during a period when the faith in technology and the human "conquest" of nature reached heights never before attained, only to lead to disillusionment and crisis beginning with the 1960s. Developing an environmental sociology as an integral part of sociology as a whole thus requires that we reach back into past theories in order to develop the intellectual means for a thoroughgoing analysis of the present. For environmental sociology the crucial issue today is to abandon the "strong constructionism" of most contemporary sociological theory, which tends to view the environment as simply a product of human beings, and to move toward a more "cautious constructionism" that recognizes that there is a complex metabolic relation between human beings and society (Dunlap 1997, pp. 31–32, 35; Dickens 1996, p. 71). Surprisingly, this is turning out to be an area in which the classical sociology of the mid-19th and early 20th centuries still has much to teach us as we enter the 21st century—a century that is bound to constitute a turning point for good or ill in the human relation to the environment.

ENDNOTES

1. I would like to express my gratitude to Joan Acker, Paul Burkett, Michael Dawson, Michael Dreiling, Charles Hunt, John Jermier, Robert McChesney, Fred Magdoff, Harry Magdoff, John Mage, David Milton, Robert O'Brien, Christopher Phelps, Ira Shapiro, Paul Sweezy, Laura Tamkin, and Ellen Meiksins Wood for creating a climate of intellectual exchange and support without which this work would not have been possible. I would also like to express my gratitude to the *AJS* reviewers, all of whom contributed in positive ways to this article.

2. The issue of sustainability, or the notion that basic ecological conditions need to be maintained so that the ability of future generations to fulfill their needs will not be compromised, is the leitmotif of most contemporary environmental thought.

3. Environmentalists sometimes use the terms "dark green" and "light green" to refer to the same division as that between "deep ecology" and so-called "shallow ecology." In both cases, the nature of the distinction is the same: between what is thought of as an "anthropocentric" perspective versus a more "ecocentric" one—though such distinctions are notoriously difficult to define. For a sympathetic account of deep ecology, see McLaughlin (1993).

4. Thompson (1968) designates the second agricultural revolution as occurring over the years 1815–80, that is, commencing with the agricultural crisis that immediately followed the Napoleonic Wars. I have narrowed the period down to 1830–80 here in order to distinguish between the crisis that to some extent preceded the second agricultural revolution and the revolution proper, for which the turning point was the publication of Liebig's *Organic Chemistry* in 1840 followed by J. B. Lawes's building of the first factory for the production of synthetic fertilizer (superphosphates) a few years later.

5. Marx highlighted the methodological importance of the concept of "material exchange [*Stoffwechsel*] between man and nature" in his *Notes on Adolph Wagner,* his last economic work, written in 1880 (1975, p. 209). As early as 1857–58 in the *Grundrisse,* Marx had referred to the concept of metabolism (*Stoffwechsel*) in the wider sense of "a system of general social metabolism, of universal relations, of all-round needs and universal capacities...formed for the first time" under generalized commodity production (1973, p. 158). Throughout his later economic works, he employed the concept to refer both to the actual metabolic interaction between nature and society through human labor, and also in a wider sense to describe the complex, dynamic, interdependent set of needs and relations brought into being and constantly reproduced in alienated form under capitalism, and the question of human freedom that this raised—all of which could be seen as being connected to the way in which the human metabolism with nature was expressed through the organization of human labor. Marx thus gave the concept of metabolism both a specific ecological meaning and a wider social meaning. It makes sense therefore to speak of the "socioecological" nature of his concept.

6. This translation has been altered slightly in conformity with the better known International Publishers edition, in which the term "successive" appears before "generations." See Marx (1967, p. 617).

7. On this later phase of Marx's analysis, in which he addressed the agricultural concerns of the Russian populists, see Shanin (1983).

8. Marx and Engels's complex relation to Darwin's work—which neither denied a relation between society and biology nor reduced one to the other—may also have something to say about why they never used the term "ecology," coined by Darwin's leading German follower Ernst Haeckel in 1866, the year before the publication of volume 1 of *Capital.* Although the concept of ecology only gradually came into common usage, Marx and Engels were very familiar with Haeckel's work and so may have been aware of his coinage of this concept. Yet, the way that Haeckel, a strong social Darwinist, originally defined the term was unlikely to have predisposed them to its acceptance. "By ecology," Haeckel had written, "we mean the body of knowledge concerning the economy of nature...in a word, ecology is the study of all those complex interrelations referred to by Darwin as the conditions of the struggle for existence" (Golley 1993, p. 207).

9. In saying there was no exploitation of agriculture in law of value terms, Kautsky was arguing that transactions here, as in other areas of the economy, were based on equal exchange. Nonetheless, he insisted that "material exploitation" (related to use values) was present insofar as the soil was being impoverished. Marx too argued that the soil was being "robbed" or "exploited" in the latter sense and connected this to the fact that the land under capitalism was regarded as a "free gift" (as Malthus had contended) so that the full costs of its reproduction never entered into the law of value under capitalism.

10. In referring to the "biosphere," Bukharin drew upon V. I. Vernadsky's *The Biosphere,* first published in 1922, which was one of the great works in ecological science of the 20th century and was extremely influential in Soviet scientific circles in the 1920s and early 1930s. Vernadsky was "the first person in history to come [to] grips with the real implications of the fact that the Earth is a self-contained sphere" (Margulis et al: 1998, p. 15). He achieved international renown both for his analysis of the biosphere and as the founder of the science of geochemistry (or biogeochemistry) (Vernadsky [1922] 1998).

11. Uranovsky was one of the first scientists to be arrested, in 1936, in the Stalinist purges (Medvedev [1971] 1989, p. 441). Accompanying Bukharin as a member of the Soviet delegation to the Second International Conference of the History of Science and Technology, London 1931, was also the brilliant plant geneticist N. I. Vavilov (one of the greatest figures in the history of ecological science), founder and first president of the Lenin Agricultural Academy, who applied a materialist method to the question of the origins of agriculture with the support of early Soviet science (Vavilov 1971). Like Bukharin and Uranovsky, he fell prey to the Stalinist purges.

REFERENCES

Altvater, Elmar. 1993. *The Future of the Market.* London: Verso.

Bacon, Francis. (1620) 1994. *Novum Organum.* Chicago: Open Court.

Bailes, Kendall. 1990. *Science and Russian Culture in an Age of Revolutions.* Bloomington: Indiana University Press.

Beck, Ulrich. 1995. *Ecological Enlightenment.* Atlantic Highlands, N.J.: Humanities Press.

Benton, Ted. 1989. "Marxism and Natural Limits." *New Left Review* 178:51–86.

———. 1994. "Biology and Social Theory in the Environmental Debate." Pp. 28–50, in *Social Theory and the Global Environment,* edited by Michael Redclift and Ted Benton. New York: Routledge.

Benton, Ted, and Michael Redclift. 1994. "Introduction." Pp. 1–27 in *Social Theory and the Global Environment,* edited by Michael Redclift and Ted Benton. New York: Routledge.

Bing, Franklin C. 1971. "The History of the Word 'Metabolism.'" *Journal of the History of Medicine and Allied Sciences* 26 (2):158–80.

Brock, William H. 1997. *Justus von Liebig.* Cambridge: Cambridge University Press.

Bukharin, Nikolai. 1925. *Historical Materialism: A System of Sociology.* New York: International.

———. 1971. "Theory and Practice from the Standpoint of Dialectical Materialism." Pp. 11–33 in *Science at the Crossroads.* London: Frank Cass.

Burch, William. 1971. *Daydreams and Nightmares.* New York: Harper & Row.

Burkett, Paul. 1997. "Nature in Marx Reconsidered." *Organization and Environment* 10 (2):164–83.

Buttel, Frederick. 1986. "Sociology and the Environment." *International Social Science Journal* 109:337–56.

———. 1987. "New Directions in Environmental Sociology." *Annual Review of Sociology* 13:465–88.

———. 1996. "Environmental and Resource Sociology." *Rural Sociology* 61 (1):56–76.

Caneva, Kenneth. 1993. *Robert Mayer and the Conservation of Energy.* Princeton, N.J.: Princeton University Press.

Carey, Henry. 1858. *Letters to the President on the Foreign and Domestic Policy of the Union.* Philadelphia: M. Polock.

———. (1858–59) 1867. *Principles of Social Science,* vol. 2. Philadelphia: J. B. Lippincott.

———. (1847) 1967a. *The Past, the Present and the Future.* New York: Augustus M. Kelley.

———. (1853) 1967b. *The Slave Trade Domestic and Foreign.* New York: Augustus M. Kelley.

Catton, William. 1982. *Overshoot.* Urbana: University of Illinois Press.

Catton, William, and Riley Dunlap. 1978. "Environmental Sociology: A New Paradigm." *American Sociologist* 13:41–49.

Churchill, Ward. 1996. *From a Native Son.* Boston: South End.

Clark, John. 1989. "Marx's Inorganic Body." *Environmental Ethics* 11:243–58.

Cohen, Stephen. 1980. *Bukharin and the Bolshevik Revolution.* Oxford: Oxford University Press.

Darwin, Charles. (1859) 1968. *The Origin of Species.* Middlesex: Penguin.

Deléage, Jean-Paul. 1994. "Eco-Marxist Critique of Political Economy," pp. 37–82 in *Is Capitalism Sustainable?* edited by Martin O'Connor. New York: Guilford.

Dickens, Peter. 1992. *Society and Nature.* Philadelphia: Temple University.

———. 1996. *Reconstructing Nature.* New York: Routledge.

———. 1997. "Beyond Sociology." Pp. 179–92 in *International Handbook of Environmental Sociology,* edited by Michael Redclift and Graham Woodgate. Northampton, Mass.: Edward Elgar.

Dryzek, John. 1997. *The Politics of the Earth.* Oxford: Oxford University Press.

Dunlap, Riley. 1997. "The Evolution of Environmental Sociology." Pp. 21–39 in *International Handbook of Environmental Sociology,* edited by Michael Redclift and Graham Woodgate. Northampton, Mass.: Edward Elgar.

Dunlap, Riley, and William Catton. 1979. "Environmental Sociology." Pp. 57–85 in *Progress in Resource Management and Environmental Planning,* vol. 1. Edited by Timothy O'Riordan and Ralph D'Arge. New York: John Wiley & Sons.

———. 1994. "Struggling with Human Exceptionalism." *American Sociologist* 25 (1):5–30.

Dunlap, Riley, and Kenneth Martin. 1983. "Bringing Environment into the Study of Agriculture." *Rural Sociology* 48 (2):201–18.

Durkheim, Émile. (1911–12) 1983. *Pragmatism and Sociology.* Cambridge: Cambridge University Press.

———. (1893) 1984. *The Division of Labor in Society.* New York: Free Press.

Durkheim, Émile, and Marcel Mauss. 1963. *Primitive Classification.* Chicago: University of Chicago Press.

Eckersley, Robyn. 1992. *Environmentalism and Political Theory.* New York: State University of New York Press.

Engels, Friedrich. (1874–80) 1940. *The Dialectics of Nature.* New York: International.

———. 1964. "Outlines of a Critique of Political Economy." Pp. 197–226 *The Economic and Philosophic Manuscripts of 1844,* edited by Dirk J. Struik. New York: International.

———. (1872) 1975. *The Housing Question.* Moscow: Progress.

Ernle, Lord. (1912) 1961. *English Farming Past and Present.* Chicago: Quadrangle.

Ferkiss, Victor. 1993. *Nature, Technology and Society.* New York: New York University Press.

Feshbach, Murray, and Arthur Friendly, Jr. 1992. *Ecocide in the U.S.S.R.* New York: Basic.

Fischer-Kowalski, Marina. 1997. "Society's Metabolism." Pp. 119–37 in *International Handbook of Environmental Sociology,* edited by Michael Redclift and Graham Woodgate. Northampton, Mass.: Edward Elgar.

Foster, John Bellamy. 1997. "The Crisis of the Earth." *Organization and Environment* 10 (3):278–95.

Gardner, Gary. 1997. *Recycling Organic Wastes.* Washington, D.C.: Worldwatch.

Geertz, Clifford. 1963. *Agricultural Involution.* Berkeley: University of California Press.

Georgescu-Roegen, Nicholas. 1971. *The Entropy Law in the Economic Process.* Cambridge, Mass.: Harvard University Press.

Giddens, Anthony. 1981. *A Contemporary Critique of Historical Materialism.* Berkeley and Los Angeles: University of California Press.

Giradet, Herbert. 1997. "Sustainable Cities." *Architectural Design* 67:9–13.

Goldblatt, David. 1996. *Social Theory and the Environment.* Boulder, Colo.: Westview.

Golley, Frank. 1993. *A History of the Ecosystem Concept in Ecology.* New Haven, Conn.: Yale University Press.

Gould, Stephen Jay. 1987. *An Urchin in the Storm.* New York: W. W. Norton.

Grundmann, Reiner. 1991. *Marxism and Ecology.* Oxford: Oxford University Press.

Harvey, David. 1996. *Justice, Nature and the Geography of Difference.* New York: Blackwell.

Hayward, Tim. 1994. *Ecological Thought.* Cambridge, Mass.: Polity.

Hillel, Daniel. 1991. *Out of the Earth.* Berkeley and Los Angeles: University of California.

Horkheimer, Max, and Theodor Adorno. 1972, *The Dialectic of Enlightenment.* New York: Continuum.

Jacobs, Michael. 1994. "The Limits to Neoclassicism." Pp. 67–91 in *Social Theory and the Environment,* edited by Michael Redclift and Ted Benton. New York: Routledge.

Järvikoski, Timo. 1996. "The Relation of Nature and Society in Marx and Durkheim." *Acta Sociologica* 39 (1):73–86.

Johnston, James. 1851. *Notes on North America.* London: William Blackwood & Sons.

Kautsky, Karl. (1899) 1988. *The Agrarian Question,* 2 vols. Winchester, Mass.: Zwan.

Komarov, V. L. 1935. "Marx and Engels on Biology." Pp. 190–234 in *Marxism and Modern Thought.* New York: Harcourt, Brace.

Lebowitz, Michael. 1992. *Beyond Capital.* London: Macmillan.

Leiss, William. 1974. *The Domination of Nature.* Boston: Beacon.

Lenin, V. I. 1961. *Collected Works,* vol. 5. Edited by Victor Jerome. Moscow: Progress.

Liebig, Justus von. 1859, *Letters on Modern Agriculture.* London: Walton & Maberly.

———. 1863. *The Natural Laws of Husbandry.* New York: D. Appleton.

———. 1865. *Letters on the Subject of the Utilization of the Metropolitan Sewage.* London: W. H. Collingridge.

———. (1842) 1964. *Animal Chemistry or Organic Chemistry in its Application to Physiology and Pathology.* New York: Johnson Reprint.

Magdoff, Fred, Less Lanyon, and Bill Liebhardt. 1997. "Nutrient Cycling, Transformations and Flows." *Advances in Agronomy* 60:1–73.

Malthus, Thomas. 1970. *Pamphlets.* New York: Augustus M. Kelley.

Margulis, Lynn, et al. 1998. Foreword to *The Biosphere,* by V. I. Vernadsky. New York: Copernicus.

Marshall, Alfred. 1920. *Principles of Economics.* London: Macmillan.

Martinez-Alier, Juan. 1987. *Ecological Economics.* Oxford: Basil Blackwell.

Marx, Karl. (1847) 1963. *The Poverty of Philosophy.* New York: International.

———. (1863–65) 1967. *Capital,* vol 3. New York: International.

———. (1875) 1971a. *Critique of the Gotha Programme.* Moscow: Progress.

———. (1861–63) 1971b. *Theories of Surplus Value,* pt. 3. Moscow: Progress.

———. (1857–58) 1973. *Grundrisse.* New York: Vintage.

———. 1974. *Early Writings.* New York: Vintage.

———. 1975. *Texts on Method.* Oxford: Basil Blackwell.

———. (1867) 1976. *Capital,* vol. 1. New York: Vintage.

———. (1865–70) 1978. *Capital,* vol. 2. New York: Vintage.

———. (1863–65) 1981. *Capital,* vol. 3. New York: Vintage.

Marx, Karl, and Friedrich Engels. (1848) 1967. *The Communist Manifesto.* New York: Monthly Review.

———. 1975a. *Collected Works.* New York: International.

———. 1975b. *Selected Correspondence,* edited by S. W. Ryazanskaya. Moscow: Progress.

Mayumi, Kozo. 1991. "Temporary Emancipation from the Land." *Ecological Economics* 4 (1):35–56.

McConnell, Campbell. 1987. *Economics,* New York: McGraw Hill.

McLaughlin, Andrew. 1990. "Ecology, Capitalism, and Socialism." *Socialism and Democracy* 10:69–102.

———. 1993. *Regarding Nature.* Albany: State University of New York Press.

Medvedev, Roy. (1971) 1989. *Let History Judge.* New York: Columbia University Press.

Milton, Kay. 1996. *Environmentalism and Cultural Theory.* New York: Routledge.

Murphy, Raymond. 1994. *Rationality and Nature.* Boulder, Colo.: Westview.

———. 1996. *Sociology and Nature.* Boulder, Colo.: Westview.

Norgaard, Richard. 1994. *Development Betrayed.* New York: Routledge.

Nove, Alec. 1987. "Socialism." Pp. 398–407 in *The New Palgrave Dictionary of Economics,* vol. 4. Edited by John Eatwell, Murray Milgate, and Peter Newman. New York: Stockton.

O'Connor, James. 1998. *Natural Causes.* New York: Guilford.

Odum, Eugene. 1969. "The Strategy of Ecosystem Development." *Science* 164:262–70.

Opschoor, J. B. 1997. "Industrial Metabolism, Economic Growth and Institutional Change." Pp. 274–86 in *International Handbook of Environmental Sociology,* edited by Michael Redclift and Graham Woodgate. Northampton, Mass.: Edward Elgar.

Pannekoek, Anton. 1912. *Marxism and Darwinism.* Chicago: Charles H. Kerr.

Parsons, Howard, ed. 1977. *Marx and Engels on Ecology.* Westport, Conn.: Greenwood.

Perelman, Michael. 1988. "Marx and Resources." *Environment, Technology and Society* 51:15–19.

———. 1993. "Marx and Resource Scarcity." *Capitalism, Nature, Socialism* 4 (2):65–84.

Peterson, D. J. 1993. *Troubled Lands.* Boulder, Colo.: Westview.

Pigou, A. C. 1920. *The Economics of Welfare.* London: Macmillan.

Quaini, Massimo. 1982. *Marxism and Geography.* Totowa, N.J.: Barnes & Noble.

Redclift, Michael. 1984. *Development and the Environmental Crisis.* New York: Methuen.

Redclift, Michael, and Graham Woodgate. 1994. "Sociology and the Environment." Pp. 51–66 in *Social Theory and the Global Environment,* vol. 1. Edited by Michael Redclift and Ted Benton. New York: Routledge.

Ricardo, David. 1951. *Piinciples of Political Economy and Taxation.* Cambridge: Cambridge University Press.

Sauer, Carl. 1963. *Land and Life.* Berkeley: University of California Press.

Schmidt, Alfred. 1971. *The Concept of Nature in Marx.* London: New Left.

Schnaiberg, Allen. 1980. *The Environment.* Oxford: Oxford University Press.

Shanin, Teodor. 1983. *Late Marx and the Russian Road.* New York: Monthly Review.

Skaggs, J. M. 1994. *The Great Guano Rush.* New York: St. Martin's.

Thompson, F. M. L. 1968. "The Second Agricultural Revolution, 1815–1880." *Economic History Review* 21 (1):62–77.

Uranovsky, Y. M. 1935. "Marxism and Natural Science." Pp. 136–74 in *Marxism and Modern Thought.* New York: Harcourt, Brace.

Vavilov, N. I. 1971. "The Problem of the Origin of the World's Agriculture in the Light of the Latest Investigations." Pp. 97–106 in *Science at the Crossroads.* London: Frank Cass.

Vernadsky, V. I. (1922) 1998. *The Biosphere.* New York: Copernicus.

Weber, Max. (1904–5) 1930. *The Protestant Ethic and the Spirit of Capitalism.* London: Unwin Hyman.

Weiner, Douglas. 1988a. *Models of Nature.* Bloomington: Indiana University Press.

———. 1988b. "The Changing Face of Soviet Conservation." Pp. 252–73 in *The Ends of The Earth,* edited by Donald Worster. New York: Cambridge University Press.

Wolman, Abel. 1965. "The Metabolism of Cities." *Scientific American* 213 (3):179–90.

World Commission on Environment and Development. 1987. *Our Common Future.* New York: Oxford University Press.

Chapter 3

Environmental Justice within and between Countries

5. Anatomy of Environmental Racism and the Environmental Justice Movement*

ROBERT D. BULLARD

Communities are not all created equal. In the United States, for example, some communities are routinely poisoned while the government looks the other way. Environmental regulations have not uniformly benefitted all segments of society. People of color (African Americans, Latinos, Asians, Pacific islanders, and Native Americans) are disproportionately harmed by industrial toxins on their jobs and in their neighborhoods. These groups must contend with dirty air and drinking water—the byproducts of municipal landfills, incinerators, polluting industries, and hazardous waste treatment storage, and disposal facilities.

Why do some communities get "dumped on" while others escape? Why are environmental regulations vigorously enforced in some communities and not in others? Why are some workers protected from environmental threats to their health while others (such as migrant farmworkers) are still being poisoned? How can environmental justice be incorporated into the campaign for environmental protection? What institutional changes would enable the United States to become a just and sustainable soci-

ety? What community organizing strategies are effective against environmental racism? These are some of the many questions addressed.... The pervasive reality of racism is placed at the very center of the analysis.

INTERNAL COLONIALISM AND WHITE RACISM

The history of the United States has long been grounded in white racism. The nation was founded on the principles of "free land" (stolen from native Americans and Mexicans), "free labor" (cruelly extracted from African slaves), and "free men" (white men with property). From the outset, institutional racism shaped the economic, political, and ecological landscape, and buttressed the exploitation of both land and people. Indeed, it has allowed communities of color to exist as internal colonies characterized by dependent (and unequal) relationships with the dominant white society or "Mother Country." In their 1967 book, *Black Power*, Carmichael and Hamilton were among the first to explore the "internal" colonial model as a way to explain the racial inequality, political exploitation, and social isolation of African Americans. As Carmichael and Hamilton (1967:16–17) write:

> The economic relationship of American black communities [to white society]...

*Excerpted from Robert D. Bullard, editor. 1993. *Confronting Environmental Racism: Voices from the Grassroots* (Boston, MA: South End Press), 15–23. Reprinted by permission of the publisher.

reflects their colonial status. The political power exercised over those communities goes hand in glove with the economic deprivation experienced by the black citizens.

Historically, colonies have existed for the sole purpose of enriching, in one form or another, the "colonizer"; the consequence is to maintain the economic dependency of the "colonized."

Generally, people of color in the United States—like their counterparts in formerly colonized lands of Africa, Asia, and Latin America—have not had the same opportunities as whites. The social forces that have organized oppressed colonies internationally still operate in the "heart of the colonizer's mother country" (Blauner 1972:26). For Blauner, people of color are subjected to five principal colonizing processes: they enter the "host" society and economy involuntarily; their native culture is destroyed; white-dominated bureaucracies impose restrictions from which whites are exempt; the dominant group uses institutionalized racism to justify its actions; and a dual or "split labor market" emerges based on ethnicity and race. Such domination is also buttressed by state institutions. Social scientists Omi and Winant (1986:76–78) go so far as to insist that "every state institution is a racial institution." Clearly, whites receive benefits from racism, while people of color bear most of the cost.

ENVIRONMENTAL RACISM

Racism plays a key factor in environmental planning and decisionmaking. Indeed, environmental racism is reinforced by government, legal, economic, political, and military institutions. It is a fact of life in the United States that the mainstream environmental movement is only beginning to

wake up to. Yet, without a doubt, racism influences the likelihood of exposure to environmental and health risks and the accessibility to health care. Racism provides whites at all class levels with an "edge" in gaining access to a healthy physical environment. This has been documented again and again.

Whether by conscious design or institutional neglect, communities of color in urban ghettos, in rural "poverty pockets," or on economically impoverished Native-American reservations face some of the worst environmental devastation in the nation. Clearly, racial discrimination was not legislated out of existence in the 1960s. While some significant progress was made during this decade, people of color continue to struggle for equal treatment in many areas, including environmental justice. Agencies at all levels of government, including the federal EPA, have done a poor job protecting people of color from the ravages of pollution and industrial encroachment. It has been an up-hill battle convincing white judges, juries, government officials, and policymakers that racism exists in environmental protection, enforcement, and policy formulation.

The most polluted urban communities are those with crumbling infrastructure, ongoing economic disinvestment, deteriorating housing, inadequate schools, chronic unemployment, a high poverty rate, and an overloaded health-care system. Riot-torn South Central Los Angeles typifies this urban neglect. It is not surprising that the "dirtiest" zip code in California belongs to the mostly African-American and Latino neighborhood in that part of the city (Kay 1991). In the Los Angeles basin, over 71 percent of the African Americans and 50 percent of the Latinos live in areas with the most polluted air, while only 34 percent of the white population does (Mann 1991; Ong and Blumenberg 1990). This pattern exists nationally as well. As researchers Wernette and Nieves (1992:16–17) note:

In 1990, 437 of the 3,109 counties and independent cities failed to meet at least one of the EPA ambient air quality standards…57 percent of whites, 65 percent of African Americans, and 80 percent of Hispanics live in 437 counties with substandard air quality. Out of the whole population, a total of 33 percent of whites, 50 percent of African Americans, and 60 percent of Hispanics live in the 136 counties in which two or more air pollutants exceed standards. The percentage living in the 29 counties designated as non-attainment areas for three or more pollutants are 12 percent of whites, 20 percent of African Americans, and 31 percent of Hispanics.

Income alone does not account for these above-average percentages. Housing segregation and development patterns play a key role in determining where people live. Moreover, urban development and the "spatial configuration" of communities flow from the forces and relationships of industrial production which, in turn, are influenced and subsidized by government policy (Feagin 1988; Gottdiener 1988). There is widespread agreement that vestiges of race-based decisionmaking still influence housing, education, employment, and criminal justice. The same is true for municipal services such as garbage pickup and disposal, neighborhood sanitation, fire and police protection, and library services. Institutional racism influences decisions on local land use, enforcement of environmental regulations, industrial facility siting, management of economic vulnerability, and paths of freeways and highways.

People skeptical of the assertion that poor people and people of color are targeted for waste-disposal sites should consider the report the Cerrell Associates provided the California Waste Management Board. In their 1984 report, *Political Difficulties Facing Waste—to-Energy Conversion Plant Siting,* they offered a detailed profile of those neighborhoods most likely to organize effective resistance against incinerators. The policy conclusion based on this analysis is clear. As the report states:

All socioeconomic groupings tend to resent the nearby siting of major facilities, but middle and upper socioeconomic strata possess better resources to effectuate their opposition. Middle and higher socioeconomic strata neighborhoods should not fall within the one-mile and five-mile radius of the proposed site (Cerrell Associates 1984:43).

Where then will incinerators or other polluting facilities be sited? For Cerrell Associates, the answer is low-income, disempowered neighborhoods with a high concentration of nonvoters. The ideal site, according to their report, has nothing to do with environmental soundness but everything to do with lack of social power. Communities of color in California are far more likely to fit this profile than are their white counterparts.

Those still skeptical of the existence of environmental racism should also consider the fact that zoning boards and planning commissions are typically stacked with white developers. Generally, the decisions of these bodies reflect the special interests of the individuals who sit on these boards. People of color have been systematically excluded from these decisionmaking boards, commissions, and governmental agencies (or allowed only token representations).

Grassroots leaders are now demanding a shared role in all the decisions that shape their communities. They are challenging the intended or unintended racist assumptions underlying environmental and industrial policies.

TOXIC COLONIALISM ABROAD

To understand the global ecological crisis, it is important to understand that the poisoning of African Americans in South Central Los Angeles and of the Mexicans in border *maquiladoras* have their roots in the same system of economic exploitation, racial oppression, and devaluation of human life. The quest for solutions to environmental problems and for ways to achieve sustainable development in the United States has considerable implications for the global environmental movement.

Today, more than 1,900 *maquiladoras*, assembly plants operated by American, Japanese, and other countries, are located along the 2,000-mile U.S.-Mexico border (Center for Investigative Reporting 1990; Sanchez 1990; Zuniga 1992). These plants use cheap Mexican labor to assemble products from imported components and raw materials, and then ship them back to the United States (Witt 1991). Nearly half a million Mexicans work in the *maquiladoras*. They earn an average of $3.75 a day. While these plants bring jobs, albeit low-paying ones, they exacerbate local pollution by overcrowding the border towns, straining sewage and water systems, and reducing air quality. All this compromises the health of workers and nearby community residents. The Mexican environmental regulatory agency is understaffed and ill-equipped to adequately enforce the country's laws (Working Group on Canada-Mexico Free Trade 1991).

The practice of targeting poor communities of color in the Third World for waste disposal and the introduction of risky technologies from industrialized countries are forms of "toxic colonialism," what some activists have dubbed the "subjugation of people to an ecologically destructive economic order by entities over which people have no control" (Greenpeace 1992:3). The industrialized world's controversial Third World dumping policy was made public by the release of an internal, December 12, 1991, memorandum authored by Lawrence Summers, chief economist of the World Bank. It shocked the world and touched off a global scandal. Here are the highlights:

> *"Dirty" Industries: Just between you and me, shouldn't the World Bank be encouraging MORE migration of the dirty industries to the LDCs [Less Developed Countries]? I can think of three reasons:*
>
> *1) The measurement of the costs of health impairing pollution depends on the forgone earnings from increased morbidity and mortality. From this point of view a given amount of health impairing pollution should be done in the country with the lowest cost, which will be the country with the lowest wages. I think the economic logic behind dumping a load of toxic waste in the lowest wage country is impeccable and we should face up to that.*
>
> *2) The costs of pollution are likely to be non-linear as the initial increments of pollution probably have very low cost. I've always thought that under-polluted areas in Africa are vastly UNDER-polluted; their air quality is probably vastly inefficiently low compared to Los Angeles or Mexico City. Only the lamentable facts that so much pollution is generated by non-tradable industries (transport, electrical generation) and that the unit transport costs of solid waste are so high pre-*

vent world welfare-enhancing trade in air pollution and waste.

3) The demand for a clean environment for aesthetic and health reasons is likely to have very high income elasticity. The concern over an agent that causes a one in a million chance in the odds of prostate cancer is obviously going to be much higher in a country where people survive to get prostate cancer than a country where under 5 [year-old] mortality is 200 per thousand. Also, much of the concern over industrial atmosphere discharge is about visibility impairing particulates. These discharges may have very little direct health impact. Clearly trade in goods that embody aesthetic pollution concerns could be welfare enhancing. While production is mobile the consumption of pretty air is a non-tradable.

The problem with the arguments against all of these proposals for more pollution in LDCs (intrinsic rights to certain goods, moral reasons, social concerns, lack of adequate markets, etc.) could be turned around and used more or less effectively against every Bank proposal…

BEYOND THE RACE VS. CLASS TRAP

Whether at home or abroad, the question of who *pays* and who *benefits* from current industrial and development policies is central to any analysis of environmental racism. In the United States, race interacts with class to create special environmental and health vulnerabilities. People of color, however, face elevated toxic exposure levels even when social class variables (income, education, and occupational status) are held constant (Bryant and Mohai 1992). Race has been found to be an independent factor, not reducible to class, in predicting distribution of 1) air pollution in our society (Freeman 1971; Gianessi, Peskin, and Wolf 1979;

Gelobter 1988; Wernette and Nieves 1990); 2) contaminated fish consumption (West, Fly, and Marans 1990); 3) the location of municipal landfills and incinerators (Bullard 1983, 1987, 1990. 1991); 4) the location of abandoned toxic waste dumps (United Church of Christ Commission for Racial Justice 1987); and 5) lead poisoning in children (Agency for Toxic Substances and Disease Registry 1988).

Lead poisoning is a classic case in which race, not just class, determines exposure. It affects between three and four million children in the United States—most of whom are African Americans and Latinos living in urban areas. Among children five years old and younger, the percentage of African Americans who have excessive levels of lead in their blood far exceeds the percentage of whites at all income levels (Agency for Toxic Substances and Disease Registry 1988:1–12).

The federal Agency for Toxic Substances and Disease Registry found that for families earning less than $6,000 annually an estimated 68 percent of African-American children had lead poisoning, compared with 36 percent of white children. For families with incomes exceeding $15,000, more than 38 percent of African-American children have been poisoned, compared with 12 percent of white children. African-American children are two to three times more likely than their white counterparts to suffer from lead poisoning independent of class factors.

One reason for this is that African Americans and whites do not have the same opportunities to "vote with their feet" by leaving unhealthy physical environments. The ability of an individual to escape a health-threatening environment is usually correlated with income. However, racial barriers make it even harder for millions of

African Americans, Latinos, Asians, Pacific Islanders, and Native Americans to relocate. Housing discrimination, redlining, and other market forces make it difficult for millions of households to buy their way out of polluted environments. For example, an affluent African-American family (with an income of $50,000 or more) is as segregated as an African-American family with an income of $5,000 (Denton and Massey 1988; Jaynes and Williams 1989). Thus, lead poisoning of African-American children is not just a "poverty thing."

White racism helped create our current separate and unequal communities. It defines the boundaries of the urban ghetto, *barrio,* and reservation, and influences the provision of environmental protection and other public services. Apartheid-type housing and development policies reduce neighborhood options, limit mobility, diminish job opportunities, and decrease environmental choices for millions of Americans. It is unlikely that this nation will ever achieve lasting solutions to its environmental problems unless it also addresses the system of racial injustice that helps sustain the existence of powerless communities forced to bear disproportionate environmental costs.

THE LIMITS OF MAINSTREAM ENVIRONMENTALISM

Historically, the mainstream environmental movement in the United States has developed agendas that focus on such goals as wilderness and wildlife preservation, wise resource management, pollution abatement, and population control. It has been primarily supported by middle- and upper-middle-class whites. Although concern for the environment cuts across class and racial lines, ecology activists have traditionally been individuals with above-average education, greater access to economic resources, and a greater sense of personal power (Bachrach and Zautra 1985; Bullard 1990; Bullard and Wright 1987; Buttel and Flinn 1978; Dunlap 1987; Mohai 1985, 1990; Morrison 1980, 1986).

Not surprisingly, mainstream groups were slow in broadening their base to include poor and working-class whites, let alone African Americans and other people of color. Moreover, they were ill-equipped to deal with the environmental, economic, and social concerns of these communities. During the 1960s and 1970s, while the "Big Ten" environmental groups focused on wilderness preservation and conservation through litigation, political lobbying, and technical evaluation, activists of color were engaged in mass direct action mobilizations for basic civil rights in the areas of employment, housing, education, and health care. Thus, two parallel and sometimes conflicting movements emerged, and it has taken nearly two decades for any significant convergence to occur between these two efforts. In fact, conflicts still remain over how the two groups should balance economic development, social justice, and environmental protection.

In their desperate attempt to improve the economic conditions of their constituents, many African-American civil rights and political leaders have directed their energies toward bringing jobs to their communities. In many instances, this has been achieved at great risk to the health of workers and the surrounding communities. The promise of jobs (even low-paying and hazardous ones) and of a broadened tax base has enticed several economically impoverished, politically powerless communities of color both in the United States and around the world (Bryant and Mohai 1992; Bullard 1990; Center for Investigative Reporting

1990). Environmental job blackmail is a fact of life. You can get a job, but only if you are willing to do work that will harm you, your family, and your neighbors.

Workers of color are especially vulnerable to job blackmail because of the greater threat of unemployment they face compared to whites and because of their concentration in low-paying, unskilled, nonunionized occupations. For example, they make up a large share of the nonunion contract workers in the oil, chemical, and nuclear industries. Similarly, over 95 percent of migrant farmworkers in the United States are Latino, African-American, Afro-Caribbean, or Asian, and African Americans are overrepresented in high-risk, blue-collar, and service occupations for which a large pool of replacement labor exists. Thus, they are twice as likely to be unemployed as their white counterparts. Fear of unemployment acts as a potent incentive for many African-American workers to accept and keep jobs they know are health threatening. Workers will tell you that "unemployment and poverty are also hazardous to one's health." An inherent conflict exists between the interests of capital and that of labor. Employers have the power to move jobs (and industrial hazards) from the Northeast and Midwest to the South and Sunbelt, or they move the jobs offshore to Third World countries where labor is even cheaper and where there even are fewer health and safety regulations. Yet, unless an environmental movement emerges that is capable of addressing these economic concerns, people of color and poor white workers are likely to end up siding with corporate managers in key conflicts concerning the environment.

Indeed, many labor unions already moderate their demands for improved work-safety and pollution control when-ever the economy is depressed. They are afraid of layoffs, plant closings, and the relocation of industries. These fears and anxieties of labor are usually built on the false but understandable assumption that environmental regulations inevitably lead to job loss (Brown 1980, 1987).

The crux of the problem is that the mainstream environmental movement has not sufficiently addressed the fact that social inequality and imbalances of social power are at the heart of environmental degradation, resource depletion, pollution, and overpopulation. The environmental crisis can simply not be solved effectively without social justice. As one academic human ecologist notes, "Whenever [an] in-group directly and exclusively benefits from its own overuse of a shared resource but the costs of that overuse are 'shared' by out-groups, then in-group motivation toward a policy of resource conservation (or sustained yields of harvesting) is undermined" (Catton 1982)....

REFERENCES

Agency for Toxic Substances and Disease Registry. 1988. *The Nature and Extent of Lead Poisoning in Children in the United States: A Report to Congress.* Atlanta: U.S. Department of Health and Human Services.

Bachrach, Kenneth M. and Alex J. Zautra. 1989. "Coping with Community Stress: The Threat of a Hazardous Waste Landfill." *Journal of Health and Social Behaviour* 26:127–141.

Blauner, Robert. 1972. *Racial Oppression in America.* New York: Harper and Row.

Brown, Michael H. 1980. *Laying Waste: The Poisoning of America by Toxic Chemicals.* New York: Pantheon Books.

———. 1987. *The Toxic Cloud: The Poisoning of America's Air.* New York: Harper and Row.

Bryant, Bunyan and Paul Mohai. 1992. *Race and the Incidence of Environmental Hazards.* Boulder, CO: Westview Press.

Bullard, Robert D. 1983. "Solid Waste Sites and the Black Houston Community." *Sociological Inquiry* 53:273–288.

———. 1987. *Invisible Houston: The Black Experience in Boom and Bust.* College Station: Texas A&M University Press.

———. 1990. *Dumping in Dixie: Race, Class, and Environmental Quality.* Boulder, CO: Westview Press.

———. 1991. "Environmental Justice for All." *EnviroAction,* Environmental News Digest for the National Wildlife Federation (November).

Bullard, Robert D. and Beverly H. Wright. 1987. "Blacks and the Environment." *Humboldt Journal of Social Relations* 14:165–184.

Buttel, Frederick and William L. Flinn. 1978. "Social Class and Mass Environmental Beliefs: A Reconsideration." *Environment and Behavior* 10:433–450.

Carmichael, S. and C. V. Hamilton. *Black Power.* New York: Vintage.

Catton, William. 1982. *Overshoot: The Ecological Basis of Revolutionary Change.* Urbana: University of Illinois Press.

Center for Investigative Reporting. 1990. *Global Dumping Grounds: The International Trade in Hazardous Waste.* Washington, D.C.: Seven Locks Press.

Cerrell Associates, Inc. 1984. *Political Difficulties Facing Waste-to-Energy Conversion Plant Siting.* California Waste Management Board, Technical Information Series. Prepared by Cerrell Associates, Inc. for the California Waste Management Board. Los Angeles: Cerrell Associates, Inc.

Denton, Nancy A. and Douglas S. Massey. 1988. "Residential Segregation of Blacks, Hispanics, and Asians by Socioeconomic Class and Generation." *Social Science Quarterly* 69:797–817.

Dunlap, Riley E. 1987. "Public Opinion on the Environment in the Reagan Era: Polls, Pollution, and Politics." *Environment* 29:6–11, 31–37.

Feagin, Joe R. 1988. *Free Enterprise City: Houston in Political and Economic Perspective.* Englewood Cliffs, NJ: Prentice Hall.

Freeman, Myrick A. 1971. "The Distribution of Environmental Quality." In *Environmental Quality Analysis,* edited by Allen V. Kneese and Blair T. Power. Baltimore: Johns Hopkins University Press for Resources for the Future.

Gelobter, Michel. 1988. "The Distribution of Air Pollution by Income and Race." Paper presented at the Second Symposium on Social Science in Resource Management, Urbana, Illinois, June.

Gianessi, Leonard, H. M. Peskin, and E. Wolff. 1979. "The Distributional Effects of Uniform Air Pollution Policy in the U.S." *Quarterly Journal of Economics* (May):281–301.

Gottdiener, Mark. 1988. *The Social Production of Space.* Austin: University of Texas Press.

Greenpeace. 1992. "The 'Logic' Behind Hazardous Waste Export." *Greenpeace Waste Trade Update* (First Quarter):1–2.

Jaynes, Gerald D. and Robin M. Williams, Jr. 1989. *A Common Destiny: Blacks and American Society.* Washington, D.C.: National Academy Press.

Kay, Jane. 1991. "Fighting Toxic Racism: L.A.'s Minority Neighborhood is the 'Dirtiest' in the State." *San Francisco Examiner* (7 April):A1.

Mann, Eric. 1991. *"L.A.'s Lethal Air: New Perspectives for Policy, Organizing, and Action.* Los Angeles: Labor/Community Strategy Center.

Mohai, Paul. 1985. "Public Concern and Elite Involvement in Environmental Conservation." *Social Science Quarterly* 66:820–838.

———. 1990. "Black Environmentalism." *Social Science Quarterly* 71:744–765.

Morrison, Denton E. 1980. "The Soft Cutting Edge of Environmentalism: Why and How the Appropriate Technology Notion is Changing the Movement." *Natural Resources Journal* 20:275–298.

———. 1986. "How and Why Environmental Consciousness Has Trickled Down." Pp. 187–220 in *Distributional Conflict in Environmental Resource Policy,* edited by Allan Schnaiberg, Nicholas Watts, and Klaus Zimmerman. New York: St. Martin's Press.

Omi, Michael and Howard Winant. 1986. *Racial Formation in the United States: From the 1960's to the 1980's.* New York: Routledge, Kegan and Paul.

Ong, Paul and Evelyn Blumenberg. 1990. "Race and Environmentalism." Paper read at Graduate School of Architecture and Urban Planning, 14 March, at UCLA.

Sanchez, Roberto. 1990. "Health and Environmental Risks of the Maquiladora in Mexicali." *Natural Resources Journal* 30:163–186.

United Church of Christ Commission for Racial Justice. 1987. *Toxic Wastes and Race in the United States, A National Report on the Racial and Socio-Economic Characteristics of Communities with Hazardous Waste Sites.* New York: United Church of Christ.

Wernette, D. R. and L. A. Nieves. 1992. "Breathing Polluted Air." *EPA Journal* 18 (March/April):16–17.

West, Pat C., F. Fly, and R. Marans. 1990. "Minority Anglers and Toxic Fish Consumption: Evidence from a State-Wide Survey of Michigan." Pp. 108–122 in *The Proceedings of the Michigan Conference on Race and the Incidence of Environmental Hazards,* edited by B. Bryant and P. Mohai. Ann Arbor: University of Michigan School of Natural Resources.

Witt, Matthew. 1991. "An Injury to One Is an Gravio a Todo: The Need for a Mexico-U.S. Health and Safety Movement." *New Solutions, A Journal of Environment and Occupational Health Policy* 1 (March):28–33.

Working Group on Canada-Mexico Free Trade. 1991. "Que Pasa? A Canada-Mexico 'Free' Trade Deal." *New Solutions, A Journal of Environmental and Occupational Health Policy* 2 (January):10–25.

Zuniga, Jo Ann. 1992. "Watchdog Keeps Tabs on Politics of Environment along the Border." *Houston Chronicle* (24 May):22A.

6. The Hazardous Waste Stream in the World-System*

R. SCOTT FREY

...the history of risk distribution shows that, like wealth, risks adhere to the class pattern, only inversely: wealth accumulates at the top, risks at the bottom.
—ULRICH BECK (1992:35)

Wealth (in the form of raw materials and energy) flows from the resource-rich countries of the periphery to the industrialized countries of the core (Caldwell 1977). This resource stream (commodity chain [Gereffi and Korzeniewicz 1994] or dissipative structure [Clark 1998] as some prefer to call it) has become the subject of increased interest to world-system scholars. They have focused attention on the political-economic forces, physical principles, and consequences underlying resource extraction from the periphery and transport to the core for industrial production (e.g., Bunker 1985, 1994; Bunker and Ciccantell 1995). As yet, however, little attention has been directed to the end product of this process: the disposal of the antiwealth (or hazardous wastes[1]) produced in the core. Core wastes must go somewhere and part

of them end up in a stream flowing to the periphery.[2]

This paper begins such a discourse by examining several issues surrounding the process by which the core dissipates entropy by transporting it to distant sinks located in the periphery. Discussion of this particular form of core-periphery reproduction proceeds in five steps. The first section examines the scope of the hazardous waste stream problem. The second section provides a brief overview of the political-economic forces underlying the transport of hazardous wastes to the periphery. The third section contains a discussion of the vulnerabilities created in the periphery by hazardous waste imports. The fourth section examines the policy regimes that have emerged to deal with the hazardous waste stream problem. The paper concludes with a discussion of what should be done to close the "global escape valve."

SCOPE OF THE HAZARDOUS WASTE STREAM

Core countries (which consume more than half of the world-system's natural resources

---

*Revised version from Paul S. Ciccantell and Stephen G. Bunker, editors. 1998. *Space and Transport in the World-System* (Westport, CT: Greenwood Press), 84–103. © 1998, Paul S. Ciccantell and Stephen G. Bunker. Reproduced with permission of Greenwood Publishing Group, Inc., Westport, CT.

and energy) produce 90 percent of the world's hazardous wastes (Sachs 1996; World Resources Institute 1994:3–26). This waste is recovered/recycled, treated, and disposed of in various ways (including landfill, storage in surface impounds, deep well injection, and incineration), but an undetermined proportion of it is exported to the periphery of the world-system (see, e.g., Anyinam 1991; Center for Investigative Reporting 1990; Greenpeace 1994; Hilz 1992; Stebbins 1992; Third World Network 1988; Vallette 1989; Vallette and Spalding 1990).[3] U.S. Greenpeace (Vallette, 1989; Vallette and Spalding 1990), for instance, has documented over 1,000 legal and illegal attempts between 1986 and 1988 by core countries to export over 160 million tons of hazardous wastes to countries of Eastern Europe and the former Soviet Union, Asia, Latin America and the Caribbean, and Africa and the Middle East. Although many of these attempts failed, Greenpeace claims that at least 3.1 million tons of hazardous wastes were transported to the periphery during this period (Vallette 1989). Exported wastes included substances that are costly to dispose of: PCBs, acids, sludge, used car (lead acid) batteries, paint solvents, plastics, heavy metals (lead and mercury), dioxin-contaminated incinerator ash, and radioactive waste (Vallette and Spalding 1990). Destinations of core wastes in the 1980s tended to be countries located in Africa, the Caribbean and Latin America, but in the 1990s the destinations shifted to countries located in Eastern Europe, the former Soviet Union, and Asia (Anyinam 1991; Greenpeace 1994; International Environment Reporter 1994; Leonard 1993). Between 1989 and 1994, there were 299 documented cases of hazardous waste exports to Eastern Europe and the former Soviet Union, 239 in Asia, 148 in Latin America and the Carib-

bean, and 30 in Africa (Greenpeace 1994, cited by Sachs 1996:144).

It is not possible to estimate how much hazardous waste finds its way to sinks located in the periphery because much of the waste leaving the core is unregulated and unmonitored. Incompatible national definitions make it difficult to determine the amount of hazardous wastes produced and the amount flowing to the periphery from the core. The true scope of the problem is therefore unknown. Selected incidents of hazardous waste exports are reported below by major shipping route to illustrate the problem.

Eastern Europe and the former Soviet Union

- The Schoenberg dump in the former East Germany has been accepting 1 million metric tons of hazardous wastes (including heavy metals and chloridized hydrocarbons) annually from West Germany and other European countries since 1981. The 150-acre waste dump is surrounded by several drinking water sources (Nunez-Muller 1990). Numerous other sites located in the old eastern zone contain the hazardous wastes of Europe (Cezeaux 1991).

- The former Soviet Union has accepted spent nuclear fuel from various European countries for years (Katasonov 1990:30). There is no way of determining how much spent fuel is delivered annually to the country or what is done with it.

- Between 1988 and 1989, 10,000 barrels of hazardous wastes (including chlorinated solvents and PCB-contaminated oils) were shipped to Poland from Austria (Cutter 1993:138). In 1992 alone, 1,322 improper waste shipments from Germany were intercepted in Poland (Coll 1994).

Asia

- In the mid-1980s, West Germany, Austria, Switzerland, and the U.S. expressed interest in storing nuclear waste in remote areas of the Chinese Gobi Desert. Rumors have persisted about continued Chinese interest in the venture (Vallette 1989; Vallette and Spalding 1990).
- Since the late 1980s, large amounts of lead scrap and lead acid batteries have been shipped from the United States to southern China, India, Pakistan, the Philippines, Malaysia, and Taiwan for recycling (Center for Investigative Reporting 1990:78–82; *International Environment Reporter* 1994; Leonard 1993).
- Since the late 1980s, plastic wastes from West Germany, the United States, and several other countries have been incinerated in remote desert locations in China (Center for Investigative Reporting 1990:78–82). Plastic wastes are also regularly shipped to other Asian countries for "recycling" (which includes incineration and landfilling in Bangladesh, Hong Kong, India, Indonesia, Malaysia, Pakistan, and the Philippines) [*International Environment Reporter* 1994; Leonard 1992, 1993]). Between 1990 and 1993, 1,931,090 metric tons of plastic waste were sent to India (*International Environment Reporter* 1994:114). In January 1993 alone, the United States sent 1,985.5 tons of plastic waste to India (Leonard 1993:23).
- Four U.S. companies mixed 1,000 tons of hazardous waste (including lead and cadmium) into a shipment of fertilizer bound for Bangladesh. Reports indicate that one-third of the fertilizer was applied to fields (often by children) before the contamination was discovered (Green-peace 1992a; Leonard 1993:22).

Latin America and the Caribbean

- U.S. waste generators sent 27,803 tons of hazardous waste to Mexico in 1989. This figure reflects only legally exported wastes. Mexican *maquiladoras* have proven to be an important front for smuggling U.S. hazardous wastes for cheap disposal in Mexican waterways, sewers, municipal landfills, and numerous private property sites (Barry 1994; Center for Investigative Reporting 1990:51–62; Sanchez 1990).
- In 1992, four Philadelphia universities (Penn, Widener, Drexel, and Temple) approached representatives of Bermuda, Barbados, and the British Virgin Islands for permission to dispose of a jointly owned waste incinerator (Greenpeace 1992a:25).
- In 1988, 4,500 tons of toxic ash from the garbage incinerators of Philadelphia were unloaded from the ship *Khian Sea* on a Haitian beach (Center for Investigative Reporting 1990:17–32).
- In 1992 it was reported that imports received by a petroleum recycling plant in the port of Esmeralda, Ecuador, consisted of hazardous wastes (Biggs 1994:349).

Africa and the Middle East

- The fishing village of Koko, Nigeria became the subject of world attention in 1988 when 8,000 drums of toxic waste were discovered. The wastes (exported by an Italian firm for several European countries and the United States) included methyl melamine, dimethyl formaldehyde, ethylacetate formaldehyde, and about 150 tons of PCBs. The deal had been arranged by an Italian trader with a Nigerian citizen, who received $100 a month to store the wastes on a dirt lot (Anyinam 1991:762–763).

- In 1988 an Italian firm (Jelly Wax) shipped 2,000 barrels of toxic wastes to Beirut, Lebanon. Reports indicate that part of the waste was burned, some was dumped in the sewers, and the remainder was buried at different locations in the country (Samhoum 1989).
- Greenpeace (1992a) reported in 1992 that a Swiss firm planned to construct and operate a million ton-a-year toxic waste incinerator in Mozambique.
- A U.S. company and several European companies have shipped tons of mercury waste to a British reprocessing plant located at Cato Ridge, South Africa, just outside the homeland of Kwa Zulu. Villagers located downstream from the facility on the Mngeweni River have used the river for drinking, bathing, and washing. Mercury levels in the river have been reported to be 1,000 to 1,900 times higher than the World Health Organization's (WHO) recommended level (Greenpeace 1992b:12–13).
- Between 1984 and 1986, radioactive waste from the former Soviet Union was illegally dumped in Canna and Dan, Benin. The problem was discovered in 1989 after contaminated groundwater was found (Cutter 1993:137).

THE POLITICAL ECONOMY OF THE HAZARDOUS WASTE STREAM

Political and economic forces characterizing relations within and between countries of the core and periphery have created the hazardous waste flow to the periphery (Covello and Frey 1990; Hilz 1992; Puckett 1992). The often-contradictory demands be-

tween capital accumulation and environmental quality within the core have created a tendency for hazardous wastes to be transported to sinks located in the periphery. The economic problems facing many peripheral countries have in turn led them to accept wastes for hard currency.

Contradictory Forces in the Core

A set of interrelated political and economic forces within the core underlie the flow of hazardous wastes. They include increased levels of hazardous waste production and reduced disposal capacity, increased environmental awareness and more stringent state regulatory control on hazardous waste disposal, and increased economic and political pressures on the waste generators.

Affluence and Hazardous Effluence.   Reliable data on the production of hazardous wastes do not currently exist, but there is consensus that the production of hazardous wastes has grown substantially since World War II (Ayers 1994; Commoner 1992; Schnaiberg 1980). This has been attributed to market forces requiring economic growth through increased consumption, as well as technological changes in the production of petroleum, chemicals, electronics, pharmaceuticals, and related products. From an annual production of 15 million tons in the early 1940s, the world-system currently produces annually anywhere from 300 to 600 million tons of hazardous wastes (Gourlay 1992; Postel 1987:9).[4] Conservative estimates indicate that the United States is the largest single producer of hazardous wastes; it is estimated to produce 238 million tons each year, or about 1 ton per capita. Although the European countries produce less hazardous waste than the United States because of greater production efficiency, they do produce millions of tons. The 12 members of the European Community (EC) produce 30 to 40 million tons of hazardous waste each year. The remaining countries of the world-system produce 35 to 40 million tons annually (Cutter 1993:113 and World Resources Institute 1990).[5] The production of hazardous wastes in the core has been so great in the past several decades that the ability of many countries to dispose of it (whether through landfilling, treatment, or incineration) has declined substantially.

Increased Environmental Awareness and State Regulation. Scientific and public concern with the health and environmental risks associated with hazardous wastes emerged as an important issue in the core during the 1970s (Brickman, Jasanoff, and Ilgen 1985; Hays 1987). This concern gave rise to increased regulatory controls on waste disposal in the United States (Fiorino 1995; Szasz 1994). These regulatory efforts represent a combination of federal statutes and administrative agency-promulgated rules. The U.S. Resource Conservation and Recovery Act (RCRA) of 1976 was a comprehensive piece of legislation creating standards for the classification, hauling, and disposal of hazardous wastes and a system for tracking wastes. Subsequent legislation such as the 1980 Comprehensive Environmental Response, Compensation, and Liability Act (CERCLA and commonly known as Superfund), the 1984 amendment to RCRA, and the 1986 Superfund Amendments and Reauthorization Act (SARA) have significantly curtailed the haphazard disposal of hazardous wastes into the air and water and increased the amount of wastes earmarked for specialized disposal. (Prior to Superfund in 1980, there was little need to export waste since "more than 90%

of all wastes were indiscrimately and... cheaply dumped in nearby pits, ponds, and lagoons all over the U.S." [Biggs 1994: 337].) Increased regulation is thought to have forced half of the 4,600 waste facilities to close in the 1980s (S. Murphy 1994:30). Similar legislation was enacted in Europe and Japan (Brickman et al. 1985).

Increased Economic and Political Pressures. The outcome of these interrelated trends is increased disposal costs in the core. In the United States, for instance, landfill disposal costs (which currently range from $250 to $300 per ton of hazardous waste) grew 16-fold in the last 20 years and incineration costs (which currently cost at least $1,500 and as much as $3,000 per ton) increased threefold in the last decade. European countries have experienced similar cost increases (Hilz 1992:44–46).

Few communities in the core countries want hazardous waste repositories because of the health and environmental risks associated with such facilities. Not-In-My-Backyard (NIMBY) behavior of core communities has grown dramatically since the discovery of sites (such as Love Canal and Times Beach) where wastes were dumped haphazardly. Environmental groups monitoring waste disposal have created public pressure against haphazard waste dumping. These forces have made it more difficult for companies to dump wastes in the core (see Brown and Mikkelsen 1990; Bullard 1994; Szasz 1994).

Waste generators have responded to these economic and political pressures by hiring brokers to export hazardous wastes to the periphery through various "trash for cash" schemes that are much cheaper than domestic disposal and recycling (Hilz 1992; Vallette 1989; Vallette and Spalding 1990). Current export practices include what several analysts have called "compliant waste handling," "sham" and "dirty" recycling, and "criminal activity" (Hilz 1992:24–30; Puckett 1994).[6] Compliant waste handling refers to hazardous waste exports that are legal and meet local, national, and international restrictions. Sham recycling is the dumping of hazardous waste in the periphery under the guise of recycling that never takes place. Dirty recycling, on the other hand, results in some waste recuperation but it is a process that is hazardous to human health and the environment. Criminal activity consists of waste smuggling and other illegal practices that endanger human health and the environment.

Costs of waste disposal are considerably less in the periphery because of lower wages and limited state control of the environment and the health, safety, and well-being of its citizens. Waste can be dumped in the periphery for as little as $5 to $50 per ton (Anyinam 1991; Logan 1991). Furthermore, international bulk flow container costs have declined substantially in the past decade, reducing the cost of shipping wastes to sinks located in the periphery (Shin and Strohm 1993). The reduced costs of transporting entropy to the periphery enhance the competitiveness of waste generators at the national and international levels and contribute to capital accumulation in the core.

Crisis in the Periphery

Many peripheral countries face economic pressures to accept hazardous wastes from the core even though they have limited expertise in treating, storing, and disposing wastes. They are confronted with poverty, debt, low agricultural and mineral commodity prices, and a world-system that does not allow them to participate fully in economic production and exchange. An illustrative example is the case of Guinea-Bissau which was offered a deal in 1988 (which it rejected) to store 15 million tons of hazardous waste for a sum of cash that was four times larger than its gross domestic product and two times larger than its foreign debt (Puckett 1994:53). Not only does the economic situation of many peripheral countries push them to swap hazardous wastes for cash but also their political situation puts them in a weak bargaining position in negotiations with core waste brokers over the terms of hazardous waste exchanges. Corrupt and politically unaccountable state officials often sanction and negotiate the terms surrounding waste shipments from the core (Puckett 1994).

VULNERABILITIES GENERATED BY THE HAZARDOUS WASTE STREAM

Hazardous wastes (like many hazardous substances) can damage the environment and adversely affect human health through dispersion in the soil, water, and air or in the form of explosions and fires (World Health Organization 1988). Peripheral countries are particularly vulnerable to such risks because of a low level of public awareness of risks and limited technical and regulatory capabilities for adequately regulating and disposing of hazardous wastes, handling accidents, and monitoring the environment (Covello and Frey 1990). In addition to potentially serious environmental and human health consequences associated with hazardous wastes, there are a number of other undesirable consequences; these include various social costs and reduced efforts to curb the generation of hazardous wastes in the core (Asante-Duah et al. 1992; Center for Investigative Reporting 1990; Daly 1993; Hilz 1992).

Environmental Effects

The improper disposal, treatment, and storage of hazardous wastes in the periphery can contribute to the risk of environmental damage (Hilz 1992; Third World Network 1988). Environmental damage includes soil contamination, ground water pollution, biodiversity loss, contamination of rivers and coastal regions, air pollution, and threats to plant and animal health. Most research done on the environmental effects of hazardous wastes is limited to the temperate climates of the core countries, but the effects of hazardous wastes in the tropical regions of the periphery may be very different and far more severe (Logan 1991). Importing countries that improperly dispose of waste may also put surrounding countries at risk by contaminating rivers and aquifers, as well as polluting oceans and air (see Barry 1994). Since reliable data do not exist on the full breadth and nature of hazardous waste disposal in the periphery, it is not possible to estimate the extent of environmental damage. Such damage is a potentially important problem because it could deplete important natural resources, destabilize ecosystems, and threaten human health.

Human Health Effects

The actual health consequences associated with exposure to improperly disposed wastes in the periphery are not fully known. Given the experiences of the core countries and random reports from several peripheral countries (Brown and Mikkelsen 1990; Center for Investigative Reporting 1990; Gourlay 1992; National Research Council 1991; Third World Network 1988), improperly disposed wastes pose a threat to those experiencing environmental expo-

sure. Those exposed to contaminated water, food, or air are at substantially increased risk of death and disease because of their increased susceptibility to various site-specific cancers, skin irritation, respiratory problems, neurobehavioral problems, birth defects and miscarriages, genetic changes and damage to the immune system, and acute and chronic damage to specific organs of the body. In turn, disposal of hazardous wastes in food-producing countries of the periphery can affect human health in the core through contaminated food exports. On the other hand, those living near hazardous waste storage and disposal sites are at increased risk of death and injury from fires and explosions. Since reliable data do not exist on the number of people exposed to improperly disposed wastes in the periphery, it is not possible to estimate the actual number of deaths or cases of disease and injury that can be attributed to waste exports, but one thing is clear: peripheral countries are at far greater risk than their core counterparts (Logan 1991).

Social Effects

The distribution of the benefits and costs associated with hazardous waste exports is unequal. Most benefits go to the core countries that generate and export the wastes; importing countries bear most of the costs. Losses within importing countries are distributed in an unequal fashion, because some groups and regions are able to capture benefits and others bear the costs. Surrounding countries may bear some of the costs as wastes move across national boundaries through the air, water, and food. And future human generations may bear costs without enjoying any of the benefits associated with the export of hazardous wastes (Logan 1991).

Reduced Pressure for Hazardous Waste Reduction in the Core

If core-based waste generators have the option of exporting their hazardous wastes to the periphery, there is little incentive for them to curb hazardous wastes through recycling or source reduction strategies (Daly 1993). In turn, the effectiveness of current waste reduction strategies in the core may be weakened if the export option remains a viable alternative for waste generators. The export option, therefore, reduces waste minimization efforts in the core and represents a means for core-based waste generators to maintain inefficient and waste-generating production practices.

A Cost-Benefit Assessment

The short-term economic benefits associated with hazardous waste transfers from the core to the periphery must be considered in light of the long-term (tangible and intangible) costs (Daly 1993; Logan 1991). The costs associated with the future cleanup of contaminated sites and improperly disposed wastes are potentially high for countries of the core and periphery, but even more so for countries of the periphery. (The estimated cost of cleaning up Koko, Nigeria, for instance, was over one million dollars, but the entire environmental budget of the country in 1987 was $255,000 [Donald 1991:446, note 140].) The treatment and compensation of victims of hazardous waste exposure in the periphery are potentially very costly. Destruction of important natural resources such as marine life, biodiversity, and soil, water and air quality is also likely to be a costly outcome of hazardous waste exports. The costs surrounding inequalities in the exposure to hazards and the failure to reduce hazard-

ous waste production in the core are also likely to be great.

Despite suggestions and efforts to the contrary (Asante-Duah et al. 1992; Logan 1991), there is no accepted factual or methodological basis for adequately identifying, estimating, and valuating the costs and benefits associated with the flow of hazardous wastes to the periphery. Comments of former World Bank chief economist Lawrence Summers (*The Economist* 1992:66) are worth quoting here because they illustrate some of the difficulties and contradictory outcomes of traditional economic reasoning:

> *The measurement of the costs of health-impairing pollution depends on the foregone earnings from increased morbidity and mortality. From this point of view a given amount of health-impairing pollution should be done in the country with the lowest cost, which will be the country with the lowest wages. I think the economic logic behind dumping a load of toxic waste in the lowest wage country is impeccable and we should face up to that.*

Such economic reasoning is based on the belief that not all humans are of equal value: human lives in the periphery are worth less than those in the core. Thus, although most costs are borne by the periphery (and most benefits are captured by the core), the costs to the periphery are deemed minimal and acceptable because life is defined as worth so little. Or, as Herman Daly (1993:57) has noted: "By separating the costs and benefits of environmental exploitation, international trade makes them harder to compare." Even if the total economic costs and benefits could be meaningfully estimated and valued, it is doubtful that the benefits accruing to the periphery would cover the immediate and most tangible costs associated with hazardous waste imports (see Logan 1991).

POLICY REGIMES

Various unilateral, bilateral, and multilateral actions have been proposed to deal with the problem of hazardous waste exports to the periphery (Allen 1995; Kitt 1995; Krueger 1999; S. Murphy 1994; Puckett 1992; Wynne 1989). These proposals emphasize actions of core and periphery states, international organizations, and non-government organizations. Proposed actions for the core states have included policy efforts to implement cleaner production practices, the establishment of restrictions on the export of hazardous wastes, the dissemination of information about hazardous wastes to importing countries, and banning the export of all hazardous wastes to the periphery. It has been proposed that peripheral states ban hazardous waste imports, develop risk assessment and management capabilities, and develop liability laws protecting victims and providing criminal liability for certain export practices. Recommended actions for international organizations have included the dissemination of risk information, technical assistance in the establishment of monitoring and management programs in the periphery, and the establishment of restrictions on hazardous waste dumping through various conventions and liability and compensational regimes. Recommendations for core and periphery nongovernment organizations include investigation of the problem of hazardous waste exports and the attendant health and environmental risks, as well as the economic and political consequences of hazardous waste exports (Kitt 1995; S. Murphy 1994; Puckett 1992, 1994; Third World Network 1988; Wynne 1989).

Many obstacles stand in the way of the effective implementation of these and related proposals. These include limited funding; questions surrounding the importing country's national sovereignty; issues regarding who should be responsible for disseminating risk information, monitoring wastes, and enforcing regulations; GATT free trade policies; and disclosure of corporate practices (Krueger 1999; Susskind 1994). Despite such obstacles, several regimes have been adopted that attempt to restrict the hazardous waste flow to the periphery (Allen 1995; Donald 1992; Hilz 1992; Kitt 1995; Kummer 1992; Krueger 1999; Puckett 1992, 1994). Selected examples include:

- The United Nations Environment Programme's Basel Convention (the Basel Convention on the Control of Transboundary Movements of Hazardous Wastes and their Disposal) was signed by 118 countries in March 1989. This convention was the first attempt to systematically regulate the international transport and disposal of hazardous waste at the global level. It established some control on the international transfer of hazardous wastes, including the requirement that exporting countries receive prior informed consent from the importing country before wastes are shipped. Under this convention, nations can forbid waste importation or require more information before consenting to accept wastes. A subsequent amendment to the Convention in March, 1994 further restricted the export of hazardous wastes to peripheral countries by core countries (Allen 1995; *International Environment Reporter* 1995a; Krueger 1999; Kummer 1995).
- The Lome IV Convention adopted on December 15, 1989 by the 12 European

Community (EC) countries and 69 African, Caribbean, and Pacific (ACP) countries bans the movement of EC hazardous wastes to the ACP countries (Puckett 1994).

- The Organization of African Unity (consisting of all African countries except Morocco and South Africa) adopted the Bamako Convention (the Bamako Convention on the Ban of the Import into Africa and the Control of Transboundary Movement and Management of Hazardous Wastes within Africa) regulating waste movement among African nations and banning the importation of all radioactive and hazardous wastes into the African Continent. The Bamako Convention was adopted because many of the African nations did not think that the Basel Convention met their needs (Donald 1992).

- The Walgani Convention (the Convention to Ban the Importation into Forum Island Countries of Hazardous and Radioactive Wastes and to Control the Transboundary Movement and Management of Hazardous Waste within the South Pacific Region) bans imports of hazardous and radioactive wastes from outside the convention area in the developing countries of the Pacific Islands (*International Environment Reporter* 1995b, 1995c).

- As of late 1992 nearly 90 nations had banned imports of hazardous wastes (Puckett 1994).

These and subsequent attempts to curb the hazardous waste flow to the periphery have been subjected to numerous criticisms (see, e.g., Krueger 1999). Efforts to control and regulate the waste flow through regimes such as the Basel Convention have been dismissed as nothing more than attempts to legalize core dumping practices (Cusack 1990; Donald 1992; Kitt 1995; Puckett 1992, 1994; Wynne 1989). If a nation consents to accept hazardous wastes for disposal but does not have the capacity to control and monitor such wastes, the prior informed consent rule is not likely to lead to the handling of the wastes in a safe and environmentally sound manner. Even efforts like the 1994 amendment to the Basel Convention outlawing hazardous waste exports to the periphery are unlikely to be enforced fully. Furthermore, there is no regulatory mechanism for adequately controlling the transfer of hazardous waste-generating industries to the periphery and there are few liability and compensation provisions (Frey 1998, 1999). On the other hand, peripheral country efforts to prohibit hazardous waste imports are unlikely to be effective, because of the limited regulatory capacity of the peripheral countries and the fact that waste traders will find dumping sites as long as hazardous wastes are produced and the economic incentives remain for trash and cash swaps. There is, as Krueger (1999:15) recently noted, "...the spectre of a challenge to the Basel ban [and other conventions] at the World Trade Organization (WTO), which administers the GATT treaty." Existing policy regimes have done little to dismantle the dissipative structure of the world-system.

CODA

The image of ghost ships laden with hazardous cargo traveling from the core to the periphery is a disturbing one. Unlike the Flying Dutchman, however, many of these "gypsy vessels" have reached port and deposited their cargoes of PCBs, cyanide, paint solvents, dioxin-contaminated incinerator ash, and lead acid car batteries on unsuspecting populations in Mexico, Nigeria, the homelands of South Africa, China, the Sudan, the former Soviet Union, South Korea, East Germany, and many unknown spots throughout the world (Center for Investigative Reporting 1990; Greenpeace 1994; Krueger 1999; Third World Network 1988; Vallette 1989; Vallette and Spalding 1990). These export practices have been described as racist (Alston and Brown 1993; Bullard 1993b; Mpanya 1992), but they represent something much more: the unequal power relations underlying interaction patterns between countries occupying different positions in the world-system. Centrality in the world-system allows countries to engage in not-in-my-backyard-behavior and impose their entropy on the periphery.

The problem can be usefully framed in terms of responsibility: those who create hazardous waste and benefit from its production should bear the costs associated with its disposal (R. Murphy 1994). Failure to accept this responsibility (because of the belief that the international waste trade is economically efficient, legal, safe, beneficial for those put at risk, or based on the consent of those put at risk) is ethically suspect (Shrader-Frechette 1991). Acceptance of this responsibility leads to the conclusion that the export of hazardous wastes to the periphery should be outlawed and strong measures should be taken to ensure that such a ban is fully implemented. Such a policy would make it difficult for the core countries to externalize their entropic costs on the periphery and pressure them to adopt production practices generating fewer hazardous wastes. Until the global political authority exists to effectively monitor and control the global waste trade, these two goals will remain elusive. But closure of the "global escape valve" is unlikely as long as the core countries are able to control a majority of the wealth generated in the world-system.

ENDNOTES

1. Hazardous waste is typically defined as waste (possessing chemical, physical, or biological characteristics) that threatens the environment or human health. Hazardous wastes can take the form of solids, liquids, sludges, or gases that are ignitable, corrosive, reactive, as well as toxic, including carcinogenic (cancer-causing), mutagenic (mutation-causing), and teratogenic (birth-defect causing) (Dowling and Linnerooth 1987; Gourlay 1992:20–22; World Health Organization 1988). Defining hazardous wastes is not as clear cut as suggested here, because there are many social, political, and economic factors involved in defining hazardous wastes (Dowling and Linnerooth 1987; Kitt 1995:494–495; Wynne 1987).

2. Hazardous products and production processes also flow from the core to the periphery (e.g., Barry 1994; Castleman and Navarro 1987; Covello and Frey 1990; Frey 1995, 1996, 1997). There is also increased concern with the movement of pollutants from the core to the periphery through the air, soil, and water, as well as the pollution of the global commons by the core countries (e.g., Barry 1994; Huq 1994; Majone 1985).

3. Some of this waste is dumped in poor and minority communities within the core countries (Bryant and Mohai 1992; Bullard 1993a, 1994; Camacho 1998; Cutter 1993:121–132; Szasz and Meuser 1997).

4. Most estimates of the amount of hazardous waste produced refer to those generated by commercial and industrial interests, but the military also produces a substantial amount of hazardous waste (Shulman 1992).

5. The bivariate correlations between GDP/capita and the production of hazardous wastes (including heavy metals, carbon dioxide, CFCs, and the like) for a sample of 70 core and peripheral countries in the early 1990s are all 0.7 or greater, suggesting that affluence promotes effluence. (See also Bergesen and Parisi [1999], Huq [1994], and Moomaw and Tullis [1994].)

6. Some industries that generate hazardous wastes have relocated to the periphery, where health, safety, and environmental standards are

lax (see, e.g., Barry 1994; Castleman and Navarro 1987; Covello and Frey 1990; Frey 1998, 1999; Leonard 1988).

REFERENCES

Allen, Mark E. 1995. "Slowing Europe's Hazardous Waste Trade: Implementing the Basel Convention into European Union Law." *Colorado Journal of International Law and Policy* 6:163–182.

Alston, Dana and Nicole Brown. 1993. "Global Threats to People of Color." Pp. 179–194 in *Confronting Environmental Racism: Voices from the Grassroots,* edited by Robert D. Bullard. Boston, MA: South End Press.

Anyinam, Charles A. 1991. "Transboundary Movements of Hazardous Wastes: The Case of Toxic Waste Dumping in Africa." *International Journal of Health Services* 21:759–777.

Asante-Duah, D., D. Kofi, F. F. Saccomanno, and J. H. Shortreed. 1992. "The Hazardous Waste Trade: Can It Be Controlled?" *Environmental Science and Technology* 26:1684–1693.

Ayers, Robert U. 1994. "Industrial Metabolism: Theory and Policy." Pp. 21–37 in *The Greening of Industrial Ecosystems,* edited by Braden R. Allenby and Deanna J. Richards. Washington, D.C.: National Academy Press.

Barry, Tom. 1994. *The Challenge of Cross-Border Environmentalism: The U.S.-Mexico Case.* Albuquerque, NM: Resource Center Press.

Beck, Ulrich. 1992. *Risk Society: Towards a New Modernity.* London: Sage.

Bergesen, Albert J. and Laura Parisi. 1999. "Ecosociology and Toxic Emissions." Pp. 43–57 in *Ecology and the World-System,* edited by Walter L. Goldfrank, David Goodman, and Andrew Szasz. Westport, CT: Greenwood Press.

Biggs, Gonzado. 1994. "Latin America and the Basel Convention on Hazardous Wastes." *Colorado Journal of International Environmental Law and Policy* 5:333–368.

Brickman, R. S. Jasanoff, and T. Ilgen. 1985. *Controlling Chemicals: The Politics of Regulation in Europe and the United States.* Ithaca, NY: Cornell University Press.

Brown, Phil and Edwin J. Mikkelsen. 1990. *No Safe Place: Toxic Waste, Leukemia, and Community Action.* Berkeley: University of California Press.

Bryant, Bunyan and Paul Mohai, editors. 1992. *Race and the Incidence of Environmental Hazards: A Time for Discourse.* Boulder, CO: Westview Press.

Bullard, Robert D., editor. 1993a. *Confronting Environmental Racism: Voices from the Grassroots.* Boston, MA: South End Press.

———. 1993b. "Anatomy of Environmental Racism and the Environmental Justice Movement." Pp. 15–39 in *Confronting Environmental Racism: Voices from the Grassroots,* edited by Robert D. Bullard. Boston, MA: South End Press.

———. 1994. *Dumping in Dixie: Race, Class, and Environmental Quality.* (Second Edition.) Boulder, CO: Westview Press.

Bunker, Stephen G. 1985. *Underdeveloping the Amazon: Extraction, Unequal Exchange, and the Failure of the Modern State.* Champaign: University of Illinois Press.

———. 1994. "The Political Economy of Raw Material Extraction and Trade." Pp. 437–450 in *Industrial Ecology and Global Change,* edited by R. Socolow, C. Andrews, F. Barkhout, and V. Thomas. New York: Cambridge University Press.

Bunker, Stephen G. and Paul S. Ciccantell. 1995. "Restructuring Space, Time, and Comparative Advantage in the Capitalist World Economy: Japan and Raw Material Transport after World War II." Pp. 109–129 in *A New World Order? Global Transformations in the Late Twentieth Century,* edited by David A. Smith and Jozsef Borocz. Westport, CT: Greenwood Press.

Caldwell, Malcolm. 1977. *The Wealth of Some Nations.* London: Zed Press.

Camacho, David E., editor. 1998. *Environmental Injustices, Political Struggles: Race, Class, and the Environment.* Durham, NC: Duke University Press.

Castleman, B. I. and V. Navarro. 1987. "International Mobility of Hazardous Products, Industries and Wastes." *Annual Review of Public Health* 8:1–19.

Center for Investigative Reporting. 1990. *Global Dumping Ground: The International Traffic in Hazardous Waste.* Washington, D.C.: Seven Locks Press.

Cezeaux, Andrea. 1991. "East Meets West to Look for Toxic Waste Sites." *Science* 251 620–621.

Clarke, Robert P. 1998. "Bulk Flow Systems and Globalization." Pp. 196–209 in *Space and Transport in the World-System,* edited by Paul S. Ciccantell and Stephen G. Bunker. Westport, CT: Greenwood Press.

Coll, Steve. 1994. "Free Market Intensifies Waste Problem." *Washington Post* (March 23):A26.

Commoner, Barry. 1992. *Making Peace with the Planet.* New York: The New Press.

Covello, Vincent T. and R. Scott Frey. 1990. "Technology-Based Environmental Health Risks in Developing Nations." *Technological Forecasting and Social Change* 37:159–179.

Cusack, M. M. 1990. "International Law and the Transboundary Shipment of Hazardous Waste to the Third World: Will the Basel Convention Make a Difference?" *American University Journal of International Law and Policy* 5:393–423.

Cutter, Susan L. 1993. *Living with Risk: The Geography of Technological Hazards.* London: Edward Arnold.

Daly, Herman E. 1993. "The Perils of Free Trade." *Scientific American* 262 (November):50–57.

Donald, J. Wylie. 1992. "The Bamako Convention as a Solution to the Problem of Hazardous Waste Exports to Less Developed Countries." *Columbia Journal of Environmental Law* 17:419–458.

Dowling, M. and J. Linnerooth. 1987. "The Listing and Classifying of Hazardous Wastes." Pp. 114–119 in *Risk Management and Hazardous Waste: Implementation and the Dialectics of Credibility,* edited by B. Wynne. Berlin: Springer-Verlag.

The Economist. 1992. "Let Them Eat Pollution." *The Economist* (February 8):66.

Fiorino, Daniel J. 1995. *Making Environmental Policy.* Berkeley: University of California Press.

Frey, R. Scott. 1995. "The International Traffic in Pesticides." *Technological Forecasting and Social Change* 50:151–169.

———. 1997. "The International Traffic in Tobacco." *Third World Quarterly* 18:303–319.

———. 1998. "The Export of Hazardous Industries to the Peripheral Zones of the World-Economy." *Journal of Developing Societies* 14:66–81.

———. 1999. "The Migration of Hazardous Industries to the *Maquiladora* Centers of Northern Mexico." Paper presented at the 1999 annual meeting of the American Sociological Association, Chicago, IL.

Gereffi, Gary and Miguel Korzeniewicz, editors. 1994. *Commodity Chains and Global Capitalism.* Westport, CT: Greenwood Press.

Gourlay, K. A. 1992. *World of Waste: Dilemmas of International Development.* London: Zed Books.

Greenpeace. 1992a. *Greenpeace Toxic Trade Update,* 5.1.

———. 1992b. *Greenpeace Toxic Trade Update,* 5.2.

———. 1994. "Database of Known Hazardous Waste Exports from OECD to non-OECD Countries, 1989-March 1994." Washington, D.C., prepared for the Second Conference of Parties to the Basel Convention, March 21–25, 1994, Geneva.

Hays, Samuel P. 1987. *Beauty, Health, and Permanence: Environmental Politics in the United States, 1955–1985.* Cambridge, UK: Cambridge University Press.

Hilz, Christoph. 1992. *The International Toxic Waste Trade.* New York: Van Nostrand Reinhold.

Huq, Saleemui. 1994. "Global Industrialization: A Developing Country Perspective." Pp. 107–113 in *Industrial Ecology and Global Change,* edited by R. Socolow, C. Andrews, F. Berkhout, and V. Thomas. Cambridge, UK: Cambridge University Press.

International Environment Reporter. 1994. "Greenpeace Report Says Asian Countries Being Used as a Dumping Ground for Waste." *International Environment Reporter* 17 (February 9):113–114.

———. 1995a. "Ban on Waste Exports Outside OECD Pushed Through Basel Treaty Meeting." *International Environment Reporter* 18 (October 4):753–754.

———. 1995b. "South Pacific Forum Finalizes Draft Convention on Hazardous Waste." *In-*

ternational Environment Reporter 18 (May 3):327.

———. 1995c. "South Pacific Forum Countries Sign Regional Hazardous Waste Convention." *International Environment Reporter* 18 (September 20):709–710.

Katasonov, Valentin. 1990. "The Price of Capitalism: Dumping on the Soviet Union." *Multinational Monitor* 11 (December):30–31.

Kitt, Jennifer R. 1995. "Waste Exports to the Developing World: A Global Response." *Georgetown International Environmental Law Review* 7:485–514.

Krueger, Jonathan. 1999. "What's Become of Trade in Hazardous Wastes?" *Environment* 41 (November):10–21.

Kummer, Katharina. 1992. "The International Regulation of Transboundary Traffic in Hazardous Wastes: The 1989 Basel Convention." *International Comparative Law Quarterly* 41:530–562.

Leonard, Anne. 1992. "Plastics: Trashing the Third World." *Multinational Monitor* 13 (June):26–31.

———. 1993. "South Asia: The New Target of International Waste Traders." *Multinational Monitor* 14 (December):21–24.

Leonard, H. Jeffrey. 1988. *Pollution and the Struggle for the World Product: Multinational Corporations, Environment, and International Comparative Advantage.* New York: Cambridge University Press.

Logan, Bernard I. 1991. "An Assessment of the Environmental and Economic Implications of Toxic-Waste Disposal in Sub-Saharan Africa." *Journal of World Trade* 25:61–76.

Majone, G. 1985. "The International Dimension." Pp. 40–56 in *Regulating Industrial Risks: Science, Hazards, and the Public Protection,* edited by H. Otway and M. Peltu. London: Butterworths.

Moomaw, William and Mark Tullis. 1994. "Charting Development Paths: A Multi-country Comparison of Carbon Dioxide Emissions." Pp. 157–172 in *Industrial Ecology and Global Change,* edited by R. Socolow, C. Andrews, F. Berkhout, and V. Thomas. Cambridge, UK: Cambridge University Press.

Mpanya, Mutombo. 1992. "The Dumping of Toxic Wastes in African Countries: A Case of Poverty and Racism." Pp. 204–214 in *Race and the Incidence of Environmental Hazards,* edited by Bunyan Bryant and Paul Mohai. Boulder, CO: Westview Press.

Murphy, Raymond. 1994. *Rationality and Nature: A Sociological Inquiry into a Changing Relationship.* Boulder, CO: Westview Press.

Murphy, Sean. 1994. "Prospective Liability Regimes for the Transboundary Movement of Hazardous Wastes." *American Journal of International Law* 88:24–75.

National Research Council. 1991. *Environmental Epidemiology: Volume I—Public Health and Hazardous Wastes.* Washington, D.C.: National Academy Press.

Nunez-Muller, Marco. 1990. "The Schoenberg Case: Transfrontier Movements of Hazardous Wastes." *Natural Resources Journal* 30:153–161.

Postel, Sandra. 1987. *Defusing the Toxic Threat: Controlling Pesticides and Industrial Waste.* Washington, D.C.: Worldwatch Institute.

Puckett, James. 1992. "Dumping on Our World Neighbors: The International Trade in Hazardous Wastes, and the Case for an Immediate Ban on all Hazardous Waste Exports from Industrialized to Less-Industrialized Countries." Pp. 93–106 in *Green Trade,* edited by H. O. Bergesen, M. Norderhaug, and G. Parmann. New York: Oxford University Press.

———. 1994. "Disposing of the Waste Trade: Closing the Recycling Loophole." *The Ecologist* 24 (March/April):53–58.

Sachs, Aaron. 1996. "Upholding Human Rights and Environmental Justice." Pp. 133–151 in *State of the World, 1996,* edited by Lester R. Brown, Janet Abramowitz, Chris Bright, Christopher Flavin, Gary Gardner, Hal Kane, Anne Platt, Sandra Postel, David Roodman, Aaron Sachs, and Linda Starke. New York: W. W. Norton.

Samhoum, R. 1989. "Lebanon: The Toxic Waste Scandal." *World Marxist Review* 32:87–88.

Sanchez, Roberto A. 1990. "Health and Environmental Risks of the Maquiladora in Mexicali." *Natural Resources Journal* 30:163–186.

Schnaiberg, Allan. 1980. *The Environment: From Surplus to Scarcity.* New York: Oxford University Press.

Shin, Roy W. and Laura A. Strohm. 1993. "Policy Regimes for the International Waste Trade." *Policy Studies Review* 12:226–243.

Shrader-Frechette, K. S. 1991. *Risk and Rationality: Philosophical Foundations for Populist Reforms.* Berkeley: University of California Press.

Shulman, S. 1992. *The Threat at Home: Confronting the Toxic Legacy of the U.S. Military.* Boston, MA: Beacon Press.

Stebbins, Kenyon Rainier. 1992. "Garbage Imperialism: Health Implications of Dumping Hazardous Wastes in Third World Countries." *Medical Anthropology* 15:81–102.

Susskind, Lawrence E. 1994. *Environmental Diplomacy: Negotiating More Effective Global Agreements.* New York: Oxford University Press.

Szasz, Andrew. 1994. *EcoPopulism: Toxic Waste and the Movement for Environmental Justice.* Minneapolis: University of Minnesota Press.

Szasz, Andrew and Michael Meuser. 1997. "Environmental Inequalities: Literature Review and Proposals for New Directions in Research and Theory." *Current Sociology* 45:99–120.

Third World Network. 1988. *Toxic Terror: Dumping of Hazardous Wastes in the Third World.* Penang, Malaysia: Third World Network.

Vallette, J. editor. 1989. *The International Trade in Wastes: A Greenpeace Inventory.* (Fourth Edition.) Washington, D.C.: Greenpeace.

Vallette, J. and H. Spalding, editors. 1990. *The International Trade in Wastes: A Greenpeace Inventory.* (Fifth Edition.) Washington, D.C.: Greenpeace.

World Health Organization. 1988. "Examples of Toxic Waste." Pp. 102–110 in *Toxic Terror: Dumping Hazardous Wastes in the Third World,* edited by Third World Network. Penang, Malaysia: Third World Network.

World Resources Institute. 1990. *World Resources, 1990–91.* New York: Oxford University Press.

———. 1994. *World Resources, 1994–95.* New York: Oxford University Press.

Wynne, B. 1987. *Risk Management and Hazardous Waste: Implementation and the Dialectics of Credibility.* New York: Springer-Verlag.

———. 1989. "The Toxic Waste Trade: International Regulatory Issues and Options." *Third World Quarterly* 11:120–146.

7.   Principles of Environmental Justice

THE FIRST NATIONAL PEOPLE OF COLOR
ENVIRONMENTAL LEADERSHIP SUMMIT

OCTOBER 24–27, 1991

WASHINGTON, D.C.

PREAMBLE

WE, THE PEOPLE OF color, gathered together at this multinational People of Color Environmental Leadership Summit, to begin to build a national and international movement of all peoples of color to fight the destruction and taking of our lands and communities, do hereby re-establish our spiritual interdependence to the sacredness of Mother Earth; to respect and celebrate each of our cultures, languages and beliefs about the natural world and our roles in healing ourselves; to ensure environmental justice; to promote economic alternatives which would contribute to the development of environmentally safe livelihoods; and to secure our political, economic, and cultural liberation that has been denied for over 500 years of colonization and oppression, resulting in the poisoning of our communities and land and the genocide of our peoples, do affirm and adopt these Principles of Environmental Justice:

1. Environmental justice affirms the sacredness of Mother Earth, ecological unity and the interdependence of all species, and the right to be free from ecological destruction.

2. Environmental justice demands that public policy be based on mutual respect and justice for all peoples, free from any form of discrimination or bias.

3. Environmental justice mandates the right to ethical, balanced and responsible uses of land and renewable resources in the interest of a sustainable planet for humans and other living things.

4. Environmental justice calls for universal protection from nuclear testing, extraction, production and disposal of toxic/hazardous wastes and poisons and nuclear testing that threaten the fundamental right to clean air, land, water, and food.

5. Environmental justice affirms the fundamental right to political, economic, cultural, and environmental self-determination of all peoples.

6. Environmental justice demands the cessation of the production of all toxins, hazardous wastes, and radioactive materials, and that all past and current producers be held strictly accountable to the people for detoxification and the containment at the point of production.

7. Environmental justice demands the right to participate as equal partners at

every level of decision-making including needs assessment, planning, implementation, enforcement and evaluation.

8. Environmental justice affirms the right of all workers to a safe and healthy work environment, without being forced to choose between an unsafe livelihood and unemployment. It also affirms the right of those who work at home to be free from environmental hazards.

9. Environmental justice protects the right of victims of environmental injustice to receive full compensation and reparations for damages as well as quality health care.

10. Environmental justice considers governmental acts of environmental injustice a violation of international law, the Universal Declaration On Human Rights, and the United Nations Convention on Genocide.

11. Environmental justice must recognize a special legal and natural relationship of Native Peoples to the U.S. Government through treaties, agreements, compacts, and covenants affirming sovereignty and self-determination.

12. Environmental justice affirms the need for urban and rural ecological policies to clean up and rebuild our cities and rural areas in balance with nature, hon-

oring the cultural integrity of all our communities, and providing fair access for all to the full range of resources.

13. Environmental justice calls for the strict enforcement of principles of informed consent, and a halt to the testing of experimental reproductive and medical procedures and vaccinations on people of color.

14. Environmental justice opposes the destructive operations of multinational corporations.

15. Environmental justice opposes military occupation, repression and exploitation of lands, peoples and cultures, and other life forms.

16. Environmental justice calls for the education of present and future generations which emphasizes social and environmental issues, based on our experience and an appreciation of our diverse cultural perspectives.

17. Environmental justice requires that we, as individuals, make personal and consumer choices to consume as little of Mother Earth's resources and to produce as little waste as possible; and make the conscious decision to challenge and reprioritize our life-styles to insure the health of the natural world for present and future generations.

Chapter 4

Driving Forces
of Environmental Problems

8. Rethinking the Environmental Impacts of Population, Affluence, and Technology[1]*

THOMAS DIETZ

EUGENE A. ROSA

HUMAN-ENVIRONMENT INTERACTIONS

How might we better understand the linkages between population, resources, and environmental impacts? How might we proceed to develop organized research programs to examine these linkages? How might we discipline our conceptual models with empirical tests? In this paper, we address these three questions, focusing on anthropogenic environmental change. We suggest that an adaptation of the widely known **IPAT** model (Commoner 1972, 1992; Ehrlich and Ehrlich 1990; Ehrlich and Holdren 1971, 1972; Holdren and Ehrlich 1974), modified to meet statistical testing requirements, is one strategy for addressing these questions. We provide a brief historical account of scholarly discourse bearing on the questions posed above. We note that the social sciences, on the one hand, and the biological and environmental sciences, on the other hand, have addressed them in parallel, but generally separately—and often antagonistically. Then, we describe the original **IPAT** model

and our proposed modifications, evaluating the respective strengths and weaknesses of both. We map our guidelines for further modification, elaboration, and testing of the model. Finally, we sketch some suggestions for superseding the **IPAT** model.

History of an Idea

The idea that population growth affects environmental resources and human welfare is perhaps as old as written history itself.[2] Herodotus, writing in the 5th century before Christ, noted how the population of the Lydians had outpaced production leading to a prolonged famine that lasted eighteen years (*The History*, Book I: 22–23).[3] And Seneca the Younger writing in the first decades of the Christian era (*Naturales Quaestiones*) noted a connection between population and pollution in Rome.[4] He traced pollution to the growth of household cooking fires and the increased traffic on the dusty streets of the city, and also to the burning of dead bodies just outside the city limits. Despite this early recognition, connections between population and environment were anecdotal and unsystematic in classical writings.

The idea of a causal link between population and resources developed into a

*This is a slightly revised version of an article that first appeared in *Human Ecology Review* 1 (1994): 277–300, and is reprinted here by permission of the Society for Human Ecology.

more concrete form in the eleventh century. In 1086, William the Conqueror commissioned an enumeration of the population and its landed wealth, recording the results in the *Domesday Book* (the word "domesday" being a corruption of the word doomsday, the final day of judgment ([Weeks 1986]). This accounting was instrumental in carrying forward the idea that there was a link between population and resources. But it wasn't until the eighteenth century, with the writing of the classical economists, particularly, Thomas Robert Malthus, that the population-resource link received systematic attention. Malthus posed a pivotal question in his first essay that gave structure to an inchoate idea: What effect does population growth have on the availability of resources needed for human welfare? (1960[1798]). His answer, known by nearly every educated person for the past two centuries, was that "geometric" growth (exponential growth in modern parlance) in population would eventually outstrip the "arithmetic" growth (or linear growth) in the means of subsistence. In other words, unless population was held in check, the inevitable outcome would be perpetual misery and poverty.

Malthus is considered a classical economist because his writings appeared during the period (the late 18th and early 19th century) when the practice of economics was crystallizing into a recognizable social science discipline.[5] While the foundation he laid was social scientific in origin, its more general applicability to the problem of species-to-environments interactions and dependency on finite resources was soon recognized. Charles Darwin experienced an intellectual "aha" upon reading Malthus. As a result, he developed his theory of evolution in *The Origin of Species* (1859) around

the same basic idea: species have the tendency to overproduce with the result that only those most "fit" to their environmental circumstances survive and reproduce.[6] Thus population pressure on critical environmental resources drives evolutionary change.

The important point to note here is the convergence of the social and biological sciences to a common problem, but with each side looking through the same lens with a different eye. Even in Malthus' time, disciplinary specialization that separated the social from the biological sciences was evident. By the late 19th century, sharp boundaries were drawn between the social sciences and the biological sciences, and even between disciplines within the social sciences. One consequence of specialization was a prolonged debate about population and human welfare that lasted over 200 years, though its intensity waxed and waned. Not much has really changed since. In the nineteenth and especially the twentieth centuries, the discipline of ecology would take the pattern of relations between organisms and environments as the focus of its investigations. Even so, it did not systematically bring the social and biological sciences into a common focus, a human ecology, but instead added a third eye to the common perspective, often ignoring systematic investigation of human-environment interrelations. This intellectual history set the stage for the current state of affairs: the investigation of a common problem along parallel, but separate tracks and with narrowly specialized foci. It also set the stage for the rekindling of the two-centuries old debate. In the last three decades, the upturn in the intensity of the debate is due to an increased concern with anthropogenic changes in the physical and biological environment.

Revisiting IPAT

We view anthropogenic environmental change as a real and challenging problem, in need of systematic investigation. The IPAT model, first proposed three decades ago, represented the efforts of population biologists, ecologists and environmental scientists to formalize the relationship between population, human welfare, and environmental impacts. Here we revisit the IPAT model that postulates that environmental impact (I) is the product of population (P), per capita affluence (A), and technology (T). Why revisit the model in the context of global environmental change? First, because it has been adopted as the orienting perspective for much of the discussion about the principal factors, called "driving forces," of global environmental change. Population is theorized to be a key driving force, along with economic activity, technology, political, and economic institutions, and attitudes and beliefs (Stern et al. 1992). Second, a number of treatments of population (e.g., Green 1992), including the award winning work of Paul Harrison (1992–1993, 1994) have likewise used it as an orienting perspective. But, third, there has been little effort to discipline the model with empirical tests since its inception three decades ago. In particular, social scientists have generally ignored the model, while biological, ecological and other physical and environmental scientists, by generally assuming the model to be true, have not been motivated to test it rigorously.[7] We propose the adoption of the IPAT model as one, but by no means the only, procedure for addressing the global change problem systematically. We also argue that the IPAT model may be an effective device for operationally bridging the perspectives—social sciences and biological sciences—around this con-temporary environmental problem. That is, the IPAT model may be an effective way to examine the problem from an human ecological point of view. It can thus serve our ultimate goal, namely to generate more disciplined research instead of debate that is ungrounded in empirical research.

The IPAT model has appealing features. It has structured much of the debate about the effects of population, affluence and technology on the environment, and has been a widely adopted perspective in ecology. But, the model also has serious limitations. Key among these is that in its current form it does not provide an adequate framework for disentangling the various driving forces of anthropogenic environmental change. As a consequence, the IPAT model stifles efforts toward cumulative theory development and empirical findings. We propose a stochastic reformulation of the model that renders it amenable to empirical "disentangling." Once we describe the theoretical and empirical advantages of our reformulation, we go on to sketch alternative ways of conceptualizing the driving forces of anthropogenic change.

Population and Economic and Social Change

The *causes* of population and economic change have been addressed in a literature too vast to cite, let alone review. Indeed, the causes of population and economic change are central topics of demography and economics. There is also a substantial literature on the *social consequences* of population and economic change.[8] For example, one of the founders of sociology, Emile Durkheim (1964[1893]) argued that leaps in population growth lead to an increased competition for environmental resources which, in turn, leads to the division of labor in society.

An early, modified effort to organize these various factors into a coherent conceptualization was the POET model proposed by sociologist Otis Dudley Duncan (1964). Duncan sought to alert social scientists to the importance of ecology, arguing that an ecological framework could enrich the theoretical understanding of societies. In particular, because the four components— population, technology, social organization, and physical environment—are constituent to the operation of literally all societies, an examination of their interactions could be the foundation of cumulative social theory. While useful for pointing a social scientific lens toward the environment, and while influential as a foundation for theory, the model has generated very little empirical research. The principal reason is not hard to discern: it is very difficult to map the framework into operational procedures. According to POET, everything is connected to everything else, with the consequence that the framework—in the language of statistical modeling—is badly underidentified.[9]

Recently there has been a focus on the impacts of population growth on resource availability and environmental impacts. The overwhelming majority of this work has examined problems of resource (especially food) shortages and human welfare. While optimists and pessimists persist, a consensus view today probably is close to that offered by Coale and Hoover (1958) in their pioneering study of India.[10] Production increases driven by price increases can keep rough pace with population growth and thus prevent the misery envisioned by Malthus. But rapid population growth retards capital accumulation and improvements in standard of living.

An even more optimistic tradition is usually traced to Boserup (1965, 1980) and holds that population growth and concen-

tration lead to economic growth, not, as Malthus would have it, the other way around. Simon (1981) is the strongest advocate of the view that population growth leads to enhanced welfare.[11] He argues that potential shortages of any key resource or necessity of life generate creative responses that increase productivity and the efficiency of resource use. Thus population growth produces innovation that ultimately enhances welfare.

This body of work has focused on agriculture, food production, employment, and per capita income. Another tradition examines the effects of growth on the supply of renewable resources such as forests and fisheries and non-renewable resources, such as minerals and energy.[12] It comes to roughly the same conclusion as the literature following Coale and Hoover on growth and welfare: while population growth generates some problems, price mechanisms and human ingenuity provide the solutions to those problems. Slower population growth might improve the efficiency of resource use. But the worst fears of Malthus have not been realized, and factors other than population growth, particularly institutional arrangements, are more important than population size in determining the adequacy of resource supplies.

Of course, scholars in the field remain cautious about the empirical evidence supporting these conclusions. For example, the editors of a recent U.S. National Research Council study (Johnson and Lee 1987:xi) note: "drawing firm conclusions about the overall impact of slower population growth is difficult because the research base is inadequate. Studies completed to date are often on limited samples and data of poor quality, as well as on only partial and occasionally inappropriate conceptual models and statistical techniques." But whatever the concerns about the quality of evidence, and whatever the remaining disputes and dissension, the relationship between population and human welfare has been far more carefully studied than the effects of population growth on the biophysical environment.

THE CHARACTER OF ENVIRONMENTAL DEGRADATION

Our understanding of the role of population in anthropogenic change is far from complete. Nevertheless, some impacts are better known than others and it will be useful to distinguish the kinds of impacts that have been relatively well researched from those that have not. Malthus' First Essay was concerned with the ability of agricultural productivity to keep pace with population growth. As classical economics developed, factors of production were clarified, and thus population became one element in studies of growth. This literature viewed land and raw materials (the classical concepts closest to current notions of environment) simply as other factors of production. To a substantial degree, the question of population impacts posed by Malthus is a question of whether or not growth in output and productivity can keep pace with population growth (cf. Ricardo 1891 [1917]).

Starting in the 1960s, increased concern with environmental problems made scholars aware of the broad character of human interactions with the physical and biological environment. In particular, concerns were raised about environmental "services" that were collective goods not given a market value, and with the "externalities" of production processes that may have adverse effects on the environment and thus on the ability of ecosystems to provide critical services. For simplicity, we will refer to these effects as environmental impacts.[13] Here we will focus on the global environmental change complex: greenhouse climate change, acid precipitation, species loss, deforestation, desertification, and the broad dispersion of toxics. But, *ceteris paribus*, the argument applies equally well to less global problems such as local air and water pollution.

Environmental impacts of these sorts are different in two ways from the problem of resource shortages and production shortfalls that have been analyzed in the literature cited above. First, these problems involve the environment as a collective good. And unlike some common property resources that have been well studied, such as fisheries, no market value is assigned to the environmental benefits that are threatened by negative environmental impacts. Climate is a factor of production, but unlike land, minerals, fish catch or other renewable and non-renewable resources, it is not subject to the pricing mechanisms that underlie the logic of previous research on population, welfare, and resources. In effect, climate is treated as a free good.

Of course, the goods and services provided by the environment do have real value whether or not prices are assigned to them. For example, Pimentel (1992; Pimentel and Hall 1989) has argued for the critical importance of "ecosystem services" to even the most highly managed agricultural systems. But because they are non-market collective goods their value is not reflected in price mechanisms. It may be possible to find institutional arrangements that will allow prices to be assigned to ecosystem services. This could be accomplished through either a market for the relevant goods and services, as in the air basin experiments currently being conducted in the U.S., or a Pigouvian tax on the activities that generate environmental degradation.[14] But the point for the present discussion is that conclusions about the effects of population growth on human welfare have assumed that welfare and its determinants have prices. Those conclusions do not necessarily apply to unpriced goods and services. Or to put it differently, whatever the policy mechanisms used to address current environmental impacts, cumulative impacts have evolved under conditions in which no economic value is assigned to ecosystem services. Thus, while existing work on population growth and welfare is tantalizingly suggestive we have a far from perfect understanding of the driving forces of global environmental change.

Second, the fact that population growth may not retard economic growth is little comfort to those concerned about anthropogenic environmental change. It has been argued that economic growth is not tightly coupled to human welfare on the one hand (e.g., Nussbaum and Sen 1993; Scotvsky 1976; Sen 1993; Rosa et al. 1982). Yet even without advancing welfare, increased per capita consumption and the attendant generation of residuals is a cause of environmental impacts. Thus concern with the biophysical environment leads to questions about the impacts of economic growth as well as of population growth. Indeed, much of the debate of the last twenty years centers around the relative importance of economic growth and population growth in generating environmental impacts.

POPULATION, AFFLUENCE, AND THE ENVIRONMENT

In the late 1960s and early 1970s the argument that population growth would have a strong adverse effect on human welfare was revisited (e.g., Ehrlich 1968; Meadows et al. 1972). The reaction to these analyses was forceful, stimulating a debate that continues today. While population growth seems not to have had the catastrophic effects on human welfare suggested by Malthus, the effects of population and economic growth on environmental degradation have not been extensively researched.[15] Indeed, only a handful of papers offer empirical or conceptual analyses of the human driving forces of environmental change. The U.S. National Research Council (1986), in a report that generally rejects the Malthusian thesis noted above, also states that there is "no evidence" about the effects of population growth on the environment. In a later report, the National Research Council concluded that research on the driving forces of global environmental change should be one of the highest priorities in "human dimensions" research efforts (Stern et al. 1992:238–241). The approach proposed here is intended as an initial step towards building a better understanding of the effects of population growth on the environment. Of course, to understand the effects of population growth, it is necessary to consider the direct and indirect effects of population on the environment and on other driving forces. It is also necessary to understand how these impacts vary across temporal, spatial, socio-cultural, and technological contexts.

There are at least four distinct positions regarding the effects of population and economic growth on the environment. They parallel the positions held on population growth and welfare. One view, held most notably by Ehrlich and his collaborators, suggests anticipated population growth will have very severe, even catastrophic, impacts on the natural environment and human welfare (Daily and Ehrlich 1992; Ehrlich 1968; Ehrlich and Ehrlich 1990; Ehrlich and Holdren 1971, 1972; Holdren and Ehrlich 1974; Holdren 1991). (See also Catton, 1982; Green, 1992). A second position, derived in part from the work of Boserup (1965, 1980), acknowledges that population growth and economic growth create increased demand for resources. But the resulting perceived or anticipated scarcity drives technological progress and with it the search for substitutes and increased efficiency. Thus the net effect of population and economic growth on resource scarcity, human welfare and the state of the environment is neutral or even positive. According to Simon (1981), the most forceful advocate of this position, the effect of growth is invariably positive. A third position suggests that technologies used as part of growth are often selected without regard to their environmental impact (Barkin 1991; Commoner 1992; O'Connor 1988, 1989; Schnaiberg 1980; Schnaiberg and Gould 1994). Thus adverse environmental impacts are more a function of the political economy of technological choice than of population or economic growth *per se*. To the extent population has an effect on the environment, it is an indirect effect that could be mollified by institutional or technological change. The fourth position, rather like the consensus on the relationship between economic welfare and population, is a middle ground. Population is seen not as the dominant driving force, but as a contributor to environmental impact acting in consort with affluence, technological choice, institutional arrangements, and other factors (Keyfitz 1991a, 1991b, 1993; Ridker 1972, 1979, 1992; Ridker and Cecelski 1979).

How are these four positions sustained? As noted above, there has been little empirical work on the impacts of population on the environment. The most extensive literature is found in a series of papers prepared for the U.S. Commission on Population Growth and the American Future (U.S. Commission on Population Growth and the

American Future 1972; Ridker 1972). The general conclusion of the editor of these papers and of the Commission itself was that population growth contributes to environmental degradation, but that the impact of population is generally less than the impact of economic growth (Ridker 1972:19). Ridker also notes that the effects of both kinds of growth can be mitigated by the appropriate choice of policies, technologies, and institutions. Thus the conclusion is generally consistent with the line of work following from Coale and Hoover's study.

Methodologies

Three methodologies were employed in the Population Commission report and subsequent studies of population, affluence, and the environment. The most common is a simulation/projection (S/P) approach. Resource demand or pollution generation is estimated as a function of per capita income. Projections of population and income are then used to estimate future resource demand or pollution. In the more sophisticated models, such as those used for the Population Commission studies, input-output analysis is used to account for intersectoral demand for goods and services (Herzog and Ridker 1972). These demands are also translated into impacts on resources and pollution generation. Typically, the final estimated outputs from each sector of the economy are multiplied by coefficients representing the impact per unit output at the most recent point in time for which data are available. In some models, these coefficients can be adjusted to take account of environmental policies or increased efficiency resulting from technological improvement. The S/P model is used to project environmental impacts under various scenarios of population and economic growth. These projections then provide the basis for determining the effects of population and economic growth.

The basic logic of the S/P model is to first establish a linkage between total economic activity (per capita activity multiplied by population) and environmental impact. Then alternative scenarios of population and economic growth are projected to assess environmental impacts. In some models, like the *Limits to Growth* study (Meadows et al. 1972), the structure is very simple—a set of linked differential equations and multipliers. In others, such as the models used for the Population Commission, and some successor studies to *Limits to Growth* (Barney 1980; Mesarovic and Pestel 1974), the linkages become much more complex. Also, they disaggregate economic activity in terms of sector by sector output.[16] But all S/P models make assumptions about environmental impacts per unit output and then extrapolate into the future under different scenarios of growth. Thus they do not provide a historical or comparative assessment of the contribution of various driving forces but rather a projection of what may happen, given the simplifying assumptions of the model. In other words, S/P models are used to ask "What if?" questions.

The conclusions drawn vary across the several S/P models. The Population Commission results suggest only moderate impact of population growth on the environment. The "Limits to Growth" models and their successors see far greater population impact. Bongaarts (1992) partitions CO_2 emissions into components for population, affluence, energy intensity due to affluence and the carbon intensity of energy. He finds that in the less developed nations, affluence changes will dominate the growth in emissions, with population growth the second most important factor. In the more developed countries, growing affluence also drives emissions but changes in energy intensity are more important than changes in population. Kolsrud and Torrey (1992) reach similar conclusions regarding population when they examine scenarios for future commercial energy consumption.

The second common approach is an accounting analysis (A/A). The most commonly used form is the **IPAT** model itself (Commoner 1972; Ehrlich and Holdren 1971, 1972; Holdren and Ehrlich 1974). This model postulates that:

$$I = P*A*T$$

where **I** is environmental impact, **P** is population, **A** is per capita economic activity (referred to as affluence), and **T** is the impact per unit economic activity (referred to as technology).

In typical applications, data are obtained on impact, population and affluence and the equation is solved for **T**

$$T = I/(P*A)$$

This approach has also been applied to the CO_2 efficiency and energy efficiency of economies (Stern et al. 1992:60–67).[17] Recently, Mazur (1994) has used a similar approach—though not **IPAT** itself—in assessing the relative contribution of population and all other factors in the growth of energy consumption in the U.S.[18]

When the model is used to assess the relative impact of population and affluence as driving forces, data for two points in time are usually translated into percentage increases for each term in the model. Change in **I** is then allocated to percentage changes in **P, A,** and **T**. For example, Commoner (1992:155) calculates that the use of synthetic organic pesticides in the U.S.

increased by 266% from 1950 to 1967 (a 1967 to 1950 ratio of 3.66).[19] During that same period, population grew 30% (a ratio of 1.30), crop production per capita by 5% (a ratio of 1.05), and pesticide consumption per unit crop production—the technology factor for Commoner—by 168% (a ratio of 2.68). That is

$$3.66 = (1.30)*(1.05)*(2.68).$$

Thus he attributes most increase in the use of synthetic pesticides to technological change, with increased consumption per capita and increased population each responsible for a smaller share in the increased value of I—here the use of synthetic pesticides.

The key problem with this approach is that the relationship is definitional. Once three of the variables are fixed, the fourth is also fixed. Thus Ehrlich and Holdren (1972:369–371) suggest that Commoner's calculations underestimate the effect of population on the environment by attributing to the T term changes that could more properly be allocated to P or A. The accounting model is useful for developing efficiency or intensity measures, but does not provide an adequate basis for testing hypotheses about the human driving forces of environmental change.

The third approach uses historical or cross-sectional data on I, P, A, and T to assess impacts. In its simplest application, this analysis takes the form of simple graphs of either bivariate relationships between I and driving forces or historical trends (Bilsborrow 1992; Bilsborrow and Geores 1991; Peierls et al. 1991; Simon 1981). More sophisticated approaches formulate stochastic models of impact as a function of other independent variables. The use of such stochastic models has substantial advantages,

as we will note below. But it has seen little use to date. For example, in Ridker (1972), only one paper uses this approach. Hoch's analysis (1972) uses regression models to estimate the effects of the population size and density of U.S. urban areas on air pollution levels, wages, and crime rates. His analysis fits into a small tradition that attempts to determine urban size effects in sociology, geography, and economics (Applebaum 1978; Appelbaum et al. 1976; Duncan 1951; Singer 1972). He finds that both population size and density have adverse effects on these variables. The stochastic modeling (S/M) approach has been used most often in studies of deforestation (Allen and Barnes 1985; Dietz, Kalof, and Frey 1991; Rudel 1989). Despite using slightly different specifications and data sets, all three of these studies find that population size, growth rate, or density has a stronger effect on deforestation than does economic activity. Rudel (1989) also finds population growth to have a stronger effect than a common measure of trade dependency. These preliminary applications and their findings suggest that the stochastic approach to assessing the impacts of population, affluence, technology, and other factors on the environment is a useful way to ground the debate about driving forces in stronger theory and empirical evidence.

A REFORMULATION OF THE IPAT MODEL

Despite the paucity of strong evidence regarding the effects of population and economic growth on the environment, strong conclusions about the relative importance of the driving forces still appear. For example, a recent, unprecedented joint statement by the Royal Society of London and the U.S. National Academy of Sciences (1992) asserts that population growth is a major threat to human well-being. Yet, there is little empirical evidence to support their claim (Stern 1993).

In order to move the debate to more solid ground, it will be necessary to reformulate the **IPAT** model in six ways.[20] First it must be considered a stochastic model rather than an accounting scheme so that it can be used, not as a balancing rule, but to test hypotheses. Second, it would be helpful to employ a variety of indicators of environmental impact and consider the possibility of creating general indices from individual indicators. Third, modeling should incorporate effects of the rate or pace of growth, population distribution, and the composition of the population in addition to the effects of population size. Rate or pace of growth, distribution, and composition may have greater effects than size per se. Fourth, alternatives to gross national and gross domestic product such as distributional measures should be considered as measures of affluence. Fifth, technology needs to be assessed directly, rather than as the residual of the accounting format. One approach should incorporate operational measures of technology, such as the efficiency of energy conversion. Another should reconceptualize technology to include a variety of candidate driving factors that influence how human activity affects the environment, including culture, social structure, and institutional arrangements. Sixth, because the various driving forces interact in complex ways, it ultimately will be necessary to move from a single equation model—one that estimates only direct effects net of other variables in the model—to a systems model that estimates both direct and indirect effects of driving forces. That is, the model must acknowledge that the driving forces influence each other. While some of the earliest formulations of the **IPAT** model

acknowledge this (e.g., Ehrlich and Holdren 1971, 1972; Holdren and Ehrlich 1974), there has been no elaboration of how these interactions may work.

With all these modifications, it may seem that the **IPAT** model is being altogether abandoned. Eventually, the elaboration of theory about the forces driving anthropogenic environmental change may lead to models that have little relationship to **IPAT**. Nevertheless, **IPAT** is a useful starting point for theory building and testing for three reasons. First, any viable theory of anthropogenic environmental change must consider population, affluence, and technology as factors of environmental change. There are other potentially important driving forces and key effects of them may be indirect. But **P, A,** and **T,** almost everyone would agree, must be part of any serious effort to understand human impacts on the environment. Second, the **IPAT** model is at the heart of debates regarding driving forces. Research that elaborates on it is more likely to influence those debates than research that rejects it. Third, the **IPAT** model is a general framework that can structure both research and discussion, thus providing a means for integrating disparate literatures.

A STOCHASTIC REFORMULATION

The **IPAT** model can easily be reformulated in stochastic form:

$$I - aP^bA^cT^de$$

where **I, P, A,** and **T** remain environmental impact, population size, per capita economic activity, and impact per unit economic activity. Now a, b, c, and **d** are parameters and e a residual term. Data on **I, P, A,** and **T** can be used to estimate a, b, c, d, and e using standard statistical methods such as regression analysis and its kin. This reformulation of the model requires multiple observations (over units, overtime or both) on **I, P, A,** and **T.** This is an important distinction from the accounting model where one term is derived from the values of the other three and thus requires data on any three of the four variables for one or a few observational units. But the advantage of this reformulation is that it converts the **IPAT** accounting model into what is certainly the most standard formulation for quantitative social research—the general linear model. As a result, the substantial array of statistical tools used in quantitative social research can be applied to the problem of assessing the importance of each of the driving forces. Assertions about the driving forces can be converted into hypotheses that are specific to the impact (e.g., CO_2 loads) and the spatial (e.g., nation states) and temporal (e.g., a decade) context under study. The stochastic version preserves the original model in that the accounting model is nothing more than a special case in which $a = b = c = d = e = 1$.[21] Early tests of the reformulated stochastic version of **IPAT** can be undertaken by operationalizing the components with readily available indicators for well defined social units, such as the nation state. For example, first approximation of the relative effects on a given impact (**I**), such as yearly CO_2 loads, could be assessed by plugging total population (**P**), gross national product per capita (**A**), and energy efficiency (**T**) into the model. Or the model could be estimated with the exact same operational indicators, except for technology (**T**), which can be treated as part of the residual term. Some work takes these various approaches (Dietz and Rosa 1997).

A key consideration in the application of the reformulated **IPAT** is the proper units of analysis. Previous applications of the **IPAT** model have used data for a single country at two or three points in time. Simulation/projection models have been applied more widely to single countries, the world as an aggregate, and world regions. The stochastic reformulation we suggest allows even broader scope for units of analysis. The world as a whole should be considered at least for exploratory efforts.[22] But because of the limited data available, and the marginal quality of some of what is available, most analyses must rely either on the nation states or on subnational units such as states, provinces or counties, as a unit of analysis. Broad cross-sectional analyses have long been used for comparative analysis in economics, political science, and sociology (e.g., Bollen et al. 1993; Jackman 1985; Mazur and Rosa 1974). These can be supplemented by individual country time series analyses where data are available, and by pooled cross-section time series analysis when short time series are available for a moderate number of cross-sectional units. The cross-national and pooled approaches offer the critically important advantage of contextualizing the **IPAT** model—that is, of acknowledging that the effects of driving forces may vary over time and across nations or regions. Time series, cross-sectional, and pooled data sets allow the estimation of models in which the coefficients of a model change over time, across cross-sectional units or both (Judge et al. 1980). This permits analyses that are sensitive to the effects of socio-economic structure and social, economic, and technological change on the relationship between driving forces and environmental change. Indeed, we believe a major advantage of the stochastic model is that it places work on driving forces squarely in the methodological tradition of quantitative social science, and allows the application of a powerful repertoire of well-developed tools.

REFORMULATING I

Examining Impacts Rather Than Human Activity

Most research on human driving forces has taken measures of human inputs into the natural environment as the impact measure rather than examining the resultant environmental change. Thus in the example noted above, Commoner (1992) examines the use of inorganic nitrogen fertilizer, synthetic organic pesticides, synthetic fibers, and phosphorous based detergents rather than the effects of these compounds on human health or on ecosystem structure and function. Ehrlich and Holdren (1971, 1972; Holdren and Ehrlich 1974; Holdren 1991) have examined energy consumption rather than environmental effects *per se*. Most work on greenhouse climate change uses CO_2 emissions rather than the change in atmospheric concentration of CO_2 (Dietz and Rosa 1997). The use of human action as an impact measure is a reasonable first approximation, and to some extent dictated by the availability of data on human activities and paucity of data on actual environmental change. But it does have the disadvantage of ignoring the capacity of natural systems to absorb impacts, and the (probably non-linear) limits of those abilities. Over the last decade, there has been a sharp increase in the availability of data on the natural environment. While some of this data is of only poor to moderate quality (for example data on deforestation rates are notoriously unreliable, and data for extinction rates are even more flawed), other measurements such as atmospheric gas concentrations are very reliable. Work on the **IPAT** model should eventually move toward the use of vari-

ables that describe the physical and biological systems of concern, not just the human inputs to those systems. Only by studying the links can we expect to monitor and understand the non-linear responses that are so troubling.

Creating an Impact Indicator

Most studies to date have examined only one or a few impacts. When comparisons are made using a single indicator, results may be misleading due to the "Netherlands" effect (Ehrlich and Holdren 1971, 1972).[23] Much of the environmental impact of a nation state may be displaced across its borders due to the mix of imports and exports and to the international division of labor (Frey 1998). This can be compensated for in part by taking account of imports and exports of high environmental consequence.

The single indicator approach is also flawed because it ignores substitutions within a social system. For example, a nation might have relatively low CO_2 emissions per unit affluence because it makes extensive use of nuclear and/or hydroelectric power rather than fossil fuels. But the disposal of nuclear waste and the disruption of riparian ecosystems are also environmental problems. Thus an adequate environmental indicator should take account of such trade-off effects as well as the possibility of displacing impacts.

In the social sciences, it is commonplace to have problems of measurement where no single indicator is adequate to capture a concept and where each indicator is subject to measurement error. Often there is no obvious *a priori* method for assigning weights to indicators. Standard measurement theory can be used to develop multi-dimensional models of environmental impact. Also, environmental impacts can be treated as latent variables, while specific indicators such as CO_2 emissions, tropical wood imports, or species endangerment serve as observed indicators or proxies linked to the latent variables. Standard structural equation modeling methods allow tests of hypotheses about the links between latent variables and manifest indices and the construction of indicators that pool individual measures (Bollen 1989). Analyses of this type will aid in the detection of tradeoffs among types of impact and can assess the role of impact displacements in a nation's overall effect on the global environment.

REFORMULATING P

Most examinations of population impacts use population size as the indicator of that driving force. This oversimplifies population impacts in a number of important ways. First, the distribution of population may be as important or even more important than size and needs to be considered (see, e.g., Day and Day 1973). A few studies of deforestation have examined the impact of rural population growth, population density, and intra-national migration (Allen and Barnes 1985; Dietz et al. 1991; Rudel 1991). Hoch's (1972) work considers urban density. But more sustained work on impacts due to the spatial distribution of population deserves a high priority in **IPAT** analyses.

Second, because children may produce substantially less impact than adults, age structure of the population should also be considered in assessing population impacts. As the populations of the low fertility nations of the world (the most affluent nations, the newly industrializing nations, and some exceptional non-industrial nations) grow older, resource consumption patterns may shift radically. We know, for example, that age/cohort is one of the best predictors of environmental concern in the U.S.

(Jones and Dunlap 1992). In the high fertility nations, the next few decades will see very sharp increases in the number of people in dependent age groups and even sharper increases in the size of the population forming families and seeking work.

Third, and perhaps most important, the pace of population growth influences a nation's ability to develop innovations and institutions. The research on population and human welfare reviewed above suggests that population growth is only a moderate detriment to human welfare and resource adequacy. This research also notes that the more rapid the growth, the more likely the effects are to be detrimental and that very rapid growth can be very detrimental (see especially U.S. National Academy of Sciences 1971). Very rapid growth exacerbates the kind of socio-economic disarticulation proposed by Amin (1974, 1976, 1977; Stokes and Anderson 1990). Thus it is plausible to hypothesize that the pace of population growth will in itself contribute to environmental impact over and above any effects of population size.[24]

REFORMULATING A

National income figures, especially gross national product per capita or gross domestic product per capita, are the usual measures of economic activity in **IPAT** models, although some simulations use output disaggregated by sector of the economy.[25] For assessing the effects of economic growth on the environment, these very standard and relatively well measured variables are appropriate. But the last few decades have also seen criticisms of these indicators as measures of human welfare. Other indicators of welfare, such as health, don't always correlate highly with economic measures (Mazur and Rosa 1971; Sen 1993). A number of alternatives have been proposed, such as the "physical quality of life index" (PQLI) that combines infant mortality, literacy, and life expectancy (Morris 1979; London and Williams 1988). An important line of sociological research has shown that welfare is no longer tightly coupled to energy consumption (Mazur and Rosa 1971; Rosa, Keating, and Staples 1980; Olsen 1992). Preliminary work suggests that for a number of nations CO_2 emissions have also decoupled from welfare, while the correlation persists in other industrial nations (Rosa 1997). Researchers have also begun to develop alternative measures of economic activity that correct gross production for consumption of non-renewable resources, military spending and other activities perceived as neither renewable or productive.[26] All this work, critical of standard national economic accounts as indicators of human welfare, suggests that alternatives to gross domestic or national product should be explored as measures of affluence.

The disadvantage of the PQLI and similar measures is that their units are quite arbitrary (Sen 1993). A better alternative to measuring affluence lies in life expectancy at birth. Life expectancy at birth is a function of the age specific mortality rates occurring in a population, and thus can reasonably be interpreted as a key quality of life indicator.[27] Life expectancy has the additional advantage that, when multiplied by population, the product represents the number of years of life that can be expected for members of a nation under their current living conditions. Thus it holds a strong parallel to the multiplication in the **IPAT** model of population by economic activity per capita to produce total economic activity.

REFORMULATING T

Most students of environmental issues would acknowledge that it is reasonable to

examine the role of population and affluence in generating environmental impact, whatever the relative importance of these two factors may be. But most social scientists are frustrated by the truncated vision of the rest of the world offered by the **T** in the **IPAT** model. As noted above, if **IPAT** is taken as an accounting model, then the normal practice is to solve for **T**. In that sense **T** captures not just technology in the narrow sense, but everything else not included in the model: attitudes, values, institutional arrangements etc. of the population. All of these must be considered as driving forces.[28]

The stochastic model estimates the effect of **T** independent of **I**, **P**, and **A**. Generating these estimates first requires an operational definition of **T**. Once accomplished, researchers can offer specific hypotheses about **T** and test those hypotheses with the operational indicators. For example, the common hypothesis that values are the key determinant of environmental impact can be tested using cross national or time series data on indicators of values, such as environmental attitudes. Arguments that a shift to a service economy will reduce environmental impacts can be tested using data on the distribution of labor or gross product across economic sectors. Ultimately, it is possible to substitute a vector of cultural, political, and social structural variables for **T** and examine the net effect of each on **I**. To do so, we must develop a human ecological model of environmental impact.

A HUMAN ECOLOGICAL MODEL OF ENVIRONMENTAL IMPACT

We have argued that the **IPAT** model is a useful framework for directing the investigation of anthropogenic environmental impacts. Such investigations are likely to shed light on an issue that more often attracts heat. Yet, it is also useful to think beyond

IPAT. We are so far from a fully articulated model of environmental impact that many may despair and retreat to the relatively robust initial formulation of **IPAT.** But population and affluence effects cannot be properly estimated if they are included in a model that is badly mis-specified. Thus it is useful to propose some first steps towards a social model of environmental impact. There are a number of variables that can be reasonably hypothesized to influence anthropogenic environmental change, and a number of ways to operationalize each. Parsimony suggests a sharp delimitation. We propose the following concepts and operationalizations.

Culture

Culture has been posited as a driving force of environmental change at least since White's (1967) classical essay. While the argument for cultural forces is plausible, existing evidence is equivocal (Tuan 1968). We suggest three operationalizations. First, *public opinion* data measuring environmental values and attitudes for a number of nations (circa 1991) are now available from the Gallup "Health of the Planet Survey" (Dunlap et al. 1993). These can be used to develop a crude indicator of public environmental concern. Such concern may influence technological choice.

Second, *social movements* are the mechanisms by which public concern is translated into policy, and thus one of the means by which the environmental impacts of nations and regions are transformed (Brulle 1993). Dietz and Kalof (1992) have developed a measure of environmentalism for nation states and find it related to some measures of state action on the environment. But there are few empirical comparisons of the environmental movement across a diversity of nations. We would expect that a strong environmental movement would, *ceteris paribus*, lead to policies that reduce the environmental impact of consumption and population.

Third, the *cultural history* of a nation may shape current actions toward the environment. Since White (1967) posited religion as a critical determinant of environmental impact, religious heritage of a nation is a candidate indicator. The work by Lenski and Nolan (Lenski and Nolan 1984; Lenski 1986; Nolan and Lenski 1985) on the technological/ecological heritage of a nation suggests that pre-colonial mode of agriculture may continue to have important ramifications for social and economic organization.

Political Economy

Many scholars have suggested that political economy is a key determinant of environmental impact. The problem is finding a conceptualization of political economy that is sufficiently parsimonious that it can be operationalized. We suggest three dimensions: *position in the global economy, democracy,* and *government involvement in the economy.*

The two most commonly used concepts of position in the global economy are investment dependence and position in the world system. A small literature has examined the impacts of dependency and world system position on the environment (Covello and Frey 1990; Bunker 1984, 1985; Evans 1979; Frey 1998; Hecht 1985; Rudel 1989). It suggests that adverse environmental impacts will be greatest in dependent nations that are in the periphery of the world economy. Other arguments suggest that institutional arrangements may have an important influence on environmental quality. Congleton (1990) reviews these arguments, and suggests that democratic governments may be more concerned with environmental quality than authoritarian governments. There may also be a relationship between government involvement in the economy and environmental degradation, but the direction of the effect is difficult to predict.

Social Structure

The social structure of a nation may also have an influence on environmental impact. For example, Inglehart (1990) suggests that *poverty* and *inequality* reduces concern with environmental quality. Analyses by Dunlap et al. (1993) do not support this argument, but further analysis is needed. Poverty is to some extent captured by national product per capita. But distribution of income and land may be more important that aggregate income. Amin's (1972, 1974, 1977; Stokes and Anderson 1990) concept of *disarticulation* is closely related to inequality (it is usually conceptualized as sectoral inequality) and is likely to have a strong link to environmental impact. Finally, there is substantial evidence for gender differences in environmental concern at the individual level (Dietz, Stern, and Kalof 1993), and this may translate into a link between gender stratification and the environmental policy of nation states.

Model Structure

Of course, there is no reason to limit analysis to a single equation that estimates only net effects. The stochastic approach allows estimates of the effects of driving forces on each other and thus can take account of direct effects (e.g., the effects of affluence on CO_2 emissions directly via consumption of fossil fuels in driving) and indirect effects (e.g., the effect of affluence on CO_2 emis-

sions indirectly by lowering fertility and thus reducing long term population size). Such simultaneous equation models underpin the analysis of the link between population growth and human welfare. In these models growth generates scarcity, which in turn generates a price signal that fosters efficiency, substitution, and innovation. To account for such simultaneity, it may be useful to embed the stochastic version of **IPAT** in a larger structural model that allows all elements of the expanded **IPAT** model to affect each other over time.

As noted above, the effects of independent variables on environmental impacts may vary across contexts. A series of methods allow for increasingly complex models with this variation. The time series and pooled methods noted above, as well as generalized least squares applied to correct for heteroscedasticity in cross-sectional models capture variation over time and across units in disturbance terms. Dummy variables (multipliers in the multiplicative form) allow for shift effects across units. Interaction models allow parameters to vary across units. Time-varying coefficient models can be applied with long time series to estimate secular trends in the effects of the independent variables, though we anticipate that the time series available for these analyses are not sufficiently long to allow the use of this method. Our general point is that a stochastic version of the **IPAT** model opens the way for the application of a rich array of conceptual and statistical tools.

CONCLUSIONS

We wish to emphasize that standard social science research methods can take us a long way towards better understanding of the human driving forces of environmental change. What we lack are theoretical frameworks that adequately conceptualize human-environment interactions. We believe the **IPAT** model, despite its limitations, provides a useful starting point for developing a better framework and for structuring empirical tests of theoretical arguments.

The recognition that humans are having untoward impacts on the bio-physical environment, a perception once confined to the industrial nations, has now reached virtually the entire globe (Dunlap et al. 1993). No one would deny the importance of deepening our understanding of the anthropogenic linkages and causes of environmental impacts. But while there is a singular vision of a common knowledge destination, there continues to be considerable debate about the best route to get there. Part of the debate stems from the "trained incapacity" of scholars working within a discipline to recognize affinities in other disciplines, and part stems from the fact that a defining feature of different disciplines is a difference in metatheoretical assumptions. Such tacitly accepted presuppositions about the proper approach to comprehending a problem allow knowledge to advance within a domain of inquiry, but block attempts to integrate and to learn at the intersection between disciplines. Split-level dialogues between the social and biological sciences on the topic of population growth have been taking place for over a century. This is precisely why an integrative, human ecological approach is needed.

In this paper we have suggested that the **IPAT** model provides a useful, if fallible, compass for setting us on our journey toward a deeper understanding of anthropogenic environmental change. The model is simple, systematic, and robust: simple because it incorporates key anthropogenic driving forces with parsimony; systematic because it specifies the mathematical rela-

tionship between the driving forces and their impacts; and robust because it is applicable to a wide variety of environmental impacts. We have suggested a reformulation of the model to stochastic form, so that it can be tested readily with conventional statistical procedures. First approximations for some impacts, such as CO_2 emissions and deforestation, can be obtained immediately with the application of these statistical procedures to available data. We also recognize that key challenges for the model remain, such as the choice of the most appropriate indicators for the model's main variables and limitations on the availability of relevant data as well as quality problems of existing data. We outlined some strategies for meeting these challenges. Our deep intent in this effort has been to prod us on the journey toward a deeper understanding of one of the most challenging intellectual problems of our age: anthropogenic environmental change.

AFTERWORD

Since this paper was published, empirical work has begun to address the issues we raise and there have been some explorations of IPAT in the context of climate change (Rosa and Dietz 1998). A number of researchers have suggested that the relationship between affluence and environmental impact will look like an inverted "U" with environmental impact increasing as affluence increases up to a point where the curve flattens out. Further increases in affluence lead to a reduction of environmental impact. This theory is sometimes called the "environmental Kuznets curve" because Simon Kuznets hypothesized that the trajectory of income inequality in a nation undergoing economic growth will follow this pattern: income inequality will increase with growth up to some level of affluence and as a nation becomes even richer, income inequality will decline. (For a review of this literature see Nordstrom and Vaughan [1999] and the special issue of *Ecological Economics,* vol. 25, #2, 1998). However, Roberts and Grimes (1997) argue that this pattern of decreased impact at high levels of affluence only applies to the richest nations that dominate the world economy. Consistent with these arguments our analysis of the effects of population and affluence on national CO_2 emissions suggests that the turning point for affluence is at very high income levels and that nations vary greatly in the value of the T (technology) variable (Dietz and Rosa 1997).

In a series of papers, Cramer (1997, 1998) has suggested that the composition of population may be a more important driver of environmental impact than population size. In particular, he notes that air pollution generated by automobiles may be more closely related to the number of households in an area than the number of people. In our analysis, we find that there may be a "diseconomy" of scale associated with the largest population sizes, with more environmental impact than one would expect from the largest nations (Dietz and Rosa 1997). In an extensive review of the literature on population growth and deforestation, Palloni (1994) argues that population growth may be an important driver of some kinds of deforestation but not of others.

ENDNOTES

1. This work was supported in part by U.S. National Science Foundation grants SES-9109928 and SES-9311593, by the Northern Virginia Survey Research Laboratory of George Mason University and by John Pierce, Dean of the College of Liberal Arts at Washington State University.

We thank Linda Kalof, William Catton, and Riley Dunlap for their very helpful comments on an earlier draft.

2. The history of research on the link between population and human welfare recently has been given thoughtful review by Keyfitz (1991a,b, 1993). See also Overbeek (1977) and Teitelbaum and Winter (1989).

3. Herodotus further writes that during this period the method of adjustment of the Lydians was to invent a number of games, including dice, and "to engage in games one day entirely so as not to feel any craving for food, and the next day to eat and abstain from games" (*The History,* Book I:22). Eventually, because scarcities continued and conditions worsened, the King decreed that half the population should emigrate to Smyrna, the choice of movers and stayers determined by lot. Thus Herodotus tells us something about not only population and resources, but also about the role of risk and uncertainty in human affairs.

4. Lucius Annaeus Seneca, c. 4 B.C.–65 A.D., the second son of the Roman educator and author, Seneca the Elder, is considered the most brilliant thinker and writer of his time, the age of Nero.

5. The contributions of Malthus, while usually acknowledged to be part of the classical tradition, have been overshadowed by Adam Smith, David Ricardo, John Stuart Mill, and others. John Maynard Keynes, an ardent admirer of Malthus, sought to correct this historical neglect. Calling him "the first of the Cambridge economists" (1933:144), Keynes lavished unabashed praise on Malthus: "If only Malthus, instead of Ricardo, had been the parent stem from which nineteenth-century economics proceeded, what a much wiser and richer place the world would be today" (1933:120).

6. Wallace's independent discovery of evolution through natural selection was also inspired by a reading of Malthus. Note that the phrase "survival of the fittest" was developed by the sociologist Herbert Spencer, rather than by either Darwin or Wallace. In some sense, Spencer was one of the last scholars who had major influence within a discipline who could also be considered

interdisciplinary or transdisciplinary. Unfortunately, one of his legacies is "Social Darwinism," recently revisited as a "vulgar sociobiology." This crude caricature of Darwin's thought has given a bad name to the evolutionary thinking that is essential to form adequate links between the social and biological sciences (Burns and Dietz 1992; Dietz et al. 1990; Rosa 1979)

7. As we will see later in the discussion, the lack of motivation may stem from the typical use of the model as an accounting equation, which is true by definition, thereby making statistical testing unnecessary.

8. See, for example, King (1987), U.S. National Research Council (1986), Schultz (1987), United Nations (1973), and World Bank (1984).

9. For modifications and elaborations of the POET framework, see Dunlap et al. (1994).

10. More recent studies that reach the same general conclusion include Ahlburg (1987), Binswanger and Pingali (1985), Birdsall (1988), Hayami and Ruttan (1987a, b), Kelley (1988), King (1987), Mason (1987), McNicoll (1984), Pingali and Binswanger (1987), Ridker (1979), and Srinivasan (1987, 1988). While these studies differ in the sectors of the economy modelled, the nations or regions considered and the methods employed, the findings are remarkably robust and remain roughly consistent with the general findings of Coale and Hoover (1958).

11. Closely related to this argument is the early work of Geertz (1963) on "agricultural involution" and the "induced innovation" analysis of Ruttan and his collaborators (Binswanger and Ruttan 1978; Hayami and Ruttan 1985a, b; see also the classic treatment by Hicks (1932) and its revival by Fellner (1961) and Kennedy (1964)). It is interesting to note that Simon (1981) seems unaware of Geertz's detailed analysis of agricultural development in Java and the problems associated with it. He does not cite any of the key work on induced innovation even though that work provides a rigorous model for some of the effects he posits.

12. Again, this literature is vast, incorporating much of resource economics and of research on common property resources. The classic reference on resource economics is Barnett and

Morse (1963). More recent reviews include Dasgupta and Heal (1979), MacKellar and Vining (1987), Repetto (1986), Ridker (1979), and Slade (1987). Common property issues are reviewed in Ostrom (1990).

13. Normative issues enter into discussions of the environment in subtle ways. The term degradation implies a change from a more desirable to a less desirable state. In economic analysis, the desirability of a state of the environment must be considered in terms of the ability of that state to produce utility through its use in production processes, its existence value, or some other function related to human welfare. The environmental changes of current political concern, such as climate change, ozone depletion, loss of biodiversity, accumulation of toxics, etc. are usually discussed in terms of their adverse effects on human welfare. But there is a philosophical position that argues some states of the environment have intrinsic worth independent of humans (e.g., Devall and Sessions 1985; see also Stern et al. 1993; Dietz 1992). The issue is further complicated by differences in preferences. For example, some may consider an undisturbed wilderness the ideal recreational site, others may prefer walkways or roads to make access more convenient.

In this discussion we will avoid these thorny issues by focusing on environmental changes that are part of the global environmental change complex: greenhouse climate change, ozone depletion, species loss, deforestation, desertification, dispersal of toxics. It may be that the actual effects on human welfare of some of these changes are minimal (e.g., Nordhaus, 1992) but all are considered at least potential threats to both the "state of nature" and human welfare.

14. The literature on "optimal pollution" follows this logic. The classic works that underpin this approach are Pigou (1920) and Coase (1960). See Baumol (1988) or Randall (1987) for a more recent discussion. Note that although Coase (1960) provides an argument about how efficient levels of externalities like pollution *might* be achieved, he offers no proof that these mechanisms actually operate.

15. Of course, those who argue that rapid population growth is very harmful emphasize the problem of tipping points and non-linearities. Current data and models may be derived from experience with a linear part of a relationship that is actually non-linear. If the biosphere or specific ecosystems are approaching asymptotes or discontinuities, key relationships embedded in existing models will change abruptly. Under such conditions existing models may not be an adequate guide to the future.

16. For a recent review of such models, see Toth, Hizsnyik, and Clark (1989).

17. The energy efficiency (**PA/I=1/T** the affluence per unit environmental impact) or energy intensity (**T=I/(P*A)**, impact per unit affluence) of nation states follow directly from the formula.

18. In particular, Mazur differentiates the following identity:

$$dE=edP+Pde,$$

where **E** equals total energy consumption, **e** is per capita energy consumption, and **P** equals total population.

19. Between 1950 and 1987 the percent increase is 484% (Commoner 1992:85–86).

20. Doubtless some scholars will be cautious about using such a simplified model to capture the myriad factors—with complex linkages and feedbacks—underlying anthropogenic environmental change. On the one hand, we are sympathetic to and share that caution. On the other hand, we note that many scientific endeavors begin with first approximations based upon crude heuristics and, further, that many scientists accept Ockam's razor as a useful convention for proceeding with their work.

Models are, after all, crude approximations to reality. They are abstractions of the real world that are stated in sufficient detail to be realistic, but have omitted the inessential detail that would complicate them needlessly as vehicles for focusing our attention in a disciplined way. Stated in analytic form, such as mathematics, they permit a systematic examination of the relationships postulated by the model.

Expectations about models conjure the time-worn image of blind scholars feeling around an elephant. The ideal model would simultaneously maximize generality, realism, and precision. Unfortunately, it is literally impossible for a model to simultaneously maximize all three at once. This unavoidable fact prompted Levins (1966) to suggest the following set of compromises: (1) sacrifice generality to realism and precision; (2) sacrifice realism to generality and precision; or (3) sacrifice precision to realism and generality. Our argument for the utility of the **IPAT** model in understanding anthropogenic environmental change is one that begins with Levin's compromise (2), then hopes to elaborate our understanding by modifying the model to accommodate compromises (1) and (3).

21. If **T** is derived as **I/PA** as in the accounting model and entered into the regression, the estimated values for **a, b, c, d,** and **e** will equal 1 and the R^2 value will also equal 1. This indicates the limit of the accounting model. It assumes each driving force has equal impact in the sense that the **impact** elasticity (the percentage change in **I** accompanying a percentage change in **P, A,** or **T**) of the driving forces are assumed equal. For example, a 1% change in population is assumed to produce a 1% change in impact.

22. While global level time series analyses may seem the ideal method, the data quality, and methodological problems are formidable. Data are limited, most of the essential time series data are highly collinear, and for some variables (for example, energy intensity of the world economy) year to year fluctuations are more likely a result of measurement error than real structural change. In addition, lack of attention to problems of functional form and cointegration can lead to spurious inferences (Engle and Granger 1991). Global analysis aggregates across contexts and thus may miss important influences of institutions, culture, and the political economy that are context specific. While the stochastic model does not make these problems disappear, its engagement with an existing methodological literature makes us aware of pitfalls that might otherwise trap unwary researchers.

23. The term "Netherlands effect" derives from the fact that the environmental impacts for nations such as Holland appear to be low for their

level of population and affluence. This is because international trade places the impacts of some Dutch consumption elsewhere (e.g., deforestation to produce wood does not take place within Dutch borders; pesticide use on food crops takes place in food exporting nations rather than in Holland, etc.).

24. It appears that in the 21st century migration will continue to be a very important determinant of population change. Migration can lead to very rapid transformations of population size, distributions, and structure. Thus migration streams may have a critical effect on the environment. And in turn, some migration is certainly driven by environmental conditions; indeed, migration may be the most common human response to adverse environmental change.

25. The original logic of the **IPAT** model uses the term "affluence" as a convenient abbreviation for consumption patterns and some measure of national income as the indicator of affluence. It is clearly consumption patterns and the associated forms of production that drive environmental impact. Here we are suggesting two ways of reconceptualizing **A.** One is to dissaggregate the "affluence/consumption" variable in ways that reflect actual consumption and production practices. Another is to consider the link between environmental impact and quality of life.

26. This literature has its origins in Nordhaus and Tobin (1973), Nordhaus (1977), and Zolotas (1981). Recent efforts include Daly and Cobb (1990: 401–455) and Repetto et al. (1989).

27. It has sometimes been suggested that life expectancy is an inappropriate quality of life measure because it incorporates the later years of life. Current life extension technologies, while adding years do not always add quality to human existence. While this argument is well founded with regard to medical ethics, the marginal additions to life span afforded by heroic technologies have almost no effect on either cross-section or time series comparisons of life expectancy. Indeed, since infant mortality is a component of life expectancy at birth, two of the three variables that compose the widely used PQLI measure are in fact components of life expectancy.

28. Ehrlich and Holdren (1970, 1971; Holdren and Ehrlich 1974) are aware of the complexity of **T**, but little has been done to elucidate the complexity of this part of the model. We have little social theory to suggest how to specify and measure **T**.

REFERENCES

Ahlberg, Dennis A. 1987. "The Impact of Population Growth on Economic Growth in Developing Nations: The Evidence from Macroeconomic-Demographic Models." Pp. 479–522 in *Population Growth and Economic Development: Issues and Evidence.* Madison: University of Wisconsin Press.

Allen, Julia C. and Douglas F. Barnes. 1985. "The Causes of Deforestation in Developing Countries." *Annals of the Association of American Geographers* 75:163–184.

Amin, Samir. 1974. *Accumulation on a World Scale.* New York: Monthly Review Press.

———. 1976. *Unequal Development.* New York: Monthly Review Press.

———. 1977. *Imperialism and Unequal Development.* New York: Monthly Review Press.

Appelbaum, Richard P. 1978. *Size, Growth and U.S. Cities.* New York: Praeger.

Appelbaum, Richard P., Jennifer Bigelow, Henry P. Kramer, Harvey Molotch, and Paul M. Relis. 1976. *The Effects of Urban Growth: A Population Impact Analysis.* New York: Praeger.

Barkin, David. 1991. "State Control of the Environment: Politics and Degradation in Mexico." *Capitalism, Nature, Socialism* 2:86–108.

Barnett, Harold and C. Morse. 1963. *Scarcity and Growth: The Economics of Natural Resource Availability.* Baltimore, MD: Johns Hopkins University Press.

Barney, Gerald O. 1980. *Global 2000: The Report to the President. Entering the 21st Century.* Washington, D.C.: U.S. Government Printing Office.

Baumol, William J. 1988. *The Theory of Environmental Policy.* (Second Edition.) Cambridge, UK: Cambridge University Press.

Bilsborrow, Richard E. 1992. "Population Growth, Internal Migration and Environmental Degradation in Rural Areas of Developing Countries." *European Journal of Population* 8:125–148.

Bilsborrow, Richard E. and Martha Geores. 1991. "Population, Land Use and the Environment in Developing Countries: What Can We Learn from Cross-National Data?" Paper presented at the U.S. National Research Council Workshop on Population Change and Land Use in Developing Countries, Washington, D.C., 5–6 December 1991.

Binswanger, Hans P. and Prabhu Pingali. 1985. "Population Growth and Technological Change in Agriculture." Pp. 62–89 in *Proceedings of the Fifth Agricultural Sector Symposium: Population and Food.* Washington, D.C.: World Bank.

Binswanger, Hans P. and Vernon W. Ruttan. 1978. *Induced Innovation: Technology, Institutions and Development.* Baltimore, MD: Johns Hopkins University Press.

Bollen, Kenneth A. 1989. *Structural Equation Models with Latent Variables.* New York: John Wiley and Sons.

Bollen, Kenneth A., Barbara Entwisle, and Arthur S. Alderson. 1993. "Macrocomparative Research Methods." *Annual Review of Sociology* 19:321–351.

Bongaarts, Jon. 1992. "Population Growth and Global Warming." *Population and Development Review* 18:299–319.

Boserup, Ester. 1965. *The Conditions of Agricultural Growth.* Chicago: Aldine.

———. 1980. *Population and Technological Change: A Study of Long-Term Trends.* Chicago: University of Chicago Press.

Bunker, Stephen G. 1984. "Modes of Extraction, Unequal Exchange and the Progressive Underdevelopment of an Extreme Periphery: The Brazilian Amazon, 1600–1980." *American Journal of Sociology* 89:1017–1064.

———. 1985. *Underdeveloping the Amazon: Extraction, Unequal Exchange and the Failure of the Modern State.* Urbana: University of Illinois Press.

Burns, Tom R. and Thomas Dietz. 1992. "Cultural Evolution: Social Rule Systems, Selec-

tion and Human Agency." *International Sociology* 7:259–283.

Catton, William R., Jr. 1982. *Overshoot: The Ecological Basis of Revolutionary Change.* Urbana: University of Illinois Press.

Coale, Ansley J. and Edgar M. Hoover. 1958. *Population Growth and Economic Development in Low-Income Countries.* Princeton, NJ: Princeton University Press.

Coase, Ronald. 1960. "The Problem of Social Costs." *Journal of Law and Economics* 3:1–44.

Commoner, Barry. 1972. "The Environmental Cost of Economic Growth." Pp. 339–63 in *Population, Resources and the Environment.* Washington, D.C.: U.S. Government Printing Office.

———. 1992. *Making Peace with the Planet.* New York: The New Press.

Congleton, Roger D. 1990. *Political Institutions and Pollution Control.* Fairfax, VA: Center for the Study of Public Choice, George Mason University.

Covello, Vincent and R. Scott Frey. 1990. "Technology-Based Environmental Health Risks in Developing Nations." *Technological Forecasting and Social Change* 37:159–179.

Cramer, James C. 1997. "A Demographic Perspective on Air Quality: Conceptual Issues Surrounding Environmental Impacts of Population Growth." *Human Ecology Review* 3:191–196.

———. 1998. "Population Growth and Air Quality in California." *Demography* 35:45–56.

Daily, Gretchen C. and Paul R. Ehrlich. 1992. "Population, Sustainability and Earth's Carrying Capacity." *BioScience* 42:761–771.

Daly, Herman E. and John B. Cobb Jr. 1989. *For the Common Good: Redirecting the Economy Toward Community, the Environment and a Sustainable Future.* Boston: Beacon Press.

Darwin, Charles. 1958[1859]. *The Origin of Species.* New York: New American Library.

Dasgupta, P. S. and G. M. Heal. 1979. *Economic Theory and Exhaustible Resources.* Cambridge, England: Cambridge University Press.

Day, Alice Taylor and Lincoln H. Day. 1973. "Cross-National Comparisons of Population Density." *Science* 181:1016–1023.

Devall, Bill and George Sessions. 1985. *Deep Ecology: Living as if Nature Mattered*. Salt Lake City, UT: Gibbs M. Smith.

Dietz, Thomas. 1992. "The Challenge of Global Environmental Change for Human Ecology." Pp. 30–45 in *Human Responsibility and Global Change*, edited by Lars O. Hansson and Britta Jugen. Göteborg, Sweden: University of Göteborg.

Dietz, Thomas, Tom R. Burns, and Frederick H. Buttel. 1990. "Evolutionary Theory in Sociology: An Examination of Current Thinking." *Sociological Forum* 5:155–171.

Dietz, Thomas and Linda Kalof. 1992. "Environmentalism among Nation-States." *Social Indicators Research* 26:353–366.

Dietz, Thomas, Linda Kalof, and R. Scott Frey. 1991. "On the Utility of Robust and Resampling Procedures." *Rural Sociology* 56:461–474.

Dietz, Thomas and Eugene A. Rosa. 1997. "Effects of Population and Affluence on CO_2 Emissions." *Proceedings of the National Academy of Sciences, USA* 94:175–179.

Duncan, Otis Dudley. 1951. "Optimum Size of Cities." In *Readings in Urban Sociology*. Glencoe, IL: Free Press.

———. 1964. "From Social System to Ecosystem." *Sociological Inquiry* 31:140–149.

Dunlap, Riley E., George H. Gallup, Jr., and Alec M. Gallup. 1993. "Of Global Concern: Results of the Health of the Planet Survey. *Environment* 35(9), 7–15, 33–39.

Dunlap, Riley E., Loren A. Lutzenhiser, and Eugene A. Rosa. 1994. "Understanding Environmental Problems: An Environmental Sociology Perspective." Chapter 2 in *Socio-Economic Approaches to the Environment*, edited by Beat Burgenmeier. Armonk, NY: M. E. Sharpe.

Durkheim, Emile. 1964[1893]. *The Division of Labor in Society*. New York: Free Press.

Ehrlich, Paul R. 1968. *The Population Bomb*. New York: Ballantine.

Ehrlich, Paul R. and Ann H. Ehrlich. 1990. *The Population Explosion*. New York: Simon and Schuster.

Ehrlich, Paul R. and John P. Holdren. 1971. "Impact of Population Growth." *Science* 171: 1212–1217.

———. 1972. "Impact of Population Growth." Pp. 365–77 in *Population, Resources and the Environment*. Washington, D.C.: U.S. Government Printing Office.

Engle, R. F. and C. W. J. Granger, editors. 1991. *Long-Run Economic Relationships: Readings in Cointegration*. Oxford: Oxford University Press.

Evans, Peter. 1979. *Dependent Development: The Alliance of State, Local and Multinational Capital in Brazil*. Princeton, NJ: Princeton University Press.

Fellner, W. 1961. "Two Propositions on the Theory of Induced Innovations." *Economic Journal* 6:305–308.

Frey, R. Scott. 1998. "The Hazardous Waste Stream in the World-System." Pp. 84–103 in *Space and Transport in the World-System*, edited by Paul S. Ciccantell and Stephen G. Bunker. Westport, CT: Greenwood Press.

Geertz, Clifford. 1963. *Agricultural Involution: The Processes of Ecological Change in Indonesia*. Berkeley: University of California Press.

Green, Cynthia P. 1992. "The Environment and Population Growth: Decade for Action." *Population Reports* 10:1–31.

Harrison, Paul. 1992–1993. *The Third Revolution: Population, Environment and a Sustainable World*. London: Penguin Books.

———. 1994. "Sex and the Single Planet." *Human Ecology Review* 1(2):265–276

Hayami, Yujiro and Vernon W. Ruttan. 1987a. *Agricultural Development: An International Perspective*. (Revised Edition.) Baltimore, MD: Johns Hopkins University Press.

———. 1987b. "Population Growth and Agricultural Productivity." Pp. 57–101 in *Population Growth and Economic Development: Issues and Evidence*. Madison: University of Wisconsin Press.

Hecht, Susanna B. 1985. "Environment, Development and Politics: Capital Accumulation and the Livestock Sector in Eastern Amazonia." *World Development* 13:663–684.

Herodotus. 1952[464–447 B.C.] *The History*. Pp. 1–341 in *Great Books of the Western World*, Vol. 6, edited by Robert Maynard. Chicago: Encyclopedia Britannica.

Herzog, H. W., Jr. and Ronald G. Ridker. 1972. "The Model." Pp. 301–11 in *Population, Resources and the Environment*. Washington, D.C.: U.S. Government Printing Office.

Hicks, J. R. 1932. *The Theory of Wages*. London: Macmillan and Company.

Hoch, Irving. 1972. "Urban Scale and Environmental Quality." Pp. 231–284 in *Population, Resources and the Environment*. Washington, D.C.: U.S. Government Printing Office.

Holdren, John. 1991. "Population and the Energy Problem." *Population and Environment* 12:231–255.

Holdren, John P. and Paul R. Ehrlich. 1974. "Human Population and the Global Environment." *American Scientist* 62:282–292.

Inglehart, Ronald. 1990. *Culture Shift in Advanced Industrial Society*. Princeton, NJ: Princeton University Press.

Jackman, Robert W. 1985. "Cross-National Statistical Research and the Study of Comparative Policy." *American Journal of Political Science* 29:161–182.

Johnson, D. Gale and Ronald D. Lee, editors. 1987. *Population Growth and Economic Development: Issues and Evidence*. Madison: University of Wisconsin Press.

Jones, Robert Emmet and Riley E. Dunlap. 1992. "The Social Bases of Environmental Concern: Have They Changed Over Time?" *Rural Sociology* 57:28–47.

Judge, George G., William E. Griffiths, R. Carter Hall, and Tsoung-Chao Lee. 1980. *The Theory and Practice of Econometrics*. New York: John Wiley and Sons.

Kelley, Allen C. 1988. "Economic Consequences of Population Change in the Third World." *Journal of Economic Literature* 26:685–728.

Kennedy, C. 1964 "Induced Bias in Innovation and the Theory of Distribution." *Economic Journal* 74:541–547.

Keyfitz, Nathan. 1991a. "Population and Development within the Ecosphere: One View of the Literature." *Population Index* 57:5–22.

———. 1991b. "Toward a Theory of Population-Development Interaction." Pp. 295–314 in *Resources, Environment and Population: Present Knowledge, Future Options*, edited by Kingsley Davis and Mikhall Berstan. New York: Oxford University Press.

———. 1993. "Population and Sustainable Development: Distinguishing Fact and Preference Concerning the Future Human Population and Environment." *Population and Environment* 14:441–462.

Keynes, John Maynard. 1933. *Essays in Biography*. London: Macmillan.

King, Elizabeth M. 1987. "The Effect of Family Size on Family Welfare: What Do We Know?" Pp. 373–412 in *Population Growth and Economic Development: Issues and Evidence*. Madison: University of Wisconsin Press.

Kolsrud, Gretchen and Barbara Boyle Torrey. 1992. "The Importance of Population Growth in Future Commercial Energy Consumption." pp. 127–141 in *Global Climate Change: Linking Energy, Environment, Economy, and Equity*, edited by James C. White. New York: Plenum.

Lenski, Gerhard. 1986. "Trajectories of Development: A Further Test." *Social Forces* 65:794–795.

Lenski, Gerhard and Patrick D. Nolan. 1984. "Trajectories of Development: A Test of Ecological Evolutionary Theory." *Social Forces* 63:1–23.

Levins, Richard. 1966. "The Strategy of Model Building in Population Biology." *American Scientist* 54:421–431.

London, Bruce and Bruce A. Williams. 1988. "Multinational Corporate Penetration, Protest and Basic Needs in Non-Core Nations: A Cross-National Analysis." *Social Forces* 66:747–773.

MacKellar, F. Landis and Daniel R. Vining, Jr. 1987. "Natural Resource Scarcity: A Global View." Pp. 259–329 in *Population Growth and Economic Development: Issues and Evidence*. Madison: University of Wisconsin Press.

Malthus, Thomas R. 1960[1798]. *On Population*. New York: Modern Library.

Mason, Andrew. 1987. "National Savings Rates and Population Growth: A New Model and New Evidence." Pp. 373–412 in *Population Growth and Economic Development: Issues and Evidence*. Madison: University of Wisconsin Press.

Mazur, Allan. 1994. "How Does Population Growth Contribute to Rising Energy Consumption in America?" *Population and Environment* 15:371–378.

Mazur, Allan and Eugene A. Rosa. 1974. "Energy and Life-Style: Cross-National Comparisons of Energy Consumption and Quality of Life Indicators." *Science* 186:607–610.

McNicoll, Geoffrey. 1984. "Consequences of Rapid Population Growth: An Overview and Assessment." *Population and Development Review* 10:177–240.

Meadows, Donella H., Dennis L. Meadows, Jorgen Randers, and William I. I. Behrens. 1972. *The Limits to Growth.* New York: Potomac Associates.

Mesorvic, M. and E. Pestel. 1974. *Mankind at the Turning Point.* New York: E. P. Dutton.

Morris, Morris David. 1979. *Measuring the Condition of the World's Poor: The Physical Quality of Life Index.* New York: Pergamon.

Nolan, Patrick D. and Gerhard Lenski. 1985. "Technoeconomic Heritage, Patterns of Development and the Advantage of Backwardness." *Social Forces* 64:341–358.

Nordhaus, William. 1977. "Metering Economic Growth." Pp. in *Prospects for Growth,* edited by Kenneth D. Wilson. New York: Basic Books.

———. 1992. "An Optimal Transition Path for Controlling Greenhouse Gases." *Science* 258:1315–1319.

Nordhaus, William and James Tobin. 1973. "Is Growth Obsolete?." Pp. 509–532 in *The Measurement of Economic and Social Performance.* New York: National Bureau of Economic Research.

Nordstrom, Hakan and Scott Vaughn. 1999. *Trade and Environment.* Geneva, Switzerland: World Trade Organization. (http://www.wto.org/wto/new/press140.htm)

Nusbaum, Martha and Amartya Sen. 1993. *The Quality of Life.* Oxford, England: Oxford University Press.

O'Connor, James. 1988. "Capitalism, Nature, Socialism: A Theoretical Introduction." *Capitalism, Nature, Socialism* 1:11–38.

———. 1989. "Political Economy of Ecology of Socialism and Capitalism." *Capitalism, Nature, Socialism* 3:93–106.

Olsen, Marvin E. 1992. "The Energy Consumption Turnaround and Socioeconomic Well-Being in Industrial Societies in the 1980s." Pp. 197–234 in *Advances in Human Ecology,* edited by Lee Freese. Greenwich, CT: JAI Press.

Ostrom, Elinor. 1990. *Governing the Commons: The Evolution of Institutions for Collective Action.* Cambridge, England: Cambridge University Press.

Overbeek, Johannes, editor. 1977. *The Evolution of Population Theory.* Westport, CT: Greenwood Press.

Palloni, Alberto. 1994. "The Relation between Population and Deforestation: Methods for Drawing Causal Inferences from Macro and Micro Studies." Pp. 125–165 in *Population and Environment: Rethinking the Debate,* edited by Arizpe Lourdes, M. Priscilla Stone, and David C Major. Boulder, CO: Westview.

Peierls, Benjamin L., Nina F. Caraco, Michael L. Pace, and Jonathon Cole. 1991. "Human Influence On River Nitrogen." *Nature* 350:386–387.

Pigou, A. C. 1920. *The Economics of Welfare.* London: Macmillan.

Pimentel, David. 1992. *World Soil Erosion and Conservation.* Cambridge, England: Cambridge University Press.

Pimentel, David and C. W. Hall, editors. 1989. *Food and Natural Resources.* San Diego, CA: Academic Press.

Pingali, Prabhu L. and Hans l Binswanger. 1987. "Population Density and Agricultural Intensification: A Study of the Evolution of Technologies in Tropical Agriculture." Pp. 27–56 in *Population Growth and Economic Development: Issues and Evidence.* Madison: University of Wisconsin Press.

Randall, Alan. 1987. *Resource Economics: An Economic Approach to Natural Resources and Economic Policy.* New York: John Wiley and Sons.

Repetto, Robert. 1986. *World Enough and Time: Successful Strategies for Resource Management.* New Haven, CT: Yale University Press.

Repetto, Robert, William Magrath, Michael Wells, and Christine Beer. 1989. *Wasting Assets: Natural Resources in the National Income Accounts.* Washington, D.C.: World Resources Institute.

Ricardo, David 1891[1817]. *The Principles of Political Economy and Taxation.* London: G. Bell and Sons.

Ridker, Ronald G., editor. 1972. *Population, Resources and the Environment.* Washington, D.C.: U.S. Government Printing Office.

———. 1979. "Resource and Environmental Consequences of Population and Economic Growth." Pp. 99–123 in *World Population and Development: Challenges and Prospects.* Syracuse, NY: Syracuse University Press.

———. 1992. "Population Issues." *Resources* (Winter):11–14.

Ridker, Ronald G. and E. W. Cecelski. 1979. "Resources, Environment and Population: The Nature of Future Limits." *Population Bulletin* 34(3):1–43.

Roberts, J. Timmons and Peter E. Grimes. 1997. "Carbon Intensity and Economic Development 1962–1971: A Brief Exploration of the Environmental Kuznets Curve." *World Development* 25:191–198.

Rosa, Eugene A. 1979. "Sociobiology, Biosociology, or Vulgar Biologizing." *Sociological Symposium* 27:28–49.

———. 1997. "Cross National Trends in Fossil Fuel Consumption, Societal Well-Being and Carbon Releases." Pp. 100–109 in *Environmentally Significant Consumption: Research Directions,* edited by Paul C. Stern, Thomas Dietz, Vernon W. Ruttan, Robert H. Socolow, and James L. Sweeney. Washington, D.C.: National Academy Press.

Rosa, Eugene A., Kenneth M. Keating, and Clifford Staples. 1980. "Energy, Economic Growth and Quality of Life: A Cross-National Trend Analysis." Pp. 258–264 in *Proceedings of the International Congress on Applied Systems Analysis Research and Cybernetics, Vol. I,* edited by G. E. Lasker. New York: Pergamon Press.

Rosa, Eugene A. and Thomas Dietz. 1998. "Climate Change and Society: Speculation, Construction and Scientific Investigation." *International Sociology* 13:421–455.

Royal Society of London and U.S. National Academy of Sciences. 1992. *Population Growth, Resource Consumption and a Sustainable World.* Washington, D.C.: U.S. National Academy of Sciences.

Rudel, Thomas K. 1989. "Population, Development and Tropical Deforestation: A Cross-National Study." *Rural Sociology* 54:327–338.

Schnaiberg, Allan. 1980. *The Environment: From Surplus to Scarcity.* New York: Oxford University Press.

Schnaiberg, Allan and Kenneth Alan Gould. 1994. *Environment and Society: The Enduring Conflict.* New York: St. Martin's Press.

Schultz, T. Paul. 1987. "School Expenditures and Enrollments, 1960–1980: The Effects of Income, Prices and Population Growth." Pp. 413–76 in *Population Growth and Economic Development: Issues and Evidence.* Madison: University of Wisconsin Press.

Scotvsky, Tibor. 1976. *The Joyless Economy.* New York: Oxford University Press.

Sen, Amartya. 1993. "The Economics of Life and Death." *Scientific American* 208(5):40–47.

Seneca, Lucius Annaeus. 1971[62 A.D.]. *Naturales Questiones.* In *The Loeb Classic Library, Vol. VII,* edited by E. W. Warrington. Cambridge, MA: Harvard University Press.

Simon, Julian L. 1981. *The Ultimate Resource.* Princeton, NJ: Princeton University Press.

Singer, S. Fred, editor. 1972. *Is There an Optimum Level of Population?* New York: McGraw-Hill.

Slade, Margaret. 1987. "Natural Resources, Population Growth, and Economic Well-Being." Pp. 331–369 in *Population Growth and Economic Development: Issues and Evidence.* Madison: University of Wisconsin Press.

Srinivasan, T. N. 1987. "Population and Food." Pp. 3–26 in *Population Growth and Economic Development: Issues and Evidence.* Madison: University of Wisconsin Press.

———. 1988. "Population Growth and Economic Development." *Journal of Policy Modeling* 10:1.

Stern, Paul C. 1993. "A Second Environmental Science: Human-Environment Interactions." *Science* 260:1897–1899.

Stern, Paul C., Thomas Dietz, and Linda Kalof. 1993. "Value Orientations, Gender and Environmental Concern." *Environment and Behavior* 25:322–348.

Stern, Paul C., Oran R. Young, and Daniel Druckman, editors. 1992. *Global Environmental Change: Understanding the Human*

Dimensions. Washington, D.C.: National Academy Press.

Stokes, Randall G. and Andy B. Anderson. 1990. "Disarticulation and Human Welfare in Less Developed Countries." *American Sociological Review* 55:63–74.

Teitelbaum, Michael S. and Jay M. Winter, editors. 1989. *Population and Resources in Western Intellectual Tradition.* Cambridge, England: Cambridge University Press.

Toth, Ferenc L., Eva Hizsnyik, and William C. Clark, editors. 1989. *Scenarios of Socioeconomic Development for Studies of Global Environmental Change: A Critical Review.* Laxenburg, Austria: International Institute for Applied Systems Analysis.

Tuan, Yuan-Fu. 1968. "Discrepancies between Environmental Attitudes and Behavior: Examples from Europe and China." *The Canadian Geographer* 12:176–191.

United Nations. 1973. *Determinants and Consequences of Population Trends.* New York: United Nations.

U.S. Commission on Population Growth and the American Future. 1972. *Population and the American Future.* New York: Signet.

U.S. National Academy of Sciences. 1971. *Rapid Population Growth: Consequences and Policy Implications.* Baltimore, MD: Johns Hopkins University Press.

U.S. National Research Council. 1986. *Population Growth and Economic Development: Policy Questions.* Washington, D.C.: National Academy Press.

Vallette, Jim and Heather Spalding, editors. *The International Trade in Wastes.* Washington, D.C.: Greenpeace U.S.A.

Weeks, John R. 1986. *Population: An Introduction to Concepts and Issues.* Belmont, CA: Wadsworth.

White, Lynn Jr. 1967. "The Historical Roots of Our Ecological Crisis." *Science* 155:1203–1207.

World Bank. 1984. *World Development Report.* Washington, D.C.: World Bank.

World Resources Institute. 1992. *World Resources, 1992–93.* New York: Oxford University Press.

Zolotas, Xenophon. 1981. *Economic Growth and Declining Social Welfare.* New York: New York University Press.

9.   Uneven and Combined Development and Ecological Crisis: A Theoretical Introduction*

No one has systematically theorized the ecological and human effects of the combined and uneven development of capitalism. However, based on new studies and a growing knowledge of ecological conditions and capitalist social formations in various parts of the globe, and guided by the general theory of uneven and combined development, we can hazard some provisional conclusions.** But before turning to this it is necessary to recap briefly and crudely the salient features of both uneven and combined development.

Uneven development is usually defined in political, economic, and sociological terms. Namely as the historically produced, uneven, spatial distribution of industry, banking, commerce, wealth, consumption, labour relations, political configurations and so on. Some writers use the categories 'development' and 'underdevelopment' to describe the polarities between, for example, industrial zones and those supplying raw materials; rich and poor countries; countries with and without developed forms of wage labour and/or liberal democratic institutions. At a more theoretical level, uneven development is the exploitative relationship between town and country (center/periphery; developed/underdeveloped country) as the basis for the reproduction of global capitalism as a whole.[1]

Combined development may be defined as the combination of economic, social and political forms characteristic of 'developed' regions with those found in 'underdeveloped' regions—a combination of new and older forms (where 'older forms' are understood as economic and social forms historically produced at some time in the past). Put simply, combined development means that capital, always seeking to maximise profits, combines advanced technology, industrial organisation and division of labour and so forth, with low-paid, disciplined and sweated labour. In effect, it is the combination of nineteenth century labour conditions and political forms with

*This essay first appeared in *Race and Class* 30, 3 (Jan–Mar 1989), 1–11, and is reprinted here with the permission of the publisher, The Institute of Race Relations.

**I stress at the outset that the present account of the problem is one-sided. This article does not address the ways that capitalism's and imperialism's destruction of natural and human ecologies is a form of self-destruction—that is, has the unintentional effects of raising costs, limiting variability of labour and capital, and so on. Nor does it address the crucial problem of social and political resistance to ecological degradation, which is almost everywhere associated with poverty, social movements and social action, and national liberation struggles, which themselves have powerful, independent effects on the costs of capital, flexibility of capital, and so on.

twenty-first-century technology. Combined development puts together the most profitable features of development and underdevelopment in a new unity which maximises profit increases.

The discussion which follows looks at, first, uneven development and the different forms of pollution; second, uneven development and the depletion of resources; third, combined development and pollution and resource depletion; fourth, the way that resources are depleted indirectly as a result of pollution; fifth, and conversely, the way that pollution is an indirect result of depletion of nature. The treatment of the subject here is suggestive, not exhaustive, and tentative, not conclusive.

One thing seems certain, though. The worst human and ecological disasters as a rule occur in the Third World and the 'internal colonies' of the First World. The human victims of ecological degradation are typically the rural poor—the land-poor and landless masses for whom ecological questions are a matter of life and death—and the unemployed and underemployed in the cities, as well as the oppressed minorities and poor in the First World. Examples of the effects of depletion of soils are the mass poverty and starvation in the African Sahel, and the overexploitation of water resources by Israel causing their rapid depletion and salinisation at the expense of the Palestinians and (ultimately) Israel itself. Examples of the effects of pollution on the oppressed of the world are the poisoning of Native American uranium miners; the decimation of farm labourers from Mexico, who are sick and dying from pesticide poisoning; the killing of dozens of people in Mexico City (November 1984) when 80,000 barrels of liquified gas exploded; the killing of thousands in Bhopal, India (December 1984) as a result of leakages of methyl isocyanate

used to make pesticides in Union Carbide's plant in that city (thousands more were made sick; the poison poured out from underground storage tanks; the plant was located in the middle of the slum part of the town; the plant itself was only five years old). Examples of 'natural disasters' which hit the poor and helpless much harder than those better-off materially are the earthquake in Mexico City in 1985 and the tragedy in Colombia, which killed thousands, mostly poor, whom the government left unprotected from the possibility of volcanic eruptions; or again, the flooding of the Mississippi and other rivers, which typically hits poor blacks living along the river edge much harder than the well-to-do who settle on the high ground.

UNEVEN DEVELOPMENT AND POLLUTION

In capitalist economy, 'nature' is the point of departure for production but typically not a point of return. Yet industrial, municipal and household *waste,* and industrial, municipal and household *pollution* are two different concepts. Waste may be potentially harmful, but waste levels may be so small that they may be naturally recycled back into nature without danger to ecological systems or human beings—for example, cigarette smoke out of doors. Or waste may be of a type which makes it easy to recycle back into nature without harmful effects even if it exists in large quantities—for example, stubble from crops.

In either case, the volume of waste (or by-products of industry and consumption) which becomes highly concentrated spatially, sooner or later becomes pollution—in other words, natural recycling cannot occur. Perhaps the separation between town and country that developed in feudal

Europe in the eleventh century was the first major interference with natural recycling since the epoch of ancient slavery. It follows that the greater the uneven development of capital, the greater will be the spatial concentration of industry, households and urban populations, and the more likely it will be that given volumes of waste will be transformed into dangerous pollution. In the USA, the biggest source of air pollution and noise pollution is automobiles in the urban regions; perhaps the biggest source of aesthetic pollution is the strips of urban America; the biggest source of water pollution (excepting agriculture) is municipal sewerage in the big industrial zones, where manufacturing and related activities and also population are heavily concentrated (about 40 per cent of this waste consists of discharge from industry). The highly spatially concentrated electronic industry (for example, Silicon Valley) transforms many waste products into toxic pollution simply because the wastes are geographically concentrated. Another example of the effects of uneven development on pollution can be drawn from the experiences of the chemical and petrochemical industries. According to the Environmental Protection Agency, there are about 6,000 plants in the USA producing dangerous chemicals. Many, if not all, of these plants are concentrated in working-class living districts, especially minority or black working-class areas. Leakages and waste from these plants are spatially concentrated and have proved dangerous to human beings and natural systems (for example, the petrochemical complex in New Jersey flatlands and in Richmond, north San Francisco Bay). The implications are clear: decentralise industry and population and everything else being the same (which in fact it isn't), some dangerous pollution will automatically be transformed into harmless waste.

UNEVEN DEVELOPMENT AND DEPLETION/EXHAUSTION OF RESOURCES

The theory of uneven development and the destruction of nature was first put forth in simple outline by Marx himself. He argued that under capitalism there is inevitably a bigger and bigger division between the city and the countryside—a division of labour between town and country—which disturbs the basic metabolism between human beings and the earth, that is, the return to the soil of the elements consumed by human beings, animals, and so on. He claimed that this division of labour violated natural conditions for lasting soil fertility. History seems to have proved him correct. Uneven development is not only the concentration of industrial production, commerce, population, and so on, in developed zones, but also the concentration of agriculture and raw material extraction in underdeveloped zones in which the 'basic metabolism' between people and nature has also been disturbed.

In most of these zones, there is a highly developed system of agricultural specialisation, or monoculture—that is, concentration on a particular crop or handful of crops for the export market. It is not too much to say that balanced, integrated, industrial structures concentrated in the First World and in the industrial zones of the Third World require or presuppose imbalanced, specialized and fragmented economies in the Third World. At least the historical facts pertaining to nineteenth-century economic development and development in the first half of the twentieth century are consistent with this view, especially with regard to English capitalism.

One effect of uneven development in terms of resource depletion—one effect of the uncontrolled expansion of monoculture—has been to ruin soil conditions. A famous example is the uncontrolled expansion of sugar production in north east Brazil in the sixteenth and seventeenth centuries which ruined the land and pushed the region into deep poverty, from which it has never recovered. A well-known contemporary example is the Sahel in Africa. This forms a large part of the old French West Africa and French Equatorial African territories where the environment has been ruined by a conjuncture of crop specialisation for export, the pushing back of subsistence agriculture by export agriculture to more ecologically fragile lands and less land availability for cattle grazing. This has led to overgrazing and starvation of the cattle. In times of drought, the well-intentioned French government sank wells for the cattle—with the effect that the areas around these wells were destroyed by the concentration of cattle. The result has been the growing fragility of the environment and the economy, and the mass impoverishment of a people who once had a well-integrated and regulated subsistence economy based on exchange between farmers and cattle-raisers. The latter were permitted to graze their cattle on the stubble on the former's farms in return for manure—the main source of fertilizer. There are other raw material export economies, specializing in one or a few crops, which have paid little attention to soil management during export booms—so hungry are the governments to earn foreign exchange—only to pay for this later in declaring productivity and poverty, as has happened in Central America.

A second effect of uneven development is deforestation, the leading contemporary example being the rapid destruction of tropical rain forests and the flora and fauna which rain forests nurture. In the age of imperialism, the nineteenth century, under the aegis of colonialism and of mindless economic expansion, a vast deforestation of the world took place. In the USA, the destruction of forests is well known; they simply disappeared, along with prairies and prairie life (the last real prairie in Texas is now threatened by development) and an abundant wildlife. Deforestation came about for two general reasons, both related to the rapid growth of industry, trade and international capital exports in the eighteenth century. Least important was the direct exploitation of timber resources, such as hardwoods in rain forest zones, for export (there were exceptions, such as Burma's hardwood teak forests, which were so valuable that the British crown put a stop to their uncontrolled commercial exploitation—to this day, they remain protected and high-yielding). The most important reason was the clearing of forest land for grazing and agriculture oriented to exports to the industrial countries. Forest clearing (for example, in the USA and in Burma, where the British cleared lowland forests to make room for a peasant-based export agriculture) was important in relation to supplies of cheap raw materials and foodstuffs for the developed capitalist world. Deforestation, and the droughts, flooding and silting of rivers, etc., which invariably result, were crucial elements in the golden age of capitalism—an age which saw the mass production of commodities and mass drought and floods and starvation. In short, in place of integrated agriculture-silviculture systems, permanent or sustainable yield forestry and a respect for the diversity of life, uneven development and underdevelopment resulted in stripping the world of most of its forest cover. Only in the industrial countries, especially in Europe, did forest management prevent much, if not all, potential damage (the first attempts to reforest the Alps were made in the early nineteenth century).

The third effect of uneven development has been the rapid exploitation of fossil fuels in the underdeveloped and developed countries. The combined effect of imperialism and colonial domination together with the great power of the energy monopolies has meant that energy resources have been exploited much faster than would have been the case in a world in which nature was a point of return, not only a point of departure, for material production—in a world, that is, which paid attention to municipal waste as a source of energy, to wind power and solar energy, and so on. Imperialism, the oil monopolies and blind state policies all militated against rational energy policies. In Britain, the equivalent of six million metric tons of coal is dumped into landfills annually (representing about one-half of Britain's industrial demand for energy, excluding energy used in the production of electricity, iron and steel). In the USA, there are only 120 refuse energy recovery plants operating or in the planning stage. Ninety-five per cent of municipal wastes goes into landfills—about 150 million tons yearly, or about four pounds per person per day of solid wastes. The energy equivalent is about 56 million tons of coal or 225 million barrels of oil.

Japan and, to a lesser degree, western Europe are more careful. In Japan, municipal wastes going to landfill declined from 42 per cent of total refuse in 1976 to 32 per cent in 1981. Energy and land costs, hence costs of capital, are so high in Japan that conservation is essential; in this way, some of the effects of uneven development on the depletion of energy supplies are mitigated. Thus the effect of the exponential growth of energy demand during the past 100 years (coal has been mined for about 800 years; 50 per cent of all coal produced in history was produced between 1940 and 1970) on fossil fuel depletion/exhaustion has been partly offset by a combination of capitalist spatial concentration and physical spatial limits and state planning.

The ecological consequences of uneven development have been great not only as a result of soil degradation and loss, deforestation, drought and aridisation, and mineral depletion, but also because of the effects on raw material zones of the out-migration of labour as people seek work in the industrial zones. In the farmlands, hills and mountains in regions where industrial capital is concentrated, typically land is neglected; labour shortages prevent traditional land management; there is little money for good crop practices; and there is extreme poverty. A good example is north Portugal where male workers migrate to industrial Europe or the Lisbon area in search of jobs; another example is the hilly and mountain areas around Lombardy in Italy, which are turning into deserts.

A more complex model of uneven development and the degradation of nature could be applied to countries or regions which specialize in both agricultural and mineral production for export and in which pollution from tailings or waste or smoke from mining facilities results in agricultural degradation and soil depletion. The Falconbridge Corporation of Canada, for example, owns nickel mines in the Bonao district of the Dominican Republic and local farmers claim that smoke from the mines has adverse effects on soils and crop yields. Conversely, floods and droughts from deforestation (that is, resource depletion) may have the effect of increasing forms of pollution.

In the raw material zones, the situation in many regions has been summarised by an African ecologist, Calestous Juma, this way: (1) The rapid growth of Third World export agriculture pushes subsistence farming into marginal, more fragile lands. The 'worst case' is Haiti, where subsistence peasants are crowded on barren mountain slopes, while agribusiness owns the best valley lands. Export agriculture concentrates land in the hands of agribusiness. (2) The worsening terms of trade between the Third World and developed countries (that is, the worsening price of raw materials compared with the price of manufactured goods) means that Third World countries have to export more and more to maintain given levels of imports. (3) This means that land under export crops is used more intensively, with more chemical fertilizers and pesticides applied to it, together with a greater use of human labour power. This results in more serious occupational health problems (the chemical poisoning of farm workers is confined mostly to the export sector where the majority of chemicals are used). (4) At the same time, the expansion of export crops requires more deforestation, as well as the transfer of fertile land from the poor to the rich, which forces landless and land-poor peasants into even more marginal areas with fragile ecosystems. (5) Within a particular under-developed country, more and more resources are consumed in urban areas, especially in Africa. (6) Low food prices maintained to keep social order among the urban working classes create constant pressure on farmers producing local food crops to expand production—thus producing more environmental degradation. (7) All of this has produced terrible social changes—for example, the recent resurgence of parasitic infections and chronic diseases of one kind or another. Intensive agricultural systems have accelerated the prevalence of malaria and schistosomiasis. All in all, world capitalism, given uneven development, has been a disaster for tens of millions of people.

Uneven capitalist development, we may conclude then, causes mass pollution in the industrial zones and mass degradation of land, soils, plant life and so on in the raw material zones. It also causes overpopulation, in the sense of overproletarianisation and mass poverty, in the underdeveloped zones which accelerates the degradation of nature (meanwhile, in the developed countries agriculture becomes more energy-intensive). In the context of movements of the world economy as a whole, it may be true that, ecologically speaking, too much is produced during boom periods, while during economic hard times export agriculture and subsistence producers attempt to maintain their incomes by expanding production, hence pushing nature more against its ecological limits.

What has happened, historically, and is happening still, is that the soils and resources of the Third World and raw material zones of the First World were and are, in part, exported through the vehicle of commodity production and exchange and capital accumulation, only to make their appearance in the industrial zones in the form of waste and pollution. It is interesting to speculate about the possibility that industrial pollution is indirectly or directly a form of physical matter which once assumed the form of rich soils, fossil fuels, minerals, forests and so on, in the raw material zones. In this way, soil exhaustion, the depletion of forests, etc., and pollution and mass Third World poverty constitute a single historical process—'one big fact'.

COMBINED DEVELOPMENT: POLLUTION AND RESOURCE DEPLETION

Combined development means that capital seeks to combine social and economic forms in the most profitable way, for example, twenty-first-century First World technology with nineteenth-century Third World labour/political conditions. This occurs in two ways simultaneously: first, there is the migration of landless and land-poor people from the Third World countryside to the city and from the Third World to the First World—also a feature of uneven development. Second, there is the outmigration of industrial and related capital and technology seeking cheap, disciplined labour in countries where governments are only too happy to repress unions, ignore environmental regulations and so forth in the interests of attracting capital. In the USA, the state so far has encouraged combined development through the internationalization of capital. On 12 May 1986, 'a Federal court issued a decision that gives U.S. multinational corporations the freedom to deploy their factories overseas regardless of the hazards they pose to the people there…the judge also sent a clear signal that other multinationals can avoid full responsibility for deleterious global practices by hiding behind subsidiaries, partnerships, and various economic and technological agreements'.[2]

In the first case, cheap labour, illegals and workers without rights are drawn into the older industrial zones; wages tend to fall for everyone; work conditions tend to deteriorate; unions are weakened; occupational health and safety problems grow and environmental conditions tend to get worse. Meanwhile, rural zones are deprived of more of their best young workers, both men and women, leading to more land neglect and ecological damage generally. The Lombardy countryside and north Portugal have already been noted; parts of rural Turkey and Appalachia in the USA can also be mentioned in this connection.

In the second case, the out-migration of capital creates new zones of industry in labour surplus (in other words, cheap labour) regions or capitalises agriculture. First World pollution is 'exported' to the Third World. Dangerous chemicals banned in the First World find their way into industrial and agricultural production in the Third World. Older and more exploitative styles of labour relations are used. Occupational health and safety are neglected. Urbanindustrial zones grow out of control, creating housing, waste disposal, traffic and other problems.

Air pollution levels in Third World cities (such as Ankara, Bangkok, Bombay, Buenos Aires, Cairo, Calcutta, Caracas, Manila, Mexico City, Rio, São Paulo, Seoul and Teheran) are worse than those of large cities in the developed world. Engine exhaust fumes are the worst culprit. The use of wood, dung and charcoal for cooking and heating intensifies the problem. Some cities suffer thermal inversions and a lack of air circulation. In Korea, Seoul, with its eight million people, suffers because of the high sulphur exhausts produced by more than 250,000 cars; from briquette gas from household smokestacks and from the use of bunker-C oil as heating fuel in high-rise buildings and factories. The city allocated only $200,000 for antipollution efforts in 1982.

In cases where, for example, advanced management, methods of finance and technology are combined with more traditional methods of agricultural production in the export sector, combined development deepens uneven development with attendant ecological damage. The 'green revolution' is the best-known example. The capitalization of Third World agriculture under the sign of the green revolution means that farmers 'pick the "best" seeds, plant uniformly over the largest area possible, and dose with chemical fertilizers. The reduction of agriculture to this simple formula leaves crops open to attack and soils highly vulnerable to deterioration…Such reductionist agriculture turns chemical fertilizers and pesticides into necessities to cover for its built-in vulnerabilities.'[3] High-yielding seeds need much water and fertilizer, are less resistant to disease than 'native' seeds and are more sensitive to drought and flood conditions.

In sum, combined development means the export of pollution and the export of dangerous products—both the means of production and the means of consumption. In other words, what is transferred from the First World to the Third World is not just the technology but also the social and environmental costs. If we view the world as an arena of capital accumulation in which both forms of combined development occur within the context of uneven development, we can make the following tentative hypothesis. First, low-wage, unorganized, state-controlled labour in the Third World and weakened labour organizations in the First World are unable to resist environmental destruction and harm to workers' and others' health. Second, the combination of high technology with cheap labour increases 'social costs' and externalities and the rate of exploitation globally, hence the rate of profit, hence the speed at which resources are used and destroyed and also the rate of pollution in all its forms. The result is a self-perpetuating spiral of ecological and human destruction.

CONCLUSION

In any particular country or region of the globe, there is a particular, unique pattern of nature destruction. Hence, to understand the causes of ecological damage in any part of the world, a 'concrete analysis of the concrete situation', is needed, and no generalization, no matter how theoretically sophisticated, will capture the uniqueness of particular situations. Specifically, the effects of the rate and pattern of capitalist accumulation, the size and organization of capitalist firms, the kind of technologies used, as well as the particular form of uneven and combined development that manifests itself in any given region—these and more 'factors' need to be taken into account. Puerto Rico is arguably the classic example of the effects of uneven and combined development together. Here there is soil degradation and loss, deforestation, air and water pollution, massive public health and urban sewerage problems, oil spills, toxic waste dangers, pesticide poisoning, and all the rest. Uneven development has resulted in the destruction of natural resources; combined development has added pollution, toxic waste problems, etc. When uneven and combined development of capital are themselves combined, it would appear that super-pollution in industrial zones may be explained by super-ecodestruction of land and resources in raw material zones, and vice versa. Depletion and exhaustion of resources and pollution depend on one another; they are the necessary result of the same universal process of capital 'valorisation'.

Depletion/exhaustion and pollution are thus not independent issues. The natural wealth of the world is depleted and turned into garbage, often dangerous garbage, through global capital accumulation. And the unwanted by-products—pollution—have the effect of depleting/exhausting resources. Put formally, the greater the profit rate, the greater the accumulation rate, the greater the rate of depletion/exhaustion which indirectly leads to a greater rate of pollution. For example, oil extraction and production depletes fossil fuel resources; oil is turned into petrochemical products which harm people and nature. Uranium mining depletes resources and damages the health of miners and others, meanwhile resulting indirectly in more pollution (for example, through leakages from nuclear plants). Also, theoretically speaking, the greater the profit and accumulation rates, the greater the direct pollution, and the greater the indirect depletion and exhaustion of nature.

ENDNOTES

1. This article is based on a simple development/underdevelopment model. For a more complex, concrete model of dependent development and disarticulated accumulation, see Daniel Faber, 'Dependent development, disarticulated accumulation and ecological crisis in Central America', *Capitalism, Nature, Socialism: a journal of socialist ecology* No. 1, Fall, 1988 (1803 Mission St, Santa Cruz, CA 95060, USA).

2. Larry Everest, 'More Bhopals', in *The Nation* (21 June 1986).

3. Frances Moore Lappe, *Food First: beyond the myth of scarcity* (Boston, 1977), p. 164.

PART II

Human Responses
to Environmental Problems

Chapter 5

Environmental Beliefs and Attitudes

10. The Social Bases of Environmental Concern: Have They Changed Over Time?*

ROBERT EMMET JONES AND RILEY E. DUNLAP

INTRODUCTION

The nature of environmental problems and issues, as well as the larger societal context in which they are viewed, has undergone substantial change over the past two decades (Hays 1987). It therefore seems reasonable to assume not only that the degree of public support for environmental protection may have changed, but that the sectors of society from which this support is drawn may have changed as well. In particular, it has often been hypothesized that environmental concern has diffused throughout the public over the years, resulting in a broadening base of support for environmental protection (e.g., Morrison 1986). An alternative argument is that a broadening of the social bases of environmental concern is contingent upon economic conditions, and that during hard times those who are most economically disadvantaged will disproportionately shift their priorities from environmental quality to economic well-being (Buttel 1975). The economic contingency hypothesis suggests that any observed broadening of the socioeconomic bases of

environmental concern should have slowed, and possibly even reversed, as the nation's economy deteriorated through the late 1970s into the early 1980s. This paper examines the broadening base and economic contingency hypotheses of that period, a timespan encompassing varying economic conditions and sociopolitical climates and characterized by different environmental problems and varying levels of public concern over these problems.

It has been over a decade since Van Liere and Dunlap (1980) first summarized available studies of the general public in an effort to establish empirical generalizations concerning the social bases of environmental concern. In the process of examining the two hypotheses, we will determine whether the key sociopolitical correlates of environmental concern—age, education, and political ideology—have remained stable over time; in other words, whether younger adults, the well-educated and political liberals remain more environmentally concerned than their counterparts, as generally assumed (Stern 1992). In addition, we will also examine whether other variables found to be related to environmental concern in various cross-sectional studies conducted in the 1980s, such as race (Taylor 1989) and gender (Hamilton

*Reprinted from *Rural Sociology* 57 (1992):28–47 by permission granted by the Rural Sociological Society.

1985; Blocker and Eckberg 1989), have become more consistent correlates over time and hold for the general population.

We will first briefly review available evidence on trends in public concern for environmental quality over the past two decades to demonstrate that the National Opinion Research Center data we employ are compatible with other available longitudinal data. Next we will discuss the broadening base and economic contingency hypotheses in detail and briefly review the results of the small number of earlier studies of them. Then, after describing the data used in our analysis, we will report the results of our examination of the sociopolitical correlates of environmental concern from 1973 through 1990 and the implications we draw from them for the two hypotheses.

TRENDS IN ENVIRONMENTAL CONCERN

A recent in-depth review of all known longitudinal data on public concern with environmental quality over the last quarter century concluded that these data paint a fairly consistent picture (Dunlap 1991a). Public awareness of environmental problems and support for environmental protection rose dramatically in the last half of the 1960s and reached a peak in 1970, when celebration of the first "Earth Day" was accompanied by large majorities of the public expressing concern about environmental quality. While the early 1970s saw some decline in environmental concern, it remained at impressive levels through 1973, when the energy crisis first hit. Then, in contrast to the expectations of some analysts, support for environmental protection remained surprisingly strong throughout the rest of the decade and declined only

modestly despite the continuing pressures of energy shortages and a deteriorating economy. The result was that by the end of the decade observers were claiming that environmental quality had become "…one of our more enduring social concerns" (Mitchell 1979:55).

Underestimating the continuing strength of public concern over the environment, the Reagan administration attempted to reduce the burden of environmental regulations on industry and, in general, give economic growth priority over environmental quality. The strategy apparently backfired. Apprehension over inadequate environmental protection by government, along with increased societal attention to environmental problems such as toxic wastes and ozone depletion, led to a significant resurgence of public support for environmental protection in the 1980s (see Dunlap 1991a; Dunlap and Scarce 1991).

One indicator of environmental concern that illustrates this pattern is an item measuring public support for spending on behalf of environmental quality used in the NORC's General Social Surveys (GSS). Beginning in 1973 NORC included "improve and protect the environment" as one of the problem areas respondents were given after being read the following:

> We are faced with many problems in this country, none of which can be solved easily or inexpensively. I'm going to name some of these problems and for each one, I'd like you to tell me whether you think we're spending too much money on it, too little money, or about the right amount.

The item has been included in every GSS since 1973 (which NORC has conducted annually, except for 1979 and 1981). It was shortened to "the environment" for sub-samples beginning in 1984; a study by Rasinski (1989) reported no significant differences between the results obtained with the two versions of the environmental spending item. The NORC data cover the longest time-span of any available set of frequently measured trend data on environmental concern.

Results from the NORC surveys, based on nationwide probability samples of approximately 1,400 each year, are reported in Table 5.1. It is clear that these data conform closely to the pattern found with other available trend data (Dunlap 1991a; Dunlap and Scarce 1991). This convergence increases our faith in the validity of this indicator of environmental concern, while the relatively modest variations from year to year (despite the long-term trends)

suggest that the indicator possesses a fair amount of reliability. In our mind these factors partially offset the well-known limitations of single-item indicators (Babbie 1989). This, along with the fact that there is no other comparable body of longitudinal data (covering such a long time period and collected with such frequency) available, has led us to select the NORC spending item as the dependent variable for our examination of possible changes in the socio-political correlates of environmental concern over time.

THE TWO HYPOTHESES

The Broadening Base Hypothesis

The possibility of change in the social bases of public concern for environmental quality

TABLE 5.1 Trends in Public Support for Spending on the Environment 1973–1990[a]

Percent responding that amount spent is	1973	1974	1975	1976	1977	1978	1980	1982
Too little	61.1	59.0	53.4	54.8	47.5	52.4	47.9	49.7
About right	25.8	26.6	30.8	31.3	34.3	32.8	31.0	32.4
Too much	7.4	7.7	9.7	9.3	11.0	9.6	15.4	11.5
Don't know[b]	5.7	6.6	6.2	4.6	7.2	5.2	5.7	6.4
N	1,498	1,476	1,490	1,494	1,524	1,528	1,465	1,504

Percent responding that amount spent is	1983	1984	1985	1986	1987	1988	1989	1990
Too little	54.3	57.8	58.4	58.4	61.2	64.7	70.1	70.8
About right	31.3	31.0	29.1	29.5	26.7	25.8	20.4	20.5
Too much	8.2	7.2	7.6	6.2	6.0	4.6	4.4	4.1
Don't know[b]	6.2	4.1	4.8	5.8	6.1	5.0	5.1	4.7
N	1,592	1,453	1,527	1,457	1,466	1,464	1,525	1,352

[a]Data from NORC's General Social Surveys, conducted annually except in 1979 and 1981.
[b]The small number of "no answers" are treated as missing data.

was raised early on by Buttel and Flinn (1974) in a trend study of the sociopolitical correlates of environmental concern in Wisconsin from 1968 to 1970. After finding that the relatively strong positive associations that existed between environmental concern and both income and education in 1968 had diminished considerably by 1970, Buttel and Flinn (1974:66) concluded that: "Environmental concern spread downward into the class structure...." These findings, plus the fact that in 1970 environmental concern was also distributed more evenly across rural-urban residence, led them to conclude that from 1968 to 1970 "...the supportive publics [for environmental quality] swelled and were drawn from *broader bases* of social structure" (Buttel and Flinn 1974:67; emphasis added).

Building upon Buttel and Flinn's analysis, Grossman and Potter (1977) formulated the broadening base hypothesis as an explicit model of the evolution of public concern for environmental quality. They argued that this hypothesis is not limited to socioeconomic status, but predicts that environmental concern will diffuse throughout all population subgroups—age, gender, racial, residential, and political as well as socioeconomic. This is important because the Van Liere and Dunlap (1980) review concluded that a majority of studies from the 1970s found environmental concern to be spread fairly evenly across income levels. Whether this reflects the fact that a significant broadening of the socioeconomic bases of environmental concern did indeed occur in the late 1960s and very early 1970s, as suggested by Buttel and Flinn's Wisconsin data, or whether environmental concern at the national level was never associated as strongly with socioeconomic status as initially assumed is not clear. However, the broadening base hypothesis

suggests that environmental concern has diffused throughout all sectors of society.

Although not spelled out clearly by Grossman and Potter, it has often been assumed that as environmental problems become more obvious, ubiquitous, and threatening to human health, awareness and concern about them will be less and less limited to any given sector of society (Morrison 1986; Dunlap 1991a). The recent emergence of environmentalism within minority communities lends credence to this assumption (Bullard and Wright 1990). However, the broadening base hypothesis suggests that sociopolitical variables in general, and not just socioeconomic variables, will become poorer predictors of environmental concern through the years. For example, over time the less educated, residents of rural areas, older adults, and political conservatives should become as concerned about environmental quality as are their counterparts. More specifically, Grossman and Potter (1977) noted that the broadening base hypothesis predicts that the bivariate correlations between sociopolitical variables and environmental concern will decline in magnitude over time, and that—by implication—the amount of variation in environmental concern explained by such variables in combination will likewise decline over time.

The Economic Contingency Hypothesis

Ironically, it was a 1972 followup study in Wisconsin by Buttel (1975) that also provided the first empirical support for the alternative economic contingency hypothesis. Not only did Buttel find an overall decline in the level of environmental concern from 1970 to 1972, but he found that the decline was most pronounced among those with lower education. The result was that in 1972 the association between education and environmental concern was stronger than in 1970, and nearly as strong as it had been in 1968. While income data were apparently not available for 1972, Buttel concluded that the initial broadening of the socioeconomic base of environmental concern had already reversed itself. Buttel's (1975:61) explanation of his results provided the seeds of the economic contingency hypothesis:

> ...*the lower strata are most directly and dramatically affected when the economy stagnates, and the occurrence of relative austerity in the U.S. economy following the mass environmental movement [marked by the 1970 Earth Day] appears to have convinced these strata that environmental problems must wait upon solutions until more basic economic problems have been handled.*

In short, Buttel followed the lead of Morrison et al. (1972) in arguing that when economic conditions worsen, or at least are perceived as worsening, those who are economically disadvantaged will be the first to withdraw their support for environmental protection and give priority to economic goals. While it has never been previously labeled as such, we think it makes sense to term this idea the economic contingency hypothesis.

Although worsening economic conditions were often cited as the cause of the overall societal decline in environmental concern observed in the early 1970s, it should be emphasized that the economic contingency hypothesis goes beyond this; it implies that the decline in environmental concern should have occurred *disproportionately* among the lower socioeconomic strata and, by extension, other economically vulnerable sectors of society, such as racial minorities and women. Specifically, the hypothesis predicts that as economic conditions worsen the correlations between environmental concern and socioeconomic status, race, and possibly gender will increase as the lower strata, minorities, and women have to give priority to economic well-being over environmental quality.

We should emphasize that we do not see the economic contingency hypothesis as contradicting the broadening base hypothesis, but rather as qualifying it. The economic contingency hypothesis suggests that a broadening of the social bases of environmental concern is contingent upon economic conditions. Presumably, should the economy seriously deteriorate, any trend toward broadening would be halted, and possibly even reversed, according to the economic contingency hypothesis.

Evidence from Previous Studies

Besides the two studies in Wisconsin (Buttel 1975; Buttel and Flinn 1974), we have found only four other studies that report data relevant to these two hypotheses—three at the national level (Grossman and Potter 1977; Honnold 1981; Howell and Laska 1992) and one in North Carolina (Marsh and Christenson 1977).

Two of the national studies examined the sociopolitical correlates of the NORC environmental spending item, Grossman and Potter through 1976 and Honnold through 1978. Although they employed different data analytic techniques, both studies came to conclusions similar to those reached by Van Liere and Dunlap (1980). In addition, both studies found gender and race to be significant predictors of environmental concern at times, with women in 1975 and 1978 and nonwhites in 1974 being more supportive of increased spending on the environment than men and whites, respectively.

Grossman and Potter (1977) explicitly evaluated the broadening base hypothesis. Focusing on trends in the bivariate correlations, they observed "…no systematic movement toward zero" (1977:14) but ignored a slight decline in the multiple correlation coefficients from 1973 and 1974 to 1975 and 1976. While not evaluating any overall hypothesis, Honnold's (1981) description of trends in the predictors of environmental concern noted the decline in predictability in 1975 and 1976 and its subsequent rise in 1977 and 1978. She (1981:73) suggested that the 1973–1974 energy crisis may have been a turning point in the public's view of environmental protection, resulting from "…both a decline in environmental concern and a slight decrease (in 1975–1976) in polarization of opinion along sociopolitical lines," a decrease that apparently disappeared by 1977.

In short, neither Grossman and Potter nor Honnold found clear evidence of a broadening base of sociopolitical support for environmental concern from 1973 onward, as the modest tendency in that direction observed in 1975 and 1976 reversed itself the next two years. Further, given that the economic downturn stimulated by the dramatic increase in oil prices reached a temporary low-point in 1975–1976 (Hawley 1986; Wilkins 1986), the fact that these were the years in which the sociopolitical variables in general—and the socioeconomic variables in particular—explained the least variance in environmental concern fails to support the economic contingency hypothesis.

In a recent study employing Michigan National Election Survey (NES) data covering 1980 to 1988, Howell and Laska (1992) also examined correlates of support for en-

vironmental spending. They reported some noticeable changes in the social bases of environmental concern over the eight years, finding that the associations decreased for residence and education but increased for political party, ideology and education. Howell and Laska do not explicitly address either hypothesis, and the mixed pattern of changing correlates reported by them does not appear to directly support either the broadening base or economic contingency hypothesis.

More importantly, we believe that for several reasons Howell and Laska's (1992) findings should be viewed with caution. First, the wording of the spending item used as their dependent variable changed each year—very noticeably from 1980 to 1984. Second, the responses to these items varied greatly across the eight years and in 1980 and 1984 departed substantially from results obtained with the NORC spending item; only 35 percent favored increased spending on the environment in the 1984 NES survey, while 58 percent did so in that year's NORC survey. Third, their results are based on only three time points, and some of the apparent changes in the correlates of environmental spending stem from abnormally high or low associations for only a single year. Finally, and perhaps stemming from the previous problems, some of their results concerning the correlates of environmental concern are quite anomalous (see Van Liere and Dunlap 1980). For example, education was found to be *negatively* associated with environmental concern in the 1980 and 1984 surveys, an exceptionally rare occurrence, while the associations for age were also strikingly low in 1984 and 1988. For such reasons, we think that the NES results must be viewed cautiously, and that Howell and Laska may have been premature in concluding that there was significant change in the social base of the environmental coalition during the change in the social bases of the environmental coalition during the 1980s.

Although covering only 1973 to 1975, the Marsh and Christenson (1977) study in North Carolina is nonetheless especially relevant because they examined possible changes in the social bases of support for both environmental protection and economic development. However, during a period that saw a dramatic downturn in the economy, thus making the economic contingency hypothesis especially applicable, Marsh and Christenson not only failed to find evidence of a disproportionate decline in environmental concern among the lower socioeconomic strata, but they also failed to find evidence of a disproportionate rise in support for economic growth within this strata.

Before drawing conclusions about the validity of either of the two hypotheses from these studies, it seems clear that it would be preferable to extend the analysis over a much longer time period. Doing so will enable us to take advantage of greater fluctuations in economic conditions, including the economic crisis from approximately 1979 to 1982 (when the United States was described by economist Lester Thurow as "an economy that no longer performs" [quoted in Wilkins 1986:230]) and the subsequent major rebound from 1983 onward. This should allow for a much stronger test of the economic contingency hypothesis, as well as a better evaluation of the broadening base hypothesis independent of its economic decline contingency.

NORC DATA

The dependent variable in our analysis is the NORC environmental spending item, annual results for which were reported in Table 5.1. The environmental spending item was coded such that a high score indicates a higher level of environmental concern, with responses that "too much" was being spent on the environment given a 1, "about right" given a 2, and "too little" given a 3. "No answer" and "don't know" were treated as missing values and excluded from the analysis.[1] We included 11 independent variables in an effort to examine the full range of sociopolitical variables that have frequently been suggested as being important predictors of environmental concern: age, gender, race, education, income, occupational prestige, industrial sector, current residence, residence at age 16, political ideology, and party affiliation.[2] Theoretical rationales as to why younger adults, women, those with higher socioeconomic status (education, income, and occupational prestige), those employed outside of extractive industries, urbanites, liberals, and Democrats have been expected to have above-average levels of environmental concern are given in Van Liere and Dunlap (1980). Hershey and Hill (1977–1978) have argued that whites should have higher levels of concern than nonwhites.

For each year that data were available we examine the bivariate and partial relationships between the spending item and the sociopolitical variables. For our purposes the bivariate correlations are more important than the standardized regression coefficients (reflecting the effect of each independent variable while controlling for all the other ones). Our primary interest is in whether higher-than-average levels of environmental concern do in fact exist among various sectors of the population, and whether these patterns have changed over time, rather than sorting out the relative effects of the independent variables. In addition, we examine multiple correlation coefficients each year to gauge whether environmental concern becomes more or less predictable in general.

RESULTS

The bivariate and standardized regression coefficients, the multiple correlation coefficients and the coefficients of determination for the regression of the environmental spending item on the 11 sociopolitical variables for each year for which data are available are reported in Table 5.2. The significance levels for these coefficients are also shown, although given the relatively large sample sizes involved, coefficients of very small magnitude reach statistical significance. For each sociopolitical variable the bivariate correlation coefficients are reported in the top row and the standardized regression coefficients in the bottom row. The sociopolitical variables are rank ordered in terms of their mean bivariate correlations with environmental spending across the 16 years.

Beginning with the bivariate correlations, a number of general patterns can be discerned among the 174 individual correlation coefficients. First, it is apparent that age is clearly the best predictor of environmental concern—judged in terms of magnitude as well as consistency of correlations—with younger adults being more concerned than their counterparts, as expected. In every year except 1989 age has been the strongest correlate of environmental concern, and the magnitude of the correlations has remained remarkably stable. These results confirm the findings of prior research on the importance of age as a predictor of environmental concern (Buttel 1979; Mohai and Twight 1987), although it must be emphasized that the correlations

are certainly not strong, ranging from 0.16 to 0.28.

Political ideology, education, and residence at age 16 are the next best predictors of environmental concern and are generally similar to one another. Not only are the magnitudes of their correlations lower (typically in the 0.10 to 0.20 range) than those for age, but they are also less consistent predictors. Yet, each performs as expected, with liberals, the well-educated, and those raised in urban areas having somewhat higher levels of environmental concern than their counterparts.

The next three variables—current residence, party affiliation, and industrial sector—have some utility as predictors of environmental concern over the years, although the magnitudes of their correlations are quite modest. Nonetheless, urban residents, Democrats, and those not employed in primary (resource extractive) industries are consistently, albeit only slightly, more environmentally concerned than their counterparts.

The remaining four variables—race, gender, family income, and occupational prestige—emerge as relatively poor predictors of environmental concern, both because their correlations are typically not significant and because they are quite inconsistent. However, in the few years where differences emerge it is the non-whites who arc generally found to be more environmentally concerned than are whites, in contrast to Hershey and Hill's (1977–1978) and Taylor's (1989) conclusions. When significant gender differences emerge, women are found to be more environmentally concerned than are males, as recent studies suggest (Hamilton 1985; Blocker and Eckberg 1989).

In short, we find that the strongest correlates of environmental concern across the

TABLE 5.2   Sociopolitical Correlates of Support for Spending on the Environment 1973–1990[a]

Year	1973	1974	1975	1976	1977	1978	1980	1982	1983
Age	−0.253*	−0.258*	−0.225*	−0.246*	−0.251*	−0.260*	−0.246*	−0.280*	−0.205*
	−0.201	−0.202*	−0.198*	−0.188*	−0.228*	−0.245*	−0.214*	−0.227*	−0.188*
Political ideology[b]	—	0.149*	0.152*	0.117*	0.193*	0.142*	0.218*	0.180*	—
	—	0.082°	0.097*	0.071†	0.129*	0.075†	0.157*	0.113*	—
Education	0.173*	0.173*	0.088°	0.154*	0.106*	0.078°	0.064°	0.142*	0.095*
	0.104°	0.080°	0.004	0.026	0.005	0.016	0.028	0.102°	0.035
Residence at 16	0.139*	0.161*	0.115*	0.154*	0.130*	0.135*	0.128*	0.136*	0.105*
	0.067†	0.071†	0.045	0.092°	0.085°	0.050	0.063†	0.045	0.052
Current residence	0.079†	0.145*	0.110*	0.101*	0.064°	0.134*	0.099*	0.141*	0.077°
	0.004	0.055	0.075†	0.016	0.000	0.068†	0.034	0.073†	0.029
Political party	0.122*	0.075°	0.090*	0.031	0.095*	0.085†	0.114*	0.066°	0.133*
	0.128*	0.042	0.053	0.009	0.061†	0.043	0.069†	0.027	0.147*
Industrial sector	0.065†	0.065†	0.051†	0.093*	0.056†	0.109*	0.053†	0.107*	0.094*
	0.020	0.009	−0.019	0.052	0.015	0.041	0.009	0.055	0.055
Family income	0.093*	0.059†	0.039	0.135*	0.004	−0.063†	−0.033	0.028	0.021
	0.020	−0.030	−0.013	0.083°	−0.064†	−0.105°	−0.054	−0.021	−0.010
Gender	0.022	−0.014	0.087°	0.020	0.011	0.112*	0.086°	0.069°	0.024
	0.014	−0.038	0.094*	0.027	0.008	0.091°	0.076*	0.062†	0.015
Race	0.018	0.073°	0.030	0.020	0.051†	0.107*	0.096*	0.089*	0.029
	0.010	0.050	−0.014	0.014	0.011	0.036	0.039	0.006	−0.017
Occupational prestige	0.046†	0.073°	0.018	0.037	0.034	−0.005	−0.039	−0.037	0.020
	−0.005	0.034	0.037	−0.011	0.055	0.024	−0.038	−0.101°	0.017
Multiple R	0.312	0.326	0.292	0.301	0.322	0.346	0.349	0.361	0.273
R^2	0.098*	0.106*	0.085*	0.091*	0.103*	0.120*	0.122*	0.130*	0.074*
N[c]	1,247	1,237	1,267	1,264	1,302	1,318	1,247	1,279	1,357

[a]For each variable, bivariate correlation coefficients are in the top row and standardized regression coefficients are in the bottom row.
[b]In 1973 the question of political ideology was not asked in the General Social Survey; in 1983 it was asked of only half of the sample.
[c]The Ns represent the total number of respondents used in the multivariate analysis.
*$p < 0.001$.
°$p < 0.01$.
†$p < 0.05$.

1973–1990 time-span are basically the same as those suggested by the studies reviewed by Van Liere and Dunlap (1980), although age clearly out-performs education and political ideology, and residence at age 16 approximates the latter two in strength. Thus, we do not concur with Howell and Laska's (1992) conclusion that the sociopolitical base of the environmental coalition changed in the 1980s.

In view of the generally low bivariate correlations, it is not surprising that the

TABLE 5.2   Continued

Year	1984	1985	1986	1987	1988	1989	1990	Mean 1973–1990
Age	−0.195*	−0.209*	−0.229*	−0.234*	−0.209*	−0.162*	−0.214*	−0.23
	−0.177*	−0.186*	−0.182*	−0.172*	−0.147*	−0.124*	−0.186*	−0.19
Political ideology[b]	0.103*	0.145*	0.123*	0.129*	0.105*	0.081°	0.116*	0.14
	0.041	0.077†	0.086°	0.091°	0.059†	0.044	0.072†	0.09
Education	0.106*	0.127*	0.149*	0.206*	0.173*	0.187*	0.197*	0.14
	0.044	0.093°	0.077†	0.155*	0.133*	0.129*	0.107*	0.07
Residence at 16	0.085°	0.098*	0.110*	0.139*	0.147*	0.077°	0.087°	0.12
	0.020	0.045	0.048	0.049	0.094°	0.034	0.022	0.06
Current residence	0.066°	0.089*	0.075°	0.131*	0.087°	0.039	0.030	0.09
	0.032	0.058	0.019	0.060	0.023	−0.001	0.015	0.03
Political party	0.125*	0.117*	0.063†	0.106*	0.056†	0.058†	0.018	0.08
	0.127*	0.126*	0.049	0.110*	0.057	0.085°	0.042	0.07
Industrial sector	0.065†	0.060†	0.075°	0.118*	0.062†	0.085°	0.154*	0.08
	0.026	0.024	0.043	0.044	0.013	0.039	0.105*	0.03
Family income	0.020	0.001	0.048†	0.063†	0.086°	0.121*	0.107*	0.05
	−0.012	−0.047	0.020	−0.015	0.030	0.054	0.001	−0.01
Gender	0.047†	0.007	−0.039	0.019	0.007	0.027	0.004	0.03
	0.048	−0.003	−0.039	0.023	0.017	0.045	0.018	0.03
Race	0.011	0.009	0.045†	0.037	−0.003	−0.029	−0.081†	0.03
	−0.030	−0.049	0.015	−0.020	−0.052	−0.052	−0.100°	−0.01
Occupational prestige	0.054†	0.014	0.031	0.057†	0.015	0.080°	0.098*	0.03
	0.040	0.045	−0.010	−0.031	−0.077†	−0.013	0.013	0.00
Multiple R	0.262	0.295	0.280	0.332	0.285	0.259	0.313	0.31
R^2	0.069*	0.087*	0.079*	0.110*	0.081*	0.067*	0.098*	0.09
N[c]	1,269	1,344	1,266	1,277	1,282	1,300	1,170	

multiple correlation coefficients obtained by predicting environmental concern with all 11 sociopolitical variables simultaneously are not terribly high—averaging under 0.31—nor that the sociopolitical variables typically explain only about 10 percent of the variance in environmental concern, which is compatible with prior findings (Van Liere and Dunlap 1980).

Of secondary interest are the standard-ized regression coefficients obtained from the multivariate analysis. Briefly, these results indicate, as one would expect, that the relationships for all of the variables are attenuated when controlling for the other ones, but that age remains the primary predictor of environmental concern. The effects of the two political variables, ideology and party affiliation, persist surprisingly well, because we would expect them to cancel one another to some degree, given that they are substantially correlated; but the effects of education, both residence variables, and industrial sector are all diminished considerably in the multivariate analyses. These results are generally consistent with findings from studies conducted on samples other than those from NORC's GSS (e.g., Mohai and Twight 1987).

Recall that the broadening base hypothesis suggests that over time the bivariate correlations between the sociopolitical variables and environmental concern would move toward zero and, by implication, that these variables would explain less and less variation in environmental concern. The data in Table 5.2 do not confirm these predictions. On one hand, there is no clear trend for the correlations between environmental concern and any of the sociopolitical variables to have moved toward zero over the long time–span, especially for the key predictors. Although there was movement in this direction for the three socioeconomic variables—education, income, and occupational prestige—during the 1970s (as noted by Honnold 1981), this was reversed in the 1980s. Equally important, there is no long-term trend for older adults becoming as environmentally concerned as younger adults, those who live in or come from rural areas becoming as environmentally concerned as their urban counterparts, nor for conservatives and Republicans becoming as environmentally concerned as their political counterparts. In

short, we find no evidence of a broadening base of environmental concern in the bivariate correlations.

Similarly, there is also no clear tendency for environmental concern to have become less predictable overall from the sociopolitical variables. The amount of variation in environmental concern explained by these 11 variables dipped a bit in 1975–1976 (as noted by Honnold 1981), then rose through 1982, declined in 1983–1986, rose again in 1987, dipped the next two years, and rose again in 1990. Such an irregular pattern may be indicative of sampling variability; it certainly does not reflect a broadening of the sociopolitical bases of environmental concern.

Equally contrary results are evident for the economic contingency hypothesis, which implies that during an economic downturn the correlations between the three socioeconomic variables, as well as race and gender, will increase—as the lower strata, non-whites and women disproportionately shift their support away from environmental protection in favor of economic growth. Precisely how one should define an economic downturn is, of course, ambiguous. However, in retrospect it is apparent that, with some ups and downs, overall the economy tended to go down-hill after the 1973–1974 Arab oil embargo (Wilkens 1986) and reached crisis proportions after the second oil shortage in 1979 when inflation soared to 13.5 percent (Hawley 1986). Reagan's anti-inflationary policies, in turn, contributed to rapidly rising unemployment rates which peaked in 1982 at 9.7 percent. Clearly, then, the economic downturn reached a nadir in 1979–1982 that greatly exceeded the severe recession that occurred toward the end of Marsh and Christenson's (1977) 1973–1975 comparisons and made the relative austerity that had begun between Buttel's (1975) 1970 and 1972 comparisons pale in comparison. In short, if one were ever to find a positive correlation between socioeconomic status and environmental concern, and significantly higher levels of environmental concern among whites and males, it would surely have been during the 1979–1982 period.

Unfortunately, NORC did not conduct a GSS in 1979 or 1981. However, the 1980 and 1982 data should provide an adequate test of the economic contingency hypothesis, and it is clear that they fail to confirm the hypothesis. For education, the most important socioeconomic variable, the correlation was erratic, being abnormally low in 1980 and then a bit higher than normal in 1982. For the other two socioeconomic variables, family income and occupational prestige, the bivariate correlations for the two years are negligible but slightly negative for income in 1980 and for occupational prestige in both 1980 and 1982. The results are more stark for race and gender. In contrast to their normal patterns, they are significantly correlated with environmental concern in both years but in the opposite direction predicted by the economic contingency hypothesis! In both 1980 and 1982 non-whites are significantly more environmentally concerned than are whites, and females significantly more so than males.

Ironically, then, when the economy hit bottom there was a slight but significant tendency for those who are presumably most likely to be economically disadvantaged to become more supportive of government spending on the environment relative to their more advantaged counterparts. This departure from the expected pattern is all the more striking because the significant gender and racial differences largely disappeared once the economy

picked up in the 1980s. Thus, the overall results from 1973 to 1990, covering a gradual downturn, major bottoming out, and then significant rebound in the economy, clearly seem to be contrary to any reasonable expectations derived from the economic contingency hypothesis.[3]

SUMMARY AND CONCLUSIONS

In sum, the results of our analysis of the sociopolitical correlates of public support for environmental spending over an 18-year period call into question the validity of the broadening base and economic contingency hypotheses, both of which were put forth to account for short-term changes in the social bases of environmental concern observed nearly two decades ago (in Wisconsin) and which have had continuing appeal to analysts of environmental concern (Morrison 1986). First, we found no evidence in nearly two decades of a broadening of the social bases of such concern, judged either in terms of trends in the bivariate correlations for individual sociopolitical variables or in terms of the multiple correlation of these variables and environmental concern. Second, even though enormous fluctuations occurred in the economy over the 18 years, we found no evidence of a tendency for the economically disadvantaged sectors of society to disproportionately reduce their levels of environmental concern during hard economic conditions nor for the reverse during good economic times. Indeed, the observed correlates of environmental concern were remarkably robust across varying economic conditions.

Of course, we must not lose sight of the fact that in 1973, the first year for which NORC data were available, public support for spending on the environment (like other indicators of environmental concern) was not spread that unevenly across the major social, economic, and political sectors of our society, as indicated by the relatively low correlations between sociopolitical variables and environmental concern observed in numerous studies (Van Liere and Dunlap 1980) as well as in the NORC surveys. While it is possible that the social bases of environmental concern had already broadened from the late 1960s to 1973, what we find striking is the tremendous stability of the (admittedly modest) sociopolitical correlates of environmental concern over approximately 20 years of empirical research. Whatever led younger, urban, well-educated, politically liberal, and Democratic adults employed outside of primary industries to be somewhat more concerned about environmental protection than their counterparts two decades ago seems to have persisted through the 1980s. Indeed, Marsh and Christenson's (1977:106) conclusion, based on their study covering only two years, that "...once a pattern of support for environmental controls emerges throughout the socioeconomic structure, it does not easily dissipate," appears to have held up for nearly two decades.

In concluding that the social bases of environmental concern have remained very stable, we must acknowledge an important qualification—that we are speaking about attitudinal concern for environmental quality (and a particular type, support for spending on behalf of the environment, at that) and not actual behavior nor activism on behalf of environmental protection. It may well be that environmental activism, especially the emergence of small community groups concerned with local environmental problems such as toxic wastes, has, to use Morrison's (1986) phrase, "trickled down" into lower socioeconomic strata to a greater degree than is true of membership in national organizations such as the Sierra

Club. In fact, one might expect that fear of perceived health hazards in one's backyard would override the relatively low levels of political efficacy that often inhibit environmental activism and sociopolitical participation in general among the lower socioeconomic strata (Mohai 1985; Bullard and Wright 1990).

Furthermore, even if we limit attention to environmental attitudes, one must be cautious about generalizing from the results of our analysis of the NORC item. In addition to being a single-item indicator, the NORC spending item taps a specific type of environmental attitude—support for governmental spending on the environment—and is focused on protecting and improving the environment at the national level. As noted previously, there is evidence to suggest that the manner in which environmental concern is conceptualized affects its correlations with sociopolitical variables (Stern 1992; Van Liere and Dunlap 1981). Thus, caution is called for in generalizing the results obtained with the NORC item to environmental concern in general. For example, we would not be surprised if studies of concern about toxic contamination at the local level find such concern to have a somewhat different sociopolitical base that in the national-level NORC surveys, as was the case in Hamilton's work (1985) and as suggested by Bullard and Wright (1990).

These qualifications notwithstanding, the results of our analysis of correlates of the NORC environmental spending item suggest that, at least at the national level, the social bases of support for environmental protection have remained remarkably stable over an 18-year period. This finding promises to have growing significance as environmental problems increasingly become crucial issues in political campaigns and policy battles (Dunlap 1991b). For example, the continuing minor importance of socioeconomic status as a predictor of environmental concern undermines the efficacy of charges of environmental elitism, used frequently by opponents of environmental regulations (Morrison and Dunlap 1986), while the modest liberal/Democratic cast of environmental support has obvious electoral implications.

ENDNOTES

1. While it seems reasonable to assume that "too much" and "too little" differ equally from "about right," technically the item is an ordinal variable. Nonetheless, we will employ it as a dependent variable using ordinary least-squares regression (OLS). While debate over employing ordinal dependent variables in regression analysis has a long history, Labovitz (1970) and others (e.g., Asher 1976) have argued that in most instances doing so does not yield distorted results. This is especially so when one can assume that the true underlying metric of a variable is continuous and when the number of cases is quite large (Kim 1975), both of which seem reasonable in this case. Further, the most likely distortions would be attenuation of the correlations between the spending item and the independent variables (Kim 1975), thus providing more conservative tests of the two hypotheses. More generally, Asher (1976:66) noted that: "There has been ample Monte Carlo work that suggests that in many instances the violation of the interval assumption is not very consequential." Finally, Achen (1982:36–67) stated that "…the strength of ordinary regression is its great resilience…. Regression will tend to the right answer under reasonable practical circumstances, even if a great many of the classical postulates are violated." For all of these reasons, we will employ OLS to examine the two hypotheses, as have prior analyses of the correlates of the NORC environmental spending item we are replicating and extending (Grossman and Potter 1977; Honnold 1991). The fact that techniques such as logistic regression, technically more appropriate for use with our dependent variable, yield unwieldy results and do not provide an easily interpretable summary measure analogous to the multiple correlation coefficient is another reason for our decision to use OLS regression.

2. The sociopolitical variables were coded as follows (for more detail see Davis and Smith [1987]): Age: number of years; Gender: (1) male, (2) female; Race: (1) white, (2) non-white; Education: highest grade attained, up to eight years of college (1–20); Family income: total family income from all sources prior to taxes in prior year, ranging from 12 to 20 categories over the years (adjusted periodically by NORC); Occupational prestige: prestige scores for male head of household, if present, and for respondent in case of female head of household; Industrial sector: three-digit industrial classification code used by the U.S. Bureau of the Census was recoded into: (1) primary industries: agriculture, forestry, fisheries and mining, (2) secondary industries: construction, manufacturing, and textiles, and (3) tertiary or service industries. (We assigned the relative rankings to this variable based on the assumption that primary industries generally have the greatest impact on the environment.) Other codes included: Residence at age 16: (1) farm or open country, (2) small city, (3) medium size city, (4) suburb near a large city, and (5) large city; Current residence: (1) rural (counties having no towns of 10,000 or more), (2) counties with small cities (over 10,000), (3) suburbs of large SMSAs, (4) suburbs of largest 12 SMSAs, (5) central cities of large SMSAs, and (6) central cities of largest 12 SMSAs; Party affiliation: seven-point scale ranging from (1) for strong Republican to (4) for Independent to (7) for strong Democrat; and Political ideology: seven-point scale ranging from (1) for extremely conservative to (4) for middle of the road to (7) for extremely liberal.

3. Primarily to determine whether the results for race would be significantly affected by examining support for environmental spending relative to support for spending on the other programs, we repeated the analysis reported in Table 5.1 using relative environmental concern. We did this by computing the difference between support for spending on environmental protection and mean scores for each respondent on support for spending on the other 10 funding

areas examined by NORC during the entire 15-year period (possible scores for this variable range from +2 to –2). Overall, the results obtained with this relative measure were quite consistent with those reported in Table 5.2 for the absolute spending item, which is not surprising given the 0.90 mean correlation between the two measures. Not only were the same variables (age, education, ideology, party preference, residence, and occupational sector) the best predictors of relative environmental concern, but the amount of variation stayed generally stable, although it was consistently less than that for absolute environmental concern reported in Table 5.2, averaging only 6 percent. In short, the results of our analysis of relative environmental concern do not clearly support the broadening base hypothesis. The one difference obtained in the analysis was that on average race was a stronger and more consistent predictor of relative environmental concern than of absolute environmental concern, as whites were found to be significantly more supportive of environmental spending than non-whites in 10 of the 16 years. Thus, although non-whites were found to be significantly more supportive than whites of absolute environmental spending for six of the years, as noted in Table 5.2, when it came to spending on the environment relative to other programs, whites were consistently more supportive (also see Honnold 1981; Lowe et al. 1980). These findings do not, however, seem to support the economic contingency hypothesis, since no significant differences were found for race in 1980 or 1982, when economic conditions were at their worst, as the hypothesis would predict.

REFERENCES

Achen, Christopher H.
  1982 Interpreting and Using Regression. Beverly Hills, CA: Sage.

Asher, Herbert B.
  1976 Causal Modeling. Beverly Hills, CA: Sage.

Babbie, Earl
  1989 The Practice of Social Research, 5th ed. Belmont, CA: Wadsworth.

Blocker, T. Jean, and Douglas Lee Eckberg
  1989 "Environmental issues as women's issues: general concerns and local hazards." Social Science Quarterly 70:586–93.

Bullard, Robert E., and Beverly H. Wright
  1990 "The quest for environmental equity: mobilizing the African-American community for social change." Society and Natural Resources 3:301–11.

Buttel, Frederick H.
  1979 "Age and environmental concern: a multivariate analysis." Youth and Society 10:237–56.
  1975 "The environmental movement: consensus, conflict, and change." Journal of Environmental Education 7:53–63.

Buttel, Frederick H., and William L. Flinn
  1974 "The structure of support for the environmental movement, 1968–1970." Rural Sociology 39:56–69.

Davis, James A., and Tom W. Smith
  1987 General Social Surveys, 1972–1987: Cumulative Codebook. Chicago: National Opinion Research Center.

Dunlap, Riley E.
  1991a Trends in public opinion toward environmental issues: 1965–1990." Society and Natural Resources 4:285–312.
  1991b "Public opinion in the 1980s: clear consensus, ambiguous commitment." Environment 33 (October):10–15, 32–37.

Dunlap, Riley E., and Rik Scarce
  1991 "The polls—poll trends: environmental problems and protection." Public Opinion Quarterly 55:713–34.

Grossman, Gary M., and Harry R. Potter
  1977 "A trend analysis of competing models of environmental attitudes." Working Paper No. 127. West Lafayette, IN: Dept. of Sociology and Anthropology, Purdue University.

Hamilton, Lawrence C.
  1985 "Concern about toxic wastes: three demographic predictors." Sociological Perspectives 28:463–86.

Hawley, Ellis W.
  1986 "Challenges to the mixed economy: the state and private enterprise." Pp. 159–86 in H. Bremner, G. W. Reichard, and R. J. Hop-

kins (eds.), American Choices: Social Dilemmas and Public Policy Since 1960. Columbus: Ohio State University Press.

Hays, Samuel P.
1987 Beauty, Health, and Permanence: Environmental Politics in the United States, 1955–1985. New York: Cambridge University Press.

Hershey, Marjorie Randon, and David B. Hill
1977–1978 "Is pollution 'a white thing'? racial differences in preadults' attitudes." Public Opinion Quarterly 41:439–58.

Honnold, Julie A.
1981 "Predictors of public environmental concern in the 1970s." Pp. 63–75 in D. E. Mann (ed.), Environmental Policy Formation. Lexington, MA: Lexington Books.

Howell, Susan E., and Shirley B. Laska
1992 "The changing face of the environmental coalition: a research note." Environment and Behavior 24:134–44.

Kim Jae-On
1975 "Multivariate analysis of ordinal data." American Journal of Sociology 81: 261–97.

Labovitz, Sanford
1970 "The assignment of numbers to rank-order categories." American Sociological Review 35:515–24.

Lowe, George D., Thomas K. Pinhey, and Michael D. Grimes
1980 "Public support for environmental protection: new evidence from national surveys." Pacific Sociological Review 23:423–45.

Marsh, C. Paul, and James A. Christenson
1977 "Support for economic growth and environmental protection, 1973–1975." Rural Sociology 42:101–07.

Mitchell, Robert Cameron
1979 "Silent spring/solid majorities." Public Opinion 2(August/September):16–20, 55.

Mohai, Paul
1985 "Public concern and elite involvement in environmental-conservation issues." Social Science Quarterly 66:820–38.

Mohai, Paul, and Ben W. Twight
1987 "Age and environmentalism: an elaboration of the Buttel model using national

survey evidence." Social Science Quarterly 68:798–815.

Morrison, Denton E.
1986 "How and why environmental consciousness has trickled down." Pp. 187–220 in A. Schnaiberg, N. Watts, and K. Zimmerman (eds.), Distributional Conflict in Environmental-Resource Policy. New York: St. Martin's Press.

Morrison, Denton E., and Riley E. Dunlap
1986 "Environmentalism and elitism: a conceptual and empirical analysis." Environmental Management 10:581–89.

Morrison, Denton E., Kenneth E. Hornback, and W. Keith Warner
1972 "The environmental movement: some preliminary observations and predictions." Pp. 259–79 in W. R. Burch, Jr., N. H. Cheek, Jr., and L. Taylor (eds.), Social Behavior, Natural Resources, and the Environment. New York: Harper & Row.

Rasinski, Kenneth A.
1989 "The effect of question wording on public support for government spending." Public Opinion Quarterly 53:388–94.

Stern, Paul
1992 "Psychological dimensions of global environmental change." Annual Review of Psychology 43:269–302.

Taylor, Dorceta E.
1989 "Blacks and the environment: toward an explanation of the concern gap between blacks and whites." Environment and Behavior 21:175–205.

Van Liere, Kent D., and Riley E. Dunlap
1980 "The social bases of environmental concern: a review of hypotheses, explanations and empirical evidence." Public Opinion Quarterly 44:181–97.

1981 "Environmental concern: does it make a difference how it's measured?" Environment and Behavior 13:651–76.

Wilkins, Mira
1986 "America and the world economy." Pp. 219–46 in R. H. Bremner, G. W. Reichard, and R. J. Hopkins (eds.), American Choices: Social Dilemmas and Public Policy since 1960. Columbus: Ohio State University Press.

11. Culture and the Environment in the Pacific Northwest*

RICHARD J. ELLIS AND FRED THOMPSON

Empirical studies of environmental attitudes often ask what people want (Dunlap, Gallup, and Gallup 1993; Dunlap and Scarce 1991) but less frequently ask why. Perhaps it is because the answer seems straightforward, even simple. People want cleaner air and water, wilderness and species preservation, habitat protection, and a healthier, safer earth because these are so obviously desirable. Environmentalism would seem to be one preference that needs no explanation.

Attempts to explain environmental preferences and concerns in terms of standard demographic variables have generally not fared well (Jones and Dunlap 1992, Van Liere and Dunlap 1980).[1] Perhaps this is because the almost universal support that environmentalism now commands leaves little variance to be explained. Or perhaps we have been looking in the wrong places, asking the wrong questions.

In this paper, building upon the so-called cultural theory of Douglas (1970, 1982a) and Wildavsky (1987; Thompson, Ellis, and Wildavsky 1990), we investigate the cultural sources of environmental atti-

tudes and beliefs. What values and beliefs, if any, underlie environmental commitments? What sorts of people defending what sorts of social relationships tend to become environmentally active? When environmental activists urge us to conserve energy or recycle plastics, what else if anything are they trying to tell us about how we should live with one another?

The Douglas-Wildavsky theory of cultural bias posits four basic ways of organizing and justifying social and political life: egalitarian, individualistic, hierarchical, and fatalistic. Each of these cultural biases is "a point of view, with its own framing assumptions and readily available solutions for standardized problems" (Douglas 1997, 128). Adherents of each cultural bias construct their policy preferences so as to bolster their preferred pattern of social relationships. Perceptions about environmental risks and dangers, in this view, are embedded in cultural orientations, rather than being merely a fiction of the level of information about the safety of particular technologies, or a product of generalized psychological predispositions, such as risk acceptance or aversion (Dake and Wildavsky 1990, Douglas 1975, Douglas and Wildavsky 1982, Rayner 1992).

Environmental activists, according to this cultural theory, are worried about the

*This essay, which was first published in the *American Political Science Review* 91(4):885–897, is reprinted here by permission of the American Political Science Association.

greenhouse effect or deforestation, for example, not only because they are concerned about the fate of the earth but because they desire to transform how human beings live with one another in an egalitarian direction. To accept that nature is fragile and that the slightest misstep may result in cataclysmic consequences for the human species helps egalitarians to justify a politics that would dramatically curtail the activities of the restless entrepreneur in the name of the collectivity. Competitive individualists construct a view of nature as forgiving as resilient because it makes it easier for them to justify laissez-faire and to resist those who would enhance centralized, governmental control. Or, to take another example, the idea of resources as nonrenewable and rapidly depleting is hypothesized as appealing to egalitarians because it enables them to justify regulating and redistributing limited resources. In order to resist these encroachments on the process of bidding and bargaining, adherents of a competitive individualistic culture counter by focusing on the "resource-full" nature of individual entrepreneurs (Thompson, Ellis, and Wildavsky 1990, 26–7, 62). The debate about nature, in this view, is also fundamentally a contest over cultures.

This thesis has attracted widespread attention in the area of risk analysis (see Rayner 1992), understandably so since it challenges a number of settled beliefs about the perception of environmental dangers. It runs counter to the seductively simple idea that people worry about environmental harms because they are harmful. Environmental activism, in this view, has little or nothing to do with culture and everything to do with the sorry state of the environment. Alternatively, we are often told that people begin to worry about the environment when they reach a higher stage of

consciousness, either because they have at last been educated about the real harms confronting the environment, or because they have satisfied their primary subsistence and economic needs. The Douglas-Wildavsky cultural thesis, by insisting that perceptions of environmental harm are "defined, perceived, and managed" (Rayner 1992, 84) according to a cultural bias, is unsettling to many received ideas about risk perception. For the most part, however, challenges to the theory and the contestation surrounding it have remained at a theoretical level.[2]

Among the ideas that the Douglas-Wildavsky hypothesis challenges head-on is the widespread belief that environmentalism transcends conventional political ideology. The view that environmentalism is "inherently neither left nor right" has been cogently argued in Paehlke's important book, *Environmentalism and the Future of Progressive Politics* (1989, 177). Paehlke suggests that we need to draw "a distinction between the 'distributive' politics of the traditional political spectrum and environmental politics" (p. 178). Distributive politics, as he defines it, "is concerned with distribution and redistribution of the products and other intended benefits of economic activity." The ethical debate in this sphere is "carried out in terms of equity." Environmentalism, according to Paehlke's autonomy thesis, offers a totally separate discourse; an ideology that is altogether apart from the conventional left-right continuum (p. 7). Environmental politics, Paehlke explains, "competes with the whole distributional agenda" (p. 189). To map the contemporary ideological spectrum properly, he argues that one needs two dimensions. The first is the familiar left-right dimension that turns on distributive economic concerns; the second is completely independent and runs from pro- to anti-environmentalism (p. 190, also p. 178; cf. Cotgrove 1982, 112, and Milbrath 1984, 24).

A related but different version of the autonomy thesis is argued by students of the "New Politics." Largely drawing upon data derived from Western Europe, they agree with Paehlke that environmentalism is "orthogonal" to the materialistic, equity-based politics of the Old Left, but unlike Paehlke these scholars embed environmentalism in the emergence of a new left-right framework pivoting around "postmaterial" issues, such as participation and individuals freedom (Dalton 1994, esp. 121–34; Inglehart 1977, 1990). The environmental movement, like other "new social movements," such as the peace and the women's movement, is said to be driven by a new "elite-challenging" as opposed to "elite-directed" style of politics (Inglehart 1977, 3). In this view it is citizen participation and opposition to elite authority, more than equal distribution of resources, that is the motive power behind environmental commitment.[3]

A third and dramatically different alternative to the Douglas-Wildavsky cultural hypothesis is offered by Kempton Boster, and Hartley in their study, *Environmental Values in American Culture* (1995). Whereas Douglas and Wildavsky argue that environmental activism is strongly joined to egalitarianism, Kempton and his colleagues counter that there is a "single cultural consensus" on environmental values and beliefs, and those few who do not share this consensus do not adopt a coherent and consistent alternative. By "cultural consensus" they do not mean that every last person agrees with each and every environmental value or belief; instead, they mean that "there is only one set of culturally agreed upon answers" (p. 211; also 196–7). The general public, in this view, closely resem-

bles environmental activists. Even members of the radical environmental group, Earth First!, have "more or less the same beliefs and values as other Americans." What differentiates environmental activists from the general public, according to Kempton et al., is less what they believe and value than their willingness to make personal sacrifices for their values and beliefs (p. 209). Far from being part of an egalitarian challenge to dominant American values and institutions, environmental activism is the American cultural mainstream.

DATA AND METHODS

To test these rival hypotheses, we carried out several surveys. The first went to the northwestern U.S. membership of three environmental groups: Audubon Society, Sierra Club, and the Earth Island Institute. The first two are well-known mainstream environmental groups, while the third is an avowedly nonmainstream organization that defines itself as working at the intersection of social justice and ecology issues.[4] For comparative purposes, we sent the same survey to a small group of leaders in the Sierra Club and Earth Island Institute. We also mailed a much shorter version to a random sample of residents in Oregon's capital, Salem, and the adjacent, largely rural, Yamhill County. On occasion, for comparative purposes only, we also draw upon a survey of members of the radical environmental group, Earth First! More specific information on sampling methods and the nature of each sample is given in Appendix A.

Respondents were offered a series of statements designed to measure egalitarian, individualistic, and hierarchical cultural biases as well as a range of environmental attitudes and beliefs.[5] For each item, respondents were asked to place themselves on a seven-point Likert-type scale, ranging from strongly agree to strongly disagree. *Egalitarianism, Individualism* (which we also call *Market Individualism*), and *Hierarchy* were each measured by three-item scales (see Appendix B for the items used in this and other scales, as well as for the reliabilities of all scales). To measure support for the environment, in both samples we used a single item: "We are spending too little money on improving and protecting the environment."

In the environmental group sample,[6] we also constructed a ten-item scale modeled on the New Environmental Paradigm pioneered by Dunlap and Van Liere (1978) and used by Milbrath (1984) and others. The central elements of this paradigm that we attempted to measure are anti-anthropocentrism and the beliefs that there are limits to growth, nature is fragile, the possibility of ecological catastrophe is imminent, and a fundamental transformation is needed in the way we live our lives (Dunlap et al. 1992, 4, 6; Mibrath 1984, 44–8). For the Salem-Yamhill general public, we constructed a five-item scale designed to measure level of environmental concern.

IS ENVIRONMENTALISM IDEOLOGICALLY AUTONOMOUS?

We begin by testing whether environmental attitudes and beliefs constitute a relatively autonomous sphere of ideas or are embedded in cultural biases and/or in the conventional left-right ideological spectrum. First, we examine the correlations between egalitarian or distributive concerns, on the one hand, and environmental commitments, on the other. Second, we look at the relationship between environmentalism and the participatory, "elite-challenging" New Politics. Finally, we investigate the relationship between market individualism and environmentalism.

Equality

If Paehlke is correct that environmentalism constitutes a relatively autonomous sphere of ideas, then we would expect to find a weak relationship between environmentalism and egalitarianism. If Douglas and Wildavsky's theory of cultural bias is correct, then the correlation should be strong. As Table 5.3 shows, among both environmental activists and the Salem-Yamhill general public there are consistently robust relationships between egalitarianism and environmentalism. Those concerned about inequality are substantially more likely to show concern about environmental degradation and to favor spending more on environmental protection.[7]

Paehlke's autonomy thesis does not fare well, even if we use the conventional liberal-conservative self-designation (see Table 5.3). Among both activists and the public, there are generally strong correlations between environmental attitudes and ideological *Self-designation,* as well as between environmental attitudes and *Party Identification* (also see Guth et at. 1995, esp. 372; and Dunlap et al. 1992, 10). Liberals and Democrats are more likely to express ecological consciousness, show strong environmental concern, and support spending for environmental protection.

If ideological self-designation and party identification account for environmental attitudes so well, then why introduce the concept of egalitarianism? To test whether egalitarianism contributes to our understanding of environmentalism, we looked at the partial correlation between the two, controlling for liberal-conservative self-identification and party identification. In

TABLE 5.3   Correlates of Environmentalism

	Environmental Activists		Salem-Yamhill Public	
	New Ecological Consciousness	Spending on Environment	Environmental Concern	Spending on Environment
Egalitarianism	.39**	.36**	.53**	.47**
	(.31**)	(.19**)	(.38**)	(.33**)
Individualism	−.34**	−.36**	−.43**	−.37**
Hierarchy	−.09*	−.13**	−.16**	−.13*
Ideology	.29**	.36**	.39**	.38**
Party ID	.24**	.34**	.38**	.37**
Partcipation	.09*	−.02	NA	NA
Age	−.08*	−.10**	−.06	−.03
Education	−.02	.10**	.05	.09
Gender	−.06	.00	−.21**	−.08
Income	−.13**	−.04	−.04	.07

Note: Correlation coefficients are Pearson's *r*. In parentheses are partial correlations, controlling for ideology and party identification. Variables are coded so that positive values indicate liberal, Democrat, and male. $*p < .05$; $**p < .01$; two-tailed test.
NA = Not asked in the survey.

both populations, as Table 5.3 shows, egalitarianism explains significant additional variance in environmental attitudes even after controlling for ideological self-designation and party identification.

Participation and Authority

The New Politics argument rests on three distinct claims: (1) The New Politics issues of participation and authority are independent of the Old Politics issues of redistribution; (2) environmental attitudes and beliefs are autonomous from the old redistributive politics; and (3) environmental attitudes and beliefs are embedded in the New Politics issues of participation and authority. We have already seen that the second of these claims is not correct, but what about the other two? The theory still could

be vindicated if the relationship between environmentalism and the New Left value of participation is greater than the relationship between environmentalism and the Old Left value of equality.

The environmental activists were offered a classic New Politics statement: "We should all participate in each decision that directly affects us."[8] Consistent with the New Politics argument, *Participation* is only weakly related to egalitarianism (Pearson's $r = .14$), and it is completely unrelated to ideological self-designation and party identification. But contrary to the New Politics argument, as Table 5.3 shows, the importance respondents attach to participation also shows no relationship with support for environmental spending and virtually none with the ten-item measure of ecological consciousness. The value activists place on participation, in short, has little or nothing to do with their environmental beliefs or attitudes. [9]

Another way to test the New Politics thesis that environmentalism is distinguished by its "elite-challenging" character is to examine the relationship between environmentalism and our hierarchy scale, which includes such statements as "one of the problems with people today is that they challenge authority too often" and "society works best when people strictly obey all rules and regulations." The elite-challenging hypothesis leads us to expect a strong inverse relationship between hierarchy and environmental support. Table 5.3 does show a consistently inverse relationship, but it is uniformly weak. Elite-challenging attitudes, then, do not appear to be strongly related to environmental attitudes, either among the general public or among activists. [10]

Market Individualism

What about attitudes toward the market? Is the new environmentalism at bottom the old antimarket impulse? (Or, looked at differently, is opposition to environmentalism grounded in traditional promarket attitudes?) Among both the Salem-Yamhill public and activists, Table 5.3 shows, there is a strong inverse relationship between support for market individualism and support for environmentalism. It is, in fact, almost the mirror image of the relationship between egalitarianism and environmentalism, which raises the question whether individualism and egalitarianism are not better conceived as opposite ends of a continuum rather than separate dimensions. Certainly the egalitarianism and individualism scales are inversely correlated (Pearson's $r = -.48$ in the activist sample and $-.44$ in the Salem-Yamhill public). [11] May it not be more appropriate, then, to combine the items into a single scale? One way of addressing this question is to enter egalitarianism and individualism in a regression equation simultaneously to determine whether any unique additional variance in environmental attitudes is explained by including a second measure of cultural bias. As Table 5.4 reports, both individualism and egalitarianism help explain significant unique variance in environmental attitudes. Moreover, in both samples, adding any one of the individualist items to the three-item egalitarian scale reduces the reliability of the scale. Finally, in both samples, factor analysis with varimax rotation revealed two distinct factors, one comprising all three egalitarian items, the other composed of the tree individualist items. (see Appendix C). Thus, the two measures'

TABLE 5.4 Standardized Partial Regression Coefficients for Egalitarianism and Individualism

	Environmental Activists		Salem-Yamhill Public	
	New Ecological Consciousness	*Spending on Environment*	*Environmental Concern*	*Spending on Environment*
Egalitarianism	.28	.24	.42	.38
Individualism	−.21	−.23	−.25	−.21

Note: All relationships are significant at $p < .01$; two-tailed test.

factor structure, internal consistency, and nonredundant predictive power justify treating them as measures of distinct albeit related constructs.

The explanatory importance of market individualism and egalitarianism holds up even when we enter these two cultural bias variables into a regression equation together with the standard demographic variables (*Age, Income, Gender, and Education*) as well as party identification, ideological self-designation, and the hierarchical cultural bias. In both the environmental activist and general public sample, as Table 5.5 documents, egalitarianism and market individu-

alism consistently emerge as the variables that explain the greatest amount of variance in environmental attitudes. This is further support for the Douglas-Wildavsky cultural thesis.

IS THERE A CULTURAL CONSENSUS AROUND ENVIRONMENTALISM?

Kempton, Boster, and Hartley's (1995) cultural consensus thesis leads us to expect relatively small differences between the public and activists in both environmental attitudes and cultural biases. Douglas and Wildavsky's cultural bias thesis, in contrast,

TABLE 5.5   Standardized Partial Regression Coefficients for Cultural Bias, Political Self-Identification, and Demographic Traits

	Environmental Activists		Salem-Yamhill Public	
	New Ecological Consciousness	*Spending on Environment*	*Environmental Concern*	*Spending on Environment*
Cultural bias				
Egalitarianism	.28**	.14**	.31**	.28**
Individualism	−.22**	−.19**	−.22**	−.22**
Hierarchy	.14**	.08	−.11*	−.05
Political self-identification				
Ideology	.08	.14*	.07	.10
Republican	−.05	−.14**	−.11	−.14
Democrat	−.13*	−.07	−.02	−.01
Demographic traits				
Age	−.01	−.02	−.02	.03
Education	−.04	.06	−.01	.02
Gender	−.09*	.01	−.04	.06
Income	−.01	.04	−.05	.02
Multiple R	.44	.42	.61	.56
Standard error	.88	.98	1.20	1.55
R^2, All variables	.20	.18	.37	.32
R^2, Egalitarianism and Individualism only	.18	.17	.33	.25
R^2, Egalitarianism only	.15	.13	.28	.22

*$p < .05$; **$p < .01$; two-tailed test.

leads us to expect large differences (Wildavsky 1991). Moreover, Douglas and Wildavsky's cultural theory also leads us to predict that the more egalitarian the environmental group, the more environmentally concerned the members of that group will be, whereas the consensus thesis leads us to expect environmental groups, even the more radical among, to be quite similar in attitudes.

Previous research has consistently shown widespread support for environmental protection among the general public (Brick, Hannigan, and Krueger 1995; Dunlap and Scarce 1991). Our results are consistent with those findings. Generally, as Table 5.6 documents, the Salem-Yamhill respondents show high levels of environmental concern. Although the public clearly worries about environmental degradation and values environmental protection, it is not surprising that they are less intensely concerned than activists. Only about one in eight Salem-Yamhill respondents, for instance, agrees in the strongest possible terms that we will soon experience an ecological catastrophe, compared to about half of the Earth Island sample and one in three Audubon and Sierra Club respondents. These findings seem to support the consensus thesis that there is a general proenvironmental sentiment, and what separates activists from the public is primarily the intensity with which they hold a belief rather than what they believe.

Other items, however, measuring attitudes toward science and technology and "deep ecology," reveal sharper differences, not only between the public and the activists but also among the activists themselves. Table 5.6 shows that Salem-Yamhill respondents have a strong faith in the promise of science and technology to solve human problems, a faith largely shared by Audubon and Sierra Club members. Earth Islanders and especially members of Earth First! take a far more jaundiced view of science and technology (cf. Milbrath 1984, 31). There is also nothing approaching a cultural consensus on issues of deep ecology. While activists generally feel we would be better off with a dramatic population reduction, the public does not. And the core deep ecology tenet that humans are no more important than any other species divides environmentalists, while the public decisively rejects such a notion. In fact, one-third of the Salem-Yamhill sample disagrees in the strongest possible terms. The substantial divergence on questions of deep ecology and technology suggests that beneath broadly shared environmental concerns are often quite different conceptions of how human beings should relate to nature and how environmental problems should be handled.[12]

The consensus thesis fares particularly poorly when we compare the cultural biases of the general public with those of environmental activists.[13] As Table 5.6 documents, the public is far less egalitarian and far more supportive of both hierarchy and market individualism. Moreover, this cultural gap becomes more pronounced as one moves toward greater activism and leadership. In each of the three environmental groups survey, as Table 5.7 shows, the more active members consistently express greater antipathy to individualism, greater support for egalitarianism, and more distrust of hierarchical authority relations.

THE POLICY IMPLICATIONS OF CULTURAL DISSENSUS

What does the divergence in cultural bias between environmental activists and the general public mean for environmental policymaking? Having pronounced the discovery of a "pervasive and strong" commitment to environmental values among the

TABLE 5.6 Percentage Endorsing Environmental and Cultural Statements

	Salem-Yamhill	Audubon Society	Sierra Club	Earth Island	Sierra Leaders	Earth Island Leaders	Earth First!
Environmental concern							
1. If things continue on their present course, we will soon experience a major ecological catastrophe.	64	81	86	91	100	93	NA
2. The oceans are gradually dying from oil pollution and dumping of waste.	67	75	87	92	84	86	95
3. We are fast using up the world's natural resources.	78	94	95	97	100	93	NA
4. We are spending too little money on improving and protecting the environment.	57	86	93	96	100	97	94
Technology and deep ecology							
1. Science and technology provide the human race with its best hope for the future.	61	56	55	34	45	21	17
2. Humans are no more important than any other species.	32	51	53	60	61	52	NA
3. We would be better off if we dramatically reduced the number of people on this earth.	40	63	68	76	88	83	NA
Cultural bias							
1. What our country needs is a fairness revolution to make the distribution of goods more equal.	32	38	41	59	47	70	71
2. The world would be a more peaceful place if its wealth were divided more equally among nations.	33	48	53	72	50	86	64
3. We need to dramatically reduce inequalities between the rich and the poor, whites and people of color, and men and women.	66	80	82	89	85	97	NA
4. Competitive markets are almost always the best way to supply people with the things they need.	76	59	47	28	34	34	17
5. Society would be better off if there was much less government regulation of business.	55	31	12	10	9	7	NA
6. People who are successful in business have a right to enjoy their wealth as they see fit.	76	38	34	24	27	17	13
7. Society works best when people strictly obey all rules and regulations.	65	50	31	26	30	7	15
8. Respect for authority is one of the most important things that children should learn.	87	72	46	39	42	24	NA
9. One of the problems with people today is that they challenge authority too often.	44	26	13	10	3	3	NA

NA = Not asked in the survey.

TABLE 5.7   Mean Score on Cultural Bias Scales

	Egalitarianism	Hierarchy	Individualism
Salem-Yamhill	−.13	.77	.92
Audubon			
Inert (*N* = 47)	.32	.49	.50
Active (*N* = 101)	.57	.19	−.24
Highly active (*N* = 61)	.46	−.17	−.45
Sierra Club			
Inert (*N* = 46)	.41	−.37	−.27
Active (*N* = 99)	.63	−.64	−.56
Highly active (*N* = 53)	.73	−.58	−.74
Leaders (*N* = 33)	.73	−.84	−1.14
Earth Island			
Inert (*N* = 24)	.63	−.69	−.40
Active (*N* = 103)	.95	−.78	−.96
Highly active (*N* = 162)	1.60	−1.00	−1.37
Leaders (*N* = 29)	1.87	−1.63	−1.41

Note: Earth cultural bias scale runs from −3 (strongly disagree) to +3 (strongly agree).

American public, Kempton et al. are led to ask: "Why is there not more environmental action? Why don't people act collectively to strengthen environmental laws, build infrastructure with reduced environmental impact, or institute incentives for behavior change?" (1995, 220). In other words, why, if Americans share the same basic values as environmentalists, do they not behave more like environmentalists? Kempton et al. explain this puzzle by focusing on the "barriers to action" that prevent widely shared environmental values from being transformed into "environmentally beneficial actions" (p. 220). Among these barriers are misinformation (the mistaken belief, for example, that cutting down rainforests is causing global warming), "structural constraints" (that we lack a strong public transit system or bikeway system, for instance), "fundamental incentive structures" (for instance, that capitalist "companies earn more

by producing and selling more, not by making people more satisfied with life"), as well as "divergent individual and group self-interests" (pp. 220, 212).

Our findings of cultural dissensus suggest that the impediments to environmental actions go well beyond institutional constraints, self-interest, or inadequate information. Or, rather, each of these is itself shaped by cultural commitments. Americans do not behave more like environmental activists because culturally they are quite unlike them. To begin with, the general public overwhelmingly believes in markets, business, and capitalism, while the activists generally do not. Most Americans do not see a lot wrong with a system that enables one to acquire more goods rather than being content with only a few. For environmental activists committed to an egalitarian culture, living with less is not just a sacrifice for the sake of the environment but a concrete expression of their commitment to an egalitarian way of life and their rejection of the acquisitive life of competitive individualism. To pose the issue in terms of self-interest versus altruism is to miss the rival value systems that undergird environmental policy debates.

Our point is not that activists want environmental amenities that the general public does not value—quite the contrary. Both want cleaner air and water, wilderness and species preservation, habitat protection, and a healthier, safer earth. Both are concerned about environmental degradation and are uneasy about the prospect of environmental catastrophe. But the divergence in their cultural biases is important because these biases shape the means activists choose to realize shared environmental goals. More specifically, since many or perhaps most activists do not trust markets, believing it unjust that resource allocations should reflect willingness and ability to pay, they may spurn policies that rely on markets to solve problems. Our evidence suggests that the public may be more willing to accept such market-based solutions to environmental problems.

IMPLICATIONS FOR "CULTURAL THEORY"

The strong relationships reported in this article between egalitarian and antimarket cultural biases, on the one hand, and environmental attitudes and beliefs, on the other, cast serious doubt on Paehlke's ideological autonomy thesis. Our evidence regarding the New Politics thesis is more mixed. Individual-level correlations show little or no relationship between an elite-challenging outlook and environmental attitudes; yet, the environmental activists are far more elite-challenging than are the Salem Yamhill public. The dramatic difference

in cultural biases between activists and the public undercuts the cultural consensus thesis, as do the substantial differences in cultural bias between radical and mainstream environmental groups. Our findings, then, refute the autonomy and consensus theses, but do they vindicate Douglas and Wildavsky's cultural theory?

Our results support the claim that environmental attitudes are embedded in broader sociocultural orientations. Moreover, Douglas, Wildavsky, and their various collaborators appear to be correct in arguing that the value one places on equality and markets is an important determinant of environmental attitudes and beliefs. Furthermore, these cultural theorists, together with theorists of the New Politics, appear to be correct in their view that environmental activists often adhere to cultural orientations markedly divergent from those of the general public. Nevertheless, our findings hardly demonstrate the indisputable triumph of cultural theory. Proponents of that theory posit four distinct cultural biases and four distinct attitudes toward nature, yet we found the environmental debate to be primarily a dispute between egalitarians and individualists (cf. Cotgrove 1982). Although we did not test for fatalism, the other cultural bias we tested, hierarchy, proved to be only weakly and inconsistently related to environmental attitudes.

This muddled empirical result mirrors a theoretical muddle about how hierarchical attitudes toward environmental issues are supposed to differ from individualistic attitudes (see especially Dake and Wildavsky 1991, 17). At times, cultural theorists collapse market individualism and hierarchy into a single "establishment" or "center" culture that downplays environmental and technological risks (Douglas and Wildavsky, 1982, chapter 5); at other times, they suggest that hierarchists will be somewhere in between the environmental alarmism of egalitarians and the unbridled optimism of competitive individualists (Thompson, Ellis, and Wildavsky 1990, 26–7). Although we found that the hierarchy and individualism scales were intercorrelated,[14] our results are more consistent with the latter than the former hypothesis. The relationship between hierarchy and environmentalism is radically different from that between individualism and environmentalism. Although hierarchial attitudes toward the environment can be distinguished from individualistic attitudes, it is hard to say positively what *is* the hierarchical conception of the environment.

Moreover, we found that ideological self-designation on the liberal-conservative scale correlates highly with both egalitarianism and market individualism, which suggests that these cultural biases are conceptually similar to the conventional left-right ideological continuum (cf. Dake and Wildavsky 1991).[15] Would it not be better, then, to speak of ideology rather than cultural bias? The difference may be largely semantic; indeed, Wildavsky often seems to use the terms "cultural bias" and "ideology" almost interchangeably (1987, 13, and 1988, 593, 594; also see Fine 1995, 130, 132; Wilson 1992, chapter 1). Ideology, as Todd Gitlin has said, is but "contested culture" (Swidler 1986, 279, n14). Wildavsky tends to prefer "culture" to "ideology," however, because, as Geertz (1973, esp. 196–200) pointed out more than thirty years ago, the term "ideology" connotes psychologically "deformed" or "distorted" thought. Wildavsky, following Douglas, prefers the term "cultural bias" because he means to insist that all preferences, not just those with which he disagrees, are "mired in bias" (Wildavsky 1984, 25).

The problem with using "culture" when not referring to entire nations or linguistic, religious, or ethnic groups is that this is at odds with standard usage (Laitin 1988, 589). For Douglas and Wildavsky, however, the key gauge of culture is not a shared language, god, or flag but whether the same people consistently line up on the same side of seemingly unrelated issues (Wildavsky 1988, 593, 595). Our survey did not probe attitudes beyond the environmental domain, but research on new social movements has consistently demonstrated the overlap between the personnel, methods, and ideology of the environmental, peace, antinuclear, feminist, and consumer protection movements (Johnston and Klandermans 1995a; O'Riordan 1995, 5). Douglas and Wildavsky's cultural theory implies that those who are active across a range of social movements will share the same cultural bias or, if you must, ideology or even "ideoculture" (Johnston and Klandermans 1995b, 12).

The suitability of the term "culture" is especially problematic when one relies, as we have, on attitudinal data alone. A full test of the Douglas-Wildavsky cultural theory would incorporate ethnographic data detailing social and institutional relations within environmental groups (Marris, Langford, and O'Riordan 1996, 6; Gross and Rayner 1985; cf. Laitin 1988, 591–2). If we found, for example, that groups whose members share egalitarian preferences (Earth Island and Earth First! in our surveys) are also organized in a more egalitarian manner, then we would be more justified in referring to "culture" rather than "ideology," since shared social relations as well as values and beliefs would be involved.

In an exchange with Wildavsky in the pages of this journal, Laitin objected that Wildavsky's cultural theory "does not answer his question about the source of preferences but merely pushes it back one step" (Laitin 1988, 590; also Friedman 1991, 346). Egalitarianism explains a substantial amount of variation in environmental preferences, but what explains the preference for egalitarianism? This is an important question, but to concede that Wildavsky's cultural theory pushes the question of preference formation back a step is not to deny the utility of cultural explanations (cf. Ellis 1993, 106–7). As a logical matter, there can be *no* value or preference about which one cannot ask a further "but why?" question. Laitin's objection, then, is not specific to the Douglas-Wildavsky version of cultural theory; it

applies to all attempts to explain specific beliefs or attitudes in terms of more general and stable values or worldviews.[16] Douglas and Wildavsky freely admit that their cultural theory "has very little to say about people's choices between social forms" (Douglas 1982b, 7; also Wildavsky 1987, 4, 6). What their cultural theory does say is that once an individual opts for a particular set of ideas and institutions, a wide range of other attitudes and behaviors follow. Predicting a lot from a little is our idea of a powerful theory.

APPENDIX A
Sample Information and Methods

ENVIRONMENTAL ACTIVISTS/MEMBERS

The Audubon sample was obtained from an August 1994 membership list of the Salem Audubon Society. We selected a systematic sample of 400 names from a list of more than 800. Although the majority of the chapter lives in Salem, members also reside in a number of smaller towns in the area. Of the 400 surveys sent out in May 1995, 36 were returned undeliverable; the 214 surveys returned completed represent a response rate of 59% (214/364). The Sierra Club sample was randomly drawn by club officials from the membership lists of the Oregon chapter, which counts approximately 14,000 members. Surveys were mailed in June 1995. Three were returned undeliverable, and 202 were completed and returned on time, for a response rate of 51% (202/397). The Earth Island sample was drawn by obtaining a list of members in Oregon and Washington. We sent the survey to each of the 246 Oregon members and randomly selected 254 of the 410 Washington members in May 1995. Of these 500 surveys, 16 were returned undelivered; the 290 completed surveys represent a response rate of 60% (290/484). One follow-up mailing was used for each group.

SALEM-YAMHILL PUBLIC

In December 1995, we mailed a shorter version of the survey to residents of Yamhill County and Salem, Oregon. Systematic probability samples of 400 households in the county and 400 households in Salem-Keizer were drawn from the respective phone books. For Salem-Keizer, 24 surveys were undeliverable, and the 197 surveys returned and completed yielded a response rate of 52% (197/376). For Yamhill County, 15 surveys were undeliverable, and the 180 surveys returned and completed represented a response rate of 47% (180/385). The total response rate for the two surveys was 50% (377/761). Two follow-up mailings were made. To compensate for a pronounced gender imbalance (almost two males to every one female), we weighted the sample for gender in calculating mean scores and frequencies for the Salem-Yamhill data.

Demographically, the Salem-Yamhill respondents have substantially lower education levels than do members of the three environmental groups, who tend to be extremely well educated. Almost three-quarters of the environmentalists claim to have college degrees, as compared to 43 percent of the public sample (46% in Salem, 38% in Yamhill). In age and household income, the two samples look remarkably similar, with environmentalists slightly more affluent and no different in average age. Within the environmental groups, however, there was substantial age variation. Audubon respondents are substantially older than either Sierra Club or Earth Island respondents. Among the former, for instance, 36% are over age 65, and only 22% are under age 45, compared to 22% and 43% for the latter two.

ENVIRONMENTAL LEADERS

In late summer 1995, the same version of the environmental survey was sent to 50 leaders in both the Sierra Club and the Earth Island Institute. The latter list was obtained from the projects given on the inside cover of a recent issue of the group's magazine, in consultation with Mary Houghteling, Earth Island's Development Director. The Sierra Club leadership list was compiled by Bob Frenkel, chair of the Oregon chap-

ter. We received 33 surveys from the Sierra Club and 29 from Earth Island, for a response rate of 66% and 58%, respectively. No follow-up letter was sent.

EARTH FIRST!

The sample was obtained from Dan Metz's (1995) survey of the Portland-based group, the Voluntary Human Extinction Movement. The group's motto, "May we live long and die out," expresses its leader's belief that only by voluntarily halting human reproduction can the earth and its creatures recover and flourish. The questionnaire, which included a number of the same items used in the environmental survey, was sent in April 1995 to all U.S. subscribers of the group's newsletter, *These Exit Times*. Only two were returned as undeliverable. The response rate, with no follow-up mailing, was 58% (219/375). The survey included a question asking respondents whether they belonged to Earth First! Seventy-nine respondents (36%) reported that they did.

APPENDIX B
Measurement and Scale Construction

For the first seven categories below, reference is made to a seven-point scale: strongly disagree (–3), disagree (–2), somewhat disagree (–1), neither agree nor disagree (0), somewhat agree (+1), agree (+2), strongly agree (+3).

NEW ECOLOGICAL CONSCIOUSNESS

The scale is scored as an average of the ten items in Table 5.8. Each item was scored on a seven-point scale. Standard deviation and the internal consistency of items are reported in Table 5.8.

ENVIRONMENTAL CONCERN

The scale is scored as an average of the five items in Table 5.9. Each item was scored on a seven-point scale. Standard deviation and the internal consistency of items are reported in Table 5.9. Scoring on items 2 and 5 was reversed.

EGALITARIANISM

The scale is scored as an average of the three hierarchy items in Table 5.10. Each item was scored on a seven-point scale.

TABLE 5.8   **New Ecological Consciousness**

	Valid N	Standard Deviation	Item-to-Total Correlation	Alpha If Item Deleted
1. If things continue on their present course, we will soon experience a major ecological catastrophe.	704	1.30	.64	.80
2. What human beings are currently doing to nature can be fairly characterized as an "ecoholocaust."	700	1.50	.65	.80
3. Humans are no more important than any other species.	701	2.00	.42	.82
4. We would be better off if we dramatically reduced the number of people on this earth.	697	1.78	.43	.82
5. No wild place will be safe from us until we reconsider our devout belief that economic growth is always good.	700	1.47	.55	.81
6. We can only save the planet by radically transforming our social lives with each other.	698	1.61	.46	.82
7. Unrelenting exploitation of nature has driven us to the brink of ecological collapse.	702	1.51	.60	.80
8. We have reduced natural beauty to postcard prettiness, just another commodity for our consumption.	697	1.63	.58	.80
9. Human happiness and human reproduction are less important than a healthy planet.	694	1.67	.43	.82
10. The oceans are gradually dying of oil pollution and dumping of waste.	703	1.21	.49	.82
Ten-item New Ecological Consciousness Scale	663	.99	NA	NA
Cronbach's alpha = .83				

NA = Not applicable.

Standard deviation and the internal consistency of items are reported in Table 5.10.

HIERARCHY

The scale is scored as an average of the three hierarchy items in Table 5.9. Each item was scored on a seven-point scale.

Standard deviation and the internal consistency of items are reported in Table 5.9.

INDIVIDUALISM

The scale is scored as an average of the three individualism items in Table 5.10. Each item was scored on a seven-point scale. Standard

TABLE 5.9   Environmental Concern

	Valid N	Standard Deviation	Item-to-Total Correlation	Alpha If Item Deleted
1. If things continue on their present course, we will soon experience a major ecological catastrophe.	376	1.88	.80	.82
2. The problems of the environment are not as bad as most people think.	376	1.77	.68	.85
3. The oceans are gradually dying from oil pollution and dumping of waste.	377	1.73	.71	.84
4. We are fast using up the world's natural resources.	375	1.69	.69	.85
5. People worry too much about human progress harming the environment.	377	1.88	.63	.86
Five-item Environmental Concern Scale Cronbach's alpha = .87	373	1.46	NA	NA

NA = Not applicable.

deviation and the internal consistency of items are reported in Table 5.10.

SPENDING ON THE ENVIRONMENT

Item wording was: "We are spending too little money on improving and protecting the environment." The item was scored on a seven-point scale. In the activist sample, standard deviation = 1.18; in the unweighted Salem-Yamhill sample, standard deviation = 1.87.

PARTICIPATION

Item wording was: "We should all participate in each decision that directly affects its." The item was scored on a seven-point scale. Standard deviation = 1.49. The item was not used in the Salem-Yamhill survey.

POLITICAL ACTIVITY

Environmental group members were asked: "Which, if any, of the following activities have you engaged in during the past four years? (1) Written a letter to a member of Congress or the state legislature about an environmental issue. (2) Written a letter to the editor about an environmental issue. (3) Boycotted a company's products because of its record on the environment. (4) Done volunteer work for an environmental group. (5) Attended a meeting of an environmental group." In Table 5.7 in the text, those who reported performing one or fewer of these activities were scored as "inert"; those performing two or three were scored as "active"; and those performing four or five were scored as "highly active."

PARTY IDENTIFICATION

"Do you think of yourself as closer to the Republican Party or Democratic Party." Values ranged from 0 (Republican) to 1 (Democrat), with "Neither" as a third option. Standard deviation = .33 in activist sample, .50 in unweighted Salem-Yamhill sample. In

TABLE 5.10   Cultural Biases

	Sample	Valid N	Standard Deviation	Item-to-Total Correlation	Alpha If Item Deleted
Egalitarianism					
1. The world would be a more peaceful place if its wealth were divided more equally among nations.	Activist	701	1.78	.61	.70
	Public	374	1.85	.55	.75
2. We need to dramatically reduce inequalities between the rich and the poor, whites and people of color, and men and women.	Activist	699	1.49	.60	.71
	Public	370	1.90	.61	.68
3. What our country needs is a fairness revolution to make the distribution of goods more equal.	Activist	695	1.66	.63	.67
	Public	370	1.75	.65	.64
Three-item Egalitarianism Scale	Activist	689	1.37	NA	NA
	Public	368	1.52	NA	NA
Cronbach's alpha = .77 in both populations.					
Hierarchy					
1. One of the problems with people today is that they challenge authority too often.	Activist	700	1.54	.55	.69
	Public	375	1.83	.45	.56
2. Society works best when people strictly obey all rules and regulations.	Activist	700	1.63	.59	.64
	Public	372	1.61	.49	.49
3. Respect for authority is one of the most important things that children should learn.	Activist	703	1.74	.58	.65
	Public	375	1.35	.43	.58
Three-item Hierarchy Scale	Activist	698	1.33	NA	NA
	Public	370	1.23	NA	NA
Cronbach's alpha = .75 in activist sample and .64 in Salem-Yamhill public sample.					
Individualism					
1. Competitive markets are almost always the best way to supply people with the things they need.	Activist	700	1.70	.44	.57
	Public	377	1.50	.41	.59
2. Society would be better off if there was much less government regulation of business.	Activist	701	1.65	.45	.55
	Public	374	1.82	.46	.54
3. People who are successful in business have a right to enjoy their wealth as they see fit.	Activist	700	1.73	.47	.53
	Public	373	1.53	.49	.49
Three-Item Individualism Scale	Activist	693	1.30	NA	NA
	Public	372	1.24	NA	NA
Cronbach's alpha = .64 in both populations.					

NA = Not applicable.

the regression analysis reported in text Table 5.5 and the partial correlations reported in text Table 5.3, dummy variables were created for Republican and for Democrat.

IDEOLOGY

"In general, when it comes to politics, do you usually think of yourself as...Strongly Conservative, Conservative, Somewhat Conservative, Somewhat Liberal, Liberal, Strongly Liberal, None of the Above." Standard deviation = 1.17 in activist sample, 1.15 in unweighted Salem-Yamhill sample.

AGE

Responses were coded in six categories, from under age 25 (1) to over age 65 (6). Standard deviation = 1.48 in activist sample, 1.40 in unweighted Salem-Yamhill sample.

EDUCATION

Responses were coded in six categories, from some high school (1) to graduate degree (6). Standard deviation = 1.37 in activist sample, 1.52 in unweighted Salem-Yamhill public.

GENDER

Responses were coded female (0) or male (1). Standard deviation = .50 in activist sample, .47 in unweighted Salem-Yamhill sample.

HOUSEHOLD INCOME

Responses were coded in six categories, from less than $20,000 (1) to more then $100,000 (6). Standard deviation = 1.49 in activist sample, 1.41 in unweighted Salem-Yamhill sample.

APPENDIX C
Rotated Factor Matrices

	Factor 1	Factor 2
Salem-Yamhill		
Peaceful place	.77343	–.16219
Reduce differences	.78429	–.24657
Fairness revolution	.85439	–.14971
Competitive markets	–.20150	.69237
Less regulation	–.05738	.81803
Enjoy wealth	–.30116	.71093
Environmentalists		
Peaceful place	.79551	–.19512
Reduce differences	.79781	–.20145
Fairness revolution	.82797	–.19571

	Factor 1	Factor 2
Environmentalists		
Competitive markets	–.32272	.64730
Less regulation	–.07675	.81083
Enjoy wealth	–.21482	.74243

Note: In each sample, an initial principal components extraction produced two factors with eigenvalues greater than one. The eigenvalue of the first factor was 2.78 (46.4% of the variance) in the Salem-Yamhill sample and 2.85 (47.6% of the variance) in the environmentalist sample; the eigenvalue of the second factor was 1.06 (17.6% of the variance) in the Salem-Yamhill sample and 1.00 (16.7% of the variance) in the environmentalist sample. Subsequent common factor analysis retaining these two factors, with varimax rotation, yielded the factor loadings reported in this table.

ENDNOTES

1. Surveying National Opinion Research Center data on support for spending on the environment from 1973 to 1990, Jones and Dunlap (1992) found that age, education, income, gender, race, residence at age 16, current residence, occupational prestige, industrial sector, as well as political ideology and political party, taken all together, could not explain more than about 9% of the variance. Only age (Pearson's $r = -.23$) and to a much lesser extent education ($r = .14$) and ideology ($r = .14$) showed much of a relationship with support for environmental spending.

2. Recently, there has been closer empirical scrutiny. See, for example, Marris, Langford, and O'Riordan 1996; Grendstad and Selle 1997.

3. Environmentalism was originally no more than a passing footnote to Inglehart's "postmaterialism" thesis (1971,1012), but the environmental movement is now generally considered "the archetypical example of postmaterial politics" (Dalton 1994, xiii).

4. Our original plan was to survey at least one mainstream and one nonmainstream group. We chose these three primarily because they were the ones that granted us access to their membership list. We also hoped to survey a so-called wise-use group, but we were not successful in gaining access to its membership list.

5. We made no effort to measure Wildavsky's fourth category, "fatalism," largely because previous survey research (Jenkins-Smith 1994a, 16) has found it to be inconsequential in understanding environmental attitudes.

6. Throughout this article, we often refer to the Sierra Club, Earth Island, and Audubon members surveyed as "environmental activists." Although not all members of environmental groups are activists in the usual sense of that term, the great majority of our respondents deserve that label. During the past five years, more than 60% had attended an environmental group meeting; slightly more than half had done volunteer work for an environmental group; almost three-fourths had written a letter to a legislator regarding an environmental issue; and 80% participated in a product boycott because of the

company's record on the environment. The only political activity reported by less than a majority was writing a letter to the editor about an environmental issue, done by fewer than one-third. Of these five political activities, at least two were reported by 83% of respondents and four or five were reported by 40%.

7. The stronger relationship for the Salem-Yamhill group is likely due largely to the less restricted range of environmental responses among the public as compared to the activists. The standard deviation on the environmental spending item was 1.18 among the activists, compared to 1.87 for the public. Similarly, the standard deviation on the ten-item measure of ecological consciousness was 0.99, in contrast to 1.50 for the five-item measure of environmental concern used in the general public survey. The standard deviation for each item used in these scales is reported in Appendix B.

8. One of Inglehart's (1977, 399–400) two measures of "postmaterialism" is: "Give the people more say in important governmental decisions." Because our participation item proved to be so weakly related to environmental attitudes and beliefs, we dropped the item in the Salem-Yamhill survey.

9. Nor can the weakness of this relationship be attributed simply to the restriction of range on the participation item. The range and standard deviation (1.49) on the participation item are identical to those for another item: "We need to dramatically reduce inequalities between the rich and the poor, whites and people of color, and men and women" (see Table 5.10). Yet, the Pearson's r correlation between this egalitarian measure and the environmental spending item is .33, and the correlation with the new ecological consciousness scale is .28.

10. When one controls for other variables, as Table 5.5 shows, these weak relationships are even further at attenuated or, as is the case among activists, reversed.

11. These results are virtually identical to those found by Marris, Langford, and O'Riordan (1996, Table 6.2).

12. It is possible that there is an emerging consensus on biocentrism (Kempton, Boster, and

Hartley 1995, 224.) Such a claim is difficult to test since it involves the future direction of change. It is possible to say, however, that judging by our data, no such consensus has yet emerged. Moreover, to the extent that environmental attitudes remain tied to contested egalitarian and individualistic cultural biases, we would expect that it will be difficult for such a consensus to emerge.

13. Caution is necessary in generalizing from the Salem-Yamhill sample, which differs in a number of important ways from the nation or even the Pacific Northwest. Tables 5.6 and 5.7 likely overstate to some extent the differences in cultural bias between activists and the public. Two surveys by Jenkins-Smith (1994b) in New Mexico and the United States used an item virtually identical to one of ours: "What our country needs is a fairness revolution" (Jenkins-Smith used "society" rather than "country"). He found mean sores of –.14 for the state and –.22 for the nation. While those scores are still slightly less egalitarian than those of Audubon (–.06) and Sierra Club members (.03), they are more egalitarian than for the Salem-Yamhill sample (–.47). For another similar item, "People who are successful in business have a right to enjoy their wealth as they see fit." (Jenkins-Smith's item was, "People who get rich in business have a right to keep and enjoy their wealth,") he found that the public overwhelmingly endorsed this individualistic measure (mean scores of 1.33 and 1.40) in ways that seem comparable to the Salem-Yamhill sample (1.20) and quite unlike our activists. Obviously, larger national surveys are needed to gauge more accurately the attitudinal gap between activists and th general public.

14. The Pearson's *r*, correlation coefficient between hierarchy and individualism is .45 in the activist sample and .27 in the general public sample. These intercorrelations, however, are substantially less strong than previous research (using different items) has found. In Dake and Wildavsky (1991, 21), the intercorrelation between market individualism and hierarchy is .54; in Marris, Longford, and O'Riordan (1996, Table 6.2; also see 27) it is .65 or .53, depending on the items used.

15. For egalitarianism and ideological self-designation, Pearson's *r* is .52 among activists and .45 among the Salem-Yamhill public. The correlation between market individualism and ideology is –.63 among activists and –.45 among the general public. The correlation between hierarchy and ideology is –.49 in the activist sample but only –.23 among the general public.

16. A more troubling question remains, however. According to Wildavsky (1988, 6), what matters most to people is how they live with one another, but how do we know this is true? What matters most to some people could be how they live with nature. It is by no means obvious that cultural bias is primary and environmental commitment secondary or derivative. The strong relationship we uncovered between cultural bias and environmental values and beliefs is consistent with the Wildavsky-Douglas hypothesis, but it is also consistent with a model that portrays people deriving their cultural biases from their ecological concerns. Judging between these alternative models calls for further research into the relative stability of cultural biases and environmental values and beliefs as well as their temporal development.

REFERENCES

Brick, Phil, Pat Hannigan, and Ian Krueger. 1995. "Common Goals, Divided Communities: A Survey of Attitudes about Economic Change and Natural Resources in the Hells Canyon Region." Department of Politics, Whitman College, Walla Walla, WA. Typescript.

Cotgrove, Stephen. 1982. *Catastrophe or Cornucopia: The Environment, Politics and the Future.* Chichester, Eng: John Wiley.

Dake, Karl, and Aaron Wildavsky. 1990. "Theories of Risk Perception: Who Fears What and Why?" *Daedalus* 119(Fall):41–60.

Dake, Karl, and Aaron Wildavsky. 1991 "Individual Differences in Risk Perception and Risk-Taking Differences." In *The Analysis, Communication and Preception of Risk,* ed. B. John Garrick and Willard C. Gekler. New York: Plenum Press.

Dalton, Russell J. 1994. *The Green Rainbow: Environmental Groups in Western Europe.* New Haven, CT: Yale University Press.

Douglas, Mary. 1970. *Natural Symbols: Explorations in Cosmology.* London: Barrie and Rockliff.

Douglas, Mary. 1975. "Environments at Risk." *Implicit Meanings: Essays in Anthropology.* London: Routledge.

Douglas, Mary. 1982a. "Cultural Bias." *In the Active Voice.* London: Routledge.

Douglas, Mary. 1982b. "Introduction to Grid/Group Analysis." In *Essays in the Sociology of Preception,* ed. Mary Douglas. London: Routledge.

Douglas, Mary. 1997. "The Depoliticization of Risk." In *Culture Matters: Essays in Honor of Aaron Wildavsky,* ed. Richard J. Ellis and Michael Thompson. Boulder, CO: Westview Press.

Douglas, Mary, and Aaron Wildavsky. 1982. *Risk and Culture: An Essay on the Selection of Technological and Environmental Dangers.* Berkeley: University of California Press.

Dunlap, Riley F., George H. Gallup, Jr., and Alec M. Gallup. 1993. "Of Global Concern: Results of the Health of the Planet Survey." *Environment* 35(November):7–15, 33–40.

Dunlap, Riley E., and Rik Scarce. 1991. "The Polls—Poll Trends: Environmental Problems and Protection." *Public Opinion Quarterly* 55 (Winter):651–72.

Dunlap, Riley E., and Kent D. Van Liere, 1978. "The 'New Environmental Paradigm.'" *Journal of Environmental Education* 9(Summer):10–19.

Dunlap, Riley E., Kent D. Van Liere, Angela Mertig, William R. Catton, Jr., and Robert E. Howell. 1992. "Measuring Endorsement of an Ecological Worldview: A Revised NEP Scale." Paper presented at the sixth meeting of the Society for Human Ecology, Snowbird, Utah.

Ellis, Richard J. 1993. "The Case for Cultural Theory: Reply to Friedman." *Critical Review* 7 (Winter):81–128.

Fine, Gary Alan. 1995. "Public Narration and Group Culture: Discerning Discourse in Social Movements." In *Social Movements and Culture,* ed. Hank Johnston and Bert Klandermans. Minneapolis: University of Minnesota Press.

Friedman, Jeffrey. 1991. "Accounting for Political Preferences: Cultural Theory vs. Cultural History." *Critical Review* 5(Spring):325–51.

Geertz, Clifford. 1973. "Ideology as a Cultural System." *The Interpretation of Cultures.* New York: Basic Books.

Grendstad, Gunnar, and Per Selle. 1997. "Cultural Theory, Postmaterialism, and Environmental Attitudes." In *Culture Matters, Essays in Honor of Aaron Wildavsky,* ed. Richard J. Ellis and Michael Thompson. Boulder, CO: Westview Press.

Gross, Jonathan L., and Steve Rayner. 1985. *Measuring Culture: A Paradigm for the Analysis of Social Organization.* New York: Columbia University Press.

Guth, James L., John C. Green, Lyman A. Kellstedt, and Corwin E. Smidt. 1995. "Faith and the Environment: Religious Beliefs and Attitudes on Environmental Policy." *American Journal of Political Science* 39(May):364–82.

Inglehart, Ronald. 1971. "The Silent Revolution in Europe: Intergenerational Change in Post-Industrial Societies." *American Political Science Review* 65(December):991–1017.

Inglehart, Ronald. 1977. *The Silent Revolution: Changing Values and Political Styles among Western Publics.* Princeton, NJ: Princeton University Press.

Inglehart, Ronald. 1990. *Culture Shift in Advanced Industrial Society.* Princeton, NJ: Princeton University Press.

Jenkins-Smith, Hank C. 1994a. "Stigma Models: Testing Hypotheses of How Images of Nevada Are Acquired and Values Are Attached to Them." University of New Mexico, Albuquerque. Typescript.

Jenkins-Smith, Hank C. 1994b. "Frequency Report: USA and NM Samples Combined." Probabilistic Risk Assessment Project, Institute for Public Policy, University of New Mexico. Typescript.

Johnston, Hank, and Bert Klandermans, eds. 1995a. *Social Movements and Culture.* Minneapolis: University of Minnesota Press.

Johnston, Hank, and Bert Klandermans. 1995b. "The Cultural Analysis of Social Movements." In *Social Movements and Culture,* ed. Hank Johnston and Bert Klandermans. Minneapolis: University of Minnesota Press.

Jones, Robert Emmet, and Riley Dunlap. 1992. "The Social Bases of Environmental Concern: Have They Changed Over Time?" *Rural Sociology* 57 (Spring):28–47.

Kempton, Willett, James S. Boster, and Jennifer A. Hartley. 1995. *Environmental Values in American Culture.* Cambridge, MA: MIT Press.

Laitin, David. 1988. "Political Culture and Political Preferences." *American Political Science Review,* 82(June):589–93.

Marris, Claire, Ian Langford, and Timothy O'Riordan. 1996. "Integrating Sociological and Psychological Approaches to Public Perceptions of Environmental Risks: Detailed Results from A Questionnaire Survey." CSERGE Working Paper GEC 96-07. University of East Anglia, Norwich, England.

Metz, Dan. 1995. "Dissecting the Voluntary Human Extinction Movement." Willamette University, Salem, Oregon. Typescript.

Milbrath, Lester W. 1984. *Environmentalists: Vanguard for a New Society.* Albany: State University of New York Press.

O'Riordan, Timothy. 1995. "Frameworks for Choice: Core Beliefs and the Environment." *Environment* 37(October):4–9, 25–9.

Paehlke, Robert C. 1989. *Environmentalism and the Future of Progressive Politics.* New Haven, CT: Yale University Press.

Rayner, Steve. 1992. "Cultural Theory and Risk Analysis." In *Social Theories of Risk,* ed. Sheldon Krimsky and Dominic Golding. Westport, CT: Praeger.

Swidler, Ann. 1986. "Culture in Action: Symbols and Strategies." *American Sociological Review* 51(April):273–86.

Thompson, Michael, Richard Ellis, and Aaron Wildavsky. 1990. *Cultural Theory.* Boulder, CO: Westview Press.

Van Liere, Kent D., and Riley E. Dunlap. 1980. "The Social Bases of Environmental Concern: A Review of Hypotheses, Explanations and Empirical Evidence." *Public Opinion Quarterly* 44(Summer):181–97.

Wildavsky, Aaron. 1984. "From Political Economy to Political Culture, or Rational People Defend Their Way of Life." University of California, Berkeley. Typescript.

Wildavsky, Aaron. 1987. "Choosing Preferences by Constructing Institutions: A Cultural Theory of Preference Formation." *American Political Science Review* 81(March):3–21.

Wildavsky, Aaron. 1988. "Political Culture and Political Preferences." *American Political Science Review* 82(June):593–6.

Wildavsky, Aaron. 1991. *The Rise of Radical Egalitarianism.* Washington, DC: American University Press.

Wilson, Richard. 1992. *Compliance Ideologies: Rethinking Political Culture.* New York: Cambridge University Press.

12.   Global Concern for the Environment: Is Affluence a Prerequisite?*

RILEY E. DUNLAP AND ANGELA G. MERTIG

Conventional wisdom has long held that concern about environmental quality is limited primarily to residents of the wealthy, highly industrialized nations located primarily in the Northern hemisphere, as residents of the poorer, nonindustrialized nations are assumed to be too preoccupied with economic and physical survival to be concerned about environmental problems (e.g., Beckerman, 1974, p. 89). This assumption was apparent in media reports concerning the 1992 UN Conference on Environment and Development in Rio de Janeiro (e.g., Elmer-Dewitt, 1992) and, interestingly, it is present in social science theorizing regarding environmentalism.

When accounting for the development of green parties and public support for environmental protection, political scientists typically argue that environmentalism stems from the emergence of "postmaterialist values" (Inglehart, 1990). Such values, it is argued, have resulted from post-World War II affluence in the industrialized nations, and represent a growing concern for quality of life over economic welfare among younger generations that take the latter for granted. Underlying the materialist/

postmaterialist distinction is the assumption of a hierarchy of human needs and values as suggested by Maslow; thus, it is not surprising that this perspective is compatible with that of psychologists who argue that environmental concern is unlikely to develop in societies where basic human needs are poorly met (Leff, 1978, p. 50). Similarly, sociologists typically view environmentalism as an exemplar of the "new social movements" (e.g., the environmental, peace, antinuclear, and feminist movements) that have arisen within the wealthy, industrialized societies to pursue lifestyle and quality-of-life goals rather than economic interests (Buttel, 1992). Finally, economists widely regard environmental quality as a "luxury good" that is likely to be of concern only to those who do not have to worry about food, housing, and economic survival (Baumol & Oates, 1979). Since the emergence of postmaterialist values (and higher order needs) and the development of the new social movements that espouse them are viewed as dependent upon widespread, sustained affluence, these convergent theoretical perspectives all suggest that residents of the poor, nonindustrialized nations will be less concerned about environmental problems and less supportive of environmental protection than are their counterparts in the wealthy nations.

*This essay was first published in *Journal of Social Issues* 51(4)1995:121–137, and is reprinted here by permission of Blackwell Publishers.

The early emergence of environmentalism and green parties in the industrialized world (primarily North America and Europe) lends support to the above perspectives, as did the wary reaction to the 1972 UN Conference on the Human Environment in Stockholm among nonindustrialized nations. However, the more enthusiastic participation of the developing nations in the 1992 Earth Summit in Rio, a follow-up to the previous UN conference (Haas, Levy, & Parson, 1992), and especially the gradual emergence of environmental activism throughout much of the nonindustrialized world (Durning, 1989; Finger, 1992), clearly pose challenges to conventional wisdom. It could be argued, however, that these phenomena are atypical, and represent only the responses of government elites or tiny portions of residents of the poorer nations. In other words, conventional wisdom concerning rich–poor national differences in environmental concern might hold true at the level of the general public.

Because existing surveys of public opinion toward environmental issues tend to be confined to North America and Europe (which vary only moderately in levels of affluence), very little is known about the general public's views of environmental issues in nonindustrialized nations (a previous survey by Louis Harris & Associates, 1989, covering several less developed nations, was plagued by inadequate sampling). Consequently, it has heretofore not been possible to test the assumption that residents of poor nations are less environmentally concerned than are their counterparts in the wealthy nations. This situation has changed as a result of a recent international environmental opinion survey sponsored by the George H. Gallup International Institute.

METHODOLOGY

Sampling and Data Collection

The Health of the Planet (HOP) survey, coordinated by the George H. Gallup International Institute, was conducted in 24 economically and geographically diverse nations by members of the worldwide network of Gallup affiliates. The selection of countries was dependent upon the existence of a Gallup affiliate (or willing partner) and the availability of adequate funding. While the poorer, less economically developed nations (especially African nations) are consequently underrepresented, the intent was *not* to conduct a worldwide survey whose results could be generalized to the entire world (an unrealistic goal). Rather, the goal was to compare the public's views of environmental issues across a wide range of nations, in terms of both geographic location and level of economic development. As shown in Table 5.11, the 24 nations included in the HOP include 6 classified as "low" income nations, 7 as "medium" income nations, and 11 as "high" income nations by the World Bank on the basis of per capita gross national product (World Bank, 1992). Comparing citizens' views of environmental issues across such a wide range of nations should provide a reasonable test of the assumption that public concern for environmental quality is much stronger among the wealthy, industrialized nations than among their less-economically developed counterparts.

Each affiliate was responsible for translating the questionnaire into the appropriate language(s) for their nation, and then the Gallup International Institute had them "back-translated" into English to ensure comparability. The surveys were conducted via face-to-face, in-home interviews (thus minimizing problems of illiteracy), and all

TABLE 5.11   Per Capita GNP and Sample Size by Nation

Country/economic level	Per Capita GNP	Sample Size
Low income		
Nigeria	290	1195
India	350	4984
Philippines	730	1000
Turkey	1630	1000
Poland	1690	989
Chile	1940	1000
Middle income		
Mexico	2490	1502
Uruguay	2560	800
Brazil	2680	1414
Hungary	2780	1000
Russia	3200	964
Portugal	4900	1000
Korea (Rep.)	5400	1500
High income		
Ireland	9550	928
Great Britain	16,100	1105
Netherlands	17,320	1011
Canada	20,470	1011
United States	21,790	1032
Denmark	22,080	1019
Germany (West)	22,320	1048
Norway	23,120	991
Japan	25,430	1434
Finland	26,040	770
Switzerland	32,680	1011

Note: Per capita GNP based on World Bank (1992) categorization.

were completed during the first four months of 1992. Nationally representative samples were used in all nations but India, where rural areas and regions experiencing terrorism were underrepresented (and thus caution must be used in generalizing the results to the nation as a whole). As can be seen in Table 5.11, sample sizes ranged from a low of 770 in Finland to nearly 5000 in India, and most were within the 1000–1500 range—yielding results that should have margins of error of approximately 3% for the respective national populations.

Measurement of Variables

The HOP survey examined a wide range of topics related to environmental issues (Dunlap, Gallup & Gallup, 1993a, 1993b), and drew upon existing environmental opinion and attitude research to ensure that key substantive domains and theoretical conceptualizations of environmental attitudes were employed (Dunlap & Scarce, 1991; Van Liere & Dunlap, 1981). In particular, we went beyond existing sociological and political science studies that have focused narrowly on "environmental activism" (e.g., Inglehart, 1990) by employing a wide range of indicators of public concern about environmental quality. We will examine several dealing with the perceived seriousness of environmental problems (at various geographical levels), personal concern about these problems, and support for environmental protection to provide a detailed examination of conventional wisdom about differences between residents of poor and wealthy nations. Some of our variables are single items, while others are multi-item composites. The variables, item(s) on which they are based, and coding procedures are reported in detail in Table 5.12 (frequency distributions for all items are reported in Dunlap et at., 1993a).

For each of the 14 environmental variables, we created national-level aggregate scores for every nation by computing the national mean of all responses. We did this because our concern is with *national-level* differences in environmental concern—specifically, in determining whether levels of concern are positively correlated with national affluence as commonly assumed. To measure the latter we used per capita gross national product, as reported in Table 5.11. In future analyses we plan to examine a variety of indicators of national affluence and quality of life, but since per capita gross national product (GNP) is the most widely used (albeit imperfect) measure of national affluence it provides the most direct test of conventional wisdom. Eventually we will also conduct individual-level analyses that

examine the relationships between socio-economic status and environmental concern within individual nations, as well as contextual analyses to explore possible variation in the social bases of environmental concern across nations, but such analyses are beyond the scope of this paper.

Data Analysis

Although conventional wisdom and social science theorizing hold that public concern for the environment is higher in wealthy nations than in poor nations, the precise nature of the relationship expected between national affluence and citizens' levels of environmental concern has not been specified. While the implicit assumption seems to be that such concern increases more or less linearly with affluence, some have argued for a more dramatic increase once a nation becomes highly industrialized—i.e., limited variation among poorer nations and among wealthy nations, but a vast difference in citizen concern between the two types of nations (Brechin & Kempton, 1994). Given the ambiguous nature of the expected positive relationship between national affluence and citizens' environmental concern, we conducted two types of analyses. First, we computed Pearson's correlation coefficients between per capita GNP and each of the 14 dependant variables for the 24 nations (in future analyses we will employ more robust techniques as recommended by Dietz, Kalof, & Frey, 1991), since at a minimum the conventional view leads us to expect positive relationships between affluence and environmental concern. Second, we also ran scattergrams for each correlation, in order to examine visually whether the observed relationships were obviously nonlinear. Because none of the relationships appears to reflect a sharp increase in environmental

TABLE 5.12   Description of Variables

Perceived Seriousness of Environmental Issues in Nation
Question wording: "I'm going to read a list of issues and problems currently facing many countries. For each one, please tell me how serious a problem you consider it to be *in our nation*.... Environmental Issues." *Coded as:* 1 = Not at all serious, 2 = Not very serious, 3 = Somewhat serious, 4 = Very serious. (Not sure, don't know and refused were deleted from analysis.)

Perceived Seriousness of Environment Relative to Other National Problems
Question wording: Same as prior item. Other National Problems: Hunger and homelessness; Crime and violence; Poor health care; The high cost of living; Racial, ethnic, or religious, prejudice and discrimination. *Coded as:* Score for prior item minus the mean rating of the other five national problems.

Personal Concern about Environmental Problems
Question wording: "How concerned are you personally about environmental problems?" *Coded as:* 1 = Not at all, 2 = Not very much, 3 = A fair amount, 4 = A great deal. (Not sure and refused deleted from analysis.)

Perceived Quality of Nation's Environment
Question wording: "Overall, how would you rate the quality of the environment in our *nation*?" *Coded as:* 1 = Very good, 2 = Fairly good, 3 = Fairly bad, 4 = Very bad. (Not sure, don't know and refused were deleted from analysis.)

Perceived Quality of Community Environment
Question wording: "Overall, how would you rate the quality of the environment here in your local *community*?" *Coded as:* Same as prior item.

Perceived Quality of World's Environment
Question wording: "Overall, how would you rate the quality of the environment of the *world* as a whole?" *Coded as:* Same as prior item.

Perceived Health Effects of Environmental Problems at Present
Question wording: "Please tell me—how much, if at all, you believe environmental problems now affect your health?" *Coded as:* 1 = Not at all, 2 = Not very much, 3 = A fair amount, 4 = A great deal. (Not sure, don't know and refused were deleted from analysis.)

Perceived Health Effects of Environmental Problems in the Past
Question wording: Please tell me—how much, if at all, you believe environmental problems affected your health in the past—say 10 years ago?" *Coded as:* Same as prior item.

Perceived Health Effects of Environmental Problems in the Future
Question wording: "Please tell me—how much, if at all, you believe environmental problems will affect the health of our children and grandchildren—say over the next 25 years?" *Coded as:* Same as prior item.

Average Perceived Seriousness of Six Community Environmental Problems
Question wording: "Here is a list of environmental problems facing many *communities*. Please tell me how serious you consider each one to be here *in your community*.... Poor water quality; Poor air quality; Contaminated soil; Inadequate sewage, sanitation and garbage disposal; Too many people, overcrowding; Too much noise." *Coded as:* 1 = Not at all serious, 2 = Not very serious, 3 = Somewhat serious, 4 = Very serious. (Not sure and refused were deleted from analysis, and individuals with fewer than four items with valid data were deleted from analysis.) *Standardized alphas* for each country range from .74 (Uruguay) to .89 (Finland, Norway).

TABLE 5.12   Continued

Average Perceived Seriousness of Seven World Environmental Problems
Question wording: "Now let's talk about the *world as a whole*. Here is a list of
environmental issues that may be affecting the world as a whole. As I read each one,
please tell me how serious a problem you *personally* believe it to be in the *world*…or you
don't know enough about it to judge?… Air pollution and smog; Pollution of rivers,
lakes, and oceans; Soil erosion, polluted land, and loss of farmland; Loss of animal and
plant species; Loss of the rainforests and jungles; Global warming or the "greenhouse"
effect; Loss of ozone in the earth's atmosphere." *Coded as:* Same as prior item. (Can't
judge and refused were deleted from analysis, and individuals with fewer than five
items with valid data were deleted from analysis.) *Standardized alphas* for each country
range from .72 (India) to .90 (Mexico).

Average Level of Support for Six Environmenbd Measures
Question wording: "Here are some actions our government could take to help solve our
nation's environmental problems. *Keeping in mind that there are costs associated with these
actions,* please tell me—for each one I read—whether you would strongly favor,
somewhat favor, somewhat oppose, or strongly oppose this action…. Make stronger
environmental protection laws for business and industry; Make laws requiring that all
citizens conserve resources and reduce pollution; Provide family planning information
and free birth control to all citizens who want it to help reduce birth rates; Support
scientific research to help find new ways to control pollution; Limit exports of our
natural resources to other nations; Ban the sale of products that are unsafe for the
environment." *Coded as:* 1 = Strongly oppose, 2 = Somewhat oppose, 3 = Somewhat
favor, 4 = Strongly favor. (Not sure, don't know, and refused were deleted from analysis,
and individuals with fewer than four items with valid data were deleted from analysis.)
Standardized alphas for each country range from .46 (Nigeria) to .86 (Poland), with the
majority ranging from .60 to .69.

Preferred Trade-Off Between Environmental Protection and Economic Growth
Question wording: "With which one of these statements about the environment and the
economy do you *most* agree? Protecting the environment should be given priority, even at
the risk of slowing down economic growth; Economic growth should be given priority,
even if the environment suffers to some extent." *Coded as:* 1 = Economic growth given
priority, 2 = Equal priority (if volunteered), 3 = Environment given priority. (Not sure was
coded as equal priority and refused was deleted from the analysis.)

Willingness to Pay Higher Prices for Environmental Protection
Question wording: "Increased efforts by business and industry to improve environmental
quality might lead to higher prices for the things you buy. Would you be willing to pay
higher prices so that industry could better protect the environment, or not?" *Coded as:*
1 = Not willing; 2 = Not sure/Don't know; 3 = Yes, willing. (Refused was deleted from
the analysis.)

concern once a threshold of affluence is
reached, and given our space limitations,
the scattergrams are not shown here (but
are reported in Dunlap & Mertig, 1994).

Some analysts have argued for using the
logarithm of per capita GNP, on the assump-

tion that differences of a few hundred dollars, for example, mean more among poorer
nations than among wealthy
nations (Brechin & Kempton, 1994). We therefore
conducted parallel analyses using both per
capita GNP and log of per capita GNP, and

report correlations for both. And finally, because we know that the sample for India is unrepresentative of rural areas, and because we have to employ a rough estimate of per capita GNP for the Republic of Russia, we also repeated the analyses with India and Russia deleted. However, since the deletion of these two countries had no substantial effect on any of the reported correlations, and certainly not on our overall conclusions, we will not report the results of this analysis.

RESULTS

Perceived Seriousness and Personal Concern

A criticism of U.S. environmental polls is that they often fail to examine environmental issues within the context of other important issues, and thus elicit misleadingly strong indications of public concern about environmental quality (Dunlap, 1995). To deal with the problem we began the HOP survey by asking a couple of questions about national-level problems *before* respondents were aware that the major focus of the survey was on environmental issues. We first asked an open-ended item, "What do you think is the most important problem facing our nation today?" The results are not used in the paper because this item yields a dichotomous variable (volunteered environmental problems or not) inappropriate for use in correlational analysis, but are reported elsewhere (Dunlap et al., 1993a, 1993b). Overall, residents of the wealthier nations are somewhat more likely to volunteer environment as their nation's "most important problem," but the results reveal that environmental quality is a surprisingly salient public issue throughout the 24 nations—and thus a meaningful topic for opinion surveys in all of them. While in some countries only 1 or 2% volunteer en-

vironmental problems as their nation's "most important problem," in over half of the countries environmental problems are volunteered by 10% or more—a level seen only rarely in the U.S. (Dunlap, 1995).

We then gave respondents a list of six national-level problems and issues, including environment, and asked them to rate the seriousness of each one on a 4-point scale. As shown in Table 5.13, there is a slightly negative (albeit insignificant) relationship between GNP/capita and *Perceived Seriousness of Environmental Issues in Nation*—the opposite of what conventional wisdom predicts. It is also important to emphasize that large majorities of citizens in all 24 nations tend to see environmental problems as at least "somewhat serious" (percents reported in Dunlap et al., 1993a).

Since all six national problems/issues were rated as more serious in the poorer nations, we created a new variable to measure the perceived seriousness of environment *relative* to the other problems by subtracting the mean rating for these five from that given to environment. The correlation between GNP/capita and *Perceived Seriousness of Environment Relative to Other National Problems* is strong and highly significant, indicating that environmental issues are rated as *relatively* less serious in low-income nations. It should be noted, however, that even in a majority of the poorer countries (i.e., those with GNP/capita of $5000 or less) environment is rated *above average* for these issues in seriousness (Dunlap & Mertig, 1994, Fig. 2)

Which of the above two variables is the better indicator of the perceived seriousness of environmental issues is debatable, but the results seem clear: Residents of low-income nations are slightly more likely to rate environment as a serious problem, but significantly less likely to rate it as serious

TABLE 5.13   **Correlations between National-Level Measures of Environmental Awareness and Concern and Per Capita GNP and Log of Per Capita GNP**

Variable	GNP/Capita	Log GNP/Capita
Perceived Seriousness of Environmental Issues in Nation	−0.18	−0.13
Perceived Seriousness of Environment Relative to Other National Problems	0.69***	0.73***
Personal Concern about Environmental Problems[a]	−0.49*	−0.48*
Perceived Quality of Nation's Environment	−0.56**	−0.47*
Perceived Quality of Community Environment	−0.61**	−0.55**
Perceived Quality of World's Environment	0.41 *	0.63**
Perceived Health Effects of Environmental Problems at Present	−0.69***	−0.66***
Perceived Health Effects of Environmental Problems in the Past	−0.26	−0.33
Perceived Health Effects of Environmental Problems in the Future	−0.54**	−0.47*
Average Perceived Seriousness of Six Community Environmental Problems	−0.52**	−0.58**
Average Perceived Seriousness of Seven World Environmental Problems	0.05	0.30
Average Level of Support for Six Environmental Protection Measures	−0.79***	−0.67***
Preferred Trade-Off Between Environmental Protection and Economic Growth	0.55**	0.73***
Willing to Pay Higher Prices for Environmental Protection	0.50*	0.66***

[a]Poland deleted.
*$p < .05$.
**$p < .01$.
***$p < .001$.

relative to other national problems, than are their counterparts in high-income nations. Citizens in all 24 nations, however, tend to see the environment as a relatively serious problem.

A more direct indicator of personal concern about environmental quality was used in the HOP after we had informed respondents of our particular interest in environmental issues (as explained below). We employed a standard measure of environmental concern by asking respondents directly—"How concerned are you personally about environmental problems?"—and allowing them to respond on a 4-point scale. (In Poland the item was incorrectly trans- lated as "How much attention do you give to environmental problems?" and we have deleted the Polish data for this variable.) The correlation between *Level of Personal Concern about Environmental Problems* and per capita GNP is surprisingly the opposite of that predicted by conventional wisdom, as residents of low-income nations tend to express higher levels of concern about environmental problems than do those of high-income nations.

Ratings of Environmental Quality

To get a sense of why people around the world are concerned about environmental problems, the HOP survey asked them to rate the quality of the environment at the national, local and world levels. This question also provided a transition to the specifically environmental focus of the questionnaire (it was asked immediately *prior* to the "personal concern" item just discussed) and as a means of clarifying exactly what we meant by "environment." After defining what we meant by environment (see Dunlap et al., 1993a, 1993b) we asked respondents to "rate the quality of the environment" for their nation, then for their local community and finally for the world as a whole. Consistent with prior research, we found that in most nations the world environment was rated the worst and the community environment the best, with the national environment in between.

The pattern of correlations between per capita GNP and ratings of environmental quality at these three geographical levels is quite interesting. The relationships are significantly negative for both the national and community levels (*Perceived Quality of Nation's Environment* and *Perceived Quality of Community Environment*), indicating that the poorer the nation the more likely residents are to rate their local and national environments badly. The relationship is reversed for *Perceived Quality of World's Environment*, however, as residents of high-income nations are more likely to see the world environment as being in bad shape than are those in low-income nations.

The results provide another indication that conventional wisdom about national differences in environmental concern is misguided. Citizens of poorer nations not only rate their community environment as significantly worse than do their counterparts in richer nations (which may not be so surprising, given the high levels of pollution found in many Third World cities) but the same

pattern holds for the national environment as well. It is only when we focus on the worldwide environment that we find residents of wealthy nations more likely to offer negative ratings. At a minimum, these results reflect the importance of specifying the geographical referent when discussing differences in public concern about environmental problems across nations.

Environmental Problems as Health Threats

At the time of the 1972 Stockholm conference, environmental problems were widely viewed as primarily aesthetic issues or threats to the beauty of nature. This likely contributed to the cool reception given to environmental protection by the poorer nations at that time (Founex Report, 1982). A major change in the past two decades has been a growing awareness that environmental problems pose threats to human health, and this appears to have contributed to the rising concern over environmental deterioration observed in the U.S. and Europe.

To investigate the perceived health effects of environmental problems in the HOP, we asked respondents to indicate how much, if at all, they believe environmental problems *now* affect their health, and then asked them if it affected their health *10 years ago* and if they thought it would affect the health of their "children and grandchildren—say over the *next 25 years*." We found a strong increase in reported health effects over time. While majorities in only 4 nations report that environmental problems affected their health at least "a fair amount" ten years ago, majorities in 16 nations report such health effects at present and majorities in all 24 countries expect them over the next 25 years (Dunlap et al., 1993b).

In all three cases—*Perceived Health Effects of Environmental Problems at Present, Perceived*

Health Effects of Environmental Problems in the Past, and *Perceived Health Effects of Environmental Problems in the Future*—the relationship between perceiving health effects from environmental problems and national affluence is negative, although it fails to reach significance for past health effacers. It is especially notable that people in poor nations are more likely than their counterparts in wealthy nations to foresee negative health impacts from environmental degradation a quarter century from now.

That residents of poorer nations are significantly more likely to feel their present (and future) health is being (or will be) negatively affected by environmental problems provides insight into their previously noted higher levels of personal concern about such problems. Conventional wisdom should acknowledge that environmental problems are no longer viewed as just a threat to quality of life, but as a fundamental threat to human welfare. This threat is especially great in poor nations, where people often depend directly on the immediate environment for sustenance (food, water, fuel, and building materials) and environmental degradation therefore threatens their very survival.

Perceived Seriousness of Specific Environmental Problems

Besides asking respondents to rate the quality of the environment at various geographical levels, as noted above, we wanted to learn what types of environmental problems they viewed as most serious at each level. For the national level we used an open-ended question that asked respondents to volunteer what they considered to be the most important environmental problem (see Dunlap et al. 1993a, p. 18), but at the community and world levels we gave

them lists of potential problems and asked them to rate the seriousness of each one.

For the community we used a list of six types of problems, and computed the mean of their ratings to create an overall indicator of *Average Perceived Seriousness of Six Community Environmental Problems.* There is a significant negative relationship between national affluence and the overall perceived seriousness of environmental problems (e.g., air and water pollution) at the community level. Residents of the poorer nations are significantly more likely to see their local community as suffering from various forms of environmental degradation, just as they were more likely to rate the quality of their community environment as lower (as noted previously).

We also computed the mean of respondents' ratings of seven worldwide environmental problems to create a measure of *Average Perceived Seriousness of World Environmental Problems.* Unlike the previously noted ratings of the quality of the world environment, the relationship is not the reverse of that for perceived seriousness of community environmental problems. Indeed, there is no relationship ($r = .05$) between national affluence and the average perceived seriousness of specific environmental problems at the world level (although residents of poorer nations are more likely to respond that they "don't know enough…to judge" these problems—see Dunlap et al., 1993a). However, this is the one variable for which the results differ notably depending on whether one uses GNP/capita or log of GNP/capita, as in the latter case the correlation is more sizable (.30) even though it still fails to reach significance. The at-best weak relationship between national affluence and citizens' perceptions of problems such as global warming and ozone depletion as serious will come as a surprise to those committed to conventional wisdom.

Support for Environmental Protection Measures

In addition to inquiring about respondents' perceptions of the seriousness of environmental problems and their levels of personal concern about such problems, we wanted to examine levels of support for specific environmental protection measures that various nations might take. We included a list of six rather diverse measures in the HOP (their diversity accounts for the relatively low alphas for this measure), and asked respondents whether they favored or opposed each one. To obtain an indicator of overall support for environmental protection, we computed the mean of the ratings given to these items. The resultant correlation between *Average Level of Support for Six Environmental Protection Measures* and per capita GNP provides one of the most striking contradictions to conventional wisdom, as it is highly negative. Even though most of these measures are favored by majorities in most of the nations, residents of the low-income countries are clearly more likely to favor them than are residents of high-income countries. This result strongly reinforces the previously reported negative relationships, and indicates that residents of poorer nations not only tend to see environmental problems as more serious, but are also more supportive of efforts to ameliorate them, than are their counterparts in the wealthier nations.

Environmental Protection and Economics

Despite the increasing emphasis being placed on the goal of sustainable development, or the achievement of economic growth without environmental deterioration, environmental protection is still widely viewed as conflicting with economic growth. Although aware of the potential shortcomings of questions that put the environment and economy in opposition, we nonetheless included a couple of items that forced respondents to make trade-offs between the two because they have been so widely used in the U.S. In posing these questions we expected that residents of low-income countries might of necessity be less willing to make economic sacrifices, even if they were as concerned as their counterparts in wealthier nations about environmental quality. In fact, using results from the Louis Harris multinational survey noted above, Brechin and Kempton (1994) computed the relationship between log per capita GNP and two forms of "willingness to pay" for environmental quality—paying higher taxes and volunteering two hours per week of community work on behalf of the environment. They found a modest but insignificant positive correlation ($r = .21$) between national affluence and willingness to pay higher taxes, but a strong and highly significant negative correlation ($r = -.78$, $p < .001$) between affluence and willingness to volunteer time.

Our first item posed the environment vs. economy trade-off at the societal level by asking respondents to choose between giving priority to environmental protection or to economic growth. The second item focused on the more personal level by asking respondents if they would "be willing to pay higher prices so that industry could better protect the environment." Not surprisingly, the correlations between both *Preferred Trade-Off Between Environmental Protection and Economic Growth* and *Willingness to Pay Higher Prices for Environmental Protection* and per capita GNP are significantly positive. Residents of the wealthier nations are understandably (in view of their higher incomes) more likely to favor environmental protection over economic growth and to express a willingness to pay higher prices than are residents of the poorer nations.

A couple of important features about responses to these two items should be mentioned. First, *majorities* in 21 nations and pluralities in 2 (India and Turkey) choose environmental protection over economic growth, and only in Nigeria does economic growth receive even plurality support. Second, majorities in 17 nations and pluralities in 4 more express a willingness to pay higher prices for environmental protection, with only Nigeria, the Philippines, and—interestingly—Japan having pluralities expressing an unwillingness to pay higher prices (Dunlap et al., 1993b). In short, although we find the expected positive relationships between national affluence and willingness to make economic trade-offs on behalf of the environment, we cannot ignore the fact that priority is still given to environmental protection in a majority of the low-income countries. And, quite importantly, Brechin and Kempton's (1994) analysis suggests that we might have found a negative relationship had we employed a nonmonetary measure of willingness to pay (or sacrifice) for environmental quality.

SUMMARY AND CONCLUSION

If it were true that generalized public concern about environmental quality is far more prevalent in the wealthy, industrialized nations than in poorer nations—as conventional wisdom has long suggested—then all of the correlations reported in Table 5.13 should be positive. However, only four of the environmental attitude variables are positively and significantly related to per capita GNP, while seven are negatively and significantly correlated with national affluence (three are not significantly correlated). Two of the positive correlations are for variables measuring environment–economic trade-offs, measures for which residents of poorer nations are inherently disadvantaged, and a third is for the perceived seriousness of environmental problems relative to other national problems such as hunger and homelessness (which are surely more pressing in poor nations). The only other variable positively correlated with per capita GNP is rating of the quality of the world's environment. In contrast, the seven variables that are negatively correlated with GNP/capita cover a wide range of areas, including personal concern about environmental problems, perceived quality of community and national environments, perceived health effects from environmental problems (now and in the future), perceived seriousness of community environmental problems, and support for environmental protection measures. Clearly, then, the preponderance of evidence contradicts the widespread view that citizens of poor nations are less environmentally concerned than are their counterparts in wealthy nations.

Our results not only challenge "lay" wisdom, but also conventional social science analyses of environmentalism. The idea that environmental quality is a luxury affordable only by those who have enough economic security to pursue quality-of-life goals is inconsistent with the observed correlations, as well as with the overall high levels of environmental concern found among residents of the low-income nations in the HOP. Our results are thus compatible with growing evidence of strong, grass-roots' environmentalism in much of the Third World (Durning, 1989; Finger, 1992), and suggest that such activism likely reflects broad-based concern for environmental quality in these nations rather than the anomalous acts of small minorities.

It appears that conventional social science perspectives on global environmentalism are in need of revision. Theories premised on the emergence of postmaterialist values and new social movements appear useful for explaining environmentalism within most wealthy, industrialized nations (although Pierce, Lovrich, Tsurutani, & Abe, 1987, question their applicability in Japan), but seem unable to account for the emergence of grass-roots environmentalism and widespread public concern for environmental quality in poorer nations. In part this may stem from the fact that environmental degradation is increasingly seen, especially in poor nations, not as a postmaterialist quality-of-life issue but as a basic threat to human survival (as suggested by Ladd, 1982). In other words, environmental quality seems to be moving from a "higher order" value to a "lower order" need in Maslowian terms.

Future research on citizen concern about the state of the environment might benefit from paying more attention to people's direct experience with local environmental degradation (which will often be more visible in poor nations) as well as to growing awareness of global environmental threats to human welfare (such as ozone depletion). It seems possible that awareness of the threats posed by environmental degradation at local, national, and global levels—stimulated and reinforced by activists, scientists, and media as well as some degree of personal observation—are beginning to reinforce one another. In some cases, this may stimulate a homocentric concern with the welfare of one's self, family, and descendants, but in other cases it may lead to a more ecological perspective that recognizes that human welfare is inextricably related to that of the environment (Oates, 1989; Stem & Dietz, 1994).

Regardless of the nature and sources of public concern about environmental quality (which will no doubt vary across as well as within nations), the findings of the Health of the Planet survey should come as welcome news to those eager to move toward a more sustainable future. The old assumption that nonindustrialized nations will not worry about environmental protection until they have achieved economic development is incorrect. Citizens of these nations are clearly concerned about environmental quality; the question thus becomes whether or not the wealthy, highly industrialized nations (which have contributed disproportionately to worldwide environmental degradation) will assist them in translating their concern into the achievement of truly sustainable development (Jordan, 1994). Facilitating sustainable development within the nonindustrialized world, along with modifying our own ecologically unsustainable ways of life, should become a top priority for the wealthy, industrialized nations.

REFERENCES

Baumol, W. J., & Oates, W. E. (1979). *Economics, environmental policy, and the quality of life.* Englewood-Cliffs, NJ: Prentice-Hill.

Beckerman, W. (1974). *Two cheers for the affluent society.* New York: St. Martin's Press.

Brechin, S. R., & Kempton, W. (1994). Global environmentalism: A challenge to the post-materialism thesis? *Social Science Quarterly, 75,* 245–269.

Buttel, F. H. (1992). Environmentalization: Origins, processes, and implications for rural social change. *Rural Sociology, 57,* 1–27.

Dietz, T., Kalof, L., & Frey, R. S. (1991). On the utility of robust and resampling procedures. *Rural Sociology, 56,* 461–474.

Dunlap, R. E. (1995). Public opinion and environmental policy. In J. P. Lester (Ed.). *Environmental politics and policy* (2nd ed., pp. 63–113). Durham, NC: Duke University Press.

Dunlap, R. E., Gallup, G. H., Jr., & Gallup, A. M. (1993a). *Health of the planet.* Princeton, NJ: George H. Gallup International Institute.

Dunlap, R. E., Gallup, G. H., Jr., & Gallup, A. M. (1993b, November). Of global concern: Results of the health of the planet survey. *Environment, 35,* 6–15, 33–39.

Dunlap, R. E., & Mertig, A. G. (1994, July). *Global environmental concern: A challenge to the postmaterialism thesis.* Paper presented at the International Sociological Association's XIII World Congress of Sociology, Bielefeld, Germany.

Dunlap, R. E., & Scarce, R. (1991). The polls—polls trends: Environmental problems and protraction. *Public Opinion Quarterly. 55,* 651–672.

Durning, A. (1989). Mobilizing at the grassroots. In L. R. Brown (Ed.), *State of the world 1989* (pp. 154–173). New York: Norton.

Elmer-Dewitt, P. (1992, June 1). Rich vs. poor: Summit to save the earth. *Time,* pp. 42–58.

Finger, M. (1992). The changing green movement—A clarification. In M. Finger (Ed.), *The Green movement worldwide* (pp. 229–246). Greenwich, CT: JAI Press.

Founex Report. (1982). Environment and development. *International Conciliation, 586,* 1–84.

Haas, P. M., Levy, M. A., & Parson, E. A. (1992, October). Appraising the earth summit: How should we judge UNCED's success? *Environment, 34,* 6–11, 26–33,

Inglehart, R. (1990). *Culture shift in advanced industrial society.* Princeton, NJ: Princeton University Press.

Jordan, A. (1994, April). Financing the UNCED agenda: The controversy over additionality. *Environment. 36,* 16–20, 26–33.

Ladd, E. C. (1982, February/March). Clearing the air: Public opinion and public policy on the environment. *Public Opinion, 5,* 16–20.

Leff, H. L. (1978). *Experience, environment, and human potentials.* New York: Oxford.

Louis Harris & Associates. (1989). *Public and leadership attitudes to the environment.* New York: Louis Harris and Associates.

Oates, D. (1989). *Earth rising: Ecological belief in an age of science.* Corvallis: Oregon State University Press.

Pierce, J. C., Lovrich, N. P., Jr., Tsurutani. T., & Abe, T. (1987). Vanguards and rearguards in environmental politics: A comparison of activists in Japan and the United States. *Comparative Political Studies. 18,* 419–447.

Stem, P. C., & Dietz, T. (1994). The value basis of environmental concern. *Journal of Social Issues, 50*(3), 65–84.

Van Liere, K. D., & Dunlap, R. E. (1981). Environmental concern: Does it make a difference how it's measured? *Environment and Behavior, 13,* 651–676.

World Bank. (1992). *World development report 1992.* Washington, DC: World Bank.

Chapter 6

The Environmental Movement

13. Environmental Discourse and Social Movement Organizations: A Historical and Rhetorical Perspective on the Development of U.S. Environmental Organizations*

ROBERT J. BRULLE

Truth is a thing of this world: it is produced only by virtue of multiple forms of constraint. And it induces regular effects of power. Each society has its regime of truth, its 'general politics' of truth: that is, the types of discourse which it accepts and makes function as true.
—M. FOUCAULT (1980, p. 131)

Environmental organizations, such as the Sierra Club and Greenpeace, are virtually synonymous with the idea of the environmental movement in the United States. They are central to the environmental movement, since they serve as developers and carriers of its identity. These organizations are also major actors in environmental politics. Finally, the messages they develop have an important influence on the formation of individual attitudes and behaviors toward the natural environment. While the importance of these organizations is generally recognized in social movements research, the study of environmental organizations remains underdeveloped.

There are two major groupings of studies of these social movement organizations. The first group uses a qualitative examination of one or two movement organizations. These analyses provide in-depth knowledge of the discourse and practices of a subset of environmental organizations (Scarce 1990; Krauss 1993). The second major group of studies examines the aggregate patterns of organizational behavior. Focused on the top ten to twenty national environmental organizations in a country, these studies examine the patterns of environmental collective action (Mitchell, Mertig, and Dunlap 1992). But because of their self-limited nature, no collective image of environmental movement organizations emerges. In addition, while there is some attempt to place the development of these organizations into a historical perspective, most of these studies are not connected to the literature developed by environmental historians. Finally, the belief systems that form the identity of these organizations have typically been studied via essentialistic or structural linguistic forms of analyses. In these modes of analysis, the social scientist imputes some core structure that underlies the surface expressions of movement participants. Linguistic structuralism has been robustly criticized as being arbitrary, and reductive because it replaces the complex of meaning that is constantly shaped and changed in communicative action with an abstract construction of the social scientist (Bleicher 1982, pp. 88–104, Norris 1982, p. 52; Worster 1985, p. 258).

To expand the study of environmental organizations, an adequate theoretical perspective must (1) encompass the entire range of environmental organizations, (2) link the development of these organizations to historical studies of the environmental movement, and (3) develop a nonessentialist analysis of the beliefs that form the identity of these organizations. The use of discourse analysis can contribute to developing this theoretical perspective. First, the mapping of existing environmental discourses can provide an overall perspective on the environmental movement. Second, an examination of the historical embeddedness of environmental discourses and organizations can provide a link to the historical analysis of the environmental movement. Finally, the analysis of environmental belief systems in environmental philosophy provides a means for examining the discourses that form the identity of environmental organizations.

This article attempts to develop this form of analysis. In the first section, the role that language plays in constructing social order is briefly reviewed. Then the role of discourse in social movements and the implications of this perspective for the study of environmental organizations is discussed. In the second section, discourse analysis is

used to examine the environmental movement in the United States. Through a reading of the philosophical and historical literature on environmental discourses, and through an examination of the founding documents of exemplary environmental organizations, the links between the development of environmental discourses and the historical formation of environmental organizations are identified. In the third section this analysis is summarized and demonstrated through the use of data compiled on forty-four major environmental organizations in the United States. The article concludes with a discussion of the applications of this framework to further study of the environmental movement.

LANGUAGE AND THE CONSTRUCTION OF SOCIAL ORDER

Social organizations can be seen as the realization of historically developed discourses in networks of collective action. Following the linguistic and postmodern turn in social theory (Brown 1990; Simon 1990), collective action in a human community is based upon a commonly held version of reality, or discourse, that constitutes the legitimate definition of the situation. The establishment of a legitimate discourse is a rhetorical achievement that constructs social reality and constitutes social order. *Discourse* is the term used to describe the historically specific world-views that serve as the basis for formulation of collective social action. A discourse is "a formation constituted by all that is said, written or thought in a determinate field" (Teymur 1982, p. 2). A discourse has an internal logic that defines regular relationships between different types of statements or concepts, which provides a basis for common interpretations of meanings. The logical structures of discourses are "contingent social logics which…acquire their meaning in precise conjunctural and relational contexts" (Laclau and Mouffe 1985, pp. 142–143). Thus discourse analysis makes no assumption that there is a pre-defined structure regarding the internal logic of the discourse, or the relation of a discourse with other discourses. Instead, in a social order, there are multiple discourses that are the historical creations of social actors. This shifts the locus of the analysis from consolidating the various viewpoints into some constructed logic to describing the multiple realities that have been proposed, contested, negotiated, and eventually defined by the actors themselves. The logic of discourse analysis is that "plurality is not the phenomenon to be explained, but the starting point of the analysis" (Laclau and Mouffe 1985, p. 140).

A discourse is not a static or refined structure that exists apart from the practices of interaction. They are the cultural constructions that the actors use to define their community (Emirbayer and Goodwin 1994, p. 1440). Communication establishes an operative reality that forms the basis for a regularized social practice (Brulle 1994). By using this image of social reality, the members have a basis for acting together in an organized manner (Brown 1978). Contained in this "definitions of the situation" is a commonly held stock of practical social know-how, including rules and paradigmatic examples of how to enact different social roles (Dietz and Burns 1992).

The establishment of a discourse and the formation of a network of communicative action are cogenerative of one another (Emirbayer and Goodwin 1994, p. 1438). Organizations result from the development and realization of a discourse as a legitimate reality in a bounded network of action. To maintain predictable social obligations, both the applicable discourse and membership in the organization must be defined. The creation of linguistic boundaries is achieved through establishing one version of reality as the legitimate and binding definition of the situation (Foucault 1980, p. 131). Membership is defined according to a series of criteria regarding who is included and who is excluded from the group.

To establish a social institution, the negotiation of discursive and membership boundaries must come to at least partial closure. Closure is created through a combination of consensus or conflict. The consensus version stresses the role of rational argumentation in creating mutual understanding. The conflictual position sees symbolic closure as the end result of a contest of power. These two images of language form the extreme points on a spectrum regarding how linguistic closure is achieved. Using these positions, one can view historical situations as being composed of varying levels of conflict and consensus, without privileging either perspective (Brulle 1994). It is through the establishment and maintenance of boundaries that legitimate social relations are realized (McLaughlin 1994) and networks of interaction are formed that in turn constitute organizations (Bittner 1965).

Symbolic closure has two effects (Brulle 1994). The first effect is the creation of discourse, as a comprehensible social reality, and definition of membership boundaries, which enables the production of social organization. In addition, while affirming one reality, symbolic closure must inherently reject the other alternative definitions of the situation. Thus the second effect of closure is the exclusion of the alternative realities, and the creation of subjugated discourses. These discourses take the form of "a whole set of knowledges that have been disqualified as inadequate to their task or insufficiently elaborated; naive knowledges, located low down on the hierarchy, beneath the required level of cognition or scientificity" (Foucault 1980, p. 82). The delegitimation of alternative realities identifies these discourses and its membership as standing "outside" of the official, i.e., institutional, practices of society.

Discourse and Social Movements

The maintenance and change of symbolic discourse is the focus of political struggle. Changes in social structure are brought about through a redemption of what constitutes the common sense embodied in the everyday practices of society. This allows us to see the symbolic dynamics of the political community as being based on the interaction between the dominant and subjugated discourses (Brulle 1994). The application of discourse analysis to social movements examines the process by which "collective actors strive to create a group identity within a general social identity whose interpretation they contest"(Cohen 1985. P. 694). Because social movements enable human societies "to develop their own orientations and to alter them" (Touraine 1977, p. 59), political struggles in the form of social movements can be seen as attempts to alter social structures through the promotion of an alternative discourse (Eder 1985). From this perspective, then, social movements are creative activities of society remaking itself.

The development of a social movement's identity originates in the delegitimation of the dominant model of reality. This results in an expression that takes the form of a rhetoric of discontinuity that justifies a need for a dramatic change in society due to the problem situation. For a social movement to gain an identity, a new narrative of society must be created. This voicing of a new representation of the social world is

the act of identity formation of a social movement. The rhetorical process of voicing a new representation of the social world creates a definable discourse of a social movement that contains

(1) diagnoses that identify problematic dimensions of power relations that are in need of amelioration, (2) prognoses that articulate an alternative vision of power arrangement, (3) compelling rationales for changing power relations and participating in movement drama and (4) strategic and tactical direction delineating the most effective means to obtain power. (Benford and Hunt 1992, p. 39)

Movement discourse also provides a link between collective action and individual beliefs and actions, since in the process of becoming a member of a social movement, individuals experience a transformation in their perceptions of society. A new narrative of the self is adopted that reconstitutes individuals in a new symbolic reality. By providing a rhetoric that supports such a personal sequence of transformation, a movement's discourse serves as a means to restructure experience and constitute a new self (Hermans, Kempen, and van Loon 1992). The individual is socialized into a given world through a rhetorical reconstitution of self. This then results in the commitment by individuals of their resources to support group action (Gamson 1992).

Discourse and the Study of Environmental Organizations

A discursive analysis of social movement organizations focuses on the historical creation of different discourses, and the realization of these discourses into networks of communication with both a definable identity and boundary. In viewing the environmental movement in the United States from this perspective, one is confronted with a number of different discourses and organizations that were formed in unique historical circumstances. This is not surprising, as this movement is the product of over a hundred years of collective action. As different environmental discourses developed into organizations, they created specific communities. Through time, these communities interacted with each other, some expanding, others contracting, and modifying in an evolutionary manner. This creates an image of several partially overlapping historical communities that form the current environmental movement in the United States. These different discourses form the basis for the variety within the current environmental movement.

DEVELOPMENT OF U.S. ENVIRONMENTAL DISCOURSE AND ORGANIZATIONS

An initial step in identifying these discourses and networks of action is to carry out a hermeneutic and historical analysis of the development of different environmental discourses and organizations. One place to start to identify the current environmental discourses is to turn to the field of environmental philosophy. Here there appears to be a building consensus on what discourses are present in the U.S. environmental movement. The most widely agreed-upon discourses are (1) Conservationism, (2) Preservationism, (3) Ecocentrism, (4) Political Ecology, (5) Deep Ecology, and (6) Ecofeminism. The primary source of the discourse categories used is the book *The Idea of Wilderness* (Oelschlaeger 1991).[1] In addition, the discourse of Manifest Destiny is also included in the analysis to form a contrasting point of view for environmental discourses.

The definition and development of environmental discourses in the United States are summarized in Table 6.1. In the left-hand column of Table 6.1 the key components of each discursive frame are identified. In the next column, some of the key texts that defined this discourse are presented. The historical events that mark the realization of this discourse into collective behavior are then listed. Finally, some of the current social movement organizations based on this discourse are shown. It is important to note that the discourses identified here are not ideal types. Instead they are typifications of the belief systems of movement participants. They are similar to shorthand descriptions of different religious faiths, such as Catholicism, Buddhism, Judaism, and so forth. Hence one criterion of accuracy of these discourse summaries is the authentication of the discourses by movement participants as accurate representations of their worldviews.

One means of examining the viability of this scheme is through an assessment of its ability to integrate a wide variety of literature on the environmental movement in the United States from a variety of sources. To test the adequacy of Table 6.1, a series of short descriptions of the development and realization of each discourse in a social movement organization follow. The analysis proceeds through an examination of environmental discourses, the specific historical events involved in the creation of environmental organizations, and the founding of exemplary paradigmatic environmental organizations as shown in these organizations' documents.

Manifest Destiny

To understand the development of environmentalism in the United States, a short review of the dominant discourse that

TABLE 6.1   Environmental Discourses and Social Movement Organizations

Definition of discursive frame	Key texts in development of frame	Defining social movement events	Examples of movement organizations
Manifest Destiny Nature has no intrinsic value. Human welfare is based on development of the natural environment. The natural environment is unproductive and valueless without development. Human labor transforms the natural environment into useful commodities. The production of commodities for human use is good. There are abundant natural resources available for human use. Humans have a right to use the natural environment to meet their needs.	Manifest Destiny speech, 1845	Stanfield Rebellion, 1920s Sagebrush Rebellion, 1979–1983 Wise Use Agenda adopted, 1988	Center for the Defense of Free Enterprise American Property Rights Alliance
Conservation Nature is a collection of parts that function like a machine. Humans need to use natural resources to maintain society. Nature can be managed through use of technical knowledge by professionals. The proper management philosophy for nature is to realize the greatest good for the greatest number of people over the longest period of time.	*Man and Nature* (Marsh 1864)	American Forestry Association founded, 1875	National Arbor Day Foundation Izaak Walton League
Preservation Natural systems are self-creating evolutionary wholes that cannot be reduced to the sum of their parts. Hence nature is an intact organism. Human actions can impair the ability of nature systems to maintain themselves. Wilderness and wildlife are important components in supporting both the physical and spiritual life of humans. Human values go beyond economics to include preservation of wilderness. Existence of wilderness is critical to the well-being of humanity.	*Walden* (Thoreau 1854)	Appalachian Mountain Club founded, 1876 Sierra Club founded, 1892	Wilderness Society Nature Conservancy World Wildlife Fund
Ecocentrism Natural systems are the basis of all organic existence, including humanity. Human survival is linked to ecosystem survival. Human ethics requires ecologically responsible actions. Proper use of natural sciences can guide the relationship between humanity and its natural environment.	*Silent Spring* (Carson 1962)	Smoke Prevention Association of America founded, 1907 Environmental Defense Fund founded, 1967	Natural Resources Defense Council Cousteau Society Zero Population Growth

TABLE 6.1 Continued

Definition of discursive frame	Key texts in development of frame	Defining social movement events	Examples of movement organizations
Political Ecology Domination of humans by other humans leads to domination of nature. The economic system and nation-state are the core structures of society that create ecological problems. Commoditization and market imperatives force consumption to continually increase in the developed economy. Environmental destruction in low-income/racially distinct communities, or Third World countries, originates in the exploitation of the people who live in these areas by the dominant social institutions. Resolution of environmental problems requires fundamental social change based on empowerment of local communities.	*Counterrevolution and Revolt* (Marcuse 1972) *Post-Scarcity Anarchism* (Bookchin 1971) *Dumping in Dixie* (Bullard 1990)	Environmental Action founded, 1970 Citizen's Clearinghouse for Hazardous Waste founded, 1981 People of Color Environmental Summit, 1991	Government Accountability Project Labor–Community WATCHDOG
Deep ecology The richness and diversity of all life on earth have intrinsic value. Human relations to nature endanger the richness and diversity of life. Human life is privileged only to the extent of satisfying vital needs. Maintenance of the diversity of life on earth mandates a decrease in human impacts on the natural environment and substantial increases in the wilderness areas of the globe. Changes affecting basic economic, technological, and cultural aspects of society are required to realize this goal.	*Shallow & the Deep* (Naess 1972) *Turtle Island* (Snyder 1974) *Monkey Wrench Gang* (Abbey 1975)	Planet Drum founded, 1977 Earth First! founded, 1981	Rainforest Action Network Sea Shepherd Conservation Society Wild Earth
Ecofeminism Earth is home for all life and should be revered and nurtured. Ecosystem abuse is rooted in androcentric concepts and institutions. Relations of complementarity rather than superiority between culture/nature, human/nonhuman, and male/female are desirable. The many problems of human relations, and relations between the human and nonhuman worlds, will not be resolved until androcentric institutions, values, and ideology are eradicated.	*Euthenics* (Richards 1912) *New Woman, New Earth* (Ruether 1975) *Death of Nature* (Merchant, 1980)	Conference on "Woman and Life on Earth," 1980 World Women in Defense of the Environment founded, 1982	Women in Environment and Development

preceded the emergence of both Conservationism and Preservationism is helpful.
From the time of the first Puritan settle-
ments in 1620, and throughout the eighteenth century and up to the middle of the
nineteenth century, the dominant discourse
that guided the U.S. relationship with the
natural environment can be characterized as
Manifest Destiny. This is not to say that
there was only one discourse toward nature
present at this time. As Burch (1971) shows,
there were multiple discourses in existence
during this time period. However, this one
discourse had a profound influence on social
behavior for several hundred years.

Nash (1967) describes Manifest Destiny
as a moral play in which "civilizing the New
World meant enlightening darkness, order-
ing chaos, and changing evil into good. In
the morality play of westward expansion,
wilderness was the villain, and the pioneer,
as hero, relished its destruction" (p. 24).
This attitude toward nature was defined in
an 1845 article by John Louis O'Sullivan:
"Our manifest destiny is to overspread the
continent allotted by Providence for the
free development of our yearly multiplying
millions" (in Bartlett 1968, p. 676). Coupled with free-market ideology, this made
exploitation of the natural environment
into a duty.

The discourse of Manifest Destiny has
continued to animate collective behavior
regarding the environment throughout the
twentieth century. A prominent manifestation of this discourse is the movements
against the expansion of government environmental protection efforts in the western
United States. The history of western lands
struggles shows that there have been a
number of these conflicts. The first such
struggle was the resistance to the development of national parks and forests between
1907 and 1916 (Maughan and Nilson 1993.
p. 2). Later, protests against the restriction

of grazing in the national forests in the
"Stanfield Rebellion" occurred in the 1920s
(Cawley 1993), and a similar protest took
place after the enactment of the Taylor
Grazing Act of 1934 (Maughan and Nilson
1993). Recently this type of protest recurred
from 1979 to 1983. Its initial identity was
fixed by the term "Sagebrush Rebellion,"
which began in July 1979, when the Nevada state legislature approved a resolution
that demanded the return of 49 million
acres of federal land to state control (Short
1989, p. 13).

Toward the end of the late 1980s under
a more comprehensive movement know as
the Wise Use Movement (Cawley 1993,
p. 166) we see a movement that combines
the ideas of manifest destiny, states' rights,
and property rights to call for the reversal of
environmental restrictions. The Wise Use
movement formed as a collective actor at a
meeting in August 1988 in Reno, Nevada.
At this meeting, the *Wise Use Agenda* (Gottlieb 1989) was produced, listing the top
twenty-five goals of the movement. Included are such items as "all public lands including wilderness, and national parks shall
be open to mineral and energy production"
(Gottlieb 1989, p. 6), and amending the Endangered Species Act to allow for differential treatment of "relic species in decline
before the appearance of man" (Gottlieb
1989, p. 12). In this movement, the discourse of Manifest Destiny plays an active
role as one key component of their worldview. This discourse provides an image from
which the development of the various environmental discourses can be seen as significantly different.

Conservationism

The first environmental discourse to
emerge in the United States was Conservationism. This discourse defines a utilitarian

and technical/managerial perspective regarding nature. The conservationist discourse began in the United States with publication of *Man and Nature* by George Perkins Marsh in 1864. Marsh argued that humanity was "a destabilizing environmental force whose impacts portended an uncertain future" (Oelschlaeger 1991, p. 107) and, therefore, humanity must develop a stewardship of natural resources. Marsh's ideas took root in the technical, managerial, and professional elites as a perceived need for control over the exploitation of natural resources (Nash 1967, pp. 265–276). The Conservation movement took the form of a top-down effort to ensure the continued availability of natural resources to sustain economic development. The result was a more professional and technically managed economy. The guiding idea of this effort was "the use of foresight and restraint in the exploitation of the physical sources of wealth as necessary for the perpetuity of civilization, and the welfare of present and future generations" (Hays 1959, p. 123). Under the leadership of Giffort Pinphot, several political initiatives were taken to form government programs of action based on this viewpoint (McCormick 1989, p. 16).

The founding of the first environmental organization in the United States was based on this discourse. In 1875, the American Forestry Association was founded, with the following objective: "The forests of the country should be made to yield the greatest possible benefits to present and future generations, both by producing timber crops and by less direct means" (*The Forester,* January 1899, Vol. 5, No. 1). This organization's purpose has changed little in the last century. Its current bylaws list the primary objective of the association to be "to bring about more efficient conservation and development of forests and other natural re-

sources toward realization of the maximum value of these resources in the economic, industrial, and social progress of the nation" (American Forests Bylaws, November 7, 1992). Organizations based on this discourse define their objective as rationally developing natural resources to meet long-term human needs.

Preservationism

The second environmental discourse to emerge in the United States was Preservationism. Preservationism defines a spiritual and psychological relationship between humans and the natural environment. This discourse had a long period of gestation. Its origins can be traced through the transcendentalism of Emerson to the writings of Thoreau. By the time Thoreau wrote *Walden* in 1854, the identity of this discourse was firmly established. Combining the imagery of a return to the Garden of Eden in nature with the Arcadian Myth of the inherent goodness of pastoral rural life over urban life, Thoreau developed a vision of the good life as being carried out with "simplicity and humility in order to restore man to a peaceful coexistence with nature"(McCormick 1989, p. 2).

The development of a social movement based on the Preservationist discourse was fostered by urbanization and appreciation of the natural beauty of the United States. First, as urbanization and its associated problems were documented by the muckrakers of the late nineteenth century, there arose a quest for wilderness as an alternative to urban life. Second, in contrast to the cultural developments of Europe, the natural beauty of the United States was developed as a source of unique "American" pride. To be able to enjoy this beauty was the mark of a refined person. The idea of self-renewal in the wilderness also led to a quest for rural and gentle life, and a search for solitude in nature (Nash 1967).

Out of this general milieu, two early Preservationist organizations were formed. The first was the Appalachian Mountain Club. Formed in 1876, its objectives were to "explore the mountains of New England and the adjacent regions, both for scientific and artistic purposes; and, in general, to cultivate an interest in geographical studies" (Appalachian Mountain Register for 1948). The second organization was the Sierra Club. Founded in 1892 by John Muir, its purpose was "To explore, enjoy, and preserve the Sierra Nevada and other scenic resources of the United States,... to educate the people with regard to the national and state forests, parks, monuments, and other natural resources of special scenic beauty and to enlist public interest and cooperation in protecting them" (Sierra Club Articles of Incorporation, June 4, 1892). These two organizations mark the beginnings of collective action based in a Preservationist discourse. Organizations based on this discourse define their objective as preserving wilderness, including physical areas, and all of the plants and wildlife that inhabit those areas.

Ecocentrism

The third environmental discourse is Ecocentrism. Based in the natural sciences, and the notion of humanity as part of natural ecosystems, it links human survival to ecosystem survival. This discourse originated in the same historical era as Conservationism and Preservationism. However, as a consequence of professional appropriation, it took more than a century for Ecocentrism to attain anywhere near the status of the other two early discourses. Following the Civil War, there was a rising concern with urban living conditions and their effect on public health. At that time, the filth theory of disease (Tarr 1985, p. 520) prevailed, which was that unsanitary conditions caused disease (Rosen 1958, pp. 240–286). Hence the foremost concern of urban reformers was the development of the infrastructure to protect human health (Melosi 1985, pp. 494–515).

Concern over the urban environment took the form of the Sanitary Movement as a response to community health problems. Its aim was to improve urban living conditions, and it dealt with problems such as sanitary water supplies, sewage systems, garbage, and air pollution (Tarr 1985, pp. 516–552). One of the first organizations that was founded to promote the improvement of the urban environment was the Smoke Prevention Association of America. Founded in 1907, its purpose was to "foster the control of atmospheric pollution and improve sanitation of the air by promoting the abatement and/or prevention of atmospheric pollution affecting health and/or damage to property, nuisance to the public, and wasting natural resources" (Bylaws, Smoke Prevention Association of America, 1951).

Beginning around the turn of the twentieth century, the germ theory of disease, which saw disease caused by bacteria instead of unsanitary conditions, replaced the filth theory of disease. Treatment for public health was redefined as a medical specialty, not a public issue. Once concern over the urban environment was relegated to a professional activity (O'Brien 1983, p. 135), the Ecocentric discourse failed to be realized as a social movement until the 1960s.

Ecocentrism's long static period ended with the publication in 1962 by Rachel Carson of *Silent Spring*. Her book reunited the conservationist and preservationist concerns about natural ecosystems with the long-dormant public health concerns. The result redefined the form of human–nature interaction and founded modern environmental discourse (O'Brien 1983, pp. 17–18). It is commonly accepted that the founding of the Environmental Defense Fund (EDF) in 1967 marked the beginning of the wave of new environmental organizations based on the ecocentric discourse (Mitchell, Mertig, and Dunlap 1992, p. 14). It was founded following the successful actions of an informal team of lawyers and biologists working on behalf of the Audubon Society to halt the spraying of DDT on Long Island. The objective of EDF is "to encourage and support the wise use of natural resources, and the maintenance and enhancement of environmental quality" (EDF Bylaws, 1994). The pattern established by the EDF consisted of using scientific research and legal action to protect the environment and human health. EDF serves as the exemplar for many other organizations that followed, including the Natural Resources Defense Council and the Friends of the Earth. Organizations based in this discourse identify their organizations' purpose as protecting Earth's ecosystem and human health.

Political Ecology

The fourth environmental discourse is Political Ecology. This perspective sees the source of ecological problems in the structure of our society. The origins of Political Ecology can be traced to the turn of the century works of Kropotkin (1899). Kropotkin argued that "industrialism is unsustainable because of its excessive strains on the natural environment" (Roussopoulos 1993, p. 16). From its earlier origins, Political Ecology developed into three distinct discursive subcommunities. Regardless of

their specific focus, all three types of organizations define their objective as changing the social order in some manner to solve environmental problems. The means to carry out this goal range from holding government and corporations accountable through democratic processes to ending racial, ethnic, or economic exploitation.

The first subcommunity is based on an idea known as social ecology. This term first appeared in *Post Scarcity Anarchism,* by Murray Bookchin (1971). He later defined social ecology as "the conviction that the very concept of dominating nature stems from the domination of human by human. As long as hierarchy persists, the project of dominating nature will continue to exist and inevitably lead our planet to ecological extinction"(Bookchin 1980, p. 59). One important U.S. organization based on this discourse is the Green Party (Merchant 1992, p. 170), founded as the Green Committees of Correspondence in 1984. Based on the success of the West German Green Party, the Green Party in the United States has attempted to form a unified environmental political party in the United States. The purpose of the organization is to "facilitate the organization of local Green groups and confederations for the purpose of creating a sustainable, just society based on the Ten Key Values" (Charter U.S. Greens, Final Edition, October 22, 1991).

The second subcommunity based on this discourse is the decentralized environmental movement based on multiple local community groups collectively known as the Environmental Justice Movement. Using the idea of environmental justice, this movement focuses on the social creation of environmental problems. The Environmental Justice movement is based on the disregard of community health and environmental needs by government and corporations.

Disadvantaged groups based on class, race, and gender differences bear the brunt of ecological problems in the form of degraded living conditions, high levels of pollution, inadequate public services, and the dumping of toxic wastes in their communities (Taylor 1993). The development of collective action based on this discourse originated in local struggles over pollution from toxic wastes that endangered people's health in local communities (Freudenberg and Steinsapir 1992).

A key example of this development is the community that lived on the abandoned toxic waste dump site known as Love Canal in New York state (Cable and Cable, 1995, pp. 75–84). Organizing itself as the Love Canal Homeowners Association, and originally dealing with the local problem, this organization served as the inspiration for the founding of a national-level environmental organization, the Citizen's Clearinghouse for Hazardous Waste (CCHW). Founded in 1981 by Lois Gibbs, a leader in the original Love Canal Homeowners Association, CCHW serves as an information center and support for community organizing for more than 24,000 local environmental groups nationwide. Its stated purpose is to facilitate the development of local environmental organizations by

> *supporting, encouraging and providing assistance to members and citizens generally who would seek to initiate, develop and conduct programs within and/or increase public and professional and understanding of the problems faced within the fields of hazardous waste, toxic chemicals, and related environmental concerns. (Bylaws, Citizen's Clearinghouse for Hazardous Waste, 1982)*

The third component of Political Ecology is the People of Color Environmental Movement. While it shares a great deal of commonality, and also aligns its identity, with the environmental justice movement, this component of the environmental movement has developed its own unique discourse, identity, and organizations. This movement's first action had to do with the filing, in Houston in 1979, of the first lawsuit that involved racial discrimination in the location of a toxic waste landfill. The suit was followed by a minority community protest in 1982 against a toxic landfill in North Carolina. The protest was based in the local black continuity, and was led and organized by a local church (Lavelle and Coyle 1993, p. 139). Following these initial protests, a series of studies, culminating in Robert Bullard's *Dumping in Dixie* (Bullard 1990), documented the correlation between race, poverty, and toxic dumping. Bullard has succeeded in defining the impact as evidence of environmental racism in the United States.

The People of Color Environmental Movement emerged as a collective actor at a meeting in October 1991 in Washington, D.C., where the Principles of Environmental Justice were written. The document lists seventeen Principles of Environmental Justice, including

> *"the rights to be free from ecological destruction, cessation of the production of all toxins, hazardous wastes, and radioactive materials, and enforcement of strict accountability of the producers of these materials, and the right of political, economic, cultural and environmental self-determination of all peoples."* (Merchant 1994, p. 371)

Unlike previous environmental movements, the People of Color Environmental Movement has not resulted in just the formation of new groups. A significant component of this movement has involved the reorientation of existing civil rights and community organizations to include environmental concerns (Bullard and Wright 1992, p. 47).

Deep Ecology

The fifth environmental discourse is Deep Ecology. At the core of this perspective is the belief that "intuition about the intrinsic value of all nature…will ground a respectful way of living in and with the natural, non-human world" (Rothenberg 1992, p. 50). Deep Ecologists maintain that a change in mindsets and worldviews will result in a change in the social order. The development of this discourse was foreshadowed by the publication of Aldo Leopold's *Sand County Almanac* in 1949. In his classic essay, "The Land Ethic," Leopold argues for the extension of ethics to include the relationship between humans and the natural environment (Leopold 1949). The identity of Deep Ecology emerged with the publications of *The Shallow and the Deep, Long-Range Ecology Movement: A Summary* by Arnie Naess (1972), and *Turtle Island* (Snyder 1974).

Deep Ecology inspired collective action in the early 1980s. Growing out of a rejection of reform environmentalism, and inspired by the novel *The Monkey Wrench Gang* (Abbey 1975), Earth First! was founded in 1980 by David Foreman, marking the development of the ideas of Deep Ecology into collective action (Scarce 1990, p. 57; Manes 1990, pp. 1–7). Earth First!'s first action, symbolically "cracking" the Glen Canyon Dam in 1981, was the first instance of a call by an environmental group in the United States for the reversal of development (Devall 1992). Earth First! has described its beliefs as being based on Deep Ecology. In a 1987 information handout, Earth First!

maintains that there are two key aspects to their beliefs. First is the idea of the interconnectedness of all life. To make this point, they offer a quote from Aldo Leopold that says that a thing is right when it tends to preserve the integrity, stability, and beauty of the biotic community. It is wrong when it tends otherwise. The second point is that all natural things have intrinsic value, or inherent worth. Organizations based in Deep Ecology generally define their objectives as acting to preserve the rights of all nonhuman beings to a natural existence.

Ecofeminism

The sixth environmental discourse, Ecofeminism ties the development of a patriarchal society, and the domination of women by men, to the domination of nature by humanity. The initial involvement of women in environmental issues in the United States can be traced to the late 1800s (Wolf 1994) when women activists were involved in environmental issues. Among them was Dr. Ellen H. Richards, the first female graduate of MIT and author of several books on the connection between health and the environment, including *Euthenics: The Science of Controllable Environment* (Richards 1912).

The development of Ecofeminism as a distinct environmental discourse was under way throughout the 1970s in several works such as *Is Female to Male as Nature is to Culture?* (Ortner 1974), and *New Woman, New Earth* (Ruether 1975). With the publication of *The Death of Nature* (Merchant 1980) and the holding of a major conference on Ecofeminism (Merchant 1992, p. 184) in 1980, the identity of Ecofeminism as a distinct environmental discourse was established. This was followed by the founding of the first Ecofeminist organization, World Women in Defense of the Environment, in

1982. Later renamed WorldWIDE, the purpose of this organization is to "promote the inclusion of women and their environmental perceptions in the design and implementation of development and environmental policies;... and to mobilize and support women, individually and in organizations, in environmental and natural resource programs" (Bylaws, WorldWIDE Network, October 1992).

In addition to establishing such organizations as WorldWIDE, women have spearheaded the grassroots movement against toxic wastes. Their activism "grows out of their concrete, immediate experiences" (Krauss 1993, p. 248). In the process of challenging the traditional belief systems, women involved in toxic waste struggles move beyond particular problems to challenge the wider issues of "race, class and gender" (Krauss 1993, p. 259). Hence women play an important role both specifically in Ecofeminist organizations and overall in the movement for environmental justice.

HISTORICAL ORIGINS OF ENVIRONMENTAL ORGANIZATIONS AND DISCOURSE

If historical conditions prepare for the development of certain environmental discourses and their manifestation in specific organizations, we may expect to find an intersection of distinct historical eras and the founding of different types of environmental organizations. To test this statement, I turned to a detailed data set regarding forty-four major environmental organizations established between 1875 and 1987. These forty-four major environmental organizations were selected through a consensus process among myself and two other environmental sociologists from a listing of

1,151 environmental organizations in the United States. These major environmental organizations play a significant role in the environmental movement, because of size, perceived political influence, use of a unique set of activities or tactics, or a distinct issue focus.

Detailed quantitative and qualitative information was then gathered on each of the forty-four environmental organizations. For each organization, two Internal Revenue Service forms were obtained. The first form was IRS form 1023, "Application for Recognition of Exemption," which is filed by an organization to obtain a tax-exempt status. It is a one-time filing and must include a copy of the organization's bylaws, a description of its major activities, and its reasons for engaging in these activities. The other form was IRS form 990, the "Return of Organization Exempt From Income Tax." Filed annually, this form contains detailed information regarding income, expenses, and activities for each organization. In addition to these IRS forms, a number of publications, information brochures, and magazines were collected on each organization. This collection of documents on each organization constituted the qualitative data on which the coding was based. I coded each organization according to my estimation of the most dominant discourse in their official documents.

To ensure reliability of the coding scheme of an organization's discourse, a random selection of the files of five organizations and coding instructions were provided to two sociology professors. They were then asked to independently code the discourse of each organization. The results of this coding were then compared with the author's coding scheme. This comparison yielded a Perreault's I (estimate of reliability) of .85. This is considered to be an acceptable level of intercodal reliability (Perreault and Leigh 1989, p. 146). The results of this coding are shown in Table 6.2.

With a few interesting exceptions, a general trend is apparent. Environmental organizations can generally be seen as originating in one of three distinct historical periods. The first period, starting in 1875 and lasting until the early 1960s, was when the majority of Conservationist and Preservationist organizations were founded. The second period was from the mid-1960s to the mid-1970s. This was when most ecocentric organizations were founded. From the late 1970s to the present the organizations founded have been based on Political Ecology, Deep Ecology, or Ecofeminism.

The historical, organizational, and discursive development of the U.S. environmental movements is summarized in Figure 6.1. This diagram combines the discourse, organizations, and history into a view of the development of the environmental movements in the United States. In this diagram, time runs from left to right (not to scale). It summarizes the argument in this article that the environmental movement is composed of multiple and historically developed discourses, realized in organizations. This diagram identifies the key points in the development and realization of each discourse. On the left side of each discourse box, there is a text whose publication is recorded by historians of environmental ideas as pioneering presentation of a unique discursive position. On the right side of each discourse box, there is a collective action that marks the realization of this discourse in institutions. Each of the events noted is a significant collective action in the development of the environmental movement in the United States.

While this figure is instructive on the historical development of distinct environmental discourses in the United States, it also is a simplification of the discourses as though they were linear and unchanging entities through time. Significant cross-discourse interaction and internal modification of these discourses also occurred, such as the role of feminist ideas in the environmental justice movement. The important point is that distinct historical periods in the development of environmental discourses are realized in the founding of particular types of environmental organizations.

CONCLUSION

Environmental organizations can be seen as the result of a number of historically developed discourses that have been realized in collective action. The use of discourse analysis can contribute to our understanding of the development of environmental organizations. The use of this perspective enabled the development of an overall perspective on the environmental movement through the mapping of the discourses of this movement. Also, this form of analysis connected environmental philosophy with the historical development of environmental organizations. The development of environmental discourses in philosophy and literature is the initial step toward their realization in collective behavior. The formation of unique discourses enables new forms of social organization. Environmental discourses are not disembodied conceptual systems. Instead, they are language games, embedded in human communities, that define and enable a series of practices

This essay presents an initial identification of these networks of communicative action through a hermeneutic analysis of several different environmental discourses. The proposed discursive scheme can integrate a wide variety of literature on the

TABLE 6.2   Organizational Discourse and Founding Date

Year	Discourse	Name of organization
1875	Conservation	America Forests
1876	Preservation	Appalachian Mountain Club
1892	Preservation	Sierra Club
1897	Ecocentric	Audubon Naturalist Society
1905	Preservation	National Audubon Society
1907	Ecocentric	Air and Waste Management Assoc.
1919	Preservation	National Parks and Consv. Assoc.
1922	Conservation	Izaak Walton League of America
1923	Ecocentric	League of Women Voters
1935	Preservation	Wilderness Society
1936	Conservation	National Wildlife Federation
1946	Preservation	Nature Conservancy
1947	Preservation	Defenders of Wildlife
1953	Conservation	Keep America Beautiful
1961	Preservation	World Wildlife Fund
1965	Ecocentric	Rachel Carson Council
1966	Ecocentric	Chesapeake Bay Foundation
1967	Ecocentric	Environmental Defense Fund
1968	Ecocentric	Zero Population Growth Inc.
1969	Ecocentric	Friends of the Earth
1970	Preservation	Treepeople
1970	Ecocentric	Environmental Action
1970	Ecocentric	League of Conservation Voters
1970	Ecocentric	Sierra Club Legal Defense Fund
1970	Ecocentric	Natural Resources Defense Council
1970	Ecocentric	Greenpeace
1971	Conservation	National Arbor Day Foundation
1971	Ecocentric	Clean Water Action Project
1973	Deep Ecology	Planet Drum Foundation
1973	Ecocentric	Cousteau Society
1973	Ecocentric	Population–Environment Balance
1974	Ecocentric	Worldwatch Institute
1974	Ecocentric	Inst. for Local Self-Reliance
1975	Political Ecology	Govt. Accountability Project
1976	Political Ecology	Clamshell Alliance
1977	Deep Ecology	Sea Shepherd Conservation Soc.
1979	Preservation	Mono Lake Committee
1980	Deep Ecology	Earth First!
1981	Political Ecology	Citizen's Clearinghouse
1982	Ecofeminism	WorldWIDE
1982	Ecocentric	Earth Island Institute
1983	Deep Ecology	Elmwood Institute
1984	Political Ecology	Green Party USA
1987	Preservation	Conservation International

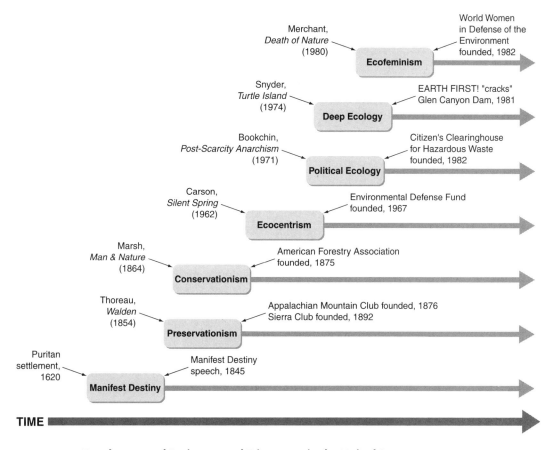

FIGURE 6.1   Development of Environmental Discourses in the United States.

environmental movement. While suggestive of its viability, further testing is needed. Herneneutic fidelity is not a sufficient demonstration of the adequacy of this scheme to describe existing communities of communicative action. The discourses identified in this essay are proposed as typifications of worldviews in the environmental movement. Accordingly, authentication of the discourses by movement participants as accurate representations of their worldview is needed. In addition, since the different environmental discourses should create networks of communicative action that define a specific pattern of interaction and membership, future network analysis of these communities would provide another empirical test of the existence of communities based on a common discourse (Phillips 1991; Dietz and Rycroft 1987, pp. 77 101).

The use of discourse analysis can provide an additional dimension to the study of environmental organizations. The historical process of development forms the basis for the many different forms of action, organization, and objectives that are found within the current environmental movement. To understand how the current environmental movement came to exist in its current configuration requires both historical and empirical research. A useful analogy might be to see discursive communities in the same manner as biological species. There is a vast array of different species in existence in the natural world. They exist in particular settings, and interact with other species in a wide variety of relationships, from competition to mutual symbiosis and so forth. To explain how a particular species developed, a detailed analysis of the ecological conditions is needed. In a similar manner, specific discursive communities developed out of their intentions with their external social and natural environments and each other in an evolutionary manner. On the basis of unique historical circumstances and opportunity structures, social movement organizations expand, contract, or are modified. The result of this historical process is the several partially overlapping communities that form the current environmental movement in the United States.

The research project defined by such an evolutionary perspective would seek to understand how these different communities came into existence and changed over time. This would require focusing on the acquisition of members, material resources, and legitimacy in a particular historical context. This raises a number of questions, including such items as the following: What are the economic sources of support of different environmental communities? How has this hindered or helped the growth of different environmental communities? Are there differences in the saliency of environmental discourse among different groups in society?

In addition, a discursive perspective could provide a means to disentangle the development of environmental politics. Social movement organizations are significant actors in the development of environmental policies. Because these organizations are based in different discourses, they will focus on and advocate distinct issues. By examining the mobilization capacity of these different discursive communities, an understanding of why some environmental issues are addressed, and others ignored, can be developed.

Finally, this perspective may be able to unravel the process by which environmental attitudes are formed. Environmental deterioration does not automatically translate into collective action. New discourses have to be created, and the public mobilized to support these alternatives. Social movement organizations play a major role in the development and transmission of these alternative ideas. From examination of the ability of these discourses to gain access to the public and of their saliency among the population, the development of environmental attitudes can be linked to the actions of both social movement organizations and the media.

This form of analysis may hold the potential to unite the previously separate literatures of environmental history, environmental philosophy, and environmental sociology into an enlarged and comprehensive framework. As this article suggests, a viable and testable perspective can be developed that will encompass the wide variety of discourses and types of organizations that make up the environmental movement. This perspective also shows promise to link the development of these organizations to both theories of social change and the development of individual beliefs, without being based on an essentialist framework. Finally, the development of these discourses, and their realization as social movement organizations, can both inform and link the theoretical literature on the processes of social change with the historical development of environmental organizations.

ENDNOTE

1. Other authors have developed similar listings. For example, there is virtual accord in the environmental history community (Nash 1967; Hays 1959) that the two earliest environmental discourses in the United States were Conservationism and Preservationism. A discourse similar to what is labeled Ecocentrism is mentioned by several authors (O'Brien 1983; McCormick 1989; Scheffer 1991). In addition, Deep Ecology, Political Ecology, and Ecofeminism have been recently identified as significant perspectives in U.S. environmentalism (Merchant 1992; Roussopoulos 1993; Zimmerman 1994). It is important to note that this listing does not preclude the possibility of including other discourses. Some possible candidates include the discourse of spiritual ecology, bioregionalism and alternative technology. There is nothing in the theoretical framework that would disallow their inclusion. However, whether these discourses serve to animate a significant level of collective behavior is an open question. Accordingly, only the six major environmental discourses are examined.

REFERENCES

Abbey, Edward. 1975. *The Monkey Wrench Gang.* New York: Avon.

Bartlett, John. (1968). *Familiar Quotations.* Boston: Little Brown.

Benford, Robert. D., and Scott A. Hunt. 1992. "Dramaturgy and Social Movements: The Social Construction and Communication of Power." *Sociological Inquiry* 62, no. 1(Feb): 36–55.

Bittner, E. 1965. "The Concept of Organization." *Social Research* 32:239–255. Reprinted in Roy Turner. 1974. *Studies in Ethnomethodology.* Baltimore: Penguin, 1974, pp. 69–82.

Bleicher, Josef. 1982. *The Hermeneutic Imagination: Outline of a Positive Critique of Scientism and Sociology.* Boston: Routledge and Kegan Paul.

Bookchin, Murray. 1980. *Toward an Ecological Society.* Montreal: Black Rose.

———. 1971. *Post-Scarcity Anarchism.* San Francisco: Ramparts.

Brown, Richard Harvey. 1990. "Rhetoric, Textuality, and the Postmodern Turn in Sociological Theory. *Sociological Theory* 8, no. 2 (Fall):188–197.

Brown, Richard Harvey. 1978. "Bureaucracy as Praxis: Toward a Political Phenomenology of Formal Organizations." *Administrative Science Quarterly* 23 (Sept.):365–382.

Brulle, Robert J. 1995. *Agency, Democracy, and the Environment: An Examination of U.S. Environmental Organizations from the Perspective of Critical Theory.* Ph.D. Dissertation. Department of Sociology, George Washington University, Washington DC.

Brulle, Robert J. 1994. "Power, Discourse, and Social Problems: Social Problems from a Rhetorical Perspective." *Current Perspectives in Social Problems* 5:95–121.

Bullard, Robert D. 1990. *Dumping in Dixie: Race, Class and Environmental Quality.* Boulder, CO: Westview.

Bullard, Robert D., and Beverly H. Wright. 1992. "The Quest for Environmental Equity: Mobilizing the African-American Community for Social Change." Pp. 39–49 in *The U.S. Environmental Movement, 1970–1990,* edited by Riley Dunlap and Angela G. Mertig. Washington, DC: Taylor and Francis.

Burch, W. R. 1971. *Daydreams and Nightmares.* New York: Harper and Row.

Cable, S., and C. Cable. 1995. *Environmental Problems, Grassroot Solutions.* New York: St. Martin's.

Carson, Rachel. 1962. *Silent Spring.* Cambridge, MA: Riverside.

Cawley, R. McGreggor. 1993. *Federal Land, Western Anger: The Sagebrush Rebellion and Environmental Politics.* Lawrence: University Press of Kansas.

Cohen, Jean L. 1985. "Strategy or Identity: New Theoretical Paradigms and Contemporary Social Movements." *Social Research* 52, no. 4(Winter):663–716.

Devall, Bill. 1992. "Deep Ecology and Radical Environmentalism." Pp. 51–62 in *The U.S.*

Environmental Movement, 1970–1990, edited by Riley Dunlap and Angela G. Mertig. Washington, DC: Taylor and Francis.

Dietz, T., and T. R. Burns. 1992. "Human Agency and the Evolutionary Dynamics of Culture." *Acta Sociologica* 35:187–200.

Dietz, T., and R. W. Rycroft. 1987. *The Risk Professional.* New York: Russel Sage.

Eder, Klaus. 1985. "The New Social Movements: Moral Crusades, Political Pressure Groups, or Social Movements?" *Social Research* 52 (4):869–900.

Emirbayer, Mustafa, and Jeff Goodwin. 1994. "Network Analysis, Culture, and the Problem of Agency." *American Journal of Sociology* 99(6):1411–1454.

Foucault, M. 1980. *Power/Knowledge.* New York Pantheon.

Freudenberg, N., and C. Steinsapir. 1992. "Not in Our Backyards: The Grassroots Environmental Movement." Pp. 27–38 in *The U.S. Environmental Movement, 1970–1990*, edited by Riley Dunlap and Angela G. Mertig. Washington, DC: Taylor and Francis.

Gamson, W. A. 1992. "The Social Psychology of Collective Action." Pp. 53–76 in *Frontiers in Social Movement Theory*, edited by Aldon D. Morris and Carol McClurg Mueller. New Haven, CT: Yale University Press.

Gottlieb, A. 1989. *The Wise Use Agenda.* Bellevue, WA: Free Enterprise Press.

Hays, Samuel P. 1959. *Conservation and the Gospel of Efficiency. The Progressive Conservation Movement, 1890–1920.* New York: Athenaeum.

Hermans, J. M., H. Kempen, and R. van Loon. 1992. "The Dialogical Self." *American Psychologist,* 47, no. 1 (January):23–33.

Krauss, Celene. 1993. "Women and Toxic Waste Protests: Race, Class and Gender as Resources of Resistance." *Qualitative Sociology* 16(3):247–262.

Kropotkin, P. [1899] 1993. *Fields, Factories and Workshops.* Montreal: Black Rose.

Laclau, Ernesto, and Chantal Mouffe. 1985. *Hegemony and Socialist Strategy: Towards a Radical Democratic Politics.* London: Verso.

Lavelle, M., and M. Coyle. "Unequal Protection: The Racial Divide in Environmental Law." Pp. 136–143 in *Toxic Struggles: The Theory and Practice of Environmental Justice,* edited by R. Hofrichter. Philadelphia: New Society.

Leopold, Aldo. 1949. *Sand County Almanac.* New York: Ballantine.

Manes, Christopher. 1990. *Green Rage.* Boston: Little, Brown.

Marcuse, Herbert. 1972. *Counterrevolution and Revolt.* Boston: Beacon.

Marsh, George Perkins. 1864. *Man and Nature: Earth as Modified by Human Action.* Cambridge: Harvard University Press.

Maughan, Ralph, and Douglas Nilson. 1993. "What's Old and What's New About the Wise Use Movement." Paper presented at the Western Social Science Association Convention, April.

McCormick, John. 1989. *Reclaiming Paradise: The Global Environmental Movement.* Bloomington: Indiana University Press.

McLaughlin, Paul. 1994. "Essentialism, Nominalism and Population Thinking: Towards a New Organizational Ecology." Paper presented at the annual meeting of the American Sociological Association, August 9.

Melosi, M. 1985. "Environmental Reform in the Industrial Cities: The Civic Response to Pollution in the Progressive Era." Pp. 494–515 in *Environmental History: Critical Issues in Comparative Perspective,* edited by K. Bailes. New York: University Press of America.

Merchant, C. 1994. *Key Concepts in Critical Theory: Ecology.* Atlantic Highlands, NJ: Humanities Press.

———. 1992. *Radical Ecology: The Search for a Livable World.* New York. Routledge.

———. 1980. *The Death of Nature, Women, Ecology, and the Scientific Revolution.* San Francisco: Harper and Row.

Mitchell, Robert Cameron, Angela G. Mertig, and Riley E. Dunlap. 1992. "Twenty Years of Environmental Mobilization: Trends Among National Environmental Organizations." Pp. 11–26 in *The U.S. Environmental Movement, 1970–1990*, edited by Riley Dunlap and Angela G. Mertig. Washington, DC: Taylor and Francis.

Naess, Arne. 1972. "The Shallow and the Deep, Long-Range Ecology Movement: A Summary." *Inquiry* 16:95–100.

Nash, R. 1967. *Wilderness and the American Mind.* New Haven: Yale University Press.

Norris, C. 1982. *Deconstruction: Theory and Practice.* New York: Methuen.

O'Brien, Jim. 1983. "Environmentalism as a Mass Movement: Historical Notes." *Radical America* 17 (March–June):7–27.

Oelschlaeger, Max. 1991. *The Idea of Wilderness: From Prehistory to the Age of Ecology.* New Haven: Yale University Press.

Ortner, S. 1974. "Is Female to Male as Nature Is to Culture?" in *Women, Culture, and Society,* edited by M. Rosaldo and L. Lamphere. Stanford: Stanford University Press.

Perreault, William D., and Laurence E. Leigh. 1989. "Reliability of Nominal Data Based on Qualitative Judgements." *Journal of Marketing Research* 26 (May):135–148.

Phillips, Susan D. 1991. "Meaning and Structure in Social Movements: Mapping the Network of National Canadian Women's Organizations." *Canadian Journal of Political Science* 24 (4):755–782.

Richards, Ellen H. 1912. *Euthenics: The Science of Controllable Environment.* Boston: Whitcomb and Barrows.

Rosen, George. 1958. *A History of Public Health.* New York: MD Publications.

Rothenberg, David. 1992. "Does the Ecology Movement Have a Philosophy?" *Social Policy* Winter, pp. 49–55.

Roussopoulos, Dimitrios II. 1993. *Political Ecology.* New York: Black Rose.

Ruether, Rosemary Radford. 1975. *Sexism and God-Talk: Toward a Feminist Theology.* Boston: Beacon.

Scarce, Rik. 1990. *Eco-Warriors: Understanding the Radical Environmental Movement.* Chicago: Noble.

Scheffer, Victor B. 1991. *The Shaping of Environmentalism in America.* Seattle: University of Washington Press.

Short, C. Brant. 1989. *Ronald Reagan and the Public Lands.* College Station, TX: Texas A&M University Press.

Simon, Herbert W. 1990. *The Rhetorical Turn: Invention and Persuasion in the Conduct of Inquiry.* Chicago: University of Chicago Press.

Snyder, Gary. 1974. *Turtle Island.* New York: New Directions.

Tarr, Joel A.1985. "The Search for the Ultimate Sink: Urban Air, Land and Water Pollution in Historical Perspective." Pp. 516–552 in *Environmental History: Critical Issues in Comparative Perspective,* edited by Kendall E. Bailes. New York: University Press of America.

Taylor, Dorceta E. 1993. "Environmentalism and the Politics of Inclusion." Pp. 53–62 in *Confronting Environmental Racism: Voices from the Grassroots,* edited by Robert D. Bullard. Boston: South End.

Teymur, Necdet. 1982. *Environmental Discourse: A Critical Analysis of Environmentalism: In Architecture, Planning, Design, Ecology, Social Sciences and the Media.* London: ?uestion Press.

Thoreau, Henry David. 1862. *Walden, A Story of Life in the Woods.* Boston: Ticknor and Fields.

Touraine, A. 1977. *The Voice and the Eye.* New York: Cambridge University Press.

Wolf, Hazel. 1993–1994. "The Founding Mothers of Environmentalism." *Earth Island Journal* Winter:36–37.

Worster, Donald. 1985. "Comment: Hays and Nash," in *Environmental History: Critical Issues in Comparative Perspective,* edited by Kendall E. Bailes. New York: University Press of America.

Zimmerman, Michael E. 1994. *Contesting Earth's Future: Radical Ecology and Postmodernity.* Berkeley: University of California Press.

14. Development, Poverty and the Growth of the Green Movement in India*

JAYANTA BANDYOPADHYAY AND VANDANA SHIVA

A characteristic of Indian civilization has been its sensitivity to natural ecosystems. Vital renewable natural resources, like vegetation, soil, water and air, were managed and used according to well-defined social norms that respected known ecological processes. Indigenous cultures were sensitive to the limits to which natural resources could be exploited. It is said, for example, that the codes of conduct for pilgrims visiting such important religious centres as Badrinath in the Himalayas included a maximum stay of one night so that the temple area would not put excess pressure on local natural resources.

Before the pre-colonial era, indigenous economic processes placed few demands on natural resources and the impact of economic activity was too low to result in drastic environmental problems. Social norms, which applied to commoners and kings alike, safeguarded the environment and the destructive use of resources invariably met with public protest.

The advent of the British brought a major change in the pattern and nature of re-source use. Instead of being used to satisfy local needs, the natural wealth of India was exploited to meet the demands of western-Europe. Natural resources, like water, forests, minerals, etc, which had traditionally been managed as commons were taken over by the colonial authorities. Large areas of land were taken over to supply the raw materials for the British textile industry—the flagbearer of the industrial revolution. In Bengal and Bihar, peasants were forced to cultivate indigo; in Gujarat and the Deccan, cotton. Forests in the sensitive mountain ecosystems of the Western Ghats and the Himalayas were felled to build battleships or to meet the requirements of the expanding railway network, wood from the forests of the Bengal-Bihar-Orissa region being used to fuel the first locomotives. In the final stages of colonial rule, control over the use of resources was so complete that even water supplies were monopolized, access to such water sources as Sambhar lake in Rajasthan or the Damodar canal in Bengal being severely restricted.

Colonial intervention in the management of India's natural resources led to conflicts over such vital renewable resources as water and forests and induced new forms of poverty and deprivation, resulting in several protest movements as local people sought to regain—and retain—control over

---

*This excerpted essay was published in *The Ecologist* 19(3): 111–117, and is reprinted by permission of *The Ecologist*, Unit 18 Chelsea Wharf, 15 Lots Road, London, UK.

their natural resources. Such movements included the Indigo movement in eastern India; the Deccan movement for land rights; and forest movements in the Western Ghats, the central Indian hills and the Himalayas.

With the collapse of colonial rule internationally, and the emergence of sovereign independent states throughout the Third World, the conflicts over the control over local resources could have been resolved. But, in India as elsewhere, political independence vested the control over natural resources with the state. External colonialism may have ended but the new quest for "economic development" ensured that the colonial framework of natural resource management remained essentially unchanged. The same institutions which had been nurtured and developed by the colonial rulers with the specific aim of ensuring the permanent occupations of the colonies and the undermining of the local "natural economy"[1] were now entrusted with the responsibility of satisfying the basic needs of local people. That the nature of the institutions—and the ideology that lay behind them—made this goal impossible was never given serious thought.

GHANDI: EXPLODING THE MYTH OF RESOURCE-INTENSIVE DEVELOPMENT

The inexorable logic of resource exploitation, exhaustion and alienation integral to classical models of economic development based on resource-intensive technologies led Ghandi to seek an alternative path of development for India. He wrote:

"God forbid that India should ever take to industrialism after the manner of the west. The economic imperialism of a single tiny island kingdom (England) is today keeping the
world in chains. If an entire nation of 300 million took to similar economic exploitation, it would strip the world bare like locusts."[2]

Ghandi's critique gave advance warning of the future problems attendant on following the classical path of resource-intensive development. But at the time of Independence, no clear and comprehensive plan for realizing the Ghandian alternative for a resource-prudent development strategy, aimed at satisfying basic needs, existed. The issue of resource constraints on economic development were scarcely discussed, partly due to the tremendous pressure to "develop" that arose from the enhanced aspirations of a newly independent nation, and partly because natural resource parameters did not feature within the framework of conventional economics.

As the scale of economic development activities escalated from one five-year plan to another, the disruption of the ecological processes that maintain the productivity of the natural resource base started becoming more and more apparent. The classical model of economic development resulted in the growth of urban-industrial enclaves where commodity production was concentrated, as well as the rapid exhaustion of those "internal colonies" whose resources supported the enhanced demands of these enclaves.

The pressure to relieve poverty accelerated the pace of development—but instead of living standards improving for the mass of people, poverty simply increased. The commercialization of forestry provides a case in point. Commercial forestry companies increased their revenues by making more timber and pulpwood available in the market, but in the process they reduced biomass productivity or damaged the hydrology of the forest. People dependent on the non-timber biomass outputs of the forests like leaves, twigs, fruits, nuts, medicines, oils, etc, were thus unable to sustain themselves. The changed hydrological regime of the forests affected both the microclimate and the stream flows, disturbing hydrological stability and affecting agricultural production. There are similar examples from all parts of the country, related to almost all the massive developmental interventions in India's natural resource systems.

The ecological degradation and economic deprivation generated by the insensitivity and intensity of resource use resulted in environmental conflicts, an understanding of which is necessary for the reorientation of our current development priorities and concepts. Increasingly, it is becoming clear that the educated minority elite is the main beneficiary of the "development" process. In the context of a limited resource base and unlimited development aspirations, the ecology movements have initiated a new politics for safeguarding the interests and survival of the poor and the marginalised, among whom are women, tribals and poor peasants.

ECOLOGY MOVEMENTS: PRESSING FOR SURVIVAL

The number and range of ecology movements in independent India have increased as the predatory exploitation of natural resources to feed the process of development has intensified. This process has been characterized by the huge expansion of energy and resource-intensive industrial activity and by major development projects, such as big dams, forest exploitation, mining, energy-intensive agriculture, etc. The resource demand of development has led to the narrowing down of the natural resource base for the survival of the economically poor and powerless, either by the direct transfer of resources away from basic needs or by the destruction of the essential ecological processes that ensure the renewability of life-supporting natural resources.

The ecology movements arose as the peoples' response to the new threat to their survival and in order to demand the ecological conservation of vital life-support systems. Beyond clean air, the most significant of these systems are the common property resources of water, forests and land, on which the majority of the poor people of India depend for survival.

Among the various ecology movements in India, the Chipko movement…is the best known.[3] It started as a movement of the hill people in the state of Uttar Pradesh to save the forest resources from exploitation by contractors from outside. It later evolved into an ecological movement that was aimed at the maintenance of ecological stability in the major upland watersheds of India. Spontaneous popular resistance to save vital forest resources took place in the Jharkhand area on the Bihar-Orissa border region, as well as in the Bastar area of Madya Pradesh where there were plans to convert the mixed natural forests to plantations of commercial tree species, to the complete detriment of the local tribal people. In the southern part of India, the Appiko movement, which was inspired by the success of the Chipko movement in the Himalayas, is actively involved in stopping illegal felling of the forests and in replanting forest lands with multi-purpose broadleaved tree species. In Himachal Pradesh, Chipko activists have concentrated their opposition on the expansion of the monoculture plantation of commercial chir pine (*pinas roxburghii*). In the Aravalli hills of Rajasthan, there has been a massive programme of tree planting to give employment to those hands which were hitherto engaged in felling trees.

The exploitation of mineral resources, in particular open-cast mining in the sensitive watersheds of the Himalayas, the Western Ghats and central India, have also caused a great deal of environmental damage. As a result, environmental movements have arisen in these regions to oppose the mining operations. Most successful among them is the movement against limestone quarrying in the Doon Valley in Uttar Pradesh. Here the volunteers of the Chipko movement have led thousands of villagers in peaceful resistance against the limestone quarries which are seen by the people as a direct threat to their economic and physical survival.[4]

While popular opposition to quarrying in the Doon Valley has a long history, and a major Supreme Court order has restricted the area of quarrying to a minimum, examples of such successes are rare.[5] Popular ecology movements against mineral exploitation in neighbouring Almora and Pithoragarh still seem to be ignored, probably due to their relative geographical isolation. Beyond the Himalayas, the movement in the Ghandhamardan hills in Orissa against the ecological havoc of bauxite mining has gained momentum. The Bharat Aluminium Company (BALCO) mining project in the Gandhamardan hills is being opposed by local youth organizations and by tribal people whose survival is directly under threat. The peaceful demonstrators have claimed that the project could be continued only "over our dead bodies".[6] The situation is more or less the same in large parts of the Orissa-Madhya Pradesh region, where rich mineral and coal deposits are being opened up for exploitation and thousands of people are being pushed into destitution. This re-

gion includes the coal mining areas around the energy capital of the country in Singrauli…. In these interior areas of central India, movements against both mining and forestry are increasing and popular resistance is growing.

OPPOSITION TO WATER PROJECTS

Large river valley projects, the numbers of which are rapidly increasing in India, are another group of development projects against which ecology movements have arisen. The large scale submersion of land, a prerequisite for these projects, invariably takes a heavy toll on dense forests and the best food-growing areas. Such areas have been usually provided the material basis for the survival of a large number of people, especially tribals. The Silent Valley dam project in Kerala was opposed by the ecology movement on the grounds that it was a threat, not to the survival of the people directly, but to the gene pool of the tropical rain forests threatened with submersion. The movement against the Tehri high dam in Uttar Pradesh in the Himalayas exposed the possible threat to the people living both above and below the dam site through large-scale destabilisation of land by seepage and by the strong seismic movements that could be induced by impoundment. The Tehri Dam opposition committee has appealed to the Supreme Court against the proposed dam on the grounds that it threatens the survival of all the people living near the river Ganges up to West Bengal.[7] Popular movements have also emerged against dams at Bedthi, Inchampalli, Bhopalpatnam, Narmada, Koel-Karo and Bodhghat.[8] In-the-context of already overused land resources, the proper rehabilitation on a land-to-land basis of millions of people displaced through the construction of dams seems impossible.[9] The cash compensation given instead is inadequate in all respects for providing an alternate livelihood for the majority of the displaced. Destitution is thus the first and foremost precondition for starting large dam projects.

While the process of the construction of the dams itself invites opposition from ecology movements, the functioning of the water projects dependent on the dams goes on to create further ecological disasters. Popular movements against widespread water-logging, salinisation and resulting desertification in the command areas of many dams have been growing. Among the projects which have spawned ecological protest are those at Tawa, Kosi, Gandak, Tungabhadra, Malaprabha, Ghatprabha, and the canal irrigated areas of Punjab and Haryana. Elsewhere, in the arid and semi-arid regions of India, the improper and unsustainable use of water has also generated ecology movements. The anti-drought and anti-desertification movement is becoming particularly strong in the dry areas of Maharashtra, Karnataka, Rajasthan, Orissa, etc. Ecological water use for survival is being advocated by movements like Pani Chetana, Pani Panchayat and Mukti Sangharsh.[10]

Another major movement, which is spreading along the 7,000 km coastline of India, is the movement of small fishing communities against the destruction caused by mechanized fishing, the instant profit motive of which is destroying the long term biological productivity of the coasts.

No account of the threat to survival in India from environmental hazards can be complete without a reference to the Bhopal tragedy. Several thousand people died and several hundreds of thousands were affected by the poisonous gas released by the explosion at the Union Carbide plant. A popular movement for clean air and water is now growing throughout the country in reaction this disaster.

DEVELOPMENT AND THE DISPOSSESSED

Though the ecology movements relate to issues that are geographically localised, like forests or water pollution, their reverberations are national and even global in import. This macro-micro dichotomy results from the existence of "the two Indias".[11] Development activities invariably have a need for natural resources. In the context of limited quantities of resources, (limited either by non-renewability or by ecological limits to renewability), the resource needs of the two Indias are bound to compete with each other. In this unequal competition, the survival of the less powerful but more populous micro-economy is directly threatened. This threat may come either by resource transfer or by resource degradation.

Yet the significance of the ecology movements does not merely lie in the fact that they are voices for the dispossessed who are the victims of the highly unequal sharing of the costs of the development process. The positive feature of these movements lies in the manner in which they make visible the invisible externalities of development and reveal its inherent injustice and non-sustainability. The recognition of these inadequacies, and the imperatives arising from the right to survival, creates another direction for development which ensures justice with sustainability, equity with ecological stability.

The ecology movements can no longer be considered flash-in-the-pan protests. They are an expression of the universal socioecological impacts of a narrowly conceived development strategy based only on the short-term commercial criteria of exploitation. The impact of ecology movements cannot be assessed merely in terms of the impact of the particular development projects they originate from. The impact in the final analysis is on the very fundamental categories of politics, economics, science and technology which together have created the classical paradigm of development and resource use. The emerging threat to survival arising from the development process demands a reevaluation not just of some individual projects and programmes which have been shown to be ecologically destructive, but of the very conception and paradigm of development that generates such projects. The ecology movements are revealing how the resource-intensive demands of current development have ecological destruction and economic deprivation built into them. They are also stressing that the issue involves not merely a tradeoff of costs and benefits, because the cost of destruction of the conditions of life and well-being is not merely a matter of money, it is a matter of life itself. The most important and universal feature of ecology movements is that they are redefining the concepts of development and economic values, of technological efficiency, of scientific rationality—they are creating a new economics for a new civilization.

GROWTH AGAINST SURVIVAL

The ideology of the dominant pattern of development derives its driving force from a linear theory of progress, from a vision of historical evolution created in eighteenth and nineteenth century Western Europe and universalised throughout the world especially in the post-war development decades. The linearity of history pre-supposed in this theory of progress created an ideology of development that equated development with economic growth, economic growth

with expansion of the market economy, modernity with consumerism and non-market economics with backwardness. The diverse traditions of the world, with their distinctive technological, ecological, economic, political and cultural structures were driven by this new ideology to converge into a homogeneous monolithic order modelled on the particular evolution of the west....

MARKET ECONOMICS VERSUS THE ECONOMICS OF NATURE AND SURVIVAL

The dominant ideology of development has been classically concerned only with the use of natural resources for commodity production and capital accumulation. It ignores the resource processes that are responsible for regenerating natural resources. It also ignores the vast resource requirements of the large number of people whose needs are not being satisfied through market mechanisms. The neglect of these two vital economies—the economy of natural resources and natural processes and the economy of survival—has been the reason why ecological destruction and the threat to human survival have remained hidden negative externalities of the development process.

The words ecology and economy have emerged from the same Greek word "oikos" or the household. Yet in the context of market-oriented development they have been rendered contradictory. "Ecological destruction is an obvious cost for economic development," the ecology movements are told. Natural resources are produced and reproduced through a complex network of ecological processes. Production is thus an integral part of the economy of nature but today the concepts of production and productivity have been exclusively identified with industrial production for the market.

Organic productivity in forestry or agriculture has also been defined narrowly in terms of marketable produce alone. This has resulted in vast areas of resource productivity—like the production of humus by forests, the regeneration of water resources, or the natural evolution of genetic products—remaining beyond the scope of economics.

Similarly, modern economic theory and current concepts of development ignore the greater part of the history of economic production. For thousands of years, the "survival economy" has enabled human societies to derive their livelihoods directly from nature. Sustenance and the satisfaction of basic needs are the organizing principles behind natural resource use in the survival economy. By contrast, the exploitation of resources in the market economy rests on profits and capital accumulation.

While the diversion of resources, like the diversion of land from multipurpose community forests to monoculture plantations of industrial tree species, or the diversion of water from staple food crops and drinking water needs to cash crops, are frequently proposed as programmes for economic development in the context of the market economy, they create economic underdevelopment in the economies of nature and survival.

It is to these threats to survival that the growing ecological movement is opposed. Thus, in the Third World, ecology movements are not the luxury of the rich but are an imperative for the majority of the people whose survival is not taken care of by the market economy but is threatened by its expansion.

TECHNOLOGICAL CHOICE AND HOLISTIC ECOLOGY

Perceived from within the framework of the market economy, technology is assumed to lead to control over larger and larger quantities of natural resources, thus turning scarcity into abundance and poverty into affluence. Technology, accordingly, is viewed as the motive force for development and the vital instrument that guarantees freedom from dependence on nature. The affluence of the industrialized west is assumed to be associated exclusively with this capacity of modern technology to generate wealth.

Most resource-intensive technologies operate in urban enclaves, with enormous amounts of various resources coming from diverse ecosystems which are normally far away. This indirect and spatially diffuse process of resource transfer is made possible by energy-intensive long-distance transportation and leaves invisible the real material demands of the technological processes of development.

The spatial separation of resource exhaustion and the manufacture of products has also considerably shielded the tendencies of modern technologies to create inequalities. Further, it is simply assumed that the benefits of economic development based on these modern technologies will automatically percolated down to the poor and the needy, and that growth will ultimately take care of the problems of distributive justice. This would, of course, be the case, if growth and surplus were in a sense absolute and purchasing power existed in all socio-economic groupings. This is not so, however. Surplus is often generated at the cost of the ecological productivity of natural resources or at the cost of exhausting the capital of non-renewable resources. For the poor, the only impact of such economic activity is the loss of their resource base and thus their livelihood.

It is, thus, no accident that the modern, efficient and "productive" technologies created within the context of growth in market economic terms are associated with heavy social and ecological costs. The resource and energy intensity of the production processes they give rise to demands ever-increasing resource withdrawals the natural ecosystems. These excessive withdrawals in the course of time disrupt essential ecological processes and results in the conversion of renewable resources into non-renewable ones. A forest provides inexhaustible supplies of water and biomass, including wood, over time if its capital stock, diversity and hydrological stability are maintained and it is harvested on a sustained yield basis. The heavy and uncontrolled market demand for industrial and commercial wood, however, requires continuous over-felling of trees which destroys the regenerative capacity of the forest ecosystems and ultimately converts the forests to non-renewable resources. Sometimes the damage to nature's intrinsic regenerative capacity is impaired not directly by over exploitation of a particular resource but indirectly by the damage caused to other related natural resources. Thus, under tropical monsoon conditions, the over-felling of trees in the catchment areas of streams and rivers destroys not only forest resources, but also stable, renewable sources of water.

DISTORTED CONCEPTS OF EFFICIENCY

In the context of the market economy, the indicators of technological efficiency and productivity make no differentiation between the satisfaction of basic needs and the satisfaction of luxury requirements, or between resources extracted by ecologically sensitive technologies and ecologically insensitive ones. Indeed, economic growth *depends* on the production and consumption of non-vital products, thus leading to the further diversion of vital natural resources. For example, the water intensive produc-

tion of flowers or fruits for the lucrative export market often results in water scarcity in low rainfall areas. The high powered purchasing capacity of the rich of the world can extract resources at the expense of resource scarcity and resulting conflicts for the poor.

Guided by a narrow distorted concept of efficiency and supported by subsidies of all types, technological change in the context of market-oriented development continues in the direction of intensive resource use, labour displacement and ecological destruction. The long-term continuation of such processes will lead to the destruction of the resource base of the survival economy and to human labour being rendered dispensable in the production processes of the market economy.

THE MARKET PUSH TOWARDS ECOLOGICAL DESTRUCTION

In the absence of a deeper understanding of the economy of natural processes and the survival economy, the critique of the market economy presented by the ecology movement is naively construed as a critique of development *per se*, technology *per se* and against any form of intervention in nature. Natural resource conflicts and ecological destruction are seen as separate from the economic crisis, and the proposed solution to the ecological crisis is seen to lie in the further expansion of the market system. As a result, instead of programmes of gradual ecological regeneration of natural resources, their immediate and enhanced exploitation with higher capital investment is prescribed as a solution to the crisis of survival. Mr. Clausen, when president of the World Bank, for example, recommended that "a better environment, more often than not, depends on continued economic growth".[12] In a more recent publication, Chandler (1986) further renews the argument in favour of a market-oriented solution for ecological problems and believes that concern for conservation can only come through the market.[13]

Such solutions are funadamentally flawed. To begin with, the global market economy has no internal mechanism for ensuring the ecological rehabilitation of the natural resources destroyed by the market itself. The costs of ecological destruction are left to be borne by the residents of the areas which have been destroyed, people who must participate in the survival economy on the same land. Under these conditions the market is incapable of responding to the requirements of the economy of nature and the economy of survival.

Secondly, calls for further growth are based on the assumption that the expansion of the market will lead to development and poverty alleviation. But what constitutes "poverty"? In the ideology of the market, people are defined as poor if they do not participate overwhelmingly in the market economy and do not consume commodities produced for and distributed through the market—even though they might satisfy those needs through self-provisioning mechanisms. They are perceived as poor and backward if they eat self-grown millets and not commercially produced, commercially distributed processed foods. They are seen as poor and backwards if they live in self-built housing from local natural resources, like bamboo, stone or mud instead of cement and concrete bought from a market. They are seen as poor and backward if they wear indigenous handmade garments of natural fibre instead of mechanically manufactured clothes made of man-made fibres.

Rudolph Bahro quotes an African writer who differentiates poverty and misery.[14] The "poverty" associated with non-western modes of consumption is often mistaken to be misery. Culturally perceived poverty is not materially rooted poverty or or misery. Millets, or maize, the common non-western staple, are nutritionally far superior to processed foods and are again becoming popular in the west as health foods. Huts built with local materials represent an ecologically more evolved method of providing shelter to human communities than concrete houses. Natural fibres and local costumes are far superior in satisfying the region-specific need for clothing than manufactured nylon and terelene clothing, especially in the tropical climate.

The new poverty that we see around the world is no longer cultural and relative however. It is absolute, threatening the very survival of millions on this planet. At its root lies an economic paradigm which is governed by the forces of the market. It cannot assess the extent of its own requirements for natural resources, and it cannot assess the impact of this demand on ecological stability and survival. As a result economic activities that are most efficient and productive within the limited context of the market economy often become inefficient and destructive in the context of the economies of nature and survival.

The logic of the market by itself is not adequate to change the patterns of resource use that threaten ecological destruction and survival, especially in the context of independent nation states. Development as an ideology allows the indirect entry of global market domination. It creates a need for international aid and foreign debt which provide the capital for the development projects that commercialize or privatize resources. Control over local resources thus increasingly shifts, from the hands of local communities, and even national governments, into the hands of international financial institutions. The conditions for loans determine the mode of natural resource use. The pressure of repayment and servicing of debts further consolidates the globalization. Total integration with the global market economy thus marginalizes the concern for the economy of natural processes and the survival economy. In the resulting anarchy of resource use, the visible enclaves of economic development with their elite minority residents get a disproportionately high access to resources and the invisible hinterlands of economic underdevelopment, the homes of the silent majority, are left with shrinking access to a shrinking resource base.

CO-OPTING THE ALTERNATIVE MOVEMENT

The need for development that will improve standards of living, not undermine them, that will create ecological stability, not instabilities, is clear. The various dimensions of social movements, for survival, for democratic values, for decentralised decision-making are all components of the emerging ecology movement. While at the local level they may demand better management of forests in mountain catchments or better conservation of water in drought-prone areas, on the whole they are slowly progressing towards defining an alternate model for economic development—a new economics for a new civilization.

The agencies of the classical model of development have responded by turning 'environmental' overnight, and an attempt at co-option has begun. The time for the ultimate battle between the traditional concepts of development and the new ecological development paradigm is drawing nearer. The new packaging of old development model is characterized by purloining the language of the ecological movement to dress up old development programmes guided by the market and biased in favour of those who already enjoy economic superiority. New forestry programmes, for example, are being handed over to the NGO sector, as if leaving matters to the NGOs means a new conceptual framework for development. It is forgotten that so long as the development programmes are framed within the limits of the market economy and do not internalize the economy of natural processes and the economy of survival, the results cannot be different. The fundamental difference between hollow, decorative environmentalism and deep ecology must be understood because a new contradiction is being created to confuse the critics of market-oriented development.

Protagonists of hollow environmentalism argue that deep ecological arguments can wait: what cannot wait is instant environmental action. In this way much of the activism of the ecology movement is being frittered away in micro-level actions while their challenges at the macro-conceptual level get diffused. The task of the ecology movements is to face both challenges in a co-ordinated manner.

The issue is not simply one of planting trees here or protecting a tiger there. The issue is related to a fundamental change in human concepts about life, about development, about civilization. It is time that the old development strategy be replaced by a new one based on a holistic principles. It is on the ecology movements of the world that the task of evolving humane and sustainable development policies has fallen.

REFERENCES

1. R. Luxemberg, *The Accumulation of Capital,* Routledge and Kegan Paul, London, 1951, 370.
2. M. K. Gandhi, *Young India,* December 20 1928, 422.
3. J. Bandyopadhyay and V. Shiva, "Chipko: Rekindling India's Forest Culture", *The Ecologist,* Vol. 17, No. 1, 1987, 26–34.

4. V. Shiva, 'How Green was My Valley', *The Illustrated Weekly of India,* October 21 1986: *see also,* S. Jain, *Hindustan Times,* December 11 1986.

5. J. Bandyopadhyay and V. Shiva, 'Conflicts over Limestone Quarrying in Doon Valley', *Environmental Conservation,* Vol. 12, No. 2, 131–139.

6. Usha Rai, *The Times of India,* December 28 1986.

7. Usha Rai, *The Times of India,* September 9 1986.

8. Medha Paktar *The Times of India.* December 11 1986: *see also,* A. Gandhi and A. Kumar, *Economic and Political Weekly,* Vol. XXI, No 22, May 31 1986.

9. J. Bandyopadhyay *in* Edward Goldsmith and Nicholas Hildyard (eds.), *The Social and Environmental Effects of Large Dams,* Volume 2, Wadebridge Ecological Centre, 1985, 209–213.

10. Gail Omvedt, *Economic and Political Weekly,* Vol. XXI, No. 18, 1986: *see also,* B. M. Parandare, *The Times of India,* September 17 1986.

11. R. Kothari, *Dossier of International Foundation for Development Alternatives,* No 52, 1986, 4–14.

12. Edward Goldsmith, 'The World Bank: Global Financing of Improverishment and Famine', *The Ecologist,* Vol. 15, Nos. 1/2, 1985.

13. W. D. Chandler, *Worldwatch Paper* 72, Worldwatch Institute, Washington DC, 1986.

14. R. Bahro, *From Green to Red,* Verso, London, 1984, 211.

15. Science, Nature, and the Globalization of the Environment, 1870–1990*

DAVID JOHN FRANK

Between 1870 and 1990, the natural environment became a highly visible node of discourse and activity in world society (Frank et al. 1998; Robertson 1992; Yearley 1996). There are many indicators of this change. In 1870, "global" environmental problems were virtually unknown. Now people around the world regard the seriousness of such problems as ozone depletion (first asserted in the early 1970s), climate change (broadly recognized in the late 1970s), and declining biodiversity (codified in the middle 1980s) (Dunlap 1994; Mazur & Lee 1993). Likewise, in the late 1800s, there were few world-oriented environmental associations, but now such associations are abundant with the list including the World Wide Fund for Nature (founded in 1961), Greenpeace (1971), and Friends of the Earth (1971). There were similarly few intergovernmental environmental organizations at the turn of the century. Now there are more than 100, such as the International Whaling Commission (established in 1946) and the United Nations Environment Pro-

gramme (established in 1972) (Meyer et al. 1997). The recent rise of world-level discourse and activity concerning the natural environment has been dramatic.

One important indicator of the overall change is the proliferation of international environmental treaties.[1] Such treaties are central to the new global environmental imageries. They offer coordinated solutions to the new worldwide problems, and appear to provide at least some direct benefits to the environment (Dietz & Kalof 1992; Haas, Keohane & Levy 1993; Roberts 1996). The number of international environmental treaties rose exponentially between 1870 and 1990, as shown in Figure 6.2. The five-year moving average of annual treaty formations experienced slow growth before World War II. Then it began a steep increase, which continued through the 1970s. Finally in the 1980s, the average number of treaty formations began to decline. A total of 156 international environmental treaties were established between 1870 and 1990, beginning in 1878 with a treaty to slow the spread of the phylloxera louse.

Few social scientists have found the recent rapid expansion of world-level discourse and activity concerning the environment to be problematic to explain. For many, it appears to have been straightforwardly driven by the growing scope and

*Reprinted from *Social Forces* 76 (December 1997): 409–435. "Science, Nature, and the Globalization of the Environment, 1870–1990" by David John Frank. Copyright © The University of North Carolina Press.

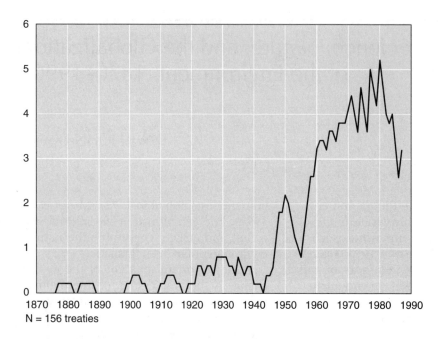

FIGURE 6.2   International Environmental Treaties—Smoothed Average of Yearly Foundings, 1870–1990

scale of degradation of the environment (Choucri 1993; Nanda 1983; Sprinz & Vaah-toranta 1994; Thomas 1992; Young 1989). While intuitively appealing, this functionalist explanation fails to account for the fact that over the course of human history, even massive episodes of environmental degradation have rarely elicited the widespread intervention-oriented activity that is now routine (see Turner et al. 1992).

I argue that the rise of the environment in world society was catalyzed in part by a conceptual reconstitution of the entity "nature." There has been a shift away from conceptions of nature as a realm of chaos and savagery, and away from conceptions of nature as a cornucopia of resources, and toward conceptions of nature as a universal, life-sustaining "environment" or ecosys-

tem. The new conception is that of a natural system with planet-wide interdependencies, encompassing *Homo sapiens* and providing most fundamental sustenance for this species. This redefinition of nature, championed by scientists and environmental activists, facilitated the striking level of world mobilization that has emerged.

The core argument of the article is thus twofold. The first contention is that nature was scientifically reconstituted over the course of the last century, being increasingly rendered as a physically sustaining global ecosystem. The second contention is that this reconstitution facilitated world-level discourse and activity concerning the environment. Both pieces of the argument can be examined with data from international environmental treaties, however they require using two different kinds of information about these treaties. First, I examine the *themes* of international environmental treaties in order to demonstrate the qualitative world-level shift in dominant depictions of nature. Then I perform event-history analyses on the *formation rate* of international environmental treaties to demonstrate the catalyzing effect of the redefinition on world-level discourse and activity.

THE CASE FOR THE RISE OF THE MODEL OF NATURE AS AN ECOSYSTEM

A rich historical and sociological literature has established that dominant conceptions of nature vary dramatically over time and space (Brulle 1996; Freudenberg, Frickel & Gramling 1995; Kempton, Boster & Hartley 1995; Nash 1982; Pepper 1984; Thomas 1983). In the West, one may distinguish two broad trends between 1870 and 1990, both driven by science. First, there was a process of functionalization, in which nature acquired an expanding array of utilities (Caldwell 1990; Frank 1994; McCormick 1989). At the beginning of the period, nature was noticeable to humans mainly for instrumental (primarily economic) reasons. By the end of the period, nature was conceived as the biogeophysical undergirding of human life itself (Lowenthal 1990; Pepper 1984). Thus, the same mountain that was a wartlike excrescence in the early modern period, and a store of iron in 1870, may now be considered a vital part of the biogeophysical support system, performing critical roles in the hydrological cycle, for example, and hosting an irreplaceable genetic pool (Freudenberg, Frickel & Gramling 1995; Nicolson 1959; Thomas 1983). In addition to functionalization, there was a process of physicalization, in which nature lost its primary connections to God and the spirit world (nature as creation) and gained connections to the physical laws of the universe (Lowenthal 1990; Weber 1946). Thus, the same lightning that embodied punishment and wrath in the early modern period may embody only universal physical laws in the contemporary one. The "scientizing" shifts were pronounced, and laid the foundations for the nature-as-ecosystem concept.[2]

Counterposing the two dimensions of change, i.e., functionalization and physicalization, suggests a typology delineating six alternative models of nature, shown in Figure 6.3 (see also the topologies in Brulle 1996; Catton & Dunlop 1980; Sack 1990).[3] Along one dimension, the typology differentiates three levels of functionality: one in which nature is separate from and opposed to human society, and essentially counterfunctional (the mountain as barrier); one in which nature is connected and subordinate to human society, providing narrow services (the mountain as mineral); and one in which nature is integrated with human society, pervasively bound into vital processes (the mountain as life-support system).

FIGURE 6.3   A Typology of Models of Nature

	Separation: Nature Against Society	Connection: Nature Subordinate to Society	Integration: Nature United with Society
Spiritual	Savage	Edenic	Rights
Physical	Feral	Resource	Ecosystem

Along the other dimension, the typology differentiates spiritual nature, directly motivated by the divine (lightning as wrath), from physical nature, directly motivated by universal laws (lightning as discharge of electricity).

Like any typology, this one places boundaries where there is intermixing, and presents differences where there are similarities. In the real world, nature is almost always multivocal (sometimes in ways not even represented by the typology, as when "humans" and "nature" are indistinguishable). Still, the typography is heuristically useful. It delineates a set of alternatives to the currently dominant ecosystem model, and thereby facilitates the investigation of the rise of that model.

I contend that ecosystem models of nature, based in scientific thought and publicized by environmentalists, arose between 1870 and 1990. Other models of nature remained stable or declined (Luhmann 1989; Pepper 1984).[4] To gather evidence in support of this argument and to establish shifts in the definition of "nature" over time, I determined the characteristics of each model in the typology, coded the main theme of each international environmental treaty, and determined the total number of environmental treaties employing each model as a function of time.[5]

The procedure for coding the main themes of the international environmental treaties is as follows. First I identified each treaty's primary goal, which appeared in the title or preamble: for example, to control locusts or conserve whale stocks. Then I followed a simple set of coding rules to locate the treaty's main theme on the typology.[6]

The results of this coding effort are summarized in Figures 6.4 and 6.5. Two facts are immediately apparent. One is that only two models of nature have received

substantial play on the world stage: nature as resource and nature as ecosystem. The second is that the rise of international discourse and activity around nature between 1870 and 1990 consisted, in substance, of an early increase in international coordination around resource issues and then, more recently and dramatically, an increase in coordination around ecosystem issues. I discuss the pattern in greater detail below.

(1) Savage Model: The first cell of the typology contains models that pose a spiritualized nature separate from and opposed to human society. For convenience, I call this the savage model of nature.

Such models are important in many cultural settings. For example, the Ewe of southwest Africa are taught to avoid the forests, which are ruled by nature devils ill-disposed towards humans (Pettersson 1961; cf. Douglas 1966). Likewise, modern Westerners are taught to avoid sexual relations with "beasts," which, though physically inconsequential, constitute grave violations of the moral order. Both examples pose a nature that harbors spiritual forces, dangerous to civilized society. In both, nature has the capacity to "pollute" humans—a stark reversal of the relationship as posed by the ecosystem model.

Savage models have framed no international environmental treaties.

(2) Edenic Model: In the second cell of the typology, models depict a spiritual nature that is connected but subordinate to human society. These may be called edenic models of nature.

Edenic models are employed, for example, in Islam, in which nature appears as a direct manifestation of God, embodying the Creator and bearing

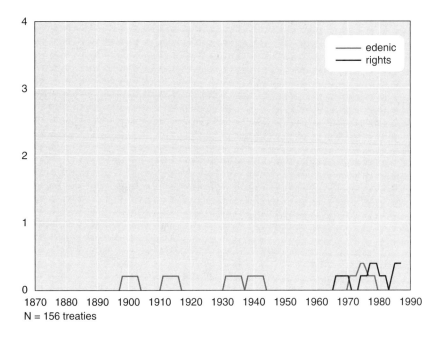

N = 156 treaties

FIGURE 6.4   International Environmental Treaties by Model of Nature, Spiritual—Smoothed Average of Yearly Foundings, 1870–1990

spiritual lessons for humankind (Ba Kader et al. 1983). Similarly in transcendentalism, nature appeared as a rejuvenating spiritual tonic, wherein Americans could retreat from the stupefying effects of overwork to wash off the "sins and cobweb cares of the devil's spinning in all-day storms on mountains" (Muir 1898:483; see also Grove 1992; Nash 1982; Pepper 1984). Both examples envision nature as spiritually beneficial to human society.

A few treaties are framed by edenic models. For example, the Convention on Nature Protection and Wildlife Preservation in the Western Hemisphere, signed in Washington, D.C., in 1940, endeavors to preserve areas of extraordinary beauty, striking formation, and aesthetic value. Its provisions include

the establishment of national parks, reserves, and "nature monuments." The treaty is focused on nature that inspires wonder and awe (as opposed, say, to nature that is economically or ecologically valuable).[7] Not many international treaties have employed the edenic model, as Figure 6.4 reveals, and they have become even less common in the most recent period.

(3) *Rights Model:* Some models pose nature as spiritually or morally integrated with human society. These may be called rights models of nature (although "rights" here should be read in the broadest sense, as moral holism).

Rights models appear in many social contexts. In Jainism, for example, even parasites can, "with the right prompting...achieve rebirth in heaven"

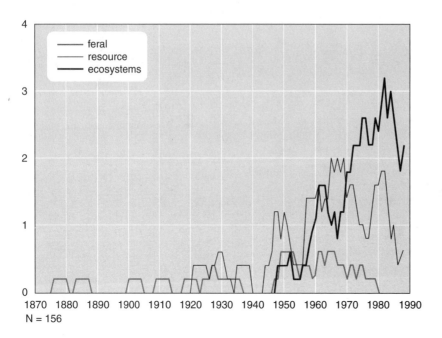

FIGURE 6.5   International Environmental Treaties by Model of Nature, Physical—Smoothed Average of Yearly Foundings, 1870–1990

(Dundas 1992:91). Likewise in the animal rights movement, even the lowest of animals are deemed inherently valuable individuals with a right to life on Earth (Jasper & Nelkin 1992).[8] Underlying both examples is a conception that nature and humanity are essentially integrated at the spiritual or moral level.

Rights models of nature show up in several recent treaties, such as the 1987 European Convention for the Protection of Pet Animals, which seeks to protect pet animals from pain, suffering, distress, and abandonment. The treaty bridges the radical separation between nature and culture, and animals (especially those that have been joined to human society as pets) are seen to warrant a level of deference and kindness that befits sentient, conscious beings.

Nature, in this scenario, is integrated with human society in a single moral community, and humans are thus obligated to treat animals "ethically." Figure 6.4 reveals that some recent environmental treaties have embodied the rights model of the human/nature relationship. Clearly the currency of this model has been boosted by the shift toward integrated conceptions of nature. Nevertheless, the rights model has remained a minor theme in international discourse, as would be expected from the spiritual basis of its claims.

Savage, edenic, and rights models all depict nature in spiritual terms. The difference between them consists in the extent to which nature is functionally integrated with human society. The feral, resource, and ecosystem models all depict nature in physical terms, with differences in functional integration parallel to those of the spiritual models.

(4) *Feral Model:* In the fourth cell of the typology are those models that pose nature as physically separate from and opposed to human society. I designate these with the term feral.

Nature is often conceived as a dangerous physical entity (e.g., Burton, Kates & White 1978). In much of the contemporary world, insects (such as locusts and cockroaches), animals (like rats and coyotes), and even plants (especially those called "weeds"), are considered to hinder or threaten human society. So too are geophysical processes such as earthquakes, meteorological phenomena such as hurricanes, and so forth. All of these examples embody the basic notion that the incursion of nature on human society is endangering.

A number of international treaties have used the feral model. There is, for example, the International Plant Protection Convention, signed at Rome in 1951. The objective of the treaty is to control the spread of pests and diseases that affect crops and livestock. The aspects of nature on which the treaty is focused, i.e., pests that eat, kill, or otherwise destroy, are depicted in opposition to the physical well-being of human society. A fair number of feral model treaties have appeared, especially just after the founding of the United Nations, as seen in Figure 6.5. By the 1970s, however, such treaties had all but disappeared.

(5) *Resource Model:* In the fifth cell fall those models that depict nature as a physical entity that is connected and subordinate to human society. These may be called resource models of nature.

Resource models have often held sway. They turn trees into timber; cows into livestock; rocks into gravel; and fast-running rivers into hydraulic power. Thoreau criticized the resource model, contrasting it with the edenic. He wrote of the farmer:

> *I respect not his labors, his farm where everything has its price, who would carry the landscape, who would carry his God to market…on whose farm nothing grows free .. whose fruits are not ripe for his till they are turned to dollars. Give me poverty that enjoys true wealth ([1854] 1974:145).*

The resource model authorizes human society to exploit nature to satisfy human needs and desires. At its root, the resource model asserts that the physical aspects of nature exist for use by human society.

The resource model has frequently framed international environmental treaties. For example, the 1946 International Convention for the Regulation of Whaling aims to "safeguard for future generations the great natural resources represented by whale stocks" (UNEP 1991a:5). This treaty depicts whales— for food, for oil, for commerce—as components of a physical nature subservient to society, to be used at human will for human benefit. A great many international environmental treaties have framed nature as a resource, as shown in Figure 6.5. A significant increase in the number of such treaties followed the founding of the United Nations. But the foundings peaked, flattened out, and even declined in recent times, with the rise of the ecosystem model (Frank 1994).

(6) Ecosystem Model: In the sixth cell are models that depict nature as physically integrated with human society. I call these ecosystem models.

In the contemporary world a "scientized" version of the ecosystem model is increasingly dominant (Caldwell 1990; Dunlap & Mertig 1992; McCormick 1989). According to it, each component of nature is dependent on the larger natural system for exchanges of energy and matter. *Homo sapiens* is but one species in the larger biosphere, which itself is subsumed within a larger physical universe (Lovelock 1988; Stern, Young & Druckman 1992; Vernadsky 1929). The basic notion in the ecosystem model is that nature, including a naturalized human society, constitutes an integrated physical system.

A great number of international environmental treaties have employed models, though none before the founding of the United Nations in 1945. For example the 1985 Convention for the Protection of the Ozone layer is intended to stop human activities that destroy the ozone layer, in order to protect the health of humans and other species. The model contains a system loop: humans damage the ozone layer and then, in turn, suffer the consequences. Nature and human society are a physical, interdependent whole. This model of nature was very prominent in recent international treaties, as shown in Figure 6.5. In the last two decades, nature-as-ecosystem has surpassed every other model, becoming dominant in international environmental treaty discourse.

Overall, Figures 6.4 and 6.5 reflect a fundamental shift. Out of many available models of nature, one became predominant in the latter half of the twentieth century: the ecosystem model. Driven by science, nature was decoupled from God and coupled to rationalized human society, becoming increasingly tied into the everyday workings—and the very survival—of human life on Earth. Thus the savage, feral, edenic, resource, and rights models were all upstaged in international discourse and activity by a scientific model of nature-as-ecosystem, in which nature is conceived as a physical entity that follows laws and includes humans as an integral part.[10]

HYPOTHESES LINKING THE ECOSYSTEM CONCEPT TO INTERNATIONAL ACTIVITY CONCERNING NATURE

The redefinition of nature shifted the cultural framework to allow the environment to be conceived and rendered as consequential to world society, thus promoting the dramatic expansion in international environmental discourse and activity. In constructing a concept of nature that is pervasively bound up with human life processes, regardless of national boundaries, the redefinition of nature as a global ecosystem provided a powerful rationale for international coordination around nature. In addition to this cultural change, two organizational changes between 1870 and 1990, namely, the structuration of the world polity and the consolidation of an official intergovernmental environmental domain, also affected the amount and form of international discourse and activity around nature.

In the following, I argue these assertions and then test them empirically in a series of event-history analyses on the rate at which international environmental treaties were formed.

Redefinition of Nature

The redefinition of nature in rationalized and scientific terms functional to human society played an important role in the proliferation of international environmental treaties over time.

Culturally, the rise of "scientized' models of nature distilled a compelling logic for international coordination of discourse and activity.[11] With redefinition, nature acquired an expanding portfolio of purposes, such that it came to be seen as the unique physical envelope capable of generating and sustaining human life. In presenting the entity nature as global, malleable, and of paramount importance to ongoing human survival, the ecosystem model of nature issued a forceful call for international discourse and activity, including international environmental treaties.

By contrast, formerly dominant models, such as those depicting nature as a realm of enchantment or danger (e.g., Douglas 1966; Hultkrantz 1961), provided less powerful logics for internationally coordinated activities. In such cases, other courses of action, such as direct supplications or boundary enhancement, were more obvious approaches to the natural world.

Organizationally, the redefinition of nature involved, both as antecedent and consequence, the rise of a number of international associations that also played a role in generating international discourse and activity around nature. These associations included groups of scientists, such as the International Union of Geodesy and Geophysics, which began collecting data on the distribution and intensity of ozone in the atmosphere in the 1950s; and groups of social movement activists, such as the World Conservation Union, first proposed in 1913, which has mobilized activity around scientific findings. International associations have often been the first to demand and the first to draft environmental treaties, and their counsel, support, and technical advice frequently have propelled the treaty formation process (e.g., see Haas, Keohane & Levy 1993; Hayden 1942; McCoy & McCully 1993).

Formerly dominant depictions of nature were less likely to produce international associations. For example, models that characterized nature as local and idiosyncratic were ill-suited to world-level coordination (e.g., Douglas 1966; Hultkrantz 1961).

Together, these cultural and organizational aspects of the redefinition of nature took the form of "epistemic communities" in which accepted facts and frameworks facilitated agreed-upon paths to environmental protection (Haas 1989). The emergence of a global epistemic community around nature consolidated both new rationales for founding international environmental treaties and new authorities to promote them. This leads to a first hypothesis:

> Hypothesis 1. *The redefinition of nature should increase the rate at which international environmental treaties are formed.*

This effect should hold both generally (for all kinds of environmental treaties), and for the two main types of environmental treaties (resource and ecosystem), since both present nature in rationalized terms functional to human society. The effect should be greatest, however, for the ecosystem treaties, which are the most extensively functionalized.

Structuration of the World Polity

The structuration of a world polity composed of juridically equal nation-states provided a framework within which all kinds of international discourse and activity could occur.

Culturally, the structuration of the world polity created an institutional forum within which issues gained world meaning and substance (Meyer 1987, 1994; Robertson 1992). A world level of society was scarcely visible in the late nineteenth century. Since then, the "world" has been richly elaborated and articulated, with concepts such as human rights, world population, and the global environment. All kinds of international discourse and activity have gained much from this movement, including the environmental (Boli & Thomas 1997; Forsythe 1991; Smith 1997).[12]

Organizationally, the structurated world offered built-in for a for the administration of global matters. Before the institutionalization of the main intergovernmental organizations, treaties were initiated by hegemons, such as Britain and France (see Hayden 1942 for examples). Later these roles were performed increasingly by the major intergovernmental organizations, such as the United Nations, and international associations (Boli & Thomas 1997; McNeely 1995). Around environmental matters, these bodies formulated discrete and actionable problems out of what had previously appeared only as "noise" (Luhmann 1989). They publicized these problems, drafted treaties to deal with them, and organized conferences to attract the support of potential parties. Finally, international organizations and associations encouraged treaty ratification with funding, technical advice, and a variety of other incentives (e.g., Haas 1989). The structuration of the world polity greatly facilitated all kinds of organizational processes leading to international discourse and activity.[13]

The essential point is that the structurated world polity that developed has catalyzed international treaties. A world alternatively organized, such as a global empire, world state or religious system, would be less likely to use treaties and more likely, for example, to rely on edicts, top-down regulations or rules.

In short, the type of structuration of the world polity that has occured both confirmed the importance of "world" issues and provided an organizational apparatus for acting on them. This leads to a second hypothesis.

> Hypothesis 2. *The structuration of the world polity into a coordinated assembly of juridically equal nation states should increase the rate at which international environmental treaties are formed.*

Official Intergovernmental Environmental Domain

Finally, and emerging partly as a result of the ongoing redefinition of nature and structuration of the world polity, there was a recent consolidation of a permanent and centralized intergovernmental environmental domain, which slowed the growth in the number of international environmental treaties.[14]

Culturally, the consolidation of a permanent and centralized intergovernmental environmental domain established a set of fundamental world-level understandings about nature, derived mainly from the ecosystem model. Once these understandings were set in place, they established a foundation that could be extended or modified without resorting to the transactional treaty stage. An example of this is the set of understandings concerning ozone put into place in the 1970's (Benedick 1991). By contrast, in the absence of crystallized understandings around nature, there would be no alternative but to identify concerns and negotiate understandings ad hoc. Under such conditions, international environmental treaties would have to be forged around even the most basic issues.

Organizationally, with the consolidation of a permanent and centralized intergovernmental environmental domain (through such organizations as the United Nations Environment Programme established in 1972), a routinized organizational mode began to supersede the transactional treaty mode; as new environmental issues appeared, they were addressed by existing organizations rather than producing treaty-type transactions and new structures.[15] Scientists and activists, instead of advocating the genesis of new treaties, simply promoted the expansion of the existing organizational structure. Existing organizations often vied for control over new issues to expand their resources and enlarge their authorized domains (for examples, see Haas 1993).

In short, the consolidation of a permanent and centralized intergovernmental environmental domain solidified a base of understandings around nation-state environmental interests, and it provided a ready-made apparatus for dealing with them. This leads to a third hypothesis:

Hypothesis 3. *The consolidation of an official intergovernmental environmental domain should decrease the rate at which international environmental treaties are formed.*

These ideas guide the event-history analyses that follow.

MODELING THE RATE OF FORMATION OF INTERNATIONAL ENVIRONMENTAL TREATIES

The empirical analyses were guided by the three hypotheses above. To test for the existence of the expected relationships, I employed event-history analysis.

The event-history analysis determines the effect of the independent variables on the limiting probability per unit of time that an event occurs given that a risk of the event exists (Tuma & Hannan 1984). In this case the event is the formation of an international environmental treaty. Here the event is recurrent, so the dependent variable is the transition rate from a treaty count of N to (N + 1). I used a constant-rate model, which assumes that the transition rate does not depend directly on time but rather depends on time only through the time-varying independent variables. All independent variables were measured yearly. When more than one treaty formation occurred in a year, the year was split into equal spells. I used the RATE program to estimate the parameters (Tuma 1992).

There are no conventional ways to measure the three main independent variables: the redefinition of nature in world society, the structuration of the world polity, and the consolidation of a permanent and official intergovernmental environmental domain. Thus, I used three sets of indicators, from which I extracted three factors to use in the event-history analyses.

Redefinition of Nature

I used three indicators to measure the world-level redefinition of nature in rationalized terms functional to human society. The indicators are highly intercorrelated, averaging .89.

The first indicator is the cumulative number of international ecology associations, from the *Yearbook of International Organizations* (UIA 1994). The *Yearbook* is indexed by keywords in organizational titles and descriptions. The keyword "ecology" was used to construct a list of potentially relevant international nongovernmental associations, which was then pared to include only those with ecology as a main concern. The founding dates of ecology associations indicate the rise of the scientific nature-as-ecosystem framework. The first such association was formed in 1910; by 1990, there were 27.

The second and third indicators measure the amount of international scientific discourse and activity since scientists are the professional agents of the most highly functional model of nature. One indicator is the cumulative number of unions associated with the International Council of Scientific Unions (ICSU) (International Research Council 1922–52; ICSU 1954–90). Founded in 1919 as the International Research Council, the ICSU has been the central umbrella organization for the world's natural science unions, such as the International Union of Geodesy and Geophysics, and it has been prominently involved in international discourse and activity around nature (e.g., Caldwell 1990; McCormick 1989). There are now 20 unions in the ICSU.

The third indicator is the cumulative number of international science associations, logged, from the *Yearbook of International Organizations* (UIA 1994). It is based on the keywords "science" "fundamental science," and "research" as above (see Schofer forthcoming). The founding dates of these organizations measure the increase in international scientific discourse and activity over time. The first international science association appeared in 1881 and by 1990 there were 224.[16]

Structuration of the World Polity

I used four indicators to create a factor measuring the overall structuration of the world polity. The variables are substantially intercorrelated, averaging .87.

The first two indicators measure the amount of intergovernmental organization. First there is the cumulative number of intergovernmental organizations, minus environmental intergovernmental organizations, from the *Yearbook of International Organizations* (UIA 1994). These organizations, such as NATO, numbered 2 in 1870. By 1990, there were 1,463. Second there is the level of general world organization. The indicator is 0 before the League of Nations; 1 during the League; and 2 after the founding of the United Nations in 1945 (see note 17).

Next, I gauged the number of agreements between nation-states: the cumulative number of multilateral treaties, minus environmental treaties (Bowman & Harris 1984,1993; Mostecky 1965). In 1870, 169 non-environmental treaties existed; by 1990 the number had grown to 7,559.[17]

Finally, to measure the diffusion of the nation-state model, and thus the extension of the basis for the world polity, I included the cumulative number of independent nation-states (*Europa Yearbook* 1990). In 1870, there were 46 independent nation-states; by 1990, there were 174.[18]

Official Intergovernmental Environmental Domain

Three indicators make up the factor measuring the consolidation of a permanent and centralized intergovernmental environmental domain. Their average intercorrelation is .91.

The first indicator is the cumulative number of intergovernmental environmental organizations, from the *Yearbook of International Organizations* (UIA 1994). Ten keywords (such as nature, environment) were used, as above, to identify intergovernmental environmental organizations, including both those organizations promoting the protection of the environment and those promoting its rational exploitation. It turns out that 113 intergovernmental environmental organizations appeared by 1990, the first in 1945.

Second, there is the staff size of the United Nations Environment Programme (UNEP), founded in 1972. UNEP is the master intergovernmental environmental organization, providing support services for smaller environmental organizations and assuming secretariat functions that independent organizations would otherwise undertake. Even more than the smaller intergovernmental environmental organizations, UNEP indicates the institutionalization of the environment as a routine nation-state concern in world society. The professional staff size measures the growth of UNEP over time. It numbered 254 by 1990.

The third indicator measures the change of the nation-state structure to include the environment as a core concern. It is the cumulative number of nation-states with environmental ministries (*Statesman's Year-Book* 1960–1989). All ministries with the words environment, conservation, or ecology in their titles were included. The first environmental ministry appeared in 1971. By 1990, there were 26.[19]

Degradation of the Environment

In addition to these three main independent variables, I included two other variables to insure that the effects posited stand up to a functionalist alternative, which asserts that international discourse and activity around nature arose in response to increasing population pressure and environmental degradation. I introduce as a variable the natural log of world population, in order to test the notion that a more populous world is a more resource-scarce world (Ehrlich 1968), the pressures of which would catalyze international envi-

ronmental treaties. I also include an industrial pollution degradation factor in order to test the notion that the despoliation wrought by industrialization spurs international environmental treaties.[20] The two indicators of the industrial degradation factor, correlated at .96, are anthropogenic carbon dioxide emissions, logged (Keeling et al. 1989; UNEP 1991b), and chloroflouroicarbon emissions, logged (Council on Environmental Quality 1991).

Results

The maximum likelihood estimates of the hazard rate of environmental treaty formation appear in Table 6.3. Each column contains one complete model, including the chi-squared goodness of fit statistic.

Throughout the analyses, there is high multicollinearity, as all of the independent variables increased significantly over time (although clearly not at the same rate). Models 1–5 show this to be the case. When entered alone, each one of the three main variables (measuring the redefinition of nature, the consolidation of the intergovernmental environmental domain, and the structuration of the world polity) had a positive and significant effect on the rate at which international environmental treaties were formed from 1870–1990 (models 1–3). So did world population and the measure of environmental degradation (models 4–5).

However, the results are somewhat different when the independent variables are entered together (models 6–7). Then the predicted patterns emerge.

The rise of the nature-as-ecosystem model in world society positively affected the rate at which international environmental treaties were formed during 1870–1990. In both models 6 and 7, in spite of multicollinearity, the redefinition effect was positive and significant. The scientization of

TABLE 6.3 Maximum Likelihood Estimates of the Hazard Rate at Which Envirommental Treaties Are Formed in the World, 1870–1990

Variable	1	2	3	4	5	6	7
Redefinition of Nature in World Society	1.04** (.09)					2.13* (.99)	2.07* (.99)
Consolidation of Official Intergovernmental Environmental Domain		0.46** (.05)				−0.75** (.16)	−0.58* (.30)
Structuration of World Polity			0.88** (.07)			1.70* (.87)	1.67* (.87)
Industrial Degradation				1.19** (.10)			0.72 (1.15)
Population					2.58** (.22)	−4.90 (3.33)	−6.89 (4.62)
Constant	−0.31** (.12)	0.11 (.09)	−0.21* (.11)	−0.44** (.14)	−2.39** (.28)	3.39 (2.68)	5.01 (3.75)
χ^2 improvement over baseline	169.05**	65.50**	156.78**	187.32**	167.04**	200.41**	200.81**
χ^2 improvement over last model, if nested						33.36**	.40
(N = 156 treaties)							

Note: Standard errors are in parentheses.

Indicators

a Cumulative no. international ecological associations
  Cumulative no. unions in International Council of Scientific Unions
  Cumulative no. international science associations, logged
b Cumulative no. intergovernmental environmental organizations
  Cumulative no. national environmental ministries (constant cases)
  Staff of United Nations Environment Programme
c Cumulative no. international treaties (nonenvironmental)
  World organization (0=pre-League, 1=League; 2=UN)
  Cumulative no. intergovernmental organizations (nonenvironmental)
  Cumulative no. independent nation-states
d Global annual CO_2 emissions from anthropogenic sources, logged
  Global annual CFC emissions, logged
e World population in millions, logged

* $p < .05$ ** $p < .01$ (one-tailed test)

nature, whereby it was seen increasingly as a lawlike physical system providing basic life support to *Homo sapiens,* appears to have provided a powerful cultural and organizational impetus to international discourse and activity concerning the environment.

The effect was especially strong on ecosystem treaties. I compared the results of two event-history analyses that included the three main independent variables: one on resource treaties ($n = 64$) and another on ecosystem treaties ($n = 64$) (results not shown). The positive effect of the redefinition of nature was *ten times* greater on ecosystem than on resource treaties, and both effects were significant ($p < .05$). The transformation of the entity nature not only promoted all kinds of environmental treaties but promoted ecosystem treaties in particular.[21]

The results in Table 6.3 also suggest that the consolidation of an official intergovernmental environmental domain negatively affected the rate at which international environmental treaties were formed overall. In both models 6 and 7, the consolidation variable is negative and significant. The official intergovernmental domain began to bureaucratize and routinize international environmental space. Existing apparatuses expand more easily than new treaties are formed, and thus the official intergovernmental environmental domain began to supersede international environmental treaties.

The results in Table 6.3 also support the notion that the overall structuration of the world polity positively affected the rate at which international environmental treaties were formed between 1870 and 1990. In both models 6 and 7, the world structuration variable is positive and significant. The structuration of the world polity provided a general cultural and organizational infrastructure—a "world" in the fullest sense—that supported international discourse and activity concerning nature.

Finally, the results in models 6 and 7 of Table 6.3 undermine the hypotheses that population pressure and industrial degradation positively affected the rate at which international environmental treaties were formed between 1870 and 1990. Indeed, net of the other effects, the population parameter is negative, and the chi-squared statistic reveals that adding the industrial degradation factor in model 7 provides no additional explanatory power. Perhaps it is not environmental problems *per se* that drive international discourse and activity concerning nature but rather their formulation and articulation in an organized world.

In the face of high multicollinearity, I took one further step to check the robustness of the findings. I disaggregated the three main independent variables back into single indicators, and then ran each one of the indicators against every pair of indicators for the other two variables. This produced a total of 36 event-history analysis of the hazard rate of international environmental treaty formation (these indicators of redefinition times three indicators of consolidation times four indicators of structuration).

The indicator for the redefinition of nature in world society positively affected the international environmental treaty founding rate in 31 of 36 equations; it was significant in 30 of these ($p < .05$, one-tailed test). The indicator for the consolidation of an official intergovernmental environmental domain negatively affected the international environmental treaty founding rate in 31 of 36 equations; it was significant in 17 of these. The indicator for the structuration of the world polity positively affected the international environmental treaty founding rate in 32 of 36 equations; it was significant in 12 of these.

The directions of the effects are stable and have the expected signs. The significance levels are encouraging. Overall, the results are consistent with the findings in Table 6.3 and suggest the basic soundness of the results.

CONCLUSION

The entity nature was transformed by science over the last 120 years, becoming conceptually integrated into the routine physical functions of human society. The transformation is evident in the world social definition and organization of nature as ecosystem. A seemingly endless array of interdependencies was discovered, and the cultural and organizational apparatus of the ecosystem welded human society and nature together as one. As pointed out by Pepper (1984), humanity is now viewed as but one natural species, encompassed within and dependent on a wider nature.[22]

One major consequence of this transformation was a global efflorescence in discourse and activity concerning nature. Now huge sums of money and legions of the most highly educated professionals plumb the Earth's core and explore the heavens to ascertain the workings of the ecosystem and humanity's place within it. Society increasingly feels the need to know what the ecosystem bodes for the future viability of the human species.

My first task here was to show the redefinition of the concept of nature at the level of world society in the period 1870–1990. By coding the main themes of international environmental treaties and then charting them over time, I demonstrated the world-level rise and consolidation of the scientific ecosystem model of nature in the post-World War II period. Increasingly, the conception of nature was institutionalized as an Earth-wide system of organisms, including human organisms, together with their physical environment. Meanwhile, other models of nature—savage, feral, edenic, resource, and rights—declined in relative importance.

My next task was to demonstrate that this redefinition was itself consequential to the amount of international discourse and activity concerning nature. In a series of event-history analyses of the rate at which international environmental treaties were formed between 1870 and 1990, I showed this to be the case. A factor built from three indicators of the redefinition of nature in world society consistently had a positive and signifiant effect on the founding rate of environmental treaties. The rise of the scientific ecosystem model involved the creation of a powerful rationale and an elaborate organizational machinery for the promotion of international discourse and activity around nature.

Two world-level organizational factors also showed effects on the rise of international discourse and activity around nature. First, the structuration of the world polity exhibited a significant effect on the rate at which international environmental treaties were formed during the period. Globalization, both in terms of meaning and in terms of organization, provided a setting within which international environmental issues were sensible and actionable. Second, the recent consolidation of an official intergovernmental environmental domain demonstrated a significant negative effect on the rate at which international environmental treaties were formed. Environmental treaties, as a transactional *form* of international discourse and activity, began to be superseded by more permanent and routine organizational arrangements (Meyer et al. 1997).

Based on this evidence, it is clear that the institutionalization of a new model of nature—nature as ecosystem—had profound consequences for discourse and activity in world society. Apparently the world social system includes not only economic (Chase-Dunn 1989; Wallerstein 1974) and military and political (Ruggie 1993; Tilly 1990) dimensions. It also includes important institutional dimensions (Boli & Thomas 1997; Meyer 1994; Robertson 1992; Smith 1997; Steinmetz 1997; Thomas et al. 1987), in which dynamic cultural and organizational orders provide the central catalysts for change.

NOTES

1. International environmental treaties are formal, often binding, agreements between three or more nation-states to regulate some aspect of the natural environment (cf. Mostecky 1965). For example, both treaties regulating river resources and those protecting the atmosphere are included in the analyses here. Excluded are agricultural treaties (which deal with crops, not naturally appearing plants), health treaties, weapons-proliferation treaties, and scientific-research treaties: nature is not their focal concern. Most environmental treaties are listed in the registries of the United Nations Environment Programme (Kiss 1983; Rummel-Bulska and Osafo 1991; UNEP 1991a). Burhenne (1974–1993) contains some others, predominantly from the pre-United Nations era. See Frank (1994) for a complete list and description.

2. At once, a single natural object or process may be framed by multiple models—dangerous and ecosystemically vital, for example. I argue that there are broad trends in the prominence of such models.

3. The cell labels are meant to be suggestive, not definitive.

4. The "ecosystem" model employed by scientists and environmentalists is not exactly the same. Although the environmentalist version of the ecosystem model builds on scientific research, it is both out of date and more conservative than the latest scientific orthodoxy (Kempton, Boster & Hartley 1995).

5. The "models" discussed here are similar to discursive frames, which have received much sociological attention from social-movement theorists (e.g., Brulle 1996; Snow et al. 1986).

6. Treaties seeking to subordinate spiritual aspects of nature to human society are savage; treaties seeking to subordinate nature's physical aspects are feral (for example, a treaty to stop the spread of phylloxera). Treaties seeking to preserve nature on spiritual grounds for the benefit of human society are edenic (such as a treaty to save magnificent landscapes); treaties seeking to preserve nature on physical grounds are resource (a treaty to conserve tuna stocks). Treaties seeking to integrate nature and human society on spiritual or moral grounds are rights (e.g., a treaty setting treatment standards for livestock); treaties seeking to integrate nature and society on physical grounds are ecosystem (a treaty to stop the pollution of seas). For comparable efforts to code international discourse, see Berkovitch (1998), Barrett and Frank (1998). Most treaties embody more than one model of nature: the effort here is code the dominant model.

7. Recent research reveals that many of the early United States national parks, though awesome, are relatively barren from the ecological point of view (Chadwick 1995).

8. A related but broader view, called deep ecology, claims that all of nature deserves moral consideration (eg., Bergesen 1995), including plants, which fruitarians believe to be sentient beings (Harris 1985).

9. One need not go back far in time to see a whole different array of species and processes—many now rehabilitated—in feral roles. See, for example, provisions to eradicate baboons and large birds of prey in the 1900 Convention for the Preservation of Wild Species in Africa.

10. The rise of the ecosystem model suggests a paradigm shift (Kuhn 1962), in which the gulf distinguishing human society from nature was bridged by a latticework of physical interdependencies. The term *ecosystem* was coined in 1935, but "a cybernetic systems concept of the basic unit of ecology did not take form until after World War II" (Haraway 1989:391). The imagination and global institutionalization of nature-as-ecosystem have fundamentally altered humankind's relationship to the universe, welding humans and nature into a unified and mutually supporting whole.

11. Many others have made similar points, although typically in the language of scientific discovery rather than institution building. See, for

examples, Ashby (1978); Caldwell (1990); Haas (1989); McCormick (1989); Taylor and Buttel (1992).

12. International treaties, as a specific form of international activity, rely on the fact that the world was structurated as a *liberal* polity, dependent on the voluntaristic cooperation of its component nation-states. Treaties assume that nation-states are elemental actors, sovereign, and at least juridically equal (Jackson & Rosberg 1982; Thomas et al. 1987; Ruggie 1993; Strang & Meyer 1993).

13. For finer grade analysis of the relationship between intergovernmental organizations, international nongovernmental organizations, and international treaties, see Frank (1994), Meyer et al. (1997).

14. To some extent, the intergovernmental sector arises as a result of international environmental treaties. See Meyer et al. (1997).

15. For example, at the ninth meeting of the parties to the Convention on International Trade in Endangered Species, China, India, Indonesia, Japan, Malaysia, Nepal, the Republic of Korea, Singapore, and Thailand agreed to implement a set of tiger protections, such as anti-poaching and public awareness campaigns. A new treaty was not created: the agreement occurred within the existing structure.

16. Using a slightly different set of indicators for the redefinition of nature has little effect on the results reported below. (1) The cumulative number of nation-states with at least one national park may be substituted for ecology associations, and (2) any one of the three indicators may be dropped, with no substantial change in the findings.

17. In the absence of a single source for the whole period, I used two sources which employ different criteria for counting treaties (cf. Lechner 1991). To render the two compatible, I calculated, for a 10-year period of overlap, the average multiplier that made the more exclusive source equal to the more inclusive source. Then I used the multiplier to adjust the remaining years of the exclusive source.

18. Three alternative world structuration variables, in which (1) the trichotomous indicator measuring the general level of world organization is replaced by two dichotomous variables, one each for the League and UN, (2) the cumulative number of nation-states indicator is dropped, and (3) the cumulative number of nonenvironmental multilateral treaties is dropped, performs similarly to the variable described.

19. Confirmatory factor analyses (Bentler 1991) offered partial support for the main factors described above. In the most demanding test, all ten indicators were detrended by time. The three residualized indicators of the official environmental domain had high standardized loadings, above .85. Three of the four residualized indicators of the world polity had high standardized loadings, above .95, but the residual of the world organization trichotomy had a weak, negative loading (−.15): it measures a more foundational dimension of world structuration. Among the three residualized indicators of the redefinition of nature, the two general science measures held together, but diverged from the ecology measure: the two general indicators tap a process that led to the later formation of ecology associations.

20. An alternative measure of natural degradation—the cumulative number of mammal and bird species extinctions—and a variable that simultaneously serves as an indirect measure of pollution and as a measure of world development—the United Nations global manufacturing index—perform similarly to the industrial degradation factor described.

21. In contrast, the strength of the negative effect from the consolidation of an official intergovernmental environmental domain and the strength of the positive effect from the structuration of the world polity were very similar for resource and ecosystem treaties.

22. The shift is expressed in recent calls for sociologists to include physical environmental factors in their explanations. See, for examples, Dunlap and Catton (1994); Laska (1993).

REFERENCES

Ashby, Eric. 1978. *Reconciling Man with the Environment.* Stanford University Press.

Ba Kader, Abou Bakr Ahmed, Abdul Latif Tawfik El Shirazy Al Sabbagh, Mohamed Al Sayyed Al Glenid, and Mouel Youself Samarrai Izzidien. 1983. *Islamic Principles for the Conservation of the Natural Environment.* Gland, Switzerland: International Union for the Conservation of Nature and Natural Resources.

Barrett, Deborah, and David John Frank. 1998. "Population-Control for National Development: From World Discourse to National Policies." In *World Polity Formation Since 1875,* edited by John Boli and George M. Thomas. Stanford University Press.

Benedick, Richard Elliot. 1991. *Ozone Diplomacy.* Harvard University Press.

Bentler, P. M. 1991. *EQS: A Structural Equation Program.* Los Angeles: BMDP Statistical Software.

Bergesen, Albert. 1995. "Deep Ecology and Moral Community." Pp. 193–213 in *Rethinking Materialism,* edited by Robert Wuthnow. Eerdmans.

Berkovitch, Nitza. 1998. "The Emergence and Transformation of the International Women's Movement." In *World Polity Formation Since 1875,* edited by John Boli and George M. Thomas. Stanford University Press.

Boli, John, and George M. Thomas. 1997. "World Culture in the World Polity: A Century of International Non-Governmental Organization." *American Sociological Review* 62:171–90.

Bowman, M. J., and David John Harris. 1984. *Multilateral Treaties: Index and Current Status.* London: Butterworths.

Bowman, M., and David John Harris. 1993. *Multilateral Treaties: Index and Current Status. Cumulative Supplement.* London: University of Nottingham Treaty Centre.

Brulle, Robert J. 1996. "Environmental Discourse and Social Movement Organizations: A Historical and Rhetorical Perspective on the Development of U.S. Environmental Organizations." *Sociological Inquiry* 66:58–83.

Burhenne, W. E. (ed.). 1974–93. *International Environmental Law,* volumes 1–6. Berlin: Erich Schmidt Verlag.

Burton, Ian, Robert W. Kates, and Gilbert F. White. 1978. *The Environment as Hazard.* Oxford University Press.

Caldwell, Lynton Keith. 1990. *International Environmental Policy,* 2d ed. Duke University Press.

Catton, Wiffiam R., Jr., and Riley E. Dunlap. 1980. "A New Ecological Paradigm for Post-Exuberant Sociology." *American Behavioral Scientist* 24:15–47.

Chadwick, Douglas H. 1995. "The Endangered Species Act." *National Geographic* March: 2–41.

Chase-Dunn, Chrisopher. 1989. *Global Formation: Structures of the World-Economy.* Basil Blackwell.

Choucri, Nazli. 1993. *Global Accord.* MIT Press.

Council on Environmental Quality. 1991. *Environmental Quality: 22nd Annual Report.* U.S. Government Printing Office.

Dietz, Thomas, and Linda Kalof. 1992. "Environmentalism Among Nation-States." *Social Indicators Research* 26:353–66.

Douglas, Mary. 1966. *Purity and Danger.* Penguin.

Dundas, Paul 1992. *The Jains.* Routledge.

Dunlap, Riley E., 1994. "International Attitudes Towards Environment and Development." Pp. 115–26 in *Green Globe Yearbook 1994,* edited by H. O. Bergesen and G. Parmann. Oxford University Press.

Dunlap, Riley E., and William R. Catton Jr. 1994. "Toward an Ecological Sociology." Pp. 11–31 in *Ecology, Society and the Quality of Social Life,* edited by William V. D'Antonio, Masamichi Sasaki, and Yoshio Yonebayashi. Transaction Publishers.

Dunlap, Riley E., and Angela G. Mertig. 1992. "The Evolution of the U.S. Environmental Movement from 1970 to 1990: An Overview." Pp. 1–10 in *American Environmentalism,* edited by Riley E. Dunlap and Angela G. Mertig. Taylor & Francis.

Ehrlich, Paul R. 1968. *The Population Bomb.* Ballantine Books.

Europa Yearbook. 1990. *The Europa World Yearbook.* London, England: Europa Publications Limited.

Forsythe, David P. 1991. *The Internationalization of Human Rights.* Lexington Books.

Frank, David John. 1994. "Global Environmentalism: International Treaties in World Society." Unpublished Ph.D. diss. Department of Sociology, Stanford University.

Frank, David John, Ann Hironaka, John W. Meyer, Evan Schofer, and Nancy Brandon Tuma. 1998. "The Rationalization and Organization of Nature in World Culture." In *World Polity Formation Since 1875,* edited by John Boli and George M. Thomas. Stanford University Press.

Freudenberg, William R., S. Frickel, and Robert Gramling. 1995. "Beyond the Nature/Society Divide: Learning to Think Like a Mountain." *Sociological Forum* 10:361–92.

Grove, Richard H. 1992. "Origins of Western Environmentalism." *Scientific American* 267:42–47.

Haas, Peter M. 1989. "Do Regimes Matter? Epistemic Communities and Mediterranean Pollution Control." *International Organization* 43:377–403.

———. 1993. "Protecting the Baltic and North Seas." Pp. 133–81 in *Institutions for the Earth,* edited by Peter M. Haas, Robert O. Keohane, and Marc A. Levy. MIT Press.

Haas, Peter M., Robert O. Keohane, and Marc A. Levy (eds). 1993. *Institutions for the Earth.* MIT Press.

Haraway, Donna. 1989. *Primate Visions.* Routledge.

Harris, Martyn. 1985. "The Animal Rights Brigade." *New Society* 31:168–71.

Hayden, Sherman Strong. 1942. *The International Protection of Wild Life.* Columbia University Press.

Hultkrantz, Ake (ed.). 1961. *The Supernatural Owners of Nature.* Stockholm: Almquist & Wiskell.

International Research Council. 1922–52. *Reports of Proceedings of the General Assembly.* London: International Research Council.

International Council of Scientific Unions (ICSU). 1954–90. *Year Book.* Paris: ICSU Secretariat.

Jackson, Robert, and Carl Rodberg. 1982. "Why Africa's Weak States Persist: The Empirical and the Juridical in Statehood." *World Politics* 35:1–24.

Jasper, James M., and Dorothy Nelkin. 1992. *The Animal Rights Crusade: The Growth of a Moral Protest.* Free Press.

Keeling, C. D., R. B. Bacastow, A. F. Carter, S. C. Piper, T. P. Whorf, M. Heimann, W. G. Mook, and H. Roeloffzen. 1989. "A Three Dimensional Model of Atmospheric CO_2 Transport Based on Observed Winds." *Geophysical Monograph* 55:165–236.

Kempton, Willett, James S. Boster, and Jennifer A. Hartley. 1995. *Environmental Values in American Culture.* MIT Press.

Kiss, Alexandre. 1983. *Selected Multilateral Treaties in the Field of the Environment,* Vol. 1. Nairobi: United Nations Environment Programme.

Kuhn, Thomas S. 1962. *The Structure of Scientific Revolutions.* University of Chicago Press.

Laska, Shirley Bradway. 1993. "Environmental Sociology and the State of the Discipline." *Social Forces* 72:1–17.

Lechner, Frank J. 1991. "Religion, Law, and Global Order." In *Religion and Global Order,* edited by Roland Robertson and William R. Garrett. Paragon House.

Lovelock, James. 1988. *The Ages of Gaia.* W. W. Norton.

Lowenthal, David. 1990. "Awareness of Human Impacts: Changing Attitudes and Emphases." Pp. 121–35 in *The Earth as Transformed by Human Action,* edited by B. L. Turner II, W. C. Clark, R. W. Kates, J. F. Richards, J. T. Mathews, and W. B. Meyer. Cambridge University Press with Clark University.

Luhmann, Niklas. 1989. *Ecological Communication.* University of Chicago Press.

Mazur, Allan, and Jinling Lee. 1993. "Sounding the Global Alarm: Environmental Issues in the US. National News." *Social Studies of Science* 23:681–720.

McCormick, John. 1989. *Reclaiming Paradise.* Indiana University Press.

McCoy, Michael, and Patrick McCully. 1993. *The Road From Rio: An NGO Action Guide to Environment and Development.* Utrecht: International Books.

McNeely, Connie. 1995. *Constructing the Nation-State: International Organization and Perspective Action.* Greenwood Press.

Meyer, John W. 1987. "The World Polity and the Authority of the Nation-State." Pp. 41–70 in *Institutional Structure,* by George M. Thomas, John W. Meyer, Francisco O. Ramirez, and John Boli. Sage.

———. 1994. "Rationalized Environments." Pp. 28–54 in *Institutional Environments and Organizations,* by W. Richard Scott, John W. Meyer and Associates. Sage.

Meyer, John W., David John Frank, Ann Hironaka, Evan Schofer, and Nancy Brandon Tuma. 1997. "The Structuring of a World Environmental Regime, 1870–1990." *International Organization* 51:623–51.

Muir, John. 1898. "The Wild Parks and Forest Reservations of the West." *Atlantic Monthly* 81:483.

Mostecky, Vaclav (ed.). 1965. *Index to Multilateral Treaties.* Harvard Law School Library.

Nanda, Ved P. 1983."Global Climate Change and International Law and Institutions." Pp. 227–39 in *World Climate Change: The Role of International Law and Institutions,* edited by Ved P. Nanda. Westview Press.

Nash, Roderick. 1982. *Wilderness and the American Mind,* 3d ed. Yale University Press.

Nicolson, M. H. 1959. *Mountain Gloom and Mountain Glory.* Cornell University Press.

Pepper, David. 1984. *The Roots of Modern Environmentalism.* Croon Helm.

Pettersson, Olof. 1961. "The Spirits of the Woods." Pp. 101–11 in *The Supernatural Owners of Nature,* edited by Ake Hultkrantz. Stockholm: Almquist & Wiksell.

Roberts, J. Timmons. 1996. "Predicting Participation in Environmental Treaties: A World-System Analysis." *Sociological Inquiry* 66:38–57.

Robertson, Roland. 1992. *Globalization: Social Theory and Global Culture.* Sage.

Ruggie, John Gerard. 1993. "Territoriality and Beyond: Problematizing Modernity in International Relations." *International Organization* 47:139–74.

Rummel-Bulska, Iwona, and Seth Osafo. 1991. *Selected Multilateral Treaties in the Field of the Environment,* vol 2. Cambridge, England: Grotius.

Sack, Robert D. 1990. "The Realm of Meaning: The Inadequacy of Human-Nature Theory and the View of Mass Consumption." Pp. 659–671 in *The Earth as Transformed by Human Action,* edited by B. L. Turner II, W. C. Clark, R. W. Kates, J. E. Richards, J. T. Mathews, and W. B. Meyer. Cambridge University Press with Clark University.

Schofer, Evan. N.d. "The Rationalization of Science and the Scientization of Society: International Science Organizations, 1870–1995." In *World Polity Formation Since 1875,* edited by John Boli and George M. Thomas. Stanford University Press.

Smith, Jackie. 1997. "Characteristics of the Modern Transnational Social Movement Sector." In *Transnational Social Movements and Global Politics,* edited by Jackie Smith, Ron Pagnucco, and Charles Chatfield. Syracuse University Press.

Snow, David A., E. Burke Rochford Jr., Steven K. Worden, and Robert D. Benford. 1986. "Frame Alignment Processes, Micromobilization, and Movement Participation." *American Sociological Review* 51:464–81.

Sprinz, Detlef, and Tapani Vaahtoranta. 1994. "The Interest-Based Explanation of International Environmental Policy." *International Organization* 48:77–105.

Statesman's Year-Book. 1960–89. *Statesman's Year-Book.* St. Martin's Press.

Steinmetz, George. (ed.). 1997. *New Approaches to the State in the Social Sciences.* Cornell University Press.

Stern, Paul C., Oran R. Young, and Daniel Druckman (eds.). 1992. *Global Environmental Change.* Washington, DC: National Academy.

Strang, David, and John W. Meyer. 1993. "Institutional Conditions for Diffusion." *Theory and Society* 22:487–511.

Taylor, Peter J., and Frederick H. Buttel. 1992. "How Do We Know We Have Environmental Problems? Science and the Globalization of Environmental Discourse." *Geoforum* 23: 405–16.

Thomas, Caroline. 1992. *The Environment in International Relations.* London: Royal Institute of International Affairs.

Thomas, George M., John W. Meyer, Francisco O. Ramirez, and John Boli. 1987. *Institutional Structure: Constituting State, Society, and the Individual.* Sage.

Thomas, Keith Vivian. 1983. *Man and the Natural World.* Pantheon.

Thoreau, Henry. 1974 [1854]. *Walden,* 8th printing. Collier.

Tilly, Charles. 1990. *Coercion, Capitalism, and European States, A.D. 990–1990.* Basil Blackwell.

Tuma, Nancy Brandon. 1992. *Invoking RATE.* Palo Alto, Calif.: DMA Corporation.

Tuma, Nancy Brandon, and Michael T. Hannan. 1984. *Social Dynamics Models and Methods.* Academic Press.

Turner II, B. L., W. C. Clark, R. W. Kates, J. R. Richards, J. T. Mathews, and W. B. Meyer (eds.). 1990. *The Earth as Transformed by Human Action.* Cambridge University Press with Clark University.

Union of International Associations (UIA). 1948–95. *Yearbook of International Organizations.* Munchen: K. G. Saur.

United Nations Environment Programme (UNEP). 1991a. *Register of International Treaties and Other Agreements in the Field of the Environment.* Nairobi: United Nations Environment Programme.

———. 1991b. *Environmental Data Report.* 3d ed. Basil Blackwell.

Vernadsky, V. I. 1929. *La Biosphere.* Paris: Librairie Felix Alcan.

Wallerstein, Immanuel. 1974. *The Modern World System,* Vol. 1. Academic Press.

Weber, Max. 1946. *From Max Weber,* translated by Hans H. Gerth and C. Wright Mills. Oxford University Press.

Yearley, Steven. 1996. *Sociology, Environmentalism, Globalization.* Sage Publications.

Young, Oran R. 1989. "The Politics of International Regime Formation: Managing Natural Resources and the Environment." *International Organization* 43:349–75.

Chapter 7

Environmental Assessment and Management

16.   Risk Assessment and Management*

THOMAS DIETZ

R. SCOTT FREY

EUGENE ROSA

Increased public concern with technological risk has promoted critical scrutiny of new technologies and reevaluation of older ones. It is both a paradox and a challenge for modern societies that technologies, despite their countless benefits, are increasingly challenged by professionals and laypersons alike. The paradox resides in the generally uncritical acceptance of the benefits of technology but a simultaneous demand for a reduction in the risks of technology. The challenge resides in the difficult issue of how to assess, choose, and manage technology through democratic processes. This problem, in turn, challenges the social sciences to inform debates about technological risk, since the outcomes of these debates will broadly shape the direction of technological and social changes.

Technological risk consists of two separate but interrelated concepts: risk and hazard. Risk is a compound measure of the probability and magnitude of some event or adverse effect. Hazard refers to dangers or threats that can produce adverse effects. Technological risk, therefore, refers to the probability and magnitude of adverse effects of technological hazards on human health and safety and the environment. The adverse effects to human health and safety include death, disease, and injury, whereas the adverse effects to the environment include threats to non-human species, ecosystems, biogeochemical cycles, climate, and the biosphere as a whole. Principal technological hazards include dangers that threaten the entire biosphere, such as nuclear holocaust and global warming; the failure of large-scale technological systems, such as nuclear power plants; the use or misuse of mechanical devices, such as power lathes in factories; the misuse or release of hazardous substances, such as toxic chemical spills; and population exposure to low-level delayed-effect dangers, such as asbestos.[1]

Technological risks have been a problem throughout human history (Covello and Mumpower 1985), but have assumed greater importance in recent times because of growing public concern. Whether increased concern reflects an actual increase in the number and severity of technological

*Copyright © 2000 by Thomas Dietz, R. Scott Frey, and Eugene Rosa. Order of authorship is alphabetical. We wish to thank Chip Clarke, Riley Dunlap, Bill Freudenburg, Jim Jasper, Ed Liebow, Jim Miley, Marvin Olsen, Ortwin Renn, and Jim Short for their comments on earlier versions of this paper.

risks is a matter of debate (e.g., Bailey 1995; Commoner 1990; Douglas and Wildavsky 1982; Epstein 1998; Lancet 1992; Lichter and Rothman 1999; Proctor 1995). However, it is clear that technological risks abound in modern industrial societies. Precise estimates are difficult to obtain, but the best available data suggest that at least 20–30% of all male deaths and 10–20% of all female deaths in the U.S. each year can be attributed to technological hazards (Harriss, Hohenemser, and Kates 1985:130–143). The economic costs are also great, for Tuller (1985) estimates that in 1979 alone the economic cost of technological hazards in the U.S. (including lost productivity, property damage, and public and private sector efforts to control technological hazards) was $179–283 billion or 8–12% of the U.S. Gross National Product. Furthermore, technological hazards have hidden effects—especially to the environment—that are not captured by the market. Harriss et al. (1985:144–148), for instance, estimate that one third of the extinction and endangerment rate of bird and mammal species since 1800 can be attributed to technology, as can 75% of the land biomass decline in recent history.

Opinion polls indicate that a majority of Americans believe that life is getting riskier and that additional regulations are needed to effectively control health, safety, and environmental risks (Dunlap 1992). There is growing evidence that such concerns are global (Dunlap, Gallup and Gallup 1993; Dunlap and Mertig 1995). Confidence in institutions responsible for risk regulation and management has been eroding steadily over the past several decades (Lipset and Schneider 1983; Rosa and Clark 1999). One consequence of the convergence of these trends is the rise in political controversy over technologies (Mazur 1981; Jasper 1988, 1990; Nelkin 1992). Other conse-

quences include increased government efforts to assess and manage technological hazards (Breyer 1993; Regens, Dietz, and Rycroft 1983; Fiorino 1995), and the development of a new profession termed "risk analysis" (Crouch and Wilson 1982; Lave 1982; Lowrance 1976; Rodericks 1992).

We describe the social and political issues associated with technological risk and outline the emerging social science perspectives for examining them. We organize our discussion around four major themes: (1) formal models of risk assessment, risk evaluation, and risk management; (2) the background and current structure of the risk policy system in the United States and other nations; (3) the major social science perspectives that have emerged to understand risk; and (4) the dynamics of the political controversies surrounding risk.

RISK ASSESSMENT, RISK EVALUATION, AND RISK MANAGEMENT

A proper understanding of technological risk requires some familiarity with the vocabulary, procedures, and range of methods currently used in risk assessment, risk evaluation, and risk management (e.g., Covello and Merkhofer 1993; Environ 1988; Rodericks 1992; U.S. National Research Council 1983; U.S. Office of Technology Assessment 1981). Risk assessment is the process of identifying technological hazards and estimating and assessing the adverse consequences (e.g., death) associated with such hazards. Risk evaluation is the process of determining the acceptability of identified risks in order to guide policy decision-making. Risk management entails efforts to avoid, reduce, control, or mitigate those risks deemed unacceptable.

Proponents of risk assessment and evaluation maintain that these techniques are rational scientific tools, essential to the accurate assessment and effective management of technological risks (e.g., Breyer 1993; Crouch and Wilson 1982; Hamilton and Viscusi 1999; Lave 1982; Rodericks 1992; Russel and Gruber 1987). But critics argue that formal risk assessment and evaluation have numerous limitations that produce deeply biased and flawed risk management practices (e.g., Clarke 1988; Perrow 1984; Proctor 1995; Shrader-Frechette 1985, 1991). We will not enter this debate here, but instead describe the dominant techniques and key concepts underpinning formal risk assessment, evaluation, and management.

Risk Assessment

The U.S. National Research Council (1983:17–20) divides risk assessment into four distinct but complementary steps: hazard identification, dose–response assessment, exposure assessment, and risk characterization.

Hazard identification is the identification of technologies or features of technologies that are hazardous. Identification is based on a variety of sources: epidemiological and clinical studies, animal experiments, in vitro tests, and examination of the relationship between molecular structure and the probable molecular activity of a suspect compound (Environ 1988; Lave 1982; U.S. Office of Technology Assessment 1981; Rodericks 1992). Clinical and epidemiological studies, because they measure effects on humans directly, are probably the best sources of data for identifying technologies hazardous to humans.[2] But because of the difficulty of obtaining reliable data on human exposure levels, the lack of experimental controls, and the fact that some technologies are too new to be evaluated

with such data, the results of clinical or epidemiological studies cannot provide complete information on all potential sources of risk. As a result, data from animal experiments or other types of laboratory studies are often used as a substitute for, or supplement to, field and clinical evidence. Despite the utility of these indirect methods and data sources, they are subject to serious shortcomings, most notably the problem of external validity. For example, small doses of some substance may prove hazardous to laboratory rats but may be harmless to humans (or even mice) because of metabolic differences between species (Environ 1988; Graham, Green and Roberts 1988; Lave et al. 1988).

Dose–response assessment is the determination of the relation between the magnitude of exposure and the probability of adverse consequences. Extrapolation techniques are used to determine such a relation. For instance, in estimating human health effects of hazardous substances, a dose–response curve is calculated from epidemiological data for population groups experiencing different levels of exposure. This curve is used to determine the link between exposure to the compound and its effects. In the absence of human epidemiological data, animal data are often used in calculating the human dose–response curve. Where human or animal data are meager or nonexistent, hypothetical models are sometimes used to fill gaps in real-world data.

Such techniques are sensitive to the assumptions that underpin them and engender large uncertainties even in the best of circumstances. The problem of measurement validity at different levels of exposure is particularly vexing. On the one hand, available techniques may be insufficient to detect small exposure levels. On the other hand, aggregate dose–response data may not permit a determination of whether low exposure levels are harmless or the precise threshold between harmful and harmless levels (Environ 1988).

Exposure assessment is the determination of the nature and degree of human exposure to a hazard. It consists of determining the source, route, dose, frequency, duration, and timing of hazard exposure, as well as the identification of the types of populations exposed to the hazard. A variety of methods, including mathematical models, are used to specify population and environmental exposure. The physical, biological, and social data and models available to predict exposure are limited, so here, as elsewhere in the risk assessment process, there are serious questions about the validity of results (Lave 1982).

Risk characterization is the overall summary of what is known about the likelihood and magnitude of adverse consequences. It represents a summary of the other three steps. It often contains a quantitative estimate of the nature and degree of risk associated with exposure to a hazard and a statement of the uncertainty associated with the risk estimate.

Because of the uncertainties built into each step in the process, not only are risks not known with certainty, but the degree of uncertainty is itself highly uncertain. We refer to this problem as one of meta-uncertainty—uncertainty about the degree of uncertainty. Such meta-uncertainty pervades all work on risk. With direct threats to human health and safety such as those posed by toxic substances, the sources of uncertainty and meta-uncertainty are easy to identify. The uncertainty embedded in the new class of risks posed by the effects of toxic substances on ecosystems and by global environmental change is much more difficult to identify. It is particularly acute

around the problem of climate change. While there is general agreement among climatologists that the earth will experience anthropogenic climate change over the next century, it is difficult to translate this prediction for the planetary climate into forms that can be used to assess human response (Intergovernmental Panel on Climate Change 1996). Localized effects can be known with much less certainty than the overall global trend, and yet are far more consequential for ecosystems and for humans. The consequences of climate change for the biosphere and for humanity may be immense, but predictions about global temperature are uncertain, and predictions about the effects that have the greatest impact on the biosphere and humans are fraught with meta-uncertainty.

Risk Evaluation

Various approaches have been proposed for judging whether or not the risks associated with a technological hazard are acceptable. We discuss five major approaches: risk–benefit–cost analysis, multi-objective methods, revealed preferences, expressed preferences, and *de minimis* (Fischhoff et al. 1981; Shrader-Frechette 1985, 1991).

Risk–benefit–cost analysis is based on the logic of rational action as described by economic theory (Jaeger, Renn, Rosa, and Webler 2000); i.e., maximizing benefits while minimizing costs (Arrow et al. 1996; Bentkover, Covello, and Mumpower 1986). Technological risks are acceptable if the economic benefits of the technology outweigh the economic costs. Subject to a broad range of criticisms, this method is most vulnerable in its emphasis on assigning monetary values to all costs and benefits. Assignment of monetary values (not only to benefits such as productivity but also to costs such as human death, disease, and injury as well as environmental degradation) rests on assumptions that many critics find problematic (Baram 1980; Dietz 1988, 1994). Further, the method frequently ignores the problem of evaluating the distribution of costs and benefits across populations.

The multi-objective approach, typically some version of multi-attribute utility theory, acknowledges that the reduction of risks to a single dimension such as money is deeply flawed (Keeney and Raiffa 1976). As a corrective, this approach uses a set of procedures for identifying the key attributes of a decision (i.e., the desirable and undesirable consequences), for assigning value to those attributes (usually through a ranking or rating system or a combination thereof), and for aggregating the evaluations of the separate attributes into an overall assessment. This approach has two major weaknesses. First, the procedure is complex, and results can be sensitive to methodological assumptions whose implications are hard to determine or analyze. Second, the list of attributes evaluated must be finite, and its selection over alternative lists is always arbitrary.

The method of revealed preferences is based on the assumption that risks tolerated currently or in the past provide a standard for assessing the acceptability of new risks. Proponents of this approach (e.g., Starr 1969) maintain that the risks of a new technology are acceptable if they are no greater than the risks of existing technologies that have similar benefits. The method is problematic for several reasons (Shrader-Frechette 1985). It assumes that the political, economic, and social relations underlying extant patterns of risk are legitimate. It is also mute to the possibility that some risks tolerated in the past should be reduced because they are no longer tolerable.

The method of expressed preferences consists of asking people what risks they find acceptable (Fischhoff et al. 1981). An obvious advantage of this approach is that it is more democratic than other methods because it is based on public preferences. Proponents of the approach use opinion surveys and public hearings to elicit preferences. Major criticisms of this method are that people change their views over time, may not be well informed about complex issues surrounding technological risk, and are seldom forced in surveys to make tradeoffs among risks, costs, and benefits associated with technologies.

The method of *de minimis* risk is based on the idea that certain risks are simply too trivial to merit attention (Breyer 1993; Whipple 1987). The goal of this method is to establish thresholds to distinguish between risks that are trivial and, therefore, acceptable and risks that are nontrivial and, therefore, unacceptable. One of the most obvious problems with this approach is the difficulty of establishing threshold levels for distinguishing between trivial and nontrivial risks (Menkes and Frey 1987). In practice, the method of natural standards is typically used to establish cut-off levels. For example, natural background levels of radiation have been used as a basis for establishing standards for human exposure to radiation. The use of such standards leads to the well-known naturalistic fallacy: the flawed logic of presupposing that what is natural is "normal" and what is normal is "moral" (Shrader-Frechette 1985).

All methods of risk assessment and risk evaluation are based on key assumptions that may be unsound or tenuous. Because of these uncertainties, risk assessments and risk evaluations—despite the fact that they are frequently portrayed as "scientific"—do not lead to unequivocal regulatory or management guidance (Proctor 1995). Nor can they, whatever their scientific validity, provide an unqualified recommendation of what risks are acceptable. Risk policy controversies, therefore, often involve conflict over the normative and methodological bases for deciding which risks are to be regulated and by what means.

Risk Management

In addition to controversies about risk assessment and evaluation, controversies exist over the appropriate methods for managing risks (see, e.g., Breyer 1993; Clarke 1999; Fiorino 1995; Jasanoff 1986). Three general strategies are currently used to manage risks: direct regulation, indirect regulation, and alternatives to regulation (Breyer 1993; Hadden 1986; Kasperson, Kates, and Hohenemser 1985).

Direct regulation takes two forms: the reduction of risks to zero through the elimination of a hazard or the reduction of risks to an acceptable level through the establishment of regulatory controls on a hazard. Banning the production, sale, or use of a hazard is a strategy for reducing risks to zero. This strategy is seldom used in risk management. Instead, the reduction of risks to an acceptable level by the use of performance or process criteria is the most common form of direct regulation. Performance criteria are standards setting limits on allowable levels of risks associated with the production or use of a hazard, whereas process criteria mandate the actual methods for the production or use of a hazard (Kasperson, Kates, and Hohenemser 1985). These strategies have been criticized for reducing the liberties of producers and users of hazards and for being ineffective (Commoner 1990).

Indirect regulation consists of informing parties at risk. The parties are provided with appropriate information so that they can make their own judgments about the acceptability of risks associated with a hazard. Standard techniques include warning labels and recommended practices for safe use, storage, transport, and disposal of a hazard. This approach is often used when the benefits for producers and/or consumers of the hazard are considered to outweigh the risks, and risk acceptance is to some degree voluntary. This strategy has been criticized because it makes questionable assumptions about human behavior, seldom leads to the dissemination of adequate risk information, and is a regressive policy (Hadden 1986).

Alternatives to direct and indirect regulations take several different forms (Baram and Miyares 1986). Voluntary compliance with recommended practices for the safe production and use of a hazard is one such form. The provision of incentives for hazard substitution and the safe production and use of a hazard is another. A third form is the use of penalties such as the indemnification of those at risk through the market, courts, or taxes. The final form is the provision of insurance for those at risk. Each of these alternatives to regulation has been criticized for failing to provide effective and fair compensation to those bearing the risks of a hazard.[3]

RISK AND RISK POLICY

Technological risks generate conflict between various social constituencies and industry over state policy toward risk. Risk policy and the current structure of the U.S. policy system that promotes, critiques, and implements risk policy evolved in response to the interactions between a variety of stakeholders, each with different interests and resources. We first examine the development and current structure of the U.S. risk policy system. We then examine the responses to risk by other developed nations, less developed nations, and international organizations.

Emergence of the U.S. Risk Policy System

Public attempts to deal with risk date at least to the Code of Hammurabi and thus are, as noted earlier, at least 5000 years old (Covello and Mumpower 1985). Before the Progressive era of the late 19th and early 20th Century in the U.S., problems of environmental risk were generally defined as economic matters and were handled by the courts under tort law. By the late 19th century, social critics and their allies challenged the laissez-faire approach to state risk policy (Hofstadter 1955). Their challenges provided the impetus for increased state intervention in the market through regulation. This "old social regulation" (Weidenbaum 1977)—including the U.S. Biologics Act of 1902, the Federal Pure Food and Drug Act of 1906, and the Federal Meat Inspection Act of 1906—targeted those industries that had been the subject of reformers' concerns. These regulations were based on the idea that monopoly or market concentration prevented the efficient functioning of markets on the one hand and promoted labor abuses and other social ills on the other. State intervention was required to ensure efficiency and to mitigate the worst costs of capitalism.

The mechanisms that emerged to control risk in this period had several common characteristics. First, they were developed in response to muckraking accounts by journalists and the actions of the political left. Second, their scope was usually industry specific, which facilitated the evolution of strong ties between regulators and the regulated—the "iron triangle" of regulated industries, executive branch agencies, and legislative oversight committees. Third,

they spawned industry organizations for both self-regulation and lobbying to influence government regulation.

During this period, in addition to regulation of industry, public bodies expanded substantially to address a variety of public health and welfare concerns. Government began to bear a substantial part of the social costs of industrial production and attendant urbanization. It was during this period that the first environmental science professionals emerged in the fields of forestry, agriculture, and public health, with most of these professionals employed in government agencies or universities (Brulle 2000; Hays 1999; also see Library of Congress).

The character of the U.S. risk policy system has changed dramatically in the last 40 years for several reasons (Hays 1987). First, the growth of the petrochemical and related industries has introduced a large number of anthropogenic (human generated) compounds into the environment. As a result, the impacts of toxic substances are more pervasive and dangerous than in the past. In addition, catastrophic failure of some new technologies, such as nuclear power and large chemical plants, could harm more people than the worst anthropogenic disasters of the past. Second, the growth of scientific knowledge, particularly in the areas Schnaiberg (1980) characterizes as the "impact sciences," provided credible information on the varied, subtle, and often negative consequences of contemporary technologies. Third, some scientists, the college educated, and in some cases unionized workers took the lead in seeking increased protection from the new technological risks. Starting with the struggle against nuclear testing in the 1950s and 1960s, the environmental, consumer, and labor movements have been effective at placing risk issues on the political agenda. The interplay between these movements, industrial interests that have usually opposed further risk regulation, and government have generated the current risk policy system.

Current Structure of the U.S. Risk Policy System

Statutes, enacted in response to the environmental and allied movements of the sixties, have produced regulations written in broad language that address generic environmental issues. One consequence has been a drastic expansion in the scope of regulation, cutting across nearly all industries (Breyer 1993; Fiorino 1995; Regens, Dietz, and Rycroft 1983). For example, the Clean Air Act (1970) and the Clean Water Act (1977) empower the Environmental Protection Agency (EPA) to intervene in the operations of nearly every industry and government agency in the U.S. to curb offending activities. A second consequence, related to the broad language in the enabling statutes—such as "unreasonable risk or injury to health" or "substantial present or potential hazard"—has been the establishment of agencies with considerable discretionary authority. Agencies such as the EPA, the Nuclear Regulatory Commission, the Occupational Safety and Health Administration, and the Food and Drug Administration have great latitude in determining how regulatory decisions are to be made and enforced. This means that the details of policy implementation are crucial to all stakeholders, so they must actively participate in the policy system to ensure that their interests are reflected in risk policy.

The U.S. risk policy system presently consists of eight major types of organizational actors (Dietz and Rycroft 1987; Fiorino 1995). Executive branch agencies responsible for implementing risk regulation employ about 25% of all professionals active in the system (Dietz and Rycroft 1987). Congress and its supporting agencies employ about 10% of the active professionals. Law and consulting firms account for about 14% of those employed, whereas environmental organizations employ about 12%. Corporations and the industry associations that represent them account for about 18% of active professionals. Universities and think tanks account for about 9%, and all remaining organizations, principally those representing state government, local government or labor, employ about 12%.

Heavy emphasis on formal methods of risk analysis and risk evaluation distinguish the risk policy system from many other policy systems. About half of the core professionals have training in the natural sciences or engineering. Over 95% of those working in the system have bachelor's degrees and nearly half hold doctorates (Dietz and Rycroft 1987). Since expertise is expensive to acquire, it is found mostly in the service of government and industry. Only 8% of environmental organization employees have natural science degrees, compared to around 20% of industry employees.

This imbalance in expertise is probably a key reason why environmental organizations are suspicious of policy decisions based on formal risk analyses. Their relative lack of expertise limits their ability to critique formal risk assessments and present counter analyses based on equally formal procedures. They prefer instead to emphasize the less "scientific" features of risk policy, such as due process and a variety of qualitative considerations, which are largely ignored in formal assessments.

In contrast, industry favors formal risk analysis as the principal basis of risk policy partly because it can employ or contract for the appropriate expertise to promote its position in technical debates. The imbalance in expertise and difference in strategies that results bring into sharp focus a central if latent theme of risk policy debates: whether policy formation and regulatory guidance should be based primarily on scientific and technical evidence or whether such evidence should be balanced against other considerations, such as fairness and equity. This issue continues to structure policy debates.

Situations Outside of the U.S.

Like the U.S., other developed nations have a full range of administrative and legal mechanisms for assessing and managing technological risks. The risk policy systems of these nations differ in many ways from the U.S. policy system. For instance, Great Britain, France, Sweden, Japan, and Germany place a heavier emphasis on scientific expertise, give a smaller role to environmental organizations in public policy discussions, and are more likely to have critical decisions made "behind closed doors" than the U.S. (Brickman, Jasnaoff, and Ilgen 1985; Jasanoff 1986).

Less developed nations, on the other hand, have a limited ability to assess and manage technological risks (Covello and Frey 1990; Montgomery 1990; Smil 1993). The legislative basis for risk protection is often weak or nonexistent. In turn, existing legislation and regulations are not adequately enforced. The problem is exacerbated by the fact that less developed nations do not have enough trained operators and managers with skills necessary for managing risky technologies effectively.

Since the risks of many technological hazards transcend national boundaries, a number of international organizations and international treaties have emerged to manage these risks (see Caldwell 1990; Covello and Frey 1990; Dietz and Kalof 1992; Elliott 1998; Frank 1997, 1999; Hackett 1990; Lipschutz and Conca 1993; Mathews 1991; Porter and Brown 1996; Roberts 1996; Rummel-Bulksa 1991; World Commission on Environment and Development 1987; Young 1989). Key examples of the agencies involved include the U.N. Environment Programme, the Man and Biosphere Program of UNESCO, the World Health Organization, the International Atomic Energy Agency, and the Food and Agriculture Organization (Caldwell 1990). Examples of key treaties include the Basel Convention on Hazardous Wastes, the Lome Convention, the Rio Accords and the Vienna and Montreal Ozone Protocols. Multilateral aid agencies, such as the World Bank and the Inter-American Development Bank, are also beginning to pay attention to risk issues in project planning (Holden 1988). Other non-government organizations (NGOs) concerned with risk include the International Council of Scientific Unions, the International Trade Union Movement, and the International Union for Conservation of Nature and Natural Resources (McElrath 1988). These organizations have pursued a variety of activities, including research, dissemination of risk information, training programs, and development of international standards and restrictions on the practices of transnational corporations (Elliott 1998; World Commission on Environment and Development 1987). In addition, the international scope of many hazards has led environmental NGOs, such as Friends of the Earth, Conservation International, Earth Island Institute, Greenpeace, and the World Wildlife Federation, to expand their activities across national boundaries through advocacy networks (Cartwright 1989; Keck and Sikkink 1998:121–163; Princen and Finger 1994; Taylor 1995).

THE SOCIAL CONTEXT OF RISK

Social scientists have increasingly turned their attention to the study of risk. Four distinct social science approaches have emerged in the past few years: the psychological, sociological, anthropological, and geographic. Previous (Krimsky and Golding 1992) and more recent (Jaeger et al. 2000) volumes provide more detailed coverage of these approaches. Here we critically but briefly review each approach.

The Psychological Perspective

Until recently, the field of risk perception was dominated by a psychometric approach that focused on cognitive processes underlying risk perceptions. An impressive body of research indicates that most individuals systematically under- or overestimate risks. Indeed, these biases may reflect fundamental processes in the cognitive organization of risk perception. A number of common sense strategies, or cognitive "rules of thumb," apparently produce these biases. The *availability* heuristic is one of the most important of these rules (Tversky and Kahneman 1982). It was discovered, along with other heuristics, in research examining people's assessments of probabilities (numerical representations of risk) in both small sample studies and laboratory experiments.

In a typical study, researchers provide subjects with pairs of causes of death and ask them to judge which of the pair is most likely to occur (Lichenstein et al. 1978). For example, subjects might be asked the following question: Which cause of death is most likely to occur out of each pair? (1) Lung cancer or stomach cancer?; (2) Murder or suicide?; and (3) Diabetes or motor vehicle accident? People tend to answer that lung cancer is responsible for more deaths than stomach cancer, murder for more deaths than suicide, and motor vehicle accidents for more deaths than diabetes. In fact, aggregate data indicate that the second alternative for each pair (i.e., stomach cancer, suicide, and motor vehicle accidents) is one and one-half times more likely to occur than the first alternative. People typically err in making two out of three probability choices.

One conclusion consistent with these findings is that laypersons are not very good at assessing the risks they face. Why are layperson's judgments sometimes correct, but more often incorrect? What cognitive processes could produce such contrary results? The availability heuristic was proposed as an answer to this question (Fischhoff et al. 1981; Tversky and Kahneman 1982). The extent to which an event is cognitively available, that is, vivid and easy to recall, strongly influences the perceived probability of the event. The familiar is seen as more probable than the unfamiliar and recent events more probable than past events, other things being equal. This suggests that people will typically overestimate causes of death that are highly publicized, such as lung cancer and homicide, relative to less publicized but more frequent causes of death, such as stomach cancer and suicide. The availability heuristic produces a biased perception.

Reliance on the availability and other heuristics, however, does produce valid assessments under some circumstances. Where the vividness of events coincides with their relative frequency, a person's perceptions will be valid—as was the case where subjects judged deaths by motor vehicle accidents to be more frequent than deaths by diabetes. To the individual, the value of cognitive heuristics, and perhaps the reason for their continued use, is that they are efficient and may often be correct.

These heuristics may be useful information-processing tools, the product of adaptation through cultural and biological evolution.[4]

The discovery that people use heuristics for assessing risks stimulated an effort to determine whether or not people use them in their perceptions of technological risk. Paul Slovic, Baruch Fischhoff, Sarah Lichtenstein, and their colleagues have produced an impressive body of findings on this topic. The Slovic, Fischhoff, and Lichtenstein group (Lichtenstein et al. 1978; Fischhoff et al. 1981; Slovic 1987) have asked people to rate the risks and benefits associated with a wide variety of hazardous technologies, activities, and substances, such as nuclear power, motor vehicles, handguns, smoking, swimming, commercial aviation, and pesticides. Their work indicates that people tend to overestimate low probability, high consequence events (unlikely events like a nuclear accident that can kill thousands) and to underestimate high probability, low consequence events (like the risks associated with X-rays). Furthermore, lay judgments of risk, although sometimes consistent with those of experts, often diverge from them in systematic ways.

Several factors appear to underlie the bias in lay perceptions. As noted above, key among these factors is the availability heuristic: People tend to overestimate the frequency of unlikely events that are dramatic in their consequences because the drama of such events makes them cognitively available and thus easier to recall. This may be due to media coverage of the news that emphasizes dramatic rather than routine events, often sensationalizing unlikely but dreadful events (Combs and Slovic 1979; Sandman et al. 1987). Discrepancies between public and expert perceptions of risk are seen to reside in the sources of information about risk and in the tendency of lay-persons to stress qualitative features of risk ignored by experts. For example, risks highly dreaded by the public are those perceived to involve a lack of control, catastrophic potential, fatal consequences, or inequitable distributions of risks and benefits. Such risks are far less acceptable to the public than to experts, who give little or no consideration to these qualitative factors in their formal analyses (Slovic 1987). In effect, discrepancies in lay and expert judgments of risk are based on different definitions of risk.

If the public does view risk differently than experts, of what importance is public opinion to risk evaluation, and what is the proper role of the public in risk management? One position, often left implicit, is that the public should be excluded or otherwise disenfranchised from risk assessment and decisionmaking (e.g., Breyer 1993; Cohen 1987; Starr 1969). A second, less extreme position, proposes that laypersons' perceptions of risk should be brought into line with those of the experts. Advocates of this view call for efforts by policy makers to improve communication between agencies and the public, to educate citizens so that they are better prepared to evaluate uncertainties, and to develop better risk management strategies that include means for providing the public with accurate, understandable information on which to make reasonable decisions about risky technologies (Covello, McCallum, and Pavlova 1988). A third position begins with the recognition that nearly all risk assessments and risk management strategies are laden with uncertainty and meta-uncertainty, that experts as well as the public are subject to cognitive biases, and that an emphasis solely on technical information has political implications for the relative power of environmental groups versus corporate interests. For these reasons, laypersons should play a more central role in the process of assessing, evaluating, and managing technological risks (Brown 1992, 1997; Dietz 1987; Fischhoff 1990; Freudenburg 1988; Perrow 1984; Rosa and Clark 1999; U.S. National Research Council 1989).

The Sociological Perspective

Though only a little over decades old, sociological interest in risk has evolved to produce an incipient specialty with a variety of perspectives. Together, they seek to understand the social influences on risk perception and behavior, the importance of organizational contexts and institutional responses to risk and the role of risk in large-scale social change. They comprise four distinct research directions, though in some instances there is considerable overlap in orientation or approach. The four directions, discussed below, represent increasing levels of theoretical aggregation, from micro to meso to macro.

A first direction, stemming from the lead of psychometric research, was to reexamine and reconceptualize the psychometric finding with a sociological lens. Several sociologists and psychologists have raised questions about the saliency of risk questions to laypersons and about the external validity of the psychometric findings, citing reliance on laboratory settings and small samples of unrepresentative groups as serious limitations on the generalizability of findings (Gould et al. 1988). The work of Heimer (1988) suggests that cognitive heuristics operate in natural settings. An extensive sample survey by Gould et al. (1988) and follow-up studies in France (Bastide et al. 1989), Hong Kong (Keown 1989), Hungary (Englander et al. 1986), Japan (Kleinhesselink and Rosa 1991, 1993), and Norway (Teigen et al. 1988), generally cor-

roborate the findings of the psychometric research. But a number of conceptual and methodological problems remain. These include whether heuristics differ in their impact for trivial versus nontrivial decisions, how perceptions differ across populations facing different life chances, and whether the framing of choices stems primarily from power differences among social actors (Heimer 1988). The most serious problem is the virtual absence of research on whether risk perceptions predict actual behavior.

The second direction of sociological research offers a fundamental reconceptualization of the psychometric model. It proposes a model that examines the problem of risk perception by taking into account the social context in which human perceptions are formed (Rosa, Mazur, and Dietz 1987; Short 1984). The model proceeds from the assumption, fundamental to all social psychology, that humans do not perceive the world with pristine eyes, but through perceptual lenses filtered by social and cultural meanings transmitted via primary influences such as the family, friends, superordinates, and fellow workers. Secondary influences, such as public figures and especially the mass media, are also presumed to affect risk perceptions (Mazur 1984). All this suggests that risk perceptions may be stratified as a result of different socializations and thus may vary along lines of gender, ethnicity, and/or class.

In addition to these contextual effects, the sociological model notes that people often take actions or form attitudes about hazardous technologies and events prior to developing meaningful perceptions about them. Formal organizations such as government agencies and corporations apparently are also guilty of offering ex-post facto explanations that have little to do with the actual reasons a decision about technological risk was made (Clarke 1989, 1999). Such "after the fact" beliefs are often used as a justification for the attitude already formed or the action already taken. This common occurrence is ignored by the unidirectional emphasis of the psychometric model, but it is a central feature of the sociological model.

The third direction has been the organizational and institutional approach that emphasizes the system characteristics and context of complex technologies and the policies that develop for their use. Perrow's (1984) analysis of "normal accidents," the exemplar of this approach, demonstrates that industrial societies have produced a variety of high risk technologies in which a main source of risk is embedded in the very systems designed to ensure their safety. For many of these technological systems, the interaction of system components (including humans) makes accidents—"system accidents"—all but inevitable. Formal risk assessments of complex technologies typically involve computing the probability of failure for each of the system's components and then aggregating these into an overall estimate of accident probability. From an organizational approach, such quantitative assessments are misleadingly precise, because they cannot take into account the vast number of component interactions that could result in conjoint failures. Accidents are therefore bound to happen. This disturbing conclusion of "normal accident" theory is studded with sociological and policy implications. It means that technological risk cannot be understood completely through formal risk assessments. Rather, risks can be understood only by analyzing the way that parts of risky systems fit together (Freudenburg 1988) and the evolution of sociotechnical systems in which technologies are embedded (Burns and Dietz 1992a). Such an understanding requires a sociological fo-

cus on the organizational and institutional contexts of decision-making by corporate actors and institutional elites. Just such a focus is beginning to emerge in this line of sociological research (Jaeger et al. 2000; Short and Clarke 1992).

A stark counterpoint to "normal accident" theory is "high reliability organization" (HRO) theory, most of whose practitioners are associated with the University of California, Berkeley (LaPorte 1988; LaPorte and Consolini 1991; Roberts 1993; Rochlin, LaPorte, and Roberts 1987; Wildavsky 1988). The Berkeley group has identified organizations that perform with remarkable safety even though their operations are technologically complex and inherently risky. This remarkable performance in the face of complexity and risk leads to the label High Reliability Organizations. In several studies, the Berkeley group has produced a sustained body of empirical work demonstrating the existence of HROs. Extensive fieldwork has been conducted on three HROs: the Federal Aviation Administration's air-traffic control system, the Pacific Gas and Electric Company's power grid (PG&E is one of the largest utilities in the U.S. and includes the Diablo Canyon nuclear power plant in its grid), and the peacetime flight operations of two U.S. Navy nuclear aircraft carriers.

How are these organizations able to operate so safely? The Berkeley group holds that the development of a "high reliability culture" where safety and reliability are made a priority of the organization's top leadership is essential. Further, organizations can overcome the potential failure of hardware and humans by designing systems with redundancies: the duplication of parts and the incorporation of backup systems. Thus HRO theory argues that accidents are preventable while normal accident theory says they are not. These antithetical positions will doubtless generate further empirical research on this important issue. Indeed, a notable first effort is this direction is the work of Sagan (1993) on the management of nuclear weapons.

The fourth direction is, if not grand theory, at least macrosociological theory on a grand scale. Grounded in the European sociological tradition, the theme of this line of thinking is worldwide social change: the transformation from modernity to its successor, some form of postmodernity. Risk is the central driving force of this transformation. Key examples of such theorizing are British sociologist Anthony Giddens' *The Consequences of Modernity* (1990) and German sociologist Ulrich Beck's *Risk Society: Toward a New Modernity* (1992) and *World Risk Society* (1999). The nets of each theory are too broadly cast, the logic too carefully crafted, and the insights too finely nuanced for us to do them justice in our short compass here. Furthermore, owing to their origins in the European tradition, they have left the operational explication to others. Thus, much work remains to assess their contribution to the sociology of risk. Nevertheless, they are too important to ignore.

Key to Giddens is the observation that modernity—modes of social life and organization emerging in Europe in the 17th Century and eventually becoming worldwide—resulted in globalization. "Globalization" refers to the "intensification of worldwide social relations which link distant localities in such a way that local happenings are shaped by events occurring many miles away and vice versa" (Giddens 1990:64). With modernity, locale no longer held a leash on the range of interpersonal interactions available to the individual. People's social relations became "disembedded," in Giddens' terms. As a consequence, people everywhere interact with "absent" and distant others, others who are often never seen or known. With the approach of postmodernity this disembeddedness has second order consequences: a worldwide division of labor accompanied by a worldwide spread of risks associated with production processes; and a worldwide diffusion of consumption practices and their accompanying risks. Overlaid on this pattern of shared risks has been the appearance of globalized risks—radiation releases from nuclear accidents, global warming, destruction of the ozone layer, the broad diffusion of toxics associated with industrial activities and others—that, because they are not contained by national borders, "do not respect division between rich and poor or between regions of the world" (Giddens 1990:125). In short, postmodernity introduces new forms of global interdependence, and interdependence grounded in globalized risks. That interdependence, in turn, magnifies the importance of trust.

Beck's theoretical argument, resembling Giddens's position, was developed independently. It consists of two interrelated theses: risk and what Beck calls "reflexive modernization." To develop his first thesis Beck identifies a fundamental distinction between industrial society and contemporary society: the former is concerned with the distribution of goods, while the latter is concerned with the distribution of "bads" (danger) and is, therefore, aptly titled "the risk society." This shift produced a fundamental restructuring of social organization, from one of class to one of risk positions. It also produced a new culture of shared meaning where "in class positions being determines consciousness, while in risk positions, conversely *consciousness (knowledge) determines being*" (emphasis in the original) (1992:53). This fundamental change results in a decline in the importance of structures, like class, and the individualization of social agents (actors) who, forced to make risk decisions, reflect on the social institutions responsible for those decisions. Like Giddens, Beck delineates the globalization of risks and underscores the role of trust in dealing with them, while adding consideration of future generations.

Beck's second thesis is based on the central role of science in issues of risk, a problem emphasized by other scholars as well (Brown 1992; Burns and Dietz, 1992a; Dietz, Stern, and Rycroft 1989; Dunlap, Kraft, and Rosa 1993; Funtowicz and Ravetz 1992). Science is, on the one hand, partly responsible for the growth of risks and hazards while, on the other hand, it is the principle social institution entrusted with knowledge claims about risk. Therein lies the rub for Beck. Because risks are difficult to define and ambiguous, subject to competing interpretations and conflicting claims, "in definitions of risks *the sciences' monopoly on rationality is broken*" (emphasis in the original) (Beck 1992:29). When science is no longer privileged, how are risk societies to make knowledge claims about the increased risks that define those societies? For Beck the answer is "reflexive modernity." By this he means, in essence, a negotiation of knowledge claims between science, political interests and laypersons—in effect, negotiation between different epistemologies.

These macro-theoretical arguments are not yet well integrated with existing and emerging work on the sociology of risk. The emphasis on the special character of science in the modern world is common in the risk literature, as noted above. The globalization of risk processes is a central theme in discussions of global environmental change (Dietz 1992; Frey 1995, 1997, 1998; Roberts and Grimes 1997; Rosa and Dietz 1998; Stern, Young and Druckman 1992). The integra-

tion of scientific with other forms of knowledge has also been emphasized in some streams of the literature on technology, risk, and impact assessment (Burns and Uberhorst 1988; Dietz 1987, 1988; Dietz and Burns 1994; Freeman and Frey 1990–91). But the argument that risk is universal contradicts emerging work on risk distribution (see the next major section).

The Anthropological Perspective

An anthropological approach to risk analysis is also emerging in the risk literature. In the initial formulation of this approach, Douglas and Wildavsky (1982) argue that the selection of risks for societal attention is purely a social process with little or no linkage to objective risk or physical reality. Instead, individuals affiliate with organizations that resonate with their values. Presumably these core values are based on personality traits, institutional socialization, or other factors not fully elaborated in the model. Douglas and Wildavsky emphasize the differences between "entrepreneurs" who are comfortable with risks, and "egalitarians" or environmentalists, who are averse to risks. Entrepreneurs receive high praise because they produce affluence and freedom, whereas environmentalists are compared to cultists and witches. Douglas and Wildavsky assert that the need for organizational self-maintenance provides the basis for environmental groups' concerns with risks. By invoking a sense of "cosmic doom," the environmentalists ensure member loyalty. This perspective has been subjected to a number of strong critiques (see, e.g., Abel 1985). Central to these critiques is the idea that Douglas and Wildavsky's scholarly vision is guided by an underlying fear of social change. In addition to the ongoing theoretical debate, there have also been attempts to use this framework to guide ethnographic studies and surveys on risk (Dake 1991; Dake and Wildavsky 1991; Rayner and Cantor 1987; Ellis and Thompson 1997; Thompson, Ellis, and Wildavsky 1990).

The Geographic Perspective

Geography has a distinguished tradition of research on human responses to natural disasters and human activities that modify the landscape (e.g., White 1974). Recently this tradition has been broadened to include technological risks, producing a growing body of literature, developing a broad theoretical framework for organizing the cumulative social science literature on risk, and for pointing the way for future inquiry (Cutter 1993; Kasperson et al. 1988; Renn 1992). The framework, borrowed from communication theory and titled "Social Amplification," holds promise for deepening our understanding of the link between risk perception and behavior and for understanding risks thus far ignored in the literature (Machlis and Rosa 1990).

Classic communications theory emphasizes a source–receiver model in which signals are sent from the source to some receiver. Clusters of signals (the message) sent from source to receiver must typically first flow through intermediate transmitters. Each of the intermediate transmitters "amplifies" the message by intensifying or attenuating certain incoming signals. Thus, the cluster of signals leaving the source will be altered during transmissions to the ultimate receiver.

The social amplification of risk, according to this framework, follows similar processes. Risk events are signals. The message contained in those signals is amplified before reaching the ultimate receiver—the public. The amplification may either be toward heightening or attenuating the risk. Principal amplifiers include information processes, institutions, social milieus, and the variety of individual experiences. Because part of the amplification of risk signals is due to cognitive heuristics, the framework attempts to integrate the psychometric findings on risk perception with the institutional context of risk communication in order to better predict responses to risk.

RISK, POLITICS, AND SOCIETY

In the U.S., many of the sociologically relevant issues stem from continued conflict between key stakeholders in debates over growth and management of technology, especially between industry and social movement organizations. Several key themes emerge from those conflicts.

Public Goods, Science, and Social Movements

A critical feature of technological risk is that the benefits derived from risk reduction are public goods. All social actors potentially exposed to the risks, therefore, will benefit from reduced risks, whether they participate in the actions to reduce risk or not. Thus, actors can "free ride" on the efforts of others. Environmental, consumer, and other social movement organizations must contend with the "free rider" problem in obtaining resources and securing public support (Olson 1965). As a result, such organizations will always be comparatively short of staff, technical expertise, and funds to hire consultants or support research. In contrast, the benefits associated with many technologies are private goods, so industries that profit from the technologies typically have abundant material resources to deploy in the protection and advancement of their private interests. There are occasions when industry is subject to free rider problems (as in instances where industry trade associations rely on voluntary contributions), but these are relatively rare and generally inconsequential to their lobbying strategies (Dietz and Rycroft 1987).

Social movement organizations have difficulty acquiring and mobilizing resources in their pursuit of collective goods (Frey, Dietz, and Kalof 1992; Gamson 1990; Walsh 1981). As a result, the amount of public goods supplied, such as the reduction of risk to ideal levels, will be less than optimal. But those seeking collective goods also have a key advantage: the pursuit of private benefits, frequently thought to be a reflection of unbridled self-interest, is easily labeled as selfish, whereas moral virtue may be attributed to groups promoting public goods. Thus, despite attempts by opponents to label environmental, consumer, and other social movements as "special interests," the public and professionals within the risk policy system are generally supportive of these movements and skeptical of industry motives (Dietz and Rycroft 1987). Furthermore, technological risk and other environmental issues seem to contain a moral component that taps strong norms in most individuals (Stern, Dietz, and Black 1985–86).

Differential access to and command of resources between the proponents and opponents of technology account for the imbalance, noted earlier, of expertise among the key actors in technological controversy. Expertise is a highly prized resource in risk assessment and evaluation, because policy formulation and implementation are heavily dependent on scientific and technical evidence. Recognizing the advantage they hold by controlling expertise, industry and other promoters of technologies seek to define risk policy conflicts as scientific or technical conflicts that can be resolved with formal methods removed from the political process. Opposition groups, recognizing not only their limited control of expertise but also the importance of issues left unaddressed in formal modes of analysis (e.g., consideration of equity or public acceptability of risks), seek to define conflicts over risk as political issues (Brown 1992, 1997; Brown and Mikkelsen 1990; Dietz, Stern, and Rycroft 1989).

The preponderance of resources in the hands of industry also means that the risk policy system will underestimate risks, because industry can use expertise to generate its own risk estimates and to offer critiques of the risk estimates of others. Opponents of technology usually lack sufficient expertise to balance the technical analyses offered by industry. Thus, public risk assessments will typically be subject to extensive formal critique by those who are concerned that risks may be overestimated, but subject to less scrutiny from those concerned that risks will be underestimated.[5]

Just as environmental and other stakeholder groups are likely to be skeptical of risk policy emphasizing formal analyses, industry will likewise be skeptical of an emphasis on accountability and public preferences. Because the public is often in favor of stricter risk regulation, industry questions the importance of public views. This discrepancy between expert and lay preferences is attributed to lay ignorance, and if the public is ignorant, its views should carry little weight in the formulation and implementation of risk policy. From a sociological perspective, this position is no more or less rational and no more or less self-serving than opponent groups' skepticism of formal analysis. The point of sociological concern is that these conflicting views, stemming from a differential command of resources, set the stage for determining acceptable processes of risk policy formulation and implementation (Dietz, Stern, and Rycroft 1989).

The Media

The media play a direct role in shaping public attitudes toward risk and, thereby, indirectly affect the support for social movement organizations critical of technologies. Conservative critics complain of a liberal bias in media coverage, including coverage of risky technologies (e.g., Lichter and Rothman 1999; Rothman and Lichter 1987). Available evidence suggests that if media bias exists, it is procedural rather than political (Combs and Slovic 1979; Sandman et al. 1987). The media are inclined to cover dramatic events and those elements of news stories that are easy to convey to a mass audience. Coverage of technological risks is often in response to either a disaster, such as Love Canal or Times Beach, or in response to new and dramatic evidence about a technological risk, such as the greenhouse effect. The undramatic is not newsworthy; there is not much to report either when a technology works smoothly or when a product or substance presumed safe has been found safe by yet another study.

In addition to a preoccupation with dramatic events, the media have few specialists covering technology or environmental beats, so reports on risk lack the benefits of "insider" knowledge that come with the coverage of sports, business, or politics. This combination of circumstances means that the media are better equipped to cover the politics of risk and risk controversy than the technical details of formal risk assessments.

The links between media coverage, public opinion, and political action are not well understood, but work has evolved to fill this gap (e.g., Gamson 1990; Gamson and Modigliani 1989; Stallings 1990; Williams and Frey 1997). Although general attitudes toward technologies have been shown to fluctuate with the amount of media coverage devoted to them (Mazur 1981, 1984), it is not known how these attitudes are translated into public action. For example, it is not clear that media coverage of risky technologies or attendant controversies is the basis for growth in support for or membership in social movement organizations opposed to such technologies, nor is media coverage clearly linked to skepticism of industry practices. Indeed, Perrow (1994) has argued that public concern with technological hazards has increased because industry tends to deny the risks of serious mishaps, only to recant after a serious accident has occurred. Given a long history of this practice, it is not surprising that the public often rejects industry claims of safety and shows a growing mistrust of risk management institutions (Freudenburg 1993). But sustained sociological inquiry into the impacts of media and other institutions on public opinion about risk is clearly needed.

Distributional Impacts

All technologies generate impacts—costs and benefits borne by people and the environment. Often large numbers of individuals experiencing little or no benefit from a technology, such as neighbors of a toxic waste site, must bear the risks associated with it (Bryant 1992; Bullard 1990, 1992; Camacho 1998; Erickson 1994; Frey 1998; Szasz 1994). At the same time, smaller groups, such as investors in chemical stocks, experience great benefit and little cost (Frey 1995, 1997). Conversely, when risks are eliminated or reduced through regulation or other means, broad populations usually receive small benefits, while smaller groups—owners, managers, and workers, for example—bear costs. Because formal risk assessments are typically based on aggregate data, distributional impacts are ignored. Thus, it is quite possible that a credible risk evaluation will show a net benefit to society generally, but neglect to identify the net costs to certain individuals, neighborhoods, or communities. To those experiencing costs, especially where such costs are not compensated, the fairness of the results are clearly in question—and prevalent norms of justice and equity motivate people to participate in the now familiar NIMBY (not in my backyard) movements (Freudenberg 1984).

The issue of distributional equity reaches a second order of concern once the unfair impacts of policy proposals are identified. It is the most advantaged members of society who have financial and organizational resources to support NIMBY movements or take other effective opposition actions. The usual effect of this process is to saddle the poorest and least powerful members of society with the brunt of risks (Bryant 1992; Bullard 1990). Society faces a variety of technological hazards, such as the disposal of high level nuclear waste, that cannot be avoided and that have serious consequences for those bearing the risks. Siting controversies are unlikely to be settled without serious consideration of equity issues. Risk management procedures ensuring a fair distribution of benefits, costs, and risks are most likely to be successful in bringing closure to controversies. Indeed, such procedures may be the most effective means for turning NIMBYS into PIMBYS (put it in my backyard) (Rosa 1988). This problem plays itself out at the global level in conflicts between North and South on hazardous technologies and on global environmental change (Covello and Frey 1990;

Frey 1995, 1998). There the less affluent nations call for financial and technological assistance from the more affluent nations in return for action to reduce risks to the global or regional environment.

Science, Communication, and Public Involvement

The duration and intensity of risk controversies can also be traced to the tension between the roles of science and public participation in risk policy. On the one hand, there is no sound basis for ignoring scientific evidence, however flawed, in decisions about risk. But on the other hand, the fact that the public is often unfamiliar with this evidence does not justify dismissing public concerns. Progress toward conflict resolution requires an approach that provides a legitimate role for each and proper channels for communication. To achieve this end, discussions of risk communication should discard a unidirectional model in which the goal is "informing the public," that is, changing public perceptions and preferences to match those of experts (Covello, McCallum, and Pavlova 1988). Instead, risk communication must be viewed as a two-way process in which public views are seen as legitimate, expert views are valued but also acknowledged as fallible, and the goal of risk communication is "informing the debate" (Brown 1992, 1997; Funtowicz and Ravetz 1992; Stern 1991; Stern and Fineberg 1996; U.S. National Research Council 1989). The scientific evidence, indispensable as it is, needs to be complemented with defensible normative criteria for making value-laden decisions. Sociology already provides guidelines for accomplishing this practice. In particular, recent work in social impact assessment has outlined methods for integrating scientific analyses with normative considerations (Burns and Uberhorst 1988; Dietz 1987, 1988, 1994; Dietz and Burns 1994; Freeman and Frey 1986, 1990–1991).

The experience from social impact assessment suggests a crucial need to revise the typical process of public involvement. If the process permits public involvement only after a major policy decision has already been reached, the role left to the public is that of "veto group," and the image of the public as ignorant "nay-sayers" is reinforced. The likelihood of conflict resolution is improved considerably if all stakeholders are allowed to participate in the design of risk assessments and in devising proper management strategies. This procedure ensures that factors relevant to those impacted are included in the analysis and that compensation favored by those impacted are included in management strategies (Rosa, Mazur, and Dietz 1987). Such involvement not only engenders confidence in the analyses but, just as importantly, builds trust among key actors.

CODA

Technological risk is a topic of growing concern in contemporary societies. We have reviewed the formal procedures used to examine risk, the development of the policy systems that address risk, current social science perspectives on risk, and the dynamics of political controversies over risk. Clearly, the topic of risk contains a rich variety of challenging sociological questions. Theoretical and empirical investigations are beginning to address them. As this work progresses, we emphasize the need for integration. Current efforts range in scope from examination of individual risk perception, through analyses of organizations, institutions, and policy systems to consideration of

the transformation of societies and global environmental change. Understanding risk will require theories that can span this range from the micro to the macro and that are attentive to empirical detail. This in turn will require grounding theoretical and empirical work in specific contexts. In doing so, the sociology of risk must take up questions at the core of social science theory: rationality, agency, collective action, valuation, globalization, social order, reality construction, and socio-cultural transformation. The study of risk will in turn make contributions to that theory, recasting it in ways that are more attentive to the physical and biological environment and to the technologies humans use to interact with that environment.

ENDNOTES

1. Although this definition is widely used, it remains the subject of continued debate (see, e.g., Fischhoff, Watson, and Hope 1984; Renn 1992; Rosa 1998; U.S. National Research Council 1989). We do not discuss risks associated with natural hazards (White 1974), individual avoidance of health and safety risks (Weinstein 1987), crime risk (Short 1984), individual risk-seeking behavior (Machlis and Rosa 1990), risks of medical procedures (Kolker and Burke 1994), or the actuarial profession and industries (Heimer 1985). These are all important topics, and existing work on them is important for the study of technological risk, but space limitations preclude discussing them here. Note also that the use of the term *risk* in policy debates may be value-laden and imply that such risks should be politically acceptable (U.S. National Research Council 1989). Finally, while the effects we discuss seem to range from the global to the local, it is useful to remember that global risks such as climate change and ozone depletion manifest themselves in local effects while many technologies whose use is localized, such as nitrogen-based fertilizers, pesticides, or products containing heavy metals have cumulative effects on the biosphere

(Beck 1999; Frey 1995; Stern, Young, and Druckman 1992). Thus the global and local distinctions are somewhat arbitrary.

2. To date, most risk analyses have been about direct threats to human health and safety. Our discussion here reflects that focus. But evidence is mounting that there are subtle environmental effects of many technologies on the biosphere, ranging from climate change and ozone depletion to a broad spread of toxics throughout the biosphere. By altering major ecosystems and the biosphere itself, these technologies may in turn pose grave indirect risks to humans. These issues are discussed in more detail in Norton et al. (1992), Silver and DeFries (1992), and Stern, Young, and Druckman (1992).

3. Recently, advocates of an "industrial ecology" (or "social metabolism") approach to environmental protection have argued for examining the entire resource extraction–manufacturing– marketing–consumption–disposal cycle to identify leverage points for minimizing environmental impact (Fischer-Kowalski 1998, 1999; Socolow et al. 1994). To date, the industrial ecology literature emphasizes a systems analysis of material and energy flows and has only begun to address policies that would reduce risk (but see Andrews 1994; Griefahn 1994). In parallel, Furger (1997) suggests examining the full institutional context of firms, regulatory agencies, and industry associations in attempting to understand risk. Both of these broader approaches suggest innovative approaches to risk regulation that may ultimately prove more effective than the proposals outlined above.

4. There is some evidence that the poor performance of lay persons on such tasks may be a result of questions that are asked in a format that differs from everyday reasoning. For example, Cosmides and Tooby (1996) find that respondents perform well on probability questions posed in a frequentist form and poorly on a Bayesian formulation, while Gigerenzer (1992) provides a theory of mental models that shows the consistency of seemingly incongruous results in probability experiments. As we will note below, this psychological approach could be greatly enhanced by consideration of the social contexts in which human reasoning evolves and

develops, the environments that are the selective regimes for human decision making. Most human decision making is about social interaction, rather than about technology, and the calculus of decisions required for interaction may differ from that typically used in normative decision theory.

5. The disproportionate power of the corporate sector relative to that of social movement groups is also brought to bear in "Strategic Law Suits Against Public Participation" (SLAPPs). SLAPPs are used to silence opposition by confronting them with the threat of substantial legal fees that may be required to defend against even a frivolous suit. SLAPPs are carefully documented by Pring and Canan (1996).

REFERENCES

Abel, Richard L. 1985. "Blaming Victims." *American Bar Foundation Research Journal* 1985: 401–417.

Andrews, Clinton. 1994. "Policies to Encourage Clean Technology." Pp. 405–422 in *Industrial Ecology and Global Change,* edited by R. Socolow, C. Andrews, F. Berkhout, and V. Thomas. Cambridge, England: Cambridge University Press.

Arrow, Kenneth J., Maureen L. Cropper, George C. Eads, Robert W. Hahn, Lester B. Lave, Roger G. Noll, Paul R. Portney, Milton Russell, Richard Schmalensee, V. Kerry Smith, and Robert N. Stavins. 1996. "Is There a Role for Benefit-Cost Analysis in Environmental, Health, and Safety Regulation?" *Science* 272:221–222.

Bailey, Ronald, editor. 1995. *The True State of the Planet.* New York: Harper-Perennial.

Baram, Michael S. 1980. "Cost-Benefit Analysis: An Inadequate Basis for Health, Safety and Environmental Regulatory Decisionmaking." *Ecology Law Quarterly* 8:473–53.

Baram, Michael S. and J. Raymond Miyares. 1986. "Alternatives to Government Regulation for the Management of Technological Risks." Pp. 337–357 in *Risk Evaluation and Management,* edited by V. T. Covello, J. Menkes, and J. Mumpower. New York: Plenum Press.

Bastide, Sophie, Jean-Paul Moatti, Jean-Paul Pages, and Francis Fagnani. 1989. "Risk Perception and Social Acceptability of Technologies: The French Case." *Risk Analysis* 9:215–223.

Beck, Ulrich. 1992 [1986] *Risk Society: Toward a New Modernity.* (Translated by Mark Ritter.) London: Sage.

Beck, Ulrich. 1999. *World Risk Society.* New York: Polity Press.

Bentkover, Judith D., Vincent T. Covello, and Jeryl Mumpower, editors. 1986. *Benefits Assessment: The State of the Art.* Boston: Reidel.

Breyer, Stephen. 1993. *Breaking the Vicious Circle: Toward Effective Risk Regulation.* Cambridge, MA: Harvard University Press.

Brickman, Ronald S., Sheila Jasanoff, and T. Ilgen. 1985. *Controlling Chemicals: The Politics of Regulation in Europe and the United States.* Ithaca, NY: Cornell University Press.

Brown, Phil. 1992. "Popular Epidemiology and Toxic Waste Contamination: Lay and Professional Ways of Knowing." *Journal of Health and Social Behavior* 33:267–281.

———. 1997. "Popular Epidemiology Revisited." *Current Sociology* 45:139–156.

Brown, Phil and Edwin J. Mikkelsen. 1990. *No Safe Place: Toxic Waste, Leukemia, and Community Action.* Berkeley: University of California Press.

Brulle, Robert. 2000. *Agency, Democracy and Nature.* Cambridge, MA: MIT Press.

Bryant, Bunyan and Paul Mohai, editors. 1992. *Race and the Incidence of Environmental Hazards.* Boulder, CO: Westview Press.

Bullard, Robert D. 1990. *Dumping in Dixie: Race, Class and Environmental Quality.* Boulder, CO.: Westview Press.

———, editor. 1992. *Confronting Environmental Racism: Voices from the Grassroots.* Boston: South End Press.

Burns, Tom R. and Thomas Dietz. 1992a. "Technology, Sociotechnical Systems, Technological Development: An Evolutionary Perspective." Pp. 206–238 in *New Technology at the Outset: Social Forces in the Shaping of Technological Innovation,* edited by M. Dierkes and U. Hoffman. Frankfurt am Main: Campus Verlag.

———. 1992b. "Cultural Evolution: Social Rule Systems, Selection and Human Agency." *International Sociology* 7:259–284.

Burns, Tom R. and Reinhard Uberhorst. 1988. *Creative Democracy: Systematic Conflict Resolution and Policymaking in a World of High Science and Technology.* New York: Praeger.

Caldwell, Lynton Keith. 1990. *International Environmental Policy: Emergence and Dimensions.* (Second Edition.) Durham, NC: Duke University Press.

Camacho, David E., editor. 1998. *Environmental Injustices, Political Struggles: Race, Class, and the Environment.* Durham, NC: Duke University Press.

Cartwright, John. 1989. "Conserving Nature, Decreasing Debt." *Third World Quarterly* 11:114–127.

Clarke, Lee. 1988. "Politics and Bias in Risk Assessment." *The Social Science Journal* 25:155–165.

———. 1989. *Acceptable Risk?: Making Decisions in a Toxic Environment.* Berkeley: University of California Press.

———. 1999. *Mission Improbable: Using Fantasy Documents to Tame Disasters.* Chicago: University of Chicago Press.

Cohen, Bernard L. 1987. "Reducing the Hazards of Nuclear Power: Insanity in Action." *Physics and Society* 16:2–4.

Combs, B. and Paul Slovic. 1979. "Newspaper Coverage of Causes of Death." *Journalism Quarterly* 56:837–843, 849.

Commoner, Barry. 1990. *Making Peace with the Planet.* New York: Pantheon.

Cosmides, Leda and John Tooby. 1996. "Are Humans Good Intuitive Statisticians after All? Rethinking Some Conclusions from the Literature on Judgment under Uncertainty." *Cognition* 58:1-73.

Covello, Vincent T. and R. Scott Frey. 1990. "Technology-Based Environmental Health Risks in Developing Nations." *Technological Forecasting and Social Change* 37:159–179.

Covello, Vincent T. and Jeryl Mumpower. 1985. "Risk Analysis and Risk Management: An Historical Perspective." *Risk Analysis* 5:103–120.

Covello, Vincent T., D. McCallum, and M. Pavlova, editors. 1988. *Effective Risk Communication: The*

Role and Responsibility of Government. New York: Plenum.

Covello, Vincent T. and Miley W. Merkhofer. 1993. *Risk Assessment Methods: Approaches for Assessing Health and Environmental Risks.* New York: Plenum Press.

Crouch, Edmund A. C. and Richard Wilson. 1982. *Risk/Benefit Analysis.* Cambridge, MA: Ballinger.

Cutter, Susan L. 1993. *Living with Risk: The Geography of Technological Hazards.* London: Edward Arnold.

Dake, Karl. 1991. "Orienting Dispositions in the Perception of Risk: An Analysis of Contemporary Worldviews and Cultural Biases." *Journal of Cross-Cultural Psychology* 22:61–82.

Dake, Karl and Aaron Wildavsky. 1991. "Individual Differences in Risk Perception and Risk-Taking Preferences." Pp. 15–24 in *The Analysis, Communication and Perception of Risk,* edited by B. J. Garrick and W. C. Gekler. New York: Plenum Press.

Dietz, Thomas. 1987. "Theory and Method in Social Impact Assessment." *Sociological Inquiry* 57:54–69.

———. 1988. "Social Impact Assessment as Applied Human Ecology: Integrating Theory and Method." Pp. 220–227 in *Human Ecology: Research and Applications,* edited by R. Borden, J. Jacobs, and G. Young. College Park, MD: Society for Human Ecology.

———. 1992. "The Challenges of Global Environmental Change for Human Ecology," Pp. 30–45 in *Human Responsibility and Global Change,* edited by L. O. Hansson and B. Jungen. Göteborg, Sweden: University of Göteborg.

———. 1994. "What Should We Do? Human Ecology and Collective Decision Making." *Human Ecology Review* 1:277–300.

Dietz, Thomas and Tom R. Burns. 1994. "Environment, Technology and the Evolution of Democracy." Paper presented at the 1994 Annual Meeting of the American Sociological Association, Los Angeles, CA.

Dietz, Thomas and Linda Kalof. 1991. "Environmentalism among Nation-States," *Social Indicators Research* 26:353–366.

Dietz, Thomas and Robert W. Rycroft. 1987. *The Risk Professionals.* New York: Russell Sage.

Dietz, Thomas, Paul C. Stern, and Robert W. Rycroft. 1989. "Definitions of Conflict and the Legitimation of Resources: The Case of Environmental Risk." *Sociological Forum* 4: 47–70.

Douglas, Mary and Aaron Wildavsky. 1982. *Risk and Culture: The Selection of Technological and Environmental Dangers.* Berkeley, CA: University of California Press.

Dunlap, Riley E. 1992. "Trends in Public Opinion toward Environmental Issues," Pp. 89–116 in *American Environmentalism: The U.S. Environmental Movement, 1970–1990,* edited by Riley E. Dunlap and Angela Mertig. Philadelphia, PA: Taylor and Francis.

Dunlap, Riley E., George H. Gallup, and Alex M. Gallup. 1993. "Global Environmental Concern: Results from an International Opinion Survey." *Environment* 35 (November): 6–15, 33–39.

Dunlap, Riley E., Michael E. Kraft, and Eugene A. Rosa, editors. 1993. *Public Reactions to Nuclear Waste: Citizen's Views of Repository Siting.* Durham, NC: Duke University Press.

Dunlap, Riley E. and Angela G. Mertig. 1995. "Global Concern for the Environment: Is Affluence a Prerequisite?" *Journal of Social Issues* 51:121–137.

Elliott, Lorraine. 1998. *The Global Politics of the Environment.* New York: New York University Press.

Ellis, Richard J. and Fred Thompson. 1997. "Culture and the Environment in the Pacific Northwest." *American Political Science Review* 91:885–897.

Englander, Tibor, Klara Farago, Paul Slovic, and Baruch Fischhoff. 1986. "A Comparative Analysis of Risk Perception in Hungary and the United States." *Social Behaviour* 1:55–66.

Environ. 1988. *Elements of Toxicology and Chemical Risk Assessment.* Washington, D.C.: Environ.

Epstein, Samuel S. 1998. *The Politics of Cancer Revisited.* New York: East Ridge Press.

Erickson, Kai. 1994. *A New Species of Trouble: Explorations in Trauma and Community.* New York: W. W. Norton.

Fiorino, Daniel J. 1995. *Making Environmental Policy.* Berkeley: University of California.

Fischer-Kowalski, Marina. 1998. "Society's Metabolism: The Intellectual History of Materialism Flow Analysis, Part I, 1860–1970." *Journal of Industrial Ecology* 2:61–78.

———. 1999. "Society's Metabolism: The Intellectual History of Materials Flow Analysis, Part II, 1970–1998." *Journal of Industrial Ecology* 2:107–128.

Fischhoff, Baruch. 1990. "Psychology and Public Policy: Tool or Toolmaker?" *American Psychologist* 45:647–653.

Fischhoff, Baruch, Sarah Lichtenstein, Paul Slovic, Steven L. Derby, and Ralph L. Keeney. 1981. *Acceptable Risk.* New York: Cambridge University Press.

Fischhoff, Baruch, Stephen R. Watson, and Chris Hope. 1984. "Defining Risk." *Policy Sciences* 17:123–129.

Frank, David John. 1997. "Science, Nature, and the Globalization of the Environment, 1870–1990." *Social Forces* 76:409–437.

———. 1999. "The Social Bases of Environmental Treaty Ratification, 1900–1990." *Sociological Inquiry* 69:523–550.

Freeman, David M. and R. Scott Frey. 1986. "A Method for Assessing the Social Impacts of Natural Resource Policies." *Journal of Environmental Management* 23:229–245.

———. 1990–1991. "A Modest Proposal for Assessing Social Impacts of Natural Resource Policies." *Journal of Environmental Systems* 20: 375–404.

Freudenberg, Nicholas. 1984. *Not In Our Backyards!: Community Action for Health and the Environment.* New York: Monthly Review Press.

Freudenburg, William R. 1988. "Perceived Risk, Real Risk: Social Science and the Art of Probabilistic Risk Assessment." *Science* 242:44–49.

———. 1993. "Risk and Recreancy: Weber, the Division of Labor and the Rationality of Risk Perceptions." *Social Forces* 71:909–932.

Frey, R. Scott. 1995. "The International Traffic in Pesticides." *Technological Forecasting and Social Change* 50: 151–169.

———. 1997. "The International Traffic in Tobacco." *Third World Quarterly* 18:303–319.

———. 1998. "The Hazardous Waste Stream in the World System." Pp. 84–103 in *Space and Transport in the World-System,* edited by Paul Ciccantell and Stephen G. Bunker. Westport, CT: Greenwood Press.

Frey, R. Scott, Thomas Dietz, and Linda Kalof. 1992. "Another Look at Gamson's *Strategy of Social Protest.*" *American Journal of Sociology* 98:368–387.

Funtowicz, Silvio and Jerome R. Ravetz. 1992. "Three Types of Risk Assessment and Emergence of Post-Normal Science." Pp. 251–297 in *Social Theories of Risk,* edited by Sheldon Krimsky and Dominic Golding. Westport, CT: Praeger.

Furger, Franco. 1997. "Accountability and Systems of Self-Government: The Case of the Maritime Industry." *Law and Policy* 19:445–476.

Gamson, William. 1990. *The Strategy of Social Protest.* (Second Edition.) Belmont, CA: Wadsworth.

Gamson, William A. and Andre Modigliani. 1989. "Media Discourse and Public Opinion on Nuclear Power: A Constructionist Approach." *American Journal of Sociology* 95:1–37.

Giddens, Anthony. 1990. *The Consequences of Modernity.* Stanford, CA: Stanford University Press.

Gigerenzer, Gerd. 1992. "Cognitive Illusions Illusory? Rethinking Judgement Under Uncertainty." Working Paper 25/92. Bielefeld, Germany: Research Group on the Biological Foundations of Human Culture, University of Bielefeld.

Gould, Leroy C., Gerald T. Gardner, Donald R. DeLuca, Adrian Tiemann, Leonard W. Doob, and Jan A. J. Stolwijk. 1988. *Perceptions of Technological Risks and Benefits.* New York: Russell Sage Foundation.

Graham, John D., Laura C. Green, and Marc J. Roberts. 1988. *In Search of Safety: Chemicals and Cancer Risk.* Cambridge, MA: Harvard University Press.

Griegahn, Monika. 1994. "Initiatives in Lower Saxony to Link Ecology to Economy." Pp. 423–428 in *Industrial Ecology and Global Change,* edited by R. Socolow, C. Andrews, F. Berkhout, and V. Thomas. Cambridge, England: Cambridge University Press.

Hackett, David P. 1990. "An Assessment of the Basel Convention on the Control of Transboundary Movements of Hazardous Wastes and Their Disposal." *American University Journal of International Law and Policy* 5:291–323.

Hadden, Susan G. 1986. *Read the Label: Reducing Risk by Providing Information.* Boulder, CO: Westview Press.

Hamilton, James T. and W. Kip Viscusi. 1999. *Calculating Risks?: The Spatial and Political Dimensions of Hazardous Waste Policy.* Cambridge, MA: MIT Press.

Harriss, Robert C., Christoph Hohenemser, and Robert W. Kates. 1985. "Human and Nonhuman Mortality." Pp. 129–155 in *Perilous Progress: Managing the Hazards of Technology,* edited by Robert W. Kates, Christoph Hohenemser, and Jeanne X. Kasperson. Boulder, CO: Westview Press.

Hays, Samuel P. 1987. *Beauty, Health, and Permanence: Environmental Politics in the United States, 1955–1985.* New York: Cambridge University Press.

———. 1999. *Conservation and the Gospel of Efficiency: The Progressive Conservation Movement, 1890–1920.* (Revised Edition.) Pittsburgh: University of Pittsburgh Press.

Heimer, Carol. 1985. *Reactive Risk and Rational Action: Managing Moral Hazard in Insurance Contracts.* Berkeley, CA: University of California Press.

———. 1988. "Social Structure, Psychology, and the Estimation of Risk." *Annual Review of Sociology* 14:491–519.

Hofstadter, Richard. 1955. *The Age of Reform.* New York: Knopf.

Holden, Constance. 1988. "The Greening of the World Bank." *Science* 240:1610.

Intergovernmental Panel on Climate Change. 1996. *Climate Change: The Second Assessment Report.* Cambridge, UK: Cambridge University Press.

Jaeger, Carlo, Ortwin Renn, Eugene A. Rosa, and Thomas Webler. 2000. *Risk, Uncertainty and Rational Action.* London: Earthscan.

Jasanoff, Shelia. 1986. *Risk Management and Political Culture: A Comparative Study of Science in the Policy Context.* New York: Russell Sage.

Jasper, James M. 1988. "The Political Life Cycle of Technological Controversies." *Social Forces* 67:355–377.

———. 1990. *Nuclear Politics: Energy and the State in the United States, Sweden and France.* Princeton, NJ: Princeton University Press.

Kasperson, Roger E., Robert W. Kates, and Christoph Hohenemser. 1985. "Hazard Management." Pp. 43–66 in *Perilous Progress: Managing the Hazards of Technology,* edited by Robert W. Kates, Christoph Hohenemser, and Jeanne X. Kasperson. Boulder, CO: Westview Press.

Kasperson, Roger E., Ortwin Renn, Paul Slovic, Halina S. Brown, Jacque Emel, Robert Goble, Jeanne X. Kasperson, and Samuel Ratick. 1988. "The Social Amplification of Risk: A Conceptual Framework." *Risk Analysis* 8:177–187.

Keck, Margaret and Kathryn Sikkink. 1998. *Activists Beyond Borders: Advocacy Networks in International Politics.* Ithaca, NY: Cornell University Press.

Keeney, Ralph and Howard Raiffa. 1976. *Decisions with Multiple Objectives, Preferences and Value Tradeoffs.* New York: Wiley.

Keown, Charles F. 1989. "Risk Perceptions of Hong Kongese vs. Americans." *Risk Analysis* 9:401–405.

Kleinhesselink, Randall R. and Eugene A. Rosa. 1991. "Cognitive Representation of Risk Perceptions: A Comparison of Japan and the United States." *Journal of Cross-Cultural Psychology* 22:11–28.

———. 1993. "Nuclear Trees in a Forest of Hazards: A Comparison of Risk Perceptions between American and Japanese University Students." In *Nuclear Power at the Crossroads,* edited by G. Hineman, S. Kondo, P. Lowinger, and K. Matsui. Boulder, CO: International Center for Energy and Economic Development, University of Colorado.

Kolker, Aliza and B. Meredith Burke. 1994. *Prenatal Testing: A Sociological Perspective.* Westport, CT: Bergin and Garvey.

Krimsky, Sheldon and Dominic Golding, editors. 1992. *Social Theories of Risk.* Westport, CT: Praeger.

Lancet. 1992. "The Cancer Epidemic: Fact or Misinterpretation?" *The Lancet* 340 (August 15):399–400.

La Porte, Todd R. 1988. "The United States Air Traffic System: Increasing Reliability in the Midst of Rapid Growth." Pp. 215–244 in *The*

Development of Large Technological Systems, edited by Renate Mayntz and Thomas P. Hughes. Boulder, CO: Westview Press.

La Porte, Todd R. and P. M. Consolini. 1991. "Working in Practice but Not in Theory: Theoretical Challenges of High Reliability Organizations." *Journal of Public Administration Research and Theory* 1:19–47.

Lave, Lester B., editor. 1982. *Quantitative Risk Assessment in Regulation.* Washington, D.C.: The Brookings Institution.

Library of Congress. "The Evolution of the Conservation Movement." Available at http://lcweb2.loc gov/ammem/amrvhtml/conshome.html.

Lichtenstein, Sarah, Paul Slovic, Baruch Fischhoff, Mark Layman, and Barbara Combs. 1978. "Judged Frequency of Lethal Events." *Journal of Experimental Psychology: Human Learning and Memory* 4:551–578.

Lichter, S. Robert and Stanley Rothman. 1999. *Environmental Cancer: A Political Disease?* New Haven, CT: Yale University Press.

Lipschutz, Ronnie D. and Ken Conca, editors. 1993. *The State and Social Power in Global Environmental Politics.* New York: Columbia University Press.

Lipset, Seymour Martin and William Schneider. 1987. *The Confidence Gap: Business, Labor and Government in the Public Mind.* (Revised Edition.) Baltimore, MD: Johns Hopkins University Press.

Lowrance, William W. 1976. *Of Acceptable Risk: Science and the Determination of Safety.* Los Altos, CA: William Kaufman.

Machlis, Gary E. and Eugene A. Rosa. 1990. "Desired Risk: Broadening the Social Amplification of Risk Framework." *Risk Analysis* 10:161–168.

Mathews, Jessica Tuchman, editor. 1991. *Preserving the Global Environment: The Challenge of Shared Leadership.* New York: W. W. Norton.

Mazur, Allan. 1981. *The Dynamics of Technical Controversy.* Washington, D.C.: Communications Press.

———. 1984. "Media Influences on Public Attitudes toward Nuclear Power." Pp. 97–114 in *Public Reactions to Nuclear Power: Are There*

Critical Masses?, edited by William R. Freudenburg and Eugene A. Rosa. Boulder, CO: Westview Press.

———, editor. 1994. "Symposium on Technological Risk in the Mass Media." *Risk: Health, Safety and Environment* 5:187–282.

McElrath, Roger. 1988. "Environmental Issues and the Strategies of the International Trade Union Movement." *Columbia Journal of World Business* 23:63–68.

Menkes, Joshua and R. Scott Frey. 1987. "*De Minimis* Risk as a Regulatory Tool." Pp. 9–13 in *De Minimis Risk,* edited by Chris Whipple. New York: Plenum Press.

Montgomery, John D. 1990. "Environmental Management as a Third-World Problem." *Policy Sciences* 23:163–176.

Nelkin, Dorothy, editor. 1992. *Controversy: Politics of Technical Decisions.* Beverly Hills, CA: Sage.

Norton, Susan B., Donald J. Rodier, John H. Gentile, William H. Van Der Schalle, William W. Wood, and Michael W. Slimak. 1992. "A Framework for Ecological Risk Assessment at the EPA." *Environmental Toxicology and Chemistry* 11:1663–1672.

Olson, Mancur. 1965. *The Logic of Collective Action: Public Goods and the Theory of Groups.* Cambridge, MA: Harvard University Press.

Perrow, Charles. 1984. *Normal Accidents: Living with High Risk Technologies.* New York: Basic Books.

Porter, Garth and Janet Welsch Brown. 1996. *Global Environmental Politics.* (Second Edition.) Boulder, CO: Westview Press.

Princen, Thomas and Matthias Finger, editors. 1994. *Environmental NGOs in World Politics.* London: Routledge.

Pring, George W. and Penelope Canan. 1996. *SLAPPs: Getting Sued for Speaking Out.* Philadelphia, PA: Temple University Press.

Proctor, Richard. 1995. *Cancer Wars: How Politics Shapes What We Know about Cancer.* New York: Basic Books.

Rayner, Steve and Robin Cantor. 1987. "How Fair Is Safe Enough?: The Cultural Approach to Societal Technology Choice." *Risk Analysis* 7:3–13.

Regens, James L., Thomas M. Dietz, and Robert W. Rycroft. 1983. "Risk Assessment in the

Policy-Making Process: Environmental Health and Safety Protection." *Public Administration Review* 43:137–145.

Renn, Ortwin. 1992. "Concepts of Risk: A Classification." Pp. 53–79 in *Social Theories of Risk,* edited by Sheldon Krimsky and Dominic Golding. Westport, CT: Praeger.

Roberts, J. Timmons. 1996. "Predicting Participation in Environmental Treaties: A World-System Analysis." *Sociological Inquiry* 66:38–57.

Roberts, J. Timmons and Peter E. Grimes. 1997. "Carbon Intensity and Economic Development, 1962–1991: A Brief Exploration of the Environmental Kuznets Curve." *World Development* 25:191–198.

Roberts, K. H., editor. 1993. *New Challenges to Organizations: High Reliability Organizations.* New York: Macmillan.

Rochlin, Gene I., Todd R. La Porte, and Karlene H. Roberts. 1987. "The Self-Designing High-Reliability Organization: Aircraft Carrier Flight Operations at Sea." *Naval War College Review* 40:76–90.

Rodericks, Joseph V. 1992. *Calculated Risks.* Cambridge: Cambridge University Press.

Rosa, Eugene A. 1988. "NAMBY PAMBY and NIMBY PIMBY: Public Issues in the Siting of Hazardous Waste Facilities." *FORUM for Applied Research and Public Policy* 3:114.

———. 1998. "Metatheoretical Foundations for Post Normal Risk." *Journal of Risk Research* 1:15–44.

Rosa, Eugene A. and Donald L. Clark, Jr. 1999. "Historical Routes to Technological Gridlock: Nuclear Technology as Prototypical Vehicle." *Research in Social Problems and Public Policy,* 7:21–57.

Rosa, Eugene A. and Thomas Dietz. 1998. "Climate Change and Society: Speculation, Construction and Scientific Investigation." *International Sociology* 13:421–455.

Rosa, Eugene, Gary E. Machlis, and Kenneth M. Keating. 1988. "Energy and Society." *Annual Review of Sociology* 14:149–172.

Rosa, Eugene, Allan Mazur, and Thomas Dietz. 1987. "Sociological Analysis of Risk Impacts Associated with the Siting of a High Level Nuclear Waste Repository: The Case of Hanford." Proceedings of the Workshop on Assessing Social and Economic Effects of Perceived Risk. Seattle: Battelle Human Affairs Research Centers.

Rothman, S. and S. Robert Lichter. 1987. "Elite Ideology and Perception in Nuclear Energy Policy." *American Political Science Review* 81:383–404.

Rummel-Bulska, Iwona. 1991. *Environmental Law in UNEP.* Nairobi, Kenya: United Nations Environment Programme.

Russel, Milton and Michael Gruber. 1987. "Risk Assessment in Environmental Policy-Making." *Science* 236:286–290.

Sagan, Scott D. 1993. *The Limits of Safety: Organizations, Accidents and Nuclear Weapons.* Princeton, NJ: Princeton University Press.

Sandman, Peter M., David B. Sachsman, Michael P. Greenberg, and M. Gotchfeld. 1987. *Environmental Risk and the Press.* New Brunswick, NJ: Transaction Books.

Schnaiburg, Alan. 1980. *The Environment: From Surplus to Scarcity.* New York: Oxford University Press.

Short, James F. 1984. "The Social Fabric at Risk: Toward the Social Transformation of Risk Analysis." *American Sociological Review* 49:711–725.

Short, James F. and Lee Clarke, editors. 1992. *Organizations, Uncertainties and Risk.* Boulder, CO: Westview Press.

Shrader-Frechette, K. S. 1985. *Risk Analysis and Scientific Method: Methodological and Ethical Problems with Evaluating Societal Hazards.* Dordrecht, Holland: D. Reidel.

———. 1991. *Risk and Rationality: Philosophical Foundations for Populist Reforms.* Berkeley: University of California Press.

Silver, Cheryl Simon and Ruth S. DeFries. 1992. *One Earth, One Future: Our Changing Global Environment.* Washington, D.C.: National Academy Press.

Simon, Herbert A. 1982. *Models of Bounded Rationality.* Cambridge, MA: M.I.T. Press.

Slovic, Paul. 1987. "Perception of Risk." *Science* 236:280–285.

Smil, Vaclav. 1993. *China's Environmental Crisis: An Inquiry into the Limits of National Development.* New York: M. E. Sharpe.

Socolow, Robert, C. Andrews, F. Berkhout, and V. Thomas, editors. 1994. *Industrial Ecology and Global Change.* Cambridge: Cambridge University Press.

Stallings, Robert A. 1990. "Media Discourse and the Social Construction of Risk." *Social Problems* 37:80–95.

Starr, Chauncey. 1969. "Social Benefit versus Technological Risk." *Science* 165:1232–1238.

Stern, Paul C., Thomas Dietz, and J. Stanley Black. 1985–86. "Support for Environmental Protection: The Role of Moral Norms." *Population and Environment* 8:204–222.

Stern, Paul C. and Harvey V. Fineberg, editors. 1996. *Understanding Risk: Informing Decisions in a Democratic Society.* Washington, D.C.: National Academy Press.

Stern, Paul C., Oran R. Young, and Daniel Druckman, editors. 1992. *Global Environmental Change: Understanding the Human Dimensions.* Washington, D.C.: National Academy Press.

Szasz, Andrew. 1994. *EcoPopulism: Toxic Waste and the Movement for Environmental Reform.* Minneapolis: University of Minnesota Press.

Taylor, Bron Raymond. 1995. *Ecological Resistance Movements: The Global Emergence of Radical and Popular Environmentalism.* Albany, NY: State University of New York Press.

Teigen, Karl Halvor, Wibecke Brun, and Paul Slovic. 1988. "Societal Risks as Seen by a Norwegian Public." *Journal of Behavioral Decision Making* 1:111–130.

Thompson, Michael, Richard Ellis, and Aaron Wildavsky. 1990. *Cultural Theory.* Boulder, CO: Westview Press.

Tversky, Amos and Daniel Kahneman. 1982. "Availability: A Heuristic for Judging Frequency and Probability." Pp. 163–178 in *Judgment under Uncertainty: Heuristics and Biases,* edited by Daniel Kahneman, Paul Slovic, and Amos Tversky. Cambridge, UK: Cambridge University Press.

U.S. National Research Council. 1983. *Risk Assessment in the Federal Government: Managing the Process.* Washington, D.C.: National Academy Press.

———. 1989. *Improving Risk Communication.* Washington, D.C.: National Academy Press.

U.S. Office of Technology Assessment. 1981. *Assessment of Technologies for Determining Cancer Risks from the Environment.* Washington, D.C.: U.S. Government Printing Office.

Walsh, Edward J. 1981. "Resource Mobilization and Citizen Protest in Communities around Three Mile Island." *Social Problems* 29:1–21.

Weidenbaum, Murray. 1977. *Business, Government and the Public.* Englewood Cliffs, NJ: Prentice-Hall.

Weinstein, Neal, editor. 1987. *Taking Care: Understanding and Encouraging Self-Protective Behavior.* New York: Cambridge University Press.

Whipple, Chris, editor. 1987. *De Minimis Risk.* New York: Plenum Press.

White, Gilbert. 1974. *Natural Hazards: Local, National, Global.* New York: Oxford University Press.

Wildavsky, Aaron. 1988. *Searching for Safety.* New Brunswick, NJ: Transaction Books.

Williams, Jerry and R. Scott Frey. 1997. "The Changing Status of Global Warming as a Social Problem: Competing Factors in Two Public Arenas." Pp. 279–299 in *Research in Community Sociology, Volume 7,* edited by Dan A. Chekki. Greenwich, CT: JAI Press.

World Commission on Environment and Development. 1987. *Our Common Future.* Oxford: Oxford University Press.

Young, Oran R. 1989. *International Cooperation: Building Regimes for Natural Resources and the Environment.* Ithaca: Cornell University Press.

Chapter 8

Science, Democracy,
and the Environment

17. Popular Epidemiology and Toxic Waste Contamination: Lay and Professional Ways of Knowing*

PHIL BROWN

Medical sociology has long been concerned with differences between lay and professional ways of knowing (Fisher 1986; Roth 1963; Stimson and Webb 1975; Waitzkin 1989). Because of their different social backgrounds and roles in the medical encounter, clients and providers have divergent perspectives on problem definitions and solutions (Freidson 1970). Professionals generally concern themselves with disease processes, while laypeople focus on the personal experience of illness. For professionals, classes of disorders are central, while those who suffer the disorders dwell on the individual level (Zola 1973). From the professional perspective, symptoms and diseases universally affect all people, yet lay perceptions and experience exhibit great cultural variation. Similarly, lay explanatory approaches often utilize various causal models that run counter to scientific notions of etiology (Fisher 1986; Freidson 1970; Kleinman 1980). Medical professionals' work consists of multiple goals, among which patient care is only one; patients are centrally concerned with getting care (Strauss et al. 1964).

The study of these contrasting perspectives has centered on clinical interaction and institutional settings. Some scholars have examined lay–professional differences in occupational health (Smith 1981), community struggles over access and equity in health services (Waitzkin 1983), and genetic screening (Rothman 1986). Yet medical sociology has scarcely studied environmental and toxic waste issues.

Recently, lay perceptions on environmental health have manifested themselves in a burgeoning community activism. Following the landmark Love Canal case (Levine 1982), the childhood leukemia cluster in Woburn, Massachusetts has drawn attention to the lay–professional gap. Woburn residents were startled beginning in 1972 to learn that their children were contracting leukemia at exceedingly high rates. By their own efforts the affected families and community activists attempted to confirm the existence of a leukemia cluster and to link it to industrial toxins that leached into their water supply. They pursued a long course of action which led to a major community health study, a civil suit against W. R. Grace Chemical Corporation and Beatrice Foods, and extensive national attention.

*Revised version printed by permission of the author and the American Sociological Association from *Journal of Health and Social Behavior* 33 (September 1992): 267–281.

Building on a detailed study of the Woburn case, and utilizing data from other toxic waste sites, this paper discusses conflicts between lay and professional ways of knowing about environmental health risks. This discussion centers on the phenomenon of *popular epidemiology,* in which laypeople detect and act on environmental hazards and diseases. Popular epidemiology is but one variant of public participation in the pursuit of scientific knowledge, advocacy for health care, and public policy, as witnessed in such diverse cases as AIDS treatment, nuclear power development, and pollution control. The emphasis on ways of knowing makes sense because knowledge is often what is debated in struggles to win ownership of a social problem (Gusfield 1981, pp. 36–45).

In their popular epidemiological efforts, community activists repeatedly differ with scientists and government officials on matters of problem definition, study design, interpretation of findings, and policy applications. In examining the stages through which citizens become toxic waste activists, this paper emphasizes lay–professional differences concerning quality of data, methods of analysis, traditionally accepted levels of measurement and statistical significance, and relations between scientific method and public policy.

STUDY BACKGROUND

There were two sets of interviews with the Woburn litigants. The first (eight families) comprised open-ended questions on individual experiences with the toxic waste crisis, including personal and family problems, coping styles, and mental health effects. These were conducted in 1985 by a psychiatrist and reanalyzed in 1988 for an earlier phase of this research (Brown 1990). This reanalysis involved both the researcher and

the psychiatrist rereading the interview material several times, and then discussing what themes were most prominent. This process defined themes for discussion of the original, largely psychosocial, interviews. As well, it directed the creation of the interview schedule for the reinterview. For example, respondents in the original interviews expressed considerable anger at the corporations accused of contaminating the wells, and at the government officials who were investigating the disease cluster. This provided initial information on these important concerns, and directly yielded more specific reinterview questions. The second set of interviews in 1988 (except for one family that did not wish to participate) comprised twenty open-ended questions on residents' perceptions of community activism, the litigation, government and corporate responsibility for toxics, and the relationship between lay and scientific approaches.

Fourteen community activists, apart from the litigants, were also interviewed in 1990. In addition to basic personal data, respondents were asked nineteen open-ended questions concerning toxic waste activism, knowledge about toxic wastes and their detection and remediation, attitudes toward corporate and governmental actors, and attitudes and participation in other environmental and political concerns. Other data were obtained from interviews with, formal presentations by, and official documents provided by the families' lawyer, state public health officials, federal environmental officials, and public health researchers. Additional data came from legal documents, public meetings, archival sources, and from research on other similar sites.

Material from all interviews, documents, meetings, and other sources was coded in two ways. First, codes were devised from prior knowledge gained from the first litigant interviews, from the themes which the litigant reinterview questions and other interview questions were expected to tap, and from existing literature on toxic waste sites. Second, additional codes were identified in the process of reading through the transcripts. In this second case, a number of codes were quickly apparent, such as the pride which citizens had in their nascent scientific abilities. The coding process therefore identified the beliefs and experiences of involved parties, enabling me to make interpretations of those beliefs and experiences. In many instances, there was considerable congruence with other scholars' findings in case studies of toxic waste sites; this provided a degree of reliability.

In addition to this coding process, all data was examined in terms of its place in the historical/chronological development of the toxic waste crisis. While a clear line of unfolding events was previously apparent, the data culled from the detailed research allowed me to fill in fine-grained detail. This approach enabled me to create the stages model of popular epidemiology described in the next section. Here, too, other toxic waste studies offered support for the development of such a schema.

LAY WAYS OF KNOWING

Popular Epidemiology

Traditional epidemiology studies the distribution of a disease or condition, and the factors that influence this distribution. These data are used to explain the etiology of the condition and to provide preventive, public health, and clinical practices to deal with the condition (Lillienfeld 1980, p. 4). A broader approach, seen in the risk-detection and solution-seeking activities of Woburn and other "contaminated communities" (Edelstein 1988), may be conceptualized as *popular epidemiology.*

Popular epidemiology is the process by which lay persons gather scientific data and other information, and also direct and marshal the knowledge and resources of experts in order to understand the epidemiology of disease. In some of its actions, popular epidemiology parallels scientific epidemiology, such as when laypeople conduct community health surveys. Yet popular epidemiology is more than public participation in traditional epidemiology, since it emphasizes social structural factors as part of the causal disease chain. Further, it involves social movements, utilizes political and judicial approaches to remedies, and challenges basic assumptions of traditional epidemiology, risk assessment, and public health regulation. In some cases, traditional epidemiology may reach similar conclusions as popular epidemiology. Yet scientists generally do not become political activists in order to implement their findings, despite exceptions such as Irving Selikoff's work on asbestos diseases.

Popular epidemiology is similar to other lay advocacy for health care, in that lay perspectives counter professional ones and a social movement guides this alternative perspective. Some lay health advocacy acts to obtain more resources for the prevention and treatment of already recognized diseases (e.g., sickle cell anemia, AIDS), while others seek to win government and medical recognition of unrecognized or under-recognized diseases (e.g., black lung, post-traumatic stress disorder). Still others seek to affirm the knowledge of yet-unknown etiological factors in already recognized diseases (e.g., DES and cervical cancer, asbestos and mesothelioma). Popular epidemiology is most similar to the latter approach, since original research is necessary both to document the prevalence of the disease and the putative causation.

From studying Woburn and other toxic cases (e.g., Levine 1982; Nash and Kirsch

1986; Couto 1986; Krauss 1989; Edelstein 1988), we observe a set of stages of citizen involvement. Participants do not necessarily complete a stage before beginning the next, but one stage usually occurs before the next begins:

1. A group of people in a contaminated community notice separately both health effects and pollutants.
2. These residents hypothesize something out of the ordinary, typically a connection between health effects and pollutants.
3. Community residents share information, creating a common perspective.
4. Community residents, now a more cohesive group, read about, ask around, and talk to government officials and scientific experts about the health effects and the putative contaminants.
5. Residents organize groups to pursue their investigation.
6. Government agencies conduct official studies in response to community groups' pressure. These studies usually find no association between contaminants and health effects.
7. Community groups bring in their own experts to conduct a health study and to investigate pollutant sources and pathways.
8. Community groups engage in litigation and confrontation.
9. Community groups press for corroboration of their findings by official experts and agencies.

1. Lay Observations of Health Effects and Pollutants. Many people who live at risk of toxic hazards have access to data otherwise inaccessible to scientists. Their experiential knowledge usually precedes official and scientific awareness, largely because it is so tangible.

Knowledge of toxic hazards in communities and workplaces in the last two decades has often stemmed from lay observation (Edelstein 1988; Freudenberg 1984a).

Although the first official action—closing Woburn's polluted wells—occurred in 1979, there was a long history of problems in the Woburn water. Residents had for decades complained about dishwasher discoloration, foul odor, and bad taste. Private and public laboratory assays had indicated the presence of organic compounds. The first lay detection efforts were begun earlier by Anne Anderson, whose son, Jimmy, had been diagnosed with acute lymphocytic leukemia in 1972.

2. Hypothesizing Connections. Anderson put together information during 1973–1974 about other cases by meetings with other Woburn victims in town and at the hospital where Jimmy spent much time. Anderson hypothesized that the alarming leukemia incidence was caused by a water-borne agent. In 1975 she asked state officials to test the water but was told that testing could not be done at an individual's initiative (DiPerna 1985, pp. 75–82). Anderson's hypothesis mirrored that of other communities, where people hypothesize that a higher than expected incidence of disease is due to toxics.

3. Creating a Common Perspective. Anderson sought to convince the family minister, Bruce Young, that the water was somehow responsible, although he at first supported her husband's wish to dissuade her. The creation of a common perspective was aided by a couple of significant events. In 1979 builders found 184 55-gallon drums in a vacant lot; they called the police, who in turn summoned the state Department of Environmental Quality Engineering (DEQE). When water samples were then taken from a number of municipal wells, wells G and H showed high concentrations of organic compounds known to be animal carcinogens, especially trichloroethylene (TCE) and tetrachloroethylene (PCE). EPA recommends that the TCE be zero parts per billion and sets a maximum of 5 parts per billion; Well G had forty times that concentration. As a result the state closed both wells (Clapp 1987; DiPerna 1985, pp. 106–108).

In June 1979, just weeks after the state closed the wells, a DEQE engineer driving past the nearby Industriplex construction site thought he saw violations of the Wetlands Act. A resultant EPA study found dangerous levels of lead, arsenic, and chromium, yet EPA told neither the town officials nor the public. The public only learned this months later, from the local newspaper. Reverend Young, initially distrustful of Anderson's theory, came to similar conclusions once the newspaper broke the story. Working with a few leukemia victims, he placed an ad in the Woburn paper, asking people who knew of childhood leukemia cases to respond. Working with John Truman, Jimmy Anderson's doctor, Young and Anderson prepared a questionnaire and plotted the cases on a map. Six of the twelve cases were closely grouped in East Woburn.

4. Looking for Answers from Government and Science. The data convinced Dr. Truman, who called the Centers for Disease Control (CDC). The citizens persuaded the City Council in Decem-

ber 1979 to formally ask the CDC to investigate. Five days later, the Massachusetts DPH reported on *adult* leukemia mortality for a five-year period, finding a significant elevation only for females. This report was cited to contradict the residents' belief that there was a childhood leukemia cluster.

5. Organizing a Community Group. In January 1980 Young, Anderson, and 20 others (both litigants and nonlitigants) formed For a Cleaner Environment (FACE) to solidify and expand their efforts (DiPerna 1985, pp. 111–125). FACE pursued all subsequent negotiations with local, state, and federal agencies. It campaigned to attract media attention, and made connections with other toxic waste groups.

Community groups in contaminated communities provide many important functions. They galvanize community support, deal with government, work with professionals, engage in health studies, and provide social and emotional support. They are the primary information source for people in contaminated communities, and often the most—even the only—accurate source (Gibbs 1982; Edelstein 1988, p. 144). Through their organization, Woburn activists report pride in learning science, in protecting and serving their community, in guaranteeing democratic processes, and in personal empowerment.

6. Official Studies Are Conducted by Experts. In May 1980 the CDC and the National Institute for Occupational Safety and Health sent Dr. John Cutler to collaborate with the DPH on further study. By then, the Woburn case had national visibility due to national newspaper and network television coverage. In June 1980 Senator Edward Kennedy asked Anderson and Young to testify at hearings on the Superfund, providing further important public exposure. Five days after Jimmy Anderson died, the CDC/DPH study was released in January 1981, stating that there were 12 cases of childhood leukemia in East Woburn, when 5.3 were expected. Yet the DPH argued that the case-control method (12 cases, 24 controls) failed to find characteristics (e.g., medical histories, parental occupation, environmental exposures) that differentiated victims from nonvictims, and that lacking environmental data prior to 1979, no linkage could be made to the water supply (Parker and Rosen 1981). That report helped bolster community claims of a high leukemia rate, although the DPH argued that the data could not implicate the wells. Cutler and his colleagues argued that in addition to the absence of case-control differences and the lack of environmental water exposure data, the organic compounds in the wells were known as animal, but not human, carcinogens (Cutler et al. 1986; Condon 1991; Knorr 1991).

The government agencies and their scientific experts worked to maintain their "ownership" of the problem by denying the link with toxics, and by maintaining control of problem solution (Gusfield 1981, pp. 10–15). Activists struggled to solidify their claim to ownership of the problem, to redefine causal responsibility, and to take on political responsibility. While epidemiologists admit to the uncertainties of their work, their usual solution is to err on the side of rejecting environmental causation, whereas community residents make the opposite choice.

7. *Activists Bring in Their Own Experts.* The activists had no "court of appeals" for the scientific evidence necessary to make their case. It became FACE's mission to obtain the information themselves. The conjunction of Jimmy Anderson's death and the DPH's failure to implicate the wells led the residents to question the nature of official studies. They received help when Anderson and Young presented the Woburn case to a seminar at the Harvard School of Public Health (HSPH). Marvin Zelen and Steven Lagakos of the Department of Biostatistics became interested; working with FACE members, they designed a health study, focusing on birth defects and reproductive disorders, widely considered to be environmentally related. The biostatisticians and activists teamed up in a prototypical collaboration between citizens and scientists (Lagakos 1987; Zelen 1987). The FACE/HSPH study was more than a "court of appeals," since it transformed the activists' search for credibility. No longer did they have to seek scientific expertise from outside; now they were largely in control of scientific inquiry.

Sources of data for the Woburn health study included information on 20 cases of childhood leukemia (ages 19 and under) which were diagnosed between 1964 and 1983, the DEQE water model of wells G and H, and the health survey. The survey collected data on adverse pregnancy outcomes and childhood disorders from 5,010 interviews, covering 57% of Woburn residences with telephones. The researchers trained

235 volunteers to conduct the survey, taking precautions to avoid bias (Lagakos et al. 1984).[1]

8. Litigation and Confrontation. During this period, the DEQE's hydrogeological investigations found that the bedrock in the affected area was shaped like a bowl, with wells G and H in the deepest part. DEQE's March 1982 report thus determined that the contamination source was not the Industri-Plex site as had been believed, but rather facilities of W. R. Grace and Beatrice Foods. This led eight families of leukemia victims to file a $400 million suit in May 1982 against those corporations for waste disposal practices which led to water contamination and disease. A smaller company, Unifirst, was also sued but quickly settled before trial (Schlictmann 1987). In July 1986 a federal district court jury found that Grace had negligently dumped chemicals; Beatrice Foods was absolved. An $8 million out-of-court settlement with Grace was reached in September 1986. The families filed an appeal against Beatrice, based on suppression of evidence, but the Appeals Court rejected the appeal in July 1990, and in October 1990 the United States Supreme Court declined to hear the case (Brown 1987; 1990; Neuffer, 1988).

The trial was a separate, but contiguous struggle over facts and science. Through consultant physicians, immunologists, epidemiologists, and hydrogeologists, the families accumulated further evidence of adverse health effects. The data were not used in the trial, which never got to the point of assessing the causal chain of pollution and illness. Nevertheless, the process made the residents more scientifically informed.

9. Pressing for Official Corroboration. In February 1984 the FACE/Harvard School of Public Health data were made public. Childhood leukemia was found to be significantly associated with exposure to water from wells G and H. Children with leukemia received an average of 21.2% of their yearly water supply from the wells, compared to 9.5% for children without leukemia. Controlling for risk factors in pregnancy, the investigators found that access to contaminated water was associated with perinatal deaths since 1970, eye/ear anomalies, and CNS/chromosomal/oral cleft anomalies. With regard to childhood disorders, water exposure was associated with kidney/urinary tract and lung/respiratory diseases (Lagakos et al. 1984). If only the children that were *in-utero* at the time of exposure are studied, the positive associations are even stronger (Lagakos 1987).

Due to lack of resources, this study would not have been possible without community involvement. Yet precisely this lay involvement led professional and governmental groups—the DPH, the Centers for Disease Control, the American Cancer Society, the EPA, and even the Harvard School of Public Health Department of Epidemiology—to charge that the study was biased. The researchers conducted extensive analyses to demonstrate that the data were not biased, especially with regard to the use of community volunteers as interviewers (See note 1). Still, officials argued that interviewers and respondents knew the research question, respondents had potential recall bias, and the water model measured only household supply rather than individual consumption (Condon 1991; Knorr 1991). Thus, although activists expected the results to bring scientific support, they saw only criticism.

Having laid out the stages of popular epidemiological involvement, I now elaborate on the main lay–professional disputes: lay participation, standards of proof, constraints on professional practice, quality of official studies, and professional autonomy.

PROFESSIONAL WAYS OF KNOWING

Traditional science contains a narrowly circumscribed set of assumptions about causality, the political and public role of scientists, and corporate and governmental social responsibility (Ozonoff and Boden 1987). Political–economic approaches argue that scientific inquiry is tied to corporate, political, and foundation connections which direct research and interpretation toward support for the status quo (Dickson 1984; Aronowitz 1988). It is useful to draw on both the political–economic perspective, which provides a social context for science, and the ethnomethodological/constructivist perspective, which shows us the internal workings of the scientific community (e.g., Latour 1987). There is a dynamic relationship between these two approaches—social movement actions provide the impetus for new scientific paradigms, and those new paradigms in turn spawn further social movement action.

The critics of the Woburn health survey did not represent *all science*, since residents received help from scientists who support community involvement and who believe that contaminated communities fail to receive fair treatment. Often such scientists

have worked without compensation. Some began as critics of mainstream approaches, while others became critical only during the investigation. Some believed in a different causal paradigm, and some were critical of prevailing canons of significance levels. Others simply believed they could conduct better studies than official agencies.

Lay pressure for a different scientific approach is not directed at "pure" science. In environmental health, we are dealing with *combined* government/professional units, e.g., DPH, EPA, CDC. The end goal for activists is mainly acceptance by *government agencies*, since they have the power to act. At the same time, activists seek to become "popular scientists" who can win the support of scientific experts for the sake of knowledge.

Popular Participation and the Critique of Value-Neutrality

Activists disagree that epidemiology is a value-neutral scientific enterprise conducted in a sociopolitical vacuum. Critics of the Woburn health study argued that the study was biased by the use of volunteer interviewers and by prior political goals. Those critics upheld the notion of a value-free science in which knowledge, theories, techniques, and applications are devoid of self-interest or bias. Such claims are disputed by the sociology of science, which maintains that scientific knowledge is not absolute, but rather the subject of debate among scientists (Latour 1987). Scientific knowledge is shaped by social forces such as media influence, economic interest, political pressure, and social movement activism (Aronowitz 1988; Dickson 1984). On a practical level, scientific endeavors are limited by financial and personnel resources (Goggin 1986; Nelkin 1985); lay involvement often supplies the labor power needed to document health hazards. Science is also limited in how it identifies problems worthy of study. As an academic and official enterprise, science does not take its direction from the lay public.

Toxic activists see themselves as correcting problems not dealt with by the established scientific community. The centrality of popular involvement is evident in the women's health and occupational health movements which have been major forces in pointing to often unidentified problems and working to abolish their causes. Among the hazards and diseases thus uncovered are DES, Agent Orange, asbestos, pesticides, unnecessary hysterectomies, sterilization abuse, and black lung (Berman 1977; Rodriguez-Trias 1984; Scott 1988; Smith 1981). In these examples and in Woburn, lay activists are not merely research assistants to sympathetic scientists, but often take the initiative in detecting disease, generating hypotheses, pressing for state action, and conceiving and overseeing scientific studies.

Standards of Proof

Many scientists and public health officials emphasize various problems in standards of proof, ranging from initial detection and investigation to final interpretation of data. Assessment of public health risks of toxic substances involves four steps. Hazard identification locates the existence and extent of toxics. Dose-response analysis determines the quantitative effects of the substance. Exposure assessment examines human exposure to the substances. Risk characterization integrates the first three steps in order to estimate the numbers of people who will be affected and the seriousness of the effects. From the scientific point of view, there is considerable uncertainty about each of these steps (Upton et al. 1989).

Scientists and officials focus on problems such as inadequate history of the site,

the unclarity of the route of contaminants, determining appropriate water sampling locations, small numbers of cases, bias in self-reporting of symptoms, getting appropriate control groups, lack of knowledge about characteristics and effects of certain chemicals, and unknown latency periods for carcinogens (Condon 1991; Knorr 1991). Epidemiologists are usually not choosing the research questions they think are amenable to study, based on clear hypotheses, firmer toxicological data, and adequate sample size. Rather, they are responding to a crisis situation, engaging in "reactive epidemiology" (Anderson 1985). Traditional approaches also tend to look askance at innovative perspectives favored by activists, such as the importance of genetic mutations, immune disregulation markers, and nonfatal and nonserious health effects (e.g., rashes, persistent respiratory problems) (Ozonoff and Boden 1987; Gute 1991).

For public health officials, disputes over toxic studies arise from shortcomings in knowledge about toxic waste-induced disease. A DPH official involved in Woburn for over a decade reflected on the vast changes in knowledge, personnel, and attitudes over that period. At first, public health researchers knew little about how to investigate clusters, environmental epidemiology was a new field, the state had few qualified scientists, and officials did not know how to involve the public. The DPH was trying out new approaches as they proceeded, without clear established protocols (Condon 1991).

Activists view scientists as too concerned with having each element of scientific study as perfect as possible. Residents believe that there have been visible health effects, clear evidence of contamination, and strong indications that these two are related. From their point of view, the officials and scientists are hindering a proper study, or are hiding incriminating knowledge.

Residents observe corporations denying that they have dumped toxic waste, or that substances have no health effects. When public health agencies find no adverse health effects, many people view them as supporting corporate polluters. While residents agree with officials that cluster studies and environmental health assessment are new areas, they believe the agencies should spend more effort on what residents consider crucial matters.

The level of statistical significance required for intervention is a frequent source of contention. Many communities that wish to document hazards and disease are stymied by insufficient numbers of cases to achieve statistical significance. Some professionals who work with community groups adhere to accepted significance levels (Lagakos et al. 1984), while others argue that such levels are as inappropriate to environmental risk as to other issues of public health, such as bomb threats and epidemics (Paigen 1982). Ozonoff and Boden (1987) distinguish statistical significance from public health significance, since an increased disease rate may be of great public health significance even if statistical probabilities are not met. They believe that epidemiology should mirror clinical medicine more than laboratory science by erring on the safe side of false positives.

Hill (1987) argues that even without statistical significance we may find a clear association based on strength of association; consistency across persons, places, circumstances, and time; specificity of the exposure site and population; temporality of the exposure and effect; biological plausibility of the effect; coherence with known facts of the agent and disease; and analogy to past experience with related substances. Pointing to the above, as well as to more "provable" experimental models and dose-response curves, Hill argues that there are no hard

and fast rules for establishing causality. Given the potential dangers of many classes of materials, he believes it often wise to restrict a substance to avoid potential danger.

Epidemiologists prefer false negatives to false positives, i.e., they would prefer to falsely claim no association between variables when there is one than to claim an association when there is none. This burden of proof usually exceeds the level required to argue for intervention. As Couto (1986) observes:

The degree of risk to human health does not need to be at statistically significant levels to require political action. The degree of risk does have to be such that a reasonable person would avoid it. Consequently, the important political test is not the findings of epidemiologists on the probability of nonrandomness of an incidence of illness but the likelihood that a reasonable person, including members of the community of calculation [epidemiologists], would take up residence with the community at risk and drink from and bathe in water from the Yellow Creek area or buy a house along Love Canal.

Indeed, these questions are presented to public health officials wherever there is dispute between the citizen and official perceptions. Beverly Paigen (1982), who worked with laypeople in Love Canal, makes clear that standards of evidence are value-laden:

Before Love Canal, I also needed a 95 percent certainty before I was convinced of a result. But seeing this rigorously applied in a situation where the consequences of an error meant that pregnancies were resulting in miscarriages, stillbirths, and children with medical problems, I realized I was making a value judgment…whether to make errors on the side of protecting human health or on the side of conserving state resources.

This dispute suggests the need for a more interactive approach to the *process* of scientific knowledge-making. Applying Latour's (1987) "science in action" framework, the real meaning of epidemiological "fact" cannot be seen until the epidemiologist experiences the citizenry and the problem being studied. Conversely, the public has no clear sense of what epidemiology can or cannot do for them until they or their neighbors are part of a study sample. In addition, both parties' perceptions and actions are jointly produced by their connections with other components, such as media, civic groups, and politicians. Latour's method tells us to ask of epidemiological research: For *whose* standards, and by what version of *proof* is a "standard of proof" determined and employed?

Institutional Constraints on Professional Knowledge and Action

Professional knowledge formation is affected by various institutional constraints. Professionals rarely view public initiatives as worthy of their attention. Laypeople have fewer scientific and financial resources than government and corporations (Paigen 1982). Without an ongoing relationship with the community, professionals enter only as consultants at a single point, and are unlikely to understand the larger framework of lay claims-making.

University-based scientists, a potential source of aid, frequently consider applied community research to be outside the regular academic reward structure (Couto 1986). Further, universities' increasing dependency on corporate and governmental support has made scholars less willing to challenge established authority (Goggin 1986). Grant support from federal agencies and private foundations is less likely to fund scholars who urge community participation

and who challenge scientific canons and government policy.

Scientists ally themselves with citizen efforts often because they see flaws in official responses. For challenging state authority, they are sometimes punished as whistleblowers. When Beverly Paigen, a biologist at the New York State Department of Health (DOH), aided Love Canal residents' health studies, she was harassed by her superiors. The DOH withdrew a grant application she had written, without even telling her, and refused to process an already funded grant. She was told that due to the "sensitive nature" of her work, all grants had to go through a special review process. Her professional mail was opened and taped shut, and her office was entered and searched at night. Paigen's state tax was audited, and she saw in her file a clipping about her Love Canal work. Later, the state tax commissioner wrote her and apologized. Two officials in the regional office of the Department of Environmental Conservation were demoted or transferred for raising questions about the state's investigation (Paigen 1982). Similar cases have been documented elsewhere (Freudenberg 1984a, p. 57).

Quality and Accessibility of Official Data

Massive complaints in Massachusetts about the state's response to lay concerns over excess cancer rates in 20 Massachusetts communities (including Woburn) led to state senate (Commonwealth of Massachusetts 1987) and university (Levy et al. 1986) investigations which found that the DPH studies were poorly conceived and methodologically weak. Most lacked a clear hypothesis, failed to mention potential exposure routes, and as a result rarely defined the geographic or temporal limits of the population at risk. Methods were presented erratically and inconsistently, case definitions were weak, environmental data were rarely presented, and statistical tests were inappropriately used (Levy et al. 1986). Frequently, exposed groups were diluted with unexposed individuals, and comparison groups were likely to include exposed individuals (Ozonoff and Boden 1987). This situation is striking, since the damaging effects of the poor studies and nonresponsiveness to the community led to the resignation of the public health commissioner, Bailus Walker, then head of the American Public Health Association (Clapp 1987).

State agencies are often unhelpful. A survey of all 50 states' responses to lay cancer cluster reports found that there were an estimated 1,300 to 1,650 such reports in 1988, clearly a large number for agencies already short-staffed. Many state health departments discouraged informants, in some cases requesting extensive data before they would go further. Rather than deal specifically with the complaint, many health departments gave a routine response emphasizing the lifestyle causes of cancer, the fact that one of three Americans will develop some form of cancer, and that clusters occur at random (Greenberg and Wartenberg 1991).

Officials may withhold information on the basis that it will alarm the public (Levine 1982), that the public does not understand risks, or that it will harm the business climate (Ozonoff and Boden 1987). Many scientists oppose public disclosure on the grounds that laypersons are unable to make rational decisions (Krimsky 1984). Often enough toxic activists are called "anti-scientific," when in fact they may simply work at science in a nontraditional manner. Indeed, toxic activists express support for scientists as important sources of knowledge (Freudenberg 1984b). FACE activists report that they have become highly informed about scientific matters, and are proud of it.

A cardinal assumption of science is that its truth and validity are affirmed by widespread recognition of the findings through open access to data among members of the scientific community. Yet the Massachusetts cases were not even shared with all appropriate scientists. Local health officials typically heard of elevated cancer rates through the media, rather than from state health officials. The EPA began a secret investigation of the Woburn data, leaving out researchers and Woburn residents who had already been involved in many investigations. Formed in 1984, the study group's existence was only discovered in 1988 (Kennedy 1988). In the EPA's view, there was no intent at secrecy, merely an internal "tell us what you think of this thing" (Newman 1991).

Professionalism, Controversy, and Information Control

It is particularly ironic that epidemiology excludes the public, since the original "shoe-leather" work that founded the field is quite similar to popular epidemiology. Woburn residents' efforts are very reminiscent of John Snow's classic study of cholera in London in 1854, where that doctor closed the Broad Street pump to cut off contaminated water. Yet modern epidemiology has come far from its original shoe-leather origins, turning into a laboratory science with no room for lay input.

The combination of epidemiologic uncertainty and the political aspects of toxic waste contamination leads to scientific controversy. According to Latour (1987, p. 132), rather than a "diffusion" of ready-made science, we must study how "translations" by many parties of undecided controversies lead to a consensual reality. From the point of view of traditional epidemiologists, citizens' translations get in the way of consensual production of science. Yet in fact, the scientific community is itself disunified on most issues of environmental epidemiology, and laypeople are partaking in the related consensual production.

In this struggle, citizens use controversy to demystify expertise and to transfer problems from the technical to the political arena (Nelkin 1985). This redefinition of the situation involves a lay approach to "cultural rationality" as opposed to the scientific establishment's "technical rationality" (Krimsky and Plough 1988). This is the form of struggle described earlier when residents ask officials whether they would live in and drink water from the contaminated community. We may also view gender differences as representative of differing rationalities. Women are the most frequent organizers of lay detection, partly because they are the chief health arrangers for their families, and partly because they are more concerned than men with local environmental issues (Levine 1982; Blocker and Eckberg 1989). From this perspective, women's cultural rationality is concerned with who would be willing to drink local water, and how their families experience daily life.

BAD SCIENCE, GOOD SCIENCE, POPULAR SCIENCE

One way to look at official support for lay involvement is to view it as simply "good politics," whereby the government provides a formal mechanism for citizen participation in such areas as Environmental Impact Statements and Recombinant DNA Advisory Panels. However, public participation was limited in these cases to minor roles on panels that already had an official agenda (Jasanoff 1986; Krimsky 1984).

But, as we observe in popular epidemiology, lay involvement is not merely "good politics." It is also "good science," since it changes the nature of scientific inquiry. This involves four elements which have been addressed throughout:

1. Lay involvement identifies the many cases of "bad science," e.g., poor studies, secret investigations, failure to inform local health officials.
2. Lay involvement points out that "normal science" has drawbacks, e.g., opposing lay participation in health surveys, demanding standards of proof that may be unobtainable or inappropriate, being slow to accept new concepts of toxic causality.
3. The combination of the above two points leads to a general public distrust of official science, thus pushing laypeople to seek alternate routes of information and analysis.
4. Popular epidemiology yields valuable data that often would be unavailable to scientists. If scientists and government fail to solicit such data, and especially if they consciously oppose and devalue it, then such data may be lost.

We see these four elements in many contaminated communities, but in Woburn the lay contribution to scientific endeavor has been exceptional. The Woburn case was the major impetus for the establishment of the state cancer registry (Clapp 1987). Activism has also contributed to increasing research on Woburn: The DPH and CDC are conducting a major five-year reproductive outcome study of the city, utilizing both prospective and retrospective data, and citizens have a large role in this process. The DPH is conducting a case-control study of leukemia, and an MIT study will study genetic mutations caused by trichloroethylene (TCE) to investigate their role in causing leukemia (Latowsky 1988).

Popular epidemiology can sway government opinion over time, especially when activists doggedly stick to their own work while constantly participating with official bodies. The since-retired DPH Commissioner who took office in 1988, Deborah Prothrow-Stith, asked for a more official relationship with FACE. On visiting Woburn, the commissioner said she was "struck with how epidemiology is dependent on the role the public plays in bringing these things to light" (Mades 1988). A DPH official in 1990, going over the chronology of events, noted that the FACE/Harvard School of Public Health study found positive associations between well water and adverse reproductive outcomes, a position the DPH avoided for the preceding 6 years since the study was published (Kruger 1990). Other officials now view the study as an important source of research questions and methods, which informs the ongoing official studies, as well as a prompt to government action. Indeed, they expect that the new studies may show evidence of adverse health effects (Condon 1991; Knorr 1991).

Popular epidemiologists also provide continuity in the scientific process. As a leading activist stated, "We have been the institutional memory of studies in Woburn. We have seen agency heads come and go. We have seen project directors come and go. Our role has been to bring those efforts together and to help the researchers investigate what was going on all throughout the area" (Latowsky 1990). To understand the significance of that position, we may observe that as late as 1990 an EPA Remedial Project Manager for the Woburn site could hear a question, "Is the leukemia cluster a cause for urgency of cleanup?" and respond that "Our investigation is not concerned

with the cluster of leukemia. It's really irrelevant. We're on a schedule based on our regulations" (Newman 1990).

Ozonoff (1988) sums up the Woburn impact:

> *In hazardous waste, three names come up— Love Canal, Times Beach, and Woburn. Woburn stands far and above them all in the amount of scientific knowledge produced. All over the country, Woburn has put its stamp on the science of hazardous waste studies.*

Of particular value is the discovery of a TCE syndrome involving three major body systems—immune, cardiovascular, and neurological—which is increasingly showing up in other TCE sites.

The leukemia reanalysis provided a form of closure to FACE's major public presence. As an organization, FACE has basically reverted back to a grassroots organization that meets in people's kitchens. Leaders are still called by the DPH to review materials, and other citizen groups call each week to seek advice, but FACE does not have the public presence it once did. Donna Robbins, one of the leaders, received an award from the Massachusetts Public Health Association in 1996 for her many years of hard work on the Woburn case. Gretchen Latowsky is called on to lecture very frequently on Woburn.

Even if Woburn activists are not still in the trenches, thousands of communities around the country are in the trenches, fighting similar battles. In many cases, they know of Woburn and are inspired by the efforts of the residents, their lawyers, and their supporters. The toxic waste movement has become a major force in American political culture. Arising from that, environmental justice activists have emphasized the inequalities of race and class in exposure to toxic hazards, in obtaining Superfund status, and in assessment of fines against polluters.

In 1995 Jonathan Harr published his book, *A Civil Action*, which became a bestseller. Anyone interested in the history of the Woburn cluster will find this book an exciting, well-written approach to the complex legal issues in the case, a good capture of many personalities, and a remarkable insight into the daily actions and feelings of Jan Schlictmann, the families' lawyer. A film version starring John Travolta opened in 1999, garnering much attention. It is quite amazing that a book and film of this sort should grab so much public attention. Apparently, there are an enormous number of people who sympathize with the plight of the Woburn families and of the plight of so many others in contaminated communities around the country.

How Do We Know If Lay Investigations Provide Correct Knowledge?

It is obviously necessary to evaluate the correctness of findings which result from popular epidemiology. Such knowledge is not "folk" knowledge with an antiscientific basis. In most cases, popular epidemiology findings are the result of scientific studies involving trained professionals, even if they begin as "lay mapping" of disease clusters without attention to base rates or controls. Indeed, lay-involved surveys are sometimes well-crafted researches with defendable data. Laypeople may initiate action, and even direct the formulation of hypotheses, but they work *with* scientists, not in place of them. Thus, the end results can be judged by the same criteria as any study. But since all scientific judgements involve social factors, there are no simple algorithms for ascertaining truth. Scientific inquiry is always full of controversy; what

is different here is that laypeople are entering that controversy.

Public health officials worry that some communities might exaggerate the risks of a hazard, or be wrong about the effects of a substance. Yet if this occurs, it must be seen in the context whereby community fears have too often been brushed aside and where data has been withheld. Given the increasing cases (or at least recognition of those cases) of technological disasters, drug side effects, and scientific fraud, public sentiment has become more critical of science. In response, lay claims may be erroneous. But this is the price paid for past failures and problems, and is a countervailing force in democratic participation (Piller 1991). Exaggerated fears may be understood as signs of the need to expand public health protection, rather than justifications to oppose lay involvement. Even if a community makes incorrect conclusions, their database may still remain useful for different analyses. As mentioned before, the DPH disagrees with the Harvard/FACE conclusions, yet they are now testing those same relationships in their own study.

CONCLUSION

Causes and Implications of Popular Epidemiology

Popular epidemiology stems from the legacy of health activism, growing public recognition of problems in science and technology, and the democratic upsurge regarding science policy. This paper has pointed to the difficulties communities face due to differing conceptions of risk, lack of resources, poor access to information, and unresponsive government. In popular epidemiology, as in other health-related movements, activism by those affected is necessary to make progress in health care and health policy. In this process there is a powerful reciprocal relationship between the social movement and new views of science. The striking awareness of new scientific knowledge, coupled with government and professional resistance to that knowledge, leads people to form social movement organizations to pursue their claims-making. In turn, the further development of social movement organizations leads to further challenges to scientific canons. The socially constructed approach of popular epidemiology is thus a result of both a social movement and a new scientific paradigm, with each continually reinforcing the other.

Dramatically increasing attention to environmental degradation may make it easier for many to accept causal linkages previously considered too novel. Further, this expanding attention and its related social movements lead to the identification of more disease clusters. This may lead to the reevaluation of problems of low base rates in light of how other sciences (e.g., physics, paleontology) conduct research on low base-rate phenomena. As well, growing numbers of similar cases containing small sample sizes and/or low base-rate phenomena may allow for more generalizability. These increasing cases also produce more anomalies, allowing for a paradigm shift.

Causal explanations from outside of science also play a role. Legal definitions of causality, developed in an expanding toxic tort repertoire, are initially determined by judicial interpretation of scientific testimony. Once constructed, they can take on a life of their own, directing public health agencies and scientists to adhere to scientific/legal definitions which may or may not completely accord with basic science. At the least, they set standards by which scientific investigations will be applied to social life, (e.g., court-ordered guidelines on claims for disease caused by asbestos, nuclear testing, DES).

Lay and professional approaches to knowledge and action on environmental health risks are structurally divergent, much as Freidson (1970) conceives of the inherent differences and conflicts between patient and physician. Yet, just as modern efforts from the side of both medicine and its clientele seek an alternate model, so too does popular epidemiology offer a new path. Popular epidemiology offers a bridge between the two perspectives, a bridge largely engineered and constructed by lay activists, yet one which potentially brings citizens and scientists together.

ACKNOWLEDGMENTS

The research for this paper was supported in part by funding from the Wayland Collegium of Brown University, the Brown University Small Grants Program, and by Biomedical Research Support Grant #5-27178 from the National Institutes of Health. Robert Gay, Martha Lang, and Beth Parkhurst were very helpful as research assistants. Elizabeth Cooksey and Carol Walker assisted by transcribing audiotapes. Peter Conrad, Stephen R. Couch, Ann Dill, Sheldon Krimsky, Donald Light, Alonzo Plough, and Irving K. Zola read earlier drafts and contributed valuable comments and ideas. Richard Clapp and Gretchen Latowsky have been very helpful in looking over material that has updated this article.

ENDNOTE

1. The researchers conducted extensive analyses to demonstrate that the data were not biased. They found no differences when they compared baseline rates of adverse health effects for West Woburn (never exposed to wells G and H water) and East Woburn (at a period prior to the opening of the wells). They examined transiency rates to test whether they were related to exposure and found them to be alike in both sectors.

Other tests ruled out various biases potentially attributable to the volunteer interviewers (Lagakos et al. 1984).

REFERENCES

Anderson, Henry A. 1985. "Evolution of Environmental Epidemiologic Risk Assessment." *Environmental Health Perspectives.* 62:389–92.

Aronowitz, Stanley. 1988. *Science as Power: Discourse and Ideology in Modern Society.* Minneapolis: University of Minnesota Press.

Brown, Phil. 1987. "Popular Epidemiology: Community Response to Toxic Waste-Induced Disease in Woburn, Massachusetts." *Science, Technology, and Human Values* 12:78–85.

Brown, Phil and Edwin J. Mikkelsen. 1990. *No Safe Place: Toxic Waste, Leukemia, and Community Action.* Berkeley: University of California Press.

Berman, Daniel. 1977. "Why Work Kills: A Brief History of Occupational Health and Safety in the United States." *International Journal of Health Services* 7:63–87.

Blocker, T. Jean and Douglas Lee Eckberg. 1989. "Environmental Issues as Women's Issues: General Concerns and Local Hazards." *Social Science Quarterly.* 70:586–593.

Clapp, Richard. 1987. Interview, March 14.

Commonwealth of Massachusetts. 1987. "Cancer Case Reporting and Surveillance in Massachusetts." Senate Committee on Post Audit and Oversight. Boston, Massachusetts, September 1987.

Condon, Susanne. 1991. Interview, August 7.

Couto, Richard A. 1985. "Failing Health and New Prescriptions: Community-Based Approaches to Environmental Risks." Pp. 53–70 in Carole E. Hill, ed., *Current Health Policy Issues and Alternatives: An Applied Social Science Perspective.* Athens: University of Georgia Press.

Cutler, John J., Gerald S. Parker, Sharon Rosen, Brad Prenney, Richard Healy, and Glyn G. Caldwell. 1986. "Childhood Leukemia in Woburn, Massachusetts." *Public Health Reports* 101:201–05.

Dickson, David. 1984. *The New Politics of Science.* New York: Pantheon.

DiPerna, Paula. 1985. *Cluster Mystery: Epidemic and the Children of Woburn, Mass.* St. Louis: Mosby.

Edelstein, Michael. 1988. *Contaminated Communities: The Social and Psychological Impacts of Residential Toxic Exposure.* Boulder, CO: Westview.

Epstein, Samuel S., Lester O. Brown, and Carl Pope. 1982. *Hazardous Waste in America.* San Francisco: Sierra Club Books.

Fisher, Sue. 1986. *In the Patient's Best Interests.* New Brunswick, NJ: Rutgers University Press.

Freidson, Elliot. 1970. *Profession of Medicine.* New York: Dodd, Mead.

Freudenberg, Nicholas. 1984a. *Not in Our Backyards: Community Action for Health and the Environment.* New York: Monthly Review.

———. 1984b. "Citizen Action for Environmental Health: Report on a Survey of Community Organizations." *American Journal of Public Health,* 74:444–448.

Gibbs, Lois Marie. 1982. "Community Response to an Emergency Situation: Psychological Destruction and the Love Canal." Paper presented at the American Psychological Association, August 24.

Goggin, Malcolm L. 1986. "Introduction. Governing Science and Technology Democratically: A Conceptual Framework." Pp. 3–31 in Malcolm L. Goggin, ed., *Governing Science and Technology in a Democracy.* Knoxville: University of Tennessee Press.

Greenberg, Michael and Daniel Wartenberg. 1991. "Communicating to an Alarmed Community about Cancer Clusters: A Fifty State Study." *Journal of Community Health,* 16:71–82.

Gusfield, Joseph R. 1981. *The Culture of Public Problems.* Chicago: University of Chicago Press.

Gute, David. 1991. Interview, August 14.

Hill, Austin Bradford. 1987. "The Environment and Disease: Association or Causation." Pp. 15–20 in Kenneth Rothman, ed., *Evolution of Epidmiologic Ideas.* Chestnut Hill, MA: Epidemiology Resources, Inc.

Jasanoff, Sheila. 1986. "The Misrule of Law at OSHA." Pp. 155–178 in Dorothy Nelkin, ed.

The Language of Risk: Conflicting Perspectives on Occupational Health. Beverly Hills: Sage.

Kennedy, Dan. 1988. "EPA to Say Pollutants Caused Leukemia." *Woburn Daily Times,* May 9.

Kleinman, Arthur. 1980. *Patients and Healers in the Context of Culture.* Berkeley: University of California.

Knorr, Robert. 1991. Interview, August 7.

Krauss, Celene. 1989. "Community Struggles and the Shaping of Democratic Consciousness." *Sociological Forum* 4:227–39

Krimsky, Sheldon. 1984. "Beyond Technocracy: New Routes for Citizen Involvement in Social Risk Assessment." Pp. 43–61 in James C. Peterson, ed., *Citizen Participation in Science Policy.* Amherst: University of Massachusetts Press.

Krimsky, Sheldon and Alonzo Plough. 1988. *Environmental Hazards: Communicating Risks as a Social Process.* Boston: Auburn House.

Kruger, Elaine. 1990. "Environmental Exposure Assessment and Occurrence of Adverse Reproductive Outcomes in Woburn, Mass." Presentation at conference, Investigations in the Aberjona River Watershed. Woburn, Massachusetts. May 18.

Lagakos, Steven. 1987. Interview, April 6.

Lagakos, Steven W., Barbara J. Wessen, and Marvin Zelen. 1984. "An Analysis of Contaminated Well Water and Health Effects in Woburn, Massachusetts." *Journal of the American Statistical Association* 81:583–596.

Latour, Bruno. 1987. *Science in Action: How to Follow Scientists and Engineers through Society.* Cambridge: Harvard University Press.

Latowsky, Gretchen. 1988. Interview, May 26.

———. 1990. "FACE's Role in the Community." Presentation at conference, Investigations in the Aberjona River Watershed. Woburn, Massachusetts. May 18.

Levine, Adeline Gordon. 1982. *Love Canal: Science, Politics, and People.* Lexington, MA: Heath.

Levy, Barry S., David Kriebel, Peter Gann, Jay Himmelstein, and Glenn Pransky. 1986. "Improving the Conduct of Environmental Epidemiology Studies." Worcester, MA: University of Massachusetts Medical School,

Department of Family and Community Medicine, Occupational Health Program.

Lilienfeld, Abraham. 1980. *Foundations of Epidemiology.* (Second edition). New York: Oxford.

Mades, Nancy. 1988. "Commissioner Wants FACE-DPH Pact," *Woburn Daily Times,* April 7.

Nash, June and Max Kirsch. 1986. "Polychlorinated Biphenyls in the Electrical Machinery Industry: An Ethnological Study of Community Action and Corporate Responsibility." *Social Science and Medicine* 23:131–138.

Nelkin, Dorothy, ed. 1985. *The Language of Risk: Conflicting Perspectives in Occupational Health.* Beverly Hills: Sage.

Neuffer, Elizabeth. 1988. "Court Orders New Hearings in Woburn Pollution Case." *Boston Globe,* December 8.

Newman, Barbara. 1990. "Investigations and Remediation at the Wells G and H Site." Presentation at conference, Investigations in the Aberjona River Watershed. Woburn, Massachusetts. May 18.

Newman, Barbara. 1991. Interview, September 6.

Ozonoff, David. 1988. Presentation at conference, "Examining Woburn's Health." April 24. Trinity Episcopal Church, Woburn, Massachusetts.

Ozonoff, David and Leslie I. Boden. 1987. "Truth and Consequences: Health Agency Responses to Environmental Health Problems." *Science, Technology, and Human Values* 12:70–77.

Paigen, Beverly. 1982. "Controversy at Love Canal." *Hastings Center Report,* 12(3):29–37.

Parker, Gerald and Sharon Rosen. 1981. "Woburn: Cancer Incidence and Environmental Hazards." Massachusetts Department of Public Health, January 23.

Piller, Charles. 1991. *The Fail-Safe Society: Community Defiance and the End of American Technological Optimism.* New York: Basic.

Rodriguez-Trias, Helen. 1984. "The Women's Health Movement: Women Take Power." Pp. 107–126 in Victor Sidel and Ruth Sidel, eds., *Reforming Medicine: Lessons of the Last Quarter Century.* New York: Pantheon.

Roth, Julius. 1963. *Timetables.* Indianapolis: Bobbs-Merrill.

Rothman, Barbara Katz. 1986. *The Tentative Pregnancy: Prenatal Diagnosis and the Future of Motherhood.* New York: Viking.

Rubin, James H. 1987. "Justices Limit Right of Citizens to Sue on Water Pollution Violations." *New York Times,* December 2.

Schlictmann, Jan. 1987. Interview, May 12.

Scott, Wilbur J. 1988. "Competing Paradigms in the Assessment of Latent Disorders: The Case of Agent Orange." *Social Problems* 35: 145–161.

Smith, Barbara Ellen. 1981. "Black Lung: The Social Production of Disease." *International Journal of Health Services* 11:343–359.

Stimson, Gerry V. and Barbara Webb. 1975. *Going to See the Doctor.* London: Routledge.

Strauss, Anselm, Leonard Schatzman, Rue Bucher, Danuta Ehrlich, and Melvin Sabshin. 1964. *Psychiatric Ideologies and Institutions.* New York: Free Press.

Upton, Arthur C., Theodore Kneip, and Paolo Toniolo. 1989. "Public Health Aspects of Toxic Chemical Disposal Sites." *Annual Review of Public Health* 10:1–25.

Waitzkin, Howard. 1983. *The Second Sickness: Contradictions of Capitalist Health Care.* New York: Macmillan.

———. 1989. "A Critique of Medical Discourse: Ideology, Social Control, and the Processing of Social Context in Medical Encounters." *Journal of Health and Social Behavior* 30:220–239.

Zelen, Marvin. 1987. Interview, July 1.

Zola, Irving K. 1973. "Pathways to the Doctor—From Person to Patient." *Social Science and Medicine* 7:677–689.

18.   Science for the Post-Normal Age*

SILVIO O. FUNTOWICZ AND JEROME R. RAVETZ

Science always evolves, responding to its leading challenges as they change through history. After centuries of triumph and optimism, science is now called on to remedy the pathologies of the global industrial system of which it forms the basis. Whereas science was previously understood as steadily advancing in the certainty of our knowledge and control of the natural world, now science is seen as coping with many uncertainties in policy issues of risk and the environment. In response, new styles of scientific activity are being developed. The reductionist, analytical worldview which divides systems into ever smaller elements, studied by ever more esoteric specialism, is being replaced by a systemic, synthetic and humanistic approach. The old dichotomies of facts and values, and of knowledge and ignorance, are being transcended. Natural systems are recognized as dynamic and complex; those involving interactions with humanity are 'emergent', including properties of reflection and contradiction. The science appropriate to this new condition will be based on the assumptions of unpredictability, incomplete control, and a plurality of legitimate perspectives.

*Reprinted from *Futures* 25, "Science for the Post-Normal Age," by Silvio O. Funtowicz and Jerome R. Ravetz, 1993, with permission from Elsevier Science.

At present, there is no agreed description of what the future will bring, but there is a general sense that much of our intellectual inheritance now lies firmly in the past. 'Post-modern' is widely used as a term for describing contemporary cultural phenomena;[1] it refers to an approach of unrestrained criticism of the assumptions underlying our dominant culture, and it flirts with nihilism and despair. In contrast to this, here we introduce the term 'post-normal'. This has an echo of the seminal work on modern science by Kuhn.[2] For him, 'normal science' referred to the unexciting, indeed anti-intellectual routine puzzle solving by which science advances steadily between its conceptual revolutions. In this 'normal' state of science, uncertainties are managed automatically, values are unspoken, and foundational problems unheard of. The post-modern phenomenon can be seen in one sense as a response to the collapse of such 'normality' as the norm for science and culture. As an alternative to post-modernity, we show that a new, enriched awareness of the functions and methods of science is being developed. In this sense, the appropriate science for this epoch is 'post-normal'.

This emerging science fosters a new methodology that helps to guide its development. In this, uncertainty is not banished but is managed, and values are not presupposed but are made explicit. The model for scientific argument is not a formalized deduction but an interactive dialogue. The paradigmatic science is no longer one in which location (in place and time) and process are irrelevant to explanations. The historical dimension, including reflection on humanity's past and future, is becoming an integral part of a scientific characterization of Nature.

Our contribution to this new methodology focuses on two aspects. One is the quality of scientific information, analysed in terms of both the different types of uncertainty in knowledge and the intended functions of the information. It has hitherto been a well kept secret that scientific 'facts' can be of variable quality; and an informed awareness of this human face of science is a key to its enrichment for its future tasks. Our other contribution relates to problem-solving strategies, analysed in terms of uncertainties in knowledge and complexities in ethics. When science is applied to policy issues, it cannot provide certainty for policy recommendations; and the conflicting values in any decision process cannot be ignored even in the problem-solving work itself. For quality of information, we have developed a transparent system of notations (NUSAP) whereby the different types of uncertainty that affect scientific information can be expressed. It can thereby be communicated in a concise, clear and nuanced way, among traditional and extended peer communities alike. The NUSAP approach embodies the principle that uncertainty cannot be banished from science; but that good quality of information depends on good management of its uncertainties.[3]

We use the interaction of systems uncertainties and decision stakes to provide guidance for the choice of appropriate problem-solving strategies. The heuristic tool is a set of graphical displays of three related strategies, from the most narrowly defined to the most comprehensive. Two of them are familiar from past experience of scientific or professional practice; the last, where systems uncertainties or decision stakes are high, corresponds to the practice of the sciences of the post-normal epoch.[4] One way of distinguishing among the different sorts of research is by their goals: applied science is 'mission-oriented'; professional consultancy is 'client-serving'; and post-normal science is 'issue-driven'. These three can be contrasted with core science—the traditional 'pure' or 'basic' research—which is 'curiosity-motivated'. In the area of post-normal science the problems of quality assurance of scientific information are particularly acute, and their resolution requires new conceptions of scientific methodology.

In this new sort of science, the evaluation of scientific inputs to decision making requires an 'extended peer community'.[5] This extension of legitimacy to new participants in policy dialogues has important implications both for society and for science. With mutual respect among various perspectives and forms of knowing, there is a possibility for the development of a genuine and effective democratic element in the life of science. The new challenges for science can then become the successors of the earlier great 'conquests', as of disease and then of space, in providing symbolic meaning and a renewed sense of adventure for a new generation of recruits to science in the future.

REINVASION OF THE LABORATORY BY NATURE

The place of science in the industrialized world was well depicted by Bruno Latour,[6] when he imagined Pasteur as extending his laboratory to all the French countryside, and thereby conquering it for science and for himself. In this vision, Nature itself no longer needs to be approached as wild and threatening, but through the methodology of science it can be tamed and rendered useful to mankind. The miracle of modern natural science is that the laboratory experience, the study of an isolated piece of Nature that is kept unnaturally pure, stable and reproducible, can be successfully extended to the understanding and control of Nature in the raw. Our technology and medicine together have made Nature predictable and in part controllable, and they have thereby enabled many people to enjoy a safer, more comfortable and pleasant life than was ever before imagined in our history. The obverse side of this achievement is that it may well be unsustainable, not merely in terms of equity, but even in terms of sheer survival.

The triumph of the scientific method, deploying the technically esoteric knowledge of its experts, has led to its domination over all other ways of knowing; this applies to our knowledge of Nature, and of much else besides. Commonsense experience and inherited skills of making and living have lost their claim to authority; they have been displaced by the theoretically constructed objects of scientific discourse, which are necessary for dealing with invisible things such as microbes, atoms, genes and quasars. Although formally democratic (since there are now no formal barriers to the training for that expertise), science is in fact a preserve of those who can engage on a prolonged and protected course of education, and thereby of the social groups to which they belong. In a tradition stemming from the Enlightenment of the 18th century, the rationality of public decision making must appear to be scientific. Hence intellectuals with a scientific style (including economists *par excellence*) have come to be seen as leading authorities, indeed the possessors and

purveyors of practical wisdom. There has been a universal assumption (however superficial and laced with cynicism) that scientific expertise is the crucial component of decision making, whether concerning Nature or society.

Now the very powers that science has created have led to a new relationship of science with the world. The extension of the laboratory has gone beyond the small-scale intervention typified by Pasteur's conquest of anthrax. We do not merely observe the familiar gross disturbances of the natural environment resulting from modern industrial and agricultural practices. The methodology for coping successfully with these novel problems cannot be the same as the one that helped to create them. Much of the success of traditional science lay in its power to abstract from uncertainty in knowledge and values; this is shown in the dominant teaching tradition in science, which created a universe of unquestionable facts, presented dogmatically for assimilation by uncritical students. Now scientific expertise has led us into policy dilemmas which it is incapable of resolving by itself. We have not merely lost control and even predictability; now we face radical uncertainty and even ignorance, as well as ethical uncertainties lying at the heart of scientific policy issues.

For understanding the new tasks and methods of science, we can fruitfully invert Latour's metaphor, and think of Nature as re-invading the lab. We see this in many ways; for example, our science-based technology, which for a while appeared to be a new man-made Nature dominant over the old, is now appreciated as critically dependent on the larger ecosystem in which it is embedded; and that it risks destruction of itself if that matrix becomes seriously perturbed or degraded. Similarly, the extension of modern technology to all humanity, essential if equity between peoples is to be realized under the present system, would accelerate the self-destructive tendencies of the technological system itself. Thus Nature reasserts itself on all our scientific planning, for the technical and human perspectives alike.

There have been other episodes in history when science has been transformed, when a particularly successful problem-solving activity has displaced older forms and become the paradigmatic example of science. These transformations have been identified with the names of such great scientists as Galileo, Darwin and Einstein. They have mainly affected theoretical science, because until quite recently technology and medicine were not generally influenced in the short term by the results of scientific research. The challenges to science were largely in the realm of ideas. Now, as the powers of science have given rise to threats to the very survival of humanity, the response will be in the social practice of science as much as in its intellectual structures.

CENTRALITY OF UNCERTAINTY AND QUALITY

Now that the policy issues of risk and the environment present the most urgent problems for science, uncertainty and quality are moving in from the periphery, one might say the shadows, of scientific methodology, to become the central, integrating concepts. Hitherto they have been kept at the margin of the understanding of science, for laypersons and scientists alike. A new role for scientists will involve the management of these crucial uncertainties; therein lies the task of quality assurance of the scientific information provided for policy decisions.

These new policy issues have common features that distinguish them from traditional scientific problems. They are universal in their scale and long-term in their impact. Data on their effects, and even data for baselines of 'undisturbed' systems, are radically inadequate. The phenomena, being novel, complex and variable, are themselves not well understood. Science cannot always provide well founded theories based on experiments for explanation and prediction, but can frequently achieve at best only mathematical models and computer simulations, which are essentially untestable. On the basis of such uncertain inputs, decisions must be made, under conditions of some urgency. Therefore policy cannot proceed on the basis of factual predictions, but only on policy forecasts.

Computer models are the most widely used method for producing statements about the future based on data of the past and present. For many, there is still a magical quality about computers, since they are believed to perform reasoning operations faultlessly and rapidly. But what comes out at the end of a program is not necessarily a scientific prediction; and it may not even be a particularly good policy forecast. The numerical data used for inputs may not derive from experimental or field-studies; the best numbers available, as in many studies of industrial risk, may simply be guesses collected from experts. Instead of theories which give some deeper representation of the natural processes in question, there may simply be standard software packages applied with the best fitting numerical parameters. And instead of experimental, field or historical evidence, as is normally assumed for scientific theories, there may be only the comparison of calculated outputs with those produced by other equally untestable computer models.

Despite the enormous effort and resources that have gone into developing and applying such methods, there has been little concerted attempt to see whether they contribute significantly either to knowledge or to policy. In research related to policy for risk and the environment, which is so crucial for our well being, there has been little effort of quality assurance of the sort that the traditional experimental sciences take for granted in their ordinary practice. Whereas computers could in principle be used to enhance human skill and creativity by doing all the routine work swiftly and effortlessly, they have instead in many cases become substitutes for disciplined thought and scientific rigour.[7]

Even when there is empirical data for policy problems, it is not really amenable to treatment by traditional statistical techniques. As J. C. Bailar puts it:

> *All the statistical algebra and all the statistical computations are of value only to the extent that they add to the process of inference. Often they do not aid in making sound inferences; indeed they may work the other way, and in my experience that is because the kinds of random variability we see in the big problems of the day tend to be small relative to other uncertainties. This is true, for example, for data on poverty or unemployment; international trade; agricultural production; and basic measures of human health and survival. Closer to home, random variability—the stuff of p-values and confidence limits, is simply swamped by other kinds of uncertainties in assessing the health risks of chemicals exposures, or tracking the movement of an environmental contaminant, or predicting the effects of human activities on global temperature or the ozone layer.[8]*

Thus, by traditional criteria of scientific method, the quality of research on these policy-related problems is dubious at best. The tasks of uncertainty management and quality assurance, managed in traditional science by individual skill and communal practice, are left in confusion in this new area. New methods must be developed for making our ignorance usable.[9] For this there must be a radical departure from the total reliance on techniques, to the exclusion of methodological, societal or ethical considerations, that has hitherto characterized traditional 'normal' science.

An integrated approach to the problems of uncertainty, quality and values has been provided by the NUSAP system. In its terms, different kinds of uncertainty can be expressed, and used for an evaluation of quality of scientific information. We have to distinguish among the technical, methodological and epistemological levels of uncertainty; these correspond to inexactness, unreliability and 'border with ignorance', respectively.[10] Uncertainty is managed at the technical level when standard routines are adequate; these will usually be derived from statistics (which themselves are essentially symbolic manipulations) as supplemented by techniques and conventions developed for particular fields. The methodological level is involved when more complex aspects of the information, as values or reliability, are relevant. Then, personal judgments depending on higher-level skills are required; and the practice in question is a professional consultancy, a 'learned art' like medicine or engineering. Finally, the epistemological level is involved when irremediable uncertainty is at the core of the problem, as when computer modellers recognize 'completeness uncertainties' which can vitiate the whole exercise, or more generally in post-normal science. In NUSAP these levels of uncertainty are conveyed by the categories of spread, assessment and pedigree, respectively.

Quality assurance is as essential to science as it is to industry; and whereas in traditional research science it could be managed informally by a peer community, in the new policy issues of risk and the environment, quality of science must be addressed as a matter of urgency. The inadequacy of traditional peer review has been extensively analysed for the different areas of core science,[11] 'mandated' science,[12] and 'regulatory' science.[13] As we see, the evaluation of quality in this new context of science cannot be restricted to products of research; it must also include process and persons, and in the last resort purposes as well. This 'p-fourth' approach to quality assurance of science necessarily involves the participation of people other than the technically qualified researchers; indeed, all the stakeholders in an issue form an 'extended peer community' for an effective problem-solving strategy for global environmental risks.

PROBLEM-SOLVING STRATEGIES

To characterize an issue involving risk and the environment, in what we call 'post-normal science', we can think of it as one where facts are uncertain, values in dispute, stakes high and decisions urgent. In such a case, the term 'problem', with its connotations of an exercise where a defined methodology is likely to lead to a clear solution, is less appropriate. We would be misled if we retained the image of a process where true scientific facts simply determine the correct policy conclusions. However, the new challenges do not render traditional science irrelevant; the task is to choose the appropriate kinds of problem-solving strategies for each particular case.

Figure 8.1 involves three distinctive features. First (and this is an innovation for scientific methodology), it shows the interaction of the epistemic (knowledge) and axiological (values) aspects of scientific problems. These are depicted as the axes of the figure, representing the intensity of uncertainty and of decision stakes, respec-

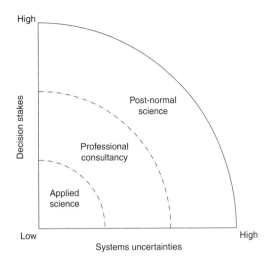

FIGURE 8.1   Problem-solving strategies

tively. We notice that uncertainty and decision stakes are the opposites of attributes which had traditionally been thought to characterize science, namely its certainty and its value neutrality (this is the second innovative feature of our analysis). Finally, the two dimensions are themselves both displayed as comprising three discrete intervals. By this means, we achieve a diagram which has three zones representing and characterizing three kinds of problem-solving strategies.

The term 'systems uncertainties' conveys the principle that the problem is concerned not with the discovery of a particular fact, but with the comprehension or management of an inherently complex reality. By 'decision stakes' we understand all the various costs, benefits, and value commitments that are involved in the issue through the various stakeholders. It is not necessary for us to attempt now to make a detailed map of these as they arise in the technical and social aspects of dialogue on any particular policy issue. It is enough for the present conceptual analysis, that it is possible in principle to identify which elements are the leading or dominant ones, and then to characterize the total systems by them.

APPLIED SCIENCE

The explanation of the diagram of problem-solving strategies starts with the most familiar strategy. We call this applied science. This is involved when both systems uncertainties and decisions stakes are low. The systems uncertainties will be at the technical level, and will be managed by standard routines and procedures. These will include particular techniques to keep instruments operating reliably, and also statistical tools and packages for the treatment of data. The decision stakes will be simple as well as small; resources have been put into the research exercise because there is some particular straightforward external function for its results. The resulting information will be used in a larger enterprise, which is of no concern to the researcher on the job. We illustrate this in Figure 8.2.

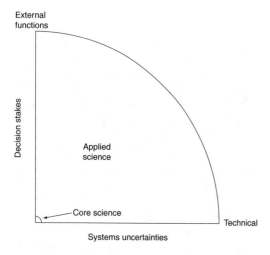

FIGURE 8.2   Applied science

In Figure 8.2, traditional 'pure', 'basic' or 'core' science can be considered as concentrated around the intersection of the axes. By definition, there are no external interests at stake in curiosity-motivated research, so decision stakes are low. Also the research exercise is generally not undertaken unless there is confidence that the uncertainties are low, that is that the problem is likely to be soluble by a normal, puzzle-solving approach. Clearly, highly innovative or revolutionary research, either pure or applied, does not lie within this category, since the systems uncertainties are inherently high, and for various reasons the decision stakes are also. Thus Galileo's astronomical researches involved the whole range of issues from astronomical technique to religious orthodoxy; so even though it was not directly applicable to industrial or environmental problems, it was definitely extreme both in its uncertainties and its decision stakes. The same could be said of Darwin's work in *The Origin of Species*. In this respect there is a continuity between the classic 'philosophy of nature' and the post-normal science that is now emerging.

We can usefully compare core science and applied science in relation to quality assurance. Where both uncertainties and external decision stakes are both low, the traditional processes of peer review of projects and refereeing of papers have worked well enough despite their known problems. However, when the results of the research exercise become important for some external function, the relevant peer community is extended beyond one particular research community, to include users of all sorts, and also managers. The situation in quality assessment becomes more like that of manufacturers and consumers, bringing different agendas and different skills to the market. For an example of how criteria of quality can differ between producers and consumers, we may consider product safety; a rare accident may be less significant to manufacturers (especially if product liability laws are lax) than for consumers. In the case of applied science, a result validly produced under one set of conditions may be inappropriate when applied to others; thus if measurements of a toxicant are given as an average over time, space or exposed populations, that may be adequate for general regulatory purposes, but that set-up could ignore damaging peak concentrations or harm to susceptible groups.

It frequently happens that the results of an applied science project are not 'public knowledge', freely available to all competent users, but rather are 'corporate know-how', the 'intellectual property' of the private business or state agency that sponsors the research exercise. If the information is relevant to some policy issue, the tasks of quality assurance may become controversial, involving conflicts over confidentiality; and the decision stakes may be raised over that non-scientific aspect. Then, the actual problem-solving strategy is no longer applied science, for the issue may involve struggles over administrative and political power, and constitutional principles of 'right to know' of citizens (for example, concerning environmental hazards or technological risks). The relevant peer community is thus extended beyond the direct producers, sponsors and users of the research, to include all with a stake in the product, the process, and its implications both local and global. This extension of the peer community may include investigative journalists, lawyers and pressure groups. Thus a problem which may appear totally straightforward scientifically can become one which transcends the boundaries of applied science, giving rise to a more complex prob-lem-solving strategy, such as 'post-normal science'. When scientists with a traditionalist outlook bemoan the bad influence of 'the media,' it is sometimes because of their difficulty in comprehending this new feature of science when it is involved in policy.

PROFESSIONAL CONSULTANCY

The diagram for professional consultancy (Figure 8.3) has two zones, with applied science nested inside. This signifies that professional consultancy includes applied science, but that it deals with problems which require a different methodology for their complete resolution. Uncertainty cannot be managed at the routine, technical level, because more complex aspects of the problem, such as reliability of theories and information, are relevant. Then, personal judgments depending on higher level skills are required, and uncertainty is at the methodological level.

The decision stakes are also more complex. Traditionally, the professional task is performed for a client, whose purposes are

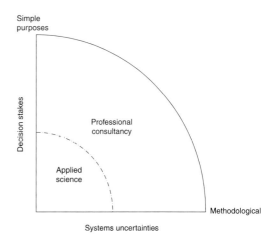

FIGURE 8.3 Professional consultancy

to be served. These cannot be reduced to a clear, perfectly defined goal, for humans are not machines or bureaucracies, and are conscious of their own purposes. In the case of risk and environmental policy issues, the professionals may experience a tension between their traditional role and new demands. For the purposes relevant to the task are no longer the simple ones of clients, but will be in conflict, involving various human stakeholders and natural systems as well.

The relation between systems uncertainties and decision stakes are well illustrated by the task of incorporation of error-costs in a decision. For exercises in applied science, these are generally subsumed implicitly in standard statistical methods. Confidence limits, and bounds for the two types of inference-errors, are normally employed at pre-set constant values, without reflection. But in professional tasks, error-costs may be so large as to endanger the continuation of a career. Hence they must be treated as risks, where some calculation may be employed but where judgment will necessarily predominate. When in a forensic situation, the professional will need to take account of the burden of proof for the particular problem, which will reflect the values of a particular society (whose harm is the more important to be prevented?). The same consideration holds for any policy issue; thus a problem of environmental pollution will be handled differently depending on whether a process is deemed safe until proved dangerous, or *vice versa*. Alternatively, we might ask whether absence of evidence of harm is interpreted as evidence of absence of harm. Although such methodological issues are quite beyond the ken of applied science, in professional consultancy they strongly condition all the work; and the simple descriptions as given here do not encompass the subtleties of burden of proof as it is used in practice.

Professional consultancy shares many features with applied science, distinguishing them both from core science. Both operate under constraints of time and resources, with projects funded and mandated by external interests; and their products frequently lie outside the 'public knowledge' domain. For much of the time professional tasks can be reduced to routine exercises, as the work becomes standardized in its technique and in the management of uncertainty. But professional consultancy involves the readiness to grapple with new and unexpected situations, and to bear the responsibility for their outcome. Engineering is on the border between the two, for most engineering work is done within organizations rather than for individual clients; and yet the problems cannot be completely reduced to a routine, so that 'engineering judgment' is a well known aspect of the work. Of engineering we could say that most routine engineering practice is a matter of empirical craft skills using the results of applied science, while at its highest levels it becomes true professional consultancy.

A contrasting intermediate case is that of the role of the 'expert'. This is normally someone who advises, but whose responsibility is defined by his position as an employee; hence it is not the client's interest that defines his role but that of his employer. In that respect, his decision stakes are simpler than those of the professional consultant, and the systems uncertainties as he sees them are correspondingly reduced. It is possible for a single individual to occupy these three roles, alternately or even (to some extent) simultaneously, giving rise to confusion among his audiences or perhaps even for himself! An academic researcher may give advice on a policy-related issue; his prestige and legitimacy derive from his reputation in research, either in core science or applied science; he assumes the authority of the professional consultant when offering his judgments; and if his research is too closely controlled by some funding organization, then in fact he might be acting as an expert on their behalf. This is why the possibility of 'conflict of interest' is raised when scientists make public pronouncements, without anyone impugning their personal integrity as perceived by themselves.

As a problem-solving strategy, professional consultancy has important differences from applied science. The outcomes of applied science exercises, like those of core science, have the features of reproducibility and prediction. That is, any experiment should in principle be capable of being reproduced anywhere by any competent practitioner, for they operate on isolated, controlled natural systems. Therefore the results amount to predictions of the future behaviour of natural or technical systems under similar conditions. By contrast, professional tasks deal with unique situations, however broadly similar they may be. The personal element becomes correspondingly important; thus it is legitimate to call for a second opinion without questioning the competence or integrity of a doctor in a medical case. Alternatively, who would expect two architects to produce identical designs for a single brief? In the same way, it would be unrealistic to expect two safety engineers to produce the same model (or the same conclusions) for a hazard analysis of a complex installation. The public may become confused or disillusioned at the sight of scientists disagreeing strongly on a problem apparently involving only applied science (and the scientists may themselves be confused!). But when it is appreciated that these policy issues involve professional consultancy, such disagreements should be seen as inevitable and healthy. The gain in clarity should more than compensate for the loss of mystique of scientific infallibility.

This last phenomenon reminds us of the differences in quality assurance that emerge when we extend from applied science to professional consultancy. We can envisage four components in the problem-solving task; the process, the product, the person and the purpose. This is the 'p-fourth' approach to quality assurance mentioned above. In core science, the main focus in the task of quality assessment is on the process; the assessment is made on the basis of the research report, and it requires a community of subject-specialism peers (who can 'read between the lines' of the research report) for its performance. In applied science, the focus of assessment extends to products, and is done by users, for it is on their behalf that the research exercises are done. Quality assurance is then not so esoteric, since the users have less need to understand the research process; and thus there is an automatic extension of the community with a legitimate participation in evaluation. In professional consultancy there can be no simple, objective criteria or processes for quality assurance (beyond simple competence). The clients become an important part of the community that assesses quality of work, although they have no relevant technical expertise. Thus in these three cases, we see an expansion of the 'peer community' involved in quality assurance. In this respect, the 'extended peer community' of post-normal science is a natural continuation of this tendency.

POST-NORMAL SCIENCE

We now consider the third sort of problem-solving strategy, where systems uncertainties or decision stakes are high (Figure 8.4).

The policy issues that drive post-normal science may include a large scientific component in their description, sometimes even to the point of being capable of expression

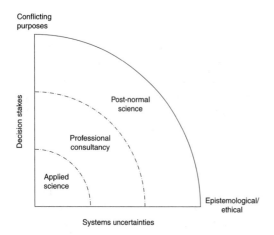

FIGURE 8.4   Post-normal science

in scientific language. In this sense they are analogous to the 'trans-science' problems first announced by Alvin Weinberg.[14] But it seems best to distinguish the problems analysed here from that earlier class; for Weinberg imagined problems that differed only in scale or technical feasibility from those of applied science. They were scarcely different from those of professional consultancy as we define it.[15] In the terms of our diagram, post-normal science occurs when uncertainties are either of the epistemological or the ethical kind, or when decision stakes reflect conflicting purposes among stakeholders. We call it 'post-normal' to indicate that the puzzle-solving exercises of normal science (in the Kuhnian sense) which were so successfully extended from the laboratory to the conquest of Nature, are no longer appropriate for the resolution of policy issues of risks and the environment. We notice that in Figures 8.2–4, applied science appears three times and professional consultancy twice. Do these labels refer to the same things when they are included in a broader problem-solving strategy as when they are standing alone? In the sense of

their routine practice, yes. But when they are embedded in a broader problem-solving strategy the whole activity is reinterpreted. The problems are set and the solutions evaluated by the criteria of the broader communities. Thus post-normal science is indeed a type of science, and not merely politics or public participation. However different from the varieties of problem solving that have now become entrenched and traditional, it is a valid form of enquiry, appropriate to the needs of the present.

Examples of problems with combined high decision stakes and high systems uncertainties are familiar from the current crop of policy issues of risk and the environment. Indeed, any of the problems of major technological hazards or large-scale pollution belong to this class. Post-normal science has the paradoxical feature that in its problem-solving activity the traditional domination of 'hard facts' over 'soft values' has been inverted. Because of the high level of uncertainty, approaching sheer ignorance in some cases, and the extreme decision stakes, we might even in some cases interchange the axes on our diagram, making values the horizontal, independent variable. A good example of such an inversion is provided by the actions that will need to be taken in preparation for mitigating the effects of sea-level rise consequent on global climate change. The 'causal chain' here starts with the various outputs of human activity, producing changes in the biosphere, leading to changes in the climatic system, then changes in sea level (all these interacting in complex ways with varying delay-times). Out of all this must come a set of forecast which will provide the scientific inputs to decision processes; these will contribute to policy recommendations that must then be implemented on a broad scale. But all the causal elements are uncertain in the extreme; to wait until all the facts are in, would be another form of imprudence. At stake may be much of the built environment and the settlement patterns of people; mass migrations from low-lying districts could be required sooner or later, with the consequent economic, social and cultural upheaval.

Such far-reaching societal policies will be decided on the basis of scientific information that is inherently uncertain to an extreme degree; even more so because plans for mitigation must be started with a long lead-time so that the huge rebuilding and resettlement programmes can get under way. The rise in sea level would not be like a slow tide, but more likely in the form of floods of increasing frequency and destructiveness. Unprepared harbour cities (as most of the world's political and financial centres) could be devastated. A new form of legitimation crisis could emerge; for if the authorities try to base their appeals for sacrifice on the traditional certainties of applied science, as on the model of Pasteur, this will surely fail. Public agreement and participation, deriving essentially from value commitments, will be decisive for the assessment of risks and the setting of policy. Thus the traditional scientific inputs have become 'soft' in the context of the 'hard' value commitments that will determine the success of policies for mitigating the effects of a possible sea-level rise. In this way we see how the 'systems' involved in environmental policy issues are truly 'emergent', comprising dimensions of cognition and value which transcend those of the systems studied by traditional systems theory and its modelling techniques. Thus post-normal science corresponds to an enriched systems theory, deriving analytical rigour from it, and providing it with experience and insights.

The traditional fact/value distinction has not merely been inverted; in post-normal science the two categories cannot be realisti-cally separated. The uncertainties go beyond those of the systems, to include ethics as well. All policy issues of risk and the environment involve new forms of equity, which had previously been considered 'externalities' to the real business of the scientific–technical enterprise, that is the production and consumption of commodities. These new policy issues involve the welfare of new stakeholders, such as future generations, other species, and the planetary environment as a whole. The intimate connection between uncertainties in knowledge and in ethics is well illustrated by the problems of extinction of species, either singly or on a global scale. It is impossible to produce a simple rationale for adjudicating between the rights of people who would benefit from some development, and those of a species of animal or plant which would be harmed. However, the ethical uncertainties should not deter us from searching for solutions; nor can decision makers overlook the political force of those humans who have a passionate concern for those who cannot plead or vote. Only a dialogue between all sides, in which scientific expertise takes its place at the table with local and environmental concerns, can achieve creative solutions to such problems, which can then be implemented and enforced. Otherwise, either crude commercial pressures, inept bureaucratic regulations, or counterproductive protests will dominate, to the eventual detriment of all concerned.

All these complexities do not prevent the resolution of policy issues in post-normal science. The diagram should not be seen statically, but rather dynamically; different aspects of the problem, located in different zones, interact and lead to its eventual solution. There is a pattern of evolution of issues, with different problem-solving strategies successively coming to prominence, which provides a means whereby dialogue can eventually contribute to their resolution. For as the debate develops from its initial confused phase, positions are clarified and new research is stimulated. Although the definition of problems is never completely free of politics, an open debate ensures that such considerations are neither one-sided nor covert. And as applied science exercises eventually bring in new facts, professional consultancy tasks become more effective. A good example of this pattern of evolution is lead in petrol, where despite the absence of conclusive environmental or epidemiological information, a consensus was eventually reached that the public health hazards were not acceptable. Such a resolution does not always come quickly or easily; some substances might be called 'yo-yo risks' because of the way they go up and down in the experts' perception; Dioxin seems to be one such. In those cases, effective public policy would be better based on an appreciation of the inherent uncertainties rather than on the illusion that this time applied science has given us the true verdict of safe or dangerous.

EXTENDED PEER COMMUNITIES

The dynamic of resolution of policy issues in post-normal science involves the inclusion of an ever-growing set of legitimate participants in the process of quality assurance of the scientific inputs. As we have seen, in applied science and professional consultancy the peer communities are already extended beyond those for core science. In post-normal science, the manifold uncertainties in both products and processes require that the relative importance of persons becomes enhanced. Hence the establishment of the legitimacy and competence of participants will inevitably involve

broader societal and cultural institutions and movements. For example, persons directly affected by an environmental problem will have a keener awareness of its symptoms, and a more pressing concern with the quality of official reassurances, than those in any other role.[16] Thus they perform a function analogous to that of professional colleagues in the peer-review or refereeing process in traditional science, which otherwise might not occur in these new contexts.

On occasion, the legitimate work of extended peer communities can even go beyond the reactive tasks of quality assessment and policy debate. The new field of 'popular epidemiology' involves concerned citizens doing the disciplined research which could, or perhaps should, have been done by established institutions but was not.[17] In such cases they may encounter professional disapproval and hostility, being criticized either for lacking certified expertise or for being much too personally concerned about the problem. The creative conflict between popular and expert epidemiology not only leads to better control of environmental problems; it also improves scientific knowledge. A classic case is 'Lyme disease', where local citizens first identified a pattern in the vague symptoms which later characterized a previously unknown, but not uncommon tick-borne disease.

When problems lack neat solutions, when environmental and ethical aspects of the issues are prominent, when the phenomena themselves are ambiguous, and when all research techniques are open to methodological criticism, then the debates on quality are not enhanced by the exclusion of all but the specialist researchers and official experts. The extension of the peer community is then not merely an ethical or political act; it can positively enrich the processes of scientific investigation. Knowledge of local conditions may determine which data are strong and relevant, and can also help to define the policy problems. Such local, personal knowledge does not come naturally to the subject-specialism experts whose training and employment predispose them to adopt abstract, generalized conceptions of genuineness of problems and relevance of information. Those whose lives and livelihood depend on the solution of the problems will have a keen awareness of how the general principles are realized in their 'back yards'. They will also have 'extended facts', including anecdotes, informal surveys, and official information published by unofficial means. It may be argued that they lack theoretical knowledge and are biased by self-interest; but it can equally well be argued that the experts lack practical knowledge and have their own unselfconscious forms of bias.

The new paradigm of post-normal science, involving extended peer communities as essential participants, is clearly seen in the case of AIDS. Here the research scientists operate in the full glare of publicity involving sufferers, carers, journalists, ethicists, activists and self-help groups, as well as traditional institutions for funding, regulation and commercial application. The researchers' choice of problems and evaluations of solutions are equally subjected to critical scrutiny, and their priority disputes are similarly dragged out into the public arena. There are some costs; thus it is no longer easy for scientists to exercise their benevolent dictatorship over passive test subjects in the 'double-blind' procedure where some get no treatment. But unless we believe it right that the sufferers from this dread disease should depend entirely on the zeal and dedication of researchers, manufacturers and regulators, they should

be included in the dialogue, however fractious it may sometimes become.

As yet, such cases are still the exception. Extended peer communities generally operate in isolation, on special policy issues in isolated localities, with no systematic means of financial support, and little training in their special skills. On many occasions, there is insufficient competence in dialogue and communication with other stakeholders.[18] Recognition of their role is very variable; in the USA, with its traditions of devolution of power to the local level, 'intervenors' in some decision processes are provided with support; in other countries they may be ignored or actively hindered. Within such extended peer communities there will be the usual tensions between those with special-interest demands, and the outside activists with a more far-reaching agenda, along with the inevitable divisions along lines of class, ethnicity, gender and formal education. However, all such confusion is inevitable, and indeed healthy, in an embryonic movement which is fostering the transition to a new era for science. It could be that the field of health, where individual 'consumer preferences' can operate more effectively on a mass scale than in environmental policy issues, the rise of post-normal science will occur more smoothly. 'Complementary medicine' could in many ways be considered a type-case for post-normal science; and in spite of the inevitable external opposition and internal confusions, it grows steadily.

It is important to appreciate that post-normal science is complementary to applied science and professional consultancy. It is not a replacement for traditional forms of science, nor does it contest the claims to reliable knowledge or certified expertise that are made on behalf of science in its legitimate contexts. The technical expertise of

qualified scientists and professionals in accepted spheres of work is not being contested; what can be questioned is the
quality of that work in these new contexts,
especially in respect of its environmental,
societal and ethical aspects. Previously the
ruling assumption was that these were 'externalities' to the work of science or technology; and that when such problems arose
an appropriate response would somehow be
invented by 'society'. Now the task is to see
what sorts of changes in the practice of science, and in its institutions, will be entailed
by the recognition of uncertainty, complexity and quality within policy-relevant
research.

As in any deep transition, the present
contains seeds of destruction as well as renewal. Some participants in environmental
struggles come to see scientists merely as
hired guns, who should provide the data
that 'we' need and consent to the suppression of the rest. Others will be personally
impervious to any arguments and evidence
that weaken their prejudged case. Are such
participants legitimate members of an extended peer community? Even traditional
science has always included such types, but
there has been an implicit ethical commitment to integrity whereby the community
as a whole has maintained the quality of its
work.[19] The maintenance of quality, without which all efforts to solve policy issues of
risk and the environment are doomed, is a
major task for the methodology of the science of the future.

CONCLUSION

In every age, science is shaped around its
leading problems, and it evolves with
them. The new policy issues of risk and the
environment are global not merely in their
extent, but also in their complexity, per-

vasiveness, and novelty as a subject of
scientific inquiry. Until now, with the dom-
inance of applied science, the rationality of
reductionist natural-scientific research has
been taken as a model for the rationality of
intellectual and social activity in general.
However successful it has been in the past,
the recognition of the policy issues of risk
and the environment shows that this ideal
of rationality is no longer universally
appropriate.

The activity of science now encom-
passes the management of irreducible uncertainties in knowledge and in ethics, and
the recognition of different legitimate perspectives and ways of knowing. In this way,
its practice is becoming more akin to the
workings of a democratic society, characterized by extensive participation and tolera-
tion of diversity. As the political process
now recognizes our obligations to future
generations, to other species and indeed to
the global environment, science also ex-
pands the scope of its concerns. We are living in the midst of this rapid and deep
transition, so we cannot predict its outcome. But we can help to create the conditions and the intellectual tools whereby the
process of change can be managed for the
best benefit of the global environment and
humanity.

The democratization of this aspect of
science is, not a matter of benevolence by
the established groups, but (as in the sphere
of politics) the achievement of a system
which despite its inefficiencies is the most
effective means for avoiding the disasters
that result from the prolonged stifling of
criticism. Recent experience has shown that
such a critical presence is as important for
the solution of the policy issues of risk and
the environment as it is for society. Let us be
quite clear on this; we are not arguing for
the democratization of science on the basis

of a generalized wish for the greatest possible extension of democracy in society. The epistemological analysis of post-normal science, rooted in the practical tasks of quality assurance, shows that such an extension of peer communities, with the corresponding extension of facts, is necessary for the effectiveness of science in meeting the new challenges of global environmental problems.

This analysis is complementary to that of our previous article on post-modernity.[20] Both deal with the loss of hegemony of a single worldview based on a particular vision of science. The post-modern phenomenon is one of a deepening disillusion and a consequent fragmentation at all levels including the ideological and the societal. One reaction, as among some leading exponents of post-modernity, is despair. Another reaction is to reassert 'normality'; thus some leading scientists claim that the solution of our ecological problems lies through funding their large programme of relevant basic research, in which uncertainty is never mentioned.[21] Indeed, the suppression of uncertainty in 'normal' science makes it compatible with quite extreme reactions to the contemporary condition; thus it has been noticed that some religious fundamentalists find no difficulty in practising scientific expertise of various sorts, as the two dogmatisms can, with appropriate boundary drawing, coexist comfortably.[22] Finally, the post-normal response is to recognize the challenge, with all its dangers and promise; and then to start towards a reintegration, through the acceptance of uncertainty and the welcoming of diversity. In a later article we will discuss these various trends.

ENDNOTES

1. S. O. Funtowicz and J. R. Ravetz, 'The good, the true and the post-modern', *Futures*, *24*(10), December 1992, pages 963–976; Z. Sardar, 'Terminator 2: modernity, postmodernism and the "Other"', *Futures*, *24*(5), June 1992, pages 493–506.

2. T. S. Kuhn, *The Structure of Scientific Revolutions* (Chicago, IL, University of Chicago Press, 1962).

3. S. O. Funtowicz and J. R. Ravetz, *Uncertainty and Quality in Science for Policy* (Dordrecht, Kluwer, 1990).

4. S. O. Funtowicz and J. R. Ravetz, 'A new scientific methodology for global environmental issues', in R. Costanza (editor), *Ecological Economics—The Science and Management of Sustainability* (New York, Columbia University Press, 1991).

5. S. O. Funtowicz and J. R. Ravetz, 'Three types of risk assessment and the emergence of post-normal science', in D. Golding and S. Krimsky (editors), *Theories of Risk* (New York, Greenwood Press, 1991).

6. B. Latour, *The Pasteurization of France* (Cambridge, MA, Harvard University Press, 1988).

7. S. Mac Lane, 'Letters', *Science, 241,* 1988, page 1144, and *242,* 1988, pages 1623–1624.

8. J. C. Bailar, *Scientific Inferences and Environmental Problems: The Uses of Statistical Thinking* (Chapel Hill, NC, Institute for Environmental Studies, The University of North Carolina, 1988), page 19.

9. J. R. Ravetz, 'Usable knowledge, usable ignorance: incomplete science with policy implications', in J. R. Ravetz, *The Merger of Knowledge with Power* (London, Cassell, 1990).

10. Funtowicz and Ravetz, *op cit*, reference 3.

11. J. Turney, 'End of the peer show?', *New Scientist, 22* September 1990, pages 38–42.

12. L. Salter, *Mandated Science* (Dordrecht, Kluwer, 1988).

13. S. Jasanoff, *The Fifth Branch* (Cambridge, MA, Harvard University Press, 1990).

14. A. Weinberg, 'Science and trans-science', *Minerva, 10,* 1972, pages 209–222.

15. A. Weinberg, 'Letters', *Science, 180,* 1972, page 1124.

16. S. Krimsky, 'Epistemic considerations on the value of folk-wisdom in science and technology', *Policy Studies Review, 3,* 1984, pages 246–262.

17. P. Brown, 'Popular epidemiology: community response to toxic waste-induced disease in Woburn, Massachusetts', *Science, Technology and Human Values, 12,* 1987, pages 78–85.

18. Salter, *op cit,* reference 12.

19. J. R. Ravetz, *Scientific Knowledge and its Social Problems* (Oxford, Oxford University Press, 1971).

20. Funtowicz and Ravetz, *op cit,* reference 1.

21. J. Lubchenko *et al,* 'The Sustainable Biosphere Initiative: an ecological research agenda (A report from the Ecological Society of America)', *Ecology, 72,* 1991, pages 371–412.

22. Z. Sardar, *Explorations in Islamic Science* (London, Mansell, 1989), chapter 2, 'Anatomy of a confusion'.

PART III

Envisioning a Sustainable and Equitable Future

Chapter 9

Toward a New Worldview

19. A New Ecological Paradigm for Post-Exuberant Sociology*

WILLIAM R. CATTON, JR.

RILEY E. DUNLAP
Washington State University

The changed ecological conditions confronting human societies seriously challenge sociology, for the discipline developed in an era when humans seemed exempt from ecological constraints. Disciplinary traditions and assumptions that evolved during the age of exuberant growth imbued sociology with a worldview or paradigm which impedes recognition of the societal significance of current ecological realities. Thus, sociology stands in need of a fundamental alteration in its disciplinary paradigm. The objectives of this article are to make explicit the "Human Exemptionalism Paradigm" implicit in traditional sociological thought, and to develop an alternative "New Ecological Paradigm" which may better serve the field in a post-exuberant age.

Specifically, we will begin by briefly tracing the historical roots of "exemptionalist" thinking in sociology, noting first its origins in Western cultural traditions, and then the unique disciplinary factors that reinforced it for sociology. Next we will describe the nature of the changed ecological conditions facing human societies that require a fundamental reorientation by sociologists, no less than of other people. Then we will turn to an explication of the emerging ecological paradigm, showing how it seems to be affecting sociological inquiry. Finally, the distinction between this new ecological paradigm and the traditional exemptionalist paradigm will be compared with more standard theoretical cleavages within sociology. This comparison will illustrate the importance of the new paradigmatic cleavage.

DOMINANT WESTERN WORLDVIEW

To understand the challenge now facing sociology, it is essential to know how deeply sociological thinking has been influenced by a worldview long prevalent in Western culture—a worldview now made increasingly obsolete by recent change. Western culture has a strong anthropocentric tradition, viewing humans as separate from and somehow above the rest of nature (White, 1967). Accumulation of scientific knowledge and the growing power of technology converted this ancient anthropocentrism

*This essay was first published in *American Behavioral Scientist* 24(1), September/October 1980: 15–47, copyright ©1980 by Sage Publications. Reprinted by Permission of Sage Publications, Inc.

into modern arrogance toward nature (Ehrenfeld, 1978; Sessions, 1974), while European expansion into the New World added a strong sense of optimism.

Profound cultural impact followed when European people gained access to a second hemisphere's carrying capacity surplus.[1] At the time Columbus embarked on the voyage that was to reveal the availability of new lands, there were about 24 acres of Europe per European. Soon afterward, however, with new continents to settle and exploit, there were suddenly some 120 acres of land per European (Webb, 1952). Using land area as a rough measure, carrying capacity was thus increased fivefold. Opportunities thereafter seemed limitless. Accordingly, the number of Europeans and the extent of their "range" expanded "exuberantly" (to use the language of the ecologist). The 400-year boom described by Webb was a human instance of the "age of exuberance" that may occur for any species population when it gains access to a substantial increment of carrying capacity. In this situation it is not surprising that an optimistic belief in "progress" developed.

Abundance, so characteristic of this age of exuberance, was especially salient for the development of American traditions, values, and expectations (Potter, 1954)—since it was in America that the new abundance was most pronounced. Yet, as extreme as it became, American optimism and faith in progress differed only in degree from that of other nations participating in the "industrial revolution." This revolution, fueled both by New World resources and new technologies providing access to the earth's seemingly vast supply of fossil fuels, created an abundance throughout the Western world previously unknown on such a large scale.

As trade and cultural diffusion among nations expanded, virtually all industrial-

ized countries came to share an optimistic worldview entailing an expectation of perpetual progress and a prodigal attitude toward nature. Thus, Watt et al. (1977: 13) describe the industrialized world's "technoculture" as "a paradigm that transcends national identity and political ideology," while Pirages (1978: 260–261) points to a "dominant social paradigm" shared by industrial nations, and Harman (1979) describes an "industrial era paradigm."

We prefer to follow Black (1970: 19–28), who speaks of a dominant "Western Worldview." While this "worldview" concept is imprecise, and its history more complex than we have been able to suggest (see Passmore, 1974: Chap. 2; Sessions, 1974), there is nonetheless considerable consensus on its basic tenets (Black, 1970: Chap. 2; Ehrenfeld, 1978: Chap. 1; Watt et al., 1977: Chap. 2; White, 1967). Although any listing must be somewhat arbitrary, we believe the Dominant Western Worldview can be represented by the following four beliefs:

(1) People are fundamentally different from all other creatures on earth, over which they have dominion.
(2) People are masters of their destiny; they can choose their goals and learn to do whatever is necessary to achieve them.
(3) The world is vast, and thus provides unlimited opportunities for humans.
(4) The history of humanity is one of progress; for every problem there is a solution, and thus progress need never cease.

Because this anthropocentric and optimistic set of beliefs is so patently unecological, it is now being challenged by recent experiences with changing conditions of life. Accordingly, several writers (e.g., Harman, 1979; Pirages, 1978; Watt et al., 1977) have begun to call for its revision to fit the changed circumstances now facing mankind.

DISCIPLINARY TRADITIONS IN SOCIOLOGY

It is not surprising that sociology, which developed in nineteenth-century Europe and prospered in twentieth-century America, reflects the optimistic anthropocentrism of the Dominant Western Worldview—for scientific endeavors are often influenced by the sociocultural milieu in which they develop (Merton, 1968: 510–542). Thus, a somewhat sophisticated version of anthropocentrism can be found in widespread sociological adherence to what Klausner (1971: 11) has called "human exceptionalism," or the "belief in an evolutionary discontinuity between man the symbolizer and other biological creatures" (also see Burch, 1971: 14–20). Similarly, an optimistic faith in social progress has been a venerable part of the heritage of sociologists, being particularly prominent in the work of the discipline's founder, Auguste Comte (Timasheff, 1967: 20–21, 27–29).

However, certain factors distinctive to sociology also contributed to its adoption of an ecologically unsound set of assumptions about human societies. In order to establish their new discipline the founders of sociology, both in Europe and America, strongly asserted the uniqueness of its subject matter and its perspectives. Of fundamental importance in this regard was the Durkheimian emphasis on the "objective reality of social facts" such as norms, groups, and institutions, and the irreducibility of such facts to the psychological properties of the individuals involved (Durkheim, 1950: Chap. 1; also see Ritzer, 1975: 25–26). As Timasheff (1967: 313–314) noted in his review of mid-twentieth-century sociology, "*social* phenomena, the subject matter of sociology, are

now commonly recognized to be *sui generis,* in other words, to be irreducible to non-social facts."

A corollary of this sui generis conception of social facts is Durkheim's (1950: 110) dictum that "The determining cause of a social fact should be sought among the social facts preceeding it." In other words, the cause of a social fact must always be another social—as opposed to psychological, biological, or physical—fact. Although Durkheim was primarily concerned with combatting the tendency to explain social phenomena with psychological variables (i.e., to *reduce* social facts to "states of individual consciousness"), what we may call his "anti-reductionism taboo" was general enough so that it also ruled out the use of biological and physical variables as explanations of social phenomena.

We can see the effects of this anti-reductionism taboo, which became normative in sociology (Timasheff, 1967: 314), by tracing the development of important conceptual distinctions among the variables that influence human behavior. At the earliest stages of social thought, it seemed human behavior was to be explained in terms of an undifferentiated concept such as "human nature" (Dewey, 1937)—i.e., people acted the way they did because it was human nature to do so. However, as biological knowledge developed sufficiently to provide a theory of heredity, it facilitated distinction between "heredity" and "environment" as sources of variation in human behavior patterns (Bernard, 1922). While this distinction did not logically require that either source be eliminated from further investigation, anti-reductionism (in the form of anti-biologism) induced sociologists to choose not to be "hereditarian."

To make further conceptual progress, sociologists had to go on to distinguish social and cultural environments from physical and biological environments (Bernard, 1925: 325–328). Again not logical necessity but an anti-reductionist taboo against "geographical (or environmental) determinism" restricted and distorted sociological recognition of the salience of physical environments (Klausner, 1971: 4–8; Choldin, 1978: 353), while the anti-biologism taboo precluded much sociological attention to the ecosystem context and consequences of human life (Burch, 1971: 14–20).

These important disciplinary developments are illustrated in Figure 9.1, where the two conceptual "forks" just described are schematically represented: first the distinction between environment and heredity, and second, the distinction between social and cultural environments, on the one hand, and biological and physical environments (or simply the "biophysical environment") on the other. Note that *moving* from left to right in the diagram represents achievement in making distinctions between one kind of causal influence and another, while *expanding* the vertical dimension represents increasing recognition of diversity in

these causal influences. Also note that advance from left to right need *not* be equated with a unidirectional (upward) shift on the vertical axis.

However, sociology, in its quest for disciplinary autonomy, has always tended to shift its attention "upward" as each conceptual distinction was made. That is, having learned to *distinguish* environmental from hereditary influences on behavior, sociologists assumed that the "lower" one was thenceforth to be *disregarded*. Again, having distinguished social and cultural environments from biophysical environments, sociologists assumed that the latter could safely be ignored. In other words, each time a conceptual distinction was made, the anti-reductionism taboo led sociologists to ignore the "lower" class of variables and focus attention on the "emergent" level. This tendency is epitomized in Stanley's (1968: 855) assertion that "the main accomplishment and direction of the social sciences to date [is] the progressive substitution of sociocultural explanations for those stressing the determinative influence of physical nature."

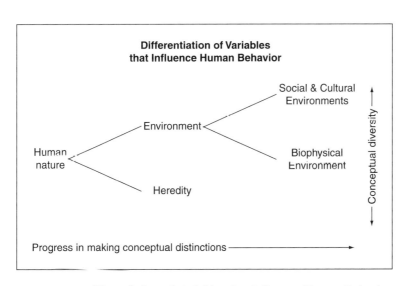

FIGURE 9.1   Differentiation of Variables that Influence Human Behavior

In addition to the Durkheimian legacy, with its emphasis on social facts and anti-reductionism, another major tradition in sociology has contributed to the discipline's tendency to ignore the biophysical environment. This tradition, inherited from Weber and elaborated by Mead, Cooley, Thomas, and others, emphasizes the importance of understanding the ways individuals "define" their situations, especially when trying to explain their actions (Ritzer, 1975: 27–28). As Choldin (1978: 353) has noted, because this perspective assumes "that the reality of a situation is in the definition attached to it by the participating actors [it] implies that the physical properties of the situation may be ignored." This can be done because an actor's "definition of the situation" is assumed to be influenced by surrounding actors rather than by the situation's physical characteristics; indeed, from this perspective physical properties become relevant *only* if they are perceived and defined as such by the actors. The strength of this "social definition" perspective, which complements the Durkheimian tradition in leading sociologists to ignore the biophysical environment, has been noted by Klausner (1971: 38): "The current tradition in sociology is to treat the environment—part of the situation of action—in terms of the meaning it has to the participants in the action rather than to some objective observer."

As a result of these historical developments within sociology, the term "environment" is typically used by sociologists to mean something quite unlike what it means in most other disciplines and in public discourse. In nonsociological parlance "the environment" means our physical surroundings—the biosphere, or a local portion of it. In contrast, within mainstream sociology "the environment" is used to refer to social and cultural influences on the entity

being examined (see, e.g., Catton and Dunlap, 1978a: 44; Choldin, 1978: 353; Dunlap and Catton, 1979a: 244–245). An individual's environment, for example, is likely to be viewed as comprising the groups to which one belongs, the institutions (economic, educational, religious) in which one participates, and the community in which one resides. Similarly, the environment of a community is likely to be conceptualized as the surrounding communities with which it interacts or the larger culture in which it is located. For sociologists, "environment" seldom denotes the physical properties of the settings in which individuals participate, or the characteristics of the biophysical region (topography, natural resources, climate, and so forth) in which communities are located.

This habit of terminology, and the disciplinary traditions behind it, imposed a set of "conceptual blinders" which made it difficult for sociologists to recognize the importance of the ecological problems that began to receive considerable public attention in our society in the late 1960s (Catton and Dunlap, 1978a: 44).

THE HUMAN EXEMPTIONALISM PARADIGM (HEP)

Given the unecological character of the dominant Western culture within which sociology developed, and the disciplinary traditions just described, it is understandable that the work of sociologists has come to rest on a profoundly unecological foundation. This foundation is largely implicit and often unconscious, and consists of what Gouldner (1970: 29–35) calls "background assumptions." While seldom made explicit, such assumptions influence the way in which sociologists approach their subject matter and practice their craft. Accordingly, to understand the discipline of sociology it is important to identify these "deepest assumptions about man and society" (Gouldner, 1970: 28).

Gouldner's analysis of the nature and role of background assumptions is quite similar to Kuhn's (1962) analysis of "paradigms," suggesting to us that a set of such assumptions can be viewed as constituting a paradigm. Although Kuhn used "paradigm" in a variety of ways, Ritzer (1975) has argued persuasively that the concept is most fertile when given a broad meaning. Specifically, Ritzer (1975: 7) offers the following comprehensive definition:

> *A paradigm is a fundamental image of the subject matter within a science. It serves to define what should be studied, what questions should be asked, how they should be asked, and what rules should be followed in interpreting the answers obtained. The paradigm is the broadest unit of consensus within a science and serves to differentiate one scientific community* (or subcommunity) *from another. It subsumes, defines, and interrelates the exemplars, theories, and methods and instruments that exist within it.*

Using this broad definition allows one to avoid the error of equating paradigms with specific theories or theoretical persuasions. This is a common practice within sociology (see, e.g., Effrat, 1972); yet, if one simply applies the label "paradigm" to theories such as "functionalism," 'Marxism," or "symbolic interactionism," little has been achieved toward understanding the intellectual impact of unstated assumptions on the field of sociology.

A few sociologists have therefore used "paradigm" in the broader and more fruitful sense. Ritzer (1975), in particular, has argued that most sociological theories can be seen as stemming from one of three broad

paradigms within the discipline: (1) the "social facts" paradigm derived from Durkheim, (2) the "social definition" paradigm derived from Weber, and (3) a newer (and, so far, less influential) "social behavior" paradigm derived from the behavioral psychologist Skinner. While we find Ritzer's analysis insightful, and feel it has considerable validity, we take him at his word when he warns that one should not "reify" paradigms. In other words, we do not take paradigms to be "real things," but "handy constructs for understanding the nature of sociology or any other field" (Ritzer, 1975: 200).

Thus, just as Ritzer was able to perceive three basic paradigms underlying the far greater diversity of theoretical persuasions seen in sociology by others (e.g., Effrat, 1972), it is possible that a still more fundamental paradigm can be discerned underlying his three.

It is our position that the vast majority of sociologists share a common (but increasingly obsolete) "fundamental image of the subject matter" of their discipline.[2] This shared image or paradigm can best be described by listing a set of background assumptions which, taken together, seem to comprise the "common core of agreement" existing among sociologists—a core that was alluded to, but not specified, by Ritzer (1975: 32, 191, 211). It must be emphasized that these assumptions are so taken for granted that they are virtually never made explicit; yet, they clearly influence the practice of sociology. Inherited from the Dominant Western Worldview (DWW) and from sociology's particular disciplinary traditions, these background assumptions can be stated (admittedly somewhat arbitrarily)[3] as follows:

(1) Humans have a cultural heritage in addition to (and distinct from) their

genetic inheritance, and thus are quite unlike all other animal species.

(2) Social and cultural factors (including technology) are the major determinants of human affairs.

(3) Social and cultural environments are the crucial context for human affairs, and the biophysical environment is largely irrelevant.

(4) Culture is cumulative; thus technological and social progress can continue indefinitely, making all social problems ultimately soluble.

Like the tenets of the DWW, of which these assumptions are sophisticated variants, they constitute a paradigm that is anthropocentric, optimistic, and profoundly unecological.

The image of human societies conveyed by these assumptions is one that emphasizes the "exceptional" nature of our species stemming from our cultural heritage, including language, social organization, and technology. For that reason we labeled an earlier (and slightly different) listing of them the "Human Exceptionalism Paradigm" (Catton and Dunlap, 1978a: 42–43). However, we hardly wish to deny that *Homo sapiens* is an "exceptional" species. What we do deny is the belief that sociologists can still afford to suppose that the exceptional characteristics of our species *exempt* us from ecological principles and from environmental influences and constraints. Thus, since the foregoing assumptions imply such exemption, we have come to call the Human Exceptionalism Paradigm the "Human Exemptionalism Paradigm" (Dunlap and Catton, 1979a: 250).

In short, we are arguing that the discipline of sociology is premised on a set of background assumptions or a paradigm that has led sociologists—regardless of their particular theoretical persuasion—to treat human societies as *if* they were exempt from

ecological constraints.[4] As part of their emphasis on the exceptional characteristics of humans, most sociologists have totally ignored the biophysical environment, as if human societies somehow no longer depend on it for their physical existence and for the means of pursuing the goals they value. These tendencies, in turn, have predisposed sociologists to accept the optimism inherent in the DWW by implicitly assuming the possibility of endless social progress.

In sociology's drive to establish its own disciplinary identity, especially its autonomy from biology, this underlying paradigm was useful. Moreover, the fact that sociology largely developed when the Western world was generally experiencing an age of abundance (as previously noted) makes the discipline's tendency to ignore ecological constraints understandable, although it is surprising that so few sociologists followed the lead provided by historians such as Webb (1952) and Potter (1954) in analyzing the social implications of ecological abundance (for an exception see Williams, 1970: Chap. 2). Also, as human societies became more urbanized and technologically sophisticated, such societies—the subject matter of most sociology—appeared further removed from the biophysical environment and seemingly able to alter that environment to suit their needs (Landis, 1949: 118). Given these conditions, it is not surprising that the vast majority of sociologists ignored the biophysical environment and felt secure working within the (unseen) confines of the HEP.

Although an occasional sociologist wrote something that challenged the HEP (see, e.g., LaPiere, 1965: Chap. 7, and the works discussed in Dunlap and Catton, 1979a: 245), the consensus regarding sociology's unseen paradigm was so great that such departures from it could be safely ignored by the larger discipline. Twentieth-century sociology—despite its great theoretical diversity—might almost be described as having been largely devoted to "fleshing out" the HEP.

However, Gouldner (1970: 34) notes that "old background assumptions may come to operate in new conditions...and thus...become boundaries which confine and inhibit" a discipline. Our contention is that in recent years human societies have begun to experience such "changed conditions," but that sociological adherence to the HEP has made it difficult for most members of the discipline to perceive the nature of these changes. For Gouldner, the rising levels of social conflict in the 1960s signaled the demise of the once-dominant functionalist theoretical perspective (with its "consensual" image of society); similarly, we see the changed ecological circumstances of human society—signaled by rising levels of pollution, resource scarcity, and other ecological problems—as necessitating rejection of the HEP and the DWW.

FROM EXUBERANCE
TO POST-EXUBERANCE

In the past few centuries the size and scale of human societies (i.e., their technological and organizational complexity as well as their actual population) tended to increase *exponentially* (Lenski and Lenski, 1978: 81–82, 97–98, 290–297). A major component of this dramatic growth involved expansion of European peoples into abundant new niches made available by two interrelated historic developments: (1) discovery of a second hemisphere that could be colonized (Webb, 1952), and (2) invention of technologies giving humans access to such "new" resources as fossil fuels (Catton, 1980: Chap. 3). Some 400-years experience with this "age of exuberance" nurtured the illusion that accelerating or exponential

growth was an endless possibility (see, e.g., Hart, 1959), but events of recent years now indicate that the trajectory of human history may be portrayed more appropriately by the logistic curve shown in Figure 9.2 than by an exponential growth curve (Ophuls, 1977; Miles, 1976).

Current awareness of the temporariness of exponential growth was no doubt stimulated by publication of *The Limits to Growth* (Meadows et al., 1972), although at least as far back as Malthus a few dissenters had seriously questioned the possibility of continuing exponential growth (Luten, 1978). In the 1970s there occurred, as part of rising awareness of ecological constraints, a dramatic revision in attitudes toward growth. A wide range of writers—including both those who were optimistic about the future (e.g., Kahn et al., 1976) as well as

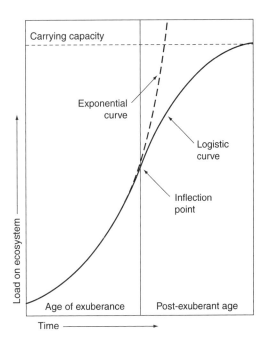

FIGURE 9.2 Exponential and Logistic Growth Models

some who were more apprehensive about it
(e.g., Ophuls, 1977)—argued that the era of
exponential growth was past (also see
Brown, 1978; Miles, 1976; Renshaw, 1976;
Wilson, 1977). In other words, the accelerating progress taken for granted until recently is now seen as having ended with the
passing of the inflection point shown in Figure 9.2. While the trajectory of human history is still generally assumed to slope
upward, there is growing acknowledgment
that the *rate of increase* is declining—with
the implication that the curve will ultimately level off.[5]

Observers have cited a variety of evidence indicating that growth no longer follows an exponential pattern, not only for
the human population per se (both in the
United States and the entire world), but for
virtually all aspects of human society. Thus,
Renshaw (1976:7–8, 30–35, 68–75), invoking a "law of diminishing returns," has
called attention to notable declines in the
rate of scientific and technological developments (such as increments in the speed of
transportation), and especially in their implementation (also see Miles, 1976: 14–15).
Likewise, several writers have noted that
the rate of increase in food production and
the discovery of natural resources (especially fossil fuels) has declined significantly
in recent years (Ophuls, 1977: Chap. 2;
Brown, 1978). Perhaps most noticeable of
all, economic growth has begun to slow, not
only among industrialized nations but
throughout most of the world (Brown,
1978: 188–191; Pirages, 1978: 223–247;
Renshaw, 1976).

In the United States, the slowdown in
growth of GNP has been attributed to declining rates of growth in capital, work
force, and particularly labor productivity
(Brown, 1978: Chap. 7; Renshaw, 1976;
Wilson, 1977: 148–150). Declining growth

in productivity, in turn, is ultimately related
to the rising cost of energy—for the latter is
leading to a much slower rate of substitution of mechanical for human energy (Renshaw, 1976:14, 28–41). And of course the
dramatic rise in the cost of energy, which
contributes to inflation and is diverting
huge amounts of capital away from other
sectors of the economy, is due to the ineluc-
table fact that petroleum is being depleted.
Indeed, there is ample evidence that despite
the economic incentives now fostering
record amounts of exploratory drilling, the
amount of additional oil and natural gas being discovered in the United States remain
less than the amount being extracted and
used (Van Slambrouck, 1980). This is, of
course, a strong indication that energy from
fossil fuels, the cornerstone of industrialism
(Miles, 1976: 29–30, 104–107), will be de-
creasingly available in the future.

If one is to describe the "post-exuberant"
age into which humanity has entered after
passing the inflection point, the concept of
"ecological scarcity" seems most apt (see the
excellent explication of this concept by
Ophuls, 1977: Chap. 3). Unlike "simple
Malthusian scarcity" of a single resource
such as food, ecological scarcity refers to the
"ensemble of separate but interacting limits
and constraints on human action" (Ophuls,
1977: 9). An understanding of this concept
is extremely useful for comprehending the
present human situation.

Ecological scarcity is a concept that allows one to see, for example, how efforts to
maintain rapidly growing use of diminishing natural resources by turning from one
substitute to another must ultimately fail.
Resource substitution almost invariably increases the amount of energy needed to
make things or do things (LaPiere, 1965:
227–228; Ophuls, 1977: 61, 69–70), and
energy availability in escalating or even

current amounts has become problematic. We have begun trying to solve energy problems by substituting one fossil fuel for another, but vast increases in the use of coal as a substitute for scarce oil threaten humanity with increasingly severe air pollution, acid rain, and ultimately the possibility of changing the earth's temperature with potentially disastrous implications (Ehrlich and Ehrlich, 1972: 233–242; Stobaugh and Yergin, 1979: Chap. 4; Likens et at., 1979; Brown, 1978: 61–65). Even the use of nuclear energy, assuming safety and cost problems of nuclear plants can be overcome, threatens humanity with accumulations of toxic wastes that cannot presently be stored in permanently safe fashion (Stobaugh and Yergin, 1979: 127–135).

Moreover, even if resource substitution could continue indefinitely and make it possible to go on increasing our rates of energy use, it would be necessary to face the fact that using energy results invariably in production of heat. Given that the second law of thermodynamics cannot be repealed and given the present scale of human activity, the production of heat can no longer be ignored—for the environmental warming resulting from increased energy use will insidiously affect climate and other aspects of the global ecosystem (Ophuls, 1977: 107–111; Ehrlich and Ehrlich, 1972: 61–63).

In short, the concept of ecological scarcity rests on a realization that the global ecosystem is finite and that it is subject to ecological laws which humans cannot permanently evade. Such "ecological facts of life" enable us to understand the importance of our recent passage into a "post-exuberant age," and to realize that the future of human society in such an age will likely differ markedly from expectations developed in the temporary age of exuberance. Successful adaptation to the changed

situations can be seriously impeded by archaic worldviews and obsolete scientific paradigms. Fortunately, there is evidence that at least some members of the public are beginning to sense that their traditional view of the world, and consequent expectations about it, are no longer valid (e.g., Dunlap and Van Liere, 1978; Yankelovich and Lefkowitz, 1980). Likewise, we see evidence that some members of our discipline have begun to recognize that sociologists must also revise their disciplinary premises. We therefore turn to a discussion of the emergence of an alternative to the Human Exemptionalism Paradigm within sociology.

THE NEW ECOLOGICAL PARADIGM

The foregoing changes in the ecological context of human societies call into question sociologists' long-held habits of thought. It was, however, a sociologist who long ago noted that a disturbance of habit evokes the response called "paying attention" (Thomas, 1909: 17). The function of attention, he said, is to establish new habits adequate to new circumstances. Or, as Kuhn (1962: 76) put it in regard to scientific paradigms faced with accumulated anomalies, "The significance of crises is the indication they provide that an occasion for retooling has arrived." The societal implications of the "ecological crisis" which became so apparent in the 1970s led some sociologists to pay attention to environmental issues and to begin a process of conceptual retooling.

The "disciplinary blinders" imposed by the HEP at first largely confined such attention to applications of traditional sociological perspectives to environmental problems. There were studies of public attitudes toward environmental issues, studies of memberships in environmental organizations, studies of problems faced by resource management agencies, and so forth. We have called such work the "sociology of environmental issues" (Dunlap and Catton, 1979a: 246–249). At the same time, however, a few sociologists (e.g., Burch, 1971; Michelson, 1970) were beginning to focus on a topic traditionally ignored in sociology: the relationship between human society and the biophysical environment. Specifically, such writers focused attention on the interaction between humans and the biophysical environment; or the impacts of human societies on the environment *and* the impact of the environment (ranging from "built" to "natural") on social organization and human behavior.

Growth of this work through the 1970s led to the recent emergence of a true "environmental sociology" (for an extensive review of this field see Dunlap and Catton, 1979a). The distinguishing feature of environmental sociology is the willingness of its practitioners to examine relationships between social and environmental variables (such as characteristics of buildings, levels of pollution, and rates of energy use), thus violating the traditional taboo against including nonsocial variables in sociological analyses. By their acceptance of environmental variables as relevant for understanding human behavior and social organization, all environmental sociologists at least implicitly (and often unknowingly) challenge the HEP (particularly the second and third assumptions in our listing).

As the 1970s brought unmistakable evidence of the unprecedented impact (both locally and globally) of human societies on the ecosystem, and particularly of the vulnerability of humans to the ecosystem's *reaction*, some environmental sociologists went beyond tacit denial of the HEP. Apparently sensing the increased salience of ecological constraints (particularly as embodied in the concept of "ecological scarcity") for human

societies in a post-exuberant age, they began to write things that contained the seeds of an alternative to the HEP (see, e.g., Burch, 1976; Buttel, 1976: 307; Catton, 1972, Dunlap and Van Liere, 1978; Morrison, 1976: 300–301; Schnaiberg, 1975).[6]

While any effort to describe a new paradigm in a few short sentences will undoubtedly be less than adequate, we think the core of this "New Ecological Paradigm" (NEP) is embodied in the set of background assumptions limited in the third column of Table 9.1 (in which the assumptions constituting the DWW and HEP are repeated to facilitate comparison with the NEP).[7] There are points in common between the NEP and HEP, but there are also significant differences between them. First, the NEP grants that humans are an exceptional species, but stresses that they should nonetheless be viewed as one among many interdependent species (depending on many other species for food, and competing for food, space, water, and so on with other species). Second, while acknowledging that human affairs were heavily influenced by social and cultural forces, the NEP stresses that human social life is also influenced by the biophysical environment, often as a reaction to human action (in the form, for example, of buildings, pollution, and climate). Third, whereas the HEP ignores the biophysical context of human activity, and stresses the determinative influence of the social-cultural "environment," the NEP calls attention to the constraints on human affairs posed by their biophysical context (e.g., human health and physical survival are possible only under certain environmental conditions). Finally, the HEP (especially when set in the context of the DWW) implies limitlessness, and expects social and technological developments to lead to perpetual progress. In contrast, the NEP recognizes that no matter how inventive

TABLE 9.1   A Comparison of Major Assumptions in the Dominant Western Worldview, Sociology's Human Exemptionalism Paradigm, and the Proposed New Ecological Paradigm

	Dominant Western Worldview (DWW)	Human Exemptionalism Paradigm (HEP)	New Ecological Paradigm (NEP)
Assumptions about the nature of human beings:	DWW_1 People are fundamentally different from all other creatures on Earth, over which they have dominion.	HEP_1 Humans have a cultural heritage in addition to (and distinct from) their genetic inheritance, and thus are quite unlike all other animal species.	NEP_1 While humans have exceptional characteristics (culture, technology, etc.), they remain one among many species that are interdependently involved in the global ecosystem.
Assumptions about social causation:	DWW_2 People are masters of their destiny; they can choose their goals and learn to do whatever is necessary to achieve them.	HEP_2 Social and cultural factors (including technology) are the major determinants of human affairs.	NEP_2 Human affairs are influenced not only by social and cultural factors, but also by intricate linkages of cause, effect, and feedback in the web of nature; thus purposive human actions have many unintended consequences.
Assumptions about the context of human society:	DWW_3 The world is vast, and thus provides unlimited opportunities for humans.	HEP_3 Social and cultural environments are the crucial context for human affairs, and the biophysical environment is largely irrelevant.	NEP_3 Humans live in and are dependent upon a finite biophysical environment which imposes potent physical and biological restraints on human affairs.
Assumptions about constraints on human society:	DWW_4 The history of humanity is one of progress; for every problem there is a solution, and thus progress need never cease.	HEP_4 Culture is cumulative; thus technological and social progress can continue indefinitely, making all social problems ultimately soluble.	NEP_4 Although the inventiveness of humans and the powers derived therefrom may seem for a while to extend carrying capacity limits, ecological laws cannot be repealed.

humans may be, their science and technology cannot repeal ecological principles such as the laws of thermodynamics; thus there are ultimate limits to the growth of human societies.

In sum, the "fundamental image" of human societies provided by the NEP is importantly different from that provided by the HEP. In sharp contrast to the anthropocentric HEP, the NEP stresses the ecosystem-

dependence of human societies. The NEP thus clearly points to the importance of considering societies' biophysical context. And, perhaps most fundamentally, it emphasizes the fact that despite their possession of exceptional characteristics, human beings are not exempt from ecological constraints.

To us, therefore, a shift from the HEP to the NEP is of "paradigmatic" proportions. As Gouldner (1970: 34) notes, "The most basic changes in any science [are] those that embody new background assumptions. They are thus changes in the way the world is seen." We contend that NEP-oriented sociologists do, in fact, "see the world" differently than do their HEP-oriented colleagues.

A true paradigm shift, of course, entails more than a shift in scientists' perceptions; it leads to differences in the way they practice their craft (Kuhn, 1962; Ritzer, 1975). Although the NEP is still in its infancy, we can see several ways it affects the work of its adherents. Most obvious, of course, is the fact that they violate the traditional sociological practice of excluding from consideration all nonsocial variables. For an NEP-adherent, a social fact such as socioeconomic status may be related in important ways to such *socially significant* facts as exposure to pollution (Burch, 1976) and vulnerability to negative impacts of petroleum shortages (Schnaiberg, 1975). Similarly, sociologists not blinded by the HEP realize the importance of investigating the interrelations between energy availability, for example, and social variables such as family privacy and housing patterns (Mulligan, 1976), the scale and form of urban life (Van Til, 1979), and lifestyle in general (Klausner, 1975). The NEP thus sensitizes sociologists to the probable societal impacts of "nonsocial" phenomena.

In addition, the NEP provides a basis for shedding new light on traditional sociological concerns. For example, sociology has long been concerned with various forms of competition (which sometimes escalates into conflict) between differing segments of society. NEP sociologists have begun to point to the likelihood that such competition and conflict will be heightened in an era of ecological scarcity. Thus, Schnaiberg (1975) and Morrison (1976) have suggested that energy scarcity will result in increased competition, and possible conflict, between

social classes, Mulligan (1978) notes emerging conflict among regions of the United States over their differential access to energy supplies, and Catton (1980: Chap. 13) points out ecological pressures toward scapegoating and even genocide.

Perhaps most importantly, the NEP leads to a concern with issues that are ignored in traditional sociological circles. For example, sociological attention to competition has heretofore been confined to competitive relations between two or more "current" factions (or, in the case of historical analyses, past factions contemporaneous with each other). That is, HEP sociology has limited itself to studying various forms of "synchronic" competition—even when it has examined age-based conflict such as that between youth and adults. In a postexuberant era, however, another form of competition becomes important—the competition *between present and future generations* for limited resources and other aspects of a finite ecosystem. This "diachronic competition" (Catton and Dunlap, 1978b: 258) is likely to become increasingly intense (Catton, 1980: Chap. 1) and will no doubt make questions of "equity" even more difficult to resolve in future decades than is the case now. We anticipate some shift of sociological attention, therefore, to problems of "intertemporal equity," a topic already under analysis in other disciplines (see, e.g., Lippit and Hamada, 1977).

The long-term perspective on human societies inherent in consideration of diachronic competition and intertemporal equity is also essential to consideration of the concept of the "steady-state" or "sustainable society." Such a society would be one that provides for successful human adaptation to a finite (and vulnerable) ecosystem on a long-term, sustainable basis. Although the characteristics of a sustainable society and the means for achieving it have received considerable attention outside sociology (e.g., Daly, 1977; Pirages, 1977), it has thus far received too little attention from sociologists (Anderson [1976] is an exception). However, the nature of such a society, particularly the forms of social organization most compatible with ecosystem maintenance, and the means for achieving those forms, certainly fall within the bailiwick of sociology (Dunlap and Catton, 1979a: 266; 1979b: 81). In dealing with this topic, scholars in any discipline should find useful a number of concepts that have been refined over several decades by biological ecologists; the "climax community," for example, is for the ecologist what the sustainable society is for social scientists (see, e.g., Odum, 1975: 10–11, 19–21, 152–154; compare Ophuls, 1977: 229, 232, 234).

THE HEP–NEP DISTINCTION VERSUS TRADITIONAL CLEAVAGES

Attempts to promote new paradigms are likely to evoke criticism, and our initial effort to distinguish the NEP from the HEP was no exception. Ironically, the major criticism has come from Buttel (1978), whose work contributed to the development of the NEP. While acknowledging that the HEP–NEP cleavage is real, Buttel (1978: 255) nonetheless argued that it is not as important as more traditional cleavages within sociology—most notably that between the "Order" (particularly structural-functionalist) and "Conflict" (particularly Marxist) theoretical perspectives. His criticism, which stems from prior efforts to explicate the importance of the Order–Conflict cleavage for the study of environmental issues (e.g., Buttel, 1976), is in a sense not surprising. As Ritzer (1975: 210, 226) has noted, most sociologists believe (incorrectly, in his view)

that the Order-Conflict debate is the "basic split" in the discipline. (Ritzer's deemphasis of this theoretical cleavage stems from his inclination to see both as representative of the "social facts" paradigm.)

An important point is raised by Buttel's criticism; we therefore want to clarify and extend our view of the relationship between the HEP–NEP distinction and the traditional Order–Conflict cleavage. Confusion arises from the fact that some sociologists view the Order and Conflict perspectives as competing *paradigms* others (such as Ritzer) see them simply as competing *theoretical perspectives*. (Buttel [1976, 1978] tends to use "paradigms" and "theories" interchangeably.) Regardless, it does appear that adherents of the Order and Conflict perspectives tend to see society rather differently. Thus, Order theorists view societies as relatively well-integrated and consensual, whereas Conflict theorists tend to see them as more competitive and coercive.

We think Dahrendorf (1958: 74) has nicely captured the "background assumptions" underlying these two "models of society." He lists the following as the "implicit postulates" of the Order model:[8]

(1) Every society is a relatively persisting configuration of elements.
(2) Every society is a well-integrated configuration of elements.
(3) Every element in a society contributes to its functioning.
(4) Every society rests on the consensus of its members.

He then lists the postulates underlying the Conflict model as follows:

(1) Every society is subjected at every moment to change: social change is ubiquitous.

(2) Every society experiences at every moment social conflict: social conflict is ubiquitous.

(3) Every element in a society contributes to its change.

(4) Every society rests on constraint of some of its members by others.

To us, the striking feature of these two "competing" models of society is that they *both* are solidly within the HEP tradition and totally neglect the ecosystem-dependence of human societal life! It is therefore not surprising that the vast majority of sociologists working with either of these models have failed to take note of humanity's changed ecological condition.

Nevertheless, as Buttel (1978: 254) notes, one can detect Order–Conflict differences among environmental sociologists whose work reflects, in varying degrees, the NEP. This is certainly understandable, as we would not expect these scholars to have shed immediately or completely their allegiance to traditional sociological theories or paradigms when they began their NEP work. Thus, while neither the Order nor the Conflict perspective has traditionally had anything to say about the ecological base of human societies, individuals schooled in one of these perspectives would naturally tend to bring it to bear on their own NEP-oriented work. One finds, for example, Schnaiberg's *The Environment: From Surplus to Scarcity* (1980) solidly in the Conflict camp, whereas Burch's *Daydreams and Nightmares* (1971) is more akin to the Order tradition. Likewise Anderson's *The Sociology of Survival* (1976) is generally Marxist in orientation, while Klausner's *On Man in His Environment* (1971) is strongly functionalist.[9]

What these few examples suggest is that the Order–Conflict cleavage (and in all likelihood other traditional theoretical cleavages in sociology) cross-cuts the HEP–NEP cleavage, resulting in new and rather complex paradigmatic/theoretical orientations among sociologists, as shown in Figure 9.3.

To illustrate the usefulness of this schema, we turn to recent work by four eminent sociologists (none of whom is regarded as an "environmental sociologist") on the probable societal impacts of ecological scarcity—particularly the impacts on the stratification system. Two of the writers, Lipset (1979) and Smelser (1979), are prominent representatives of the Order perspective, while the other two, Rainwater (1977) and Horowitz (1977), are prominent among Conflict sociologists. Despite these differences in orientation, all four writers provide quite similar analyses of the likely effects of increasing scarcity (and resultant

FIGURE 9.3   A Cross-Classification of Cleavages

	Order theory	Conflict theory
Human Exemptionalism Paradigm	HEP-order	HEP-conflict
New Ecological Paradigm	NEP-order	NEP-conflict

slowed growth) on our nation's stratification system—less mobility, regressive distribution of impacts, and increased social conflict (which will strain our democratic political system).

Nonetheless, there are some interesting differences among the four. As one might expect, Rainwater and Horowitz (the two conflict theorists) indicate a strong concern with the achievement of greater equality via redistribution, so that the burden of scarcity will be less disastrous for those at the bottom. On the other hand, one can detect a slightly keener concern on the part of the two order theorists, Lipset and Smelser, for maintaining a democratic political system (although Horowitz is also quite concerned about this). At the same time, however, there are sharp differences *within* each of these two pairs, concerning the *reality* of ecological limits. This leads us to classify one member of each pair of works into the HEP row, and one of each into the NEP row.

Thus, Lipset's analysis seems to fall into the HEP-order cell. Although he acknowledges that his belief in the possibility of continued growth is a "hope" (Lipset, 1979: 24), overall he takes a very skeptical attitude toward the idea of ecological limits, implies that a slackening of growth will result more from policy options than from ecological limits, and concludes with a classic HEP position: Since a purposeful reduction in growth will undoubtedly have negative impacts, we should opt for continued growth because

the assumption that necessity is the mother of invention, that demand will provide the impetus for new discovery in the future as in the past...offers a more beneficent prospect for the future of both the developed and underdeveloped worlds [Lipset, 1979: 34].

In sharp contrast, Smelser's somber analysis, which we would place in the NEP-order cell, is premised on a very NEPish reposition:

In the foreseeable future humanity will always be pressing against one limit or another—if it is not oil, it may be some metal in short supply and difficult to substitute for or synthesize; or it may be certain classes of foodstuffs. It is very difficult not to envision the future as a constant series of crises and diversions of resources to overcome these crises [Smelser, 1979: 222].

Analogously, Rainwater's otherwise insightful analysis of the need for substantial equality in a sustainable society HEPishly prescribes greater equality *first,* and *then* slowed growth (as if the latter were primarily a matter of choice). For this reason we would place it in the HEP-conflict cell. Appearing to doubt the reality of ecological limits, it also alludes to the future in a way that makes diachronic competition almost unrecognizable: "It would be shameful if the exigencies of saving the planet for the future of mankind became an excuse to perpetuate the injustices some men now inflict on their fellows" (Rainwater, 1977: 273).[10] In contrast, Horowitz's more realistic assessment of ecological limits leads him to the politically unpalatable conclusion that the United States must begin to accept a "revolution of falling expectations" (Horowitz, 1977: 12, 15) in order to cope with a future of increased scarcity, thus clearly qualifying for the NEP-conflict cell.

In sum, despite their differing theoretical orientations, Smelser and Horowitz share a view that departs markedly from the HEP; both believe human societies will have to change in fundamental ways to cope with ecological limits. In contrast, Lipset and Rainwater, who also perceive the negative impacts of scarcity, ultimately fall back on an eminently HEPish position—hoping the problems can be averted by maintenance of traditional patterns of growth.

Our point in all this is not to argue that the HEP–NEP cleavage supersedes traditional cleavages, but to demonstrate that it is *just as real*—and, in some instances at least, it may be more important. Thus, we anticipate that existing Conflict theories and Order theories, stemming as they both do from the traditional HEP, will undergo significant modification as their adherents attempt to ground them more explicitly within the NEP (see, e.g., Enzensberger [1974] for an attempt to reconcile Marxism with the ecological constraints acknowledged by the NEP). This, of course, raises the question of whether, for example, NEP-Marxism will have more in common with traditional HEP-Marxism, or with other NEP theoretical perspectives. Only time will tell. No paradigm is so specific that it automatically generates a full-blown theory. It only makes certain kinds of questions askable and certain kinds of hypotheses conceivable (Catton and Dunlap, 1978b).

CONCLUSION: THE PROBABLE FUTURE OF THE PARADIGMS

New kinds of questions, and previously inconceivable hypotheses, will be required of sociologists by the ecological constraints inherent in a post-exuberant age. We expect a growing number of sociologists (and other social scientists) to feel the need for shedding the blinders imposed by the HEP. Anomalies generated by recognition of the impacts of ecological constraints on a species thought to be exempt from them will exert pressure for adoption of a more ecologically realistic worldview. Our explica-

tion of the NEP is an attempt to foster the needed realism. We are heartened by evidence of the apparent penetration of this new paradigm beyond the small but growing area of environmental sociology and into the work of at least a few eminent members (e.g., Smelser and Horowitz) of "mainstream" sociology.

It would be foolhardy, however, to predict the imminent demise of the venerable HEP; when its reign seemed unchallengeable, generations of social scientists received their professional socialization according to its tenets. The tenacity with which many of its adherents will defend its implications (in the face of troublesome facts) is well illustrated in recent work of two additional eminent sociologists. For example, in a wide-ranging critique of opposition to nuclear power, an energy source that he believes necessary for continued economic growth and prosperity, Nisbet (1979) views such opposition as a manifestation of declining "faith in progress." By implication, then, continued growth and prosperity could be guaranteed (ecological scarcity notwithstanding) if only we could *restore that faith.* Similarly, Bell (1977: 18), in a strong defense of economic growth and a scathing attack on the idea of physical limits to growth, assures readers that, "If one thinks only in physical terms, then it is likely that one does not need to worry about ever running out of resources." This unecological view is consistent, of course, with his long-held vision of a "post-industrial society," premised as that view is on absence of ecological constraints such as resource scarcity (Marien, 1977). Bell does, however, acknowledge the possibility that there may be "social limits to growth." If there are limits to the development of human societies, Bell seems to be saying, they *must be social* rather than physical. This is, of course, the quintessential HEP response to the "anomalous" limits now affecting human societies.

ENDNOTES

1. An environment's *carrying capacity* for a given form of life means the amount of that life form which that environment can continue supporting indefinitely. When carrying capacity exceeds the quantity of the life form then present in that environment, the surplus can have profound consequences, fostering either population growth or quality-of-life improvement, or both. It ought to be obvious that a carrying capacity deficit would have opposite and equally profound effects. For definitions and discussion of related concepts, see Catton (1980).

2. By very different methods (a "discursive," or linguistic/phenomenological, analysis), Lemert (1979) reaches a similar conclusion—that modern sociologists share in a "homocentric" image of man.

3. A criminologist has recently discerned a similar set of background assumptions in contemporary sociology (Jeffery, 1976: 152).

4. Even sociological human ecology, despite its historical ties to biological ecology, has come to operate within the confines of the HEP (see Dunlap and Catton, 1979b: 58–59, 62–65).

5. There is disagreement, however, over whether carrying capacity is a fixed (or even still enlargeable) quantity, or has begun to decrease from environmental degradation. For the time being wc have simply sidestepped this issue; in our argument it suffices simply to show that even if carrying capacity is fixed and can be represented by a horizontal upper asymptote in the logistic model, conditions of life in post-inflection times are now increasingly recognized as differing fundamentally from pre-inflection conditions. In addition, there is disagreement—which we also sidestep here—over whether or not the ecological load imposed upon the global ecosystem by present human numbers and existing technology *already exceeds* ecosystem carrying capacity. See, for example. Kahn et al. (1976), versus Catton (1980: Chap. 15); Ophuls (1977: 131–137).

6. For an even earlier statement—which unfortunately had little immediate discernible impact—see LaPiere (1965: Chap. 7).

7. In an earlier effort to explicate this nascent paradigm, we labeled it the "New Environmental Paradigm" because it was embodied primarily in the work of environmental sociologists (Catton and Dunlap, 1978a: 44–45). However, since the essence of the NEP is its "ecological" worldview, we have subsequently come to label it the "New Ecological Paradigm" (Dunlap and Catton, 1979a: 250).

8. Dahrendorf actually purports to describe the postulates underlying "structural-functional theory." However, since this theory is the major representative of the Order perspective, his description can also be applied to the broader perspective.

9. Unlike Buttel (1978: 254), however, we do not see Klausner's book as "solidly within the 'NEP' tradition," because of an important ambiguity: it points out the "doctrine of human exceptionalism" but fails to show the unecological inferences drawn from that doctrine.

10. We do not disagree, of course, with Rainwater's moral concern for present inequities. Rather, we feel he does not sufficiently recognize the seriousness of problems of intertemporal equity.

REFERENCES

Anderson, C. H. (1976) The Sociology of Survival. Homewood, IL: Dorsey.

Bell, D. (1977) "Are there 'social limits' to growth?" pp. 13–26 in K. D. Wilson (ed.) Prospects for Growth: Changing Expectations for the Future. New York: Praeger.

Bernard, L. L. (1925) "A classification of environments." Amer. J. of Sociology 31: 318–332.

———. (1922) "The significance of environment as a social factor." Publications of the Amer. Soc. Society 16: 84–112.

Black, J. (1970) The Dominion of Man. Chicago: Aldine.

Brown, L. R. (1978) The Twenty-Ninth Day. New York: Norton.

Burch, W. R., Jr. (1976) "The Peregrine falcon and the urban poor: some sociological interrelations," pp. 308–316 in P. J. Richerson and J. McEvoy III (eds.) Human Ecology: An Environmental Approach. North Scituate, MA: Duxbury Press.

———. (1971) Daydreams and Nightmares: A Sociological Essay on the American Environment. New York: Harper & Row.

Buttel, F. H. (1978) "Environmental sociology: a new paradigm?" Amer. Sociologist 13: 252–256.

———. (1976) "Social science and the environment: competing theories." Social Sci. Q. 57: 307–323.

Catton, W. R., Jr. (1980). Overshoot: The Ecological Basis of Revolutionary Change. Urbana: Univ. of Illinois Press.

———. (1972). "Sociology in an age of fifth wheels." Social Forces 50: 436–447.

———. and R. E. Dunlap (1978a) "Environmental sociology: a new paradigm." Amer. Sociologist 13: 41–49.

———. (1978b) "Paradigms, theories, and the primacy of the HEP-NEP distinction." Amer. Sociologist 13: 256–259.

Choldin, H. M. (1978) "Social life and the physical environment," pp. 352–384 in D. Street (ed.) Handbook of Contemporary Urban Life. San Francisco: Jossey-Bass.

Dahrendorf, R. (1958) "Toward a theory of social conflict." J. of Conflict Resolution 2: 170–183.

Daly, H. E. (1977) Steady-State Economics. San Francisco: Freeman.

Dewey, J. (1937) "Human nature," pp. 531–537 in E. R. A. Seligman and A. Johnson (eds.) Encyclopedia of the Social Sciences. Vol. 7. New York: Macmillan.

Dunlap, R. E. and W. R. Catton, Jr. (1979a) "Environmental sociology." Annual Rev. of Sociology 5: 243–273.

———. (1979b) "Environmental sociology: a framework for analysis," pp. 57–85 in T. O'Riordan and R. C. d'Arge (eds.) Progress in Resource Management and Environmental Planning. Vol. 1. Chichester, England: John Wiley.

Dunlap, R. E. and K. D. Van Liere (1978) "The 'new environmental paradigm': a proposed measuring instrument and preliminary results." J. of Environmental Education 9 (Summer): 10–19.

Durkheim, E. (1950) The Rules of the Sociological Method, New York: Free Press.

Effrat, A. (1972) "Power to the paradigms: an editorial introduction." Soc. Inquiry 42: 3–33.

Ehrenfeld, D. (1978) The Arrogance of Humanism. New York: Oxford Univ. Press.

Ehrlich, P. R. and A. H. Ehrlich (1972) Population, Resources, Environment: Issues in Human Ecology. San Francisco: Freeman.

Enzensberger, H. M. (1974) "A critique of political ecology." New Left Rev. 84: 3–31.

Gouldner, A. W. (1970) The Coming Crisis of Western Sociology. New York: Basic Books.

Harman, W. W. (1979) An Incomplete Guide to the Future. New York: Norton.

Hart, H. (1959) "Social theory and social change," pp. 196–238 in L. Gross (ed.) Symposium on Sociological Theory. Evanston, IL: Row, Peterson.

Horowitz, I. L. (1977) "Social welfare, state power, and the limits to equity," pp. 1–18 in I. L. Horowitz (ed.) Equity, Income, and Policy: Comparative Studies in Three Worlds of Development. New York: Praeger.

Jeffery, C. R. (1976) 'Criminal behavior and the physical environment.' Amer. Behavioral Scientist 20: 149–174,

Kahn, H., W. Brown, and L. Martel (1976) The Next 200 Years: A Scenario for America and the World. New York: William Morrow.

Klausner, S. Z. (1975) "Forty years in the energy desert: life styles in a changing environment." Forensic Q. 49: 329–336.

———. (1971) On Man in His Environment. San Francisco: Jossey-Bass.

Kuhn, T. S. (1962) The Structure of Scientific Revolutions. Chicago: Univ. of Chicago Press.

Landis, P. H. (1949) Man in Environment: An Introduction to Sociology. Now York: Thomas Y. Crowell.

LaPiere, R. T. (1965) Social Change. New York: McGraw-Hill.

Lemert, C. C. (1979) Sociology and the Twilight of Man: Homocentrism and Discourse in Sociological Theory. Carbondale: Southern Illinois Univ. Press.

Lenski, G. and J. Lenski (1978) Human Societies: An Introduction to Macrosociology. New York: McGraw-Hill.

Likens, G. E., R. F. Wright, J. N. Galloway, and T. J. Butler (1979) "Acid rain." Scientific American 241 (October): 43–51.

Lippit, V. D. and K. Hamada (1977) "Efficiency and equity in intergenerational distribution," pp. 285–299 in D. C. Pirages (ed.) The Sustainable Society: Implications for Limited Growth. New York: Praeger.

Lipset, S. M. (1979) "Predicting the future of post-industrial society: can we do it?" pp. 1–35 in S. M. Lipset (ed.) The Third Century: America as a Post-Industrial Society. Stanford, CA: Hoover Institution Press.

Luten, D. B. (1978) "The limits-to-growth controversy," pp. 163–180 in K. A. Hammond et al. (eds.) Sourcebook on the Environment: A Guide to the Literature. Chicago: Univ. of Chicago Press.

Marien, M. (1977) "The two visions of post-industrial society." Futures 9: 415–431.

Meadows, D. H., D. L. Meadows, J. Randers, and W. W. Behrens III (1972) The Limits to Growth. New York: Universe Books.

Merton, R. K. (1968) Social Theory and Social Structure. Enlarged edition. New York: Free Press.

Michelson, W. H. (1970) Man and His Urban Environment. Reading, MA: Addison-Wesley.

Miles, R. (1976) Awakening from the American Dream: The Social and Political Limits to Growth. New York: Universe Books.

Morrison, D. E. (1976) "Growth, environment, equity and scarcity." Social Sci. Q. 57: 292–306.

Mulligan, L. (1978) "Energy regionalism in the United States: the decline of the national energy commons," pp. 1–12 in S. Warkov (ed.) Energy Policy in the United States. New York: Praeger.

———. (1976) "Energy abundance and energy scarcity: the norm of family privacy." Presented at the annual meeting of the North Central Sociological Association, Louisville, Kentucky.

Nisbet, R. (1979) "The rape of progress." Public Opinion 2 (June/July): 2–6, 55.

Odum, E. P. (1975) Ecology: The Link Between the Natural and the Social Sciences. New York: Holt, Rinehart & Winston.

Ophuls, W. (1977) Ecology and the Politics of Scarcity. San Francisco: Freeman.

Passmore, J. (1974) "Man's Responsibility for Nature: Ecological Problems and Western Traditions." New York: Scribner.

Pirages, D. C. (1978) The New Context for International Relations: Global Ecopolitics. North Scituate, MA: Duxbury Press.

———. [ed.] (1977) The Sustainable Society. New York: Praeger.

Potter, D. M. (1954) People of Plenty: Economic Abundance and the American Character. Chicago: Univ. of Chicago Press.

Rainwater, L. (1977) 'Equity, income, inequality and the steady state," pp. 262–273 in D. C. Pirages (ed.) The Sustainable Society: Implications for Limited Growth. New York: Praeger.

Renshaw, E. F. (1976) The End of Progress: Adjusting to a No-Growth Economy. North Scituate, MA: Duxbury Press.

Ritzer, G. (1975) Sociology: A. Multiple Paradigm Science. Boston: Allyn & Bacon.

Schnaiberg, A. (1980) The Environment: From Surplus to Scarcity. New York: Oxford Univ. Press.

———. (1975) "Social syntheses of the societal-environmental dialectic: the role of distributional impacts." Social Sci. Q. 56: 5–20.

Sessions, G. (1974) "Anthropocentrism and the environmental crisis." Humboldt J. of Social Relations 2 (Fall/Winter): 71–81.

Smelser, N. J. (1979) "Energy restriction, consumption, and social stratification," pp. 215–228 in C. T. Unseld et al.(eds.) Sociopolitical Effects of Energy Use and Policy. Washington: National Academy of Sciences.

Stanley, M. (1968) "Nature, culture and scarcity: foreword to a theoretical synthesis." Amer. Soc. Rev. 33: 855–970.

Stobaugh, R. and D. Yergin [eds.] (1979) Energy Future: Report of the Energy Project at the

Harvard Business School. New York: Random House.

Thomas, W. I. (1909) Source Book for Social Origins. Chicago: Univ. of Chicago Press.

Timasheff, N. S. (1967) Sociological Theory: Its Nature and Growth. New York: Random House.

Van Slambrouck, P. (1980) "US energy 'bank account' shrinks, but more slowly." Christian Science Monitor (May 8).

Van Til, J. (1979) "Spatial form and structure in a possible future: some implications of energy shortfall for urban planning." J. of the Amer. Planning Association 45: 318–329.

Watt, K. E. F., L. F. Molloy, C. K. Varshney, D. Weeks, and S. Wirosard Jono (1977) The Unsteady State: Environmental Problems, Growth, and Culture. Honolulu: Univ. Press of Hawaii, for the East-West Center.

Webb, W. P. (1952) The Great Frontier. Boston: Houghton Mifflin.

White, L., Jr. (1967) "The historical roots of our ecologic crisis." Science 155: 1203–1207.

Williams, R. M., Jr. (1970) American Society: A Sociological Interpretation. New York: Knopf.

Wilson, I. (1977) "The changing metabolism of growth," pp. 143–160 in K. D. Wilson (ed.) Prospects for Growth: Changing Expectations for the Future. New York: Praeger.

Yankelovich, D. and B. Lefkowitz (1980) "National growth: the question of the 80's." Public Opinion 3 (December/January): 44–49, 52–57.

Chapter 10

From Growth to Sustainable and Equitable Development

20. What Does Sustainability Really Mean? The Search for Useful Indicators*

ALEX FARRELL AND MAUREEN HART

Four years ago, the town of North Andover, Massachusetts, began grappling with an issue common to many communities: how to set the price for the water it supplies to residents. The town was fortunate in having a good source of clean water in a municipally-owned lake. But resident water bills had been rising steadily for several years, and many were unhappy about it. One reason for these increases was the town's new $20 million treatment plant. But town authorities had also set the water rates so as to generate a small profit—a fact that spawned a vigorous debate among residents. Some approved of this strategy, while others felt that the town should sell water at cost, and still others wanted to subsidize the water used by low-income residents.

Framing the debate solely in terms of dollars allowed a very important fact to go unnoticed however: North Andover's water use was close to exceeding the available supply, the lake's "safe yield" (the amount of water that can dependably be withdrawn

even in times of drought) was estimated to be 3.4 million gallon per day by 2000. North Andover has still not solved its water problem, but it has shifted the focus of the debate from revenues to sustainability—a change that has had some marked consequences. The town's community development director has incorporated a measure of safe yield per person into projections of the town's growth. The town manager has proposed a conservation-oriented rate structure that would charge people higher-rates the more water they use. And a developer is talking about ways to reduce the use of in-ground lawn-sprinklers one of the principal causes of increasing demand for water.

Both water revenues (the initial focus of the debate) and consumption relative to the safe yield (the current focus) are indicators of community well-being. The first pertains to the town's financial position, the second to its use of key resource. The crucial difference between them is that the revenue indicator would eventually fail—at some point, water shortages would force the town water rates to bring demand into line with supply, restricting water use, purchasing additional water elsewhere, or some other measure.

The situation in North Andover offers a concrete example of the need to ensure that human activities are sustainable. Although

*This essay was originally published in *Environment* 40(9), November 1998:4, 4–9, 26–31. Reprinted with permission of the Helen Dwight Reid Educational Foundation. Published by Heldref Publications, 1319 Eighteen St., NW, Washington, DC 20036-1802. Copyright © 1998.

the importance of sustainability is gaining acceptance in many parts of the world, furthering it poses a serious challenge to decision makers because there is no generally accepted definition of the term. Even those who support this concept disagree on its precise meaning, while those who do not support it argue that it has no meaning at all.[1] And just as there is no agreement on the meaning of sustainability, so there is no widely recognized way to measure it. As a result, researchers and organizations have been left to their own devices in formulating specific (usually qualitative) indicators of sustainability and progress toward that goal. These efforts may provide useful guides for policy in the future. But they are already significant because they provide a number of concrete definitions of sustainability—indicating that although the concept means different things to different people, it is far from meaningless.

This article explores the concept of sustainability and the derivation of sustainability indicators, focusing on some of the more prominent efforts in this area to date. There is still a long way to go to reach consensus on how to measure sustainability. However, the ongoing efforts of many organizations (ranging from local, grassroots initiatives to those of global institutions) are helping to change sustainability from a buzz word to a meaningful concept that is understandable to the lay public and that may become useful for decisionmaking.

THE CONCEPT OF SUSTAINABILITY

There are two general conceptions of sustainability, which are often seen as being in conflict. Concerns about environmental degradation and the Earth's carrying capacity[2] have led to what might be called the critical limits view of sustainability. This

view focuses on natural assets such as the ozone layer, fertile soil, and healthy wetlands, which provide services people rely on to live and which we do not know how to replace. Together, such assets constitute ecosystems that are essential to human well-being. This implies that we must preserve these ecosystems and respect the limits that they impose on the number of people in the world and their mode of living. The competing objectives view of sustainability, on the other hand, focuses on balancing social, economic, and ecological goals. It thus aims at meeting a broad range of human needs and aspirations, including health, literacy, and political freedom as well as purely material needs.[3]

These concepts differ in two important ways. First, the idea of resource limits is central to the critical limits view but entirely absent from the competing objectives view. Second, the critical limits view has a much narrower scope. It is also said to be more objective, but that assertion is questionable. Because the number of humans that the Earth can support is not readily determinable, it is not always clear which assets are critical and which are not. For example, although biodiversity is a necessary component of a healthy wetland ecosystem, it is not always clear how important each individual species is. For this reason, it is virtually impossible to ascertain the amount of resources that humans require without making some subjective judgments.

Each view, however, is very concerned about equity, both within and between generations. Intergenerational equity, of course, entails leaving future generations an ecologically viable planet with abundant resources, while intragenerational equity entails distributing the environmental costs and benefits fairly among people living now. Both forms of equity are based in part on concerns about the morality of some people living well at the expense of others. A more; pragmatic concern is that the poverty resulting from inequitable resource distribution leads to the degradation of ecosystems.[4] The destruction of local ecosystems can, of course, have global effects. For example, the global climate system depends in part on the role of rainforests, which are often clearcut due to local pressure for jobs and income. Such changes can lead to international—and possibly violent-conflicts over scarce resources, such as the recent conflict between Canada and the United States over fishing rights and disputes over water rights worldwide.

Although there is no agreement on the precise meaning of sustainability, a good working definition—one that incorporates elements of both views–might be the following: "improving the quality of human life while living within the carrying capacity of supporting ecosystems."[5] Whatever definition one choses, there is widespread agreement that sustainability is important and that indicators to measure progress toward it are needed.

INDICATORS OF SUSTAINABILITY

In general, an indicator is something that provides useful information about a physical, social, or economic system, usually in numerical terms.[6] Indicators can be used to describe the state of the system, to detect changes in it, and to show cause-and-effect relationships. For instance, the level of water in a reservoir is a state, drawdowns represent a change in that state, and comparisons of these variables over time can reveal cause-and-effect relationships such as the impact of conservation policies on water usage. Indicators thus supplement other information that we have (such as that from

theories), giving us more complete pictures of the systems in question.

The choice of a particular indicator is guided by two considerations: what one wishes to know and how the information will be used. Scientists and analysts are generally interested in seeing the raw data and interpreting it themselves.[7] Policymakers are more interested in summary information that is clearly related to policy objectives, evaluation criteria, and targets; they usually do not want to perform much analysis themselves, although they may be interested in how it is done. And members of the public, who tend to lack an analytical perspective, often just want simple, clear, unambiguous messages. Regardless of the level of detail, however, there are certain characteristics that every good indicator will have, such as relevancy and the use of reliable data.

One point should be stressed, however: Although a great deal has been written about indicators in general, much less work has been done on sustainability indicators per se. The criteria that have been proposed for such indicators suggest that they should focus on a fairly broad range of concerns, such as furthering inter- and intragenerational equity; not exceeding the carrying capacity of natural resources and ecosystems; reducing the impact that human activities have on the *environment* (particularly the rates at which renewable and nonrenewable resources are used); integrating long-term economic, social, and environmental goals; and preserving biological, cultural, and economic diversity.[8] More research is needed in this area, however. (See Box 10.1.)

In the area of sustainability, a number of different indicators have been developed. These indicators vary considerably, depending on the underlying view of sustainability they embody, the organizing framework

Box 10.1
Frameworks for Sustainability Indicator Sets

Sustainability indicator sets are generally developed within a framework that not only organizes them but also shows whether or not they are balanced, that is, whether or not they reflect the full range of sustainability concerns. There are three common frameworks in use: the topic of interest, the goals of the developers, and the pressure-state-response framework.[1] A topic-based framework groups indicators by specific topic areas, such as the economy, the ***environment,*** transportation, pollution, and so forth. With this framework, one can readily determine the degree of balance by looking at the number of indicators used for each topic, but it has the disadvantage of tending to use traditional indicators that sometimes conflict. For example, traditional measures of economic growth fail to reflect the increases in pollution that generally accompany growth. Thus, topic-based frameworks make it hard to see the linkages between areas and provide no impetus for the development of better indicator sets.

The goal-based framework organizes indicators into a matrix showing how each indicator relates to all the different sustainability goals of a particular community or other entity. As long as the goals adequately represent the desires of the community, this framework ensures that the indicator set reflects the full range of desires. It also shows the links between goals, as certain indicators can measure progress toward multiple goals. For example, "the number of acres of sustainably managed farmland" could measure progress toward the sustainable use of a natural resource (land) as well as that toward a healthy economy. The disadvantage to this framework is that if the goals are not representative, the resulting indicator set will not be representative either.

The pressure-state-response framework was developed by the Organisation for Economic

Cooperation and Development as a way of analyzing environmental indicators. (The United Nations Commission on Sustainable Development has since modified this framework by substituting the concept of "driving forces" for "pressure" to include the social, economic, and institutional factors that affect sustainability.[2]) This framework focuses on those human activities (the pressures) that lead to particular environmental conditions (the states) and ultimately to remedial actions (the responses). Poor air quality, for example, is a state, one of the contributing pressures for which is automobile emissions; one possible response is to establish automobile emissions standards. This framework is very useful for describing the causes of problems and for understanding the linkages between the economy, the ***environment,*** and society. One disadvantage is that it can be difficult to apply to social and economic indicators. For example, "the number of people driving cars" is a pressure with respect to air quality, a state with respect to transportation, and a response indicator with respect to land use patterns. Although such an indicator has the virtue of highlighting the links among several different aspects of sustainability, one must be clear how such an indicator is used in any specific case and whether an increase or decrease is preferred.

1. V. Maclaren. Developing Indicators of Urban Sustainability: A Focus on the Canadian Experience (Toronto: International Committee on Urban and Regional Research Press, 1996).

2. United Nations Department of Economic and Social Affairs. Division of Sustainable Development, "Measuring Changes in Consumption and Production Patterns" (background paper for the Workshop on Indicators for Changing Consumption and Production Patterns, New York, 2–3 March 1998).

they employ, and the interests and goals of their creators (see the box on page 8 for a description of the frameworks most commonly used for indicators). Specific examples include energy use and emissions of greenhouse gases (total and per capita); the percent of harvested forest that is successfully replanted; environmentally adjusted measurements of economic activity; the hours of work (at the average wage) that are required to satisfy basic needs; the income disparity between the top and bottom segments of the population; and the number of college graduates who are able to return home and find appropriate employment.

Indicators are generally reported in one of three ways: individually, as part of a set, or in the form of a composite index that combines various individual indicators into a single number. As a rule, individual indi-

cators are of limited use—a balanced set of indicators is needed to adequately represent a complex system. A well-chosen suite of indicators can also be very educational, particularly for the lay public. Then too, a single, aggregated number can be very useful in communicating information to the public and decision makers, although the appropriate methods to use in achieving such aggregation remain very controversial. (See Box 10.2 for examples of the indicators identified by the United Nations Commission on Sustainable Development and Box 10.3 for further details on aggregation.)

The organizations that are developing sustainability indicators range from the international to the very local, from corporations to national and municipal governments. Not only have they produced different kinds of indicators, they have

---

Box 10.2
Selected Indicators

United Nations Commission on Sustainable Development
Income inequality
Population growth rate
Difference between male and female school enrollment rates
Per capita consumption of fossil fuels for transportation
The ratio of the average house price to average income
Living space (floor area) per person
Environmentally adjusted net domestic product
Energy consumption
The intensity of materials use
Percentage of the population with adequate excreta disposal facilities

Share of renewable energy resources consumed
Annual withdrawals of ground and surface water
The ratio of debt service to export earnings
Amount of new funding for sustainable development
The maximum sustained yield for fisheries
Changes in land use
Percent of arable land that is irrigated
Energy use in agriculture
Percentage of forest area that is protected
Emissions of greenhouse gases
Waste recycling and reuse
Access to information
The representation of major groups on national councils for sustainable development

NOTE: The United Nations Commission on Sustainable Development has identified a total of 134 indicators of sustainability (see gopher://gopher.un.org/00/esc/cn17/1997-98/pattern/mccppS-9.txt).

Box 10.3
Sustainability Indices

An index is a single measure that combines many individual pieces of information by means of a precise mathematical formula. A familiar example is the Consumer Price Index, which is a weighted average of the prices for individual goods and services where the weights are the relative shares of those goods and services in consumer purchases overall. Sustainability indices, however, pose a problem that economic indices generally do not, namely, finding a common unit by which to measure all of the variables in which analysts are interested. There are two basic solutions to this problem: to use monetary equivalents or to use some common physical parameter.

Monetary Measures

Monetary measures of sustainability are essentially modifications of well-known economic indicators designed to measure growth. They represent an attempt by economists to incorporate the concept of sustainability into an existing theoretical framework so that they can bring familiar techniques and insights to bear on the issue. Another important rationale for this approach is that it gives decision makers environmental information in a form with which they are familiar and in which it can readily be compared with other types of information. Monetary indices are of two general types, those pertaining to "green national accounting" and those that attempt to measure general well-being.

Green national accounting entails modifying the System of National Accounts (SNA) to include environmental factors. The SNA framework was developed by the United Nations. It sets the standards for measuring gross domestic product (GDP) and other parameters needed to understand a nation's economy, such as the current account balance, wealth, and government income and expenditures. Such parameters, of course, are crucial in making many policy decisions, but they tend to exclude important envi-

ronmental factors because those factors are not reflected in market activities.

Green national accounting does not replace the SNA system; rather, it attempts to bring environmental issues into the existing framework through satellite accounts.[1] These satellite accounts principally measure changes in natural resource balances and the damage caused by pollution. For example, when a forest is cleared to produce lumber, the value of the lumber would be recorded as part of GDP in the usual way, but a satellite account for forests would also show a decrease in the value of the forest itself. Analysis might then reveal that this decrease was related to the loss of other sorts of revenue (such as income from tourism), along with environmental degradation such as erosion and siltation in streams. However, green national accounting does not include reductions in ecosystem services that lie completely outside the market, such as the wildlife habitat that the forest provides. Furthermore, green national accounting does not address social issues even though such issues are central to many people's understanding of sustainability. Therefore, it is not surprising that broader indicators of well-being have emerged as well.

Perhaps the best known of these new indicators are the Index of Sustainable Economic Welfare (ISEW) and the related Genuine Progress Index (GPI), which come in the wake of a long history of efforts by economists to improve the measurement of welfare.[2] To calculate the values of these indices, one starts with a standard national accounting measure such as personal income or consumption and adjusts this for a variety of factors, including income inequality, defensive expenditures like cleaning up pollution, and environmental degradation. Calculations for the United States, Austria, the United Kingdom, and Scotland show that the ISEW is significantly lower than GDP and has not increased since about 1970.[3]

(continued)

Box 10.3   Continued

Nonmonetary Measures

Nonmonetary measures of sustainability are composite indicators that use a metric other than money, usually some sort of physical parameter such as the amount of nonrenewable energy a society uses. Nicholas Georgescu-Roegen first rigorously applied thermodynamic concepts (particularly entropy) to economic systems, and economist Kenneth Boulding extended these ideas with his notion of a "spaceship economy" in which the Earth is a spaceship that is closed materially but receives energy from the sun.[4] According to this conception, the Earth has a certain amount of stored energy in the form of fossil fuels, but once that stock is depleted it will be necessary to rely on solar inputs alone.[5] Energy-based sustainability indices reflect the critical limits view of sustainability because there is no effort to measure factors such as education or employment. Even so, it is not clear how factors like biodiversity can be meaningfully transformed into thermodynamic measurements.

A closely related and widely known measure is the "ecological footprint" developed by land-use planners William Rees and Mathias Wackernagel.[6] This indicator is based on the idea that one can assess sustainability in terms of the amount of land that is required to produce goods and services for (and absorb the pollution from) a person, city, country, or other entity. The focus of the ecological footprint is on consumption and the flow of materials and energy through human systems. Because of its simplicity, it may be a useful tool for promoting dialogue between various community group interested in sustainability or as a means of education. However, this measure is limited in that it does not address the social or economic components of sustainability very well.

A third nonmonetary indicator is the Human Development Index (HDI) published by the United Nations in its annual Human Development Report.[7] This indicator is constructed by calculating a normalized sum of life expectancy, adult literacy, education, and income.[8] One of the primary purposes of the HDI is to study how economic growth relates to other aspects of human development. Thus it reflects the competing-objectives view of sustainability even though it contains no environmental information. While some analysts find the HDI useful in fostering discussion of the appropriate forms of development, others point out that there are strong correlations among the various components and thus that little is gained by having a more extensive (and subjective) measure.[9] One limitation of this indicator is that it does not address the ecological issues pertaining to sustainability or those of equity (except when comparing different areas). Furthermore, because the HDI is additive, it implies that its components are all directly comparable and substitutable for each other (e.g., more literacy can compensate for lower income).

1. See R. Repetto, "Earth in Balance Sheet: Incorporating Natural Resources in National income "National Accounts and **Environment** Resources," **Environment** and Resource Economics 1, no. 1 (1991): 1; P. Bartelmus and J. von Tongren, "Integrated Environmental and Economic Accounting: Framework for an SNA Satellite System," review of Income and Wealth 2 (1991); and United Nations Department for Economic and Social Information and Policy Analysis, Integrated Environmental and Economic Accounting: Interim Version (New York: United Nations, 1993).

2. See H. Daly and J. Cobb, For the Common Good (Boston, Mass.: Beacon Press, 1993); C. Cobb et al., "If the GDP Is Up, Why Is America Down?," Atlantic Monthly, October 1995, 59; C. Cobb and J. Cobb, The Green National Product: A Proposed Index of Sustainable Economic Welfare (Lanham, Md.: University Press of America, 1994A); W. Nordhaus and J. Tobin, Is Growth Obsolete? (New York: Columbia University Press, 1972); and I. Moffat, "On Measuring Sustainable Development Indicators," International Journal of Sustainable Development and World Ecology 1, no. 2 (1991): 97.

3. T. Jackson and N. Marks, Measuring Sustainable Economic Welfare: A pilot Index 1950–1990 (Stockhom: Stockholm **Environment** Institute, 1994); I. Moffat and M. Wilson, "An Index of Sustainable Economic Welfare for Scotland, 1980–1991," International Journal of Sustainable Development and World Ecology 1, no. 4 (1991): 264; and E. Stockhammer et al., "The Index of Sustainable Economic Welfare (ISEW) as an Alternative to GDP in Measuring Economic Welfare:

The Results of the Austrian (Revised) ISEW Calculation 1955–1992," Ecological Economics 21, no. 1 (1992): 10.

4. N. Georgescu-Roegen, The Entropy Law and the Economic Process (Cambridge, Mass.: Harvard University Press, 1971), 145; and K. Boulding, The Economics of the Coming Spaceship Earth (Baltimore, Md.: John Hopkins University Press, 1966), 3–14.

5. H. Odum, "Energy in Ecosystems," in N. Polunin, ed., Environmental Monographs and Symposia (New York: John Wiley and Sons, 1986): C. Cleveland, "Natural Resource Scarcity and Economic Growth Revisited: Economic and Biophysical Perspective," in R. Costanza, ed., Ecological Economics (New York: Columbia University Press, 1991), 289; J. Gever et al., Beyond Oil: The Threat to Food and Fuel in the Coming Decades (Cambridge, Mass.: Harper & Row, 1986); and R. Ayres and K. Martinas, "Waste Potential Energy: The Ultimate Ecotoxic," Economic Applications 43, no. 2 (1995).

6. M. Wackernagel and W. Rees, Our Ecological Footprint: Reducing Human Impact on the Earth (Gabriola Island, B.C.: New Society Publishers, 1996).

7. United Nations Development Programme, Human Development Report 1990 (New York: Cambridge University Press, 1994).

8. The four indicators are normalized before they are added, that is, each is converted to a value between 0 and 1 using a fixed scale. The scale for life expectancy runs from 25 years (which assumes the value 0) to 85 years (which assumes the value 1). Similarly, income is measured as per capita GDP (on a purchasing power parity basis) on a scale from $200 to $40,000; adult literacy is the percentage of literate adults divided by 100; and education is measured as the average number of years of school completed from 0 to 15. All of these adjustments, however, reflect significant normative judgements that go to the heart of what sustainability means. As a result, they deserve much more scrutiny by both researchers and the public.

9. V. Rao. "Human Development Report 1990: Review and Assessment," World Development 19, no. 10 (1991): 1,454; and M. McGillivray, "The Human Development Index; Yet Another Redundant Composite Development Indicator?," World Development 19, no. 10 (1991): 1,461.

used very different processes to do so. Indeed, many participants and observers note that the process of developing a sustainability indicator set is as valuable as the set of indicators that results. The process is considered so important, in fact, that there are now guides on how to develop sustainability indicators.[9]

A good example of the advice being offered is the Bellagio principles, which were developed by an international group of researchers and practitioners in 1996.[10] These principles are built on four basic concepts: First, those developing a set of indicators must have a vision of sustainability that is appropriate for the particular place and people involved. Second, the indicators should reflect a holistic view of the linkages between the economic, environmental, and social aspects of development, they should consider both inter- and intragenerational equity, and they should consider the ecological conditions that life depends on and

have sufficient scope to address distant effects while still having practical application. Third, the process of developing indicators should be open, inclusive, and take advantage of existing techniques and technologies for effective communication. And fourth, the developers need to conduct ongoing assessments of the quality of the indicators in the set. Although the exact process has varied, many of the sustainability indicator projects undertaken to date have relied on these general principles.

CURRENT EFFORTS

National and International

Sustainability indicators are being developed at the national level in many countries, although with different levels of effort and different degrees of sophistication. For most, Agenda 21—the principal document signed at the 1992 Earth Summit—provides important motivations and guidance.[11] International efforts to develop sustainability indicator sets generally have two objectives: coordinating national and subnational efforts and evaluating global-scale processes and effects. Most of these efforts are conducted by groups of government employees (often from different departments) assisted by outside experts.

Canada was one of the earliest countries to attempt to measure sustainability, having started an environmental indicators program in 1989 and published sustainability plans as early as 1993. Sustainability indicators are now used routinely by governmental bodies in Canada from the local to the national level. The national-level indicators are organized by topic; there are also sectoral indicators for the forestry sector.

Within the U.S. government, efforts to develop sustainability indicators are guided by the report of the President's Council on Sustainable Development, a panel of business, government, and environmental leaders that met for two years to attempt to identify what sustainability meant for a broad range of issues. Their recommendations emphasize improving management practices to reduce the cost and red tape associated with environmental protection; increasing public participation in the development of environmental policy; improving social and economic opportunities; and promoting intergenerational equity.[12] An Interagency Working Group on Sustainable Development Indicators that has been at work since 1994 recently proposed an indicator set that includes 32 indicators.[13] The overall framework includes three concepts: endowments (the resources, assets, and conditions—economic, environmental, and social—that are inherited from past generations and passed on to future generations); current outputs (the

goods, services, and experiences that the current generation enjoys); and processes (activities that use endowments to produce current outputs). Although this framework is partially topic-based, it also attempts to identify pressures on the *environment* as well as the effects of policy responses. The working group states explicitly that the framework is not intended to include criteria for selecting indicators; instead, a collaborative process that "allows wide participation and achieves broad consensus" is to be used. As a result, some of the indicators that have been proposed, such as gross domestic product, have the characteristics of good indicators but are not true sustainability indicators.

In addition to this effort, several federal agencies have launched sustainability indicator programs, notably the U.S. Forest Service and the Environmental Protection Agency (EPA). The Forest Service has held a series of roundtables with forest-based communities and other federal agencies on sustainable forestry management and has begin to produce sustainability indicators, but it is not clear whether these efforts have led to changes in policy.[14] Not surprisingly, EPA has many programs related to sustainability indicators at both the national and regional levels.[15] These too are mostly in the development stage and have not led to major changes in policy. EPA's Office of Sustainable Ecosystems and Communities has even developed a training program for community leaders who would like to formulate sustainability indicator sets for their own purposes.[16]

Many European countries have undertaken extensive efforts to develop sustainability indicators as pan of their response to Agenda 21.[17] Some of these have been conducted by governments, but many are the work of research institutes and environmental organizations such as the European chapters of Friends of the Earth (FOE).[18] In 1995, FOE launched a "Sustainable Europe" campaign that has produced sustainability indicator sets for several different countries, including those usually considered green (Austria, Germany, the Netherlands, Norway, and Finland) plus Scotland.[19] The FOE approach uses the concept of "environmental space"—a critical limits approach organized by topics.

Although European efforts generally take the critical limits view of sustainability, they do tend to acknowledge the equity implications of the very large differences in standards of living in industrialized and nonindustrialized countries and they clearly show an appreciation for the value-laden nature of choosing sustainability indicators. Because FOE explicitly describes the choice of indicators and the determination of numerical targets as requiring both scientific information and value judgments, these endeavors are best described as social processes. It is somewhat surprising, therefore, to observe relatively few social and economic indicators in some of the European sustainability indicator efforts.

During the last several years, the European Union (EU) has been moving towards the adoption of sustainability as an important goal, and several member states have been pressuring the European Commission to develop sustainability indicators. Currently, the EU has an Environmental Pressure Indices program under way and is making an effort to use a set of indicators developed by the United Nations Commission on Sustainable Development. Although the recently established European Environmental Agency is largely a data-gathering organization at present, it may play a larger role in implementing sustainability indicators in the future.

Most developing nations lag behind in the implementation of sustainability indicators, though Costa Rica and the Philippines stand out as good examples of countries that have taken the first steps.[20] Most poor countries see economic development as their primary objective, and it is only in the last decade that their governments have become concerned about environmental issues like pollution. The sustainability indicator programs that do exist in such countries tend to be fairly small efforts that are usually conducted with outside funding (often from an international development agency). And poor nations face a serious challenge in developing sustainability indicators owing to the lack of reliable and comprehensive data, among other factors.

Local

Local efforts to develop sustainability indicators (usually indicator sets) have employed widely varying definitions of sustainability. While some attempt to measure sustainability per se, others focus on quality of life or the "state of the community." Most of these efforts, however, reflect the competing objectives view of sustainability, although the most thoughtful ones also focus on respecting biogeophysical limits.[21]

Perhaps the best-known such effort (at least in the United States) is the indicator set formulated by residents of Seattle, Washington.[22] This effort began in 1990, following a conference sponsored by the Global Tomorrow Coalition. It has since produced a series of reports on indicators and trends, the most recent being released in April of this year. The process entailed extensive public meetings over a period of two years, aided by a small amount of grant money for organizational and communications activities.

The definition of sustainability used by this community is "long-term health and vitality—cultural, economic, environmental, and social."[23] The indicator set includes 40 individual indicators grouped according to five main topics: the *environment* population and resources, the economy, youth and education, and health and community. Five criteria were used to identify suitable indicators. Each indicator had to be a bellwether of sustainability, that is, it had to "reflect something basic and fundamental to the long-term cultural, economic, environmental, or social health of a community over generations." It also had to be accepted by the community; attractive to local media; statistically measurable; and logically or scientifically defensible.

Although not stated specifically in the criteria, the ability of an indicator to highlight the linkages between different parts of the community was another selection factor. The indicators used by Sustainable Seattle include the number of salmon returning to spawn (compared with a 1978 baseline); the annual per capita number of vehicle miles traveled and gallons of gasoline consumed; the number of hours of work at the average wage needed to pay for basic needs; and total and per capita water consumption.

These indicators are maintained by a volunteer organization housed at the Seattle Metrocenter YMCA. Tracking and publishing the indicators from 1993 to the present has involved hundreds of area residents (more than 250 worked on the 1998 report). The main purpose of this effort is to provide education and outreach to the community on issues related to sustainability. Because Sustainable Seattle is not affiliated with any governmental organization, its reports are not used directly in policy making, though they have influenced a number of projects undertaken by area governments.[24]

Another good example of a local indicator effort comes from Fife, Scotland.[25] This community used three criteria for selecting indicators: the effect of the activities in question on future generations; the full environmental cost of those activities; and the fairness of the resulting distribution of resources and services. In addition, the entire community was encouraged to participate in the decisionmaking process. The resulting indicator set includes 20 indicators framed in terms of four topics (see Box 10.4). This set, which is typical of local efforts, is fairly balanced. However, it has at least one drawback that is common to such efforts: It does not provide adequate information for decisionmaking. For instance, the indicator "tons of fish landed at Fife ports" does not indicate the optimal level of such landings (a larger catch would provide immediate economic benefits but could also entail greater long-term harm to the *environment*). To be sure, the accompanying text notes some of the issues underlying this indicator, such as the long-term decline of fisheries, the effect of competition from large boats on small boat operators and fishing villages, and the amount of nonrenewable energy that is expended in catching fish compared with the energy gained by eating it. But it merely raises a red flag without necessarily showing which way to go.

Three general observations can be made about the formulation of sustainability indicators at the local level. First, whatever indicators are selected, the selection process is valuable because it focuses attention on the issue of sustainability. Most of the communities that have adopted indicators began with no more than a rudimentary notion of this concept and its implications for community life. However, the lengthy and sometimes difficult process of selecting indicators forced them to examine not only the environmental, economic,

---

Box 10.4
The Sustainability Indicator Set for Fife, Scotland

Basic Needs

Number of households registered as homeless

Average energy efficiency rating of homes

Number of people unemployed for more than one year

Poverty rate (number of claims for financial support)

Transportation alternatives (kilometers of bicycle routes)

Community

Average life expectancies at birth for men and women

Number of deaths in the first year of life per 1,000 live births

Reported cases of crimes of violence, burglary, and indecent assault

Number of placements in Fife Regional Council Nurseries

Number of accidents involving injury to pedestrians and cyclists

Quality of the *environment*

Number of square kilometers of land lost to development

Number of submerged plant species in selected lochs

Water quality (the concentration of nitrates in the water in boreholes)

Number of complaints to local authorities about noise

Air quality (the ratio of sulfur dioxide and smoke to the limits set by the European Community)

Use of resources

Number of people employed in agriculture

Tons of fish landed at Fife ports

Household waste per person

Percentage of population with sewage discharged to the sea untreated or partially treated

Total energy consumption

SOURCE: Department of Economic Development and Planning, Sustainability, Indicators for Fife: Measuring the Quality of Life and the Quality of the Environment in Fife (Fife, Scotland, 1995).

---

and social conditions at issue but their values as well. As a result, many people have come away with a more intuitive understanding of sustainability and what it means for them as individuals and as a community.

Second, most of the local sustainability indicator initiatives in the United States are grassroots responses to local concerns and do not refer to Agenda 21 or other concepts developed at the international level. Thus, even though those leading such efforts are familiar with international work (and most U.S. efforts are consistent with the broad outline of sustainability indicators articulated in international documents), home-grown practices and techniques developed by peers tend to dominate U.S. efforts. In a word, there seems to be no attempt to connect local sustainability indicators to anything at a larger scale or to look to organizations like the United Nations for guidance, a feature that contrasts with many local efforts elsewhere in the world.

Third, public participation features prominently in community-level sustainability indicator efforts in the United States, which is not surprising given the character of U.S. politics. Indeed, it is unlikely that such efforts could obtain popular support without significant public participation. Most local advocates of sustainability realize that the implementation of sustainability requires action by the public, either in political forums (primarily as voters) or in the marketplace (primarily as consumers). Thus, they see the generation of interest in indicators as a way to get on the path to sustainable development. Of course, the same may be true elsewhere in the world.

MOVING BEYOND THE VAGUE

Although cynics may claim that sustainability is just the latest buzz word to include in reports and project proposals, a review of the many definitions in use shows that there is a growing convergence in the meaning of this term. Three concepts in particular are reflected in many of these definitions: that natural resources are finite and there are limits to the carrying capacity of the Earth's ecosystems; that economic, environmental, and social goals must be pursued within these limits; and that there is a need for inter- and intragenerational equity.

Although there is growing consensus that development objectives have to respect the boundaries set by the biosphere, there is still a wide gap between developing and developed countries as to the relative priorities of economic and environmental goals. Developing countries still emphasize economic growth and increases in material possessions as ways to improve the quality of life. In developed countries, by contrast, quality of life is beginning to be seen less in terms of material possessions and more in terms of the quality of the time spent in various activities, the quality of personal relationships, and personal well-being.[26] Thus, while developing countries are understandably most concerned about living better, developed countries are beginning to think about living well within certain limits.

So far, the convergence on the meaning of sustainability is not being seen in the indicators used to measure progress toward it. In many cases, the indicators proposed are simply combined lists of traditional economic, environmental, and social indicators with the word sustainable added to the title. To be sure, combining different types of indicators in this way is a significant first step: It recognizes that all three areas are important and the discussions that attend it help give meaning to the somewhat abstract concept of sustainability. It is extremely important, however, that the development of indicators not stop there. Unconnected indicators encourage the same fragmented view of the world that has historically led to some of our most serious problems. Decision makers need indicators that show the links between social, environmental, and economic goals to better understand how to achieve economic growth that is in harmony with—rather than at the expense of—the natural systems within which we live. And there remains a need for criteria for evaluating indicators that can be understood by decision makers at all levels.

Questions also remain as to whether or not individual indicators can or should be aggregated. There are two issues here: how to represent the concept of sustainability meaningfully and accurately in a compact form, and how to connect different sustainability indicator sets to each other. Indices may be useful in resolving the first issue, although every index contains hidden assumptions and simplifications and so needs to be used judiciously. On the second issue, connecting indicators will not be a simple task because physical and social systems often act differently at different scales. For example, a long-term decline in the world price of petroleum would be good for the U.S. economy overall but bad for Texas and Louisiana. Similarly, a rise in sea level appears simply as faster beach erosion from a local perspective. Such difficulties, of course, complicate the job of national governments, which need to consolidate the large amounts of information available to them. (On the other hand, one-size-fits-all indicators may not suit governments at lower levels and organizations with a local, state, or regional focus.) Most importantly, before there is any attempt at aggregation, it should be clear why it is being done and what decisions will be informed by it.

Despite these problems, decision makers will often be forced to aggregate different sustainability indicators when comparing options. Similar problems attend processes that involve the public in decisionmaking. One tool that may prove useful in easing these difficulties is multicriteria analysis, which can use some or all of a community's sustainability indicators to evaluate a specific choice.[27] This technique can help a decision maker determine which indicators are most affected by the particular decision at hand and show how the different options compare in this regard. Many observers have called for such efforts, including the President's Council on Sustainable Development.[28] An approach of this type could help meet two difficult challenges: aggregating indicators without either being misleading or ignoring processes with biogeophysical limits; and appropriately weighting those objectives that do compete.

One aspect of the development and use of sustainability indicators is unsurprising: They tend to reflect the education, experience, and concerns of the organizations that produce them. Thus, there are often sharp differences between indicators developed by physical scientists and those developed by social scientists, and one frequently hears complaints that the former ignore social issues while the latter do not have enough scientific input. Of course, no one group has

the ultimate authority to define sustainability, and different individuals and organizations will continue to hold their own views on the subject. In some cases, it would be useful to recognize that sustainability cannot be a purely objective concept and will require collaboration on many levels. In other cases, however, greater reliance on technical expertise would improve efforts to measure and represent sustainability.

While sustainability indicators do not bring about change themselves, they are a valuable tool for understanding what change might be like. The idea of measuring the elusive concept of sustainability has clearly taken root, but many challenges and opportunities lie ahead. However, by moving us beyond vague—but important—discussions about sustainability in the abstract, indicators are already helping us not only to establish numerical goals and analyze trends but also to explore the full implications of this concept.

ENDNOTES

1. For representative views, see J. Pezzy, Sustainable Development Concepts: An Economic Analysis (Washington, D.C.: World Bank, 1992): A. Heyes and C. Liston-Heyes, "Sustainable Resource Use: The Search for Meaning," Energy Policy 23, no. 1 (1995): 1; and W. McKibben, "Buzzless Buzzword," New York Times, 10 April 1996. A19.

2. The carrying capacity of an ecosystem (be it a particular biome or the entire planet) is the maximum number of individuals of a given species that the ecosystem can support indefinitely. It depends on two factors: the resources that are available and the quantity of resources that individuals of that species require for survival. Any population that exceeds its resource requirements will necessarily decline, and it may seriously impair the ecosystem itself in the process. For most species, carrying capacity is a fairly

straightforward concept because the species' habitat is clearly delimited and its resource requirements are fixed. Humans are a more complex case because their requirements change dramatically over time due to technological advance (and can even decline on a per capita basis even though the standard of living is rising) and because they have the ability to effect vast changes to the natural *environment* throughout the planet.

3. See M. Sagoff, The Economy of the Earth (Cambridge, U.K.: Cambridge University Press, 1988); H. Daly and J. Cobb, Far the Common Good (Boston, Mass.: Beacon Press, 1993); World Wildlife Fund, Sustainable Use of Natural Resources (Gland, Switzerland, 1993); and United Nations Development Programme, Human Development Report (New York: Cambridge University Press, 1994).

4. World Commission on *Environment* and Development, Our Common Future (Oxford, U.K.: Oxford University Press, 1987), 6–7.

5. World Conservation Union, Caring for the Earth: A Strategy for Survival (London: Mitchell Beazley, 1993), 211.

6. See G. Gallopin, "Indicators and Their Use: Information for Decision-making," in B. Moldan and S. Billharz, eds., Sustainability Indicators (New York: John Wiley & Sons, 1997).

7. See L. Braat, "The Predictive Meaning of Sustainability Indicators," in O. Kuik and H. Verbruggen, eds., In Search of Indicators of Sustainable Development (Boston, Mass.: Kluwer Academic Publishers, 1992), 57.

8. V. Maclaren, Developing Indicators of Urban Sustainability: A Focus on the Canadian Experience (Toronto: International Committee on Urban and Regional Research Press, 1996).

9. Ibid.; M. Hart, Guide to Sustainable Community Indicators (Ipswich, Mass.: QLF/Atlantic Center for the *Environment,* 1995): Tyler Norris Associates et al., The Community Indicators Handbook: Measuring Progress toward Healthy and Sustainable Communities (San Francisco. Calif.: Redefining Progress, 1997); and R. Hardi and T. Zdan, Assessing Sustainable Development: Principles in Practice (Winnipeg, Man.: International Institute of Sustainable Development, 1997).

10. These principles are available at http://iisdl.iisd.ca/measure/bellagiol.htm.

11. Moldan and Billharz, note 6 above, contains accounts of 10 national efforts and 1 multinational one. To facilitate these efforts, the United Nations Commission on Sustainable Development has prepared a handbook that provides detailed descriptions of some 130 indicators. Each description includes the indicator's place in the overall set, its significance, recommended methods for calculating it, and information on data needs and sources. See United Nations Commission on Sustainable Development. Indicators of Sustainable Development: Framework and Methodologies (New York, 1996).

12. President's Council on Sustainable Development, Sustainable America: A New Consensus for Prosperity, Opportunity, and a Healthy *Environment* for the Future (Washington, D.C.: U.S. Government Printing Office, 1996). The council identifies some sustainability indicators on pages 15–23.

13. For details, visit http://www.hq.nasa.gov/iwgsdi.html.

14. See http://www.fs.fed.us/intro/speech/roundtable.html.

15. See, for instance, http://www.epa.gov/region03/sdwork and http://www.epa.gov/ecocommunity/.

16. For free on-line training and a downloadable version, see http://www.subjectmatters.com/indicators/HTMLSrc/IndicatorTrain.html.

17. W. Jung, "Sustainable Development in Industrial Countries: Environmental Indicators and Targets as Core Elements of National Action Plans—the German Case," Sustainable Development 3 (1998): I.

18. Ibid.: and D. Pearce, Blueprint 3: Measuring Sustainable Development (London: Earthscan, 1993).

19. FOE has worked with non-European nations as well, including China, Japan, Australia, Ghana, and Uruguay. See http://www.wx4all.nl/~foeint/suscamp.html.

20. M. Altieri and O. Masera, "Sustainable Rural Development in Latin America: Building from the Bottom Up," Ecological Economics 7,

no. 1 (1993): 93; and Moldan and Billharz, note 6 above.

21. C. Azar et al., "Socio-ecological Indicators for Sustainability," Ecological Economics 18, no. 2 (1996): 89; D. Kezell. "Development of a Decision-Support System for a Regional Energy and Environmental Sustainability Model" (master's thesis, Arizona State University, 1991); and R. Ayres, "Statistical Measures of Unsustainability," Ecological Economics 16, no. 3 (1996): 239.

22. For details, visit http://www.scn.org/sustainable/susthome.html.

23. See gopher://gopher.un.org/00/esc/cn17/1997-98/patterns/mccpp5-9.txt.

24. King County Office of Budget and Strategic Planning, King County Benchmark Report (Seattle, Wash., 1996); and Pierce County Department of Community Services, Pierce County Quality of Life Benchmarks: Annual Report (Tacoma, Wash., 1998).

25. Department of Economic, Development and Planning, Sustainability Indicators for Fife: Measuring the Quality of Life and the Quality of the *Environment* in Fife (Fife, Scotland, 1995).

26. Extensive empirical research and theoretical work on this issue has been assembled to explain this phenomenon, which is called postmaterialism. See R. Abramson and R. Inglehart, Value Change in Global Perspective (Ann Arbor, Mich.: University of Michigan Press, 1995).

27. A. Farrell, "Sustainability and the Design of Knowledge Tools," Technology & Society 15, no. 4 (1996): 11: and J. Herkert et al., "Technology Choice in a Sustainable Development Context," Technology & Society 15, no. 2 (1996): 12.

28. President's Council on Sustainable Development, note 12 above.

Chapter 11

Attaining Sustainable and Equitable Development

21.   A Declaration of Sustainability*

PAUL HAWKEN

I recently performed a social audit for Ben and Jerry's Homemade Inc., America's premier socially responsible company. After poking and prodding around, asking tough questions, trying to provoke debate, and generally making a nuisance of myself, I can attest that their status as the leading social pioneer in commerce is safe for at least another year. They are an outstanding company. Are there flaws? Of course. Welcome to planet Earth. But the people at Ben & Jerry's are relaxed and unflinching in their willingness to look at, discuss, and deal with problems.

In the meantime, the company continues to put ice cream shops in Harlem, pay outstanding benefits, keep a compensation ratio of seven to one from the top of the organization to the bottom, seek out vendors from disadvantaged groups, and donate generous scoops of their profits to others. And they are about to over-take their historic rival Häagen-Dazs, the ersatz Scandinavian originator of super-premium ice cream, as the market leader in their category. At present rates of growth, Ben & Jerry's will be a $1 billion company by the end of the century. They are publicly held, nationally recognized, and rapidly growing, in part because Ben wanted to show that a socially responsible company could make it in the normal world of business.

Ben and Jerry's is just one of a growing vanguard of companies attempting to redefine their social and ethical responsibilities. These companies no longer accept the maxim that the business of business is business. Their premise is simple: Corporations, because they are the dominant institution on the planet, must squarely face the social and environmental problems that afflict humankind. Organizations such as Business for Social Responsibility and the Social Venture Network, corporate "ethics" consultants, magazines such as *In Business* and Business Ethics, non-profits including the Council on Economic Priorities, investment funds such as Calvert and Covenant, newsletters like *Greenmoney*, and thousands of unaffiliated companies are drawing up new codes of conduct for corporate life that integrate social, ethical, and environmental principles.

Ben and Jerry's and the roughly 2,000 other committed companies in the social responsibility movement here and abroad have combined annual sales of approximately $2 billion, or one-hundredth of 1 percent of the $20 trillion sales garnered by the estimated 80 million to 100 million enterprises worldwide. The problems they are trying to address are vast and unremittingly complex: 5.5 billion people are breeding

*This essay was originally published in *Utne Render,* September/October 1993: 54–61, and is reprinted by permission of the author.

exponentially, and fulfilling their wants and needs is stripping the earth of its biotic capacity to produce life; a climactic burst of consumption by a single species is overwhelming the skies, earth, waters, and fauna.

As the Worldwatch Institute's Lester Brown patiently explains in his annual survey, *State of the World*, every living system on earth is in decline. Making matters worse, we are having a once-in-a-billion-year blowout sale of hydrocarbons, which are being combusted into the atmosphere, effectively double glazing the planet within the next 50 years with unknown climatic results. The cornucopia of resources that are being extracted, mined, and harvested is so poorly distributed that 20 percent of the earth's people are chronically hungry or starving, while the top 20 percent of the population, largely in the north, control and consume 80 percent of the world's wealth. Since business in its myriad forms is primarily responsible for this "taking," it is appropriate that a growing number of companies ask the question, How does one honorably conduct business in the latter days of industrialism and the beginning of an ecological age? The ethical dilemma that confronts business begins with the acknowledgment that a commercial system that functions well by its own definitions unavoidably defies the greater and more profound ethic of biology. Specifically, how does business face the prospect that creating a profitable, growing company requires an intolerable abuse of the natural world?

Despite their dedicated good work, if we examine all or any of the businesses that deservedly earn high marks for social and environmental responsibility, we are faced with a sobering irony: If every company on the planet were to adopt the environmental and social practices of the best companies—

of, say, the Body Shop. Patagonia, and Ben and Jerry's—the world would still be moving toward environmental degradation and collapse. In other words, if we analyze environmental effects and create an input-output model of resources and energy, the results do not even approximate a tolerable or sustainable future. If a tiny fraction of the world's most intelligent companies cannot model a sustainable world, then that tells us that being socially responsible is only one part of an overall solution, and that what we have is not a management problem but a design problem.

At present, there is a contradiction inherent in the premise of a socially responsible corporation: to wit, that a company can make the world better, can grow, and can increase profits by meeting social and environmental needs. It is a have-your-cake-and-eat-it fantasy that cannot come true if the primary cause of environmental degradation is overconsumption. Although proponents of socially responsible business are making an outstanding effort at reforming the tired old ethics of commerce, they are unintentionally creating a new rationale for companies to produce, advertise, expand, grow, capitalize, and use up resources: the rationale that they are doing good. A jet flying across the country, a car rented at an airport, an air-conditioned hotel room, a truck full of goods, a worker commuting to his or her job—all cause the same amount of environmental degradation whether they're associated with the Body Shop, the Environmental Defense Fund, or R. J. Reynolds.

In order to approximate a sustainable society, we need to describe a system of commerce and production in which each and every act is inherently sustainable and restorative. Because of the way our system of commerce is designed, businesses will not be able to fulfill their social contract with the environment or society until the system in which they operate undergoes a fundamental change, a change that brings commerce and governance into alignment with the natural world from which we receive our life. There must be an integration of economic, biologic and human systems in order to create a sustainable and interdependent method of commerce that supports and furthers our existence. As hard as we may strive to create sustainability on a company level, we cannot fully succeed until the institutions surrounding commerce are redesigned. Just as every act of production and consumption in an industrial society leads to further environmental degradation, regardless of intention or ethos, we need to imagine—and then design—a system of commerce where the opposite is true, where doing good is like falling off a log, where the natural, everyday acts of work and life accumulate into a better world as a matter of course, not a matter of altruism. A system of sustainable commerce would involve these objectives:

1. It would reduce absolute consumption of energy and natural resources among developed nations by 80 per-cent within 40 to 60 years.
2. It would provide secure, stable, and meaningful employment for people everywhere.
3. It would be self-actuating as opposed to regulated, controlled, mandated, or moralistic.
4. It would honor human nature and market principles.
5. It would be perceived as more desirable than our present way of life.
6. It would exceed sustainability by restoring degraded habitats and ecosystems to their fullest biological capacity.

7. It would rely on current solar income.
8. It should be fun and engaging, and strive for an aesthetic outcome.

STRATEGIES FOR SUSTAINABILITY

At present, the environmental and social responsibility movements consist of many different initiatives, connected primarily by values and beliefs rather than by design. What is needed is a conscious plan to create a sustainable future, including a set of design strategies for people to follow. For the record, I will suggest 12.

1. Take back the charter.

Although corporate charters may seem to have little to do with sustainability, they are critical to any long-term movement toward restoration of the planet. Read *Taking Care of Business: Citizenship and the Charter of Incorporation,* a 1992 pamphlet by Richard Grossman and Frank T. Adams (Charter Ink, Box 806, Cambridge, MA 02140). In it you find a lost history of corporate power and citizen involvement that addresses a basic and crucial point: Corporations are chartered by, and exist at the behest of, citizens. Incorporation is not a right but a privilege granted by the state that includes certain considerations such as limited liability. Corporations are supposed to be under our ultimate authority, not the other way around. The charter of incorporation is a revocable dispensation that was supposed to ensure accountability of the corporation to society as a whole. When Rockwell criminally despoils a weapons facility at Rocky Flats, Colorado, with plutonium waste, or when any corporation continually harms, abuses, or violates the public trust, citizens should have the right to revoke its charter, causing the company to disband, sell off its enterprises to other companies, and effectively go out of business. The workers would have jobs with the new owners, but the executives, directors, and management would be out of jobs, with a permanent notice on their résumés that they mismanaged a corporation into a charter revocation. This is not merely a deterrent to corporate abuse but a critical element of an ecological society because it creates feedback loops that prompt accountability, citizen involvement, and learning. We should remember that the citizens of this country originally envisioned corporations to be part of a public-private partnership, which is why the relationship between the chartering authority of state legislatures and the corporation was kept alive and active. They had it right.

2. Adjust price to reflect cost.

The economy is environmentally and commercially dysfunctional because the market does not provide consumers with proper information. The "free market" economics that we love so much are excellent at setting prices but lousy when it comes to recognizing costs. In order for a sustainable society to exist, every purchase must reflect or at least approximate its actual cost, not only the direct cost of production but also the costs to the air, water, and soil; the cost to future generations; the cost to worker health; the cost of waste, pollution, and toxicity. Simply stated, the marketplace gives us the wrong information. It tells us that flying across the country on a discount airline ticket is cheap when it is not. It tells us that our food is inexpensive when its method of production destroys aquifers and soil, the viability of ecosystems, and workers' lives. Whenever an organism gets wrong information, it is a form of toxicity. In fact, that is how pesticides work. A herbicide kills because it is a

hormone that tells the plant to grow faster than its capacity to absorb nutrients allows. It literally grows itself to death. Sound familiar? Our daily doses of toxicity are the prices in the marketplace. They are telling us to do the wrong thing for our own survival. They are lulling us into cutting down old-growth forests on the Olympic Peninsula for apple crates, into patterns of production and consumption that are not just unsustainable but profoundly short-sighted and destructive. It is surprising that "conservative" economists do not support or understand this idea, because it is they who insist that we pay as we go, have no debts, and take care of business. Let's do it.

3. Throw out and replace the entire tax system.

The present tax system sends the wrong messages to virtually everyone, encourages waste, discourages conservation, and rewards consumption. It taxes what we want to encourage—jobs, creativity, payrolls, and real income—and ignores the things we want to discourage—degradation, pollution, and depletion. The present U.S. tax system costs citizens $500 billion a year in record-keeping, filing, administrative, legal, and governmental costs—more than the actual amount we pay in personal income taxes. The only incentive in the present system is to cheat or hire a lawyer to cheat for us. The entire tax system must be incrementally replaced over a 20-year period by "Green fees," taxes that are added onto existing products, energy, services, and materials so that prices in the marketplace more closely approximate true costs. These taxes are not a means to raise revenue or bring down deficits, but must be absolutely revenue neutral so that people in the lower and middle classes experience no real change of income, only a shift in expenditures. Eventually, the cost of non-renewable resources, extractive energy, and industrial modes of production will be more expensive than renewable resources, such as solar energy, sustainable forestry, and biological methods agriculture. Why should the upper middle class be able to afford to conserve while the lower income classes cannot? So far the environmental movement has only made the world better for upper middle class white people. The only kind of environmental movement that can succeed has to start from the bottom up. Under a Green fee system the incentives to save on taxes will create positive, constructive acts that are affordable for everyone. As energy prices go up to three to four times their existing levels (with commensurate tax reductions to offset the increase), the natural inclination to save money will result in carpooling, bicycling, telecommuting, public transport, and more efficient houses. As taxes on artificial fertilizers, pesticides, and fuel go up, again with offsetting reductions in income and payroll taxes, organic farmers will find that their produce and methods are the cheapest means of production (because they truly are), and customers will find that organically grown food is less expensive than its commercial cousin. Eventually, with the probable exception of taxes on the rich, we will find ourselves in a position where we pay no taxes, but spend our money with a practiced and constructive discernment. Under an enlightened and redesigned tax system, the cheapest product in the marketplace would be best for the customer, the worker, the environment, and the company. That is rarely the case today.

4. Allow resource companies to be utilities.

An energy utility is an interesting hybrid of public-private interests. A utility gains a

market monopoly in exchange for public control of rates, open books, and a guaranteed rate of return. Because of this relationship and the pioneering work of Amory Lovins, we now have markets for "negawatts." It is the first time in the history of industrialism that a corporation has figured out how to make money by selling the absence of something. Negawatts are the opposite of energy: They represent the collaborative ability of a utility to harness efficiency instead of hydrocarbons. This conservation-based alternative saves ratepayers, shareholders, and the company money—savings that are passed along to everyone. All resource systems, including oil, gas, forests, and water, should be run by some form of utility. There should be markets in negabarrels, negatrees, and negacoal. Oil companies, for example, have no alternative at present other than to lobby for the absurd, like drilling in the Arctic National Wildlife Refuge. That project, a $40 billion to $60 billion investment for a hoped-for supply of oil that would meet U.S. consumption needs for only six months, is the only way an oil company can make money under our current system of commerce. But if the oil companies formed an oil utility and cut a deal with citizens and taxpayers that allowed them to "invest" in insulation, super-glazed windows, conservation rebates on new automobiles, and the scrapping of old cars? Through Green fees, we would pay them back a return on their conservation investment equal to what utilities receive, a rate of return that would be in accord with how many barrels of oil they save, rather than how many barrels they produce. Why should they care? Why should we? A $60 billion investment in conservation will yield, conservatively, four to ten times as much energy as drilling for oil. Given Lovins' principle of efficiency extraction, try to imagine a forest utility, a salmon utility, a copper utility, a Mississippi River utility, a grasslands utility. Imagine a system where the resource utility benefits from conservation, makes money from efficiency, thrives through restoration, and profits from sustainability. It is possible today.

5. Change linear systems to cyclical ones.

Our economy has many design flaws, but the most glaring one is that nature is cyclical and industrialism is linear. In nature, no linear systems exist, or they don't exist for long because they exhaust themselves into extinction. Linear industrial systems take resources, transform them into products or services, discard waste, and sell to consumers, who discard more waste when they have consumed the product. But of course we don't consume TVs, cars, or most of the other stuff we buy. Instead, Americans produce six times their body weight every week in hazardous and toxic waste water, incinerator fly ash, agricultural wastes, heavy metals, and waste chemicals, paper, wood, etc. This does not include CO_2, which if it were included would double the amount of waste. Cyclical means of production are designed to imitate natural systems in which waste equals food for other forms of life, nothing is thrown away, and symbiosis replaces competition. Bill McDonough, a New York architect who has pioneered environmental design principles, has designed a system to retrofit every window in a major American city. Although it still awaits final approval, the project is planned to go like this: The city and a major window manufacturer form a joint venture to produce energy-saving super-glazed windows in the town. This partnership company will come to your house or business, measure all windows and glass doors, and then re-

place them with windows with an R-8 to R-12 energy-efficiency rating within 72 hours. The windows will have the same casements, molding, and general appearance as the old ones. You will receive a $500 check upon installation, and you will pay for the new windows over a 10- to 15-year period in your utility or tax bill. The total bill is less than the cost of the energy the windows will save. In other words, the windows will cost the home or business owner nothing. The city will pay for them initially with industrial development bonds. The factory will train and employ 300 disadvantaged people. The old windows will be completely recycled and reused, the glass melted into glass, the wooden frames ground up and mixed with recycled resins that are extruded to make the casements. When the city is reglazed, the residents and businesses will pocket an extra $20 million to $30 million every year in money saved on utility bills. After the windows are paid for, the figure will go even higher. The factory, designed to be transportable, will move to another city; the first city will retain an equity interest in the venture. McDonough has designed a win-win-win-win-win system that optimizes a number of agendas. The ratepayers, the homeowners, the renters, the city, the environment, and the employed all thrive because they are "making" money from efficiency rather than exploitation. It's a little like running the industrial economy backwards.

6. Transform the making of things.

We have to institute the Intelligent Product System created by Michael Braungart of the EPEA (Environmental Protection Encouragement Agency) in Hamburg, Germany. The system recognizes three types products. The first are *consumables*, products that are either eaten, or, when they're placed on the ground, turn into dirt without any bio-accumulative effects. In other words, they are products whose waste equals food for other living systems. At present, many of the products that should be "consumable," like clothing and shoes, are not. Cotton cloth contains hundreds of different chemicals, plasticizers, defoliants, pesticides, and dyes; shoes are tanned with chromium and their soles contain lead; neckties and silk blouses contain zinc, tin, and toxic dye. Much of what we recycle today turns into toxic by-products, consuming more energy in the recycling process than is saved by recycling. We should be designing more things so that they can be thrown away—into the compost heap. Toothpaste tubes and other non-degradable packaging can be made out of natural polymers so that they break down and become fertilizer for plants. A package that turns into dirt is infinitely more useful, biologically speaking, than a package that turns into a plastic park bench. Heretical as it sounds, designing for decomposition, not recycling, is the way of the world around us.

The second category is *durables,* but in this case, they would not be sold, only licensed. Cars, TVs, VCRs, and refrigerators would always belong to the original manufacturer, so they would be made, used, and returned within a closed-loop system. This is already being instituted in Germany and to a lesser extent in Japan, where companies are beginning to design for disassembly. If a company knows that its products will come back someday, and that it cannot throw anything away when they do, it creates a very different approach to design and materials.

Last, there are *unusables*—toxins, radiation, heavy metals, and chemicals. There is no living system for which these are food and thus they can never be thrown away.

In Braungart's Intelligent Product System, unsalables must always belong to the original maker, safe-guarded by public utilities called "parking lots" that store the toxins in glass-lined barrels indefinitely, charging the original manufacturers rent for the service. The rent ceases when an independent scientific panel can confirm that there is a safe method to detoxify the substances in question. All toxic chemicals would have molecular markers identifying them as belonging to their originator, so that if they are found in wells, rivers, soil, or fish, it is the responsibility of the company to retrieve them and clean up. This places the problem of toxicity with the makers, where it belongs, making them responsible for full-life-cycle effects.

7. Vote, don't buy.

Democracy has been effectively eliminated in America by the influence of money, lawyers, and a political system that is the outgrowth of the first two. While we can dream of restoring our democratic system, the fact remains that we live in a plutocracy—government by the wealthy. One way out is to vote with your dollars, to withhold purchases from companies that act or respond inappropriately. Don't just avoid buying a Mitsubishi automobile because of the company's participation in the destruction of primary forests in Malaysia, Indonesia, Ecuador, Brazil, Bolivia, Canada, Chile, Canada, Siberia, and Papua New Guinea. Write and tell them why you won't. Engage in dialogue, send one postcard a week, talk, organize, meet, publish newsletters, boycott, patronize, and communicate with companies like General Electric. Educate non-profits, organizations, municipalities, and pension funds to act affirmatively, to support the ecological CERES (formerly *Valdez*). Principles for business, to invest intelligently, and to *think* with their money, not merely spend it. Demand the best from the companies you work for and buy from. You deserve it and your actions will help them change.

8. Restore the "guardian."

There can be no healthy business sector unless there is a healthy governing sector. In her book *Systems of Survival,* author Jane Jacobs describes two overarching moral syndromes that permeate our society: the commercial syndrome, which arose from trading cultures, and the governing, or guardian, syndrome that arose from territorial cultures. The guardian system is hierarchical, adheres to tradition, values loyalty, and shuns trading and inventiveness. The commercial system, on the other hand, is based on trading, so it values trust of outsiders, innovation, and future thinking. Each has qualities the other lacks. Whenever the guardian tries to be in business, as in Eastern Europe, business doesn't work. What is also true, but not so obvious to us, is that when business plays government, governance fails as well. Our guardian system has almost completely broken down because of the money, power, influence, and control exercised by business and, to a lesser degree, other institutions. Business and unions have to get out of government. We need more than campaign reform: We need a vision that allows us all to see that when Speaker of the House Tom Foley exempts the aluminum industry in his district from the proposed Btu tax, or when Philip Morris donates $200,000 to the Jesse Helms Citizenship Center, citizenship is mocked and democracy is left gagging and twitching on the Capitol steps. The irony is that business thinks that its involvement in governance is good corporate citizenship or at least is ad-

vancing its own interests. The reality is that business is preventing the economy from evolving. Business loses, workers lose, the environment loses.

9. Shift from electronic literacy to biologic literacy.

That an average adult can recognize one thousand brand names and logos but fewer than ten local plants is not a good sign. We are moving not to an information age but to a biologic age, and unfortunately our technological education is equipping us for corporate markets, not the future. Sitting at home with virtual reality gloves, 3D video games, and interactive cable TV shopping is a barren and impoverished vision of the future. The computer revolution is not the totem of our future, only a tool. Don't get me wrong. Computers are great. But they are not an up-lifting or compelling vision for culture or society. They do not move us toward a sustainable future any more than our obsession with cars and televisions provided us with newer definitions or richer meaning. We are moving into the age of living machines, not, as Corbusier noted. "machines for living in." The Thomas Edison of the future is not Bill Gates of Microsoft, but John and Nancy Todd, founders of the New Alchemy Institute, a Massachusetts design lab and think tank for sustainability. If the Todds' work seems less commercial, less successful, and less glamorous, it is because they are working on the real problem— how to live—and it is infinitely more complex than a microprocessor. Understanding biological processes is how we are going to create a new symbiosis with living systems (or perish). What we can learn on-line is how to model complex systems. It is computers that have allowed us to realize how the synapses in the common sea slug are more powerful than all of our parallel processors put together.

10. Take inventory.

We do not know how many species live on the planet within a factor of ten. We do not know how many are being extirpated. We do not know what is contained in the biological library inherited from the Cenozoic age. (Sociobiologist E. O. Wilson estimates that it would take 25,000 person-years to catalog most of the species, putting aside the fact that there are only 1,500 people with the taxonomic ability to undertake the task.) We do not know how complex systems interact—how the transpiration of the giant lily, *Victoria amazonica,* of Brazil's rainforests affects European rainfall and agriculture, for example. We do not know what happens to 20 percent of the CO_2 that is offgassed every year (it disappears without a trace). We do not know how to calculate sustainable yields in fisheries and forest systems. We do not know why certain species, such as frogs, are dying out even in pristine habitats. We do not know the long-term effects of chlorinated hydrocarbons on human health, behavior, sexuality, and fertility. We do not know what a sustainable life is for existing inhabitants of the planet, and certainly not for future populations. (A Dutch study calculated that your fair share of air travel is one trip across the Atlantic in a lifetime.) We do not know how many people we can feed on a sustainable basis, or what our diet would took like. In short, we need to find out what's here, who has it, and what we can or can't do with it.

11. Take care of human health.

The environmental and socially responsible movements would gain additional credibility if they recognized that the greatest amount of human suffering and mortality is caused by environmental problems that are not being addressed by environmental organizations or companies. Contaminated water is killing a hundred times more people than all other forms of pollution combined. Millions of children are dying from preventable diseases and malnutrition.

The movement toward sustainability must address the clear and present dangers that people face worldwide, dangers that ironically increase population levels because of their perceived threat. People produce more children when they're afraid they'll lose them. Not until the majority of the people in the world, all of whom suffer in myriad preventable yet intolerable ways, understand that environmentalism means improving their lives directly will the ecology movement walk its talk. Americans will spend more money in the next 12 months on the movie and tchotchkes of *Jurassic Park* than on foreign aid to prevent malnutrition or provide safe water.

12. Respect the human spirit.

If hope is to pass the sobriety test, then it has to walk a pretty straight line to reality. Nothing written, suggested, or proposed here is possible unless business is willing to integrate itself into the natural world. It is time for business to take the initiative in a genuinely open process of dialogue, collaboration, reflection, and redesign. "It is not enough," writes Jeremy Seabrook of the British Green party, "to declare, as many do, that we are living in an unsustainable way, using up resources, squandering the substance of the next generation however true this may be. People must feel subjectively the injustice and unsustainability before they will make a more sober assessment as to whether it is worth maintaining what is, or whether there might not be more equitable and satisfying ways that will not be won at the expense either of the necessities of the poor or of the wasting fabric of the planet."

Poet and naturalist W. S. Merwin (citing Robert Graves) reminds us that we have one story, and one story only, to tell in our lives. We are made to believe by our parents and businesses, by our culture and televisions, by our politicians and movie stars that it is the story of money, of finance, of wealth, of the stock portfolio, the partnership, the country house. These are small, impoverished tales and whispers that have made us restless and craven; they are not stories at all. As author and garlic grower Stanley Crawford puts it, "The financial statement must finally give way to the narrative, with all its exceptions, special cases, imponderables. It must finally give way to the story, which is perhaps the way we arm ourselves against the next and always unpredictable turn of the cycle in the quixotic dare that is life; across the rock and cold of lifelines, it is our seed, our clove, our filament cast toward the future." It is something deeper than anything commercial culture can plumb, and it is waiting for each of us.

Business must yield to the longings of the human spirit. The most important contribution of the socially responsible business movement has little to do with recycling, nuts from the rainforest, or employing the homeless. Their gift to us is that they are leading by trying to do something, to risk, take a chance, make a change—any change. They are not waiting for "the solution." but are acting without guarantees of success or proof of purchase. This is what all of us must do. Being visionary has always been given a bad rap by commerce. But without a positive vision for humankind we can have no meaning, no work, and no purpose.